*Readings for
Educational
Psychology*

Readings for Educational Psychology

Second Edition

WILLIAM A. FULLAGAR, *Dean of the College of Education,*
University of Rochester

HAL G. LEWIS, *Professor of Foundations of Education,*
University of Florida

CARROLL F. CUMBEE, *Associate Professor of Child*
Development, University of Florida

Thomas Y. Crowell Company
New York / Established 1834

Cover photo by Hays from Monkmeyer.

Library of Congress Catalog Card Number: 64-14571

FIRST EDITION

First Printing, March, 1956
Second Printing, June, 1957
Third Printing, July, 1958
Fourth Printing, March, 1959
Fifth Printing, April, 1960
Sixth Printing, January, 1962

SECOND EDITION

First Printing, May, 1964
Second Printing, December, 1964

Manufactured in the United States of America

PREFACE

College instructors, like other teachers, encourage their students to read broadly and to reflect on this reading. Often, however, they lack the time to choose worthwhile readings from the welter of educational writings. And, when time is found for this task, the selections are not readily available to students. It was with these problems in mind that the original edition of *Readings for Educational Psychology* was prepared.

In this Second Edition, sixty-eight selections by seventy-three authors from the fields of education, psychology, psychiatry, mental hygiene, and related disciplines are arranged in three parts—"Learning and Learning Theory," "Understanding the Learner," and "The Learning Situation"—which are subdivided further into ten sections. New emphasis has been given to programed learning, creativity, critical thinking, self-actualization, and measurement and evaluation. The articles or chapters, in almost every case, are printed in their entirety, with the omission only of bibliographical references when such deletion does not greatly reduce the utility of the selection.

The basic format of the first edition has been retained. An interpretive headnote and a biographical footnote at the beginning of each selection set the stage for the reader. In addition, other selections relating to the subject under discussion are listed by number before each selection. If the student follows the careful reading of a selection with an equally careful perusal of the related selections, the breadth of his understanding of the topic will be greatly enhanced. Finally, a table correlating the selections with the chapters of twenty-one educational psychology textbooks appears at the back of the book.

Thirty-nine selections from the first edition appear again here either because they are invaluable classic studies or because they exemplify viewpoints as timely today as when they were first expressed. To this central core of material have been added twenty-nine selections chosen with the following criteria in mind:

1. The readings should complement and supplement, not duplicate, the material of the basic text.
2. They should stay well within the bounds of educational psychology.
3. A balance should be maintained between the "old," as represented by certain classic statements by the leaders of yesterday, and the "new," as represented by some of today's frontier thinkers.
4. The book should be oriented toward helping prospective and in-service teachers to better meet their everyday problems.
5. The selections should be interesting and understandable, yet not superficial; challenging, yet not difficult.

Acknowledgment is made, in separate footnotes, to the authors and publishers of the selections used. The editors would like here again, however, to express their indebtedness for the privilege of reprinting these significant papers. Whatever merit this volume may possess is due to the scholarship and creativeness of the authors who generously consented to the inclusion of their previously published work.

W. A. F.

H. G. L.

CONTENTS

CONTENTS

PROGRAMED LEARNING AND TEACHING MACHINES

PART ONE

Learning and learning theory

SOME CONCEPTS
OF LEARNING

1 *The nature of learning theories*

Related selections: 2, 3, 5, 6, 7

Both the teacher and the psychologist have regarded a study of learning and of the learning process as being of prime importance. An understanding of how people learn and under what conditions they learn best has been considered by many as being the first and major contribution of psychology to pedagogy. From many experiments and studies have come several different theories of learning with numerous variations within each theory. Getting deeply involved in these differences is one sure road to confusion for beginning teachers. Dr. Hilgard here defines learning and outlines some of the differences among learning theories.

THE DEFINITION OF LEARNING

What learning includes

There are many activities which everyone will agree count as illustrations of learning: acquiring a vocabulary, memorizing a poem, learning to operate a typewriter. There are other activities, not quite as obviously learned, which easily classify as learned, once you have reflected upon them. Among these are the acquiring of prejudices and preferences and other social attitudes and ideals, including the many skills involved in the social interplay with other people.

ERNEST R. HILGARD, *Theories of Learning,* 2d ed. (New York: Appleton-Century-Crofts, 1956), pp. 2–13. Copyright © 1948, 1956, Appleton-Century-Crofts, Inc., and reprinted with their permission.

DR. HILGARD (1904–) is Executive Head of the Department of Psychology and former Dean of the Graduate Division, Leland Stanford University. He is past-president of the American Psychological Association and an eminent scholar in the field of learning.

3

Finally there are a number of activities whose acquisition is not usually classifiable as a gain or improvement because their utility, if such there be, is not readily demonstrable. Among these are tics, mannerisms, autistic gestures.

Such a pointing to illustrations of learning serves very well as a first approximation to a definition. It is, in fact, extremely difficult to write an entirely satisfactory definition. Although we are tempted to define learning as improvement with practice, or as profiting by experience, we know very well that some learning is not improvement, and other learning is not desirable in its consequences. To describe it alternatively as any change with repetition confuses it with growth, fatigue, and other changes which may take place with repetition. The following definition may be offered provisionally:

> Learning is the process by which an activity originates or is changed through reacting to an encountered situation, provided that the characteristics of the change in activity cannot be explained on the basis of native response tendencies, maturation, or temporary states of the organism (e.g., fatigue, drugs, etc.).

The definition is not formally satisfactory because of the many undefined terms in it, but it will do to call attention to the problems involved in any definition of learning. The definition must distinguish between (1) the kinds of changes, and their correlated antecedents, which are included as learning, and (2) the related kinds of changes, and their antecedents, which are not classified as learning. We can now go on to consider some of the changes that are excluded by our provisional definition.

Native response tendencies versus learning

The older catalogs of innate behavior usually included among unlearned activities the reflexes (such as pupillary constriction to light), the tropisms (such as a moth's dashing into a flame), and the instincts (such as a bird's nest-building). We may continue to acknowledge such activities as species characteristics. After a period during which it was rather emotionally tabooed, the term "instinct" is again part of the psychologist's vocabulary, referring to complex unlearned activity characteristic of a species.

The problem of instinct versus learning is not solved by attempting to classify some behavior as instinctive in its entirety and other behavior as learned in its entirety. The in-between nature of behavior with large instinctive components is well illustrated by the experiments on *imprinting*. A young duckling, for example, is prepared instinctively to accept a certain range of mother-figures, characterized by size, movement, and vocalization. Once such a mother-figure has been accepted and followed about, only this *particular* mother now satisfies the instinctive demand. The selected mother (who may be Professor Lorenz crawling on hands and knees) has become imprinted, and is the only "mother" the duckling will now follow. Imprinting is then a form of learning, but a form very closely allied to the instinctive propensities of a particular kind of organism of a particular age. (We lack at present evidence for imprinting except in fowls and other birds.) The problem of distinguishing between the instinctive and learned components of the behavior illustrated by imprinting is an experimental problem, depending for its clarification upon the ingenuity of the experimenter in designing appropriate control experiments.

Maturation versus learning

Growth is learning's chief competitor as a modifier of behavior. If a behavior sequence matures through regular stages irrespective of intervening practice, the behavior is said to develop through maturation and not through learning. If training procedures do not speed up or modify the behavior, such procedures are not causally important and the changes do not classify as learning. Relatively pure cases like the swimming of tadpoles and the flying of birds can be attributed primarily to maturation. Many activities are not as clear-cut, but develop through a complex interplay of maturation and learning. A convenient illustration is the development of language in the child. The child does not learn to talk until old enough, but the language which he learns is that which he hears. In such cases it is an experimental problem to isolate the effects of maturation and of learning. The ambiguity in such cases is one of fact, not of definition.

Fatigue versus learning

When activities are repeated in rapid succession, there is often a loss in efficiency commonly attributed to fatigue. Such changes in performance are called work decrements in the experimental laboratory. The units of a work curve are like those of a practice curve: performance plotted against trials or repetitions. Hence the experimental arrangements in obtaining a work curve are essentially those of a learning procedure and, at first sight, it appears to be a form of question-begging to define the processes involved by the results obtained. It would be question-begging, however, only if we were to equate learning or fatigue with the change in performance. Actually *both* learning and fatigue are *inferences* from the performances, and it is permissible to make such inferences as the obtained performances require or suggest. Fatigue curves tend to show decreasing proficiency with repetition and recovery with rests. Learning curves ordinarily show gains with repetitions and forgetting over rests. These typical differences between learning effects and fatigue effects are evident enough, but the inferences from performance are made on somewhat more complex evidence. It is because of the complexity of these inferences that it is difficult to state a concise definition of learning which will conserve the learning inferences from performance while eliminating the fatigue inferences. The problem is logically the same as distinguishing changes due to maturation and to learning. But again the ambiguity is one of fact, not of definition.

Learning always must remain an inference from performance, and only confusion results if performance and learning are identified. A clear illustration is provided by performance under the influence of drugs or intoxicants. The fact that learned behavior fails when the organism is in such a state does not mean that forgetting has occurred. When the normal state has been restored, the performance may return to normal levels although there has been no intervening training.

Learning and the nervous system

Some definitions of learning avoid the problem of performance by defining learning as a change in the central nervous system. So long as this change in the nervous system persists, temporary changes in state, such as those in fatigue and intoxication, affect performance but not learning. This definition asserts that learning is an inference, but it goes on to make a particular sort of inference about the role of the nervous system in learning. In view of the lack of knowledge of what actually does take place inside the organism when learning occurs, it is preferable not to include hypothetical neural processes in the definition of learning. We know that learning takes place. We should therefore be able to define what we are talking about without reference to any speculation whatever. This position does not deny that what we are calling learning may be a function of nervous tissue. It asserts only that it is not necessary to know anything about the neural correlates of learning in order to know that learning occurs.

Learning, problem-solving, and reasoning

After you have learned, there are many things which you are able to do. If you can add and subtract, you can solve many novel problems without learning anything new. Where the solution of problems is relatively mechanical (as in addition and subtraction), the problem may be thought of as merely the exercise or utilization of a learned bit of behavior. When, however, there is greater novelty, more putting of things into relationship, as in reasoning or inventiveness, the process is interesting in its own light, and is not to be described simply as the running off of old habits.

The question has been raised, especially by Maier, as to the appropriateness of including processes like reasoning within the same classification as other kinds of learning. My preference is for including them. Leaving them in does not prejudge their explanation. There may be several kinds of learning from the simpler to the more complex, not all following the same principles. If so, we have no assurance that the only sharp break comes when "reasoning" appears. Leaving the doubtful processes in simply asserts that a complete theory of learning must have something to say about reasoning, creative imagination, and inventiveness, in addition to what may be said about memorizing and retaining or about the acquisition of skill.

Definition not a major source of disagreement between theories

While it is extremely difficult to formulate a satisfactory definition of learning so as to include all the activities and processes which we wish to include and eliminate all those which we wish to exclude, the difficulty does not prove to be embarrassing because it is not a source of controversy as between theories. The controversy is over fact and interpretation, not over definition. There are occasional confusions over definition, but such confusions may usually be resolved by resort to pointing, to denotation. For the most part it is satisfactory to continue to mean by learning that which conforms to the usual socially accepted meaning that is part of our common heritage. Where distinctions have to be made with greater precision, they can be made through carefully specified types of inference from experiments.

SOME TYPICAL PROBLEMS CONFRONTING LEARNING THEORIES

The preferences of the theorist often lead him to concentrate upon one kind of learning situation to the neglect of the others. His theory is then appropriate to this situation, but becomes somewhat strained in relation to other problems of learning. A comprehensive learning theory ought to answer the questions which an intelligent non-psychologist might ask about the sorts of learning which are met in everyday life. A few such questions will be listed here, and then used later in appraising the theories which different writers present.

1. WHAT ARE THE LIMITS OF LEARNING?   Here is raised the question of the capacity to learn, of individual differences among learners of the same species and of unlike species. There are questions not only of persistent differences in capacity, but of change in capacity with age. Who can learn what? Are the limits set at birth? Do people get more or less alike with practice? These are the sorts of questions which it is natural to raise.

2. WHAT IS THE ROLE OF PRACTICE IN LEARNING?   The old adage that practice makes perfect has considerable racial wisdom behind it. Surely one learns to roller skate or to play the piano only by engaging in the activity. But what do we know about practice in detail? Does improvement depend directly on the amount of repetition? If not, what are its conditions? What are the most favorable circumstances of practice? Can repetitive drill be harmful as well as helpful to the learner?

3. HOW IMPORTANT ARE DRIVES AND INCENTIVES, REWARDS AND PUNISHMENTS?
Everybody knows in a general way that learning can be controlled by rewards and punishments, and that it is easier to learn something which is interesting

than something which is dull. But are the consequences of rewards and punishments equal and opposite? Is there a difference between intrinsic and extrinsic motives in their effect upon learning? How do goals and purposes affect the process?

4. WHAT IS THE PLACE OF UNDERSTANDING AND INSIGHT? Some things are learned more readily if we know what we are about. We are better off as travelers if we can understand a timetable or a road map. We are helpless with differential equations unless we understand the symbols and the rules for their manipulation. But we can form vowels satisfactorily without knowing how we place our tongues, and we can read without being aware of our eye movements. Some things we appear to acquire blindly and automatically; some things we struggle hard to understand and can finally master only as we understand them. Is learning in one case different from what it is in the other?

5. DOES LEARNING ONE THING HELP YOU LEARN SOMETHING ELSE? This is the problem of formal discipline, as it used to be called, or of transfer of training, to use a more familiar contemporary designation. Some transfer of training must occur or there would be no use in developing a foundation for later learning. Nobody denies that it is easier to build a vocabulary in a language after you have a start in it, or that higher mathematics profits from mastery of basic concepts. The question is really one of how much transfer takes place, under what conditions, and what its nature is.

6. WHAT HAPPENS WHEN WE REMEMBER AND WHEN WE FORGET? The ordinary facts of memory are mysterious enough, but in addition to familiar remembering and forgetting, our memories may play peculiar tricks on us. Some things we wish to remember are forgotten; some things we would be willing to forget continue to plague us. In cases of amnesia there are often gaps in memory, with earlier and later events remembered. Then there are the distortions of memory, in which we remember what did not happen, as is so strikingly demonstrated in testimony experiments. What is taking place? What control have we over processes involved?

These six questions will serve as useful ones to ask of each of the major theories. They suffice to illustrate the kinds of questions which give rise to theories of learning.

ISSUES ON WHICH
LEARNING THEORIES DIVIDE

In the preceding section we asked certain common-sense questions about learning, on the assumption that a good learning theory should have something to say about each of them. Such questions can be raised before we know anything about actual learning theories. Now we wish to turn, however, to certain issues that have arisen in the formulation of actual theories. By alerting us in this way to what is to follow, we are better prepared for some of the differences in flavor that we shall meet as we review one theory after another.

Learning theories fall into two major families: *stimulus-response* theories and *cognitive* theories, but not all theories belong to these two families. The stimulus-response theories include such diverse members as the theories of Thorndike, Guthrie, Skinner, and Hull. The cognitive theories include at least those of Tolman, the classical gestalt psychologists, and Lewin. Not completely and clearly classifiable in these terms are the theories of functionalism, psychodynamics, and the probabilistic theories of the model builders. The lines of cleavage between the two families of theories are not the only cleavages within learning theories; there are other specific issues upon which theories within one family may differ.

General issues producing a cleavage between stimulus-response and cognitive theories

The cleavages between the theorists of opposing camps are difficult to understand because many of the distinctions which at first seem to contrast sharply later are found to be blurred. All reputable theorists accept a common logic of experimentation, so that disagreements over experimentally obtained facts are readily arbitrated. In the end, all the theorists accept a common body of demonstrated relationships, at the factual or descriptive level; any theorist who denied an established fact, a reproducible experimental finding, would lose status among his scientific colleagues, and his theories would no longer command respect. The first rule that we must be prepared to accept, as we judge the relative merits of different theories, is this: *All the theorists accept all of the facts.* Some experimental findings are doubted when they are first announced and the status of findings *as fact* may for a long time be doubted; but once the status as fact is established, all accept the fact as true. Hence the difference between two theorists are primarily differences in interpretation. Both theories may fit the facts reasonably well, but the proponent of each theory believes his view to be the more fruitful. We shall be better prepared later on to discuss the ways in which theories get validated or modified after we are acquainted with them in more detail. For the present, we must be prepared to accept the historical truth that opposing theories have great survival value, and that an appeal to the facts as a way of choosing between theories is a very complex process, not nearly as decisive in practice as we might expect it to be.

We may begin by examining three kinds of preferences on which stimulus-response theorists tend to differ from cognitive theorists.

1. "PERIPHERAL" VERSUS "CENTRAL" INTERMEDIARIES. Ever since Watson promulgated the theory that thinking was merely the carrying out of subvocal speech movements, stimulus-response theorists have preferred to find response or movement intermediaries to serve as integrators of behavior sequences. Such movement-

produced intermediaries can be classified as "peripheral" mechanisms, as contrasted with "central" (ideational) intermediaries. The stimulus-response theorist tends to believe that some sort of chained muscular responses, linked perhaps by fractional anticipatory goal responses, serve to keep a rat running to a distant food box. The cognitive theorist, on the other hand, more freely infers central brain processes, such as memories or expectations, as integrators of goal-seeking behavior. The differences in preference survive in this case because both kinds of theorists depend upon *inferences* from observed behavior, and the inferences are not directly verified in either case. It is potentially easier to verify tongue movements in thinking than it is to discover a revived memory trace in the brain, but in fact such verification is not offered with the precision necessary to compel belief in the theory. Under the circumstances, the choice between the peripheral and the central explanation is not forced, and favoring one or the other position depends upon more general systematic preferences.

2. ACQUISITION OF HABITS VERSUS ACQUISITION OF COGNITIVE STRUCTURES. The stimulus-response theorist and the cognitive theorist come up with different answers to the question, What is learned? The answer of the former is "habits"; the answer of the latter is "cognitive structures." The first answer appeals to common sense: we all know that we develop smooth-running skills by practicing them; what we learn is *responses*. But the second answer also appeals to common sense: if we locate a candy store from one starting point, we can find it from another because we "know where it is"; what we learn is *facts*. A smooth-running skill illustrates a learned habit; knowing alternate routes illustrates cognitive structure. If all habits were highly mechanical and stereotyped, variable non-habitual behavior would force us to admit cognitive structures as part, at least, of what is learned. But the stimulus-response psychologist is satisfied that he can deduce from the laws of habit formation the behavior that the cognitive theorist believes supports his interpretation. Hence we cannot choose between the theories by coming up with "decisive" illustrations of what we learn, for both groups of theorists will offer explanations of all our examples. The competing theories would not have survived thus far had they been unable to offer such explanations.

3. TRIAL AND ERROR VERSUS INSIGHT IN PROBLEM-SOLVING. When confronted with a novel problem, how does the learner reach solution? The stimulus-response psychologist finds the learner assembling his habits from the past appropriate to the new problem, responding either according to the elements that the new problem has in common with familiar ones, or according to aspects of the new situation which are similar to situations met before. If these do not lead to solution, the learner resorts to trial and error, bringing out of his behavior repertory one response after another until the problem is solved. The cognitive psychologist agrees with much of this description of what the learner does, but he adds interpretations not offered by the stimulus-response psychologist. He points out, for example, that granting all the requisite experience with the parts of a problem, there is no guarantee that the learner will be able to bring these past experiences to bear upon the solution. He may be able to solve the problem if it is presented in one form and not solve it if it is presented in another form, even though both forms require the same past experiences for their solution. According to the cognitive theorist, the preferred method of presentation permits a perceptual structuring leading to "insight," that is, to the understanding of the essential relationships involved. The stimulus-response psychologist tends, by preference, to look to the past history of the learner for the sources of solution, while the cognitive psychologist, by preference, looks to the contemporary structuring of the problem. His preference for the past does not require the stimulus-response psychologist to ignore the present structuring of the problem, nor does his preference for the present require the cognitive psychologist to ignore the past. One must not assume because there is a difference in preference that either theorist is blind to the totality of the learning situation. The facts of the insight experiment are accepted by both theorists, as are the facts of skill learning. We may remind ourselves again that no single experiment will demolish either the interpretation according to trial and error or the interpretation according to insight.

These three issues—peripheral versus central intermediaries, acquisition of habits versus acquisition of cognitive structures, and trial and error versus insight in problem-solving—give something of the flavor of the differences between these two major families of theories.

Specific issues not confined to the major families

Some issues lie outside the conflict between the stimulus-response and the cognitive theories. Thus two stimulus-response psychologists may differ as to the role of reinforcement in learning, and two cognitive theorists may differ as to the necessity for a physiological explanation of learning. Three of these issues will suffice to alert us to the many problems that learning theorists face.

1. CONTIGUITY VERSUS REINFORCEMENT.   The oldest law of association is that ideas experienced together tend to become associated. This has come down in one form or another to the present day as the principle of association by contiguity, although it is now more fashionable to describe the association as between stimuli and responses rather than as between ideas. Several of our contemporary theorists accept the principle of contiguous association, notably Guthrie (a stimulus-response psychologist) and Tolman (a cognitive psychologist). Other theorists insist that learning does not take place through contiguity alone, unless there is some sort of reinforcement, some equivalent of reward or punishment.

2. ONE OR MORE KINDS OF LEARNING?   The contiguity-reinforcement dilemma may be resolved by accepting both, thus defining two varieties of learning. This solution has appealed to theorists such as Thorndike and Skinner and Mowrer. But these two varieties are not the only possibilities. Perhaps by using the com-

mon name "learning" to cover the acquisition of motor skills, the memorization of a poem, the solving of a geometrical puzzle, and the understanding of a period in history, we are deceiving ourselves by looking for common laws explanatory of processes that have little in common.

Hence the theorist has to choose between a single-factor theory and a multi-factor one. Tolman at one time pointed to the possibility of seven kinds of learning.

3. INTERVENING VARIABLES VERSUS HYPOTHETICAL CONSTRUCTS. We have already considered a contrast between two types of intermediary, the peripheral and the central types. But as theories become more refined, additional problems arise over the way in which inferred intermediaries should be specified. One kind of intermediary found in theories is a mathematical constant that reappears in various contexts, such as the acceleration of a free-falling body (g) that appears in equations describing the movement of a pendulum, the path of a projectile, or the way in which balls roll down inclined planes. Such an integrating intervening variable need have no properties other than those expressed in its units of measurement, that is, it need have no independent existence, apart from the functional relationships it has in its systematic context. This kind of integrating intermediary, without surplus meanings, is called an *intervening variable*. By contrast, some kinds of intermediaries are concrete, tangible, palpable, with properties of their own. Suppose, for example, we describe the behavior that results when a cat is confronted with a barking dog. The cat arches its back, hisses, its hair stands on end, and numerous changes take place within its digestive and circulatory system. Many of the internal changes can be *explained* by the use of a demonstrable intermediary, adrenin, the hormone of the adrenal glands. Suppose that before adrenin was isolated a theorist had inferred that some substance in the blood stream was causing the internal changes. This would have been a *hypothetical construct* at this stage, an inferred intermediary with palpable qualities. The discovery of adrenin would have then confirmed the hypothesis that such a substance in the blood stream was, in fact, causing many of the changes. Adrenin, as a substance, has other properties than those inferred from bodily changes in emotion. In this it differs from a mere intervening variable, which has no further properties beyond its systematic ones.

Those who hold with intervening variables in their learning theories are free to choose such variables as they wish, provided they serve their systematic purposes of producing a more coherent and parsimonious theory than can be produced without them. Those who prefer hypothetical constructs must seek either demonstrable movements or secretions (if they are peripheralists), or some physiological brain processes (if they are centralists). Again, the issue over intervening variables or hypothetical constructs is not confined to one or the other of the major theoretical families.

One extreme position is that we can do away with intermediaries entirely

(Skinner). Thus, on this issue as on the others, we have nearly all possible views represented.

This brief introduction to three contrasts between stimulus-response theories and cognitive theories, and three issues that are not confined to the two major families, should make it clear that what seem to be diametrically opposed points of view may turn out to be based on differences in preference, each being possible of persuasive statement, and to a point justifiable. The opposed cases are each made by intelligent men of good will. We shall have to wait until later to consider how a more unified outlook may eventually be achieved.

2 Conditioned emotional reactions

Related selections: 1, 67

Out of the experimental work of Pavlov, Watson, and others came a conditioned reflex theory of learning that had important implications for child rearing and schooling. Although many of their conclusions were later questioned and modified, one permanent contribution of this pioneer work was the placing of psychological study on a scientific basis. Students should understand the methods of this school and ask themselves if there are any kinds of learning for which it offers the best explanation. This selection reports one of a number of experiments by Watson and his associate during the first quarter of the century.

In recent literature various speculations have been entered into concerning the possibility of conditioning various types of emotional response, but direct experimental evidence in support of such a view has been lacking. If the theory advanced by Watson and Morgan to the effect that in infancy the original emotional reaction patterns are few, consisting so far as observed of fear, rage and

JOHN B. WATSON and ROSALIE RAYNER, "Conditioned Emotional Reactions," *Journal of Experimental Psychology*, III (February, 1921), 1–14. Reprinted by permission of the American Psychological Association.

PROFESSOR WATSON (1878–1958) was director of the psychological laboratory at the Johns Hopkins University for many years. He was the foremost behaviorist in this country. ROSALIE RAYNER (WATSON) collaborated with him in his research.

love, then there must be some simple method by means of which the range of stimuli which can call out these emotions and their compounds is greatly increased. Otherwise, complexity in adult response could not be accounted for. These authors without adequate experimental evidence advanced the view that this range was increased by means of conditioned reflex factors. It was suggested there that the early home life of the child furnishes a laboratory situation for establishing conditioned emotional responses. The present authors have recently put the whole matter to an experimental test.

Experimental work has been done so far on only one child, Albert B. This infant was reared almost from birth in a hospital environment; his mother was a wet nurse in the Harriet Lane Home for Invalid Children. Albert's life was normal: he was healthy from birth and one of the best developed youngsters ever brought to the hospital, weighing twenty-one pounds at nine months of age. He was on the whole stolid and unemotional. His stability was one of the principal reasons for using him as a subject in this test. We felt that we could do him relatively little harm by carrying out such experiments as those outlined below.

At approximately nine months of age we ran him through the emotional tests that have become a part of our regular routine in determining whether fear reactions can be called out by other stimuli than sharp noises and the sudden removal of support. Tests of this type have been described by the senior author in another place. In brief, the infant was confronted suddenly and for the first time successively with a white rat, a rabbit, a dog, a monkey, with masks with and without hair, cotton wool, burning newspapers, etc. A permanent record of Albert's reactions to these objects and situations has been preserved in a motion picture study. Manipulation was the most usual reaction called out. *At no time did this infant ever show fear in any situation.* These experimental records were confirmed by the casual observations of the mother and hospital attendants. No one had ever seen him in a state of fear and rage. The infant practically never cried.

Up to approximately nine months of age we had not tested him with loud sounds. The test to determine whether a fear reaction could be called out by a loud sound was made when he was eight months, twenty-six days of age. The sound was that made by striking a hammer upon a suspended steel bar four feet in length and three-fourths of an inch in diameter. The laboratory notes are as follows:

> One of the two experimenters caused the child to turn its head and fixate her moving hand; the other, stationed back of the child, struck the steel bar a sharp blow. The child started violently, his breathing was checked and the arms were raised in a characteristic manner. On the second stimulation the same thing occurred, and in addition the lips began to pucker and tremble. On the third stimulation the child broke into a sudden crying fit. This is the first time an emo-

tional situation in the laboratory has produced any fear or even crying in Albert.

We had expected just these results on account of our work with other infants brought up under similar conditions. It is worth while to call attention to the fact that removal of support (dropping and jerking the blanket upon which the infant was lying) was tried exhaustively upon this infant on the same occasion. It was not effective in producing the fear response. This stimulus is effective in younger children. At what age such stimuli lose their potency in producing fear is not known. Nor is it known whether less placid children ever lose their fear of them. This probably depends upon the training the child gets. It is well known that children eagerly run to be tossed into the air and caught. On the other hand, it is equally well known that in the adult fear responses are called out quite clearly by the sudden removal of support, if the individual is walking across a bridge, walking out upon a beam, etc. There is a wide field of study here which is aside from our present point.

The sound stimulus, thus, at nine months of age, gives us the means of testing several important factors. I. Can we condition fear of an animal, e.g., a white rat, by visually presenting it and simultaneously striking a steel bar? II. If such a conditioned emotional response can be established, will there be a transfer to other animals or other objects? III. What is the effect of time upon such conditioned emotional responses? IV. If after a reasonable period such emotional responses have not died out, what laboratory methods can be devised for their removal?

I. The establishment of conditioned emotional responses. At first there was considerable hesitation upon our part in making the attempt to set up fear reactions experimentally. A certain responsibility attaches to such a procedure. We decided finally to make the attempt, comforting ourselves by the reflection that such attachments would arise anyway as soon as the child left the sheltered environment of the nursery for the rough and tumble of the home. We did not begin this work until Albert was eleven months, three days of age. Before attempting to set up a conditioned response we, as before, put him through all of the regular emotional tests. *Not the slightest sign of a fear response was obtained in any situation.*

The steps taken to condition emotional responses are shown in our laboratory notes.

11 MONTHS 3 DAYS

1. White rat suddenly taken from the basket and presented to Albert. He began to reach for rat with left hand. Just as his hand touched the animal the bar was struck immediately behind his head. The infant jumped violently and fell forward, burying his face in the mattress. He did not cry, however.

2. Just as the right hand touched the rat the bar was again struck. Again the infant jumped violently, fell forward and began to whimper.

In order not to disturb the child too seriously no further tests were given for one week.

11 MONTHS 10 DAYS

1. Rat presented suddenly without sound. There was steady fixation but no tendency at first to reach for it. The rat was then placed nearer, whereupon tentative reaching movements began with the right hand. When the rat nosed the infant's left hand, the hand was immediately withdrawn. He started to reach for the head of the animal with the forefinger of the left hand, but withdrew it suddenly before contact. It is thus seen that the two joint stimulations given the previous week were not without effect. He was tested with his blocks immediately afterwards to see if they shared in the process of conditioning. He began immediately to pick them up, dropping them, pounding them, etc. In the remainder of the tests the blocks were given frequently to quiet him and to test his general emotional state. They were always removed from sight when the process of conditioning was under way.
2. Joint stimulation with rat and sound. Started, then fell over immediately to right side. No crying.
3. Joint stimulation. Fell to right side and rested upon hands, with head turned away from rat. No crying.
4. Joint stimulation. Same reaction.
5. Rat suddenly presented alone. Puckered face, whimpered and withdrew body sharply to the left.
6. Joint stimulation. Fell over immediately to right side and began to whimper.
7. Joint stimulation. Started violently and cried, but did not fall over.
8. Rat alone. *The instant the rat was shown the baby began to cry. Almost instantly he turned sharply to the left, fell over on left side, raised himself on all fours and began to crawl away so rapidly that he was caught with difficulty before reaching the edge of the table.*

This was as convincing a case of a completely conditioned fear response as could have been theoretically pictured. In all, seven joint stimulations were given to bring about the complete reaction. It is not unlikely had the sound been of greater intensity or of a more complex clang character that the number of joint stimulations might have been materially reduced. Experiments designed to define the nature of the sounds that will serve best as emotional stimuli are under way.

II. When a conditioned emotional response has been established for one object, is there a transfer? Five days later Albert was again brought back into the laboratory and tested as follows:

11 MONTHS 15 DAYS

1. Tested first with blocks. He reached readily for them, playing with them as usual. This shows that there has been no general transfer to the room, table, blocks, etc.
2. Rat alone. Whimpered immediately, withdrew right hand and turned head and trunk away.
3. Blocks again offered. Played readily with them, smiling and gurgling.
4. Rat alone. Leaned over to the left side as far away from the rat as possible, then fell over, getting up on all fours and scurrying away as rapidly as possible.
5. Blocks again offered. Reached immediately for them, smiling and laughing as before.

   The above preliminary test shows that the conditioned response to the rat had carried over completely for the five days in which no tests were given. The question as to whether or not there is a transfer was next taken up.
6. Rabbit alone. The rabbit was suddenly placed on the mattress in front of him. The reaction was pronounced. Negative responses began at once. He leaned as far away from the animal as possible, whimpered, then burst into tears. When the rabbit was placed in contact with him he buried his face in the mattress, then got up on all fours and crawled away, crying as he went. This was a most convincing test.
7. The blocks were next given him, after an interval. He played with them as before. It was observed by four people that he played far more energetically with them than ever before. The blocks were raised high over his head and slammed down with a great deal of force.
8. Dog alone. The dog did not produce as violent a reaction as the rabbit. The moment fixation occurred the child shrank back and as the animal came nearer he attempted to get on all fours but did not cry at first. As soon as the dog passed out of his range of vision he became quiet. The dog was then made to approach the infant's head (he was lying down at the moment). Albert straightened up immediately, fell over to the opposite side and turned his head away. He then began to cry.
9. The blocks were again presented. He began immediately to play with them.

10. Fur coat (seal). Withdrew immediately to the left side and began to fret. Coat put close to him on the left side, he turned immediately, began to cry and tried to crawl away on all fours.
11. Cotton wool. The wool was presented in a paper package. At the end the cotton was not covered by the paper. It was placed first on his feet. He kicked it away but did not touch it with his hands. When his hand was laid on the wool he immediately withdrew it but did not show the shock that the animals or fur coat produced in him. He then began to play with the paper, avoiding contact with the wool itself. He finally, under the impulse of the manipulative instinct, lost some of his negativism to the wool.
12. Just in play W. put his head down to see if Albert would play with his hair. Albert was completely negative. Two other observers did the same thing. He began immediately to play with their hair. W. then brought the Santa Claus mask and presented it to Albert. He was again pronouncedly negative.

11 MONTHS 20 DAYS

1. Blocks alone. Played with them as usual.
2. Rat alone. Withdrawal of the whole body, bending over to left side, no crying. Fixation and following with eyes. The response was much less marked than on first presentation the previous week. It was thought best to freshen up the reaction by another joint stimulation.
3. Just as the rat was placed on his hand the rod was struck. Reaction violent.
4. Rat alone. Fell over at once to left side. Reaction practically as strong as on former occasion but no crying.
5. Rat alone. Fell over to left side, got up on all fours and started to crawl away. On this occasion there was no crying, but strange to say, as he started away he began to gurgle and coo, even while leaning far over to the left side to avoid the rat.
6. Rabbit alone. Leaned over to left side as far as possible. Did not fall over. Began to whimper but reaction not so violent as on former occasions.
7. Blocks again offered. He reached for them immediately and began to play.

All of the tests so far discussed were carried out upon a table supplied with a mattress, located in a small, well-lighted darkroom. We wished to test next whether conditioned fear responses so set up would appear if the situation were markedly altered. We thought it best before making this test to freshen the reaction both to the rabbit and to the dog by showing them at the moment the

steel bar was struck. It will be recalled that this was the first time
any effort had been made to directly condition response to the dog
and rabbit. The experimental notes are as follows:

8. The rabbit at first was given alone. The reaction was exactly as
   given in test (6) above. When the rabbit was left on Albert's knees
   for a long time he began tentatively to reach out and manipulate
   its fur with forefingers. While doing this the steel rod was struck.
   A violent fear reaction resulted.
9. Rabbit alone. Reaction wholly similar to that on trial (6) above.
10. Rabbit alone. Started immediately to whimper, holding hands far
    up, but did not cry. Conflicting tendency to manipulate very evident.
11. Dog alone. Began to whimper, shaking head from side to side, hold-
    ing hands as far away from the animal as possible.
12. Dog and sound. The rod was struck just as the animal touched him.
    A violent negative reaction appeared. He began to whimper, turned
    to one side, fell over and started to get up on all fours.
13. Blocks. Played with them immediately and readily.

On this same day and immediately after the above experiment
Albert was taken into the large, well-lighted lecture room belonging
to the laboratory. He was placed on a table in the center of the
room immediately under the skylight. Four people were present.
The situation was thus very different from that which obtained in
the small darkroom.

1. Rat alone. No sudden fear reaction appeared at first. The hands,
   however, were held up and away from the animal. No positive
   manipulatory reactions appeared.
2. Rabbit alone. Fear reaction slight. Turned to left and kept face
   away from the animal but the reaction was never pronounced.
3. Dog alone. Turned away but did not fall over. Cried. Hands moved
   as far away from the animal as possible. Whimpered as long as the
   dog was present.
4. Rat alone. Slight negative reaction.
5. Rat and sound. It was thought best to freshen the reaction to the
   rat. The sound was given just as the rat was presented. Albert
   jumped violently but did not cry.
6. Rat alone. At first he did not show any negative reaction. When rat
   was placed nearer he began to show negative reaction by drawing
   back his body, raising his hands, whimpering, etc.
7. Blocks. Played with them immediately.
8. Rat alone. Pronounced withdrawal of body and whimpering.
9. Blocks. Played with them as before.
10. Rabbit alone. Pronounced reaction. Whimpered with arms held
    high, fell over backward and had to be caught.

11. Dog alone. At first the dog did not produce the pronounced reaction. The hands were held high over the head, breathing was checked, but there was no crying. Just at this moment the dog, which had not barked before, barked three times loudly when only about six inches from the baby's face. Albert immediately fell over and broke into a wail that continued until the dog was removed. The sudden barking of the hitherto quiet dog produced a marked fear response in the adult observers!

From the above results it would seem that emotional transfers do take place. Furthermore it would seem that the number of transfers resulting from an experimentally produced conditioned emotional reaction may be very large. In our observations we had no means of testing the complete number of transfers which may have resulted.

III. The effect of time upon conditioned emotional responses. We have already shown that the conditioned emotional response will continue for a period of one week. It was desired to make the time test longer. In view of the imminence of Albert's departure from the hospital we could not make the interval longer than one month. Accordingly no further emotional experimentation was entered into for thirty-one days after the above test. During the month, however, Albert was brought weekly to the laboratory for tests upon right- and left-handedness, imitation, general development, etc. No emotional tests whatever were given and during the whole month his regular nursery routine was maintained in the Harriet Lane Home. The notes on the test given at the end of this period are as follows:

1 YEAR 21 DAYS

1. Santa Claus mask. Withdrawal, gurgling, then slapped at it without touching. When his hand was forced to touch it, he whimpered and cried. His hand was forced to touch it two more times. He whimpered and cried on both tests. He finally cried at the mere visual stimulus of the mask.
2. Fur coat. Wrinkled his nose and withdrew both hands, drew back his whole body and began to whimper as the coat was put nearer. Again there was the strife between withdrawal and the tendency to manipulate. Reached tentatively with left hand but drew back before contact had been made. In moving his body to one side his hand accidentally touched the coat. He began to cry at once, nodding his head in a very peculiar manner (this reaction was an entirely new one). Both hands were withdrawn as far as possible from the coat. The coat was then laid on his lap and he continued

nodding his head and whimpering, withdrawing his body as far as possible, pushing the while at the coat with his feet but never touching it with his hands.

3. Fur coat. The coat was taken out of his sight and presented again at the end of a minute. He began immediately to fret, withdrawing his body and nodding his head as before.

4. Blocks. He began to play with them as usual.

5. The rat. He allowed the rat to crawl towards him without withdrawing. He sat very still and fixated it intently. Rat then touched his hand. Albert withdrew it immediately, then leaned back as far as possible but did not cry. When the rat was placed on his arm he withdrew his body and began to fret, nodding his head. The rat was then allowed to crawl against his chest. He first began to fret and then covered his eyes with both hands.

6. Blocks. Reaction normal.

7. The rabbit. The animal was placed directly in front of him. It was very quiet. Albert showed no avoiding reactions at first. After a few seconds he puckered up his face, began to nod his head and to look intently at the experimenter. He next began to push the rabbit away with his feet, withdrawing his body at the same time. Then as the rabbit came nearer he began pulling his feet away, nodding his head, and wailing "da da." After about a minute he reached out tentatively and slowly and touched the rabbit's ear with his right hand, finally manipulating it. The rabbit was again placed in his lap. Again he began to fret and withdrew his hands. He reached out tentatively with his left hand and touched the animal, shuddered and withdrew the whole body. The experimenter then took hold of his left hand and laid it on the rabbit's back. Albert immediately withdrew his hand and began to suck his thumb. Again the rabbit was laid in his lap. He began to cry, covering his face with both hands.

8. Dog. The dog was very active. Albert fixated it intensely for a few seconds, sitting very still. He began to cry but did not fall over backwards as on his last contact with the dog. When the dog was pushed closer to him he at first sat motionless, then began to cry, putting both hands over his face.

These experiments would seem to show conclusively that directly conditioned emotional responses as well as those conditioned by transfer persist, although with a certain loss in the intensity of the reaction, for a longer period than one month. Our view is that they persist and modify personality throughout life. It should be recalled again that Albert was of an extremely phlegmatic type.

Had he been emotionally unstable probably both the directly conditioned response and those transferred would have persisted throughout the month unchanged in form.

IV. "Detachment" or removal of conditioned emotional responses. Unfortunately Albert was taken from the hospital the day the above tests were made. Hence the opportunity of building up an experimental technique by means of which we could remove the conditioned emotional responses was denied us. Our own view, expressed above, which is possibly not very well grounded, is that these responses in the home environment are likely to persist indefinitely, unless an accidental method for removing them is hit upon. The importance of establishing some method must be apparent to all. Had the opportunity been at hand we should have tried out several methods, some of which we may mention. (1) Constantly confronting the child with those stimuli which called out the responses in the hopes that habituation would come in corresponding to "fatigue" of reflex when differential reactions are to be set up. (2) By trying to "recondition" by showing objects calling out fear responses (visual) and simultaneously stimulating the erogenous zones (tactual). We should try first the lips, then the nipples and as a final resort the sex organs. (3) By trying to "recondition" by feeding the subject candy or other food just as the animal is shown. This method calls for the food control of the subject. (4) By building up "constructive" activities around the object by imitation and by putting the hand through the motions of manipulation. At this age imitation of overt motor activity is strong, as our present but unpublished experimentation has shown.

INCIDENTAL OBSERVATIONS

(a) Thumb sucking as a compensatory device for blocking fear and noxious stimuli. During the course of these experiments, especially in the final test, it was noticed that whenever Albert was on the verge of tears or emotionally upset generally he would continually thrust his thumb into his mouth. The moment the hand reached the mouth he became impervious to the stimuli producing fear. Again and again while the motion pictures were being made at the end of the thirty-day rest period, we had to remove the thumb from his mouth before the conditioned response could be obtained. This method of blocking noxious and emotional stimuli (fear and rage) through erogenous stimulation seems to persist from birth onward. Very often in our experiments upon the work adders [1] with infants under ten days of age the same reaction appeared. When at work upon the adders both of the infant's arms are under slight restraint. Often rage appears. They begin to cry, thrashing their arms and legs about. If the finger gets into the mouth crying ceases at once. The organism thus apparently from

[1] A work adder is a work-measuring device which sums up and indicates the total amount of work done by a series of muscular contractions.

birth, when under the influence of love stimuli, is blocked to all others.[2] This resort to sex stimulation when under the influence of noxious and emotional situations, or when the individual is restless and idle, persists throughout adolescent and adult life. Albert, at any rate, did not resort to thumb sucking except in the presence of such stimuli. Thumb sucking could immediately be checked by offering him his blocks. These invariably called out active manipulation instincts. It is worth while here to call attention to the fact that Freud's conception of the stimulation of erogenous zones as being the expression of an original "pleasure" seeking principle may be turned about and possibly better described as a compensatory (and often conditioned) device for the blockage of noxious and fear- and rage-producing stimuli.

(b) *Equal primacy of fear, love and possibly rage.* While in general the results of our experiment offer no particular points of conflict with Freudian concepts, one fact out of harmony with them should be emphasized. According to proper Freudians sex (in our terminology, love) is the principal emotion in which conditioned responses arise which later limit and distort personality. We wish to take sharp issue with this view on the basis of the experimental evidence we have gathered. Fear is as primal a factor as love in influencing personality. Fear does not gather its potency in any derived manner from love. It belongs to the original and inherited nature of man. Probably the same may be true of rage although at present we are not so sure of this.

The Freudians twenty years from now, unless their hypotheses change, when they come to analyze Albert's fear of a seal skin coat—assuming that he comes to analysis at that age—will probably tease from him the recital of a dream which upon their analysis will show that Albert at three years of age attempted to play with the pubic hair of the mother and was scolded violently for it. (We are by no means denying that this might in some other case condition it.) If the analyst has sufficiently prepared Albert to accept such a dream when found as an explanation of his avoiding tendencies, and if the analyst has the authority and personality to put it over, Albert may be fully convinced that the dream was a true revealer of the factors which brought about the fear.

It is probable that many of the phobias in psychopathology are true conditioned emotional reactions either of the direct or the transferred type. One may possibly have to believe that such persistence of early conditioned responses will be found only in persons who are constitutionally inferior. Our argument is meant to be constructive. Emotional disturbances in adults cannot be traced back to sex alone. They must be retraced along at least three collateral lines—

---

[2] The stimulus to love in infants according to our view is stroking of the skin, lips, nipples, and sex organs, patting and rocking, picking up, etc. Patting and rocking (when not conditioned) are probably equivalent to actual stimulation of the sex organs. In adults, of course, as every lover knows, vision, audition, and olfaction soon become conditioned by joint stimulation with contact and kinaesthetic stimuli.

to conditioned and transferred responses set up in infancy and early youth in all three of the fundamental human emotions.

3 The laws of learning

Related selection: 1

A generation of American teachers and teachers of teachers were nurtured on the psychology of Thorndike. His books on educational psychology are monumental and were, at the time of publication, a synthesis of knowledge about learning. In the selection that follows he reviews the laws of learning from an earlier book and then sets forth the position that learning is making connections. The ideas contained in these two short excerpts shaped the practices of many teachers for years and are still an important force in American education.

The intellect, character and skill possessed by any man is the product of certain original tendencies and the training which he has received. His eventual nature is the development of his original nature in the environment which it has had. Human nature in general is the result of the original nature of man, the laws of learning, and the forces of nature amongst which man lives and learns.

In a previous volume the original tendencies of man as a species were listed and described. It was shown that these constitute an enormous fund of *connections* or *bonds* of varying degrees of directness and strength between the *situations* furnished by physical forces, plants, animals and the behavior of other men and the *responses* of which the human creature is capable. Many of these tendencies are notably modifiable; and some of them—such as vocalization, manipulation, curiosity, "doing something to have something happen," and "making a variety of responses to an annoying state of affairs which continues in spite of this, that and the other responses"—are veritable hot-beds for the growth of learned habits.

From EDWARD L. THORNDIKE, *The Psychology of Learning, Educational Psychology,* II (Teachers College, Columbia University, 1913), 1–5, 54–56. Reprinted by permission of the publisher.
PROFESSOR THORNDIKE (1874–1949) was for over thirty-five years Professor of Educational Psychology at Teachers College, Columbia University. He served as president of the American Psychological Association in 1912.

These original human tendencies include also certain ones whereby modifiability or learning itself is possible. These are best thought of in the form of the three laws of Readiness, Exercise and Effect. The Law of Readiness is: When any conduction unit is in readiness to conduct, for it to do so is satisfying. When any conduction unit is not in readiness to conduct, for it to conduct is annoying. When any conduction unit is in readiness to conduct, for it *not* to do so is annoying. By a satisfying state of affairs is meant one which the animal does nothing to avoid, often doing things which maintain or renew it. By an annoying state of affairs is meant one which the animal does nothing to preserve, often doing things which put an end to it.

The Law of Exercise comprises the laws of *Use* and *Disuse*.

The Law of Use is: When a modifiable connection is made [1] between a situation and a response, that connection's strength is, other things being equal, increased. By the strength of a connection is meant roughly the probability that the connection will be made when the situation recurs. Greater probability that a connection will be made means a greater probability for the same time, or an equal probability, but for a longer time.[2] This probability in any case would be for the recurrence of the connection, supposing all other conditions—of general health, general or special fatigue, interest, time of day, distraction by competing tendencies, and the like—to be equal. Furthermore, in certain cases, where the probability that the connection will be made as the result of the mere presence of the situation is zero, the connection still may exist with a measurable degree of strength, shown by the fact that it can be remade more readily.[3] Also, in certain cases in each of which the probability that the connection will be made is 100 per cent, the connections still may exist with different degrees of strength, shown by the fact that the probability of 100 per cent will hold for a week only or for a year; will succumb to a slight, or prevail over a great, distraction; or will otherwise show little or much strength. Thus, if the reader will read and repeat *miscob raltof* once or twice he may be apparently as able to supply the *raltof* when *miscob* is presented as if he had read and repeated these words a thousand times: but the future history of the two connections would reveal their differences in strength.

Ultimately degrees of strength of a connection in behavior will be defined as degrees of some anatomical or physiological fact whereby synapses between neurones differ in intimacy.

[1] The vigor and duration of each "making" of the connection count, as well as the number of times that it is made.
[2] Thus, a certain greater strength of the connection between the situation *"What is the square of 16?"* and the response *"256"* may mean that the probability of that response to that situation is now ninety out of a hundred instead of sixty out of a hundred; or that it is ninety-nine out of a hundred for fifty days hence instead of for twenty days hence.
[3] Thus, though a man was utterly unable to give the English equivalent of a hundred Greek words, both on January 1, 1905, and on January 1, 1910, he might have been able to relearn them in thirty minutes in 1905, but only in sixty minutes in 1910.

Varying symptoms that we now refer to the "strength" of a connection will then each appear as a consequence of this difference in the neurones concerned. For the present, greater strength has to mean either a greater percentage of occurrence under equal conditions outside of itself; or an equal percentage of occurrence for a longer time, or against greater competition; or a readier re-establishment to equal strength (tested in any of the above ways); or some even more subtle and indirect effects on behavior.

It should be borne in mind also that the connection is often a compound of several connections each having possibly a different degree of strength. Thus, the connection between the situation, *Understanding of and desire to fulfill the command, "Write that man's full name,"* and the response of writing *Jonathan Edwards Leighton* is multiple. One of the names may be remembered and the other not; the bond productive of the general structure of the name may be strong, but all the others very weak, with the result that *Timothy Williams Damon* is the best that can be done; similarly for many variations in complete-ness, spelling, and so on. The actual physiological bond in even the apparently most single connections is doubtless a compound, and subject to variation by varying unevenly in its different parts as well as by an equal strengthening or weakening of them all.

The Law of Disuse is: When a modifiable connection is *not* made between a situation and a response during a length of time, that connection's strength is decreased. The explanations and qualifications stated in connection with the Law of Use apply here also.

The Law of Effect is: When a modifiable connection between a situation and a response is made and is accompanied or followed by a satisfying state of affairs, that connection's strength is increased: When made and accompanied or fol-lowed by an annoying state of affairs, its strength is decreased. The strengthen-ing effect of satisfyingness (or the weakening effect of annoyingness) upon a bond varies with the closeness of the connection between it and the bond. This closeness or intimacy of association of the satisfying (or annoying) state of affairs with the bond in question may be the result of nearness in time or of at-tentiveness to the situation, response and satisfying event in question. "Strength" means the same here as in the case of the Law of Use.

These laws were briefly explained and illustrated in the previous volume. By their action original tendencies are strengthened, preserved, weakened, or alto-gether abolished; old situations have new responses bound to them and old responses are bound to new situations; and the inherited fund of instincts and capacities grows into a multitude of habits, interests and powers. They are the agents by which man acquires connections productive of behavior suitable to the environment in which he lives. *Adaptation, adjustment, regulative change,* and all other similar terms descriptive of successful learning, refer to their effects.

A man's intellect, character and skill is the sum of his tendencies to respond to situations and elements of situations. The number of different situation-response connections that make up this sum would, in an educated adult, run well up into the millions. Consequently, in place of any list of these detailed tendencies to make responses r_1, r_2, r_3, etc., to each particular situation, we may summarize the man in terms of broader traits or functions, such as "knowledge of German," "honesty," "speed in writing," "love of music," "memory for figures," "fidelity of visual images of faces," and the like.

In educational theories of human learning, and still more in the actual control of it by school practice, these larger traits or functions—these knowledges, powers, conducts, interests and skills—rather than the elementary connections and readinesses of which they are composed, are commonly the subjects of discussion and experiment. Psychological theory and experimentation have also been engaged with traits or functions each of which denotes a group of elementary tendencies, though the traits or functions or abilities which have been investigated by psychologists are usually narrower than those just listed. For example, amongst the functions which have been somewhat elaborately studied are "rapidity in tapping as with a telegraph key," "the delicacy of discrimination of pitch," "ability to grasp and retain a series of nonsense syllables," "skill in tossing balls," and "interest in puzzles."

Facts concerning the nature of such "traits" or "functions" or "abilities" and their improvement by practice have been accumulating very rapidly in the course of the last fifteen years. To present and interpret these facts is the second task of this volume, and the one to which the majority of its pages will be assigned.

· · · · ·

MENTAL FUNCTIONS

Learning is connecting, and man is the great learner primarily because he forms so many connections. The processes operating in a man of average capacity to learn, and under the conditions of modern civilized life, soon change the man into a wonderfully elaborate and intricate system of connections. There are millions of them. They include connections with subtle abstract elements or aspects or constituents of things and events, as well as with the concrete things and events themselves.

Any one thing or element has many different bonds, each in accordance with one of many "sets" or attitudes, which co-act with it to determine response. Besides the connections leading to actual conduction in neurones, there are those which lead to greater or less readiness to conduct, and so determine what shall satisfy or annoy in any given case.

The bonds productive of observable motor responses—such as speech, gesture, or locomotion—are soon outnumbered by those productive, directly and at the time, of only the inner, concealed responses in the neurones themselves to which what we call sensations, intellectual attention, images, ideas, judgments, and the like, are due. The bonds productive of motor responses also include a far richer equipment than we are accustomed to list. Man's life is chock-full of evanescent, partly made, and slurred movements. These appear in so-called "inner" speech, the tensions of eyes and throat in so-called intellectual attention, and the like.

The bonds lead not only from external situations—facts outside the man— to responses in him, and from situations in him to acts by which he changes outside nature, but also from one condition or fact or event in him to another and so on in long series. Of the connections to be studied in man's learning an enormous majority begin and end with some state of affairs within the man's own brain—are bonds between one mental fact and another.

The laws whereby these connections are made are significant for education and all other branches of human engineering. Learning is connecting; and teaching is the arrangement of situations which will lead to desirable bonds and make them satisfying. A volume could well be written showing in detail just what bonds certain exercises in arithmetic, spelling, German philosophy, and the like, certain customs and laws, certain moral and religious teachings, and certain occupations and amusements, tend to form in men of given original natures; or how certain desired bonds could economically be formed. Such would be one useful portion of an Applied Psychology of Learning or Science of Education.

The psychology of learning might also properly take as its task the explanation of how, starting from any exactly defined original nature, the bonds have been formed which cause the man in question to make such and such movements, attend to this rather than that feature of an object, have such and such ideas in response to a given problem, be satisfied with some of them and reject others, enjoy this picture, abstract numerical relations from a certain state of affairs, and so on through all the acquisitions which his life of learning comprises. Psychology might seek to list the bonds and elements of bonds which account for his habits, associations of ideas, abstractions, inferences, tastes and the rest, might measure the strength of each, discover their relations of facilitation and inhibition, trace their origins, and prophesy their future intrinsic careers and their effects in determining what new bonds or modifications of old bonds any given situation will form. As a geologist uses the laws of physics and chemistry to explain the modifications of the earth's surface, so a psychologist might use the laws of readiness, exercise, and effect to explain the modifications in a man's nature—in his knowledge, interests, habits, skill, and powers of thought or appreciation. This task is, however, one for the future.

The process of learning is one of simple making and keeping connections and readinesses to conduct, but the result is a mixture of organized and unorganized tendencies that, even in an average three-year-old child, baffles description and prophecy. No one has ever even listed the tendencies to respond of any one human creature above that age and of average capacity to learn, nor even begun to trace the history of their acquisition.

What psychology has done is to consider certain vaguely defined groups of tendencies, describing them roughly and observing how they change in certain important respects, notably in their efficiency in producing some desired result in living. The terms, *intellect, character, skill,* and *temperament,* thus more or less well separate off four great groups of connections in a man. Within the sphere of intellect, the terms, *information, habits, powers, interests* and *ideals,* go a step further in delimiting certain groups of connections. The terms, *ability to add, ability to read, interest in music, courage,* and *business honesty,* are samples of compound tendencies or groups of connections much narrower than those listed above, and cutting across them in many ways.

4 *Perception research and audio-visual education*

Related selections: 8, 9, 20

Research in perception has caused students in education to re-examine much of what they formerly believed not only in respect to use of audio-visual aids to learning but also in other aspects of learning. Although this article is chiefly concerned with the implications of perception studies for the use of audio-visual materials, it shows that perception is a governing factor in all learning. If one perceives even material objects in terms of his prior experiences, then how individualized must be his view of himself, of others, and of the complex situation in which he finds himself and others? The influence of the demonstrations described here and others like them has been felt in the development of personality theory.

Psychological research in the field of perception is obviously of great importance to the scientific development and use of visual materials in education. Visual

KENNETH NORBERG, "Perception Research and Audio-Visual Education," *Audio-Visual Communication Review*, I (Winter, 1953), 18–29. Reprinted by permission of the author and the publisher. Pictures and diagrams reprinted by permission of Franklin P. Kilpatrick, Institute for Associated Research, Princeton.

DR. NORBERG (1909–   ) is Professor of Education and Coordinator of Audio-Visual Services, Sacramento State College, California, and was formerly Director of the Audio-Visual Center, University of Chicago.

education rests upon the assumption that people learn from what they see, that visual experience influences behavior, and that instruction can be improved by enabling people to look at objects and pictures under appropriate circumstances, and in connection with other varieties of experience. We have experimental evidence to show that broadening the base of perceptual experience improves learning. Why this is so can perhaps be explained, crudely, although we are frequently inclined to take it for granted. But we still have much to learn before visual presentations can be used as precision tools in communication and teaching. In order to gain a better understanding of visual education we must first know what happens when we perceive.

Perhaps at no time in the past have psychologists shown greater and more wide-spread interest in the problem of perception. Much experimental work is going on, and along with it, much discussion of the theoretical issues involved. Various approaches and lines of development are represented. Experimental psychologists still support a constant line of interest in the physiological aspect of perception, but a recent and prominent trend seems to be toward an emphasis on a broader construction in which perception is viewed as an aspect of the total behavior of man in the course of purposeful action. One interesting and widely noted example of the broader approach to perception is the development centering in the work of the Hanover Institute and the well-known demonstrations which have grown out of the earlier experimentation of the Dartmouth Eye Institute. The Hanover Institute is located at Hanover, New Hampshire. Adelbert Ames, Jr., is the director.

It is the purpose of this article to discuss the Hanover Institute demonstrations in perception with regard to possible implications for audio-visual research. In this brief analysis we shall rely mainly on the reports and interpretative writings of a small cluster of men including Adelbert Ames, Jr., Hadley Cantril, Merle Lawrence, Earl C. Kelley, and Ross L. Mooney. These sources have been selected and used either because they were directly instrumental in the development of the demonstrations, or have been actively concerned in their interpretation and/or educational use.

Because the Hanover Institute experiments have already been widely reported there will be no attempt to present a comprehensive description here. Instead, we shall describe very briefly a few representative demonstrations, mainly for purposes of orientation, and then proceed to the interpretation.

THE "CHAIR" DEMONSTRATION

The subject looks through a peep-hole in each of three different screens, "A," "B," and "C." Behind each of the screens he sees a chair, or what appears to be one. It is noted that behind each of the three screens the observer sees an upright chair at a specific distance, of a specific size, three-dimensional in form, with legs parallel and at right angles to the seat. Now, if the observer looks behind screen "A" he will find strings arranged to give an outline of a chair. Behind screen "B" he will see a number of disconnected strings of different lengths and at different angles. Behind screen "C" he will see strings in a plane which constitutes a perspective projection of a chair-shaped object. What one sees if he looks behind each screen (what is "actually there") is quite different from what he sees as he looks through the several peep-holes. (Figure 1.)

Now, it should be noted that the Hanover Institute demonstrations are not merely experiments, in the usual sense. They are actually demonstrations designed to bring out facts of perception, and to interpret and relate these facts in a gradually developing theoretical structure. In the case of each demonstration an interpretation is offered, and the interpretations of the several demonstrations are fitted together in the cumulative development and elaboration of a theory of the nature of perception.

In the case of the "chair" demonstration the interpretations offered in the manuals and other writings connected with the Hanover Institute point out that the characteristics and qualities of the "chair" behind each of the three screens are obviously not in the object, itself, i.e., the arrangement of strings. The same stimulus pattern, or retinal image, may be produced by any one of an infinity of external conditions. Moreover, what is perceived, or seen, is not determined by the physiological stimulus pattern. Two conclusions are drawn: (a) The characteristics and qualities of things seen cannot be derived from the immediate outside world. (b) They cannot be derived from immediate physiological stimulus patterns. "This means, then, that the explanation of the nature of sensations must be looked for in the prior events that are related to the immediate events."

THE STAR-POINT DEMONSTRATIONS

In a completely dark room two star-points are viewed from a stationary position. These illuminated points are the same distance from the observer. One point is

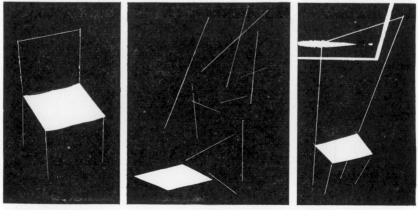

A   **B**   **C**

Figure 1

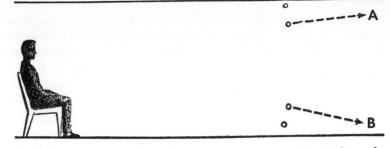

Figure 2   Although the star-points are actually equidistant from the observer, assumption from past experience causes A and B to appear more distant.

brighter. It appears to be nearer. The interpretation is that under these conditions the observer "assumes" the star-points to be identical and interprets the difference in brightness as a difference in distance from him.

In another demonstration the observer looks down (at an angle) at two star-points of equal brightness, one vertically above the other. The observer senses the upper point as farther away. If the situation is reversed so that the observer looks up at two points, the lower point will appear farther away. "The apparent explanation of this phenomenon is that when we look down there is a probability that objects in the upper part of the field are farther away than objects in the lower part. When we look up, the opposite is true." (Figure 2.)

DEMONSTRATION WITH LINES

In a darkened room two vertical lines of different length, at the same distance from the observer, appear as though the shorter line were farther away, if the lines are positioned so that their middle points are on a level, B, Figure 3. However, if the shorter line is arranged below the longer one, it will appear closer, A, Figure 3. "The apparent explanation of this phenomenon is that in the first relationship there is a greater probability that the two lines might represent identical things, e.g., telegraph poles, than in the second relationship where the longer line might represent a telephone pole and the shorter line a fence post."

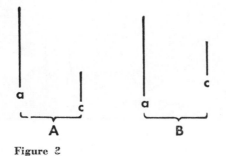

Figure 2

Now, if we repeat the first demonstration of the lines with the middle points on a common level, and give the observer a stick with a light on the end of it, directing him to touch the lines (first the shorter and then the longer) the following will result: the observer, after touching the shorter line with the end of the stick, will at first fail to touch the longer line. After some experimental trying he will be able to touch the longer line, also. But by this time the two lines will appear to be at the same distance from him.

THE DISTORTED ROOM DEMONSTRATION

A distorted room is so designed that when it is viewed with one eye through a hole at a certain position in a screen the room appears rectangular and normal. (Even if the observer has already looked behind the screen and knows the room is distorted, it will still look like an ordinary room when he views it with one eye, through the screen.) (Figure 4.)

Now, if the observer takes a stick and tries to touch a ball in the upper left hand corner of the room after touching a ball in the upper right hand corner, he will be unable to do it, at first. After repeated tries he may become fairly successful in touching both balls. As this occurs *the appearance of the room will change.*

GENERAL INTERPRETATION
OF THE DEMONSTRATIONS

Many of the Hanover Institute demonstrations have not been mentioned here. However, with this very brief introduction to the demonstrations we may now examine some of the main hypotheses which have been advanced in explanation.

1. What is perceived is not determined by objective or environmental conditions, in their own right.

2. What is perceived is not determined by the physiological stimulus pattern.

3. *Given objective conditions and associated retinal stimulation, the observer perceives whatever represents, for him, the most likely prognosis for action based upon his experience.* This prognosis is not a deliberate judgment or consciously formed hypothesis. Neither is it an arbitrary or capricious fantasy without any necessary connection to what is "there." But it is definitely something the perceiver makes for himself out of his past experience and the present circumstances. "The nature of what is experienced is not a true portrayal of the existing physical environment; it is only a 'guess' based upon all the previous experience the observer has had with the impingements he has confronted."

4. What the observer brings to any particular occasion by way of his perceptions reflects an "assumptive form world" built up out of his past experiences. This "assumptive form world" is modified as the prognoses or predictions which we call perceptions are acted upon, and thereby tested.

5. To understand perception we must look upon human behavior as a "trans-

Figure 4A

action" in which neither the individual nor the environment is regarded as an independent entity merely affecting or conditioning the other.

The functional character of perception which is brought out in the preceding statements is emphasized in the following definition of perception given by Cantril:

> On the basis of the demonstrations, not to mention everyday life observations, we may define a perception as an implicit awareness of the probable consequences an action might have for us with respect to carrying out some purpose that might have value for us. Perceptions are conceived and given birth to in purposeful action that results from value-judgments. And for whatever reason a perception may return to consciousness, it has in it implicitly the factors of action, purpose, and awareness of value.

Thus, at some risk of over-simplification we might sum up by saying that the theory of perception developed in connection with the Hanover Institute demonstrations insists first of all that perceiving be considered always in the context of purposeful behavior, and that the question "What is perceived?" must be answered as a directive for action reflecting some set of assumptions as to what will happen if such and such actions are carried out. Our perceivings are not merely guides for actions, or invitations; they are essentially phases of purposeful action, itself. They have various degrees of reliability, but they are never direct copies of some "reality" which is merely and independently "there." Hence, they are essentially dynamic attitudes in constant change.

Figure 4B

SOME POSSIBLE IMPLICATIONS

What are the implications of the Hanover Institute demonstrations for audio-visual education? This is a difficult question, and we will only attempt to suggest a partial answer. Perhaps the best answer, at this time, is to indicate some questions that seem to arise out of the Hanover Institute demonstrations and the associated theoretical development.

1. *Can we actually learn anything from visual presentations as such?* In the demonstration of the distorted room it has been noted that the observer can never get to see the room in its "true" shape just by looking at it. Merely looking, from a constant position, changes nothing—results in no change in perception, no learning. It is only when the observer changes his position of observation, looks behind the screen, or attempts to manipulate objects inside the room that some learning (involving change in perception) results. In more general terms, this would seem to mean that we do not learn by merely seeing, but in the action, or course of action, in which seeing is involved. (It should be added that this would not rule out learning *at the time* of visual presentation, nor the possibility that an appropriate visual cue might be critical to the carrying out of some action, or course of action, from which learning occurs).

Of course, if the generalization just given follows from the demonstration of the distorted room, we would have to inquire what happens when something more than a single static perception is involved. True, nothing can be learned if we continue to stare at the room from a fixed perspective; we must actively explore the situation to gain new understanding. But what if we substitute for direct and active exploration a series of still pictures taken from different points of view? In this case behavior is still limited to merely "seeing" but it is apparent that some learning—some progressive change in understanding—might occur anyway. This is not difficult to explain, nor does it seem to contradict our generalization that merely looking at something does not constitute a learning experience. Would it be appropriate to say that we learn from a "look" at something only when this "look" stands in a *series* of experiences linked together in a course of purposeful action? This would take into account the fact that perception, itself, is a form of action, and that experiences that are primarily, or merely, visual, may (and very frequently do) assume critical value in carrying forward a line of purposeful action which results in learning. To say that learning may result from a visual presentation, as such, seems consistent with the Hanover Institute demonstrations *if* we include the presentation in question in a time-series of other experiences (not necessarily or exclusively visual), in which case we assign the learning effect to the series, primarily, and to the specific visual presentation only in so far as it represents a genuine link or culmination of that series.

2. *Is perception a cause of learning, or a dimension of the learning process?* This question is really a corollary to the first question. The Hanover Institute demonstrations bear out the thesis that our perceptions are learned. They are *results* of past experiences and present concerns. This, of course, does not rule out perception as a causal factor in learning, but it does suggest that we should not think of perception *merely* as cause, *nor* merely as a result of learning. The Hanover Institute demonstrations help to remind us that learning occurs in the course of purposeful action, involving the full range of behavior, over time.

It is probably more accurate and more fruitful to think of perception as an aspect or as a *dimension* of the learning process than merely as a "cause." A simple example may help to illustrate the point. Every child learns in due course of time that certain objects are dogs. This ordinary learning process involves a series of experiences during which certain sensory-motor, lingual, emotional, and other responses are developed. During the same series of experiences the child learns to perceive and to deal with certain external events as dogs. The child does not first perceive dogs and then learn to deal with dogs, or talk about them, although he may have crude perceptions of moving things, or animals-of-some-sort, prior to perceptions of dogs in a full and meaningful sense. The development of the perception is actually concurrent with the development of the interrelated motor habits, emotions, thinking, and talking that adds up to the "dog" behavior of the child. It is evident that children would not learn about dogs without sensory contacts with this animal. But what is more important is that there must be a *continuity* of perceptional experiences over time, during which there is constant interplay of sensory experience with the full range of other factors or "levels" of experience.

The implications for audio-visual research and theoretical development should be obvious.

3. *Are our visual perceptions of things more concrete than words?* Our "common sense" tells us our perceptions, including presentations of objects and events, come closer to the "concrete" than words. The Hanover Institute demonstrations seem to throw some doubt on this assumption. (Actually, a simple logical analysis reveals that words, *in general*, can hardly be regarded as less concrete than visual perceptions *in general*.) The theory growing out of the Hanover Institute demonstrations holds that every perception is a kind of summing up, a "weighted average," of the meanings of a vast number of particular sensory impingements, or stimulus-patterns, so that what we perceive at any given moment is not just a "concrete" object, in the sense of an independently existing thing, "out there," but a meaning which we derive from the past as appropriate to the present situation. In this sense, every perception is a kind of abstraction: a *pulling out* from the available fund of past experiences (the "assumptive form world") the "weighted average" meaning which represents the present "hypothesis" for action.

Now if perception is regarded in this way, it would appear that the differences between perceptions and words, as viewed by "common sense," should be reconsidered. Ross L. Mooney has commented on this problem as follows:

> We are quite likely to assume that words and perceptions are two quite different sorts of things. However, it becomes quite clear, when we stop to think about it, that words and perceptions are the same kind of phenomena. Indeed, words are perceptions.
>
> When we hear a spoken word, our ears are receiving sound waves; when we see a written word, our eyes are receiving light rays. As children, we come to know the "meaning" of a spoken word with the same operations we use to come to know the "meaning" of a squeaking door, a barking dog, or a clap of thunder. Similarly, we come to know the "meaning" of a written word with the same operations we use to come to know the "meaning" of a red ball, a square room, or a moving human figure.

This seems to outline a significant attitude to be taken into account by audio-visual specialists and research workers when dealing with the differences between visual and verbal methods of presentation. If words and perceptions are regarded as the same kind of psychological phenomena, it would follow that we must be careful in making any general assumptions about their relative abstractness or concreteness. It may be that all perceptions, including those we call "words," involve abstraction. Also, it may be that certain levels or kinds of abstractions necessarily involve lingual expression. But it seems overly crude, and possibly misleading, to generalize that perceptions (in the limited sense) are necessarily "concrete" as opposed to words. This is a highly complex problem which cannot be discussed in the limited space available here. However, it might be noted that so long as perceptions are regarded as yielding only prognoses for action they can hardly be regarded as providing the ultimate grasp which is considered to be the concrete object. In this sense, the concrete always lies one step beyond perception. It is not the object of present perception, and can be realized only by reconstruction of some event that has already occurred in the past.

4. *What are some of the larger implications of the Hanover Institute demonstrations?* One of the most striking features of the theoretical discussion growing out of the work of the Hanover Institute is the emphasis on wider application of the principles (hypotheses) revealed by the demonstrations. It is clear that those who have been associated with the Hanover demonstrations think of perception in very broad terms, and feel that the implications of the experiments cannot be limited to some range of experience regarded as merely or purely sensory in character. Cantril, for instance, points out that our social perceptions are governed by certain requirements brought out in the demonstrations, and his whole discussion of social perceptions in *The Why of Man's Experience* seems to reflect the assumption that the attitudes involved in social behavior can be interpreted along lines suggested by the demonstrations. The same general approach is observed in Earl C. Kelley's book, *Education for What Is Real*, which deals specifically with the educational implications of the Hanover Institute demonstrations. The more general implications of the demonstrations are also mentioned by John Dewey in the foreword to Kelley's book.

> . . . There has been developed an experimental demonstration of the principles which govern the development of perceiving, principles which are formed, moreover, to operate more deeply in the basic growth of human beings in their distinctive human capacity than any which have been previously laid bare.

Thus we are reminded that perception, in this general framework of interpretation, cuts across the entire range of human behavior including the social and the symbolic, that the story of our developing perceptions is also the story of learning. We are reminded that perception is never merely an appeal to the senses, while at the same time the effective engagement of the learner in lines of continuous action, by which his perceptions are changed and enriched, calls for an optimum level of carefully selected sensory contacts with whatever is pertinent to his developing purposes and interests.

The implications for audio-visual research and practice should not be too obscure. These seem to be some of them: We cannot say what an individual will learn from any discrete visual presentation, as such, and aside from a context of other experiences, in time. Learning results from a *series* of purposeful acts carried out with continuity of purpose and direction. All action is not overt or "physical," but to maintain and carry forward a line of purposeful action, in time, requires adequate conditions of sensory contact with the environment. We learn *from* visual presentations in so far as they make it possible, or easier, for us to carry out our purposes. As we learn *from* perceptions, and *to* new ways of perceiving things, our "assumptive form world" changes and this involves the most complex organizations of our behavior including social attitudes and conceptions.

We cannot learn without acting. We cannot act without perceiving.

5 The idea of learning as development of insight

Related selections: 1, 8, 9, 65, 67

The following article by Bayles is selected from a number of articles that have centered their attention on the study of insight in learning situations and have concluded that the development of insight is the major factor in learning. Is Bayles's position adequate for all kinds of learning? Is he in conflict with those who believe strongly in programed learning methods? Compare this selection with selections 65 and 67.

Theory regarding the nature of learning lies close to the heart of teaching theory. Lack of clarity regarding the former, whether in high degree or low, leads to corresponding lack of clarity regarding the latter. This is not to say that learning theory is the whole of teaching theory; far from it. Theory regarding social organization and theory regarding the nature of subject matter are equally essential. But, with the confusion which still surrounds current professional thinking regarding the nature of learning, further discussion of the question seems much in order.

Lack of clarity of the bond theory—of psychological connectionism—was brought home to me early in the twenties. As a supervisor of practice teachers, I was supposed to help beginners achieve competence in handling the learning process. But connectionist principles always pointed to wrong procedures.

Repetitive drill was obviously wrong. Yet the path-wearing, bond-forming principle of conditioning, leading to supposedly lowered synaptic resistance

ERNEST E. BAYLES, "The Idea of Learning as Development of Insight," *Educational Theory*, II (April, 1952), 65–71. Reprinted by permission of the author and the publisher.

DR. BAYLES (1896–   ) is Professor of Education at the University of Kansas. He has written widely in the field of education and is the author of several basic texts in high school science.

along preferred neural pathways, pointed inexorably to that. Both the logic of the theory and the nature of teaching materials available at the time led inevitably to repetitive drill.

Then Gestalt theory, and relativism as a clear-cut psychological principle, began to present themselves for consideration. Threads of clarity began to penetrate the confusion in thought, and order began to emerge. The books of Koffka, Koehler, and Wheeler appeared; then Bode's penetrating *Conflicting Psychologies of Learning*. Afterwards, Thorndike reported that, on the basis of his research findings, repetition (*per se*) has little, if any, effect on learning and, although making no attempt to define the term, proposed the concept of "belongingness."

Looking at the matter through mid-twentieth century eyes, individuals appear to behave on the basis of the principle of least action; *to act in such a way as to try to achieve an adopted pattern of goals in the quickest and easiest way that they sense or comprehend as available under existing circumstances.* In other words, we seem to be inherently lazy; to seek always the easiest way to get done what appears necessary or desirable. Laziness seems no longer to be intrinsically vicious. It seems merely the wise thing to do something the easy instead of the hard way. If we see an acquaintance taking a long way home, we are likely to suspect either his motives or his judgment.

INSIGHT AND THE PRINCIPLE
OF LEAST ACTION

Reliance upon the principle of least action in the interpretation of behavior means that we base it upon three factors: *goal,* or what a person wants or intends to do; *confronting situation,* or what he will meet in proceeding to attain the goal; and *insight,* the way he sees or sizes up the situation with which he is confronted. You will note that we do not say the quickest and easiest way available; we say the quickest and easiest way which is sensed or comprehended *as* available. We do not take paths that we know nothing about.

What does this interpretation of behavior mean for learning? Learning is repeatedly defined as a change in behavior. And, when a person learns, he indeed undergoes a change in behavior. He is likely to act quite differently from before. But does every behavioral change mean learning?

A change in action or behavior will accompany a change in goal, even though no learning may have occurred. Likewise, a change in behavior will accompany a change in confronting situation, even though no learning may have occurred. Evidently, and this seems to be amply supported by experimental and experiential evidence though as yet not so recognized in psychological literature, learning represents and is confined to *a change in insight.*

The view that learning means development of insight, and that alone, is decidedly revolutionary. Very few textbooks in educational psychology yet take this stand in a clear-cut way. However, comparison of today's texts with those of a quarter-century ago or even a decade ago shows that they are coming to it. About the last step in the transition is to argue that, although conditioning may be the way in some learning situations, that kind occurs very rarely, if at all, in school work. Let us examine the idea of learning as development of insight.

THE MEANING OF "INSIGHT"

First, what do we mean by the term insight? We do not mean any linguistic expression. We refer to what lies back of any word statement; to that which one catches even before he has words to express it, such as the swing of a ball bat or an idea for which one cannot quite find the right word. Perhaps insight should be defined as *a sense of, or feeling for, pattern*. We may have words for it or we may not; it may be clear or it may be more or less confused; it may be true or it may be false, fruitful or unfruitful. It is on the basis of what we see as being required by a situation that we design behavior. That is what, for us, constitutes reality; the real basis upon which we act in any and every case of intelligent behavior.

How does learning as development of insight differ from the notion of learning as establishment or alteration of neural pathways? To wear a path requires continuous traversal of an area by way of a given line, without deviation. That is the precise meaning, neurologically speaking, of the so-called Law of Use. Through use, resistance across a given synapse is lowered and impulses cross it more easily afterwards. This point is vital to the path-wearing idea of conditioning, regardless of whether a commitment is hazarded as to the nature of the resistance. It was neural paths of this kind which Lashley sought and failed to find. Repeating a line of action always the same way until it is "stamped-in" is what the concept has to mean if it means anything. Repetitive drill is another word for it.

On the other hand, development of insight means establishment of a sense of, or feeling for, pattern. It may require looking sharply into a confronting situation, but imaginatively, in order to make the pattern "jump out at you," as when we used to look for hidden faces in a cleverly designed drawing or for stage animals in fleecy clouds. Or it may require closing the eyes and trying intently to visualize a situation, possibly not yet fully observed. Then, catching the point, we act with precision and exactitude. It is less of learning by doing and more of learning by seeing, even though with the mind's eye. Emphasis, in the process of learning, shifts from going through motions to conceptualization.

In working on a difficult violin passage, a learner needs first to study the passage, figure out fingering which will lie best for the hand, imagine the "feel" of the passage as a whole; then swing into execution. Repeatedly have I had music teachers report to me with amazement the results of tryouts of this kind on the parts of their students. It was an attack different from any used before, and the "hang" of it came with a rush that they had never before witnessed.

A workman has to get the "heft" of an object before proceeding to move it. A batsman gets the feel of his bat before advancing to the plate and a golfer the swing of his club before stepping up to the tee. A child, approaching the multiplication process, needs to "get the sense of the matter" before any attention whatsoever is given to speed in producing answers for particular combinations. The thought line probably needs to go from addition to multiplication; first see multiplication as a form of addition. If you add five fours together, how many will you have? Therefore, five fours make what? Or, five times four equals what? Take it easy; not this fast. Let each step "sink in" before taking the next. Insights do not form at the word, "Go!" although when they do form they practically always come suddenly. James employed the phrase, "flyings and perchings."

THE PLACE OF PRACTICE

But, I am asked, shall we dispense with practice? The answer is, of course, that we shall not. Because practice is to be something other than repetitive stamping-in, does not mean no practice. From the point of view of learning as development of insight, the repeated efforts of practice represent each time doing the thing differently from the way it was done before. Try it; see what happens; try to diagnose why it did not turn out as intended; modify procedure in light of the diagnosis; try it again. Each trial is distinctly different from the previous ones; a step in a search for the best way to do a thing. Once that best way is caught—done with a realization of *why* the doing achieved the desired end— then the matter may be permitted to rest for a while. Come back to it some time later—a day, two days, a week, or more—just to see whether it still goes right. If the point was really caught, later performances are very likely to be even better than that or those at the time of arrival of insight. If not, it is probable that the point was not really caught when it was thought to be.

It is not how many times a thing is done that counts. It is the grasp the learner has of it that makes the difference. And this "grasp" is very much of a mental phenomenon, whether the subject is basketball, woodwork, appreciation of an art object, or mastery of a proposition in mathematics or science. Once one "gets the hang of a thing," the feel for pattern, one does not have to repeat and repeat and repeat in order to make perfect. There may, of course, be much else yet to be learned; more work to do. But that should be analyzed in terms of the additional insights to be gained, and each subsequent insight attacked in the way just indicated. We need to get completely away from repetitive drill. The present writer feels thoroughly justified in insisting that, *whenever repetitive drill is invoked, learning will suffer.*

Practice, which represents a search for insight, means persistently working with something new. In spelling, for example, the policy of working on a particular list of words until all of the words are known is to be almost, if not completely, abandoned. Instead, particular words are always to be approached as typifying a certain spelling pattern, the pattern being what is sought rather than a word for its own sake. In the earlier stages, word-lists need to be chosen on the basis of spelling patterns which they exemplify. Study will then represent a search for the hidden pattern and, once discovered, other words will be sought which also conform. Later, words will be sought which seemingly should conform to the pattern, but do not. These, then, should be studied to see wherein they are divergent, to find why if possible, and to see whether the divergence is typical of other words as well. If so, a statement of the divergence and something of when to expect it may possibly be incorporated in the original rule; e.g., *i* before *e* except after *c*, etc.

It will be noted that this represents a return to spelling rules, a practice abandoned during the teens. It may well be that the abandonment worked to the detriment of instruction in spelling but, be that as it may, it should also be noted that there is a vital difference between former practice and the one here contemplated. Formerly, the rule was learned more or less by rote. Then the following list of words supposedly exemplifying the rule was learned, also more or less by rote. Many were the pupils who failed to note the connection between the rule and the words which followed. We propose that the words come first and that whatever rule is adopted be one worked out by the students and held only so long as it performs in a fairly satisfactory manner. When, as vocabulary expands, an adopted rule becomes unsatisfactory, a new study is inaugurated and a new rule formulated. And it must be remembered that, although we speak of "rules," we are really meaning basic insights, as previously defined.

It is true, of course, that the English language is bothersomely non-phonetic. But this is far from completely so, in spite of what many so-called experts used to insist. It is likely that at least 95 percent of words likely to be used can be handled in the above manner. If the rest must be learned by rote, so be it; but even then a sound-pattern or a visual pattern can be sought. It will be much better to learn only five percent by rote, if that be necessary, than to learn all in that manner.

We have dealt with spelling for what it typifies rather than for its own sake. Study is focused upon "getting the idea," particular cases merely serving as a vehicle by way of which an insight is gained. Once a child catches the phonetic signification of "at," he can handle "at" words whether he has met them before or not. The kind of spelling instruction inaugurated under the aegis of connectionism took a child's attention completely away from sound-letter relationships. If they were to be discovered at all, it had to be done by a child entirely on his own, in spite of his instruction rather than because of it. Small wonder we turned out a generation of poor spellers.

And here we may well inject a point of theory with reference to transfer of training. Our suggestion is that an individual will transfer previous training (insights gained) if and whenever he sees a confronting situation as presenting an opportunity for transfer, and if his purposes at the time make the transfer appear to him desirable. Thus, again, it is not how many times a thing is done that counts. We re-employ an insight whenever we discover an opportunity and are disposed to take advantage of it. Training will not transfer, even though opportunity offers, if the individual does not recognize it as an opportunity, or if indisposed to take advantage of the opportunity when recognized. Therefore, training for transfer requires, first, development of widely generalizable insights. But it requires considerably more than that. It also requires fertility of imagination, in order to wrest old learnings out of the limbo of forgotten things and see them as again useable. And it requires a set of suitable dispositions (or goals), one being the disposition to search one's memory—to be self-reliant and resourceful—when confronted with a situation seemingly new.

BELONGINGNESS AND REPETITION

Early in this paper we mentioned Thorndike's concept of *belongingness*. His proposal, early in the thirties, was that belongingness must accompany repetition; by itself, repetition has little if any effect. But what is belongingness? Thorndike did not say. That it can, and should, mean insight as we are using the term seems highly reasonable. It may, in fact, seem so reasonable or obvious that we may be thought by many as hypercritical to say or imply that its original user should have defined it. Yet here is a case which shows exactly why words need to be defined with operational clarity.

Thorndike's *operations* with reference to learning, even after his admission of belongingness, continued to include repetition—repetition in the path-wearing sense. In fact, it was *repetition with belongingness;* repetition came first, belongingness was an adjunct. Thus, the S-R,* reflex-arc principle remained intact, and connectionism remained in force.

It is exactly at this point that the insight theory parts company with connectionism, even though belongingness may be included. *Insights may be gained without repetition,* and when they do no repetition is needed. How many of us, who have sufficient insight to refuse to jump from a 50-foot height, gained that insight by even a single repetition? It may be true that we learned it from lesser jumps, but the learning was by transfer nonetheless. Moreover, this is not an isolated case. It is typical of the bulk of human activity. It represents the heart of habit-level action. Whenever a confronting situation, and its meaning in terms of desirable action, occur simultaneously in experience, correct action is possible the first time; even though the action may not be taken. If there is any validity to the truism that life is forever new—that no line of action is ever exactly twice the same—then we are continually having to act correctly the first time or be hopelessly incompetent. This is the point of R. H. Wheeler's repeated assertion that any psychology which fails to explain correct action the first time fails to explain human behavior at all.

There are many times, of course, when a situation and its meaning do not

* Stimulus-response.

occur simultaneously in experience. This is a problem-case and reflective thought is in order. Or the anticipated meaning of a situation—the line of action first considered as appropriate thereto—does not turn out as anticipated. Then an alternative has to be sought. But the procedure in each case is much more accurately described by Dewey's "complete act of thought" than by Thorndike's "trial and error" process as Thorndike originally described it. Dewey's description was of a search for insight; Thorndike's was of gradual stamping-in of a correct line of action through chance repetition of chance acts which later proved to be the right ones.

PROOF OF THE THEORY

Finally, we shall probably be asked what proof we have of the correctness of the insight theory of learning. Our answer is fairly simple. We rely upon the operational test. We deduce from the generalized theory the observable facts which, in given or particularized cases, the theory logically implies. *In the degree to which* the facts turn out as anticipated or deduced, the theory is taken as proven; proven in the sense of being demonstrated as dependable. Any theory which weathers this test better than competing theories is taken to be the better or best of those under consideration.

That the insight theory of learning has, so far, weathered this test is, I believe, a reasonable statement. Whenever, in connection with studies which have been made, sharp and precise deductions disclose the possibility of experimentally or experientially observable differences, the findings have consistently been such as to favor overwhelmingly the insight theory. It seems that the more painstaking or meticulous the analysis, the more convincing is the showing.

In summary, then, it seems that, if teaching is to be most effectual, the learning theory which should be employed is that which seeks consistently to develop insight. Procedural emphasis shifts from repetition to conceptualization, from learning by doing to learning by "seeing." Learning is not a function of the number of times an act is repeated. It is the feeling for pattern which is caught during a performance—the insight gained—that counts. Ten performances may have no effect and the eleventh one turn the trick. A teacher needs to look always for the "Oh! I see!" response in whatever form it may become manifest. And it often comes after rehearsal periods are over; during a time of no performance at all. Many a time, of course, a learner or his teacher may feel that he has it when indeed he does not. But this merely indicates a need for caution against unjustified optimism. It does not deny the principle. Learning as development of insight does not mean elimination of practice, although over-all reduction of practice time—often marked reduction—may reasonably be universally expected if repetitional procedures have previously been employed. Learning as development of insight does mean that repetitive drill shall be eliminated completely; that it shall be no more.

6 Are theories of learning helpful?

Related selections: 1, 7, 45, 53

Recently there have been numerous objections to the belief that learning theory is the major contribution of psychology to education. Teachers and students in education have maintained that because of the confusion and conflicts in learning theory, they have found it of little help in understanding how to organize a teaching-learning situation. As a result, much of our classroom method is based upon a trial-and-error technique. This article points up the task of educational psychology in selecting from all fields those data relevant to schooling.

There has been concern about learning "since the memory of man runneth not to the contrary." The volume of theories has filled many volumes of books, and shows no indication of losing momentum. After centuries of thought and millions of words, nobody really knows the nature of the learning process. Theories follow theories; contradicting, replacing, modifying, ignoring, supplementing or re-verbalizing their predecessors. Students in the field become protagonists, presenting statements that describe the phenomenon without actually explaining causes and effects. Even the best friends of these theorists are showing signs of worry. In 1948, Ernest R. Hilgard [5] closed his excellent "Theories of Learning" with these words, "The erroneous impression may be left that little is known about learning. The factual knowledge does in reality bulk large. . . . It is the consistent ordering of this voluminous material into a compact and agreed-upon systematic structure which is lacking. . . . The time is ripe for a concerted attack upon the major points of disagreement within facts and theories. The next twenty years may well lead to a clearing of issues. . . ." Six years have passed, but this hope is not being realized. It may not be feasible to attempt an attack on the learning problem along the same lines as the present studies in cancer research; but it may be time to declare a moratorium on theories and to devote more energy to experimentation, as well as to correlation of data.

It was quite logical for the early students to concern themselves with problems of *individual* learning. The person who acquires, modifies, retains and forgets

SAMUEL A. KRAMER, "Are Theories of Learning Helpful?" *Educational Forum*, XIX (January, 1955), 227–35. Reprinted by permission of Kappa Delta Pi, copyright owners.

DR. KRAMER (1906–   ) is Educationalist, Office of Higher Education, U. S. Department of Health, Education, and Welfare, Washington, D.C.

concepts is the basic unit to be studied. Since this is so obvious, the questions of learning that relate to a member of a group were overlooked until very recent years. Most psychologists and educators simply accepted the "fact" that all learning is alike, and the same laws must apply to a child in a slum area, an ape, a Comanche Indian, a laboratory rat or a research scientist. Yet, there has never been any doubt about learning differences, quantitatively and qualitatively, under varying social conditions. In 1919, Floyd H. Allport experimented with groups of upper classmen and graduate students at Harvard and Radcliffe, and found marked differences between "working alone" and "working in groups." [1] The psychologists of that period and later years completely ignored the implications of such experiments. In what, then, were these learning theories absorbed? Mainly, the answer is "Thorndike."

Although it was not the first important proposition, being preceded by the concepts of mental states and formal discipline, Thorndike's association theory is notable for its powerful and lasting impact on educational practices and related social phenomena. From 1898 to the present time, the S-R bond has been considered an integral factor in learning, as clearly a part of any animal as the digestive system. It is a peculiar but easily observable phenomenon that educators who give lip service to Gestalt and other field psychologies, write and use "How To Study" manuals that emphasize the concepts (without the language) of Thorndike's laws of readiness, exercise and effect. Further, they adopt wholeheartedly his six aids to improvement in learning: interest in the work, interest in improvement, significance of the problem, problem-attitude, attentiveness and the absence of irrelevant emotion and worry. They may now be called concentration, organization, memory, health, motivation, recreation, social adjustments and absence of personal problems; but this does not change them. Possibly there is no quarrel with this as a practical procedure, but it must be admitted that it stems directly from the educational psychology of Thorndike. His law of effect seems to have been most eagerly accepted, and to have left a lasting heritage in the form of punishments, promotions, school marks, substantive rewards and other incentive devices.

Thorndike was almost a messiah. Other doctrines developed in psychology, but at best they merely evaded his work; and, more frequently, the new schools did little more than paraphrase his findings. Until 1926, no one had the temerity to make a point-by-point refutation. Then was published "Aspects of Thorndike's Psychology in Their Relation to Educational Theory and Practice," by H. Gordon Hullfish.[7] His approach can be understood from this quotation. "How, then, can an intelligible answer be furnished to such questions as habit formation, interest, concept formation, the place of aims, and other kindred problems? The answer is necessarily colored by the underlying assumptions; and when these are not water-tight, the opinion advanced as a reply must remain questionable."

Hullfish pointed out that one important difficulty is Thorndike's vacillation between behaviorism and mentalism. On the one hand, he admits ideas, such as satisfaction, annoyance and readiness, just as the Herbartian school did. On the other hand, he insists that "Whatever exists at all exists in some amount. To know it thoroughly involves knowing its quantity as well as its quality." Hullfish comments, "There is no measure of patriotism, confusion or the concept 'dog'; there is, simply, a measurement of products of reactions to these stimulating conditions. . . . Thorndike's dictum reduces education to a proposition in physics, and those who accept the thesis must frankly admit that they are of the behavioristic school." This paper is not the place to go more deeply into the evaluative criticisms. One other interesting point denoting further inconsistencies may be quoted, however. "Tests of native ability and achievement, as actually employed, likewise lean towards the stimulus-response position. The expressed conviction that native ability is being measured connects quite naturally with the assumption that the body is the whole thing. This point of linkage, however, is not always evident . . . the assumption has been made that a certain something, quite unknown, has been measured; whereas, as the behaviorist puts it, all that has been measured is behavior. And since the tester proceeds on the basis of the S-R bond hypothesis, he has no ground for claiming that he has measured anything more than a particular response to a particular stimulus."

This definitive critique seemed to open the floodgates of attack, some direct and some circumlocutionary. Naturally, the true behaviorists were at the forefront. Now that the first well-aimed stone had been thrown, other hurlers promptly appeared. One of the first casualties in Thorndike's system was the law of exercise, when Edwin R. Guthrie [4] announced his theory concerning the relationship between stimulus and response. He started with an apparent restatement of Pavlov's conditioned reflex theory that any combination of stimuli accompanying a movement will on its recurrence tend to be followed by that movement. However, he soon reached the conclusion that, *"A stimulus pattern gains its full associative strength on the occasion of its first pairing with a response."* The italics are mine. Clearly he says that practice is a waste of time, although he hedges somewhat in the complete discarding of the value of repetitive action.

Closely following the lead of Clark L. Hull,[6] who developed a thorough and systematic presentation of behaviorism applied to learning theory, Miller and Dollard [13] have determined that there are just four factors in learning.

1. *Drive;* the strong stimulus which impels to action.
2. *Cue;* the determinant of when, where and how the response will be made, serving as a goal or signpost.
3. *Response;* the result of acceptance of a cue, so that a major task of training is so to arrange the situation that the desired response will occur.
4. *Reward;* which develops a tendency to repeat the desired response.

Transfer of training is recognized, on the ground that the more similarity there is between one stimulus and another, the more nearly it can substitute for the other in arousing conditioned responses.

One other point must be made about the behavioristic approach. Sometimes, when a situation seems to be inadequately explained, an entity is posited which, if it were not a heresy to say so, seems to be an atavism strongly pointing to mental states. B. F. Skinner, a "descriptive behaviorist," has contributed the concept of a "reflex reserve" from which operant or learned responses are emitted over a period of time. *He claims emissions can exhaust the reserve.*[14] It is not difficult to envision the army of ants emptying the warehouse of wheat when each ant takes one grain; but is this "reflex reserve" the same thing? There is no clarification of what constitutes this reserve, or where it is located. It actually seems like a "deus ex machina," which may be unusual for a behaviorist.

It must now be evident that behaviorism was not as wide a departure from Thorndike's theory of association as was claimed during the late twenties and early thirties. The S-R bonds remained unbroken as the basis of all learning, and human beings and other animals were considered as only placid receptors, reacting stolidly to the changes in environment. The most intelligent animal, therefore, was merely the one who had the highest number of receptors. Although Watson and his cultural offspring emphatically announced that they were creating a new school of thought based on "mechanism," the freshness was more obvious in the claimants than in the claim. The school did little more than present a re-emphasis of existing ideas. The concept of mental states had been effectively destroyed by Thorndike and Woodworth; and their propositions had been clearly exploded by Hullfish and others. A "coup de grace" from the behaviorists was unnecessary.

A few years before the advent of behaviorism in the United States, an entirely different approach to research in human and other animal behavior was being born in Germany. About 1910, Max Wertheimer developed the Gestalt theory which was later expanded into the school of field psychology. The significant feature of Gestaltism is the recognition that man acts with a purpose or motive and that, therefore, he develops an "insight" toward the solution of his problems. Wertheimer had an overwhelming conviction that even a complete knowledge of sensory elements and all possible combinations of these elements—numbering in the millions—must be inadequate to explain perception. The fact that he and his two assistants, W. Kohler and K. Koffka, used facts from the physical sciences as illustrations and analogies was necessary, but highly unfortunate. This mention of physical facts created misunderstanding of intent, definition and application, and presented opponents with ready-made arguments that delayed acceptance of basic principles. They started with visual sensations that were not in agreement with physical phenomena, such as "seeing" a continuous moving picture that is really a series of discrete elements. Obviously, the whole was *more* than the sum of its parts. Something new had been added. The physical scientists could describe the manifestation but could not explain it. The social scientists could observe it, but could neither describe it as a social phenomenon nor explain it by accepted psychologies. What made the discrete phenomena appear to flow together? [8]

Wertheimer clearly intended to present this case of a visual perception as a starting point or springboard for its application to psychology. However, he was not credited with this purpose, so that early scholars in the field became enmeshed in a consideration of Gestalt as a physical approach to the problem of learning.

The general viewpoint of Gestalt psychology is expressed in the statement that the laws of organization apply equally to perception and to learning. Since they have demonstrated that perception is based on past experience, their "trace theory" is significant. Its essential features are: (a) a trace is assumed to persist from a prior experience, so that it is part of the present; (b) the present process can select, reactivate or in some manner communicate with the trace; and (c) there is a resulting new process of recall or recognition.[9]

What happens when new traces are formed? The aggregate trace system resulting from repetition is constantly being transformed and preceding traces are disrupted. The value of repetition lies in the fact that the trace *systems* become consolidated even while the individual traces are being destroyed. Gestaltists refer to such consolidated trace systems as being increasingly available (much as what associationists call a habit system ready to function). They warn, however, that if this is overdone, the trace system becomes too available for one process and not available for another; as too much drill in a school subject may have a narrowing or "blinding" influence. These psychologists are not at all disturbed by the similarity to associationism, because the important distinguishing concept cannot possibly be ascribed to anyone but the Gestaltists. This is "insight," or the perception of a relationship which leads to the solution of a problem. Insight depends upon capacity, relevant previous experience, experimental arrangements to make all parts necessary to insight readily available, and finally a period of fumbling and search. Insightful solutions can be readily repeated and can be used in new situations. In memorization and retention, insight is more important than drill, this being the best alternative to trial-and-error.[10, 15]

SOCIAL PSYCHOLOGY ENTERS THE FIELD

Just as the Gestaltists created consternation among the individual psychologists by insisting that the whole is more than the sum of its parts, the social psychologists have caused a revolution by showing that the individualists are not moving forward and, probably, have been causing harm. Most expressive of this attitude is that of Solomon E. Asch, professor of psychology at Swarthmore College, who remarks on page 24 of his "Social Psychology," [2] "Modern psychology has often drawn, I suspect, a caricature rather than a portrait of man. As a result it has introduced a grave gap between itself and the knowledge of men that observation gives us and from which investigation must start." Nor is social psychology free from suspicion. As a relatively new system, it has leaned heavily toward acceptance of ideas from other sciences and popular beliefs, and has not yet fully adopted a cautious and experimental approach. However, the great value lies in its examination of the human element in social affairs, of studying man among men as something different from an ape among apes or an ape among men. In the field of learning, social psychology is *testing* the theories that have heretofore been blindly accepted or only theoretically adopted.

In his presidential address in 1950, W. J. Brogden said this to the Division of Experimental Psychology. "The advancement of knowledge in other areas of psychology depends upon the advancement of our understanding of learning. General laws of learning, then, are the goal. Although laws in the last analysis have their origin in experimental results, theory development can assist materially in such progression. A theory may organize the results of many researches, it may bring new relations to light, or it may serve as a catalyst for fruitful experimentation. On the other hand, a theory of learning may impede advancement seriously. It may fail to consider existing experimental evidence that does not support it; it may encourage research to proceed in non-productive channels; or it may define problems verbally that cannot be attacked experimentally. There are other ways in which theories can hinder advancement or accelerate it. Each of our present-day theories is probably doing both."

This danger is further emphasized by Norman R. F. Maier.[12] "Changes in an individual imply learning, and in this sense therapy becomes closely associated with learning. Problems of learning, however, are very complex and many variables influence learning progress. Hence the association of therapy with learning does not simplify the views on therapy. Rather confusion may be created because varying learning theories have given clinical theory as well as clinical practice different types of emphasis."

The individual psychologist "naturally" considers all of learning as a personal affair, since his science is rooted deeply in biological thinking. The social world is considered as a one-way street in which the individual affects society but society does not basically affect the individual. In this view, capitalism exists because people are acquisitive and not because of social conditions. Consciously departing from the theorists, the experimental psychologists have nevertheless continued this individualistic approach. People have been studied without regard to the social conditions in which they developed. It is inferred that the sum of individual responses is all that needs to be known to understand society; and that social situations are merely end results and not causal factors. It is true that a knowledge of man's perceptions and conceptions is necessary to understand how he learns; but it is not true that such studies can be made without regard to the social atmosphere. Another statement by Asch will be found helpful.[2]

"We conclude that to discover the full potentialities of men we must observe them in the social medium, that the basic problems of psychology require the extension of observation into the region of social processes. The study of social processes must base itself on what is known about the relation of individuals to the physical surroundings, but it should in turn deepen and extend this knowledge. The region of social events should provide a body of facts and a testing ground for theories formulated under more restricted conditions, but it should also furnish problems for general psychology. Only in this way will psychology achieve a unified conception of the place of man in nature and society, and realize its mission as a natural and social science."

This refutes, or at least challenges, the proposition that a study of learning is entirely or even mainly the province of the individual psychologist who paid no attention to performance under such social stimuli as mass hysteria or authoritarian compulsion. A human being cannot be understood or properly studied as a hermit or a Tarzan. This is "learning" about man in a non-human environment, and therefore is not learning about him at all. To understand *how* man learns, we must know *where, when,* and *under what conditions* he learns. This is the function of the social psychologist; to evaluate the transformation of man in and by social relationships, and to study how his apparent individual limitations have been expanded by the fact of his living among men. It will be remembered that even the Gestaltists, despite their emphasis on insight, spoke of "capacity" as being determined by age, species and individual differences within a species. Nothing was said about the effect of social interaction on capacity.

Experimentation has developed at a great pace during the last ten years, by social psychologists as well as individual psychologists. This is all to the good. If an experiment studies man in a vacuum, there will likely be another experiment producing incompatible results—and someone is bound to raise questions. The answer will probably be found in that the social conditions were different, and the perceptions could not be the same. Yet it seems difficult to escape from the individualistic approach. James J. Gibson [3] insists that learning is strictly a biological function rooted in the nervous system. This was written in 1950, and we may expect less of this as experimentation continues.

The viewpoint of the social psychologist may be judged from the questions he asks.

1. Why do different human beings perceive situations in different ways?
2. Why does a human being perceive situations in different ways at different times?
3. What needs or values drive an individual to particular perceptions?
4. Since needs and values modify perceptions, how can these modifiers (hunger, desire for success, release from tensions, etc.) be measured? This is a basic problem for the attitude researchers interested in *how* attitudes develop.
5. How can perceptions be differentiated from conception? To the

individual psychologist, this is not a problem, especially if he is a non-Gestaltist; but the social psychologist may well prefer to consider both as "cognition."

6. Is there any difference, in kind or degree, between man and other animals, and, if so, is it profitable to study animals in order to understand man?

7. Is there any original human nature, other than such simple reflexes as the patellar and salivary? Since it is now commonly accepted that most behavior is learned, and depends very little on original nature, *the method of learning becomes a dominant social problem.* For example, the desire for war may be learned, and not depend at all on innate human aggressiveness.

8. Is "learning" a single process or a group of many processes, so that different things are learned in different ways?

9. What is the importance of social and physical environments in learning? Is a man among men different from a cat among cats, or a cat among men?

10. If learning can be explained by a drive-reduction *or* a drive-increase (the more we learn the more we want to learn), what prevents these drives from being constantly reinforced to an overpowering point? Do social conditions and the institutional order prevent such an imbalance in most people?

11. If reinforcement is accepted as a central doctrine in learning theory, and people do things because they are rewarding or useful, how do persons learn to carry on survivals that have no apparent utility, beauty or other social function?

12. Is learning molar or molecular? This is simply asking whether the Gestaltists have a point.

13. Admitting that drives, needs, rewards and punishments are connected with learning among men and other animals, how does the capacity for rational thought fit into the picture?

14. With what material should we study the learning process? Krech and Crutchfield [11] claim that, "If we are interested in the general operation of the cognitive processes of one's social world, then data collected with almost any cognitive material will do." If this is true for the collection of data, does it also apply to the learning process? Is it a return to mind as an apperceptive mass?

15. Must there be any theories of learning? Would it be practicable simply to accept learning as any other behavior to be studied as a social phenomenon?

These are but a few of the questions that need answers. The inferences are clearly seen in the many writings and experiments in this field. If the proper study of mankind is man, it must now be realized that the proper place to study man is among men. This is the great task for the social experimenter, to give his work a definite and momentous import. Experimentation carried on in the social structure is possible and essential. Man is much more than a storehouse of fluid ideas or a mechanical entity dependent only upon habits formed by repetitive action. It is not enough to say that "We learn to do by doing."

From an immediate utilitarian viewpoint, a knowledge of the learning process is of the utmost importance to the educator. How has he been affected by these disputed approaches? The situation described in 1926 by Hullfish [7] still exists, although the entrance of social psychology may have made it more hopeful. He said in the preface, "The development of an educational psychology today cannot fail to be an interesting, though a precarious, undertaking. Interesting, because of increasing opportunities for research and study; precarious, because of the changes in psychology which have been taking place with a startling swiftness. There have come about radical shifts in the approach to this science; undeniable differences in fundamental positions now exist, and any educational psychology which is worthy of the name must needs account for the conflicts existing between present-day points of view. In short, the student of today who engages in a study of psychology must find that his undertaking is far from simple; must realize, indeed, that his is truly a study of psychologies and not of a psychology. . . . If the study does no more than suggest definitely, and clearly, that a basic and consistent approach is imperative, and that this must be made by first evaluating the psychologies now available, it will have served its purpose." At that time, the startling weakness of the "psychologies now available" lay in the fact that social phenomena were disregarded. Educators have a stronger support now.

An eclectic approach is probably the only feasible attack. The present knowledge of human learning requires an integration of data derived from such diverse fields as biology, sociology, chemistry, psychology, physics, education, and many more; aided by the techniques of statistics, attitudes research, mathematics and philosophy. In developing a whole picture, no aspect must be overemphasized or underestimated. There must be a fair sampling of each ingredient in the learning process. Unilateral approaches are valuable only if no fixed and pat conclusions develop, and the findings are acknowledged to be just a part of the final pattern of explanation. When this is learned by the scientists, they will be able to unfold the nature of the learning process.

BIBLIOGRAPHY

1. Allport, Floyd H. *Social Psychology*. New York: Houghton Mifflin, 1924.
2. Asch, Solomon E. *Social Psychology*. New York: Prentice-Hall, 1952.
3. Gibson, James J. "The Implications of Learning Theory for Social Psychology," in Miller, J. G., ed., *Experiments in Social Process*. New York: McGraw-Hill, 1950.

4. Guthrie, Edwin R. "Conditioning," in National Society for the Study of Education, 41st Yearbook, Part II, 1942.
5. Hilgard, Ernest R. *Theories of Learning.* New York: Appleton-Century-Crofts, 1948.
6. Hull, Clark L. *A Behavior System.* New Haven: Yale University Press, 1952.
7. Hullfish, H. Gordon. *Aspects of Thorndike's Psychology in Their Relation to Educational Theory and Practice.* Columbus: Ohio State University Press, 1926.
8. Koffka, K. *Growth of the Mind.* New York: Harcourt, Brace, 1928.
9. Koffka, K. *Principles of Gestalt Psychology.* New York: Harcourt, Brace, 1935.
10. Kohler, W. *Gestalt Psychology.* New York: Liveright, 1947.
11. Krech, D. and Crutchfield, R. S. *Theories and Problems of Social Psychology.* New York: McGraw-Hill, 1948.
12. Maier, Norman R. F. *Frustration.* New York: McGraw-Hill, 1949.
13. Miller, N. E. and Dollard, J. *Social Learning and Imitation.* New Haven: Yale University Press, 1941.
14. Skinner, B. F. *The Behavior of Organisms.* New York: Appleton-Century, 1938.
15. Wertheimer, M. *Productive Thinking.* New York: Harper, 1945.

7 Counseling as a learning process

Related selections: 6, 36, 37, 39, 56

Counseling service for pupils with personal and educational problems has become widespread in our schools. Dr. Combs states his belief that since to be effective counseling must result in learning for the counselee, counselors must study learning and how it takes place. He believes that learning theories have not been helpful in education and that educators have turned to the educational philosophers for assistance (see subsection, "Educational Philosophy and Learning"). He suggests personality theory as a substitute for learning theory not only in counseling but in teaching.

There can be little doubt that counseling is, in essence, a learning process. When counseling is successful, the client learns a new and better relationship between

ARTHUR W. COMBS, "Counseling as a Learning Process," *Journal of Counseling Psychology,* I (Winter, 1954), 31–36. Reprinted by permission of the author and the publisher.

DR. COMBS (1912–), formerly Director of Clinical Training at Syracuse University, is currently Professor of Education at the University of Florida. With Donald Snygg he is author of *Individual Behavior.* He is a Diplomate in Clinical Psychology.

himself and the world in which he lives. Counseling badly done may, equally well, result in learning a poorer, less effective way of living. Whatever happens in counseling, the client learns something from the experience, even if it is nothing more than the idea that counseling is not much help to him. In this respect, counseling is no different from any other life experience. Counseling, however, should be a situation expressly designed to assist the client to learn more effectively and efficiently than is possible in most other life experiences. If not, counselors had better close up shop.

Assuming that counseling is fundamentally a learning experience, it would appear logical that our existing theories of learning should apply to the problem. Unfortunately, this does not turn out to be the case. The fact that counseling is a learning process does not mean that existing theories of learning automatically become useful in solving the problems of counseling. The writer has been forced to the conclusion that traditional learning theories seem to have little to offer to the improvement of counseling. Indeed, the attempt to apply them to the problem of counseling may even be fraught with considerable danger.

Our existing learning theories, for the most part, are concerned with small bits of the problems encountered in counseling. They seem to have little application beyond the simplest behavior, while the behavior of clients is complex and involving entire personalities. Most of our traditional theories apply to the *process of learning* rather than to *people who learn*. Counseling is unquestionably a process of learning, but a much broader process of learning than we have usually considered under that heading. What appears to happen to clients in counseling is a matter of personality reorganization calling for much broader concepts of learning than most present theories of learning even attempt to deal with.

This discussion does not mean to suggest that existing learning theories have no application to learning in counseling. They *do* apply, but to such small and isolated aspects of the problem of personality organization as to make them almost useless for any practical purpose.

THE EXPERIENCE OF EDUCATION
WITH LEARNING THEORY

Educators have been dealing with problems of learning for a long time. Modern education has taken as its goal "the optimum development of the individual" and that objective could serve equally well as a goal for counseling. Counseling, like education, is a learning process. Perhaps we can learn something for our problem by observing the contributions traditional learning theory has made to education.

If there is any place where one would expect learning theory to have proved of value, it would be in the field of education. Yet, interestingly enough, learning theory has provided little or no leadership in solving problems of educational method. Leadership in education, almost exclusively, has come, not from learning theorists, but from educational philosophers. One looks in vain to find any great educational movement arising from learning theory. As a matter of fact, learning theory in some instances has even had a regressive effect on education. At the very time when education is moving to a holistic concept of teaching, many educators are still hammering away at methods of drill and rote learning growing out of the Ebbinghaus experiments of three generations ago. Because such learning theory seems to be "scientific," furthermore, many teachers find great comfort in continuing to teach by methods long since outdated.

Modern education has shifted its emphasis from subject matter to children, from processes to people. As a result, the theory of greatest use to educators is not learning theory but personality theory. The mental hygienists have taken over a very large share of the former functions of learning theorists in many a school of education. The unpleasant fact of the matter is that modern schools of education find little that is helpful in the average course on learning for the training of beginning teachers. Teachers have discovered long since that children are people with feelings, beliefs, attitudes, personal meanings, and convictions. Learning theory, which does not help to deal with these facets of child behavior, seems to the average teacher far out of touch with reality. She needs a broader, more inclusive approach to her problems. Education tried to gear itself to learning theory but found it to be a mistake. It would be unfortunate were we to make the same error in counseling. Counseling, too, is a problem of people rather than processes. Perhaps we have something to learn from the experience of education.

THEORY LEVEL AND APPLICATION

There is nothing sacred about theory. Theory in any field of endeavor is nothing more than a systematic explanation of events useful to the purposes one has in view. Theory, which holds for one frame of reference or one problem, may be totally inadequate, even misleading, in another. Theory can be constructed on many levels and for many different purposes, but is maximally efficient only for those levels and purposes for which it is designed. Atomic theory is useful in dealing with problems of atomic energy. At that level and for those purposes, it is relevant and essential. Theories of organic and inorganic chemistry are useful and pertinent for the pharmacist when he makes up a doctor's prescription. He knows little or nothing about atomic theory, however, and carries on his job quite effectively without it. This is not to imply that atomic theory does not hold for the chemicals with which he deals. Indeed, they do, but the pharmacist does not need to know them to carry on his profession adequately. On still another level, colleges of home economics have developed theories of cake baking quite without reference to chemical or atomic physics. While it is true that chemical and atomic theory is at work in the batter along with the hands of the cook, the cook does not need to guide her behavior by them, or even to know they exist. This is as it should be. Society needs its atomic physicists to make atomic bombs, but most of us would rather our cakes be baked by cooks!

This same relationship of theory to function is true of learning theory as well. The learning theory one finds useful for his purposes depends upon the number of variables one attempts to control in studying a process. For example, theory may be constructed for purposes of understanding what happens to a client in the counseling situation. To do this it is necessary to deal with people as they are with a large number of variables left uncontrolled. Nevertheless, it is quite possible to construct effective theories extremely helpful for our purposes. This is the kind of study many educators carry on in the classroom to discover better methods of inducing learning-in-life situations. Such studies, however, make some people very uncomfortable. Too many variables remain uncontrolled. Accordingly, one may seek to study learning on a level wherein more of the variables may be controlled. He can, for instance, study learning in the laboratory instead of the classroom, where theories of learning can be developed from experiments using tachistoscopic exposures. One can go further and control the material being learned by removing all meaning from it as in the use of nonsense syllables. In short, one can repeat the Ebbinghaus experiments and find new theories of learning applicable to the "purer" situations constructed under such laboratory conditions. It is possible to eliminate even more variables and study a single stimulus-response unit as Pavlov did with his dogs. Here, too, it will be feasible to construct learning theories applicable to the kind of situations studied. Unfortunately, when learning is examined under these restricted conditions it is no longer people who are being studied but an isolated process.

Dynamic personality theory is expressly designed to aid our understanding of behavior outside the laboratory, in free situations where few, if any, variables are likely to be in the control of the observer. The fact of many variables left uncontrolled makes some psychologists feel that such investigations are somehow less "scientific." This is an unfortunate attitude which equates science with minuteness rather than understanding. Teachers have long since discovered how inadequate minute theories are in providing guides to classroom learning. In the writer's experience, they have proved equally fruitless as approaches to understanding what happens in the counseling process.

The major problems of our time are problems of human relationships. In solving these problems, psychology must, of necessity, play an ever more important role. To do this effectively, we need theories about behavior at every level which help us understand behavior. It is difficult to conceive, however, how we can live up to our tremendous birthright by an atomistic approach to holistic problems. Too great an insistence upon such an approach may make it difficult or impossible to contribute significantly to the great social problems of these times.

Although the writer's basic training in psychology was thoroughly behavioristic, he has been increasingly disappointed in traditional approaches to learning theory as they apply to the counseling process. Though these theories have explained certain isolated aspects of what seems to be happening to clients, they have generally failed to explain the kinds of changes any counselor observes daily in the course of his practice. Even more disappointing, they do not offer much help in improving practices or in providing guides to behavior when problems arise for which no ready answers are available. The counselor must live and work in a world where variables can seldom be controlled or held constant. Theory which applies only under laboratory conditions is of little help in solving his practical problems.

PERCEPTUAL FIELD THEORY AS
A GUIDE TO COUNSELING PRACTICE

More and more the writer has been forced to adopt a field theory of personality organization based upon our growing understandings about the nature and function of perception and the concept of self. Perceptual theory seems eminently more satisfactory in explaining what we can observe about human behavior. It ssems more helpful, too, as a personal guide to behavior in our never ceasing attempts to become effective individuals whether it be in counseling or any other aspect of human relationships. This theory has been stated on several other occasions. The writer would certainly not presume to claim it as the answer to all our counseling problems. It is only an approach to personality which has proved satisfying, logical, and helpful in organizing thinking and guiding practice. That, after all, seems to be the purpose of any theory—to give meaning to the events we observe and to make possible the prediction and control of events still in the future. There is not room here for an exposition of this theoretical position. Let us, therefore, look only at its fundamental assumptions and point out a few of its implications for counseling theory.

Briefly, this theoretical position begins with the assumption that all behavior is a function of the individual's field of perceptions at the instant of behaving. In other words, people behave according to how things *seem* to them. If a man believes oysters can be eaten only in months with an R, he will avoid eating them in June and July. If he does not know about this concept, or if he does not believe in the "R" fiction, he will eat them any time. How each person behaves at any moment is a function of the organization of his perceptual field at the moment of behaving—or misbehaving.

This perceptual field has the feeling of reality to the individual and is always organized with respect to the concepts he holds of himself. As the field of perceptions changes, so, too, does behavior. When we perceive differently, we behave differently. When perceptions are vague and indistinct, behavior is correspondingly vague and inexact. When perceptions are clear and accurate, behavior is similarly precise and efficient.

This is the frame of reference within which an increasing number of psychologists are basing their thinking and research. It is a broad frame of reference capable of integrating and giving meaning and order to a large amount of our accumulated research and thinking. It is consistent with client-centered therapy and much of psychoanalysis. It seems to apply equally well to the problems of vocational and educational counseling and to the problems of classroom teaching. Many of the seemingly diverse points of view, as those of Freud, Rogers, Murphy, Allport, Snygg and Combs, Frank, and a host of others interpreted in this framework, fit into a meaningful and useful theoretical structure. A tremendous amount of recent research similarly finds effective interpretation in this setting. Research on perception, for example, is directly applicable to such a theoretical position. So, also, is a large amount of current research on such problems as threat, rigidity, discrimination, and the whole field of research on projective instruments.

If it is true that behavior is a function of perception, then the goal of counseling must be to assist the client to change his perceptions. Effective, efficient, and satisfying behavior both from the viewpoint of the client and of society requires a maximum freedom of perception. Rogers, for example, has described the adjusted person as follows: "It would appear that when all of the ways in which the individual perceives himself—all perceptions of the qualities, abilities, impulses, and attitudes of the person and all perceptions of himself in relation to others—are accepted into the organized conscious concept of self, then this achievement is accompanied by feelings of comfort and freedom from tension which are experienced as psychological adjustment."

In perceptual terms, the goal of counseling thus becomes one of aiding the client to achieve a perceptive field as rich, varied, accurate, and free of distortion as possible. If the perceptive field is organized about the concept of self, this theory would imply further that counseling must concern itself with assisting clients to clearer, more accurate perceptions of self and the relationship of self to the world in which the client lives.

If it is true that behavior is a function of perception, it follows that to change behavior it will first be necessary to find ways of changing perception. The perceptual field of the client is, however, a personal, internal organization not directly open to manipulation from outside. This means that counseling must be seen, not as a place where something is done *to* the client, but as the provision of a situation in which the client can be helped to change his ways of seeing. Counseling in this sense becomes a process of assisting, facilitating, and encouraging change in perception. It seems, furthermore, to reverse the usual doctor-patient role in which the doctor is the one who knows and the patient does not. In counseling, it is the client who knows and the counselor who does not. The counselor in this frame of reference is a catalyst in a process of growth. His task becomes one of supplying for his client a special kind of experience which will assist his client to explore and perceive a more adequate relationship of self to life.

VARIABLES OF PERCEPTION AS
THE FACTORS OF COUNSELING

Finally, if it is true that behavior is a function of perception, then the variables of the process of counseling become the factors affecting perception. To understand and control the process of counseling, it becomes necessary to understand and control the factors which encourage or impede perception. Once these factors are well understood it would seem possible to design the counseling process in the light of these understandings. There is much yet to be learned about the variables of perception, but a fine start has been made. The literature already includes a considerable body of knowledge about some of these variables and every day brings new understanding about some further aspect of perception.

To this point there are at least six variables of perception about which a good deal is already known and which have immediate bearing upon the counseling process. Applying what is known about these variables has possibilities of helping improve the counseling process. These are:

1. Perception is a function of the state of the physical organism in which the perception occurs. Perception both affects and is affected by the physical organism which serves as the vehicle for perceiving.

2. Perception takes time. Effective perception requires sufficient exposure to make perceiving possible.

3. Perception cannot occur without opportunity for experience. This opportunity for perceiving may be of a concrete character or may be purely symbolic. In any event, there must be some form of opportunity provided for perceiving to happen.

These first three variables of perception are already well known and understood. They have been more or less intensively studied for a number of years. The last three have been far less subjected to experimental study but continue to grow in importance every day. They are:

4. Perception is a function of the individual's values and goals. The values and goals of the individual have a selective effect upon the individual's field of perceptions. Other factors being equal, people perceive more sharply and effectively those aspects of themselves and of life which have greatest value for them.

5. Perception is a function of the self concept of the perceiver. The concept of self has a selective effect on the perceptual field. People perceive that which is appropriate for persons with their concepts of self to perceive. Children who perceive themselves as poor readers read poorly. We are only beginning to understand the tremendous importance of the self concept upon every aspect of human behavior. It appears to be the very core around which all the rest of our perceptions of reality are organized.

6. Perception is seriously affected by the experience of threat. These effects seem to be of two kinds: (a) When a person feels threatened his field of per-

ceptions is reduced to the object of threat producing the well-known effect of tunnel vision; and (b) when threatened, the individual seeks to defend his existing self organization. Both of these effects seem to have extremely important bearings upon the counseling process.

A good deal is already known about these six important variables. Much of this information has a direct bearing upon the kind of counseling situations we need to construct. What is already known of these variables is highly useful in guiding the counselor in his task. These seem like fruitful fields for further experimental exploration. It is conceivable that there are a number of other important variables affecting perception with equally important implications for the counseling process waiting to be uncovered.

Counseling is indeed a function of learning. Learning in counseling, however, is never an isolated process. It is *people* who learn in counseling. Counseling could not exist without them. A theoretical position which can help us very effectively in improving our understanding of the processes the counselor sets in motion or the methods he devises to help his clients must be a theory which deals with people.

Learning theory applies to some parts of the problems of counseling. We cannot afford, however, to jump to the conclusion that because it is partly applicable it is a sufficient or an adequate avenue of explanation or exploration. There seems nothing more dangerous in human thought than ideas which are partly true. The danger of theory partly right is that it encourages people by its partial provision of answers to the vain hope that with a little more effort, a little more trying, they can find answers to the whole problem. Sometimes this works but sometimes, too, it is better to find a better premise as a framework from which we may evaluate and improve our practices. An adequate theory for counseling must *include* learning theory but must also extend beyond it. This seems to require a personality theory in which traditional learning theory would play but a very minor role. The writer of this article has here indicated the direction of his own bias, but the fact of the matter seems to be that *almost any* personality theory is a more effective guide to practice than the best our traditional learning theories have so far produced.

EDUCATIONAL PHILOSOPHY AND LEARNING

8 *Experience and thinking*

Related selections: 4, 5, 9, 10, 11

Since the publication of Democracy and Education *in 1916, educators have turned to Dewey for insight into many phases of education; even for those most familiar with his work, there are new discoveries upon each rereading. Most people agree that a major objective of schooling is to teach people to think. Disagreement comes over how this is to be accomplished. In this selection Dewey sets forth the nature of thinking and how the processes called thinking and experiencing are related to each other. Beginning students may find this selection difficult, but it is worth careful reading and study. It may be helpful to organize a small group of classmates to read it and discuss its meaning.*

THE NATURE OF EXPERIENCE

The nature of experience can be understood only by noting that it includes an active and a passive element peculiarly combined. On the active hand, experience is *trying*—a meaning which is made explicit in the connected term experiment. On the passive, it is *undergoing*. When we experience something we act upon it, we do something with it; then we suffer or undergo the consequences. We do something to the thing and then it does something to us in return: such is the

JOHN DEWEY, *Democracy and Education* (New York: The Macmillan Company, 1916), pp. 163–78. Reprinted by permission of the publisher. Copyright 1916 by The Macmillan Company; renewed 1944 by John Dewey.
JOHN DEWEY (1859–1952), America's most eminent philosopher, was Head of Department of Philosophy and Education at the University of Chicago before becoming Professor of Philosophy at Columbia University. He held this latter position for over a quarter of a century. He was made Honorary Life President of the National Education Association in 1932. His writings explored all aspects of philosophy and education.

peculiar combination. The connection of these two phases of experience measures the fruitfulness or value of the experience. Mere activity does not constitute experience. It is dispersive, centrifugal, dissipating. Experience as trying involves change, but change is meaningless transition unless it is consciously connected with the return wave of consequences which flow from it. When an activity is continued *into* the undergoing of consequences, when the change made by action is reflected back into a change made in us, the mere flux is loaded with significance. We learn something. It is not experience when a child merely sticks his finger into a flame; it is experience when the movement is connected with the pain which he undergoes in consequence. Henceforth the sticking of the finger into flame *means* a burn. Being burned is a mere physical change, like the burning of a stick of wood, if it is not perceived as a consequence of some other action.

Blind and capricious impulses hurry us on heedlessly from one thing to another. So far as this happens, everything is writ in water. There is none of that cumulative growth which makes an experience in any vital sense of that term. On the other hand, many things happen to us in the way of pleasure and pain which we do not connect with any prior activity of our own. They are mere accidents so far as we are concerned. There is no before or after to such experience; no retrospect nor outlook, and consequently no meaning. We get nothing which may be carried over to foresee what is likely to happen next, and no gain in ability to adjust ourselves to what is coming—no added control. Only by courtesy can such an experience be called experience. To "learn from experience" is to make a backward and forward connection between what we do to things and what we enjoy or suffer from things in consequence. Under such conditions, doing becomes a trying; an experiment with the world to find out what it is like; the undergoing becomes instruction—discovery of the connection of things.

Two conclusions important for education follow. (1) Experience is primarily an active-passive affair; it is not primarily cognitive. But (2) the *measure of the value* of an experience lies in the perception of relationships or continuities to which it leads up. It includes cognition in the degree in which it is cumulative or amounts to something, or has meaning. In schools, those under instruction are too customarily looked upon as acquiring knowledge as theoretical spectators, minds which appropriate knowledge by direct energy of intellect. The very word pupil has almost come to mean one who is engaged not in having fruitful experiences but in absorbing knowledge directly. Something which is called mind or consciousness is severed from the physical organs of activity. The former is then thought to be purely intellectual and cognitive; the latter to be an irrelevant and intruding physical factor. The intimate union of activity and undergoing its consequences which leads to recognition of meaning is broken; instead we have two fragments: mere bodily action on one side, and meaning directly grasped by "spiritual" activity on the other.

It would be impossible to state adequately the evil results which have flowed from this dualism of mind and body, much less to exaggerate them. Some of the more striking effects may, however, be enumerated. (*a*) In part bodily activity becomes an intruder. Having nothing, so it is thought, to do with mental activity, it becomes a distraction, an evil to be contended with. For the pupil has a body, and brings it to school along with his mind. And the body is, of necessity, a wellspring of energy; it has to do something. But its activities, not being utilized in occupation with things which yield significant results, have to be frowned upon. They lead the pupil away from the lesson with which his "mind" ought to be occupied; they are sources of mischief. The chief source of the "problem of discipline" in schools is that the teacher has often to spend the larger part of the time in suppressing the bodily activities which take the mind away from its material. A premium is put on physical quietude; on silence, on rigid uniformity of posture and movement; upon a machine-like simulation of the attitudes of intelligent interest. The teachers' business is to hold the pupils up to these requirements and to punish the inevitable deviations which occur.

The nervous strain and fatigue which result with both teacher and pupil are a necessary consequence of the abnormality of the situation in which bodily activity is divorced from the perception of meaning. Callous indifference and explosions from strain alternate. The neglected body, having no organized fruitful channels of activity, breaks forth, without knowing why or how, into meaningless boisterousness, or settles into equally meaningless fooling—both very different from the normal play of children. Physically active children become restless and unruly; the more quiescent, so-called conscientious ones spend what energy they have in the negative task of keeping their instincts and active tendencies suppressed, instead of in a positive one of constructive planning and execution; they are thus educated not into responsibility for the significant and graceful use of bodily powers, but into an enforced duty not to give them free play. It may be seriously asserted that a chief cause for the remarkable achievements of Greek education was that it was never misled by false notions into an attempted separation of mind and body.

(*b*) Even, however, with respect to the lessons which have to be learned by the application of "mind," some bodily activities have to be used. The senses— especially the eye and ear—have to be employed to take in what the book, the map, the blackboard, and the teacher say. The lips and vocal organs, and the hands, have to be used to reproduce in speech and writing what has been stowed away. The senses are then regarded as a kind of mysterious conduit through which information is conducted from the external world into the mind; they are spoken of as gateways and avenues of knowledge. To keep the eyes on the book and the ears open to the teacher's words is a mysterious source of intellectual grace. Moreover, reading, writing, and figuring—important school arts—demand muscular or motor training. The muscles of eye, hand, and vocal organs accordingly have to be trained to act as pipes for carrying knowledge back out of the mind into external action. For it happens that using the muscles repeatedly in the same way fixes in them an automatic tendency to repeat.

The obvious result is a mechanical use of the bodily activities which (in spite of the generally obtrusive and interfering character of the body in mental action) have to be employed more or less. For the senses and muscles are used not as organic participants in having an instructive experience, but as external inlets and outlets of mind. Before the child goes to school, he learns with his hand, eye, and ear, because they are organs of the process of doing something from which meaning results. The boy flying a kite has to keep his eye on the kite, and has to note the various pressures of the string on his hand. His senses are avenues of knowledge not because external facts are somehow "conveyed" to the brain, but because they are *used* in doing something with a purpose. The qualities of seen and touched things have a bearing on what is done, and are alertly perceived; they have a meaning. But when pupils are expected to use their eyes to note the form of words, irrespective of their meaning, in order to reproduce them in spelling or reading, the resulting training is simply of isolated sense organs and muscles. It is such isolation of an act from a purpose which makes it mechanical. It is customary for teachers to urge children to read with expression, so as to bring out the meaning. But if they originally learned the sensory-motor technique of reading—the ability to identify forms and to reproduce the sounds they stand for—by methods which did not call for attention to meaning, a mechanical habit was established which makes it difficult to read subsequently with intelligence. The vocal organs have been trained to go their own way automatically in isolation; and meaning cannot be tied on at will. Drawing, singing, and writing may be taught in the same mechanical way; for, we repeat, any way *is* mechanical which narrows down the bodily activity so that a separation of body from mind—that is, from recognition of meaning—is set up. Mathematics, even in its higher branches, when undue emphasis is put upon the technique of calculation, and science, when laboratory exercises are given for their own sake, suffer from the same evil.

(c) On the intellectual side the separation of "mind" from direct occupation with things throws emphasis on *things* at the expense of *relations* or connections. It is altogether too common to separate perceptions and even ideas from judgments. The latter are thought to come after the former in order to compare them. It is alleged that the mind perceives things apart from relations; that it forms ideas of them in isolation from their connections—with what goes before and comes after. Then judgment or thought is called upon to combine the separated items of "knowledge" so that their resemblance or casual connection shall be brought out. As a matter of fact, every perception and every idea is a sense of the bearings, use, and cause, of a thing. We do not really know a chair or have an idea of it by inventorying and enumerating its various isolated qualities, but only by bringing these qualities into connection with something else—the purpose which makes it a chair and not a table; or its difference from the kind of chair we are accustomed to, or the "period" which it represents, and so on. A wagon is not perceived when all its parts are summed up; it is the characteristic connection of the parts which makes it a wagon. And these connections are not those of mere physical juxtaposition; they involve connection with the animals that draw it, the things that are carried on it, and so on. Judgment is employed in the perception; otherwise the perception is mere sensory excitation or else a recognition of the result of a prior judgment, as in the case of familiar objects.

Words, the counters for ideas, are, however, easily taken for ideas. And in just the degree in which mental activity is separated from active concern with the world, from doing something and connecting the doing with what is undergone, words, symbols, come to take the place of ideas. The substitution is the more subtle because *some* meaning is recognized. But we are very easily trained to be content with a minimum of meaning, and to fail to note how restricted is our perception of the relations which confer significance. We get so thoroughly used to a kind of pseudo-idea, a half perception, that we are not aware how half-dead our mental action is, and how much keener and more extensive our observations and ideas would be if we formed them under conditions of a vital experience which required us to use judgment: to hunt for the connections of the thing dealt with.

There is no difference of opinion as to the theory of the matter. All authorities agree that that discernment of relationships is the genuinely intellectual matter; hence, the educative matter. The failure arises in supposing that relationships can become perceptible without *experience*—without that conjoint trying and undergoing of which we have spoken. It is assumed that "mind" can grasp them if it will only give attention, and that this attention may be given at will irrespective of the situation. Hence the deluge of half-observations, of verbal ideas, and unassimilated "knowledge" which afflicts the world. An ounce of experience is better than a ton of theory simply because it is only in experience that any theory has vital and verifiable significance. An experience, a very humble experience, is capable of generating and carrying any amount of theory (or intellectual content), but a theory apart from an experience cannot be definitely grasped even as theory. It tends to become a mere verbal formula, a set of catchwords used to render thinking, or genuine theorizing, unnecessary and impossible. Because of our education we use words, thinking they are ideas, to dispose of questions, the disposal being in reality simply such an obscuring of perception as prevents us from seeing any longer the difficulty.

REFLECTION IN EXPERIENCE

Thought or reflection, as we have already seen virtually if not explicitly, is the discernment of the relation between what we try to do and what happens in consequence. No experience having a meaning is possible without some element of thought. But we may contrast two types of experience according to the proportion of reflection found in them. All our experiences have a phase of "cut and try" in them—what psychologists call the method of trial and error. We simply do something, and when it fails, we do something else, and keep on trying till we hit upon something which works, and then we adopt that method as a rule of thumb measure in subsequent procedure. Some experiences have very little else in them than this hit and miss or succeed process. We see *that* a certain way of acting and a certain consequence are connected, but we do not see *how* they are. We do not see the details of the connection; the links are missing. Our discernment is very gross. In other cases we push our observation farther. We analyze to see just what lies between so as to bind together cause and effect, activity and consequence. This extension of our insight makes foresight more accurate and comprehensive. The action which rests simply upon the trial and error method is at the mercy of circumstances; they may change so that the act performed does not operate in the way it was expected to. But if we know in detail upon what the result depends, we can look to see whether the required conditions are there. The method extends our practical control. For if some of the conditions are missing, we may, if we know what the needed antecedents for an effect are, set to work to supply them; or, if they are such as to produce undesirable effects as well, we may eliminate some of the superfluous causes and economize effort.

In discovery of the detailed connections of our activities and what happens in consequence, the thought implied in cut and try experience is made explicit. Its quantity increases so that its proportionate value is very different. Hence the quality of the experience changes; the change is so significant that we may call this type of experience reflective—that is, reflective *par excellence*. The deliberate cultivation of this phase of thought constitutes thinking as a distinctive experience. Thinking, in other words, is the intentional endeavor to discover *specific* connections between something which we do and the consequences which result, so that the two become continuous. Their isolation, and consequently their purely arbitrary going together, is cancelled; a unified developing situation takes its place. The occurrence is now understood; it is explained; it is reasonable, as we say, that the thing should happen as it does.

Thinking is thus equivalent to an explicit rendering of the intelligent element in our experience. It makes it possible to act with an end in view. It is the condition of our having aims. As soon as an infant begins to *expect* he begins to use something which is now going on as a sign of something to follow; he is, in however simple a fashion, judging. For he takes one thing as *evidence* of something else, and so recognizes a relationship. Any future development, however elaborate it may be, is only an extending and a refining of this simple act of inference. All that the wisest man can do is to observe what is going on more widely and more minutely and then select more carefully from what is noted just those factors which point to something to happen. The opposites, once more, to thoughtful action are routine and capricious behavior. The former accepts what has been customary as a full measure of possibility and omits to take into account the connections of the particular things done. The latter makes the momentary act a measure of value, and ignores the connections of our personal action with the energies of the environment. It says, virtually, "things are to be just as I happen to like them at this instant," as routine says in effect "let things continue just as I have found them in the past." Both refuse to acknowledge responsibility for the future consequences which flow from present action. Reflection is the acceptance of such responsibility.

The starting point of any process of thinking is something going on, something which just as it stands is incomplete or unfulfilled. Its point, its meaning lies literally in what it is going to be, in how it is going to turn out. As this is written, the world is filled with the clang of contending armies. For an active participant in the war, it is clear that the momentous thing is the issue, the future consequences, of this and that happening. He is identified, for the time at least, with the issue; *his* fate hangs upon the course things are taking. But even for an onlooker in a neutral country, the significance of every move made, of every advance here and retreat there, lies in what it portends. To *think* upon the news as it comes to us is to attempt to see what is indicated as probable or possible regarding an outcome. To fill our heads, like a scrapbook, with this and that item as a finished and done-for thing, is not to think. It is to turn ourselves into a piece of registering apparatus. To consider the *bearing* of the occurrence upon what may be, but is not yet, is to think. Nor will the reflective experience be different in kind if we substitute distance in time for separation in space. Imagine the war done with, and a future historian giving an account of it. The episode is, by assumption, past. But he cannot give a thoughtful account of the war save as he preserves the time sequence; the meaning of each occurrence, as he deals with it, lies in what was future for *it*, though not for the historian. To take it by itself as a complete existence is to take it unreflectively.

Reflection also implies concern with the issue—a certain sympathetic identification of our own destiny, if only dramatic, with the outcome of the course of events. For the general in the war, or a common soldier, or a citizen of one of the contending nations, the stimulus to thinking is direct and urgent. For neutrals, it is indirect and dependent upon imagination. But the flagrant partisanship of human nature is evidence of the intensity of the tendency to identify ourselves with one possible course of events, and to reject the other as foreign. If we cannot take sides in overt action, and throw in our little weight to help determine the final balance, we take sides emotionally and imaginatively. We desire this or that outcome. One wholly indifferent to the outcome does not follow or think about what is happening at all. From this dependence of the act of thinking upon a sense of sharing in the consequences of what goes on, flows one of the chief paradoxes of thought. Born in partiality, in order to accomplish its tasks it must achieve a certain detached impartiality. The general who allows his hopes and desires to affect his observations and interpretations of the existing situation will surely make a mistake in calculation. While hopes and fears may be the chief motive for a thoughtful following of the war on the part of an onlooker in a neutral country, he too will think ineffectively in the degree in which his preferences modify the stuff of his observations and reasonings. There is, however, no incompatibility between the fact that the occasion of reflection lies in a personal sharing in what is going on and the fact that the value of the reflection lies upon keeping one's self out of the data. The almost insurmountable difficulty of achieving this detachment is evidence that thinking originates in situations where the course of thinking is an actual part of the course of events and is designed to influence the result. Only gradually and with a widening of the area of vision through a growth of social sympathies does thinking develop to include what lies beyond our *direct* interests: a fact of great significance for education.

To say that thinking occurs with reference to situations which are still going on, and incomplete, is to say that thinking occurs when things are uncertain or doubtful or problematic. Only what is finished, completed, is wholly assured. Where there is reflection there is suspense. The object of thinking is to help *reach* a conclusion, to project a possible termination on the basis of what is already given. Certain other facts about thinking accompany this feature. Since the situation in which thinking occurs is a doubtful one, thinking is a process of inquiry, of looking into things, of investigating. *Ac*quiring is always secondary, and instrumental to the act of *in*quiring. It is seeking, a quest, for something that is not at hand. We sometimes talk as if "original research" were a peculiar prerogative of scientists or at least of advanced students. But all thinking is research, and all research is native, original, with him who carries it on, even if everybody else in the world already is sure of what he is still looking for.

It also follows that all thinking involves a risk. Certainty cannot be guaranteed in advance. The invasion of the unknown is of the nature of an adventure; we cannot be sure in advance. The conclusions of thinking, till confirmed by the event, are, accordingly, more or less tentative or hypothetical. Their dogmatic assertion as final is unwarranted, short of the issue, in fact. The Greeks acutely raised the question: How can we learn? For either we know already what we are after, or else we do not know. In neither case is learning possible; on the first alternative because we know already; on the second, because we do not know what to look for, nor if, by chance, we find it can we tell that it is what we were after. The dilemma makes no provision for *coming* to know, for learning; it assumes either complete knowledge or complete ignorance. Nevertheless the twilight zone of inquiry, of thinking, exists. The possibility of *hypothetical* conclusions, of *tentative* results, is the fact which the Greek dilemma overlooked. The perplexities of the situation suggest certain ways out. We try these ways, and either push our way out, in which case we know we have found what we were looking for, or the situation gets darker and more confused—in which case, we know we are still ignorant. Tentative means trying out, feeling one's way along provisionally. Taken by itself, the Greek argument is a nice piece of formal logic. But it is also true that as long as men kept a sharp disjunction between knowledge and ignorance, science made only slow and accidental advance. Systematic advance in invention and discovery began when men recognized that they could utilize doubt for purposes of inquiry by forming conjectures to guide action in tentative explorations, whose development would confirm, refute, or modify the guiding conjecture. While the Greeks made knowledge more than learning, modern science makes conserved knowledge only a means to learning, to discovery.

To recur to our illustration. A commanding general cannot base his actions upon either absolute certainty or absolute ignorance. He has a certain amount of information at hand which is, we will assume, reasonably trustworthy. He then *infers* certain prospective movements, thus assigning meaning to the bare facts of the given situation. His inference is more or less dubious and hypothetical. But he acts upon it. He develops a plan of procedure, a method of dealing with the situation. The consequences which directly follow from his acting this way rather than that test and reveal the worth of his reflections. What he already knows functions and has value in what he learns. But will this account apply in the case of the one in a neutral country who is thoughtfully following as best he can the progress of events? In form, yes, though not of course in content. It is self-evident that his guesses about the future indicated by present facts, guesses by which he attempts to supply meaning to a multitude of disconnected data, cannot be the basis of a method which shall take effect in the campaign. *That* is not *his* problem. But in the degree in which he is actively thinking, and not merely passively following the course of events, his tentative inferences will take effect in *a* method of procedure appropriate to *his* situation. He will anticipate certain future moves, and will be on the alert to see whether they happen or not. In the degree in which he is intellectually concerned, or thoughtful, he will be actively on the lookout; he will take steps which although they do not affect the campaign, modify in some degree *his* subsequent actions. Otherwise his later "I told you so" has no intellectual quality at all; it does not mark any testing or verification of prior thinking, but only a coincidence that yields emotional satisfaction—and includes a large factor of self-deception.

The case is comparable to that of an astronomer who from given data has been led to foresee (infer) a future eclipse. No matter how great the mathematical probability, the inference is hypothetical—a matter of probability.[1] The hypothesis as to the date and position of the anticipated eclipse becomes the material of forming a method of future conduct. Apparatus is arranged; possibly an expedition is made to some far part of the globe. In any case, some active

[1] It is most important for the practice of science that men in many cases can calculate the degree of probability and the amount of probable error involved, but that does not alter the features of the situation as described. It refines them.

steps are taken which actually change *some* physical conditions. And apart from such steps and the consequent modification of the situation, there is no completion of the act of thinking. It remains suspended. Knowledge, already attained knowledge, controls thinking and makes it fruitful.

So much for the general features of a reflective experience. They are (1) perplexity, confusion, doubt, due to the fact that one is implicated in an incomplete situation whose full character is not yet determined; (2) a conjectural anticipation—a tentative interpretation of the given elements, attributing to them a tendency to effect certain consequences; (3) a careful survey (examination, inspection, exploration, analysis) of all attainable consideration which will define and clarify the problem in hand; (4) a consequent elaboration of the tentative hypothesis to make it more precise and more consistent, because squaring with a wider range of facts; (5) taking one stand upon the projected hypothesis as a plan of action which is applied to the existing state of affairs; doing something overtly to bring about the anticipated result, and thereby testing the hypothesis. It is the extent and accuracy of steps three and four which mark off a distinctive reflective experience from one on the trial and error plane. They make *thinking* itself into an experience. Nevertheless, we never get wholly beyond the trial and error situation. Our most elaborate and rationally consistent thought has to be tried in the world and thereby tried out. And since it can never take into account all the connections, it can never cover with perfect accuracy all the consequences. Yet a thoughtful survey of conditions is so careful, and the guessing at results so controlled, that we have a right to mark off the reflective experience from the grosser trial and error forms of action.

SUMMARY

In determining the place of thinking in experience we first noted that experience involves a connection of doing or trying with something which is undergone in consequence. A separation of the active doing phase from the passive undergoing phase destroys the vital meaning of an experience. Thinking is the accurate and deliberate instituting of connections between what is done and its consequences. It notes not only only that they are connected, but the details of the connection. It makes connecting links explicit in the form of relationships. The stimulus to thinking is found when we wish to determine the significance of some act, performed or to be performed. Then we anticipate consequences. This implies that the situation as it stands is, either in fact or to us, incomplete and hence indeterminate. The projection of consequences means a proposed or tentative solution. To perfect this hypothesis, existing conditions have to be carefully scrutinized and the implications of the hypothesis developed—an operation called reasoning. Then the suggested solution—the idea or theory—has to be tested by acting upon it. If it brings about certain consequences, certain determinate changes, in the world, it is accepted as valid. Otherwise it is modified, and another trial made. Thinking includes all of these steps,—the sense of a problem, the observation of conditions, the formation and rational elaboration of a suggested conclusion, and the active experimental testing. While all thinking results in knowledge, ultimately the value of knowledge is subordinate to its use in thinking. For we live not in a settled and finished world, but in one which is going on, and where our main task is prospective, and where retrospect—and all knowledge as distinct from thought is retrospect—is of value in the solidity, security, and fertility it affords our dealings with the future.

9 *Education from a pragmatic point of view*

Related selections: 4, 5, 8, 11, 20

In this chapter from How We Learn, *Professor Bode draws upon the classic work of Koehler on the behavior of apes that demonstrated the importance of insight in learning. Bode analyzes the characteristics of this kind of learning, relates it to a conception of mind, and points out that the learner's feel for the total situation comes prior to his understanding of relationships. The implications for schooling are discussed.*

It is to be expected that [one's] conception of mind . . . will have significant bearing on educational outlook. If mind is a function, there can be no room for a faculty psychology. If this function is a function of a "field," then education cannot be a process of organizing mental states. Lastly, if this function is a process of progressively shaping up the environment so as to bring an ongoing activity to a successful termination, then education cannot be identified with a mechanistic stamping in of S-R bonds.

In approaching the problem of learning, our clue must come from the idea that mind is such a process of "progressively shaping up the environment." This process was illustrated earlier by the example of the pedestrian making his way along a difficult path. He picks and chooses, as we say; which means that a whole field, consisting of environmental relationships and bodily reactions, is in continuous reorganization. This process of reorganization is not,

BOYD HENRY BODE, *How We Learn* (Boston: D. C. Heath and Co., 1940), pp. 233–46. Reprinted by permission of the publisher.

PROFESSOR BODE (1873–1953), philosopher and teacher, was for many years Professor of Philosophy of Education at the Ohio State University. At the time of his death he was a visiting professor at the University of Florida.

indeed, the same as learning, since no new elements may be involved. The case is different if our pedestrian discovers, as a result of his experience, that clay is slippery, whereas sod or gravel affords a firm footing. He learns about clay, for example, provided that he notes the connection between the appearance of clay and what the clay does to him when he tries to walk on it. To note the connection is to learn something, and the learning takes the form of changing the experience. The clay now *looks* slippery; it has acquired meaning. Such change in an experience whereby it becomes more serviceable for the guidance of behavior is what is meant by learning.

In this illustration learning is an intellectual affair, since it is identified with the perception of significant relationships. This kind of learning naturally occupies a prominent place in formal education. Instruction in golf, for example, is possible because the reason why a beginner "hooks" his drives or fails to get distance can be analyzed out. The significant relationships can be brought to the attention of the learner. Where such analysis is difficult, instruction is correspondingly difficult, as, for example, in teaching a boy how to balance himself on a bicycle, or to wag his ears, or to be at ease in a social gathering. Such accomplishments are also classed as learning, but they are generally acquired by trial and error, and perhaps without any perception of significant relationships. The result may be achieved without any knowledge of how it was done. But, even so, the learning is a process of getting the "feel" of the thing; which is to say that the experience is changed so as to provide better control for behavior.

To what extent relationships are clearly perceived in learning is sometimes open to doubt. If a baby touches a hot stove and thereafter avoids the stove, we are tempted to assume that the baby sees the relationship between "stove" and "hot." It is evident that the experience of bing burned changes the infant's response to the stove, and the inference is warranted that there has been a change in his experience of the stove. The precise nature of this change, however, is not so clear. Psychologically there is a vast difference between seeing the stove as "stove-meaning-burn" and seeing it merely as "bad" or "hot." In the former case there is a clear distinction between the object and the thing meant or pointed to; in the latter case the meaning is so completely incorporated that there is no clear distinction. This complete assimilation of the meaning to the thing is exemplified in all cases of simple recognition. Persons seeing a lemon will sometimes "make a face"; they react to the object as sour, but they may not make the distinction which we ordinarily make when we infer that a person broken out with rash has measles or smallpox. That is, we do not distinguish between "thing" and "meaning"; we "recognize" the thing without this internal distinction. Recognition, however, implies a change in the perceived object; a lemon *looks* different after we have had experience with it. Moreover, the lemon thus seen controls behavior in terms of future consequences; we decline, for example, to bite into it. Hence the lemon exercises the function which we have identified with mind. But this is mind in its lowest terms, so to speak; the "sour" is not definitely marked off as something symbolized, or indicated, or pointed to. The function is performed, but it is not definitely intellectualized.

In the case of the lemon it is easy enough for the average person to distinguish between "lemon" and its meaning, "sour," if there is occasion to do so. There are many situations, however, where we are unable to draw a satisfactory contrast between "thing" and "meaning." An experienced physician, for example, may "sense" that a patient stands no chance, before he has even started to make a diagnosis; a lawyer may "sense" that there is something crooked about the case that is brought to him, even if it baffles him to find anything wrong. The expert has learned to "size up" situations in advance of tangible evidence. Cases of this kind are not wholly devoid of the contrast between thing and meaning; but they suggest how thing and meaning can run together and blend, and they suggest why we speak of being guided by "intuition." They also suggest the possibility that there are experiences where the *contrast* between "thing" and "meaning" is not present at all. Sometimes the contrast is lacking because it has gradually faded out. The child learns at one stage that the man in uniform *means* letters; later on he simply recognizes the man as the mailman. But there may be other instances when the experience may undergo an adaptive change without the clear intervention of this contrast at any point. The case of the baby and the stove may perhaps be explained either way.

A reference to the learning of the lower animals may serve to emphasize the fact that there are different varieties of learning and that careful interpretation is necessary. There is a story of a cat eating from a dish of codfish under which a mischievous boy had placed a large lighted firecracker. According to the story, that cat would never touch codfish again, no matter in what form it might be offered. Did the cat remember the original experience and relate the codfish specifically to explosions, or did the learning consist in a simple transformation of the experience so that the codfish did not look good any more? Then there is the familiar experiment with the pike, which was placed in a glass tank inside a larger tank, for the purpose of ascertaining whether the pike could learn to keep away from the small fish swimming around outside the glass tank. The pike finally learned, but only after countless collisions with the walls of his glass tank. In this case the learning presumably consisted simply in a change in the appearance of the small fish, so that they no longer looked inviting or appetizing. It is related that the pike did not offer to molest these fish even after the inner glass tank was removed, but that it unhesitatingly pursued other kinds of small fish when these were introduced into the tank. This bears out the supposition that the learning was confined to a change in the appearance of those kinds of fish with which its experience had been unfortunate. There was no evidence of anything resembling what, on the human level, is called analysis and generalization.

By contrast the experiments of Koehler with apes do provide evidence of this kind. These experiments were so devised as to require a comprehension or "insight" into relationships, if the apes were to solve their problem, which consisted in each case in adapting ways and means for securing tempting fruit. The situations were so arranged that the ape would at least stand a chance to "figure out" the solution. That is, the difficulty was, from a human standpoint, relatively simple, yet it required some kind of new adaptation of means to ends, such as fetching a box for the purpose of standing on it so as to reach an object overhead.

> The experiment provides a situation in which the direct way to a goal is barred, but in which an indirect way is left open. The animal is introduced into this situation, which has been so planned that it is fully comprehensible. The animal is then left to indicate by its behavior whether or not it can solve the problem by the indirect means that have been provided.[1]

It is not necessary for our purpose to do more than to make brief mention of some of these experiments. In one experiment, fruit was placed beyond reach outside the cage, but a string was attached to it which was in easy reach; in another there was no string, but a stick was placed inside the cage with which the fruit could be reached. One variation of this experiment consisted in placing in the cage, not a stick, but a part of a dead tree from which a branch could be broken off to be used as a stick. In another variation two bamboo sticks had to be fitted together by inserting one into the hollow end of the other so as to make the stick of adequate length. In still another experiment the fruit was hung from the ceiling of the cage, but so high that a box which was in the cage had to be placed under it. As a variation of this experiment the box was filled with stones which had to be taken out before the box could be moved. Again the fruit thus suspended could be reached by swinging towards it with a rope, which was likewise suspended from the ceiling at a distance of two meters. In a subsequent experiment the rope was laid on the floor, and it had to be replaced on the hook—which was accessible to the ape—before it could be used for purposes of swinging.

In struggling with these situations the apes naturally made errors, some of which Koehler calls "clever," and others he labels "stupid." For example, on one occasion an ape brought in a box and placed it against the wall above the floor where it was in a position from which the fruit could easily be reached, if only the box could be made to stick to the wall. Koehler calls this a clever error because it showed a comprehension of the problem, even though an essential factor had been overlooked. This epithet applies also to the procedure of the ape who tried to obtain the fruit by means of two short sticks, his method being to lay the two sticks endwise, instead of inserting one into the other; so

---

[1] W. Koehler, *The Mentality of Apes,* by permission of Harcourt, Brace and Company, Inc., p. 4, quoted by K. Koffka, *The Growth of the Mind,* p. 81.

that by pushing with one of the sticks he made the other stick come into contact with the fruit. In this way the ape succeeded in reaching the fruit with the sticks, although this did not help him in bringing the fruit into the cage. By contrast a stupid error is illustrated by the behavior of a cat in Thorndike's experiments. The cat had learned to pull a string so as to release itself from the cage; and having learned this it went to the same spot and made the motion of pulling the string, in spite of the fact that the string had been hung in another part of the cage.

It may be remarked that the methods by which the apes sought to solve their problems were sometimes quite unexpected. In one instance the two sticks to be fitted together were too nearly of the same size, so the ape proceeded to whittle down the end of one with his teeth, apparently for the purpose of making it fit. This resulted in his breaking off a large splinter, which caused a change of plan. The splinter was inserted into the other uninjured end of the pole, which made it long enough to serve the purpose of reaching the fruit. On another occasion the ape led the keeper by the hand under the fruit, with the evident intention of using the keeper as a stepladder by climbing on his shoulder, as he had done on previous occasions. This time, however, the keeper knelt down at the critical moment, so that, after the ape had climbed up, the fruit was still beyond reach. The ape, as Koehler tells the incident, "climbs on to the man's shoulder after he has dragged him underneath the object, and the keeper quickly bends down. The animal gets off complaining, takes hold of the keeper by his seat with both hands, and tries with all his might to push him up. A surprising way of trying to improve the human implement."

With one exception, all of the experiments mentioned, and others besides, were successfully performed by some one or more of the apes. As was perhaps to be expected, some of the apes proved to be distinctly superior to others in intelligence. The experiment in which all the apes failed required that a rope lying on the floor of the cage be hung on a hook in the roof of the cage so that it might be used as a means of swinging the animal within reach of the fruit. In these experiments there was no gradual sloping downward of the time-curve, as in the case of Thorndike's experiments with the cats, the reason being that Koehler's experiments were so arranged as to enable the animal to pick out the essential relationship beforehand. Ordinarily the successful performance meant that the animal was master of the situation at once. He could do the right thing on the next occasion with a minimum of fumbling. In terms of curves, his learning was represented, not by a gradual downward slope, but by a straight drop.

It is of interest in this connection to observe that the experiment in which stones had to be taken from a box before the box could be moved was performed in a way that exhibited a curious limitation of insight. Instead of removing all the stones, the ape took out only as many as were necessary to make the box movable. The labor involved in moving the box with a quantity of stones still left inside was considerable, but the ape apparently did not grasp the fact that his labor would be lightened by the removal of the remaining stones. The stones were regarded as an obstacle to moving the box only as long as the box was too heavy to move. As soon as the box was movable, the remaining stones were ignored.

Learning, then, is a term that covers a variety of meanings. Sometimes the emphasis is on the co-ordination that is acquired, as in the case of the batsman who learns to hit the ball safely, or the golfer who learns to correct a fault, without, in either case, knowing how it has been done. All we can say is that there is an improvement in skill, together with a difference in the "feel" of the thing. Then there is the kind of learning in which the emphasis falls on this change in the "feel" or the quality of the experience; as when we learn to judge the speed of an automobile or to distrust certain persons, without being able to specify the clues on which we rely. Lastly, there is the kind of learning which is based on some trait of fact or relationship that can be analyzed out and offered as evidence, as when we infer from the appearance of a lawn that it needs sprinkling or when we abstain from coffee because it keeps us awake at night. The clear perception of relationships is what is sometimes designated as insight.

These differences in kinds of learning derive whatever significance they may have from the fact that they are connected with corresponding differences in the procedure by which they are acquired. They are primarily differences of emphasis. It seems safe to assume, on the one hand, that all learning involves some perception of relationship, however dim, and, on the other hand, that analysis, or insight into relationship, however extensive, never keeps abreast with the adaptive changes in our experience. Mind, as Dewey has told us, is "the power to understand things in terms of the use made of them." Understanding has to do with relationships. This understanding, however, may take various forms. It seems fair to describe the experience of the benighted pike in the tank as an obscure comprehension that the little fish were "to-be-let-alone." Some such quality of "futurity," therefore, inheres in all learning. It is worth noting that the expert who devotes himself to the business of analysis or the picking out of relationships does not thereby diminish the area of his unanalyzed experience. On the contrary, he increases it; he develops a kind of sixth sense or "instinct" or "intuition" which constantly outruns his ability to make clean-cut analyses and which guides him in situations that he cannot handle adequately by analysis. In other words, the expert never gets away from a certain resemblance to the pike. All this is reminiscent of the familiar advice given by an old judge to a young colleague, to the effect that a judge should make his decisions without giving the reasons therefor, because "the decisions are likely to be right, but the reasons are bound to be wrong."

All forms of learning, then, have a common element. They all involve a change in the experiential situation which gives greater control in relation to subsequent behavior. To the boy who has learned to swim, water has become a different medium, to which he responds differently. To the veteran salesman the reactions of his "prospects" when he approaches them take on the same kind of difference. The experiential situation has changed for them as truly as for the automobile mechanic who discovers that the trouble with an automobile is due to a defective carburetor. This change finds expression in the control of behavior, whether or not there is a *specific* reference to the future, in much the same way that the visual perception of a flame as "hot" controls behavior, without any such specific relationship as "flame *means* burn." All learning, then, is a change in experience such as to provide for increased control of behavior.[2]

We can now plot the curve of learning as it ordinarily goes on. It starts on the level of everyday living and it has to do with the changes made in things by our responses. These changes are speeded up and made more extensive by the process of analysis, or insight into relationships—a process in which the relationship of meaning or "pointing" is prominent and which aims to bring new elements into the picture. With familiarity this relationship of pointing drops out; the new elements become increasingly absorbed into the original experiences; recognition takes the place of inference. The experiences as thus modified become the basis for a repetition of the process; and thus experience continues to grow or to become enriched without any assignable limit.

This process of inference giving way to recognition is exemplified rather strikingly by language. When we first start to learn a foreign language, we rely extensively on the relationship, "this means that" (e.g., *cheval* means *horse*). If we reach a point, however, where we can speak and think in terms of the new language, this relationship disappears. The words begin to *look* different and to *sound* different. This change in the quality or *feel* of words takes place in much the same way in the case of our mother tongue. As William James remarks:

> Our own language would sound very different to us if we heard it without understanding, as we hear a foreign tongue. Rises and falls of voice, odd sibilants and other consonants, would fall on our ear in a way of which we can now form no notion. Frenchmen say that English sounds to them like the *gazouillement des oiseaux* —an impression which it certainly makes on no native ear. Many of us English would describe the sound of Russian in similar terms. All of us are conscious of the strong inflections of voice and explosives and gutturals of German speech in a way in which no German can be conscious of them.[3]

The inference to be drawn is that the term "meaning" has different applica-

---

[2] "We thus reach a technical definition of education: It is that reconstruction or reorganization of experience which adds to the meaning of experience, and which increases the ability to direct the course of subsequent experience." John Dewey, *Democracy and Education*, copyright 1916 by The Macmillan Company, p. 89.

[3] From *Principles of Psychology*, vol. II, by William James. By permission of Henry Holt and Company, Inc., p. 80.

tions. In one sense the term denotes the function of pointing or symbolizing. To make a clear contrast between the thing and whatever is pointed to is to "intellectualize" the experience of the thing. When this contrast drops out, the thing is still considered to retain the meaning, but the term "meaning" is now used in a different sense. It is now a name for a certain quality of the total experience. To use an illustration, we avoid an onrushing automobile, and we ordinarily do so without the help of a specific relationship, such as "automobile means danger." The quality of danger has become a part of the automobile, in the same way as its shape or color; it remains, indeed, just as effective in the control of behavior, but meaning is now better described as "appreciation" rather than "pointing." In the language of Dewey:

> Definiteness, depth, and variety of meaning attach to the objects of an experience just in the degree in which they have been previously thought about, even when present in an experience in which they do not evoke inferential procedures at all. Such terms as "meaning," "significance," "value" have a double sense. Sometimes they mean a function: the office of one thing representing another, or pointing to it as implied; the operation, in short, of serving as a sign. In the word "symbol" this meaning is practically exhaustive. But the terms also sometimes mean an inherent quality, a quality intrinsically characterizing the thing experienced and making it worth while. . . . In the situation which follows upon reflection, meanings are intrinsic; they have no instrumental or subservient office,—because they have no office at all. They are as much qualities of the objects in the situation as are red and black, hard and soft, square and round.[4]

If we turn now to the consideration of the implications contained in this general point of view for school procedures, we are at once confronted with what Dewey calls the principle of the continuity of experience. All learning, whether in school or out of school, has to do with the transformation of experience in the interest of better control. In order to bring about this transformation, it is necessary to do something that will produce the desired change. This contradicts the familiar assumption that pupils should go to school in order to draw upon a storehouse of knowledge, in somewhat the same way that a railroad car goes to the mine in order to take on a load of coal. The school, from the present point of view, is simply a place which is especially designed to facilitate the business of securing the desired transformation of experience. It is a place where new experiences are provided in such a form as to best promote that reconstruction or reorganization of experience which is identified with education.

[4] Reprinted from *Essays in Experimental Logic* by John Dewey. By permission of the University of Chicago Press, copyright 1916 by the University of Chicago.

10   *Dewey's analysis of the act of thought*

Related selections: 8, 9, 43

Criticisms of Dewey's philosophical and educational theories have been abundant, increasing in quantity in recent years. Much of this criticism has been just a gross misunderstanding and misinterpretation of what he actually wrote and stood for. There is little doubt that his professional peers will continue to evaluate his insights and contributions. In this selection Broudy carefully and thoughtfully analyzes Dewey's description of the act of thought and raises some questions as to the adequacy of problem solving as the method of all thinking, and as the sole basis for teaching method and subject-matter organization. Study of these criticisms should follow study of selections 8 and 9.

Analyses of thought and of scientific method are not uncommon in the history of philosophy, but none of them in our time has aroused so much educational controversy as has that of John Dewey.

Without trying to probe for the causes of this phenomenon, may I put forward the hypothesis that, because of a variety of circumstances, Dewey's work was perceived as announcing great and good news (*kerygma*). This message proclaimed that a turning point in human history was at hand (*kairos*) during which a promise would be fulfilled and an emancipation accomplished.

The promise was that man, by use of science and scientific method, could weave his own destiny. Life henceforth need not be a tale told by an idiot, all sound and fury, but rather an intelligent transformation of man and his environment toward greater happiness.

The emancipation goes with the promise, but must precede it. Old beliefs, old values, old institutions must be examined and, if they cannot receive a clean bill of health from science, must be rejected. This is a hard, dangerous program, with great risks and even greater prospects. Is it any wonder that, at the close of a century filled with the tumult of industry and expansion, Dewey's message

HARRY S. BROUDY, "Dewey's Analysis of the Act of Thought," *Bulletin of the School of Education,* Indiana University, 36 (January, 1960), 15–26. Reprinted by permission of the author and the publisher.

DR. BROUDY (1905–   ) is Professor of Education at the University of Illinois. He is author of *Building a Philosophy of Education* and *Paradox and Promise.*

stirred the imagination and disturbed the thinking of those who were to live out their lives in the century about to begin?

As we enter the last four decades of that century, it is obvious that the promise was not an empty one, but that neither the promise nor the emancipation has come about as many of us would have wished. The divisions and hatred and exclusions that Dewey deplored are still with us—politically, socially, economically, and educationally.

In this paper I propose to examine the act of thought, or scientific method, or problem solving in the hope of making clear both its great power and its limitations as a formula for the reconstruction of philosophy, society, and the individual; in short, a prescription for life itself. This examination may disclose why this prescription, so successful in many ways, has nevertheless not produced the consequences envisioned for it.

THE COMPLETE ACT OF THOUGHT IN SCIENCE

Dewey says:

> The two limits of every unit of thinking are a perplexed, troubled, or confused situation at the beginning and a cleared-up, unified, resolved situation at the close. The first of these situations may be called *pre*-reflective. It sets the problem to be solved; out of it grows the question that reflection has to answer. In the final situation the doubt has been dispelled; the situation is *post*-reflective; there results a direct experience of mastery, satisfaction, enjoyment. Here, then, are the limits within which reflection falls.[1]

In between, Dewey goes on to say, are included: (1) suggestions, (2) an intellectualizing of the felt difficulty into a *problem* to be solved, (3) the use of suggestions as guiding ideas or hypotheses, (4) the mental elaboration of the idea, and (5) testing the hypothesis by overt or imaginative action.

> In the intermediate course of transition and transformation of the indeterminate situation [pre-reflective situation] discourse through use of symbols is employed as means—propositions, or terms and the relations between them, are intrinsically involved.[2]

Yet discourse is not the whole of inquiry, because in "inquiry a deliberate operation intervenes: first, to select the conditions that are operative, and secondly, to institute the new conditions which interact with the old ones."[3]

---

[1] John Dewey, *How We Think*, p. 106.

[2] John Dewey, *Logic*, p. 105.

[3] *Ibid.*, p. 289. Emmanuel G. Mesthene makes a cogent point in his article "The Role of Language in the Philosophy of John Dewey" (*Philosophical and Phenomenological Research*, 19:4, 511-517, June, 1959) that it is language that makes us think because it is by means of discourse that the indeterminate situation becomes determinate. Yet it would seem that "to institute the new conditions that would interact with the old ones" need not always be a matter of discourse; indeed, the testing of hypotheses by overt action is, whenever possible, to be preferred.

In what sense does the act of inquiry give us knowledge? Consider an inquiry that in recent years has not been uncommon in nuclear science.

It is a fundamental principle or postulate of physical science that the energy on one side of the equation describing a reaction must equal the energy on the other. Suppose a scientist finds that the sides of an energy equation do not balance. Here is a perplexing situation. We can expect that he will now observe the reaction more closely, check instrument readings and calculations, and have them rechecked by his colleagues.

If the examination fails to disclose errors of procedure, i.e., if his observations do not clear up the puzzle, he must either discard the principle of energy balance or he must account for the loss in terms of that principle.

There are crucial periods in the intellectual history of man when a fundamental principle is discarded, but it is the last rather than an early resort. Instead, the scientist will rack his brains and the knowledge of the field to make his data consistent with the principle. Now it may occur to him or a colleague that perhaps the lost energy has been used to form a new particle. If this possibility (hypothesis) is not completely absurd, although once it might have seemed so, the scientist will try to verify the guess. He will cast about for some means to detect the presence of the new particle, e.g., by tracing its path in a cloud chamber. By combining known principles of chemistry and physics with his knowledge of apparatus, he arrives at the hypothesis: If I carry on the reaction under these conditions, there ought to be a track of this dimension traveling in this direction in this cloud chamber. Let us suppose that our scientist performed the experiment and happily confirmed his hypothesis.

The scientist is now warranted in saying that a new particle was formed during the reaction *because* there is evidence for saying so. The scientist might have arrived at this conclusion by intuition or in a dream, or under the influence of drugs, but then it would not have been a *warranted* assertion, because there would have been no authority to issue the warrant.

Logically, the scientist believes his hypothesis to be probable because it accounts for or explains the facts better than any other, e.g., that his instruments were faulty or that the postulate of energy balance no longer holds. But, inasmuch as the hypothesis is the conclusion of a long chain of reasoning, all the principles and generalizations involved are also strengthened.

Psychologically, verification provides an overwhelming conviction that the hypothesis cannot be false, for we find it almost impossible to imagine how the prediction would have come true apart from the truth of the hypothesis. Yet imagine it we can, for, unlikely as it seems, it might have come about through a coincidence or for reasons we cannot now discern.

If, however, we could assert that the nature of X is to be a Y, then if anything could *unambiguously* be identified as an X, it would *certainly* be a Y. The doctrine of *infima* species made it possible for Aristotle to hope for certainty in propositions about living organisms. Definitions of matter and motion would lead to certainty for principles in physics, and a fixed human nature would provide a source for certainty in statements about the good life.

Certain fundamental principles in these areas, it was held, could be intuited as self-evident, and by sense perception certain parts of our world could be identified as members of a class or as having the properties of a class. Such principles as the end being more important than the means, the actual being prior to the potential, the laws of logic, and the principle of causation and sufficient reason were taken as self-evident. Mistakes in classification could be made, of course, but, because sense perception was basically veridical, such mistakes could be corrected. And, if sense experience was veridical, then we had to assume that in sense perception the mind through abstraction united with the object's sensible form, just as via concepts and thought it united self with its meaning, i.e., its intelligible form.

The classical search for truth was, as Dewey correctly observed, a quest for certainty—a quest for the essences or natures of things related to each other logically, so that the human mind, if it traveled the right route, would apprehend the map of reality itself.

This hope for certainty modern pragmatism in the persons of James, Peirce, and Dewey abjured in favor of the kind of warranted assertion that enabled men to predict what would happen if one did thus and so. How do things behave? not, what are their natures? is the proper question for modern science. Perhaps, argues the pragmatist, there are no essential natures to be discovered and, even if there are, how can we compare our statements about them with the objects themselves? Rather than to try to compare our experience of the world with the world as it would be apart from our experience, the pragmatist is willing to settle for a comparison of a prediction of what he will experience under certain conditions with the experience that ensues. He is willing to exchange a grasping of reality for an efficient control of it, i.e., truth for warranted assertion.

This kind of argument frees man from the fetters of traditional philosophy, science, and values and encourages him to begin his thinking with particular situations that to him seem perplexed, confusing, and indeterminate and to stop when they are cleared up.

Can we really have warranted assertion without making a truth claim about reality? Suppose, for example, that there were no reality with its own powers and properties. Or, suppose that these powers and properties changed capriciously from moment to moment. The confirmation of a scientist's prediction would be a first-rate miracle. We would honor him not as a scientist but as a magician or prophet.

Why is it that we place so much emphasis on verification of our hypotheses? Why not be satisfied with the assurance that they are not inconceivable? Why not be satisfied with their aesthetic elegance? The real, we say, is not identical with the conceivable, as fairy tales demonstrate; nor is the aesthetically pleasing a reliable index to the behavior of things, as men have learned to their dismay.

Scientific method is our way of making as sure as we can that our predictions will not come true by chance or demons or other fortuitous circumstances. But if it is not chance, nor demons, nor fortuitous circumstances, then what does make our predictions come true if not the fact that in verification we have proof that we have hit a vein of reality?

Nor does the scientific method dispense with intuition, perception, and classification—processes that the classical theory of knowledge made central, perhaps too central. At every stage of thinking we identify objects as tables, chairs, Geiger counters, or last year's hats. Indeed, scientific method, far from abandoning classification, may be regarded as our most reliable method for discovering reliable and useful classifications. For example, our fight against cancer will achieve a breakthrough once we can be sure of the class of disease processes to which it belongs.

Similarly, the act of reflection to proceed must combine the flights of inference with the perches of immediate awareness. Yet in his preoccupation with the dynamic, relational, and reconstructive features of thinking and learning, Dewey virtually forgets that without awareness of the situation from moment to moment, the thinker thinks of nothing and gets nowhere. The persistent denial of cognitive knowledge to this immediate awareness means either that it tells us nothing or that it does not provide evidence for what it reports. The latter is true, but the former is not. As Dewey says:

> Intellectual activity, science, has its phases of appreciation as truly as the fine arts. They arise whenever inquiry has reached a close that fulfills the activities and conditions which led up to it. Without these phases, sometimes intense, no inquirer would have the experiential sign that his inquiry had reached its close.[4]

One does not have to wait until inquiry reaches a close in order to achieve these "experiential signs." The flow of inference is always between patterns of concepts or *Gestalten*. Even the relation called implication ties two or more concepts together into a Gestalt that is unique and different from the Gestalt called contradiction, or cause-effect. These Gestalten have to be intuited as such or the inference does not even get started. Second, the situation that sets off the thinking process and the one in which it eventuates have certain characteristics, e.g., perplexity, clarity, determinateness, indeterminateness, etc., that have to be apprehended directly. Furthermore, at each step of the inquiry, the thinker has to judge whether the situation is changing and in what manner. Without these signs the act of thought would be directionless.

PROBLEM SOLVING AND MORAL REFLECTION

Let us now turn to problem solving in the field of value. Much of the influence of Dewey's philosophy stems from his claim that there is no fundamental difference between achieving warranted assertions about matters of fact and about

[4] *Ibid.*, p. 176.

values. Whether we are seeking a probable hypothesis about the solar system or about the good life, the act of thought is the only reliable formula for *warranted* assertion.

What kind of moral knowledge or value knowledge can the act of thought provide? Given a situation in which we desire something, the act of thought may provide warranted assertions as to the means that will achieve it. Given two or more desires that conflict, the act of thought may point to a reliable way of choosing between them on the basis of the consequences that follow from each. Thus, what in the pre-reflective situation was a *valuing* becomes in the post-reflective situation a valuing with a reason, i.e., it is transformed into a *value*.

The parallel to theoretical knowledge is clear. Just as awareness without reflection is for Dewey not knowledge, so desiring and preferring without reflection is not a value. In both types of reflection we deal with data, generalizations, hypotheses, and verification. We need never get outside of the initial human predicament and the final transformation of it.

At several points, however, the parallelism is somewhat strained. In the first place, what corresponds to the generalizations and principles that guide the inquiry into matters of fact?

Presumably in choice situations we rely on generalizations about what makes men in general happy, healthy, wise, etc., to frame our hypotheses as to what in our particular situation will make *us* happy, healthy, wise, etc. These generalizations in an enlightened age will be provided by psychology, sociology, and other sciences.

It is interesting to note that, although we often speak of *using* the knowledge of the laws of nature to control this or that operation, we never speak of changing the laws of nature. They are not that kind of law. With respect to the laws of human nature, matters, so far as pragmatic doctrine goes, stand otherwise; there are apparently no laws of human nature, because there is no human nature as such. But this means there are no generalizations and principles to guide inquiry comparable to those in physical science. The uniformity of nature is a postulate the denial of which makes science impossible, and we might conclude that a denial of the uniformity of human nature would make a scientific inquiry into value fruitless.

In the second place, what is the role of verification in the moral act of thought? Granted that sometimes the moral problem is what to do to achieve a given goal or to decide between two courses of proposed action, are there no other kinds? Often our moral problem concerns the meaning of a moral obligation on our part rather than finding the practice it demands. What, for example, does "love thy neighbor" mean? This is the moral problem rather than finding the means of loving him once we know what this signifies. How does one verify the meaning assigned to this phrase, or to democracy, or to self-realization?

An even more serious reservation about the attempt to equate moral reflection with factual inquiry comes from the Existentialist philosophers of various denominations, who regard the human predicament as something more than a state of temporary perplexity, discontinuity, and indeterminateness. On the contrary, they point out that human existence is dialectical in nature, a strange mixture of the finite and the infinite; poor in power, exalted in aspiration; longing for union with the eternal, yet doomed to be estranged from it.

Consider, by way of example, the human predicament of knowing that one will have to die some day. (What Karl Jaspers referred to as a boundary situation.) We can be both learned and shrewd in finding means for postponing death for many human beings and for ourselves. We can even wager with the insurance people that we shall die sooner than they expect. But until we can contrive existential immortality, we have been well counseled to act as if we were to live forever, and at the same time as if we were to die tonight. Presumably this advice has nothing to do with statistics on longevity or public health. It has to do, I take it, with the peculiar nature of human existence in which value makes a joke of death, and death makes a joke of value. To strive as if our existence were eternal while never forgetting that death might be lurking just outside the door—that is a mode of existence that is quite different from the mode of existence we call problem solving. There are some predicaments from which the only extrication is commitment. Every moment of life is decisive, because life is not reversible. That we can assume the problematic posture is the great human act of defiance, because in this stance we do hold up the moment of commitment, even though we cannot hold up life itself.

But how do we make our commitments? And do we really make them? How do we make them in an existential situation in which the biological urges of others impose life upon us and the cultural demands of others shape that life in their own image, whatever that may happen to be at the moment?

This is the predicament of freedom. Is freedom a problem to be solved? Is it a search for means to ends? Is it a matter of restoring compatibility to incompatible concepts? Is it, for that matter, a predicament from which we are trying to extricate ourselves? Is not freedom our expression for a predicament that *defines* human existence? For to get rid of the "ought" that weights so heavily on our hearts, or to get rid of the impatience that makes the "ought" unbearable, is to get rid of the anchors of the spring that generates the tension of human existence.

And what about the predicament of the "ought" itself? How does one deal with the tyrannical demands of the better and the best in face of our theoretical dubiety about what is the better and the best? About all of the predicaments it is, of course, possible to think. It is even possible to trace their origins and causes, and knowing these it is possible to hypothesize cures that would extricate us from these predicaments. One can always try to adjust; one can always try to reduce the demands upon oneself to what one can comfortably achieve; one can heed the call of the group without question; one can indeed fashion a civilization in which strenuousness of both body and spirit is enormously relaxed. And perhaps one can achieve all this and more by the problem-solving method. Yet when all this is done, and I see no reason for abating our efforts to do so, there is the suspicion that matters will still be as they always have been. For there are some aspects of human nature, although not all, that are defined by predicaments rather than by solutions. That is why the problem-solving attitude seems so curiously irrelevant to some of these predicaments, and why such categories as faith, guilt, sacrifice, commitment, courage, and suffering seem so curiously relevant to them.

PROBLEM SOLVING AS
A FORMULA FOR LEARNING

Just as problem solving is Dewey's design for discovering warranted assertions about matters of fact and value, so is it the design for learning. Children have their difficulties and perplexing situations, and if they proceed by problem-solving procedures they find out what will extricate them, i.e., they learn.

Like the scientist the pupil uses data, generalizations, hypotheses, and verification. As problem succeeds problem, the pupil acquires tested beliefs about his world and his choices. In addition, the problem situation demands from the pupil open-mindedness, single-mindedness, perseverance, and honesty. Scientific method has its own moral code, and its use builds character.

Problem solving when applied collectively to group problems becomes the formula for democracy, for choosing both goals and the means to achieving them.

Here, then, we have Dewey's answer to a design for learning that had developed for nearly nineteen centuries. It had had its high moments and its low ones. At the turn of the century the traditional curriculum and its methods were definitely on the down side. This was its most serious challenge; a challenge to drill, a challenge to Latin grammar, a challenge to the classical languages and literature—in short, a bold challenge to the subject-matter curriculum as a pattern for general education.

No doubt Dewey's cricitisms were sound. The gap between the mind and interest of the child and the subject matter had grown too wide, and it was even wider between the knowledge the pupil acquired and what he used in coping with the predicaments of an industrial social order.

By and large, whatever real changes have been made in American schools can be credited to Dewey's challenge. They are either attempts to conform to the Dewey formula or to evade the criticisms that it leveled against the traditional pattern. Yet curiously the results, though great, have not resulted in any wide acceptance of the problem-solving curriculum. Why not?

I submit that the slurring over of the immediate and the given in the act of thought is again responsible.

For one thing, it virtually restricted learning to the outcomes of problem solving. We learn by problem solving, but we also learn by noting, perceiving, and insight.

Because knowledge already achieved and organized is learned by insight, the Dewey formula has had the effect of belittling logically organized subject matter. Skills perfected by practice and attitudes formed by conditioning also come under the ban, because they are used without thought, i.e., without intelligence. Dewey was right, of course. Whatever we accept simply as given is taken unintelligently, and only an arch traditionalist would regard this sort of learning as the end of the educative process.

Nevertheless, we cannot escape the fact that the given is the *beginning* of the process. Without *given* knowledge, there is nothing to reconstruct; without perfected skill, problems requiring skill do not get solved. Without conditioned attitudes, there is nothing to transform into intelligent attitudes. Without valuings, there is nothing to be evaluated.

While current critics of Dewey may be wrong in detail, they are probably right in sensing the thrust of his attack, for they realize that the problem-solving theory of learning endangers the privileged position of any content and consequently of the particular content to which the critic is devoted.

If whatever is relevant to the solution of a problem constitutes subject matter, then Dewey's theory would seem to reject the systematic study of physics, history, geography, etc.

I am aware that some followers of Dewey cite his remarks about stages of subject matter in *Democracy and Education*, Chapter XIV, as evidence that this extreme deduction cannot be drawn, and that Dewey did favor study of organized subject matter in a systematic way in the later stages of the curriculum. But my reading of this material does not lead me to this conclusion. Dewey says:

> To be informed is to be posted; it is to have at command the subject matter needed for the effective dealing with a problem. . . . Informational knowledge . . . is a kind of bridge for mind in its passage from doubt to discovery. It has the office of an intellectual middleman.[5]

As regards science itself, Dewey reiterated his prior definition of it as a method of inquiry and testing. Even when regarded as a body of organized or systematized knowledge this means only that it is organized in a special way, viz., "with specific reference to the successful enterprise of discovery."[6]

On the other hand, he re-emphasized the warning that the abstractness of perfected knowledge makes scientific information ever "more exposed to the dangers attendant upon presenting ready-made subject matter than are other forms of information."

[5] John Dewey, *Democracy and Education*, p. 22.
[6] *Ibid.*, pp. 223-224.

Further:

> All information and systematized scientific subject matter have been worked out under the conditions of social life and have been transmitted by social means. But this does not prove that all is of equal value for the purpose of forming the disposition and supplying the equipment of members of present society. The scheme of a curriculum must take account of the adaptation of studies to the needs of existing community life; . . . . The things which are socially most fundamental, that is, which have to do with the experiences in which the widest groups share, are the essentials.[7]

These quotations do not, it seems to me, indicate any real departure by Dewey from the notion that knowledge ought to be an outcome of problem solving and a resource for it. Therefore, the question arises as to whether systematic knowledge of a subject is desirable, and, if so, whether the problem-solving approach will provide it.

1. If a subject is a logically organized body of concepts and relations, it is difficult to see how anything short of apprehending the total pattern would be satisfactory either for the mastery of the subject or for the use of it in problem solving.

2. It is difficult to imagine how a sufficient variety of problems could be introduced to make sure that systematic mastery ensues.

3. If it is argued that tests show that pupils using the problem approach do no worse on subject matter tests than do those studying by the more traditional method, I would respond that this may show the inefficacy of the traditional method rather than the efficacy of the problem-solving approach.

However, an even more important difficulty confronts the problem-solving approach to learning. Generalizations used in school problems may come from common sense or from systematic bodies of knowledge. If the school problems are confined to those that do not go beyond common sense, the school becomes superfluous. If, on the other hand, problems require knowledge from organized subject matter, where is the pupil to get this knowledge if he does not study it directly and systematically? That he can "raid" a logically-organized subject when he needs it is doubtful indeed.

The same line of argument could be restated for skills and attitudes. The "unthinking" efficiency of a skill or an attitude is the result of repetition and reinforcement. Problem solving must regard only the element in a situation as doubtful and to be cleared up through inquiry. It cannot doubt everything and test everything in the same act of thought. Whatever is used to solve the problem, whether it be a piece of information, a conceptual set of relations, a moral conviction, it must be steady and operate uniformly during the problem-solving procedure. It is only when the problem does not get solved that we go

[7] *Ibid.*, p. 225.

back and put in doubt an element we had taken as beyond doubt. Thus, if in a court trial doubt is raised about any of the "facts" in the case, e.g., that X signed a certain document or whether X is really sane, the major problem has to be sidetracked until these subproblems are investigated.

Whether problem solving is an adequate account of knowledge or learning depends on whether we attend to large segments of experience or their smaller constituents. What is true of problem solving as a process may not be true of each of its component parts. The act of relating these components is dynamic, flowing, and instrumental, but each component is an insight or behavioral unit with a character of its own that has to be taken for *what* it is.

In both knowing and learning, the intrinsic and the given are as strategic as the instrumental and the reconstructed. In the appraisal of Dewey's analysis of the act of thought, I have tried to point out that the balance between these two aspects has been disturbed. This, I believe, has resulted in the unhappy conflict between the *what* of life and learning and the *how*. It has resulted in a cleavage between those who regard formal schooling as the time and place for the mastery of the tested items in knowledge and value and those who believe the school is the place to achieve the habits and attitudes of problem solving. To say that we need both is to say the obvious, but it is a restatement of the problem rather than a solution of it. How to do both in a single learning act is still the paramount problem of educational method.

That Dewey himself did not intend to create a new dualism in his zeal to abolish the traditional ones is witnessed by his *Art as Experience* and a passage such as the following in *Democracy and Education:*

> As long as any topic makes an immediate appeal, it is not necessary to ask what it is good for. . . . Some goods are not good *for* anything; they are just good. Any other notion leads to an absurdity. For we cannot stop asking the question about an instrumental good, one whose value lies in its being good *for* something, unless there is at some point something intrinsically good, good for itself.[8]

Perhaps we can add that some items of knowledge are also good for no other reasons than that they are true, and some skills are good simply because they represent human achievements. Sometimes their relation to other goods is clear; sometimes not.

The quest for what is good in itself is enormously furthered by the act of thought. That it would come to be regarded as an end in itself was perhaps inevitable. Every profound philosophy is a caricature of the real in that it exaggerates the truth it has found. But every profound philosophy provokes an impulse to correct the caricature. In great minds this provocation produces new theory; in lesser souls, sound practice. History will record our debt to Dewey for both.

[8] *Ibid.,* p. 283.

11 *We learn what we live*

Related selections: 8, 9, 29

In the folk-thinking of America, there has been a disparagement of "book learning." This represents a belief that unless an endeavor is reflected in changed and improved behavior, it cannot be of much consequence. In this selection Kilpatrick sets forth the principles that learning involves changed behavior and that the change in behavior is what we learn. He also enumerates four principles as a basis for spiritual education. The statements regarding learning and those on the basis of spiritual life offer material for reflection and discussion.

What this title means may not be quite clear to all. Just what does this transitive use of the verb *to live* mean? And is the theory thus asserted psychologically true? And if true, what does it mean for teaching? These questions we shall consider in the order given.

1. What does it mean *to live* anything that is to be learned? What does it mean, for example, *to live persistence?* Can we not agree that actually *to live* persistence in any instance means (1) that one faces a life situation which itself calls for persistence; and (2) that one does then in his own heart accept the idea of persisting; and (3) accordingly does indeed so persist? When all these three things concur, then one has on that occasion *lived* persistence. If with this positive instance we contrast a negative one, the meaning may come clearer.

Certain pupils were asked to write out the words of their morning flag salute. Among the various replies received the following were noted:

I pejur legens; I plaig alegins; I pledge a legion; to the Republicans; one country invisable; one country inavisable; with liberty and jesters.

Is it not at once clear that these pupils did not adequately *live* the meaning of the words used in the salute? Whatever else they may or may not have lived, it stands clear that they did not in any full or adequate degree *live* the meanings which the words were supposed to carry.

It may be added that we can live things in many different degrees. Take feel-

WILLIAM H. KILPATRICK, "We Learn What We Live," *New York State Education,* XXXIII (April, 1946), 535–37. Reprinted by permission of the publisher.

PROFESSOR KILPATRICK (1871–) is Professor Emeritus of Education, Teachers College, Columbia, and a renowned teacher and scholar.

ings, for example; some we may live so slightly that we hardly think of them at the time, and soon forget all about them. Others we live so deeply and poignantly that we can hardly banish them to give due attention elsewhere needed.

So much for the meaning of the transitive verb *to live*.

2. Is it psychologically true that we learn what we live?

The fact of internal *acceptance* we saw as an essential part of *truly living* anything. We can now say that different people will *live* the same thing differently if they accept it differently, differently for behavior purposes. Two women hear a child scream; both so accept it, the one as the scream of an unknown child, the other as the scream of her own child. Both are concerned; but the first one does nothing overt, the other hurries to rescue her child. Each woman lived the scream as she accepted it, accepted it for behavior purposes.

What now does *learn* mean? Consider this mother. After the screaming ceased, did not the matter remain with her—remain as she had accepted it? And as accepted, did it not help determine her further behavior? And determine it appropriately?

This then is what we mean by *learn:* When, after something has been lived, it does not die, but stays with one to get back, sooner or later, appropriately into one's further behavior—when these things happen, we say learning has taken place.

The full principle of learning may thus be stated:

We learn what we live as we accept it to live by, and we learn it in the degree that we live it.

For proof of this principle the reader is asked to apply it to his own life and see whether it fits, whether it does not pick out the strong instances of learning from the weak; and also to apply it to children and their living and learning in the home and in the school. Is it not true that one learns anything *as* he accepts it? Jacob accepted that the bloody coat was Joseph's and learned—falsely as to fact, but truly as to psychological learning—that Joseph was dead: "some evil beast of the field hath devoured him." And it stayed with him; "he refused to be comforted."

As to "degree of living"—and consequently of learning—there are two sub-principles that apply. (1) We live anything in the degree we count it important to us. So Jacob lived deeply the (supposed) death of Joseph and it stayed strongly with him to affect his further behavior. (2) We live more vividly and so learn stronger anything in the degree that it fits well in with what we already know and live. If a man tells me that he has moved next door to me, I shall remember his house number easily. In general, we learn easier what we understand well.

3. What difference in teaching does this learning theory demand?

First, it demands a kind of school different from the old one of merely assigned lessons in books; this must be a school of living. If a child inevitably learns what he accepts in his heart to live by, then the quality of that living becomes the essential factor. For all he lives, even his private heart reactions, he builds at once into character; and out of his character comes all his future behavior.

It is the learning of spiritual values that here concerns us. Four typical samples will illustrate all such values: consideration for others, regard for their rights and feelings; appreciation, as for example of literature; persistence (in a worthy cause) ; and acting on thinking. If these four are to be learned they must each be lived, lived (a) in some natural setting, as in life; and lived (b) in such variety of settings that the cumulative result is a dependable trait, well founded and many sided.

Let us conclude by considering the building of the four named typical traits.

CONSIDERATION OF OTHERS.   No true regard for others can come by mere compulsion, but only as the heart's own response to how others will feel justly considered. True enough, compulsion may prevent positive habits of disregard. How now shall we stir the youthful heart to regard others? The school life must be largely shared living, with abundant opportunities at co-operative creating and effecting. Each such successfully managed instance of shared effort makes *implicitly* for mutual regard. But temptation to the contrary will arise; and besides the *implicit* regard must become *explicit* and critically judged. When, then, conflicts occur, the resourceful teacher will mobilize the impartial public opinion of the group. Nothing is more effective. Next time the temptation will be better resisted, while the discussion has helped to build the conscious ideal.

APPRECIATION.   We must of course build many appreciations; for each is in range limited. Can I build an appreciation of Whittier's "Barefoot Boy" by saying "I give you till next Monday to appreciate this, or else"? Clearly not. Appreciation, like "the quality of mercy," is "not strained." We cannot command it. The only way is to help each youth find in the poem something that "clicks" within, something that rouses appreciation in him. And the public opinion of the class must be closely watched; it can fortify and so strengthen a shared appreciation, but it can build a hurtful conformity instead of honest appreciation. And note: Many varied cumulative appreciations are necessary to build a reliable "appreciation of good literature."

PERSISTENCE.   This we discussed at the outset. How then shall we develop that crucial inner attitude, the wish to persist? Here "nothing succeeds like success and nothing fails like failure." The wise teacher will know the strength and weakness of each pupil and see that each new enterprise, while difficult enough to be challenging, still lies within the area of possible success. The appreciative regard of the others in connection is a most powerful aid, as the same wise teacher will know. Persistence here is both effect and cause, effect of past success, cause of further and stronger effort, with the still further effect of increased self-respect and felt security.

ACTING ON THINKING. If there is any one trait which best promises to take care of all spiritual values, this is it. Consideration for others, persistence, proper sensitivity, self-respect, sense of security—these and a host of other spiritual traits are likely to come out of well-directed acting on thinking. In fact, this fourth trait of acting on thinking furnishes the twin highway for building, alike, both intelligence and strength of character. It builds intelligence; for acting on thinking is practically the only process for building trustworthy knowledge, reliable conceptions, effective principles of attack and of critical judgment. Acting on thinking likewise builds strength of character; for it alone can build sound and reliable attitudes and convictions, defensible ideals, and trustworthy principles of action.

The single principle to guide all teaching is that our pupils learn what they live as they in their hearts accept it.

12 *Psychology, existentialism, and religion*

Related selections: 7, 33, 37, 38, 40

The growth of interest in existentialism in religion and philosophy, and in phenomenological or perceptual psychology during the past two decades has been marked. Some scholars regard these movements as a "retreat from reason," representing a "failure of nerve" in the face of the difficulties of the era. Others feel that the movements can afford new and promising insights into human behavior and purposes. Professor Royce has drawn upon varied sources in his attempt to establish some agreement and common concerns among religion, existentialism, and psychology. Students may have some difficulty following and evaluating his presentation. We suggest that they read first the summary at the end, and then follow the development of his ideas from the beginning of the selection.

A. INTRODUCTION

Science and religion have a long and well known history of mutual indifference and, at times, animosity. Such animosity has been most apparent whenever it has been necessary for man to incorporate a major change in his Weltanschauung.

JOSEPH R. ROYCE, "Psychology, Existentialism, and Religion," *The Journal of General Psychology*, 66 (1962), 3–16. Reprinted by permission of The Journal Press and the author.

PROFESSOR ROYCE (1921–) is Chairman, Department of Psychology, University of Alberta.

Consider, for example, the upheavals which followed the Copernican Revolution, the Darwinian Revolution, and the Freudian Revolution. In all three of these examples it was religion which received the major body blow and had to effect a recovery. It is highly significant that religion has always been able to do this.

Science, on the other hand, has been riding the crest of the wave of success. We of the twentieth century may be in the middle of an interesting switch in the science-religion controversy. For in many ways the usual roles have been reversed. Whereas in earlier centuries religion held the hearts and minds of men, and science had to struggle for recognition, now we see science emerging as the new religion in many quarters. Whereas religion had to be shown the error of its ways by the scientific insights of a Copernicus, a Darwin, and a Freud, we may now be in the situation where science has to be shown the error of its ways by religious insights. For the possible errors of science without religion have never been so obvious to man as they have since the advent of the atomic bomb.

The history of the rift between science and religion indicates that a rapprochement can occur. As in the case of other apparently contradictory approaches in life, such rapprochement follows automatically when each contender comes to the realization that his position, while formidable, is not sufficient in isolation. With the door thus opened, each is more ready to learn from the other. Each contender is thereby rendered more able to see the positive contributions of the other, and because of this, each is more ready to join forces as complementary rather than contradictory approaches to truth.

The uncooperative relationship between psychology and religion is part of the traditional science-religion controversy. Psychologists, concerned with the scientific status of their discipline, have felt that identification with a humanistic discipline such as religion would sell out psychology's cause before it had a chance to come into existence as a science. Religionists, on the other hand, followed the traditional pattern of rejecting scientific advances in psychology as further evidence of encroachment on the part of alien fields. But there are signs that the beginnings of a rapprochement between psychology and religion are occurring. Perhaps the outstanding development along these lines is that of pastoral psychology. However, it must be admitted that this development is due more to the openness of the religionists than it is to the combined effort of both disciplines. Perhaps the recent establishment of an APA committee to study relationships between religion and mental health represents an official declaration of better intentions on the part of American psychologists. It is to be hoped that these expressions of a more positive attitude on the part of both religion and psychology represent a beginning of more intensive and open study of problems of mutual interest,[1] one capable of leading to the development of an all-encom-

[1] A recent development within psychology is encouraging, namely, the establishment of a "working group" with a growing interest in studying the basic presuppositions of psychology and religion, and the relations between the two. The current membership of this group is as follows: Walter H. Clark, Charles Curran, Joseph Havens, Keith Irwin, Robert Kimball, Robert MacLeod, Paul Pruyser, and Joseph R. Royce.

passing theory of man. Such a goal will require the insights of all students of man, whether they come from the scientific or the humanistic camp.

In addition to the practical developments mentioned above, there are also certain intellectual developments which point to a convergence of thought in psychology and religion. In religion I have in mind the thinking of Paul Tillich, particularly as exemplified in his book *The Courage to Be*, and his recent article on psychoanalysis, existentialism, and theology. In psychology we have the reminders of Gordon Allport and others, such as Paul Johnson and W. H. Clark, but there has been no sustained, unified concern on the part of psychology comparable to that in religion. The psychiatrists (e.g., Jung) and social psychoanalysts (e.g., Fromm) have been much more open to religious thought than have the psychologists. However, I predict a change in psychology along these lines in the near future. This prediction is based primarily on the impact of existentialism on twentieth-century thought. There are indications that this approach to man is not being taken lightly in spite of its essentially non-systematic form, and that it contains religious insights which make sense to both religionists and scientists. The purpose of this paper is to point up the relevance of existentialism to both psychology and religion, with the idea of offering it as an intellectual bridge between the two. A major working assumption is that psychology, in its study of man's ultimate concerns,[2] will find the phenomenological approach of existentialism more palatable than the typically non-empirical approach of the religionist, and further, that it may be possible to tackle certain aspects of existential or religious questions empirically.

B. TOWARD A COMMON THEORY OF MAN

Because of the richness of each domain, the potential lines of convergence between psychology, existentialism, and religion are many. However, at the initial stage of our inter-disciplinary inquiry it must be admitted that the points of overlap are fuzzy and confused. The material which follows, therefore, is to be regarded as primarily suggestive and exploratory. Furthermore, stress will be placed on a discursive exposition of the contributions from existentialism which may be common or at least relevant to the other two. No attempt will be made to exhaustively and systematically interrelate all three domains. It should be obvi-

[2] This will be my working definition of religion, taken from Tillich. This point raises the question of what I mean by existentialism, for this domain is perhaps as chaotic as the domain of religion. Let me simply say that I do *not* mean the existential statements of any one man such as Sartre, Camus, or Kierkegaard. As a working definition I have in mind all questions and propositions concerning the meaning of life, not in the abstract, but in terms of subjective existence. Similarly, by psychology I mean the science of the behavior (which is meant to include subjective behavior or experience) of organisms, particularly man. The disunity which pervades all three disciplines here considered makes an inherently difficult task all but impossible. The writer wishes to stress the point that definitions should not bind us unnecessarily at this early point of inquiry, and should, therefore, be accepted in the spirit in which they were offered—namely, as rough, first statements which might provide a common basis for subsequent departure. For a more complete statement of the sense in which I am using the term religion, please see my paper on *The search for meaning*.

ous that even this relatively limited task is beyond the capabilities of an exponent from only one of the three domains.

Let us begin with several observations of common concern to all three approaches. Perhaps the idea which all three disciplines share most completely is that for self-realization man must live authentically. Here we are dealing with the problem of values, and what it means to live out one's life in terms of them. Perhaps this concern is most obviously identified with religion, with its traditional stress on investing in those values which have the potential of supplying sufficient meaning to sustain the full life. A similar concern, however, lies behind the therapist's goal of client self-acceptance and is perhaps best represented in psychology by Carl Roger's natural growth process, Jung's concept of individuation, and Maslow's concept of self-actualization. The existentialists deal with authenticity and value by demanding that we live our lives honestly, that we make our choices with as much consciousness as possible, that we be aware of the values that lie behind such choices, and that we not rationalize our way out of the consequences which ensue. In short, they make a plea for responsible decision making. Inter-disciplinary statements on authenticity, values, and self-realization are most clearly stated in the existential religious views of Tillich, who has written a book on the courage to become one's self, in the existential psychological views of Wolff who states that "the task of existential therapy is to give the individual insight into his existential reality, to unify his individuality, and to make him able to face the responsibilities of the existential risk," and in the psychological-religious views of Allport.

A second area of convergence deals with the importance of irrational processes as determinants of man's behavior. The prominence of Freudian psychology on this issue is obvious and pre-eminent. What is not so obvious is that existential thought on unconscious processes actually preceded that of psychoanalysis in the writings of literary men such as Dostoevsky and Tolstoy, and in the works of such philosophers as Nietzsche and Kierkegaard. The contemporary existentialist concern for the non-rational aspects of the universe in contrast to unconscious mental processes is perhaps most obvious in the works of Camus, who describes behavior which should be thought of not as a protest against reason, but as a protest against mere reason.[3] The concern for the irrational side of man in religion is best seen in its realization that human existence is impossible without some kind of faith. The religionist has long recognized the necessity for commitment in order to live, and that such commitment may not necessarily be a rational or a conscious one. Note, for example, that the commitment to rationality as a basis for living is not necessarily a rational decision. Thus, the shortcomings of *mere* rationality are implicit in the religious concern for faith. This concern represents an item of great wisdom which religion shares with psychology and existentialism in their common pointing up of the irrational in man.

[3] The same protest as Nietzsche's, in his will to power concept.

A third area of common concern is that of anxiety. While it is true that the anxiety of the existentialists and the religionists is more metaphysical than that of the psychologists it is, nevertheless, anxiety. Both the religionists and the existentialists speak of the anxiety which accompanies alienation—separation from fellow man, society, and nature. While the religionists stress the anxiety which accompanies separation from God, the existentialists speak of the threat of non-being. At this point we see the linkage with the more pedestrian anxiety of the psychologist. For the existentialist concept of non-being might be physical death, psychological inadequacy, or severe ego threat, and the immortality concern of religion might be thought of as a psychological security measure. Otto Rank has developed this point most convincingly with his suggestion that man, unable to accept physical death, unconsciously makes his bid for continued being by the creation of great works of art and science, and by the preservation of political and social ideologies. Unable to manage physical immortality, he at least transcends himself by achieving psychological or spiritual immortality. The relevance of Rank's thesis to existential and psychological anxiety is seen in his exposition of how the urge to immortality lies behind our social and political revolutions and wars, for people are willing to die on behalf of such ideologies (e.g., note the contemporary situation of communism versus capitalism) if it represents a projected self-perpetuation. At this juncture note the tie-up to our earlier discussion on authenticity. For if there is an imminent threat of non-being, that is, of not becoming what one should become in terms of one's individuality and in terms of the highest reaches of what it means to be human, then the threat to the self is severe, and dread, or anxiety, is a natural consequence. One reason for the recent emergence of existential psychotherapy is the growing realization of the legitimacy of the existential anxiety of meaninglessness in addition to the free-floating anxiety of the neurotic. Frankl speaks of such severe existential frustrations as an oögenesis or spiritual neurosis in contradistinction to a psychogenic neurosis.

Perhaps the most important example of common concern is that of symbolic processes. From the point of view of psychology it is unfortunately true that Jung has stood practically alone in his prophetic writings on the importance of symbolic manifestations for the understanding of both psychological and religious matters. His position is that modern man is in search of a soul (i.e., integrated personality) because the traditional religious symbols have lost their meaning. Jung interprets the increase of neuroticism in our time and the mass psychosis of modern totalitarianism as symptomatic of spiritual starvation. He interprets these mental disturbances as the natural compensatory activity of unconscious processes. He claims there is always an increase in "symbolizing" when the contemporary symbols fail to convey meaning. The result is an increase in symbolic representations in individual men's fantasies and dreams and an increase in mythmaking at the group or collective level. The most meaningful symbolic manifestations of man, whether observed at the individual level or in the analysis of myths, are the archetypes. These recurrent themes are so meaningful because they reflect the eternal needs of the psyche; they reflect the tendency toward wholeness, they reveal man's searching for the unity of his psyche. The most powerful of these universal expressions of psychic need is the archetypal symbol of God.

In general, the psychologists have branded Jung as mystical and have essentially ignored him as unscientific, whereas the religionists have not been too happy with his interpretation of God in symbolic rather than literalistic terms. The discipline of religion has been reluctant to see the power and the deep insight of this view, although the recent indirect support from the writings of Cassirer, Langer, and other philosophers on symbolic forms, has begun to have a very salutary impact on contemporary religious thought. Cassirer points out that all forms of knowledge, the sciences, the humanities, and the arts, are symbolic manifestations of man's cultural evolution, and that the history of the development of the human psyche lies symbolically hidden in the major myths of mankind. For example, as the content of the myth progresses from many gods to one God, man moves from relative unconsciousness to relative consciousness. In short, polytheism symbolically represents a multitude of fragmented ego projections which moves toward a more unified "self" as man's conceptualization approaches monotheism. Taken together, Jung and Cassirer present a complementary exposition of the nature of symbolic forms. Their difference comes in the fact that Cassirer gives us an essentially conscious theory of symbolization, whereas Jung gives us an essentially unconscious theory.[4]

The social psychological implications of Jungian thought is brought out in a recent book of Progoff's, who makes the major point that a living religion is the dominant force which holds a social structure together. Since it is the core around which people build the meaning of their lives, by definition its symbols represent what a people value most.

> To say that an individual has "faith" is to say, psychologically, that he can live his symbols, that they are *alive* within him; and to say that an individual is "sceptical" means that the symbols are no longer spontaneously active or alive within him.

The existential temper of this quote is obvious—without authenticity, one's religion or faith is dead. Symbols, whether religious or otherwise, must carry an existential impact in order to be effective as determinants of man's beliefs and behavior. The theologian Schaer is in complete sympathy with Jung's analysis of symbols, including the stress on unconscious processes.

> Religion is the acknowledgement of the things that consciousness fails to realize . . . religion contributes substantially to man's social

---

[4] The complementary nature of the thought of Jung and Cassirer is developed more fully in Ch. VIII, "Symbol, Myth, and Reality," of the writer's forthcoming book *The Encapsulated Man.*

structure, and a living religion is needed for full development of personality.

He accepts individuation as the essence of rebirth and suggests that "the task of religion is to do what the symbol does; bring opposites together."

But it is in the work of the existential theologian Paul Tillich, especially in his magnum opus, *Systematic Theology*, that we see the complete, integrative treatment—in terms of psychology, existentialism, and religion—of symbolism. For here we see the existential concern for the meaning which is invested in a religious symbol, the religious idolatry which is the lot of those who literalize such symbols, and the awareness that it is important not to speak psychological nonsense about such matters.

Now let us turn to several ideas which are central to existential thought, and which may be shared in part by one or both of the other two disciplines, but which are not clearly common to all three. These ideas are presented because they are fundamental to an eventual theory of man, and it may be that either or both psychology and religion ought to be more cognizant of these views. I shall present the first two points together because they are interrelated. They are as follows: (1) existence is not essence and (2) man is not a machine. First, the existential view that existence is not essence. This view holds that the way things are is not necessarily the way they ought to be, or the way they "really" are. Therefore, statistical descriptions of man's behavior, for instance, do not constitute a standard for the existentialist. Rather, the existentialist stresses the potential or the demand of what man can become.

Secondly, the existentialists say that man cannot be understood as a machine or robot. A given man at a given time does not know what he will do at the next moment, his essence is still evolving. Furthermore, he is not always rational. What's more he does not follow a certain set of rules or principles. In short, man is not a thing, and therefore, scientific prediction regarding man will not work. However, contemporary man is being treated as if he were a thing, for he is being pushed around by masses, big organizations, and urban industrialization, and he is being compartmentalized by educational and occupational specialization. Finally he gets to the point where he sees himself, not as man, a whole person with a diversity of needs and purposes, but only as a plumber, a teacher, or a salesman. That is, he sees himself functionally rather than as a human being. Such a dehumanized or fragmented man, treated essentially as a thing, is existentially dead. Man in such a state is not free, he is simply a robot. Existential man, on the other hand, is free.

These two views are interrelated by the existential assumption that man is free, not determined. Here is a position diametrically opposed to that of scientific psychology. For psychology, in order to play the scientific game, was forced to accept the assumption of determinism, and is proceeding as rapidly as possible with an electronic brain as the current model for man. While it must be admitted that psychology has learned much about man on the basis of this assumption, it must also be admitted that existentialism and religion have also gained insights into man's nature by proceeding with the opposite assumption. As so often happens with either-or dichotomies, I suspect the difficulty here arises if one insists that the answer must be one way or the other. Doesn't our best available evidence suggest that there is potent truth on both sides? Is it not truth that many aspects of man's behavior are in fact, machine-like? And is it not equally true that such an approach to man is too reductive and will leave too much unaccounted for? Does this not suggest that psychology, for example, become more humanistic, and at least go so far as to use the model of an organism rather than a machine? And isn't it also true that man as a completely free being is equally preposterous? The dilemma of freedom versus determinism as far as man's behavior is concerned is generally recognized as one of the perennial, and perhaps unresolvable, issues of philosophic thought. I see the position of both the existentialists (i.e., for complete freedom) and the scientific psychologists (i.e., for complete determinism) as extremist in that they each fly their banner in the face of obvious and overwhelming evidence to the contrary, and I have concluded that this dilemma can best be resolved by discarding both of the extreme positions, and settling for a position of probabilistic determinism.[5]

Another existential view which I want to call to your attention is the stress which is placed on the value and meaning of the immediately apprehendable aesthetic experience. This is one of the positive by-products of their protest against "mere" reason, and a further reminder of the artistic aspect of man's nature. It is related to the existentialist's stress on living in the moment, maximizing one's awareness, existing fully. This view overlaps Zen and other Eastern philosophic and religious views, and it is consistent with Northrop's plea that Western man needs to balance his identification with the rational or theoretic approach to life by the Eastern concern for the aesthetic. While it is doubtful that psychology has any objection at this point, it is also true that as a discipline it hasn't had much to say on this issue. Perhaps the only systematic exposition within psychology which has stressed the aesthetic or intuitive component is that of Jung, whose fourfold typology requires that a healthy psyche balance the rational and the intuitive along with the sensory and the feeling functions. Perhaps the main point to be made here is that Western culture, including Western therapeutic practice, could profit greatly by openness to the ancient therapeutic practices of Eastern culture.[6] Close examination of such procedures would cer-

[5] This point receives more complete development in a forthcoming paper on *Philosophy, Theory, and Psychology.*

[6] See, for example, the journal of oriental psychology *Psychologia*, especially Vol. 1, No. 4, 1958, and Vol. 2, No. 2, 1959. And what could be more consistent with recent existential and phenomenological writings than the following quote concerning the purpose of Zen training? "Such awareness is a lively attention to one's direct experience, to the world as immediately sensed, so as not to be misled by names and labels. (Samadhi) . . . is the perfection of the . . . pure experience, pure awareness. . . ." (33, p. 52.)

tainly result in confirmation of much that is being done today in psychotherapy as well as point the way to new insights which could be applied to currently over-rational, aesthetic-deprived Western man. Such an approach might even lead to a broader view of the role of the therapist, namely, as more of a sage and guide, in other words, as the archetypal "wise old man," rather than the more restrictive adjustor-to-society or mind-healer prototype which is currently the mode.

The final concept I want to bring to your attention is that of existential truth. I confess to having had great difficulty in ferreting out this view, and I'm not certain to what extent it contains my own projections. But the basic idea is clearly in the existential atmosphere. It is not stated explicitly in existential writings, but for that matter, neither are most of the other views. Just as Jacobi has done us a great service by pulling together the scattered and unsystematic writings of Jung, so somebody needs to organize existential writings into a reasonable systematic and understandable summary. Such a step will be slow in coming because of the essentially anti-systematic bias of most existentialist writers; however, it is bound to come as the non-existential professional philosophers come to grips with it more and more seriously. What is meant by existential truth? I have discussed this concept more fully in another paper, and am currently pursuing its epistemological implications at greater length elsewhere,[7] but I can summarize it as follows. Existential truth refers to those insights or awarenesses which emerge from concerns which have a transforming effect on one's existence. Conversely, if one's concerns are detrimental to life, then the implied insights are invalid. In addition to investing one's life in meaningful concerns, existential validity also requires total involvement of the individual. That is, not only the rational or the intuitive, but the sensory and the feeling functions as well. This concept is very much akin to the insightful or "aha" experience of the client who has successfully undergone psychotherapy. Such an experience reflects a new awareness, a reintegration of the personality, a more insightful understanding of the meaning of one's existence. A purely intellectual insight or the verbalization of certain psychiatric terminology does not result in a "cure." In short, the person's existence is not affected unless there is emotion or feeling at the core of his experiences. There is a requirement of total involvement or emotional reliving before the rebirth can occur. The relevance of this concept to religious inquiry is obvious. It is, in fact, crucial to the problem of religious truth, and provides as potent a foundation for truth in the religious domain as I am aware of. This is particularly true when the concept of existential truth is tied to Tillich's conceptualization of religion as ultimate concern.

C. CAN WE VALIDATE EXISTENTIAL QUESTIONS?

How can we validate existential insights? If our ultimate goal is to understand man, on what grounds shall we accept insights concerning his nature, and on

[7] In a paper in progress on "epistemology and existential validity."

what grounds shall we reject them? In spite of the existential protest concerning the over-scientizing of man, let us first examine this question from the point of view of the usual empirical criteria. That is, let us ask ourselves whether we can translate existential propositions into empirically testable procedures? Let us begin where it is easiest to answer, with the four ideas shared by psychology, existentialism, and religion, for considerable progress has already been made in these areas. Unconscious processes and anxiety, for example, have been empirically investigated at great length. Similarly, a great mass of evidence has been accumulated in the areas of symbolic processes and self-realization. While it is true that most of these observations have been made in the clinic, there actually have been laboratory experiments performed on three of the four problems, including, for example, the investigation by J. G. Miller on unconscious conditioning, the work on sub-liminal perception, the value-oriented research of Bruner on symbolic processes, and the induced anxiety procedures of Silvan Tomkins. Now there is no claim being made here that such matters as metaphysical anxiety have been experimentally studied. But we are pointing out that while this very difficult problem is currently not amenable to experimental study, it is subject to empirical observation in the clinic, and that earlier views regarding unconscious processes were similarly regarded as not subject to experimental verification. The point is very simply that we need to remain entirely open on the issue of what can and what cannot be studied empirically, including the highly philosophical propositions of existentialism, for we may be able to investigate them once we give them acceptable philosophical status.

Let us look at the four non-shared existential propositions. Perhaps the easiest of these to investigate empirically is the third one on the impact of the aesthetic experience. The small band of psychology's students of aesthetics has already made sufficient inroads in assessing aesthetic sensitivity, although they have not conducted cross cultural psychological studies of relatively "pure" aesthetic types from the East as contrasted with relatively "pure" Western rational man. The existential proposition concerning the robotizing and dehumanizing of man has also been loosely verified empirically by social psychologists such as David Riesman and social psychoanalysts such as Erich Fromm. Thus, the empirical research from the behavioral sciences and the conceptual insights of religion add weight to the existential proposition that man is not a machine. Since the proposition that existence is not essence entails concern about the difference between conditions as we find them and what one ought to become, the earlier references to the empirical researchers of Rogers, Jung, and Maslow are relevant.

The last proposition, that having to do with existential truth, moves us to consider the problem of non-empirical, or at least non-traditional-empirical, validation of truths concerning the nature of man. At this juncture we see a most important link between the highly subjective phenomena of existentialism and religion on the one hand, and the problem of verification which scientific psychology demands on the other hand. For there is overwhelming evidence from the psychological clinic to the effect that men have had experiences in therapeutic sessions (although the experiences are not necessarily public or reproducible), which have changed them—in short, there is psychological evidence for subjective or existential truth. It is in the clinic, then, where the verities of existence can best be observed and checked into, whether they be finally checked out in terms of the usual empirical criterion or the criterion of existential truth. In this connection we need to be reminded of the considerable work which has already been done in Europe under the banner of what has come to be known as existential analysis. Many astute observations concerning the psychology of existence have already been made in the psychological clinic, and one transplanted European existential psychologist, Werner Wolff, has developed a significant theoretical framework which combines existential thought with traditional therapy and the psychology and philosophy of values.

Considerations of this kind, where we mix such disparate approaches as psychology, existentialism, and religion, force us to consider the philosophic presuppositions which undergird each discipline, particularly as they relate to the problem of establishing truth. The debate within psychology on ideographic versus nomothetic laws is a case in point. If we insist on the traditional conception of the scientific enterprise we shall be forced to confine ourselves to nomothetic principles. But Gordon Allport and others have presented convincing arguments and demonstrations for ideographic principles in addition to nomothetic principles The phenomenologists have made a similar plea in their insistence that we cannot understand behavior without a clear understanding of the perceptual framework of the individual. The recent experimental research on the interrelations between projection, value, and motivation represents a firm link between personality and perception, a development which provides some degree of empirical confirmation for the phenomenological approach. The point to be made in this connection is that the perceptual, phenomenological, and ideographic currents of contemporary thought insist on getting at the inner psychology or subjective meanings of men. This means that such traditionally tabooed subjects as beauty, love, and religious behavior are not only rendered admissible, but become primary targets of investigation. In short, such currents of thought would allow the psychologist to freely and legitimately investigate existential questions, even though some of these questions cannot be handled within the usual scientific epistemology. This point of departure raises serious questions concerning the definition of psychology, and carries with it equally serious consequences for its future development.[8]

[8] Underlying this thought is the question of the adequacy and relevance of existential validity for the establishment of psychological truths. Both of these important issues, the definition of psychology, and the nature of existential validity, lie beyond the scope of the present paper and are being investigated more fully in other papers. Perhaps it will suffice at this juncture to state my bias in favor of a broad conception of psychological science, and to look with favor on the possibility of new avenues of approach via the pathway of existential validity. At the same time, I hope it has been clear that, while my position is one of openness to the insights of existentialism, I am of the opinion that psychology must continue to evaluate experience with rigor. I presume the problem is to proceed with rigor, but without rigor mortis!

D. SUMMARY AND CONCLUSIONS

Psychology and religion have a long and well known history of mutual indifference, and, at times, animosity. There are signs that the beginnings of a rapprochement between psychology and religion are occurring. The purpose of this paper is to point up the relevance of existentialism to both psychology and religion, with the idea of offering it as an intellectual bridge between the two. Four ideas or concepts are presented which are seen as being common to all three approaches. These are: (1) for self-realization each man must live authentically, (2) the importance of irrational processes as determinants of man's behavior, (3) the concept of anxiety, and (4) the problem of symbolic processes. Four additional ideas, central to existential thought, were presented as food for thought for the disciplines of psychology and religion. These are: (1) existence is not essence, (2) man is not a machine, (3) man's need for the immediately apprehendable aesthetic experience, and (4) the concept of existential truth.

The point of the paper is that existential questions, which are clearly important aspects of human nature, should be seen as central to the concerns of psychology, and that they can be validly investigated, some in accordance with the usual scientific criteria, and some according to the as yet unexplored but promising criterion of existential validity.

PART TWO

Understanding the learner

THE PROCESS OF
GROWTH AND DEVELOPMENT

13 The nature of organic wholeness

Related selections: 14, 15, 16, 57

Research in child development provides evidence that the growth of the individual tends to be unified and that the school must be concerned with the organic wholeness of children if desirable educational objectives are to be achieved. The growth demands of any child are a function of the totality of the organism and may or may not be the same as the growth demands of other children. The following selection by Professor Gilchrist clarifies the concept of organic wholeness. The entire original article, of which this selection is but the introduction, could be read with profit by students who are familiar with biological concepts and terminology.

We have become so accustomed to building toy houses of blocks, or constructing automobiles from accurately machined parts, that we think of wholes as formed by putting pieces together. It comes therefore as somewhat of a struggle to picture to ourselves a process, such as the molding of a vase from a lump of clay, in which the whole precedes the parts and gives to the parts their meaning. Yet it is this latter analogy and not the former which we must have in mind if we are to comprehend aright the nature of the organism and the processes of its becoming.

If one would understand a machine he will take it apart, either actually or in his imagination, and will study it piece by piece, noting the characteristics of each piece and the relations of each piece to each other piece. Then by synthesizing the knowledge thus obtained, he will understand the machine. On the other

FRANCIS G. GILCHRIST, "The Nature of Organic Wholeness," *The Quarterly Review of Biology*, XII (September, 1937), 251–53. Reprinted by permission of the author and the publisher.

DR. GILCHRIST (1895–   ) is Professor of Zoology at Lewis and Clark College, Portland, Oregon.

hand, if one would understand the vase or organism, he must begin by first comprehending the thing as a whole. Only then will he be able to discern the significance of the parts. Indeed, he may fail to discern discrete parts at all; yet his appreciation of the whole will not thereby be impaired.

But how does one comprehend a whole except by knowing the parts and observing their relations to one another? Can one know a whole directly? Yes. Indeed, it is the natural thing to do. The child knows a cat before it distinguishes a head. It knows its mother's face before it discerns her eyes. It would be very unnatural indeed for a child to reconstruct its concept of a face by piecing together its various anatomical structures or its characters. It is just as unnatural for a biologist to construct his concept of an organism by adding together entities of any sort, be they organs, germ layers, unit characters, cleavage cells, or organforming stuffs. It is only a habit of mind which we have acquired through familiarity with houses and machines which leads us to think that way.

But admitting that one might form some general concept of a whole before discerning parts, is it nevertheless not true that a whole is nothing more than the sum of its parts plus whatever interrelations may exist between its parts? This is indeed true with regard to some wholes; namely, the artificial wholes which men construct; but it is not true of organic wholes such as we commonly find in nature. Certainly it is not true of organisms. Let us examine this assertion from the standpoint of a part.

A thing may become a part in one or the other of two ways: (a) It may begin as a discrete and independent unit and then by integration with other units secondarily find itself a part of a whole. Thus the brick becomes a part of a house. Thus also a balance-wheel becomes a part of a watch. Houses and watches as thus fabricated are merely the sums of interrelated parts. Their wholeness, or had we not better say, their togetherness, is the result of a "creative synthesis" which has taken place. Their special properties depend upon the special relations between their constituent parts. (b) In organic wholes, on the other hand, the whole exists first, and the part arises by differentiation within the pre-existing whole. Homogeneity precedes heterogeneity. At first the parts are indistinguishable from one another except, perhaps, by future reference. Thus a "part" of a lump of clay may be described as the prospective handle of a vase, or a part of an amphiban egg may be termed "presumptive neural plate"; but the part is not yet handle, nor neural plate; nor is it entirely certain that it will become such.

Organic wholes, then, are not primarily composed of parts, or even of interrelated parts. They are not the result of an integration or of a "creative synthesis." Quite to the contrary, they precede their "parts" in time, and remain superior to them in space.

It is likely that the reader is not convinced. Perhaps he is a morphologist and is engaged in dissecting organisms and studying their structures, dead or alive. To him the organism is a definite pattern in space; or indeed a succession of such patterns, if he be an embryologist. But the morphologist's organism is, of course, not the whole organism. It is only that aspect of the organism which he has chosen to abstract and study. Perhaps the reader is a physiologist, and concerns himself with the functioning of organs or the rôles of forces. He, no doubt, has become much interested in the interrelationships of processes, and has noted the remarkable self-regulating devices within the functioning system. But his organism, like the organism of the morphologist, is an abstraction from the whole.

To study the organism as an organic whole, one must be interested not merely in the organism which is and does; but he must know also what under other conditions and in other relationships this same mass of living matter will be and do. He will want to know how and why the organism came to be what it is and to do what it does. Indeed, he will go further and will seek to comprehend, if possible, the nature of the organic wholeness in itself; that is, the wholeness which precedes the being and the doing and which gives to parts their significance.

Let us illustrate this by reference to a very primitive animal, the fresh-water polyp *Hydra*. A piece of the body stalk of this animal is morphologically only a piece of the body stalk. As such it may be killed, sectioned, reconstructed, and described. Physiologically it is an organization of more or less specialized cells carrying on the numerous functions of living. But isolate this piece of the stalk (the following is true of the central portions of the stalk), and immediately these same cells commence to reorganize themselves; and in a short time a whole new polyp has been formed. It is therefore true that what a part of a polyp is and does is a function of its position in a whole; and the whole must be understood first, if the structure and functioning of the part is to be comprehended.

14 *Concepts of growth— their significance to teachers*

Related selections: 13, 15, 16, 17, 18

If the school is to provide the experiences necessary for the optimum development of children, teachers and administrators must be concerned with appraising and understanding the growth of individual

WILLARD C. OLSON and BYRON O. HUGHES, "Concepts of Growth—Their Significance to Teachers," *Childhood Education*, XXI (October, 1944), 53–63. Reprinted by permission of the authors and The Association for Childhood Education International, 3615 Wisconsin Avenue, N.W., Washington, D.C. 20016.

DR. OLSON (1899–) is Dean of the School of Education, University of Michigan, and Professor of Education and Psychology. DR. HUGHES (1906–) is Professor of Education at the same institution.

children. The concepts of growth held by teachers will influence
both classroom practice and administrative policy. The research of
Olson and Hughes calls into serious question many of the common
practices in education, particularly those relating to comparative
making, methods of reporting, promotion policies, and attempts to
force growth.

The growing body of data and principles about human growth and development offers an ever more secure foundation for the adoption of philosophies of growth in the classrooms of the nation. On the technical side, generalizations are increasing in number and proceeding toward greater precision and scope. On the practical side, more teachers are attaining the fundamental understanding that enables them to meet new problems at a high level of professional competence and confidence.

The literature that definitely attempts to bridge the gap between the laboratory and the classroom is meager. The resources for such a literature are enormous. The writers will attempt to present concepts and illustrations that to them appear to be of peculiar importance in the classroom. The illustrations are drawn from research at the child development laboratory of the University Elementary School at the University of Michigan.

While maintaining the importance of the point of view of the child as a whole, the writers have selected examples of historical and immediate concern to teachers. This article will stress factors of significance in understanding the growth of individuals and the implications of these factors for school practices. A series of studies made in the laboratory school stress the relationships that exist among members of classroom groups. Both individual and group concepts are needed for complete understanding.

CHILDREN DIFFER IN RATE
AND LEVEL OF GROWTH

Every classroom teacher is impressed with the fact that children are not alike. If tests have been administered at any given time these impressions have been confirmed in an objective manner. Research in child development gives added knowledge of the nature of the differences and how they persist through time. By following growth in a number of characteristics more understanding of total significance is secured than by studying one attribute.

Figures 1 and 2 illustrate how two boys grew through time. Repeated measures were made and the original units were translated into an age scale as described in other publications. Thus in the figures height in inches has become height age (H.A.) ; weight in pounds, weight age (W.A.) ; number of permanent teeth erupted, dental age (D.A.) ; extent of ossification of hand and wrist bones, carpal age (Ca.A.) ; and strength of grip in kilograms, grip age (G.A.). In

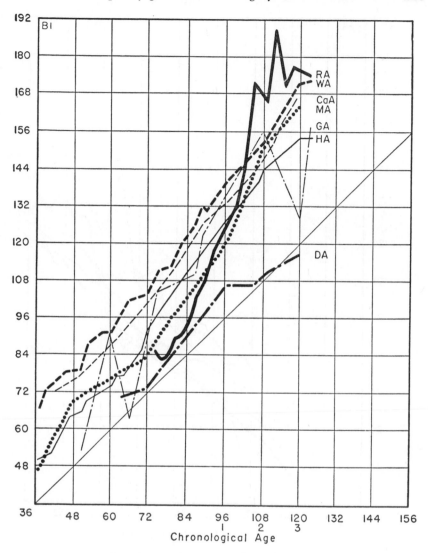

Figure 1   Growth of a boy at a high level (B1).

the conventional manner success in intelligence tests is described by mental age (M.A.), and achievement in reading by reading age (R.A.).

The figures are constructed by plotting growth ages for a particular attribute above the chronological age at which it was obtained and by connecting the points. Thus the record for the boy in Figure 1 (B1) starts at about 36 months of age in the nursery school while the record for the boy in Figure 2 (B28) starts in the kindergarten at about 60 months of age. These boys were selected because they represent the extremes in organismic age of 28 boys being given

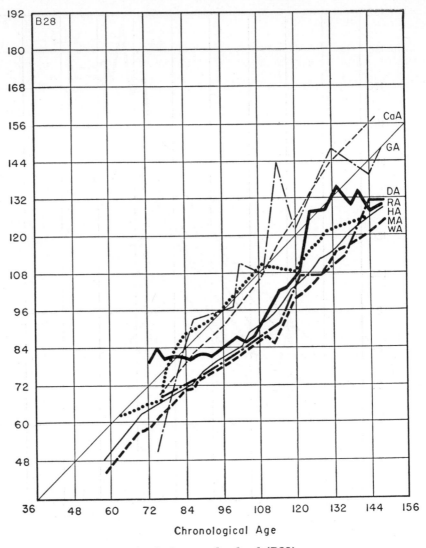

Figure 2   Growth of a boy at a low level (B28).

intensive and systematic study. Organismic age is a coined name for the average of all available growth ages at a point in time. A straight diagonal line has been drawn through the intersection of the scales for chronological and growth ages as a convenient reference point for average growth—12 months of growth for 12 months of living.

It will be observed that most of the curves for B1 remain above the line of average development throughout the period while those of B28 remain below the line. The various attributes of growth tend to cluster together and there is some continuity throughout the years. The numbers on the base line indicate that Child B1 had pubic hair at 108 months which was pigmented at 120 months. Pubic hair has not yet appeared in Child B28 at 150 months. The differences between Child B1 and B28 are deep seated. The first menstruation for the mother of B1 occurred at 11 years of age while that for the mother of B28 was at 15. B1 weighed 9 pounds at birth while B28 weighed 4¼ pounds. B1 was breast-fed 5 months and B28 not at all. B1 had his first tooth at 6 months and B28 had a tooth at 12 months. B1 reverses the trend by delaying talking until 20 months while B28 talked at 15 months.

Detailed case records are available for these boys showing interesting differences in health, behavior and personality. The inescapable fact of persistent individual differences in growth as illustrated by B1 and B28 must be taken into account in implementing a program based upon the philosophy of growth. Policies and practices that take differences into account will be elaborated elsewhere.

GROWTH HAS SOME UNITY
WHEN VIEWED AS A WHOLE

Since growth as expressed in a child is a result of the action of the environment on the potential that originally existed in a single cell, it is not surprising that some tendency toward unity continues to exist through the years of growth. The research literature has demonstrated this tendency in a number of ways. The most common method is to calculate coefficients of correlation between the various attributes of growth. Such research rather regularly reports positive intercorrelations. In a few attributes and in some samples of children, the values may drop very close to zero. An accidental negative correlation may at times appear. The trend of the evidence, however, supports the conclusion of some tendency toward unification in childhood.

The writers currently are investigating another approach to the problem in which various aspects of growth are viewed simply as interchangeable samples of total growth, finding one expression in one individual and another in another. The essential conclusion is the same, i.e., that the various attributes in an individual tend to cluster about a center of gravity of growth of that individual and that the freedom to vary is restricted. The detailed support has been worked out, but the manuscript has not been printed. The thought can be illustrated by Figures 1 and 2 by pointing out that any measure collected for B1 tends to cluster with the others and that the same is true for B28. The finding is important for education in that achievement in school, illustrated by reading in the diagrams, tends to be an expression of total growth.* Consideration of the whole child thus becomes more vital and expectancies for a given child are modified accordingly.

* The reader should note that the case illustrated by Figure 3 is atypical in that reading age lags behind all other indices of growth.

CHILDREN DIFFER IN
THE PATTERN OF GROWTH

Children vary in the growth curves that they present both in changes with time and in the arrangement of various aspects within the pattern. Thus in Figures 1 and 2, the children differ not only in the general level at which they are growing, but also in detail. In Figure 1 reading age is finally at the top of the pattern while in Figure 2 reading age is near the middle.

Figure 3 gives a more dramatic illustration of variations in pattern and the significance of these variations for education. The attributes of growth for this girl are somewhat more scattered than for most children. The physical assets are particularly high with height, weight, carpal development and strength above the line of average growth and with intellectual factors such as mental age and reading age several years below. If attention is focused on the mental age and reading, it would appear that this child has borderline intelligence. No observer is likely to reach this conclusion if the behavior as a whole is viewed. This child in the elementary period was one of the best baseball players and runners in the room, could sing well, and had artistic talents beyond the average. As she went on into high school she did well in these areas. Her organismic age is not markedly retarded and a measure of social age, not shown in the figure, is slightly above the average. She is very good at taking care of young children. She does not do well at abstract intellectual tasks. "Capitalize on strength" is an essential aspect of the philosophy and practice of a growth point of view in a classroom. It would be a sad mistake to stress competitive and comparative methods for a child growing as in Figure 3.

GROWTH WITH TIME IS
A HIGHLY INDIVIDUAL MATTER

Differences in the level of various attributes of growth have been stressed in connection with Figure 3. The changes that occur in children with time are also important in a consideration of patterns. When the results of tests secured at a particular time are made available without the growth point of view, serious mistakes of interpretation may be made. For example, in the examination of 56 individual growth curves in reading, the writers could not find a single child with a growth curve of the shape that would be described by the average values or norms.

[When we trace] the growth in ability to read in 28 boys, [and in] 28 girls, the lines are so intertwined as to be indistinguishable in detail. However, problems of level and direction become apparent. The total group of girls presents a more compact picture than the boys and it is obvious that the girls most delayed in reading tend to start upwards between 9 and 10 years. The boys who are delayed, however, may remain at low levels even to 10 or 11 years of age. It is

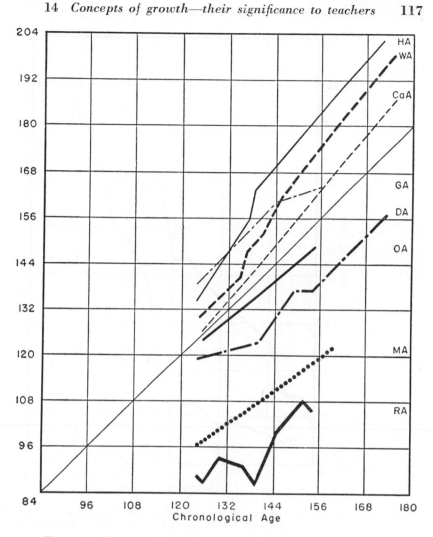

Figure 3   Pattern of growth for a socially competent, mentally re-tarded girl.

not an accident that boys supply a disproportionate number of cases for reading clinics.

A quantitative analysis of some of the reasons for the differences in the growth curves of individual children is being pursued. One of the writers has already reported in some detail on the differences between G7 and G24 called A and B in Figure 4. Although intelligence quotients have fluctuated slightly year by year, the average for each over the period is 118. Detailed study explains some of the reasons why their pattern of growth in reading has been so different. Child A

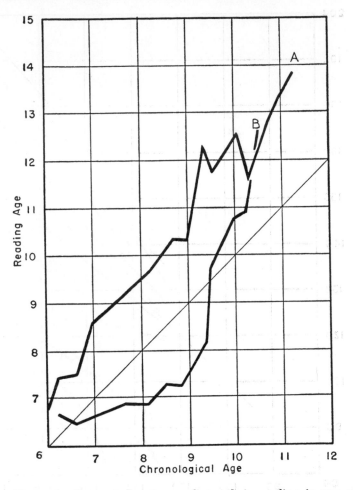

Figure 4   **Contrasted patterns of growth in reading in two girls of equal mental ability but unequal total maturity. (Reproduced by permission of the Michigan Education Association.)**

had an earlier maturing mother (menarche at age 14) and is maturing early herself. Child B had a later maturing mother (menarche at age 17) and is maturing later than Child A. When total organism is taken into account, including all of the various attributes described elsewhere, Child A is actually an older organism, age for age, than Child B. Child B rejected reading experiences violently during the period of plateau and sought them avidly during the period of spurt. According to the growth philosophy and data it would be quite incorrect to call Child B a case of "reading disability" in spite of the retardation before age 9 and the discrepancy between reading and mental age.

MEMBERSHIP IN A GIVEN FAMILY
IS INFLUENTIAL IN DETERMINING
THE PATTERN OF GROWTH

In the previous discussion the writers have noted that the reasons for differences in the growth of children are deep seated. The nature of some of these differences has been indicated in discussing the two girls of approximately the same intelligence who presented such diverse patterns of growth in reading. The writers have recently prepared the growth records in reading for 46 pairs of children where each pair comes from a given family. It becomes evident at once that a very important factor in the shape of a reading curve is membership in a family.

Pairs of curves illustrating high, intermediate and low achievement are presented in Figure 5. The chronological age of the children is on the base line and the growth in reading along the vertical axis. A and A' are brothers born 25 months apart. B, B' and B" are three brothers born at intervals of 27 and 25 months, and C and C' are brothers born at an interval of 36 months. By the longitudinal method it is possible to compare them as if they were twins advancing together. The rate and level of advancement in reading for A and A' and C and C' are, of course, strikingly similar. B and B' cling rather closely. At 10 years of age B" drops several years below in reading as compared to his older brothers and converges toward them near the close of the record.

These curves are particularly provocative to the person who may have been inclined to feel that level and rate of progress in reading were primarily a matter of instruction. It is true that these children would not read at all in a culture which did not provide the experience. The examination of the whole body of the material, however, makes it apparent that cases of extreme delay such as C and C' cannot be understood simply by assuming that instruction is at fault. While reading has been used for illustrative purposes other aspects of growth behave in similar manner.

It should be pointed out that the 7 boys in Figure 5 encountered substantially the same school environment but their reactions in reading have been strongly influenced by the fact that they came from a given family with all that that implies for differences in heredity and nurture. Teachers should not expect the same effects from the same instruction or from the best possible adaptation of instruction to the individual. The folly of a common expectancy on the part of teacher, administrator, or parent is obvious since achievement is only partially under the control of the educational process.

GROWTH HAS STABILITY AND CONTINUITY
AND MAKES ITS DEMANDS FOR NURTURE

If the reader will reexamine Figures 1 and 2 he will be impressed by the general picture of stability of the level of growth with time. Although detailed items in each pattern of growth show periods of plateau and spurt there appears to be

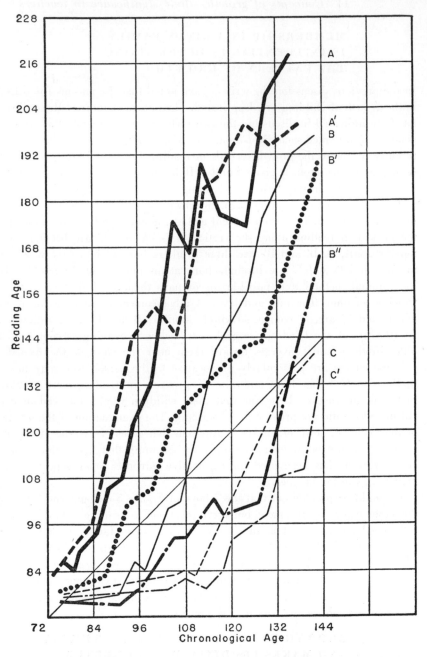

Figure 5   The growth curves for children from the same family show
a resemblance. Compare A and A'; B, B', and B''; and C and C'.

some unifying factor in rate of energy available for growth which keeps the individual on his course.

It is interesting to study the curve of growth when organismic age is taken as the best single expression available to us of the average growth for an individual. One hundred eleven curves were plotted and arranged in order of magnitude of organismic age as of chronological age 8. Children numbered 1 (Boy), 23 (Girl), 42 (Boy), 90 (Girl), and 111 (Boy) are given in Figure 6 for illustrative purposes.

It is probable that the age unit method and the use of averages make the curves unusually straight and smooth. The fact remains that the individual differences in total growth are highly predictable and continuous with time and even tell much about the achievement of the child in the years that follow the ages that have been plotted. The data also suggest some balancing mechanism which releases energy for the production of growth in an orderly fashion. Growth itself is a demanding process impelling the individual to seek nurture to supply it. A slowing down in growth alters attitudes and feelings. In a free environment in school, level of growth makes for differences in the number and difficulty of books consumed. Schools traditionally have emphasized the stimulating conditions and the learning process. Growth studies are giving a better understanding of the learner.

CHILDREN VIEWED AS WHOLES ARE MORE ALIKE THAN CHILDREN VIEWED AS PARTS

Curriculum materials and teaching methods once took an extreme swing in the direction of adaptation to individual differences in some one attribute of interest in schools. At the height of the enthusiasm many methods were proposed for the sectioning of classes, for classification according to special abilities, and for adjustment through promotion and retardation. For the most part the attempts were disappointing in that individuals with similar characteristics seemed to make the same progress regardless of the administrative plans. This is not surprising to the student of growth.

Individual differences among children are most impressive when one segment of total growth is viewed. For example, if we calculate the average deviation for reading age for the group of 56 children described elsewhere we find that it varies with age but averages 18 months. If we calculate the same measure for organismic age we find it to be only 8.5 months. Thus as we move toward the objective of total growth in the elementary period we may emphasize those things in which children are alike as well as those things in which children differ more widely.

SOME IMPLICATIONS OF GROWTH STUDIES FOR TEACHERS

"Seeking" behavior. Differences in growth among children of the same age make for differences in reaction to the environment that is supplied. The child

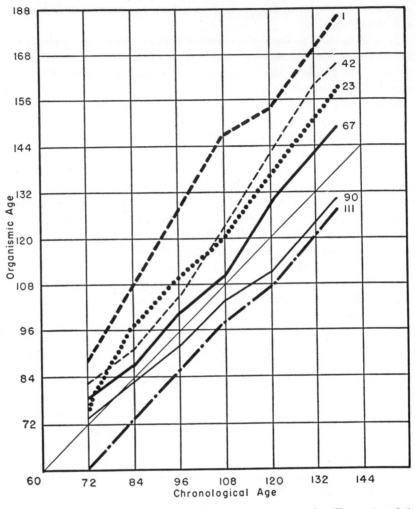

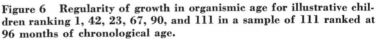

Figure 6   Regularity of growth in organismic age for illustrative children ranking 1, 42, 23, 67, 90, and 111 in a sample of 111 ranked at 96 months of chronological age.

is not a passive recipient of stimulation. He reaches out for it according to the maturity of his total and partial growth and the energy at his disposal. He reacts selectively to the surroundings that are supplied and creates his own world of experience within them. He tends to reject the experiences for which he is not ready. Teachers may make full use of "seeking" behavior by providing a school environment in which children may find suitable experiences of a wide variety in kind and difficulty. No narrowly conceived curriculum of fixed content can attain this goal.

"Seeking" behavior also underlies a principle of method—children should participate in the determination of their curriculum experiences both individually and in groups. The planning period, continuous interaction, or observation of behavior thus give the teacher her safest guide as to the experiences for which the group as a whole is ready and the way each individual may be expected to relate himself to them. These techniques on the part of the teacher also give the children experience in cooperative planning. Growth does not occur in a vacuum and "seeking" behavior and environmental stimulation are interactive processes. The problem is one of relative emphasis.

Pacing, forcing, and delaying. When the teacher insures an environment adequate to the needs of all the children and adjusts his expectancy for each child according to the level and pattern of growth the technique may be called "pacing." This simply means that the teacher meets the "seeking" level by an expectancy and experience in close harmony with it. The child's aspirations and performance are not in conflict with the expectancies of the teacher.

A segment of the general and teaching population continues to have large confidence in specific instructional techniques and experiences as a means of achieving a high level of performance in a child. This confidence was supported originally by laboratory studies of learning. According to this idea a clever teacher with a clever method, excellent material, and time and persistence can produce achievement in a child beyond that which he would attain by seeking and pacing. Thus someone might attempt to justify the early introduction of school subjects on the basis of this point of view. This is sometimes called "forcing" in the sense that there is an attempt to push up the level of the growth curve. The writers admit that the total evidence is still inadequate but they are skeptical whether a forcing method produces anything more than a temporary effect of very limited size.

Their study of the effects of special instruction, feeding, and the administration of special growth substances supports the idea that deprived children show some responsiveness to special treatment, that well-nurtured children do not, and that the special effects do not materially upset individual differences or persist for a very long period of time. They prefer "pacing" to "forcing" theory.

It has been advocated that schools should make a deliberate attempt to delay experiences. The experiments rather regularly demonstrate that the gains that subsequently follow when the experience is introduced will be very rapid and that there will be no permanent impairment of the objective desired. The more systematic studies of delayed experience in reading, stair-climbing, and language, as well as more informal studies of delay in arithmetic suggest that this will be true. The writers are more inclined to stress "seeking" and "pacing." If this results in delay, delay there should be. If on the other hand, some rapidly growing children seek reading and number experiences at an early age in nursery school and kindergarten, there seems no good reason to exclude them. Growth, after all, occurs in a context supplied by the total environment.

Administrative implications. What administrative policies and practices affecting children and parents should prevail in a school that has accepted the data, principles, and philosophy of growth? A few may be suggested for illustrative purposes. The strong tendency for achievement in school to reflect total growth and family patterns calls into question the policy of competitive and comparative marks and formal report cards. Elementary schools rapidly have been giving up such techniques as ineffective and incompatible with modern knowledge. Formal marking practices persist as a cultural survival where communities lag in in-service and parent education or where conservative and reactionary groups have attained dominance. The investment in time necessitated by the newer techniques of conferencing and mutual education brings returns in the long run. At times administrators have hoped that schools and teachers could be appraised by measuring the growth of the children. The idea sounds logical but there is nothing in the growth studies that gives much reassurance that such a measure can be used and properly interpreted.

Classification and promotion problems are of continual interest for administrative policy. Growth in achievement, just as in height and weight, appears to be independent of how children are grouped. It is obvious that a thoroughgoing growth philosophy finds the criteria for placement in the growth of the individual and his social relations rather than in arbitrary grade standards. The growth philosophy and data justify much experimentation with the nature of the groups that are to be maintained and how individuals should be placed in them. The growth philosophy tends to bring children through the elementary grades without failure. If reclassification is necessary after individual study because of extreme immaturity, retention is not thought of or acted upon as a failure on the part of the child.

It is probably fair to say that secondary schools, on the whole, have been relatively more committed to the selective philosophy than the elementary schools. The struggle of philosophies sometimes creates problems of articulation at the seventh grade level or the ninth grade level, depending on the type of school organization. There is evidence for reapproachment.

SUMMARY

Research in child development is providing working generalizations for the classroom teacher. Children differ in their rate and level of growth and the acceptance of these differences permits policies which make schools happier places for parents, teachers, and children.

Growth tends to be unified. Schools may properly take the view that they must be concerned with the whole child to accomplish even intellectual objectives.

The total competence of children is made up by different details of pattern. Building on these differences within the individual is an important aspect of curriculum planning, method, and guidance.

Growth is an individual matter and must be appraised from the point of view of the nature of the individual. There can be no common expectancy for achievement when it is conditioned by sex differences, the total maturity of the child, and the family from which he comes.

It is reassuring that growth has stability and is not easily deflected by the efforts of others to alter it. The stability of growth has great survival value for the race and the individual.

Children as they present themselves in schools have more things in common when viewed broadly than when single attributes are studied in detail. Similarities as well as individual differences deserve attention in classrooms.

The imperative demands of the organism for growth cause children to seek for the environmental supply of nurture and this behavior offers teachers an important clue to the provision of environmental experiences and the use of effective techniques.

Where the data, generalizations, and philosophy of growth have become the common property of the professional staff and patrons, classroom practices and administrative policies in the treatment of individuals and groups tend to be less rigid, competitive, and frustrating, and more flexible, social, and satisfying.

15 *Energy — basis of living and learning*

Related selections: 13, 14, 29

Children are dynamic, going energy systems that are continuously capturing, transforming, and using energy for growth and activity. Whatever affects physical health will affect this process of free-flowing energy and thus the person's ways of behaving. How the child behaves in a given situation depends in part on his energy pool. The teacher needs to recognize and understand individual variations in energy output and use. In this selection and the following Dr. Dildine discusses how energy is used in living and learning and describes some of the differences in health and physical condition which affect energy output and energy use.

GLENN C. DILDINE, "Energy—Basis of Living and Learning," *NEA Journal*, XXXIX (April, 1950), 252–53. Reprinted by permission of the author and publisher.

At the time of publication of this article, DR. DILDINE (1909–) was Project Coordinator for the Research Project in Developmental Needs of Youth, National 4-H Club Foundation of America, Washington, D.C. He was formerly a staff member of the Institute of Child Study at the University of Maryland.

Living is *action*. Anything alive moves, actively does things, responds with explosive power to changes inside and outside itself. We are fascinated to watch an amoeba purposefully flowing around a clump of bacteria, or a robin searching all day for worms for her brood, or a child taking bump after bump in his need to learn to walk alone.

Behind our fascination is wonder at ceaseless, kaleidoscopic ebb and flow of activity. What whirring, changing dynamos living creatures are!

URGE TOWARD PERFECTION

Living is reaching for perfection. The unfolding panorama of life through the ages reveals living things in increasing variety climbing toward greater complexity and directing their energy toward more effective adaptation. In individual human development, children first revel in scattered, tumbling, bubbling play. Then they push their life-given activity onward into the miracles of adolescent awakening and adult achievement.

OBTAINING AND USING ENERGY

Living is capturing, controlling, and using energy. Each human is designed to capture and transform the energy stored in foods into the complex processes of living, growing, and behaving. Every organ in the body is planned to play some essential part in a regular, intricate sequence of internal energy flow and change.

Sense organs, arms and legs, mouth and teeth help to locate and get hold of food and pass it on to the digesting organs for chemical simplification and absorption. The blood stream carries energy-rich products of digestion, together with oxygen extracted from the air by the lungs, to all parts of the body. Each organ takes up from the blood the special products and the oxygen which it needs, burns enough to carry out its particular job, and changes this freed energy into forms essential to living.

The heart changes its energy into squeezing, pumping pressure on the blood. Muscles change their energy into minutely variable amounts and directions of pull on the body's bony levers. Brain and nerves change their freed energy into pulsing currents flowing in delicately patterned channels. These currents serve to modify and direct all of the rest of the body's energy-transformations.

All processes eventually result in body activity. And because man's superb brain is capable of such complex and efficient patterning of the energy at its disposal, human behavior can become amazingly effective.

FEELING

Living is also feeling. Our deepest satisfactions come as energy surges through us and we succeed in the jobs we have set for ourselves. If living is fundamentally energy flowing in intricately controlled patterns through a highly organized system, then emotion or feeling is our personal measure of the quality of our living.

If pleasure is anticipating, remembering, or actually experiencing efficient surge of internal power, then unpleasant feeling must be our warning of blocking or breakdown of normally free channels of energy flow.

To illustrate: A healthy youngster takes life head on, gleefully putting all he has into his fun. How violently he resents and fights against us if we suddenly force him to stop and then hold him quiet! We are halting his own free use of energy which he is spending for things he needs, wants, and enjoys. Also, we can remember personal bitterness when someone stopped something we liked to do.

Even physical pain is necessary, for it throbs with warning of injury and possible breakdown in some necessary part of ourselves. So unpleasantness and pain may be nature's way of telling us, "something *here* challenges your very existence, for it threatens to disorganize or cut off vital flow of energy into and through your being."

Living depends on energy flowing on through into acting. Blocking a person's activity bottles energy up and dams it off and causes tension. Severe tension held too long gives way to inward or outward explosion, and inward explosion is breakdown or death. Energy channels have to be kept open.

URGE TO LEARN

Living is urge to learn. Being alive is really worthwhile when we feel we are growing more competent, better able to do things we want to do, learning to be the kind of person others expect. Children and adults are not naturally lazy or misbehavers.

We are coming to see that *our most basic human quality is an inborn urge and drive to push our own development and self-realization to their limits.* We long to learn to use our energy in more and more effective ways of feeling, thinking, deciding, and acting.

People of all ages, unless they have already been too severely wounded, will face up to severe physical, emotional, and mental threat for the joy of working on thru challenge toward greater competence and self-assurance. But this can happen only if the restrictions and demands from outside have not been too severe.

A child's own memory must consistently tell him, "I have succeeded more often than I have failed. The fun of growing up and learning has far outweighed the necessary pain and defeat and restriction along the way. How exciting and enjoyable it is to use my energy to grow and learn!"

What must adults have done to force so many growing children to deny this birthright? They have forced children to withdraw, already half-licked by life, into a tentative, hesitant shell for protection against any more wounding. They have forced children to become so aggressive, in tense defiance of too much blocking, that they lose much-needed affection, group acceptance, and opportunities for learning. The limitations and distortions which our culture forces onto children are a major problem.

ONLY ONE ENERGY POOL

Living requires balancing and directing the energy budget. The energy we have must be spent on several vital jobs: keeping body machinery in good working order; growing up into a maturing person; using and expanding our ability to feel; and learning to think, decide, and act more effectively. But each person has only one pool of energy to supply all these jobs—the energy he gets from the food he eats.

A grown man normally requires about 2800 calories of food energy per day, a woman about 2400. Approximately half of this is used just to keep alive— providing draft, stoking, cleaning out, carrying around, oiling and repairing the never-resting machinery of living. This maintenance energy is measured as *basal metabolism*. The other half of the energy pool is available for growing and learning.

Since all essential activities draw their energy from the common pool, they must be intimately and inseparably interrelated. We should expect that efficiency in one means more energy for the others, and that defects in one will detract from the others.

We can also anticipate that there must be some over-all control to insure that all energy available will be organized and used for the benefit and enjoyment of the whole person. From this viewpoint, the common denominator unifying all life activities is ever-flowing energy intertwined in increasingly intricate patterns, making breathing or thinking or acting from convictions or visioning the ultimate goals of man all part of a unified synthesis of flowing power.

HEALTH, GROWTH, AND BEHAVIOR

Clearly, anything affecting a child's physical health will also affect his body growth and his ways of behaving as an individual. The changes occurring in growth have to build onto and into already working organs and systems *at the same time that these parts keep on working.* (Wouldn't it be miraculous if we could remake a Model T Ford engine into a 1950 V-8 motor at the same time we were driving the car at 60 miles per hour and simultaneously keep the motor in shape for decades of hard driving?)

Physical health affects behavior, but behavior also influences health and growth. The efficiency of our ways of organizing energy in the nervous system in order to control behavior (the nervous energy patterns behind our ways of feeling and thinking, our attitudes and goals, our hopes and values for right and wrong) will play a dominating part in physical health and growth. Good psychological adjustment is associated with healthy body and top-level growth, but psychological maladjustment can actually damage health and prevent growth.

We all know that stomach ulcers and heart disease increase with severe, prolonged emotional tension, and we have each sensed our own lost initiative and pep when we are struggling with a baffling internal emotional conflict. There is startling evidence to show that emotionally disturbed children fail to grow normally.

We conclude that all phases of energy flow are inseparably interwoven in any individual. What each of us will do with his total energy pool depends partly on the mechanical efficiency of body physiology, and partly on the more complex patterns of individual psychological organization, especially on *what life has come to mean to each person.*

If we are to understand any child, we must not only gain a clear picture of his body machinery, but we must also try to discover what this condition seems like to him. We must see how what he is and does matches up with the kind of person he feels himself to be and wants to become.

16 *Motivated to learn*

This selection should be read in conjunction with the preceding one by the same author.

The first article of this discussion described human life as ever-flowing energy, power surging in infinite variation and intricate pattern through a highly developed body and brain. This dynamic idea of human life helps in understanding behavior. It focuses on the core of an individual, on each person's internal, intimately personal pattern of controlling and using his own pool of energy.

A person's outward behavior (what he will actually do) is thus the final or outgoing phase of energy use. It will depend in part on the efficiency of his own body as an energy-transforming machine (the things his body actually could do). It will depend in part on how he feels and thinks and hopes about himself as a person, the kinds of things he likes to do (whether he thinks he is strong or weak; how much he wants to put out his energy).

Thus, any discussion of the effect of physical conditions on a child's behavior

GLENN C. DILDINE, "Motivated to Learn,'" *NEA Journal*, XXXIX (May, 1950), 356–57. Reprinted by permission of the author and the publisher. For a brief biographical sketch of DR. DILDINE see the footnote for selection 15.

must include (1) knowledge of various physical processes in humans and physical conditions in a particular child, and (2) what this body seems like to the child.

HIGH VERSUS LOW ENERGY OUTPUT

It is astonishing how much more fun children become and how we improve our ways of working with them as we learn to recognize some of the reasons for differences in their energy output, their ways of using available energy, and their will to use the energy they have. For example, a child may have seemed "dull" to us, but more careful check shows that he has less energy to use than most of his classmates. Although he must go at living and learning more slowly, he shows that he can eventually learn well if we give him time.

Another child points up the gross difference in rate of living between adults and children. Not realizing that the years between have slowed our own energy output down by comparison, we may easily have described a certain child as "nervous," with a slight edge of distaste and rejection as we said it. Gradually deepening insight shows us that this child has a high energy efficiency, so his driving urge and need is to release a tremendous exuberance flowing thru a healthy body.

Realizing that his behavior is really normal and right for him, instead of trying to curb activity in order "to control nervousness," we now try to provide a variety of enjoyable and productive things for him to do. School seems more fun to him now; he is using his soaring energy productively, and we can be a little more relaxed around him.

PHYSICAL HEALTH INFLUENCES
ENERGY OUTPUT AND USE

When we are sick, we not only lose efficiency of infected parts but also have to redirect much of the reduced energy we have left toward fighting the infection and replacing damaged tissues. When we recall how listless and irritable we get when coming down with a severe cold, we can sense how ill-health will rob children of energy, and of easy control of residual energy. Listlessness and irritability may be signs that children need a doctor's care, not that they are lazy or bad.

Children react so differently to the same illness that one wonders what illness and health have come to mean to a child. Is sickness so rare that it frightens? Has previous illness been so painful or frightening that thought of nurses or doctor or sickbed is almost unbearable? Has sickness been used as a substitute satisfaction to gain attention or love? Has this child come to think of himself as a person who gets sick all the time, so he gives in easily? Is he secure, confident, and independent enough to handle both illness and its emotional threats?

PHYSICAL DEFECTS REQUIRE
REPATTERNING ENERGY USE

Injuries, defective eyes and ears, arm, leg, and spine deformities may reduce a child's actual efficiency and are often unrecognized causes for slow learning or "poor" behavior. But we all know of people with gross bodily defects who have lived satisfying, productive lives. Our bodies have amazing capacities for self-correction, for sharpening senses or strengthening the other leg.

But a child needs to know from everyday experience of being accepted, wanted, and helped that his defect does not make him shameful or ugly to others. He then finds courage and can actually mobilize his energy to struggle through toward compensation and readjustment. He needs help to see himself as a person, a bit different of course, yet able to do many things well and maybe some things even better than others.

ENDOCRINE EFFICIENCY IS
BASIC IN ENERGY CONTROL

Chemicals (hormones) from ductless glands play a controlling part in our energy level. Each gland has a special job, yet its effect is often modified by secretions of other glands.

The thyroid is a significant example. The hormone thyroxin sets the body's rate of energy release by controlling the rate of burning body fuels, thus freeing energy from foods for change into nerve impulse, heart beat and blood flow, muscle action, and all the subtle variations in energy found in living systems. If the thyroid is lazy, all body processes slow down.

Such a child may seem "lazy" because he has little energy left over from just keeping alive to use as he would like, or he may partially lose self-control and become cantankerous because he hasn't energy enough left to keep himself focused, or he may gain excess weight because extra unburned fuel is stored away as fat. Lack of enough free energy will also slow down action of other endocrines, so hormone deficiencies may appear.

A basal metabolism test reveals thyroid condition. Doctors can frequently correct a malfunctioning thyroid and many other endocrine disturbances. But the effect on a child's picture of himself may continue, depending partly on how he was treated during the upset. If he became overweight, how did other people treat him? How much failure did he go through before the cause of low energy was discovered? Is this still a part of his estimate of present ability?

ENERGY VARIES WITH PLACE IN GROWTH CYCLE

Energy output changes with age. It is very high in young children, then tapers off. It spurts again during puberty, and then gradually declines. It will require a different home and school program to enable young children to control and use up their high energy output.

For young children, this means frequent change of activity, a minimum of such physical restraints as sitting quietly at a desk or talking in low tones, and chance for variety in much enjoyable physical action. We are just beginning to realize how right play is for children, how much they learn about growing up during play, in addition to releasing pent-up energy.

During the teenager's growth spurt, so much energy is shifted into growing that often little is left for home and school jobs. A boy or girl who had been fairly self-controlled and active may now show contrasting days of boredom, disorganized restlessness, and even hostility. It is significant to realize that during this growth spurt, energy may vary over 30% within a few days, but that stability returns during later puberty and that this will be reflected then in more consistent energy output and behavior.

Adolescent bodies change and grow so fast! A child may become quite accustomed to himself during the slow changes of late childhood, but all at once, "What is happening to me now? Will my feet ever stop growing? Is this the kind of nose I'll always have? Is this what a normal man is like? or woman? Why can't I be pretty?"

Our way of life puts such a high value on a particular, limited kind of beauty or handsomeness, screaming it from radio, billboards, magazines and movies! We reject deviations so strongly. How must it feel to Al or Caroline to be just their kind of young person, right now? Their answers to these disturbing questions may show very clearly in the ways they act in class or on the playground.

FATIGUE IS RELATED TO AVAILABLE ENERGY

Children (and adults) often get into trouble near the end of the day, losing self-control as energy dwindles. "Lazy" or "slow" or "stupid" children are often dead-tired from home chores or routine late hours or an extra-late visit the night before. Energy resources and the speed at which they can be used up are limited, vary for different children, and change through time in the same child. The amount of rest and sleep and the timing of alternate activity and rest also differ.

Some regimenting is necessary in schools and can be suited to the majority in a group, but many children will still need individual adjustment to suit their rhythm and their tiredness. Even though the others are expected to be actively at work, maybe one child today really should be sleeping instead.

EACH PERSON'S REALITY
DETERMINES HIS ENERGY USE

Although many specific physical conditions vary widely between different children and in the same child at different times, these are relatively easy to discover. But what these conditions mean to a child is another matter, for each of us judges "what is real" by his own picture of it, by how it appears to him. This "seeing how things are" varies with our own peculiar psychological slant and differs for each person.

So it is hard for us to get even figuratively inside another person's skin in order to feel how they feel and see as they see. Instead, we are accustomed to interpreting any situation for others from how it would seem to us if it were happening to us. It takes time and conscious, continuous effort to develop sensitivity to the feelings of other people.

Why do so many healthy, good-looking, capable, well-coordinated, energetic young people take so little interest in schoolwork and even seem so antagonistic? Part of the answer lies in whether or not schoolwork and adult demands for behavior seem really good, worthwhile, important, and enjoyable to each child, as *he* sees it from *his* own personal feeling and ideas about himself and his own personal world.

The directions in which a child will use his energy wholeheartedly will depend on his attitudes and interests, the things he fears and hopes for, the goals he strives for, and failures he has had, all of which have been somehow included in his pattern of organizing and spending energy. The farther away his background of experience (especially at home and in his home neighborhood) is from the behavior the school expects, the less the chance that he will see much sense to the school program.

But if we can learn to tie the things we expect and demand (if only we can be sure our demands are important) to ideas and jobs that seem important to him and promise him pleasure, then he will move into the job cheerfully and profitably. He will be "motivated to learn."

17 *The fundamental needs of the child*

Related selections: 14, 18, 31

The nature of the human organism and its processes is such that every individual has certain basic needs that, in a measure, are with him continuously and that must be met if he is to develop into an adequate person. Such requirements consist of the things, the activities, the experiences, and the conditions that are basic to permanent adjustment. Lawrence K. Frank's discussion is a synthesis that draws upon the findings of many studies of physiological and psychological needs.

Every society and every generation uses children for its own purposes. It is significant that to-day we are beginning to speak of the needs of the child as

LAWRENCE K. FRANK, "The Fundamental Needs of the Child," *Mental Hygiene*, XXII (July, 1938), 353–79. Reprinted by permission of the publisher.
DR. FRANK (1890–   ), distinguished scholar and author in the field of mental hygiene of children, is the recipient of many awards and honors and has served in an advisory capacity to a score or more government and philanthropic agencies.

entitled to consideration in his nurture and education or even as the controlling factor in child care. Contrast this emerging conception of the child's nature and needs with the practices all over the world, among so-called civilized people and so-called primitive people, in which the nurture and education of children are dictated by religious, ethical, and moral ideas, by political and economic requirements, by social class lines, indeed by an extraordinary variety of ideas and purposes all more or less remote from the child himself. The children in all these cultures are molded by the dominant ideas and beliefs and the group purposes into greater or less conformity in which they may sacrifice much or little.

Consider also the variety of practices in regard to the physical make-up or form of children. Among certain Indian tribes, the infant's head is flattened to a board. Among certain African tribes, the lips or ears may be stretched or the neck encased in coils of brass. Everyone is familiar with the ancient Chinese practice of binding the feet of female infants. As children grow older, many peoples have puberty rites involving tattooing, skin incisions, various forms of mutilation of the male and female genitals, and the inculcation of rigidly prescribed motor patterns of action that may involve anatomical deformities. The catalogue of practices that deform, distort, or otherwise manipulate the physical structure is endless, but all are regarded by those who use them as essentially necessary to make over the child into the image prescribed by the culture as the only right form for a man or a woman. In their cultural context these practices and beliefs may be purposeful and valid.

Not only is the physical structure of the child made over into the patterns of the culture, but so are the physiological functions, as we see in the diverse standards imposed upon the young child by different societies. In the matter of nutrition, for example, every group teaches the child to like the food of its traditional choice, which means developing an appetite for an incredible array of foodstuffs, or supposed foodstuffs, and abhorring other foodstuffs of equal or greater nutritive value. Many of these food choices represent a wise, economical use of available animal and vegetable resources, while others are obviously dictated by various beliefs in sympathetic magic, by rigid taboos, and by religious convictions that have little or no relation to the nutritional requirements of the growing child or even of the adult. Every society, again, imposes some kind of training upon children with respect to elimination. In some cultures the requirements are minimal, but in others they may be so severe and so rigorously imposed upon the very young child as to create lifelong impairment of physiological efficiency. Even breathing, in some cultures, is subject to special training, and sleeping patterns, peculiar to each group, are inculcated at an early age.

It is safe to say that most of these traditional patterns of child training and nurture derive from ideas and beliefs and strong convictions that have little or no relevance to the immediate needs of the child. Civilized man in many cases has survived *despite*, not because of, these methods of child care, as we are now beginning to realize in the light of recent investigation.

Curious as are these practices of physical and physiological training, the variety of practices in phychological training are even more astonishing, since here we find methods and procedures for bringing up children in the most fantastic, distorted patterns of conduct and feeling. The belief in using the child for social purposes is revealed here more convincingly than in the realm of physical care, where the organic limits of deformation impose some restraint; whereas in the area of conduct and belief there apparently are no limits to the grotesque, the cruel and brutal, the diabolical ingenuity of man in warping and twisting human nature to cultural patterns which originally may have been useful or even desirable, but which have become rigid and perverse.

When we reflect upon these various beliefs and practices that are imposed upon the child to make him conform to group-sanctioned patterns, we can begin to understand how extraordinarily significant it is to-day that we are discussing the needs of the child as a basis for his nurture and education. We can also see how questions of education and training become the focus of bitter conflicts, as contending factions in a society struggle to direct the nurture of children in order to control the group life. As we meet to-day to discuss programs of education for the young child in the home and in the nursery school, we are not concerned merely with questions of technique and procedures, with this or that pedagogical device; we are faced with the major issues of the future of our culture and the direction of our whole social, economic, and political life, since an effective program of early-childhood education based upon the needs of the child will inevitably change our society far more effectively than any legislation or other social action.

We must, therefore, be humble and deliberate in our discussion, not only because of the gravity of the larger social issues involved, but also because we know so little about the needs of the child. It is safe to say that whenever you hear any person or group speaking with strong convictions about specific needs of the child and how to meet them, that person or group is probably sustained more by emotional fervor and loyalty to cultural traditions than by dependable knowledge of actual children.

Anyone who is prepared seriously and fairly to consider the question of the child's needs must begin by trying to be honest about his or her own personality bias and beliefs, emotional attitudes, religious loyalties, and social-economic and political leanings, because these often unconscious feelings and values play so large a rôle in our attitudes toward the child and in our willingness to recognize some of his needs or our strong denial of them. Probably the most general statement that we can make about the child's needs is that he should be protected from distortions, from unnecessary deprivations and exploitations by adults—parents, teachers and nurses, physicians, psychologists, and others engaged in dealing with children.

It is difficult to realize the extent of these often subtle coercions and pressures exerted upon the child. Before the infant is born, the parents may have built up a picture of the kind of child he or she is to be, with a pronounced bias toward the male or the female sex, or toward a certain kind of temperament, physique, and ability. The infant, having within him the genes of countless previous generations as well as the characteristics of his parents, enters into a family situation that even at birth may be threatening and out of harmony with his peculiar, idiosyncratic temperamental make-up and needs. Parents who are eager to minister to the infant's need for warmth, food, and safety may be doggedly determined to deny the child's sex and his many personal, temperamental characteristics, which gives rise to needs as important and urgent as the need for physical care.

It is not without reason, therefore, that we stress this primary and inalienable need of the child to be accepted as a unique individual, or, if the parents cannot or will not accord that acceptance, the need to be protected and reinforced against the destructive, warping influence of these parental biases. Every child suffers to a greater or less extent from this denial of his own personal, temperamental individuality, because even the most emancipated parents are not wholly free from the desire to see their children conform to the images they have constructed. Moreover, every teacher has these partialities, often unconscious, which incline her toward one child and away from another. Further, the child himself is subject to the strong desire to be like the parents, however out of harmony with his own make-up such an identification may be. It is interesting to see how the recognition of individual differences is resisted even by professionally trained persons, such as teachers, who will accept the fact of such differences with respect to mental capacity, as shown by standardized mental tests, but deny it with respect to personality, temperament, physical maturity, and other obvious characteristics.

The infant, as he grows into childhood and youth, faces a series of life tasks that cannot be evaded or denied. The way in which he meets those life tasks and his attempts to master them give rise to the various needs for which we to-day believe his nurture and education should provide. It is obvious that we have only a fragmentary knowledge of those needs, since we have studied so briefly the process of growth and development and the life tasks presented by our culture. But it is highly significant, as we suggested earlier, that we are genuinely concerned with understanding child growth and development and are trying to discover the child's needs, as a basis for his education and nurture.

The processes involved in living and growing create needs for warmth, nutrition, and bodily care concerning which we are gaining more knowledge and technical competence. Much of the research in the field of nutrition and its results are still in terms of uniform standardized rules based on pure-strain rat colonies, with no allowance made for individual differences in vitamin and mineral requirements, so that, in the name of scientific standards, we may create serious deficiencies in the individual child as contrasted with the standardized laboratory animal. Even rats in the same litter differ, as Streeter has recently shown, in their susceptibility to rickets. The nutritional and other physical needs of the individual child are to be viewed dynamically, not statically, in terms of continuing growth and development rather than fixed height-weight standards which are purely statistical averages. Moreover, these needs should be viewed in terms of physiological functioning, not merely of structural size and shape, since it is functional efficiency, not structure, that is important.

How many problem children, hypochondriacs, and psychoneurotics have been created by blind adherence to these standardized tables which physicians and nurses, health educators, and teachers have given to mothers as scientific laws and which mothers have then used on their children! Surely we should allow for individual differences in children and not increase parental anxiety in this area of physical needs by insisting upon these standardized height and weight tables for chronological-age groups. The child's need is for food, rest, sleep, and play, so that he will continue to grow and develop *at his own rate.* The emphasis should be upon the growing, not upon fixed dimensions for chronological ages based upon the assumption that all children grow at the same rate.

The same criticism may be made of other chronological-age standards, such as prescribed hours for sleeping, where again failure to make allowance for individual differences has created many distraught mothers and problem children. The sleep needs of children vary greatly, and the loss of a nap is often much less undesirable than conflict, rebellion, punishment, and other consequences of a rigid sleep regimen.

If we are to gain a better understanding of the child's needs in terms of the life tasks he faces, we should envisage the physiological processes involved in what we call socialization. First in order of impact upon the infant is the regularization of feeding, involving a fixed interval of three or four hours between food intake, to which the infant must adapt despite individual differences in the reduction of blood sugar that creates hunger and in the capacity to endure hunger. Prolonged hunger and crying, often while the mother keeps her eye on the clock to see when the precise minute for feeding arrives, create in the child a condition of tension that may in some cases initiate persistent personality difficulties.

In feeding we are confronted with something more than just a need for nourishment. In early infancy, the whole body of the infant is receptive and in need of comforting, cuddling warmth and opportunity to suckle. In breast-feeding these needs may be adequately filled, through the warmth of the mother and the close tactual contact with her through nourishment and suckling, wherein the baby receives much of his needed sense of security and feeling of being protected. Tactual contacts and soothing are primitive, but highly necessary, forms of reassurance. We never outgrow the need of them, but it is especially great in infancy and childhood. In this respect the human infant is like the young of all mammals, who thrive when nursed and cuddled and derive much needed emotional security from the oral activity of sucking and the close contact with the mother.

By many students of personality, it is said that if the infant is given adequate breast-feeding and affectionate cuddling, his future attitude toward the world will be outgoing, generous, and trusting, whereas if he is denied these satisfactions, he will be suspicious, niggardly, and resentful. Dr. David Levy is quoted with approval by Dr. James S. Plant as stating "that satisfactory breast-feeding [cuddling] experiences do more than whole dictionaries of later words in the establishment of security in the family group"—what Dr. Plant calls "belongingness." Since so many children nowadays are deprived of breast-feeding, it is necessary to consider the acceptance of that deprivation as a life task that is imposed upon the dependent infant, thereby creating specific needs which may persist throughout life. The seriousness of this deprivation could be diminished if the bottle-fed infant were held by the mother and cuddled while taking the bottle, so as to receive the warmth and security of her close presence during the feeding.

But even the breast-fed infant must sooner or later lose that happiness and comfort and face the process of weaning, which may create anxiety and irritability if too abruptly or roughly handled. During weaning the child needs additional reassurances and comforting to prevent acute feelings of insecurity and anxiety and to lessen the loss of sucking. Every deprivation is a threat to the child, a source of anxiety which can be mitigated by affectionate reassurance which makes him feel that the deprivation is not a punishment and that he is still loved. The important question for nursery schools to ask is what can they do for the children who have been deprived of breast-feeding or unwisely weaned, and who need to be reassured and protected, helped to outgrow their anxiety, and aided with affectionate reassurance.

Eliminations and their regularization present two more life tasks that may create persistent needs. In discussing and teaching toilet training, we are apt to forget what a profound physiological disturbance we are imposing on the child. The physiological process of elimination of urine and feces is marvelously well organized, so that automatically the sphincters of the bladder and the rectum respond to accumulated pressure within. This physiological autonomy the child is asked to surrender when toilet training begins. Instead of functioning in accordance with his physiological needs, he is asked to inhibit the sphincter response to pressure, responding instead to an external stimulus— vessel, place, and so on—presented by the adult. Furthermore, he is asked to respond at a fixed time, whether or not he needs to do so physiologically. In this training, the child is expected to subordinate his processes to outside events and times, giving up his own physiological autonomy, often months before he is sufficiently mature to make such an adjustment. Maturity does not mean chronological age or size or weight; it means that the child has had enough of an activity, such as sucking or unrestricted elimination, to be able to go on to something else without a persistent feeling of deprivation or an unsatisfied infantile longing.

The widespread prevalence of enuresis and of constipation are not unrelated to the way in which toilet training has been imposed upon children who find in this process a serious nervous and emotional strain. During toilet training the child needs constant reassurance and comforting to stand the anxiety he so often feels. When failure to be continent elicits scoldings and punishment, the emotional stresses are increased and reinforced by feelings of guilt and inadequacy, often expressed in various symptoms of misbehavior. Evidence of how precariously the little child is balanced during toilet training is seen in the relapses that follow any emotional shock or family disturbance, or in the appearance of misconduct suddenly in the midst of peaceful, engrossing play, when the child is made uneasy and restless by a full bladder of which he is not yet fully aware. The evident over-concern of parents and nurses with toilet training raises for nursery schools the question of what they can do to provide reassurance for the anxious child, and to make toilet functions an unemotional subject and action. It is probable that some nursery schools themselves are guilty of aggravating the child's insecurity by their rigid overemphasis upon toilet training and the fuss made over "slips" or the teachers' unconscious reaction toward feces.

Here it is necessary to point out that the emotional tone or attitude of parents, nurses, and teachers toward toilet training is the important thing, not their actions, for the child reacts to the tone or attitude and feels the tenseness or overemphasis or dislike in the adult's voice and handling. The importance of the manner and tone of voice lies in the child's feeling that he is being deprived by this training. Any anger or impatience, then, may become an occasion for anxiety and feelings of guilt. How else is the child to understand and interpret the adult's treatment of him? Since many adults carry over from their own childhood a feeling of anxiety or disgust at feces, it is clear that they are not able to treat the child under their care without emotional stress when faced with this process, which for the child is entirely normal and unconnected with emotion until adult interference begins. Since few children pass through toilet training without some stress, we may include among the needs of the child the need for reassurance and often for release from the effects of this process upon the personality. It is appropriate to raise the question about toilet training: Are we concerned only with character training and the conformity it implies, or are we concerned with personality development and the kind of human being we are helping to foster? We can instill good habits or foster a personality; in the latter case, the habits will usually be established without difficulty. Weaning and toilet training, as often handled, are important sources of personality twists and biases, and may give rise to persistent needs in the child.

The arrival of a younger child in the family also may create acute anxiety when the older child has not been prepared for it. The shock of waking up one morning to find the mother absent, to be told that she has gone to the hospital to have a baby, and then to have her return with an infant who engrosses her time and attention, is the unhappy fate of many children whose parents either ignore their need for preparation and reassurance or else deny it because they cannot face the questions about sex and procreation involved. So many children suffer unnecessarily from the arrival of a younger brother or sister when that arrival could be the occasion for happy expectations and enjoyment! Here we have an excellent illustration of how children are sacrificed to religious and moral traditions that insist upon denying sex and hiding procreation as something shameful and obscene.

The symptoms of sibling rivalry, often aggravated by overt favoritism for the new baby and rejection of the older child, are many and various. The young child is faced with the necessity of accepting a place and a rôle for which he needs much affection and reassurance, which he may not receive at home or at school. Often this shock comes just as the child is striving to learn toilet habits, so that he is under a double load of anxiety which may lead to "slips" or persistent enuresis.

The frequency of rejected children—children not wanted or not acceptable as personalities or temperaments to the parents—is so great that special mention should be made of the need of such children for something to compensate for their unhappy fate. In this group must be numbered the children of over-solicitous mothers who are hiding their rejection of the child under an effusive care and atoning for their guilty feeling by "smothering" the child. Nursery schools have a great opportunity to meet the acute needs of these children.

The little child is frequently disturbed physiologically by emotional reactions such as anger, rage, and grief which clamor for expression or release in overt behavior. In a very real sense these physiological disturbances or upheavals seize control of the child and often impel him to act violently and destructively against things and people and even himself. One of the most important of life tasks for the young child is to learn how to manage these emotional reactions and thereby to free himself from this overwhelming experience. It is difficult for adults to conceive or to understand the panic that these emotional reactions may arouse in the child, who finds himself helplessly carried on a tide of feeling so strong that he cannot resist it unaided. If at the same time he meets with a violent response from adults, who strike him or forcibly restrain him, the emotional disturbance may be aggravated cumulatively until terminated by exhaustion. Such an experience teaches the child nothing constructive or helpful, and it may make him so afraid of himself that he begins to be anxious about this behavior and less and less prepared to meet the next provocation. Although the adult may forcibly control the child at the moment, what the child needs is help in controlling the emotional disturbance himself, so that, instead of a persistent conflict within the child between himself and his emotions, he can bring these emotional reactions into the pattern of his own living. The situation is in many respects like that in the case of hunger and elimination, where physiological processes are initially dominant, but are gradually transformed into regulated functional activities over which the individual has, as we say, control, because those functional processes are subject to the culturally sanctioned times, places, and objects.

In other words, the emotional reactions of the child are normal psychological functions that call for regulation and patterning, so that the child may be freed from their urgency and disturbance. They are not, as our tradition teaches, moral or ethical problems, and when handled as such, they only increase the child's guilt and resentment and serve to fixate him at that infantile level, as in toilet training when it is made a moral issue. Anger and rage, like fear, have had a great biological value in the past, but in group living they may, as persistent infantile reactions, seriously interfere with the individual's capacity for peaceful, coöperative adult living, just as persistent incontinence of feces will restrict an individual's activities.

The child, then, needs help in bringing his emotional responsiveness under regulation. Some children are more prone to anger and rage, others to fear and pain, so that each child requires highly individualized help in meeting his peculiar personal reactions. Unfortunately we have little knowledge of how to provide this help in a constructive, rather than a repressive, manner, because we have treated the problems as moral issues, meeting them with threats, punishment, shame, and often equally violent emotional reactions. There is need for much experimentation here in terms of physiological processes that need to be regulated and integrated into the child's total personality make-up through the help we can give him in his handling of these internal upheavals.

Perhaps the greatest need in these situations is for sympathetic reassurance that will allay the child's panic and so help him to meet the situation more effectively. If not helped early in life, the child may go forward with a capacity for violent reaction that his increasing size and strength make potentially dangerous, especially since he may, at the same time, be developing an increasing resentment toward others because of the way frustrations and deprivations are being inflicted upon him—a resentment that may later take the form of a persistent hostility and aggression, repeatedly reinforced by the revival of the infantile emotional reactions.

Fear and grief are also difficult reactions for the child to handle, but again we usually fail to provide really constructive help and only too often aggravate these feelings by our clumsy or careless attempts to dissipate them. Both fear and grief are physiological reactions that more or less paralyze or restrict activity, unless the fear activates flight. The child needs reassurance and reinforcement in meeting the strange, unknown, and apparently threatening experiences that confront him, and if we will accept the child's view that a situation is terrifying, even if we see that it is not, we can avoid the usual mistakes. Nothing is so helpful as learning some effective method of dealing with a fear-producing situation, since a learned motor response displaces the panicky fear of helplessness, as we see in the training of firemen, policemen, soldiers, and others. But many of the fears of children are not really physiological fears, but rather a disguise for other needs which the child cannot or does not reveal. It is the insecure, anxious child, the child who is not sure of himself or his place in the family or group, who appears fearful of situations that have no terrifying character, so that our earnest explanations and reassurances of safety are wholly irrelevant. Then, too, many children are reared under a constant threat of danger, the parents instilling fear before the situation arises in their efforts to protect the child, or the environment itself may be constantly terrifying. Again, many children have suffered really shocking accidents or exposures to danger which have been indelibly impressed upon them, so that they are ever apprehensive of a repetition and live in dread. Children from such a background need a long experience of peace, of safety and security, to escape from the terror that dominates their lives. In some cases only repeated rehearsals of the shock will enable them to escape from their hysterical reactions.

In view of the frequency of fears in little children, fears that often persist throughout life and handicap the individual, we should recognize as of the utmost importance the child's need for help in dissipating them. But we must be alert to the difference between fears and the persistent anxieties that derive from ill treatment and neglect and that are exhibited as fears of specific situations only because the child must find occasional release.

Grief is another pervasive emotional response for which we have little adequate treatment. Children lose beloved parents, siblings, and nurses through death, divorce, or the inevitable changes in relationship, and something happens to them that we can only guess at, for the child has no comforting philosophy or belief to assuage the acute sense of loss. He can then only mourn, as we see a dog mourn a beloved master, inaccessible to our proffered sympathy or reassurance, because what is missed is that idiomatic, personal relationship that can rarely be regained with another. Children who are well loved can often find in the non-verbal response of those they love some comfort, but if they have lost someone of value in their lives, that loss may never be forgotten. The facing of death or deprivation, the acceptance of the inevitable, is one of the life tasks which mankind has never found a satisfactory method of meeting. To-day children are increasingly obliged to face another kind of loss that is more perplexing and difficult than death—the separation or divorce of their parents, which is so hard to explain to the child and almost impossible to render innocuous. In meeting this situation the child has needs that we can scarcely understand, but we must try to provide some kind of helpful assistance, because the experience is so devastating to the young child and so persistently disturbing throughout childhood and especially adolescence. The conflict of parents, the frequent accusations and impugning of motives, all the bitterness and the competition for the child's favor, act as a psychological poison that, especially in the case of girls, may ruin the individual's capacity for adult mating, for one of the child's great needs is to build up images of the husband and wife, the father and mother, as guides to his or her own future rôle in marriage.

Another task of the child that is a source of anxiety, creating an acute need for reassurance and understanding help, is that of accepting his or her own sex and the many taboos that surround this subject. The traditional view of childhood is that children have no awareness of sex differences and no concern over their genitals, while the cumulative clinical evidence indicates that they are often greatly worried about sex differences and puzzled, if not greatly preoccupied, by their genitals. It is hard for a child to envisage the process of procreation, to accept his maleness or her femaleness, and to see any meaning or sense in the confusing "explanations" given, at the same time striving to understand the violent reactions of adults to exposure of the genitals, manipulation, and so forth.

Little children need constant reassurance and simplified enlightenment on questions of sex and procreation if they are to escape prolonged anxiety and possible lifelong unhappiness. In so far as nursery schools and other schools can provide children with an understanding and wholesome attitude here, we can see how the education of children may change our whole culture, for undoubtedly our culture is warped and distorted by our inherited traditions of uncleanliness, obscenity, and wickedness in regard to sex. We cannot expect to dispose of the child's curiosity and concern by purely biological explanations, since, as Otto Rank has pointed out, adults themselves are not satisfied with merely biological answers. Moreover, the exigent questions about sex, for the child and the adult, are not concerned with gestation, but with the uses of sex in living, in feeling, in intimacy and affection.

It is not too much to say that the ability of men and women to marry and to find happiness in marriage and family life is largely conditioned by their experience and acceptance of their masculine or feminine rôles and sex differences during the pre-school years. If the boy is to grow up as a psychologically potent male, he must during the pre-school years develop his maleness and focus his future sex interests and needs in the genitals, since failure to do so at that time, as clinical evidence amply shows, will compromise his adolescence and prevent his achievement of a wholesome heterosexual adjustment toward women. Likewise it is clear that the little girl, during the pre-school years, must get a clear idea of her future feminine rôle, must accept her essential biological, physiological, and anatomic difference from the male and begin to look forward to her psychological differentiation as a female, with unique capacities for mating, procreation, lactation, and maternal and feminine rôles.

Children find these tasks, which should be simple, wholesome, and natural stages of pre-school development, matters of extraordinary difficulty and stress. Their parents, especially the mother, are so often suffering from anxiety, disgust, or fear about their own sex functions and needs that they cannot tolerate the child's natural curiosities and activities, nor can they permit the child's efforts to make these early life adjustments. Unfortunately many nursery-school teachers suffer from the same unfortunate conditioning, and so are unable to give the child the understanding and help he or she needs. It is not going too far to say that in some nursery schools the difference between boys and girls is ignored or rigidly suppressed, with serious consequences for the personality of the children.

As we gain more insight into the process of personality development and realize how crucial these pre-school sex interests and adjustments are for the subsequent adult life, we can and must work out nursery-school procedures designed to help the child to meet these tasks with courage and happiness, free from the distortions and anxieties that are now so prevalent, able and ready to give and to receive affection.

Another life task confronting the child is that of learning to recognize and observe the inviolabilities that every culture establishes with respect to objects, persons, places, and times. We are so accustomed to think of private property in things and animals, of the sanctity of the physical person of individuals, of the great number of special places and days consecrated to particular purposes which must not be profaned, that we fail to realize that private property and the sanctity of the person are not entities or mysterious powers, but learned ways of behaving toward things and persons, taught to children often with severe penalties for evasion or violation. These lessons as to the inviolability of things and persons are painfully learned by the young child as he begins to explore the world about him, seeking occasions for satisfying his needs and expressing his impulses, and being more or less forcibly restrained, rebuffed, and frustrated. He finds that everything and every person is protected by an invisible barrier of inviolability ("don't touch," "don't look," "don't eat," "don't go near," "don't handle") which he may not disregard except in duly sanctioned ways, such as buying and selling and making contracts or agreements. He must also learn to uphold the inviolability of his own person and property.

These lessons are not simple, since there are many fine distinctions to be made. What is freely accessible in the home is taboo outside; certain persons may be freely invaded, as in fighting with siblings, while others, such as strangers, are inviolable; certain persons are receptive to physical contact, such as parents or near relatives, while others not in the family group are untouchable; actions that may be performed in one place or at one time are forbidden in other places and at other times. Then, too, the child confronts the magical power of money, whereby small pieces of metal or paper render freely accessible what is otherwise inviolable.

These lessons are indeed formidable, and the young child struggling with the complicated customs of group life faces a heavy task for which he needs endless patience and sympathetic teaching. How often a little mistake over private property, which he is just beginning to understand, evokes sudden and immediate punishment, with accusations of "thief" and "liar" and other terrifying characterizations. When we realize that these early lessons in observing the inviolabilities are the most essential steps in preparation for group living, perhaps we shall devise more desirable and effective methods of teaching them, and shall remember to provide toleration and reassurance for the bewildered child who is attempting to assimilate the cumulative customs of thousands of years. It is little wonder that the learning of these inviolabilities, involving as they do repeated frustrations and a form of negative conditioning that inhibits the response to biologically adequate stimuli of objects and persons, should so frequently impair the child's whole adult life, causing him to face every encounter and every negotiation with timidity or anxiety, or to be intensely preoccupied with getting the better of everyone in all situations.

Besides learning to inhibit his responses to things and persons who are inviolable, the child must also learn to perform those acts which his parents insist upon as the required actions in various situations. These actions include the traditional manners and customs, the etiquette and the moral duties which the parents especially cherish and respect and which they are compelled to teach their children as the essentials of life. These lessons are difficult for the child because, like the inviolability of things and persons, the required conduct has no natural, biological relation to the situations in which it is demanded of the child. He must, therefore, be repeatedly shown what to do, and prompted and compelled to do it, with a greater or less amount of verbal and often physical punishment. The outcome of this training is the establishment of more or less automatic conduct, according to the required pattern, which is always a variation, peculiar to the family, of the general socially approved pattern.

As in the teaching of inviolabilities, parental instruction as to the performance of these required actions involves the exercise of authority, often by the father, who rarely has as close and affectionate a tie with the child as the mother and who, therefore, relies more upon coercion to exact obedience, while the mother relies upon the child's desire for her love and approval. Thus the child experiences authority and coercion for the first time, and only too often it is administered severely and arbitrarily, arousing in the child fear, resentment, and hostility toward the father.

These disturbing emotional reactions toward the parents, especially the father, are of crucial importance for the future of the child. As a member of a group, he has to learn to acknowledge and to accept authority, to recognize outside himself a regulator, controller, and arbiter of conduct that is largely traditional, not reasonable or based upon anything but custom. He must learn to observe in his conduct the repressions and frustrations required by the inviolability of things and persons; and equally he must learn to perform various acts, from small courtesies to the greater, more important duties appropriate to his sex, status, class, position, and so on, accepting all these complicated and largely ritualized acts as necessary and desirable and as duly sanctioned by the law and the prescribed rules of social living. The development of such conduct involves the constant recognition and willing acceptance of the authority of the state, which, to be really effective, must function, not in physical coercion and police supervision, but within the individual himself. Authority, then, like private property, is merely a way of behaving toward individuals and situations; it is an attitude or effective reaction toward what is expected or demanded.

Now if the young child experiences authority for the first time as coercive, severe, and brutal, as something that arouses fear, anxiety, and resentment, his socialization will be compromised. He cannot calmly and gracefully accept that which is expected or demanded, performing acts or refraining from responses, but rather he will feel tension, will resent the parental authority, and will develop a persistent hostility toward the parents, especially the father, and all others who attempt to direct his conduct.

Instead, then, of accepting the inviolabilities or the required performances, the child who has been thus treated will fail to build those conduct patterns into an integrated whole, in which his behavior and his personality are at one. He may outwardly conform to what is demanded or prohibited, but only because of fear and anxiety. The learned conduct, essential to group life, is never assimilated or made wholly automatic, and so the child becomes preoccupied with the conflict between what he must do and not do and what he feels. Often he releases his feelings in misbehavior that is difficult to understand, for it gives the child nothing of value or advantage and usually is wholly incongruous with the situation. These aberrant actions are symptoms of conflict, modes of expressing resentment or hostility against authority that has made him fearful and unhappy.

With so many children exposed to this destructive experience of authority, destined by their persistent feelings of fear and resentment to unhappy adult lives, if not to more serious outcomes in mental disorders and criminality, the nursery schools are confronted by the urgent need of these children for help in accepting authority and in escaping these initial disturbances. Can we devise experiences in the nursery school that will enable the child to accept authority and to find freedom from the emotional conflicts and resentments that his previous experiences have engendered? The need is for ways of inculcating acceptance of authority without aggravating the already serious conflicts so many children have when they come to nursery schools; and this calls for reformulation of the problem, as discussed above, so that the authority will be transferred to the situation and divested of the personal element that evokes the resentment and conflict. Paradoxically, this depersonalization of authority depends upon a personal relation of the parent to the child wherein the exercise of authority is benevolent and helpful, not antagonistic and repressive.

This brings us to another life task of the child, who must create for himself, out of his experiences and the teaching he receives, an image of himself and of the kind of person he would like to be. This ideal of self will embody all the feelings of inadequacy and guilt that the child has experienced and must somehow express. Such feelings may lead to aspirations for constructive achievement, to altruistic, helpful conduct, and to other forms of expiation and atonement which, if not exaggerated into a neurotic drive for perfection, make the individual personality into a friendly, coöperative adult. Or they may lead to hostility and aggression, which take the form of intense competitive striving or coercive conduct; to delinquency, so that the individual may obtain punishment; or to mental disorders, in which the individual punishes himself. All these adjustment patterns are exhibited in childhood, when the child already has adopted his "style of life," and if we had enough insight and understanding, these adjustments might be treated in the nursery-school group in such a way as to mitigate, if not actually to revise, these personality trends. No one can prescribe a general method or procedure for all children, but undoubtedly the largest single element in the situation is the kind and extent of affectionate personal interest shown by an adult toward the child, who thereby may find much needed help toward a constructive, not a self-defeating, ideal of self. The process of identification, wherein the child strives to emulate an admired and loved adult, makes the teacher-child relationship of crucial importance. Lack of sympathetic understanding, of tenderness and patient toleration, may turn the child toward hostility and aggression, from which he can be reclaimed only by long and difficult therapy later, if at all.

One of the most important problems facing students of personality to-day is this question whether hostility and aggression are inborn characteristics of all individuals or whether they are the reactions of individuals who, as infants and pre-school children, were deprived of needed love and affection and security and so were driven by the unrelieved pressure for socialization to hostile, aggressive, destructive conduct. This question is of the utmost importance socially and educationally, since the answer involves the future of our society and of the civilized world. If man is innately hostile and aggressive, prone to destructive antagonisms and rivalries, then the prospects for a better, more humanly desirable society are not very bright. If human nature, as theological tradition and many of our contemporary students of personality tell us, is born wicked, sinful, and hostile and must be forced to be social, coöperative, and altruistic, the task of education is essentially a coercive one, that of curbing the hostility, of teaching individuals to "handle their aggressiveness." If, on the other hand, human nature is essentially plastic, subject to educational direction toward friendliness, coöperativeness, gentleness, and genuine group or social activity, then the task of education is to prevent the early distortions and unnecessary deprivations that arouse resentment and aggressiveness, by providing as much affectionate reassurance and toleration of individual, temperamental differences as possible for the children who have been ill treated or neglected by their parents. Here pre-school education has an immense opportunity and responsibility for the future course of our culture.

But here we must ask whether we know enough now to meet this issue of resentment and aggressiveness wisely. The policy of restraint and repression in many schools may prevent fighting and disorder for the moment, but it does nothing to release the child from inner tensions and frustrations of which his aggressions are but symptoms. Perhaps we have to face a mixed answer to the earlier question and realize that tensions and resentment are probably present in all children in the early years, as a necessary consequence of the process of deprivations and coercions they undergo during socialization. Whether these tensions will become persistent, life-long hostile attitudes toward the world, or be replaced by friendly, coöperative, attitudes, may be the critical issue of pre-school education. No permanent good is achieved by a repressive policy, nor is any constructive end attained by permitting the children to fight it out, with the risk of damage to all concerned. What is needed is an imaginative, insightful handling of conflicts and aggressions on an experimental basis, addressed to the underlying anxiety, guilt, and frustrations and the need for reassurance and security. There is also need for methods of handling situations in such a way that the initial hostility or aggression of the child may be rendered unnecessary by opportunities for friendly, helpful responses. Many children do not know how to act coöperatively and need the skillful guidance of an adult to encourage them in friendly conduct and sympathetic actions. It must be realized that repeated rebuffs and frustrations may transform love into hatred and aggression, so that the child can only attack what he has most desired.

This brings us to the exigent question of freedom and self-expression, over which there has been so much controversy and often hasty action. It may help us to obtain some perspective on this question if we will remember again that the child faces a series of unavoidable life tasks, including the persistent problem of how to get along in an organized group life. To the young child the world around him is indeed precarious and ambiguous. He faces a natural world often dangerous and always puzzling even to adults; his own organism, with its many functions and needs which must conform to parental and social patterning; obscure, often unconscious, impulses that impel him to actions that frequently he cannot understand, and that others usually resent, rebuke, and often retaliate for; a social or cultural world organized into patterns of behavior and regulated by symbols, such as language, that are subtly differentiated and variable; a constellation of human relationships, in the immediate family, the wider kinship group, the neighborhood, and the school, among which he must find personality fulfillment and security despite the capricious and disparate character of all these impinging personalities; and finally an immense body of tradition and folklore, knowledge, skills, and play.

Faced with such a welter of confusing, conflicting adjustments, the young child desperately needs the security of stable, persistently uniform situations, of dependable human relations, and of endless patience and tolerance. The frequent cry against any repression of the child involves a confusion that is often tragic for the child. Every culture involves deprivations and repression, the patterning and regulation of physiological functions and human behavior, which, if wisely handled, are only redirections and modulations of impulses. The young child especially needs a wisely administered regulation or direction because he cannot sustain the immense burden of making individual decisions on all the aspects of life and of learning unaided to manage his impulses. Few adults can do this, as we see in the overwhelming need for guidance, for precepts, for legal, ethical, and religious direction. Moreover, the regularization of hunger and elimination and the respecting of the inviolabilities leaves the individual free for other activities and interests that would not be possible if he were continually driven by hunger, beset by impulses to elimination, and at the mercy of every provocative personal contact or sexual stimulus. These learned patterns and repressions are the chief factors in man's ability to go beyond a purely organic existence. It is not the ordering of life that damages the child, but the distortion, the fears, anxieties, and permanent frustrations and inhibitions that parental and educational practices unnecessarily inflict upon the child in the process of establishing these socially and individually necessary repressions.

It is also the confusion and anxiety and insecurity of capricious, vacillating teaching that damages the personality in search of something stable and constant to build upon. Children love order, regularity, repetition of the same pattern endlessly, and they need consistent adult guidance and help in learning these patterns of what is essential to their adult life and social living. But they do not need, nor can they safely endure, the fears, the anxieties, the feelings of inadequacy and of guilt that so many parents and teachers instill during this socialization process. Indeed fear seems to be the chief psychological instrument in early child-rearing—either the arousal of fears by cruel and coercive treatment or the inculcation of fears of experience, of people, of living, which cripple the child for life. Fear, and the resentment or hostility it often generates, are indeed the major emotional drives in our social life and give rise to much unsocial and antisocial behavior. What the child needs, but seldom receives, is a clear-cut definition of the situation and of the conduct appropriate therein, so that he can and will learn what conduct is permitted and what is not permitted without the emotional disturbances he now experiences during these lessons. Practically, this means that the teaching by parents and teachers should stress the desirability or undesirability of the action without imputing blame to the child, so that instead of the usual admonishment, "You are a bad, naughty boy!" the statement should be, "That action is not desirable or not kind, not generous or not permissible, and I don't like it." The important difference is in the personal imputation of guilt and the emotional disturbance it creates in the child.

As many writers have pointed out, the child accepts socialization and the inevitable frustrations and repressions involved largely because he wants love and security from the parent and teacher. The long-popular method of asking the child to do this or that "if you love me," is especially damaging because it fails to create a recognition of impersonal authority in situations. The love for parents should never be exploited to control the child whose anxiety lest he lose that love is already great. The traditional manner of teaching, by calling the child bad or wicked when it is the behavior that should be defined as undesirable, makes the child fearful, guilty, and unhappy, and, if continued, may establish a persistent feeling of guilt and inadequacy and of being rejected.

To assuage that feeling of guilt and to overcome the sense of inadequacy and rejection, the child may commit more antisocial or forbidden acts to get the punishment he needs for his guilty feelings or to prove that he is not worthless. As Dr. William Healy and Dr. Augusta Bronner have recently shown in their study, *New Light on Delinquency*, the delinquent generally has had an unhappy childhood, characterized by feelings of rejection, inadequacy, and guilt, and by lack of affection.

This point about the necessity of socialization for the child without undue emotional stress and strain during the process is being emphasized here because it has such great consequences for our social life. If we could persuade parents and teachers to avoid characterizing the child as bad or naughty, while defining the behavior, and then give the child ample reassurance when receiving such lessons, undoubtedly we could make an immense contribution to the reduction of delinquency, criminality, and other non-criminal, but socially destructive conduct on the part of those who spend their adult lives proving by the acquisition of property, prestige, and power that they are not as guilty or as worthless as they were repeatedly told in childhood.

This question of socialization of the child without distortion and emotional disturbances must be seen in the light of the great individual differences among children in intelligence, temperament, rate of maturation, and need of reassurance, so that each child may be treated individually. The professional urge to standardize, to routinize, to substitute academic training for sympathetic interest and insights into children and to look for uniformities and generalizations that will save thinking, all must be critically reëxamined by nursery-school educators who are aware of these large social responsibilities. Especially is there a need for questioning the well-established principle that nursery-school teachers should be impersonal and should repress all affective responses to and from children. This principle came into vogue in the 1920's when behavioristic theories of child-rearing were dominant. The ideal of education was seen as that of almost complete emotional anesthesia and continually rational conduct, which is the ideal of the neurotic who is afraid of life and is seeking to suppress all feelings, of which he is fearful. As we realize how much the child is in need—as indeed all adults are also—of warm personal, human relations, of affectionate interest and real concern, and of opportunities to give and receive affection and to *feel*, we must challenge this old principle as directly contrary to the deepest need of the child and as destructive of human values, which can be preserved only by sensitivity and feeling tones toward people and situations.

Here it is necessary to ask why are we so afraid to recognize that the child needs mothering, not only at home, but in the nursery school, and that nursery-school teachers, by the very nature of their work, must be mother surrogates, ready and capable of giving affection and tenderness and warm emotional response to the children and of accepting them from the children. Is it because mothering does not seem scientific that we have tried to exclude it from the nursery schools or because—and I say this in no critical spirit, but as a statement based upon the actual situation—so many of those in nursery-school education are unmarried and childless and have unconsciously projected their own personal life adjustment into the training of nursery-school teachers? When we reflect upon the number of children in all classes of society who are raised by fear, terror, punishment, and other sadistic methods, with little or no experience of love and affection, we may well ask whether mothering (not smothering) may not be the most important service the nursery school can render to little children. Mothering does not mean babying or pampering, but rather giving a feeling of being liked and wanted, of belonging to someone who cares, and of being guided in the conduct of life with benevolent interest and confidence.

Dr. David Levy, a year or so ago, told this story at a meeting of the American Orthopsychiatric Association. He said that the social workers in the Bureau of Child Guidance were having unusually successful results with problem children, just because they were being maternal to these boys and girls so frequently denied real mothering. But they gave up this procedure because, said he, it did not seem scientific and was so hard to record! Perhaps if the nursery-school teacher were to consider her function as not only educational, but clinical, it might be easier to accept what the psychotherapeutic clinician accepts—namely, the rôle of parent surrogate, who gives the child individual personal interest and attention and tries to help that child work out a design for living by providing direction and deprivation, but always with interest and helpful concern.

Finally, we must look at the question of socialization in the light of the cultural changes through which we are now living, which are bringing about the destruction of so many of our traditional ideas, beliefs, and older certainties. The men and women of to-morrow will have to live in a shifting, uncertain world, of rapidly changing ideas and conceptions, with few or no absolutes or certainties. What is to guide their lives, to help them find fulfillment and a design for living sanely, wholesomely, and coöperatively? Probably no previous generation has had to face such acute personal problems without help from religion, custom, and tradition. Either they will demand an authoritarian state because they cannot endure uncertainty or tolerate the destructive hostility and aggressions of unhappy individuals, or they will learn to seek in constructive work and recreative play, in the warm human relations of marriage, parenthood, and the family, a way of life that will permit realization of the enduring human values.

The nursery school, in close and coöperative relationship with the home and parents, is the primary agency for mental hygiene. The opportunity in preschool education to build wholesome, sane, coöperative, and mature personalities, and to determine the future of our culture, is unlimited. The discharge of that responsibility lies in helping the young child to meet the persistent life tasks and to fulfill his insistent needs. But the nursery school cannot do this alone. It must have collaboration from the kindergarten and the grade schools, and it must find some way of coöperating with the home and the family, despite the frequent blindness and resistance of the parents. If nursery-school teachers were to realize that they are like parents, with their personal peculiarities, their emotional resistance and susceptibilities, their ignorance and rigid convictions—which may be just as undesirable for the child as the home practices they deprecate—perhaps such a realization would make them more tolerant and more willing to seek a basis of collaboration in meeting the fundamental needs of the child. The family can and does provide the child with a place, a status, with "belongingness" and often much needed love and affection. Can the nursery school organize its procedures and prepare its teachers to meet these same needs and also those other educational needs which the family has difficulty in supplying?

The fundamental needs of the child are in truth the fundamental needs of society.

18 Life and learning: introduction to the developmental task concept

Related selections: 14, 17, 19, 32

A developmental task is defined by Dr. Havighurst as "a task which arises at or about a certain period in the life of the individual, successful achievement of which leads to his happiness and to success with later tasks, while failure leads to unhappiness in the individual, disapproval by society, and difficulty with later tasks." Recognition of the particular tasks upon which the child is working at any given time is essential to an understanding of individual growth and behavior and to the proper timing of educational experiences. In this selection from Human Development and Education, *Dr. Havighurst introduces the concept of developmental tasks, briefly discusses their origin, and indicates the usefulness of*

ROBERT J. HAVIGHURST, *Human Development and Education* (New York: David McKay Co., Inc., 1953), pp. 1–5. Used by permission of David McKay Co., Inc.

DR. HAVIGHURST (1900–) has been Professor of Education at the University of Chicago since 1941. In 1956–58 he was Co-director of the Brazilian Government Center for Educational Research. His professional interests include the fields of psychology, sociology, gerontology, juvenile delinquency, and child development.

the concept for educators. The reader will find the entire book valuable for getting a picture of the developmental tasks of individuals at different age levels.

Living is learning, and growing is learning. One learns to walk, talk, and throw a ball; to read, bake a cake, and get along with age-mates of the opposite sex; to hold down a job, to raise children; to retire gracefully when too old to work effectively, and to get along without a husband and wife who has been at one's side for forty years. These are all learning tasks. To understand human development, one must understand learning. The human individual learns his way through life.

The lower animals rely more than human beings do on maturation, or "doing what comes naturally," to meet the problems of growing up. Apparently, playing with a mouse comes naturally to a kitten, without learning, and so does the salmon's long journey back to the waters of his birth, and the ways of the ant to the young graduate from the larval stage to adult anthood. Human beings are not built this way, with almost fully developed action patterns emerging as their nerves and glands and muscles grow. Very little of human behavior is such a crude product of maturation unformed by learning.

Nature lays down wide possibilities in the developing of the human body, and which possibilities shall be realized depends on what the individual learns. This is true even of such crude biological realities as feeding habits and sexual relations, while the more highly social realities of language, economic behavior, and religion are almost completely the product of learning at the hands of society.

The path of learning is not one long slow uphill climb with something to learn every new day, but consists of steep places, where the learning effort is severe, interspersed with plateaus where one can spend along almost without effort. For instance, the little boy works hard to learn how to throw and catch a ball, but once he has mastered this skill he may coast along on it for years without further improvement. The little girl works hard to learn to form her letters into a neat feminine script. She learns this during the years from age five to ten, and then has mastered the task. In simple unchanging societies, the young adult has mastered most of the learning tasks of his life. He knows the solutions to most of life's problems. For him, learning is just about over. Not so in the modern changing society where social life changes so rapidly that the individual must continually learn to adapt himself to changed conditions.

Living in a modern society such as that of the U.S.A. is a long series of tasks to learn, where learning well brings satisfaction and reward, while learning poorly brings unhappiness and social disapproval.

The tasks the individual must learn—*the developmental tasks* of life—are those things that constitute healthy and satisfactory growth in our society.

They are the things a person must learn if he is to be judged and to judge himself to be a reasonably happy and successful person. *A developmental task is a task which arises at or about a certain period in the life of the individual, successful achievement of which leads to his happiness and to success with later tasks, while failure leads to unhappiness in the individual, disapproval by the society, and difficulty with later tasks.*

The prototype of the developmental task is the purely biological formation of organs in the embryo.

> In this development each organ has its time of origin and this time factor is as important as the place of origin. If the eye, for example, does not arise at the appointed time "it will never be able to express itself fully, since the moment for the rapid outgrowth of some other part will have arrived, and this will tend to dominate the less active region, and suppress the belated tendency for eye expression."
>
> After the organ has begun to arise at the right time, still another time factor determines the most critical stage of its development: "A given order must be interrupted during the early stage of its development in order to be completely suppressed or grossly modified. . . . After an organ has arisen successfully from the anlage, it may be lamed or runted, but its nature and actual existence can no longer be destroyed by interrupting the growth."
>
> The organ which misses its time of ascendancy is doomed not only as an individual, it endangers at the same time the whole hierarchy of organs. "Not only does the arrest of a rapidly budding part, therefore, tend to suppress its development temporarily, but the premature loss of supremacy to some other organ renders it impossible for the suppressed part to come again into dominance, so that it is permanently modified. . . ." The result of normal development is proper relationship of size and function among the body organs: The liver adjusted in size to the stomach and intestine, the heart and lungs properly balanced, and the capacity of the vascular system accurately proportioned to the body as a whole. Through developmental arrest one or more organs may become disproportionately small; this upsets functional harmony and produces a defective person.

These purely biological developmental tasks of the body illustrate the essentials of the bio-socio-psychological tasks with which we are concerned. If the task is not achieved at the proper time it will not be achieved well, and failure in this task will cause partial or complete failure in the achievement of other tasks yet to come.

Consider the task of learning to talk, for example. Sometime between the ages of one and two most children master the essentials of human speech and language. They still have much to learn at the end of the second year, but they are well started. *They have learned to talk.* There is some evidence, from the few cases on record of children who were denied human companionship during their first few years of life and therefore did not learn to talk, that the task of learning to talk is extremely difficult and may never be accomplished well if it is not achieved in the second year of life. This is the crucial period for this particular task. And, if the task is not learned, the failure will stand in the way of learning a series of later tasks which depend greatly upon language.

THE ORIGIN OF DEVELOPMENTAL TASKS

As the individual grows, he finds himself possessed of new physical and psychological resources. The infant's legs grow larger and stronger, enabling him to walk. The child's nervous system grows more complex, enabling him to reason more subtly and to understand the complexities of subjects such as arithmetic. The individual also finds himself facing new demands and expectations from the society around him. The infant is expected to learn to talk, the child to learn to subtract and divide.

These inner and outer forces contrive to set for the individual a series of developmental tasks which must be mastered if he is to be a successful human being.

Some tasks arise mainly from physical maturation, such as learning to walk, learning to behave acceptably to the opposite sex in adolescence, and (for women) adjusting to the menopause in middle life. Other tasks, arising primarily from the cultural pressure of society, are learning to read, and learning to participate as a socially responsible citizen in society.

There is a third source of developmental tasks—namely, the personal values and aspirations of the individual, which are part of his personality, or self. The personality, or self, emerges from the interaction of organic and environmental forces. As the self evolves, it becomes increasingly a force in its own right in the subsequent development of the individual. Already by the age of three or four the individual's self is effective in the defining and accomplishing of his developmental tasks.

Examples of tasks arising primarily from the personal motives and values of the individual are: choosing and preparing for an occupation, and achieving a scale of values and a philosophy of life.

Thus developmental tasks may arise from physical maturation, from the pressure of cultural processes upon the individual, from the desires, aspirations, and values of the emerging personality, and they arise in most cases from combinations of these factors acting together.

THE TEACHABLE MOMENT

There are two reasons why the concept of developmental tasks is useful to educators. First, it helps in discovering and stating the purposes of education in the schools. Education may be conceived as the effort of the society, through the school, to help the individual achieve certain of his developmental tasks.

The second use of the concept is in the timing of educational efforts. When the body is ripe, and society requires, and the self is ready to achieve a certain task, the teachable moment has come. Efforts at teaching which would have been largely wasted if they had come earlier, give gratifying results when they come at the *teachable moment*, when the task should be learned. For example, the best times to teach reading, the care of children, and adjustment to retirement from one's job can be discovered by studying human development, and finding out when conditions are most favorable for learning these tasks.

19 *On the theories and problems of adolescence*

Related selections: 18, 35

Is adolescence a single phenomenon the characteristics of which are much the same for all individuals, or is it a period during which many different behavior patterns are manifested? Is it, as G. Stanley Hall and later psychologists have described it, a period of emotional storm and stress? Does adolescent behavior have its origin in the biological changes occurring at puberty? Luchins believes that the so-called emotional disturbances of adolescence may be more related to factors in the social scene than to physiological maturity.

A. DISAGREEMENT CONCERNING THE MEANING OF ADOLESCENCE

When the man in the street speaks of "adolescence," he generally knows what he means by the term and is probably quite confident that the next fellow using the expression has the same referent in mind. The experts, however, are not in agreement concerning the meaning of adolescence.

ABRAHAM S. LUCHINS, "On the Theory and Problems of Adolescence," *Journal of Genetic Psychology*, LXXXV, First Half (September, 1954), 47–63. Reprinted by permission of the author and The Journal Press.

DR. LUCHINS (1914–   ), Professor of Psychology at the University of Miami, has been on the faculties at Oregon, McGill, and Yeshiva Universities. He is a Diplomate in Clinical Psychology.

1   *The period of adolescence*

Some psychologists refer to adolescence as the period between 12 and 17 years
of age, but others refer to it as the teen-age period, while still others regard it
as the entire second decade of life, or as extending until the 25th year of life, or
even later. There are psychologists who are opposed to this description in terms
of age, maintaining that adolescence begins with biological puberty.

But there are psychologists who claim that the beginning of adolescence
cannot clearly be characterized either in terms of biological maturity or
chronological age but should be characterized in terms of when the individual faces adult adjustments. Adolescence itself is then regarded as the period
of transition between childhood and adulthood. For example, in a recent text
on adolescence, Kuhlen writes that regardless of actual chronological age or
state of biological development, an individual is adolescent to the extent
that he is engaged in the process of making sexual-social adjustments, ideological adjustments, vocational adjustments, and adjustments relating to achievement of freedom from parents. One is preadolescent in the years before he
is concerned with such problems, and he is adult to the extent that he has
successfully solved these difficulties and eliminated them as problems. It must
be emphasized that even among psychologists who define adolescence as the
period between childhood and adulthood, there are differences of opinion as
to the criteria determining the cessation of childhood and those determining the
onset of adulthood.

2   *The characteristics of adolescence*

A. STORM AND STRESS.   Not only is there a lack of agreement among psychologists as to when the period of adolescence begins and when it ceases, but
there is not even general agreement concerning the *characteristics* of adolescence. One of the characteristics sometimes referred to is that of emotional
disturbance and instability. G. Stanley Hall, who pioneered in the study of
adolescence, in 1904 described adolescence as a period of emotional storm and
stress. In line with Hall's theory of recapitulation—the theory that every individual in his development parallels the history of evolution of his species—he
maintained that development in adolescence is suggestive of some ancient period
of storm and stress for the species when old moorings were broken and a higher
level attained. While the theory of recapitulation has largely been abandoned,
the notion of adolescence as a period of storm and stress has persisted to the
present day, exercising considerable influence not only on the layman's thinking
but also upon that of many psychologists.

Yet this notion has not remained unchallenged. Psychologists and anthropologists, among them Ruth Benedict and Margaret Mead, have emphasized the
differences in adolescent behavior patterns prevailing in different cultures. They
note that in some so-called primitive cultures, for example, Samoa, emotional

disturbances do not seem to accompany biological puberty or the teen-age years or the second decade of life or the attainment of adult status. On the basis of such evidence it would not be valid to generalize that adolescence is everywhere an emotionally stressful period.

One might seek to limit this generalization to adolescence in our society but even this conception has been challenged. Thus Kuhlen, after assessing the available evidence, concludes that adolescence in our society does not seem to be an unduly stressful period, that it is not a period of general storm and stress.

B. REINFORCEMENT OF SEX DRIVES.   Another supposedly general character-istic of adolescence pertains to the reinforcement of sexual drives. This aspect is emphasized by psychoanalysts who relate adolescence to the reawakening of the sex drives, particularly the drive for heterosexuality which is assumed to be rather latent in the period from about 6 to 10 years of age. A recent text by Harsh and Schrickel *defines* adolescence as that period during which sexual motivation reaches its peak, when psychosexual drives and emotions are prob-ably more intense than at any earlier or later period of life. But actual ob-servation and investigation do not support the contention that sex drives and emotions are for every individual necessarily more intense beginning with puberty or in the teens or during the second decade of life than at other periods. For some individuals, sex drives seem to become highly active before overt signs of puberty are noted or before the ages of 10 or 12 or 13 or any other of the various criteria considered to mark the beginning of adolescence; while for other individuals sex drives and emotions seem to become active or to be particularly intense only long after puberty or even after the second or third decade of life.

Thus, in this area also it does not seem possible to draw a conclusion which is generally valid.

C. CHANGES IN PERSONALITY DEVELOPMENT.   Consider now another character-istic sometimes attributed to adolescence. G. Stanley Hall emphasized that marked and rapid changes occur in all aspects of *personality development* during adolescence, the changes being so dramatic that he referred to adoles-cence as a rebirth or a new birth. This conception has been challenged on the grounds that personality development constitutes a gradual and continuous pattern which generally does not reveal any striking deviations at or about the time of adolescence. In Hollingworth's words, the notion that every child is a changeling who at puberty comes forth as a different personality is but a widespread myth.

3   The biological origin of adolescent behavior

A particularly persistent belief exists that the characteristics of adolescence are biologically generated, that they result from the biological changes occurring at puberty. This point of view was set forth by Hall and has been reaffirmed by many other psychologists. For example, Blanchard, writing from a psycho-analytically oriented point of view, concludes that reinforcement of the drive for heterosexuality, of the drive for independence, and possibly, of the drive for aggression, are *direct results* of the physiological changes accompanying puberty.

A. CROSS-CULTURAL COMPARISONS. Evidence against this viewpoint may be found in the reports of certain cultural anthropologists and psychologists. They indicate that the same physiological changes tend to be accompanied by different behavior in different cultures. They have emphasized the influence of different culturally-determined attitudes toward the same physiological and morphological characteristics. Thus, in certain parts of Africa, females desirous of becoming attractive enter a fattening house whereas in our society females having the same desire go on a starvation diet. To cite another example: Among the Carrier Indians of British Columbia at the time of the first menstruation the girl is considered to be seized by evil spirits and is treated as a social pariah who must live apart from the others, whereas among the Apache Indians the girl at puberty is considered to be possessed by good spirits and is regarded as a direct source of supernatural blessing.

B. INFLUENCE OF SOCIO-ECONOMIC CONDITIONS. The thesis of biological determinism becomes even more tenuous if we consider the results of studies of the effects of socio-economic conditions on adolescent behavior. In our own culture, the great grandfathers of our present-day youth were generally considered adults, with adult responsibilities, at an age at which the youth of today often manifests so-called adolescent behavior. Surely the average chronological age of biological puberty has not advanced. As a matter of fact, the available evidence seems to indicate that the average age of physiological maturity of the studied samples tends to be somewhat lower nowadays than it was several generations ago. Another example may be found in the general differences among adolescent behavior in urban districts as compared to rural districts when presumably the same physiological changes occur in urban youth as in rural youth.

C. PHYSICAL-BEHAVIORAL CORRELATIONS. Finally, against the thesis that behavioral phenomena of adolescence are caused by pubertal changes, I should like to present the conclusions of a psychologist such as Wayne Dennis who is admittedly strongly biologically oriented. Dennis defines the beginning of adolescence as coinciding with biological puberty and conceives the central aim and interest of the psychology of adolescence to be the portrayal of the effects of pubertal changes upon behavior. To study these effects, he examines what he describes as certain sets of mental-physical correlations, bearing on the relationship between physical maturity and such a variety of behavioral phenomena as: sexual behavior, various play activities and interests, religious activities and interests, delinquency, suicide, and so on. His finding is that the available studies are generally inconclusive with reference to the causal relationship between psychological phenomena and physiological changes accompanying puberty. It would seem that even a biologically oriented investigator can at the present time find little evidence to support the thesis that biological changes accompanying puberty *cause* any given behavioral phenomenon.

D. TO SUMMARIZE.   I have attempted thus far to show that there is a lack of agreement among psychologists with regard to the definition of the period of adolescence, the characteristics of adolescent behavior, and whether or not the behavior is biologically determined.

B.   NEGLECT OF THE INDIVIDUAL CASE

Even after allowance is made for the varying definitions of adolescence, valid generalizations holding for all adolescents seem to be rare. Perhaps this is not as unfortunate a state of affairs as it may appear at first glance. Perhaps there has been an overemphasis on the attempts to derive generalizations valid for all or most adolescents and too little emphasis on the study of the adolescent as an individual. In support of this contention I should like to review some of the major approaches to the study of adolescence and to note how their very methodology involves a neglect of the individual case.

One of the approaches, which has already been referred to, seeks to correlate behavioral phenomena and physiological phenomena. Whatever else may be said for or against this approach, it seems to be clear that the individual is of necessity lost in the correlations, that the correlations may portray *trends* but cannot portray what actually occurs in a particular case. Another approach, sometimes described as culturally-oriented, seeks to compare prevailing patterns of adolescence in one culture with that in another culture. While the merits of this approach are not denied, it must not be overlooked that it concentrates on gross cultural differences, on general patterns and attitudes which seem most prevalent in a particular culture. But the approach thereby tends to neglect or to minimize individual differences within any one culture. A third approach is concerned with the influence of various social conditions and institutions in our society on adjustment to adulthood. Adherents of this approach may note that adjustment to adulthood was somewhat different several generations ago than it is today or that even today the adjustment is somewhat different in rural than in urban districts. Noteworthy as such observations are, they do not reveal individual differences in adjustment patterns which presumably existed for young people several generations ago and which exist today, even within any particular urban or rural district.

It seems to me that it is time to cease this rather futile chase after generalizations valid for all adolescents or for all adolescents of a particular culture or generation or locality. It is perhaps time to concentrate on intensive studies of individual adolescents. It may be time to cease attempting to explain the phenomena of adolescence exclusively in terms of biology or culture or society or psychoanalysis, or what have you. Rather, we should perhaps suspend judgment as to the how and why of adolescent behavior. We should momentarily put aside our theories and hypotheses, and seek to look as unbiasedly as possible at some examples of this behavior, permitting the behavior itself to suggest possible hypotheses for explanations.

C. SOME OBSERVATIONAL DATA

I shall now turn to some observations which I made during a seven year study of a group of boys of Brooklyn, New York. The techniques used included participation with the boys in some of their activities, naturalistic observations, individual and group discussions with the boys, and discussions with their parents, teachers, siblings, and others in the neighborhood who knew them, as well as analysis of diaries kept by the boys. All the boys were of bright-normal or superior intelligence and of about the same socio-economic status.

In 1931, when the study began, their ages ranged from 10 to 14. Let us consider now the behavior manifested by three of the boys in the period between 1935 and 1936, when each of them was about 14 or 15 years of age.

1 Description of behavior

When I first met Robert he seemed to be a happy, even-tempered youngster. But at the age of 14 he was displaying what has been described as typically adolescent behavior. He was depressed, moody, irritable, emotionally unstable, and difficult to get along with. His parents and other adults frequently attributed this behavior to his adolescence. In short, Robert seemed to fit the stereotype of the adolescent in our society.

Ted at 14 was well-poised, essentially happy, and emotionally stable, showing little of the turbulence manifested by Robert. His teachers and other adults commented on his social poise and maturity.

Lester's behavior was closer to that displayed by Robert. Lester was moody, irritable with parents, siblings, and almost everyone else. He was inclined to think deeply and often about his own misery and the world's misfortunes.

2 Attempts at understanding the behavior

Should the behavior of these three boys be attributed to pubertal changes or to adjustment to adulthood or to the culture in which they live? Will any of these generalizations yield an understanding of the dynamics underlying each case? Will any of them give insight into the reasons for the differences and similarities in overt behavior?

To begin with, it should be noted that both Lester, the unhappy, brooding individual, and Ted, the happy, poised individual, were at 14 years of age manifesting an accepted sign of puberty, pigmented pubic hair, and were about equal in other signs of physical maturity. Robert, on the other hand, had at this age not yet shown any overt signs of pubertal change. Blond, slight of stature, and shorter than the others, he looked like a "kid," to use the label which members of the group sometimes applied to him in a derogatory manner.

Thus in two of the boys similar physical changes were accompanied by very different behavior patterns. Nor can the change in Robert's behavior from his earlier emotional stability to the storm and stress variety he manifested at the ages of 14 and 15 be correlated with any concomitant signs of overt physical maturity. Indeed, study of the relevant facts seem to indicate that Robert's change in behavior might more accurately be traced to his *lack* of physical maturity. Robert had previously been the acknowledged leader of the gang; but at 14 and 15, with the growing interest in females and social events, the group found him somewhat of a hindrance. They were afraid that his youthful appearance might hurt their chances with the girls and lessen their possibilities of making "pickups." Moreover, Robert's older brothers were prone to boast about their amorous exploits and Robert once told me that he wished that he were as manly-looking and attractive to girls as his older brothers.

What had happened to Robert? It might be said that he had lost status in the group, that he no longer had a sense of group-belongingness, that he no longer had a well-structured behavioral world, and that there were sharp discrepancies between his aspirations and his achievements. Incidentally, as Robert grew older and became physically mature, he joined another group, became their leader, and displayed considerably less behavior of the turbulent type. It would seem that physiological maturity in this case did not foster adolescent conflicts but was one of the factors helping to decrease emotional disturbance.

What about Lester? May his behavior be attributed to pubertal changes? As a matter of fact, acquaintance with Lester's life history reveals that he had for years been moody, irritable, concerned with the world's troubles. He had been struggling to find answers to such questions as: What is life? What is man? Who am I? He regarded as inadequate the answers given to him, directly or indirectly, by his teachers or by books he read. Although accepted and respected by members of the group, who were rather proud of his erudition, he often preferred being by himself and confided to me that he did not really feel that he belonged to the gang or that he could fully share the other members' interests. What is important to note here is that the behavioral patterns and emotional tone manifested by Lester at or about the time of puberty were not very different from those which he showed in the years preceding overt pubertal change, or, for that matter, from those which he showed in the years which followed. Until his death in World War II at the age of 22, members of the group who were then with him later told me, he was always the same moody, irritable, philosophical Lester. And yet, a psychologist attempting to study Lester's behavior only at about the time of puberty might have concluded that the moodiness and concern with ideological matters which he then revealed were a unique development accompanying biological puberty. From the vantage point of a knowledge of Lester's history for several years prior and subsequent to pubertal change, it seems to me that he was seeking for a meaning in life, that he was attempting to develop a clearly structured world, and that there were sharp discrepancies between his ideals and reality, as well as between his aspirations and achievements with regard to a purpose for man's existence.

Let us return to Ted, the third of the trio. Ted, the well-poised, emotionally stable youth was that way until about the age of 19 when a severe financial setback in his father's business necessitated his leaving college and obtaining a rather menial position to help support his family. He became irritable, argumentative, displayed extreme mood-swings and found it difficult to get along with his family and others. He was, in short, manifesting at 19 the kind of turbulent behavior which Robert had shown at 14. Analysis of my records on Ted made one thing clear. As early as his elementary school days, he had made definite vocational plans. He knew that he wanted to be a medical doctor, was confident of his mental ability and the financial support required to achieve his goal. But the financial reverses made it impossible for him to reach his goal and frustrated his ambition.

3   Inferences from the three cases

What can be inferred from these three cases? Firstly, it would seem that youths living in the same locality and having similar socio-economic backgrounds may manifest strikingly different behavior patterns. Secondly, similar physiological changes may be accompanied by different behavior patterns. Also, individuals who are far apart with regard to physical maturity may display similar behavior patterns. While the issue of whether or not pubertal changes may directly induce behavioral changes is still a moot one, it would seem that behavior may be a consequence of the *attitudes* possessed by the individual himself and others regarding physical changes or *lack* of such changes. Thirdly, the kind of emotional storm and stress which is sometimes considered as characteristic of adolescence may not be manifested at all, may occur long before or only long after pubertal changes, may be momentary or of rather limited duration, or may be generally characteristic of the individual.

As a hypothesis for future research it is suggested that emotional instability may tend to be manifested at any chronological age when the individual lacks a clear frame of reference with which to meet reality, when his behavioral world is not clearly structured, and when there are marked discrepancies between his aspirations and his achievements.

4   Conclusions drawn from study

The inferences drawn from the three cases are not sufficient to account for the behavior of the other 12 boys who were studied. Some of the boys, although behaving as typical adolescents, did not seem to have any serious emotional involvements. Rather, it seemed to me that they had simply adopted the characteristic *stereotype*. They were playing the rôle called for by this stereotype. They were exhibiting the kind of behavior which they and others expected of adolescents of this day and age. Still others of the boys behaved like impulsive children who were gorging themselves on new experiences in an irresponsible carefree manner. The behavior of one of the boys seemed to be related to a deficiency of social skills, such as the skills of dancing and getting along with girls. Once he acquired these skills, there was a noticeable change in his behavior.

In brief, adolescence does not seem to constitute one phenomenon. An analysis reveals a variety of different behavior patterns. Moreover, the different phenotypical patterns are not caused by one genotype. In other words, overtly similar behavior may be brought about by different conditions and overtly different behavior may be brought about by similar conditions. In view of this, it is not surprising to find a diversity of contemporary descriptions and explanations of adolescent behavior. One way to minimize the contemporary confusion of concepts and terminology may be to study the individual adolescent as a person instead of merely regarding him as a source of information which can confirm or infirm a hypothesis stemming from a general theory of adolescence.

D. SOME SOCIAL FACTORS WHICH MAY INFLUENCE ADOLESCENT BEHAVIOR

Regardless of the shape which future studies or theories of adolescence may take, there is an immediate and practical problem which must be faced. It is obvious to parents, teachers, and even the youths themselves that many individuals go through an adolescent stage characterized by turbulence and conflict. On the basis of the data collected in the study referred to above I was led to conclude that there are certain social field conditions which operate to produce or aggravate such turbulence and conflict. It is not denied that temperamental and experiential factors may make one more or less susceptible to the influence of these conditions. What follows should be taken as preliminary hypotheses to be tested by future research.

1 Uncertainty concerning adult status

I have already hypothesized that emotional difficulties may tend to occur under conditions in which the individual lacks a clear frame of reference with regard to his status and function. There are factors in the social scene which are conducive to an unstable frame of reference concerning the achievement of *adult status*. Unlike what occurs in some other cultures, in our society there is no one initiation rite or ceremony or fixed pattern of activities in which one must participate in order to be regarded by himself and by others as having donned the mantle of adulthood. The physically mature youth may be treated as a child by those about him, either consistently or intermittently. At other times he may be reminded that he has no business behaving as a child. Indeed, there are individuals, regardless of chronological age, who are never quite certain of whether they have attained adult status.

Whether or not the individual ever attains adult status, either subjectively or objectively, depends on a host of socio-economic factors and on the nature of his inter-personal relations. Depending upon the individual circumstances and, to some extent, on such general conditions as whether it is a time of war or of peace, of depression or prosperity, there tend to be considerable differences with regard to the age of occurrence, the ease, and the mode of locomotion involved in the crossing of that nebulous threshold leading to adulthood. The existence of such differences may help to account for the various age limits which different authorities ascribe to the adolescent period. It may also help to account for the wide variety of behavior patterns observed during adolescence. Moreover the uncertainty which often accompanies the attainment of adulthood may help to account for the prevalency of emotional difficulties during adolescence.

Incidentally, I should like to refer here to the observation that adolescence in rural districts is by and large a less stressful experience than in urban districts. This may be related to the fact that the youth on the farm may be able to attain relative independence and other signs of adult status more readily than his urban cousin. Similarly, the observation that adolescence tended to be a less stressful experience several generations ago than it is today, may be related to the fact that adult status, including marriage, was generally attained at an earlier age in former years.

2   *Institutional complexity and conflict*

There are other factors which may contribute to an unstable frame of reference, to a lack of clearly structured behavioral world. As the child becomes older, he may become more aware of contradictions between what is preached and what is practiced. He may realize that his parents and their beliefs are far from perfect. He may realize that his idols have clay feet.

Moreover, as he grows older, he comes into contact with more and more institutions and practices other than the primary institution of the home. Several generations ago the home was the center of life activities, with business, recreational, religious, educational, and vocational training activities centered in the home. Today there are separate institutions each specializing in an activity which was once the function of the home. By and large, these institutions lack the intimate, personal relationship which may have prevailed in the home. The very structure of these institutions may rule out the possibility of a warm, genuine interest in its members. The youth may be upset by what he regards as a cold, impersonal attitude towards him.

Each institution may think of the individual primarily as a tool for the fulfillment of the institution's goals and objectives. It may demand of him that he play a certain rôle regardless of the individual's own needs. Or it may be interested in the individual only in so far as he is capable of playing this rôle. A middling example of this is the practice of placing an individual into a vocational school because test results indicate that he has little chance of successfully playing the rôle of a student in an academic institution. This may occur in spite of the individual's desire to attend an academic school and in spite of social pressures exerted by family and friends that demand that he be an academic student.

The demands which one institution makes on the individual may conflict with the demands made upon him by other institutions. Moreover, the various demands may clash with the values and purposes learned in the home. Thus there may be a clash between what the home teaches and what the school teaches, what the church wants and what the street gang wants, and so on. Confronted by these conflicting demands, the individual may have some difficulty in meeting them and yet maintaining his integrity as an organized, whole being. He may have to struggle against becoming a mere collection of selves—a home self, a school self, a street self, a business self, and so on. He may be aghast at the thought that he is expected to play a rôle and be able to don and cast off rôles as one might change masks. Moreover, he may have difficulty in achieving a self-concept, in knowing just who he is. All this may contribute to adolescent conflict.

In short, the youth must learn to dance in harmony with many different tunes while still attempting to maintain some degree of harmony within himself. For some individuals, the conflicting demands may be extremely upsetting. They may find that the personal and rather clearly structured world of childhood is replaced by a cold, disorganized, and unstable world. They may not be quite certain of just who they are, whether they are being themselves or merely playing rôles, and just what rôle they are expected to play at any particular time. Herein may lie some clues to the emotional turbulence which has come to be associated with adolescence.

3 Gaps between aspirations and attainments

Reference was previously made to the possible effect on behavior of a discrepancy between aspirations and achievements. It seems to me that there are factors in our social fabric which, in some cases, make for a considerable discrepancy between the ideals and aspirations associated with adulthood and the actual achievements attained by the youth once he is "grown up." As a child he may have been led to believe that when he grows up he will be allowed entrance into the wonderland hitherto denied to him, the world of privileges, immunities, status, worthwhile responsibilities, independence, and fulfillment of numerous dreams. Yet, the physical signs of being grown up may be attained without the fulfillment of even one of the goals which had been intimately associated with being grown up.

For example, in our culture a premium is placed on economic independence.

Yet, scarcity of positions, the need for lengthy educational training or lengthy apprenticeship may make it necessary to postpone such independence for many years. In some professions, economic independence cannot be secured until one is well past the second decade of life or well into the third.

Ideals and aspirations with regard to dating, romance, and marriage are fostered by the home, movies, and magazines. But these ideals may be quite impossible of attainment or may be interfered with by finances or physical unattractiveness or simply by the fact that the available candidates for romance are quite different from those portrayed in the movies.

Youth is bombarded by stimuli which arouse or intensify various kinds of needs, particularly those involving status and sex. The radio, television, movies, magazines, newspapers, and even the home serve to over-stimulate certain needs. But at the same time there may be little or no opportunity for the youth to gratify these desires in socially accepted ways. For example, the boy or girl who is expected to abstain from sexual activity is at the same time exposed to stimuli which play up sex. The result may be that these over-stimulated desires become central in the youth's view of the situation and that obstacles to these needs loom very large. Consequently, the youth may feel that he is blocked and hemmed in on all sides. One might draw an analogy between the situation he faces and that faced by the rat in Norman R. F. Maier's experiments on neuroses. Forces arousing and over-stimulating the various needs may be compared to the airblast aimed at making the rat jump; but, like the rat, the youth may have no way of reacting to these forces without encountering punishment. It is therefore small wonder that what is akin to neurotic behavior may be noticed in some adolescents.

4 *Some other hypotheses*

Thus far I have suggested that the emotional difficulties often associated with adolescence in our culture may in part be the resultant of a gap between the youth's goals and achievements or of his lack of a stable frame of reference with which to view his rather disorganized world. It is also interesting to speculate to what extent the youth who is seemingly manifesting emotional storm and stress may simply have adopted the stereotype of behavior which he and others associate with this period. I should also like to refer to the interesting hypothesis advanced by Kuhlen—namely, that the stress commonly attributed to the adolescent may in part be a projection of the emotional stress experienced by parents and other adults dealing with youth.

E. WHAT CAN BE DONE ABOUT THE EMOTIONAL TENSIONS OF ADOLESCENTS?

I have described some social field conditions which may produce emotional tensions in the adolescent. The problem arises as to what can be done to minimize these tensions. Before dealing with this problem, I should like to draw a distinction between two kinds of tensions. Every living system experiences tensions; these are necessary for the life activities of the organism, for its development and growth, and for the attainment and maintenance of its equilibrium. The late Max Wertheimer, founder of Gestalt Psychology, used to refer to these as tensions with a small t. In contrast to the tensions with a small t, he referred to tensions with a capital T; by the latter he meant those tensions whose direction of operation is opposed to that of the organism, tensions which interfere with adequate functioning of the organism, hinder development, and even alter the organism's essential structure.

This distinction seems to me to be applicable to the tensions experienced by the adolescent. Some are related to the youth's striving toward equilibrium under changing conditions and are necessary to further his growth both as a physical organism and as a social being. Specifically, tensions may be said to have positive value insofar as they awaken the youth from a kind of lethargic slumber, arouse some self-analysis and introspection, and set him to seek for values and purposes in life. Because of tensions, the youth may be led to question, to evaluate critically, and perhaps to strike out in new directions, to find new ways of doing things. It might even be argued that the stresses and strains experienced by the younger generation help them to work for social change and social progress. To such tensions we may refer as those with small t's. But there are tensions with capital T's: tensions whose direction and nature of operation interfere with the youth's growth and development, which hamper his functioning at an adequate level, which keep him in continuous disequilibrium and may even create mental illnesses. These latter tensions are what I have in mind in what follows.

1. There is a need to decrease somewhat the gap between the youth's goals and desires, on the one hand, and what he can accomplish, on the other. Perhaps a step in this direction can be made by realistically evaluating the ideals and standards which our culture propagates with regard to adult status. For example, completion of education and economic independence on the part of the male are often regarded as prerequisites for marriage. Scholarships, fellowships, and apprenticeships may require the single status. Under present-day conditions this often means late marriage which in turn makes more difficult the satisfaction of sexual needs within moral bounds. If our society holds that present-day sex standards have definite and positive value, then something should be done to make it easier for the physically mature youth to live up to these standards. Somewhat less ballyhoo about sex in our movies, radios, magazines, may help to dim the spotlight currently focused on it and perhaps decrease the severity of youth's sex problems. Another solution might be earlier marriage. The success of married veterans who attended school after World War II seems to provide ample testimony that formal education and marriage are not necessarily incompatible. Undoubtedly early marriage will raise problems of its own, including the very pragmatic issue of finances; it may be necessary that financial assistance be given to the young couple by parents or perhaps private or government agen-

cies. Notwithstanding the above something should be done to decrease the discrepancy between youth's sexual needs and his possibilities for gratifying them in a socially acceptable manner.

There is a broader issue involved here. Many of our ethical standards may be seen by youth primarily as taboos, as limitations. But just as a road facilitates travel even though it deters the traveler from other possible paths, so a social standard is not solely a taboo but often has a positive function. Greater emphasis on the positive function of social and ethical standards rather than emphasis on their limitations to actions, as well as greater opportunity for young people to realize the positive values of these standards in their own life situations, may help to make youth more willing to accept and comply with the moral standards of our society.

It is appropriate to refer here to the matter of independence, quite aside from financial independence. The mature individual in our society is expected to stand on his own feet, to make decisions on his own. But such intellectual and emotional independence, if I may refer to it as such, does not suddenly spring into being at any one time of life. Although the capacity for such independence may be related to personal endowment, the exercise of this independence hinges on previous training and on suitable conditions. Parents must be made aware of the importance of training for emotional and intellectual independence, of allowing and encouraging ever-increasing opportunities for independent judgment on the part of the child. They must, so to speak, allow for loosening of the proverbial apron strings. Our schools can make an important contribution by placing an emphasis *not* on rote drill, memorization, and blind following, but on *understanding* and productive thinking. The child should not merely learn a collection of facts and skills but should learn to learn. Moreover, participation in the formation of value judgments in the school, as well as opportunities to evaluate these judgments, may help to create an individual who can make intelligent judgments outside of the school situation.

2. I have referred to the possible rôle of institutional conflicts in fostering emotional difficulties. Here there seems to be a decided need for discussion and coöperation among representatives of various institutions in the community, among parents, teachers, other educators, religious leaders, people who determine policies in recreational and advertising media, and so on. They should consider how they may contribute to the problems faced by adolescents. They should consider their goals and practices in relation to youth and the demands which they make of youth. The aim should be to minimize intra-institutional and inter-institutional conflict. This calls for community planning, for the utilization of social action research in the community as well as for the utilization of other group dynamic techniques which have been successfully applied by Kurt Lewin and his students to various community problems.

3. It is important to find socially useful functions for youth, socially productive uses of youth's vast sources of energies. Totalitarian movements have

made use of the potential energy in youth and have taken advantage of youth's needs for group-belongingness, and need for a definite rôle and function in life. Democracies have yet to channelize youth's energies into socially productive paths so that the young person knows and feels that he belongs and is needed. The picture of groups of teen age youngsters, lolling idly about, seeking to kill time, seems to me to symbolize our tendency to be wasteful of our human resources.

In every community, worthwhile projects can be organized in which young people, either with their peers or together with other age groups, can serve in some worthwhile socially useful activity. Such experiences might help to develop a feeling of belonging and being useful. Since our social structure is of such a nature that there seems of necessity to be a long period between childhood and adulthood, we must learn to make those who are going through this period feel more than simply in-betweens, marginal individuals who are too old to be children and who are not yet adults. These young people are capable of dealing with certain community problems and projects, precisely because they are more mature than younger children and are not yet weighed down with all the time-consuming responsibilities of adulthood. In short, adolescence can be made into a worthwhile, socially productive period of life rather than being merely a waiting period.

F.   CONCLUDING REMARK

After criticizing others for talking in generalities rather than studying specific adolescents, I too have indulged in some generalizations and theorizing. Of course there is nothing intrinsically wrong in promulgating general hypotheses concerning adolescence. But, it seems to me, only by studying the individual case will we gain deep understanding of the particular field conditions which are operating to produce the specific kind of adolescent behavior. Theorizing should not be a substitute for observation and study of the particular individual. Nor should a theory or a hypothesis or a generalization predispose the investigator to look only for or at certain aspects of the phenomenon under study. In conclusion, I should like to stress the importance—for parents, teachers, clinicians, and others who deal with adolescents—not to allow any *theory of* adolescence to blur their vision of the particular youth with whom they are dealing.

MENTAL AND
CREATIVE ABILITY

20 *Intelligence from a perceptual point of view*

Related selections: 4, 9, 21, 34, 37

Has the time-honored static conception of intelligence and human capacity proved more restrictive than constructive in educational practice? Dr. Combs suggests that it has and explores the idea of intelligence as a function of an individual's perceptions. If this view is tenable, it follows that the school, having the opportunity to influence appreciably some of the factors that affect perception, can thereby better educate most students, even those formerly believed to be operating near "capacity."

There is a growing trend in psychology toward viewing behavior as a function of perception. More and more we have come to understand that the individual's behavior is not so much a function of the physical stimulus as it is a function of his perceptions of the events to which he is exposed. It is the meaning of events to the individual rather than the externally observed nature of events which seems crucial in behavior. As a result, psychologists in increasing numbers are turning their attention to the problems of human perception and are attempting to observe behavior, not from an external point of view, but from the point of view of the individual who is behaving. This paper is an attempt to relate this method of observation to the problem of intelligence. The question we wish to explore in this paper is: "What is the nature of intelligence viewed from a perceptual or phenomenological frame of reference?"

ARTHUR W. COMBS, "Intelligence from a Perceptual Point of View," *Journal of Abnormal and Social Psychology*, XLVII (July, 1952), 662–73. Reprinted by permission of the author and the American Psychological Association.
DR. COMBS (1912–   ), formerly Director of Clinical Training at Syracuse University, is currently Professor of Education at the University of Florida. With Donald Snygg he is author of *Individual Behavior*. He is a Diplomate in Clinical Psychology.

Intelligence as a problem of perception

By the term *intelligence* we ordinarily refer to the effectiveness of the individual's behavior. In a personal frame of reference the individual's behavior is described in terms of the perceptions that he can make in his own unique perceptive field. This perceptive field has been called by Snygg and Combs *The Phenomenal Field* and has been defined by them as "the universe of experience open to the individual at the moment of his behavior." In other words, the behavior of the individual will be dependent upon the perceptions that the individual makes in his phenomenal field at the moment of action. The effectiveness of his behavior will necessarily be a function of the adequacy of those perceptions.

If an entity in the perceptive field is vague and ill defined, the behavior of the individual will be correspondingly vague and lacking in precision. Until the child has clearly differentiated that 2 plus 2 equals 4, this function is comparatively meaningless and his behavior in arithmetic is correspondingly inaccurate and ineffective. Thus, the precision and effectiveness of the individual's behavior will be dependent upon the scope and clarity of his personal field of awareness. Intelligence, then, from a perceptual point of view becomes a function of the factors which limit the scope and clarity of an individual's phenomenal field.

The perceptions that could be made of any given situation, such as looking at a stone wall, for example, are, theoretically, practically infinite in number and quality. As a matter of fact, however, we are strictly limited in our perceptions of a stone wall to those which we, as human beings, can make. The perceptions possible to us are only those that people can make. We cannot, for instance, perceive the wall as it would appear to a man from Mars, or from the interior of an atom, or as it would appear to a centipede. What is more, we cannot even perceive it as it would appear to all people. Different people will perceive different aspects of the wall differently, even at the same instant. I can only perceive the wall, and hence behave toward it, in terms of the perceptions that I, as an individual, can make regarding it. I may, for instance, perceive it as a fine, sturdy fence enclosing my property, while a stone mason friend might perceive it as having been poorly designed or as having been built with too little cement in the mortar mixture. The perceptions open to my mason friend are the result of his unique experience. I, not having such experience, am incapable of those perceptions at this moment.

Potential and functional perceptions

Before proceeding further with our discussion of the limiting factors in perception, it is necessary for us to pause for a moment to distinguish between potential and functional perceptions. By potential perceptions I mean those perceptions that exist in the individual's unique field of awareness and that, given the right circumstances at any particular moment, *could* occur. The fact that a perception is potentially possible to any individual, by no means, however, means that it would occur at the moment of action. Even those perceptions that I can make potentially may not be active for me at any given moment. Potentially, I might be able, for instance, to perceive the wall that we have just been using as an example as a barrier to be gotten over, as an eyesore to be beautified, as composed of 687 bricks costing me $80.27, or as providing pleasant shade on a hot day. These are all potential perceptions I am capable of making about the wall. They will affect my behavior, however, only when they are active or functioning in my field of perceptions. When I am beating a hasty retreat pursued by a neighbor's angry dog, perceptions about the shade, beauty, or cost of the wall, though potential, are not functional in affecting my behavior. I behave only in terms of my functioning perception of the wall as something to get over— and quickly. The fact that particular perceptions may exist potentially in the phenomenal field of an individual is by no means a guarantee that they may exist functionally at the moment of action.

While the potential intelligence of the individual is of interest in judging his capacities, it is practically always a matter impossible to measure with any degree of accuracy. We can only sample those parts of a phenomenal field that *we* happen to feel are important. Obviously the measurement of a person's potential perceptions in these terms is open to extremely grave sampling error and improves in accuracy only as the individuals tested have common experience in the materials chosen for testing. It seems probable that an intelligence test cannot accurately measure the potential differentiations that the individual can make in his phenomenal field. Rather, what we usually measure are the subject's functional perceptions. That is, we measure what differentiations he can make when confronted with the necessity to do so for one reason or another. We may define these functional perceptions as: those perceptions in the field experienced by the individual at the moment of behaving.

From a perceptual viewpoint, if intelligence is the capacity for effective behavior, *the intelligence of an individual will be dependent upon the richness and variety of perceptions possible to him at a given moment.* To understand and effectively to foster intelligent behavior, it will be necessary for us to be concerned with the limiting factors upon the perceptions of an individual. We need to know not only what the individual *could* perceive, but what he *would* perceive at a given moment of behaving.

SOME LIMITING FACTORS UPON PERCEPTION

Physiologic limitations on perception

Certainly the physical limitations upon the organism affect the differentiations possible in the phenomenal field. Some forms of prenatal anomalies, like mongolism, microcephalia, and similar disorders, indubitably reduce the level of operation at which the individual can function and seriously impair the ability of the organism to make adequate perceptions. Similarly, there seems good reason to believe that some types of mechanical or disease injury to the central nervous system may result in impaired functioning, such as occurs in cerebral palsy, birth injuries, prefrontal lobotomy, the aftermath of such diseases as encephalitis or, even, in common childhood diseases accompanied by prolonged high fever. Various forms of endocrinopathies, particularly cretinism, also appear to have limiting effects upon differentiational capacity for some individuals. Such physical or biological limitations upon the organism have been widely studied but account for only a small proportion of those persons operating at impaired intelligence levels.

Other less dramatic forms of physical handicaps may also have important effects upon the perceptions possible to the individual, however. This is particularly true of individuals suffering impairment of various sense modalities which may inhibit the clarity or even the existence of some perceptions. We need to remind ourselves, however, that such persons may have as rich and varied a perceptive field within their own limitations as we have within ours. Testing persons living in one frame of reference with tests based on those of another can easily lead us astray, a fact well known to the makers of some tests for the handicapped. The limitations imposed upon perception by such physical handicaps as the loss or impairment of locomotion or the use of arms or hands are also important in limiting certain kinds of perceptions. These people experience different, but not necessarily fewer or poorer perceptions of events than so-called "normals."

Perhaps less well recognized in their effects upon perception are such factors as malnutrition, focal infections, and chronic fatigue, which may reduce both the need for and the ability to make adequate perceptions. It is well known in industrial psychology, for example, that fatigued workers are more likely to have accidents, perhaps because of failure to make the right differentiations at the right time. It is conceivable that persons suffering from chronic fatigue over long periods similarly fail to make differentiations useful to them on later occasions.

Certainly such physical factors as these have important effects upon the ability of the individual to make adequate differentiations in his perceptive field. The more dramatic of these have often been recognized and studied. Others, such as the effects of malnutrition, fatigue, and the like, have been less adequately explored. In spite of the lack of research in respect to some of the physical limitations upon intelligence, far more work has been done in this area, however, than in some of those to be discussed below.

Environment and opportunity
as a limitation upon perception

The differentiations in the phenomenal field that an individual can make will, of course, be affected by the opportunities for perception to which he has been exposed. To appear in the perceptive field an event must have been, in some manner, experienced by the person who perceives it. Environmental effects upon perception appear to be of two types, actual or concrete and symbolic or vicarious.

EXPOSURE TO ACTUAL ENVIRONMENTAL EVENTS. In the first place the perceptions possible to any individual will be limited, in part, by the actual environmental factors to which he has been exposed. Eskimos ordinarily do not comprehend bananas, nor African Bushmen snow, since neither has had the opportunity to experience these events in their respective environments. It is not necessary to go so far afield for illustration, however. In our own country our experience with the testing of children in various parts of the nation has shown that perceptions are highly limited by the environmental conditions surrounding the individual. Mountain children, for example, often give bizarre responses on intelligence tests. Sherman and Henry found intelligence test results on such children arranged themselves in order of the opportunities provided by their environment.

There are differences also between the perceptions of rural and urban children, children from the North and children from the South, mountain and valley, seaboard and plains. Nor are such differences confined only to children. Adults, too, are limited in their perceptions by environmental factors. During the war I worked for a time in an induction station receiving men from the mountains of Kentucky, West Virginia, and southern Ohio. An intelligence test in use at this station was composed of a series of five pictures with instructions to the subject to cross out that one of each series of five objects that did not belong with the others. One set of five pictures showed four stringed instruments, a guitar, harp, violin, bass fiddle, and a trumpet. Large numbers of these back country men crossed out the harp because they had never seen one or because "all the others are things in our band." We cannot assume that these men were less able to make differentiations or had perceptive fields less rich than their examiner on the basis of these tests. We can only suggest that their perceptions are different from those who made the test. Presumably, had they made the test and administered it to the psychologist, the psychologist would have appeared rather dull!

EXPOSURE TO SYMBOLIC OR VICARIOUS EVENTS. Differentiations may occur in the perceptive field upon a symbolic basis as well as from exposure to an actual event. That is, perceptions may occur in the individual's field through indirect exposure to experience as in reading, conversation, movies, and other means of communication. Although I cannot directly perceive that it is dangerous to expose myself to rays from an atomic pile, for example, I can differentiate this notion through what others whom I respect have told me. Ideas and concepts are largely differentiations of this sort and it is probable that many of our perceptions are acquired through a symbolic rather than an actual exposure. Certainly most of our formal schooling falls in this category which may explain, in part, why so little of it is effective in our behavior.

It will be recognized at once that exposure to events in no sense completely determines the perceptions that the individual will make. Exposure to events is only one of the factors involved in determining whether or not an event will be differentiated. Even with equivalent exposure, the perceptions we make are not alike. Perception is not an all or none proposition but a selective process. The same person in the same situation at different times may perceive quite different aspects of the situation and behave accordingly. The provision of opportunity to perceive is by no means a guarantee that a particular perception will occur, a phenomenon of which teachers are only too aware. The personal field of the individual is always organized and meaningful and, even with exposure to events, only those aspects that have meaning for the individual in his own unique economy will be differentiated with permanence.

The individual in a particular culture perceives those aspects of his environment that, from his point of view, he needs to perceive to maintain and enhance his self in the world in which he lives. This does not mean he makes fewer perceptions than an individual in another culture; he makes only *different* perceptions. Thus, intelligence tests made in one culture and applied in another do not measure the ability to differentiate, nor do they measure the richness of the individual's field. Perhaps what they really measure is no more than the difference between cultures. American-made intelligence tests applied to other cultures generally show the following arrangement of nationality groups in decreasing order: British Isles, Germany, France, Italy, the Balkans, Asiatic countries. It will be noted that these nationality groups are also roughly arranged in order of the degree of commonality with our own culture.

Time as a limitation of perception

Differentiation requires time. The richness of perception, therefore, will be in part a function of how long the individual has been in touch with experiences. While it is true that a perception is possible only when confronted by an experience, it is also true that this exposure must be long enough to make differentiation possible. This principle is familiar to anyone who has looked at a painting for a period of time. The perceptions which can be made are almost limitless if one looks long enough.

In thinking of the effect of time upon differentiation, it is necessary for us to keep in mind that we are speaking of the duration of the individual's experience with an event and not of the observer's experience. Thus, while it may appear to an outside observer that an individual is confronted by an experience, from the individual's own point of view, he may have no contact with it whatever. A child may sit in school all day, apparently exposed to the curriculum, but may actually be experiencing and perceiving quite different aspects of the situation. Perception is an internal, individual phenomenon and may be quite different from that of another person, even in the same situation.

Most perceptions that the individual makes are functions of previous differentiations he has made in his phenomenal field. For example, before one can perceive the mechanics of multiplication he must have perceived addition. In the same way, before he can perceive the function of a sand dome on top of the locomotive he must differentiate the fact that locomotive wheels sometimes slip. Clearly this process of differentiation takes time. It seems axiomatic that to make differentiations an individual must have lived long enough to do so, a fact we recognize in the construction of intelligence tests calibrated for various age levels, and which teachers recognize in the concept of readiness.

Differentiations in the phenomenal field seem to be occurring continuously as the organism seeks to satisfy its needs in the myriad situations of life. In this sense, intelligence never ceases to develop but is continuously increasing so long as the individual remains alive and operating. That intelligence seems to level off at age sixteen or later is probably a mere artifact of our method of observation. So long as the individual remains in school we have at least a modicum of comparable experience which can be tested in different persons. After the school years, when individuals are free to go their separate ways, this modicum of comparable experience rapidly disappears. The older one gets, the more diverse is his experience. Intelligence tests based upon comparability of experience may thus fail to evaluate properly the effectiveness of adults.

The individual's goals and values
as a limiting factor on perception

Up to this point in our discussion we have been dealing with factors affecting perception that are widely discussed in the literature and for the most part are well understood. In the remainder of this paper let us turn our attention to several factors less well explored as they appear in a phenomenological setting. The first of these has to do with the effects of the individual's own goals and values as a limiting factor on perception.

From a phenomenological view the individual is forever engaged in a ceaseless attempt to achieve satisfaction of his need through the goals and values he has differentiated as leading to that end. These goals and values may be explicit or implicit, simple or complex, but they are always unique to the personality itself. The goals of an individual will vary in another respect as well. The individual's goals and values may be either positive or negative. That is, in the course of his experience, the person may differentiate some things as matters to be sought, while other things may be differentiated as matters to be avoided. What is more, although there is a considerable degree of stability in the major goals and values of a particular individual, there may be great fluctuations in how some goals are perceived from time to time, depending upon the total organization of the perceptual field at any moment.

The goals and values an individual seeks have a most important effect upon the perceptions he can make. Once goals have been established by the individual they continue to affect his every experience. Thus, the person who has differentiated good music as a goal to be sought, perceives music more frequently. His entire experience with music is likely to be affected. Certainly his experience will differ markedly from the person who has formulated a goal to avoid music at all costs. In the same way the experiences of children who perceive schooling as something to be sought are vastly different from those of children who try to avoid all aspects of schooling. If the fundamental thesis of this paper is accurate, that intelligence is a function of the variety and richness of the perceptive field, then the individual's goals must have a most important effect upon intelligence. A considerable body of research has been accumulating over the past several years, demonstrating this controlling effect of goals and values on the individual's perceptive experience. Such studies as those of J. M. Levine, R. Levine, Postman, and Bruner are fascinating cases in point.

This effect of goals on perception is by no means limited to the subject whose intelligence we wish to measure. It is equally true of the intelligence test constructor. It leads to the very confusing situation wherein the test constructor with one organization of goals perceives certain experiences to be marks of intelligence for another person who may or may not have similar goals. Indeed, the likelihood is that he, almost certainly, does not have similar goals. Intelligence tests thus become highly selected samplings of perception in terms of what the testers consider important. Low scores do not necessarily mean less rich and varied fields of perception; they may mean only fields of perception more widely divergent from those of the examiner. A young man whom the writer tested at an induction center during the war illustrates the point very well. This young man was a newsboy on the streets of a West Virginia city. Although he had failed repeatedly in grammar school and was generally regarded as "not bright," he appeared on a national radio hook-up as "The Human Adding Machine." He was a wizard at figures. He could multiply correctly such figures as 6235941 × 397 almost as fast as the problem could be written down. He astounded our induction center for half a day with his numerical feats. Yet, on the Binet Test given by the writer he achieved an IQ of less than 60! People in his home town, who bought his papers, amused themselves by giving him problems to figure constantly. When not so occupied this young man entertained himself by adding up the license numbers of cars that passed his corner. He was a specialist in numbers. Apparently as a result of some early success in this field, he had been led to practice numbers constantly, eventually to the exclusion of all else. This was one area in which a poor colored boy could succeed and he made the most of it. His number perceptions were certainly rich and varied but other things were not. Although he was capable of arithmetic feats not achieved by one in millions, he was classified as dull! I do not mean to argue that variety of perception is unimportant in effective behavior. I do mean to suggest the importance of goals in determining perception.

Cultural effects on goals and perceptions

We have stated here that the richness of the individual's perceptive field is in part a function of the goals he has differentiated as important or threatening to him. But, clearly these goals are themselves the result of the individual's experience. The culture one grows up in deeply affects the goals one holds. Cultures both restrict and encourage, approve and disapprove the formulation of goals in the individual. This selective effect of the culture in large measure determines the goals sought and avoided by the individual. These goals in turn must exert important effects upon the perceptions that become part of the individual's perceptive field.

I remember the Kentucky moonshiner to whom I once administered the Wechsler-Bellevue. This man could not tell me "how many pints in a quart" although he had certainly been taught this fact in his early schooling. Knowing that my client did a considerable business in bootleg liquor, I framed the question differently and asked "Well, how do you sell your liquor?" He smiled tolerantly and replied, "Oh Boss, I just sell it by the jug full!" In his community to have done otherwise would have been to risk bankruptcy. In a culture where a jug is standard container for spirits, what need to know about quarts?

It is conceivable that low intelligence may be, at least in part, no more than a function of the goals an individual is striving to reach in achieving his need satisfaction. The well-known phenomenon in which intelligence tests give best results in the school years, when experience and goals have a degree of commonality, and break down badly following those years would seem to corroborate this point. Perhaps by concerning ourselves with human goals we can affect perception, and thus intelligence, much more than we believed possible. Can it be that the child of low apparent intelligence is not so much a problem of an unfortunate heredity as an unfortunate constellation of goals or values? We could do a great deal about intelligence if that were true.

The self-concept as a factor limiting perception

We are just beginning to understand the tremendous effects of the individual's concept of self upon his perceptions and behavior. Lecky, for instance, reports the effect of a change in self-concept in improving the ability of children to spell. Other researchers have reported similar effects of the self-concept upon the perceptions which the individual may make. Clinical experience would tend to bear out such observations. Any clinician is familiar with numerous instances in which a child's conception of his abilities severely limited his achievement, even though his real abilities may have been superior to his perception of them. One needs but to go shopping with one's spouse to discover again how one's conception of himself as a male or female affects the things he sees and the things he hears.

Perception is a selective process and the conception one holds of himself is a vital factor in determining the richness and the variety of perception selected. It makes a great deal of difference, for example, how one perceives the president of our country if one conceives of himself as a democrat, a republican, or a communist. One needs but to observe a group of children to become aware that little boys perceive things quite differently from little girls. Professors do not perceive like truck drivers, although when I have had to ride with professor automobile-drivers, I have often wished they did. Thousands of people in our society avoid perceptions having to do with mathematical functions by their firm concept of themselves as people who "cannot do mathematics." The self-concepts we hold have a very vital effect in selecting the perceptions which become part of our perceptive fields. If the effectiveness of behavior is dependent on our perceptive fields, it follows that the self-concepts we hold must affect the "intelligence" of our behavior.

There is another factor in the effect of the self-concept upon perception that makes it even more important as a selector of experience. That factor is the circular effect of a given concept of self. Let us take, as an example, the child who has developed a concept of himself as "unable to read." Such a child is likely to avoid reading and thus the very experience which might change his concept of self is by-passed. Worse still, the child who believes himself unable to read, confronted with the necessity for reading, is more likely than not to do badly. The external evaluation of his teachers and fellow pupils, as well as his own observations of his performance, all provide proof to the child of how right he was in the first place! The possession of a particular concept of self tends to produce behavior that corroborates the self-concept with which the behavior originated.

Every clinician has had experience with children of ability who conceive of themselves as unable, unliked, unwanted, or unacceptable and perceive and behave in accordance with their perceptions. And this effect is not limited to children alone. It seems to me one of the great tragedies of our society that millions of people in our society perceiving themselves as able to produce only X amount, behave in these terms. Society, in turn, evaluates them in terms of this behavior and so lends proof to what is already conceived by the individual. Compared to this waste of human potential in our society, our losses in automobile accidents seem like a mere drop in the bucket. It is even conceivable in these terms that we create losses in intelligence. If, in our schools, we teach a child that he is unable and if he believes us and behaves in these terms, we need not be surprised when we test his intelligence to discover that he produces at the level at which we taught him!

It is conceivable that psychology has unwittingly contributed to this situation by the widespread publication of a static conception of intelligence and human capacities. The concept of severe limits upon the capacities of the organism simply corroborates the self-concept of the man in the street and decreases the likelihood of change in his concept of self. Even more important must be the effect upon our educational system. Teachers who believe in an unchanging character of child capacities provide the attitudes and experiences that produce and maintain a child's conception of self and his abilities. It is notorious that children's grades vary very little from year to year through the course of schooling. This continuous and little-changing evaluation must have important effects on the self-concept of the child. If the school system in which the child lives is thoroughly imbued with the notion that a child's capacities are comparatively fixed, it is even conceivable that the system may in large measure produce a child's intelligence level by the circular effect we have mentioned above.

Threat as a factor in perception

The last of the factors I should like to discuss as a possible factor in intelligence is the effect of threat upon the perceptive field. If our fundamental assumption that intelligence is a function of the richness and breadth of the phenomenal field is correct, the effect of threat on this field becomes a most important consideration. Although these effects have been so widely understood by the layman that they have been made a part of his everyday speech, it is interesting that until very recently the phenomenon has been given little attention by psychologists. The perception by the individual of threat to himself seems to have at least two major effects upon the perceptive field.

RESTRICTION OF THE PERCEPTIVE FIELD UNDER THREAT. The first of these effects is the restrictive effect that the perception of threat to self seems to have on the individual's perception. When he feels himself threatened, there appears to be a narrowing of the perceptive field to the object of threat. This has often been described in the psychology of vision as "tunnel vision." The phenomenon is extremely common and almost everyone has experienced it at some moment of crisis in his lifetime. One hears it described in such comments as "All I could see was the truck coming at us," or, "I was so scared I couldn't think of a thing." There seems reason to believe that this effect is not limited to traumatic experiences alone, but exists in lesser degree in response to milder threats as well. Combs and Taylor, for example, have demonstrated the effect under extremely mild forms of threat.

Such limiting effects on perception must certainly have a bearing upon perceptions available to the individual in his phenomenal field. Subjects who have participated in food deprivation experiments report uniformly that when threatened by hunger, food becomes an obsession. Recently, at the dinner table, I asked my young daughter what she had learned at school that day. "Oh nothing," said she with much feeling, "But was our teacher mad! Wow!" It would appear from her remarks that, feeling threatened by an angry teacher, it was difficult for her to perceive much else. Her perceptions of the day were apparently entirely concerned with the nature of anger. No doubt these are valuable perceptions to possess, but I know of no intelligence test which measures them.

I recall, too, the behavior of two little girls whose mother was taken to a mental hospital at the beginning of the summer. The matter was kept a deep secret from these two children for fear they "would not understand." The children spent most of the summer with the writer's daughter in an incessant game of "hospital." From morning to night this game went on outside our living room window. Apparently, this preoccupation was the direct outcome of the threat they felt in the loss of their mother, for with the mother's return the game ceased as suddenly as it had begun. To the best of my knowledge it has not occurred since. Under threat there seem to be severe limits imposed upon the breadth and character of perception.

DEFENSE OF THE PERCEPTIVE FIELD UNDER THREAT.   There is a second effect of threat upon the individual's perceptions. This effect has to do with the defense reactions induced in the individual on perceiving himself to be threatened. The perception of threat not only narrows the field and reduces the possibility of wide perceptions, but causes the individual to protect and cling to the perceptions he already holds. Thus, the possibility of perceptual changes is reduced and the opportunities for new perceptions or learning are decreased. Under threat, behavior becomes rigid. The fluidity and adaptation which we generally associate with intelligent behavior is vastly decreased. A number of interesting experiments in the past few years have demonstrated this phenomenon. Cowen, for example, illustrated this effect in problem solving.

Our own experiment previously mentioned also demonstrated this effect with even very mild forms of threat. This rigidity or resistance of perception to change under threat is well known to the layman and is well illustrated in some of the sayings of our culture. Such aphorisms as "Nobody ever wins an argument" or "You can lead a horse to water but you cannot make him drink" seem to be illustrations of a vague understanding of the phenomenon in the public mind. It is surprising that this principle has been so long overlooked.

I think it will be generally agreed that intelligence behavior is quite the antithesis of rigidity. In the terms we have used in this article, intelligent behavior is a function of the variety and richness of perception in the phenomenal field. Whatever produces narrowness and rigidity of perception becomes an important factor in limiting intelligence. If this reasoning is accurate, or even partly so, one is led to wonder about the effects of long-continued threat upon the development of intelligence. What of the child who has suffered serious threats to himself for long periods of his life, as in the case of the delinquent, for example? Or what of the child who has been seriously deprived of affection and warmth from those who surround him over a period of years? Is it possible that we have created low intelligence in such children? Axline has reported a number of cases in which intelligence scores improved considerably under therapy. We have observed similar changes in our own clinical practice.

It may be argued that, although threat seems to reduce perception, some people under threat apparently produce more effectively. I think, however, it is necessary for us to distinguish between "threat" and "challenge." In threat, the individual perceives himself in jeopardy and feels, in addition, a degree of inadequacy to deal effectively with the threat perceived. In challenge, the individual perceives himself threatened but feels at the same time a degree of adequacy to deal with the threat. It would appear that whether an event is perceived as threatening or challenging is a function of the individual's feeling of competence to deal with it. If this analysis is correct, it would explain why a situation that appears threatening to a person, from the viewpoint of an outside observer, might one time produce rigidity and another highly effective behavior. This description of events seems characteristic of the history of civilization as well as of individuals, if Toynbee's explanation can be given credence. He points out that the most productive (more intelligent?) societies are those in which the society faces some crisis within its capacities to cope with the situation (challenge), while societies without crisis or in which the crisis is overwhelming produce very little or collapse entirely.

SOME IMPLICATIONS OF THIS
CONCEPTION OF INTELLIGENT BEHAVIOR

If the conception of intelligence we have been discussing in this paper should prove accurate, it seems to me to raise serious questions about some of our common assumptions with respect to intelligence and, at the same time, opens some exciting new possibilities for the treatment or education of persons we have often assumed to be beyond help. It implies that our conception of the limiting factors of intelligence may have been too narrow. It would suggest perhaps that our very point of view with respect to intelligence may have resulted in our own tunnel vision, such that we have not been able to perceive other factors given little attention to this point. Perhaps we have been too impressed with the limitations upon growth and development which we observe in physical maturation. We may, for instance, have jumped too quickly to the assumption that intelligent behavior was limited as severely as physical growth and that we have explored to exhaustion other factors that may limit intelligence.

I am not suggesting that physiologic limits do not exist in respect to intelligence. I am suggesting that we may have conceded too early that we had approached those limits. There is no doubt that we can demonstrate in some cases, such as mongolism, cretinism, and the like, that physical factors severely limit intelligence. But these cases are comparatively few compared to the so-called "familial" cases of low intelligence that we often assume are hereditary in origin. What evidence do we really possess that would lead us to the position that an individual of "normal" physical condition and vigor may be limited in his capacity for effective behavior by some physical condition? We assume there must be such factors operating because we cannot explain his handicap otherwise. That biological science has not yet been able to demonstrate such physical bases has not deterred us in this. On the contrary, we have simply deplored the lack of sufficient advance in that discipline to demonstrate our conclusion! I should like to suggest that this may not be their failure but ours. Until it can be definitely established that limitations exist as biological functions, our task as psychologists is to assume that they may just as well be social or psychological in character and to work just as hard exploring the matter in our discipline as we expect the biologist to work in his.

Let us, for example, explore to the very fullest the possibility that in those cases where we cannot demonstrate biologic impairment, the limitations upon intelligence may be psychological. If it turns out not to be true, we shall find out in time. I do not believe we can afford to limit the places where we look by the pre-perceptions we have about the matter. Our responsibility here is too great. Education, to name but the most obvious of our social institutions, has in large measure predicated its goals and methods on a concept of humanity with certain static limitations on intelligence. If these limitations are not static, it is up to us as psychologists to find out. The task of the scientist is to question, not to be content with answers. We cannot afford to accept an undemonstrated point of view that prevents us from asking questions.

Some implications for intelligence testing

If the concepts of intelligence we have been discussing prove accurate, another area of psychological thought toward which we must cast a quizzical eye is the area of intelligence testing. This is particularly important at a time when our culture has come to accept these instruments as trustingly as the family doctor's prescription. If our approach to intelligent behavior as a function of the variety and richness of the perceptual field is a valid consideration, we need to ask regarding these tests at least the following questions:

1. Is our sampling of the perceptive field truly adequate? If I lived for years in a prison cell, I presume I should become expert in perceptions about that cell. Unfortunately, they would be of little value outside the prison walls, but can it truthfully be said that my perceptions are less rich or varied, or only that they are less rich and varied about things I have not had opportunity to experience? Is the delinquent, with rich and varied perceptions on how to elude the police, less intelligent or has he simply not perceived things society wishes he had?

2. Since perceptions are always closely affected by need, by whose need shall we sample perceptions—yours, mine, society's, the subject's own? I suspect that in terms of his own needs and perceptions the subject might be deemed quite brilliant, though he might or might not appear so from the point of view of society. For the most part our tests are based on the assumption that academic, upper middle-class, intellectual perceptions are important. But are they? Can we assume that the expert machinist, who can perceive things "out of this world" for most of the rest of us about a piece of stock on his lathe, is less intelligent than a diplomat who perceives many things about foreign affairs? Can we be so sure of our values as to call one bright and the other dull? Can we blame the machinist for his lack of perception about foreign affairs without asking the diplomat to be equally skilled in the machinist's field of perceptions?

3. Finally, if perceptions are affected by the factors we have discussed in this paper, is it fair to sample intelligence irrespective of the control of such factors? Shall we, for example, examine the child who has lacked opportunity to perceive, has possessed a concept of self or been so threatened over a long period

of time so as to have been unable to perceive what we wish to sample without consideration of those factors? Shall we overlook such factors and be satisfied that the perceptions important to us are not there, or shall we seek for ways to make it possible for the child to have them? Shall we assume that our failure to discover a particular perception present in the field is, *ipso facto*, evidence of lack of capacity; or seek to discover why it is not? On the positive side of the picture, if the concepts we have here been discussing are sound, there is reason to believe that intelligence may be far less immutable than we have thought. It may be that we can do far more than we have dreamed we could. Perhaps we may even be able to create intelligence!

Implications for constructive action

Who can say, for example, what results we might be able to achieve by a systematic effort to remove or decrease the effectiveness of the limitations on perception discussed in this paper? It is fascinating to speculate on the possibilities one might try in constructing a situation for a child, or adult, consciously designed to minimize the limitations imposed on perception by physical condition, environment, goals, the individual's self-concept, and the effects of perceived personal threat.

If the position we have taken is accurate, it would suggest that there is much we can do (*a*) to free individuals from the restraints upon perception and (*b*) to provide the opportunities for perception to occur.

1. First and most obviously, we should be able to discover and make available to far more people the means to achieve better physical condition. We have already done a good deal in this area but much needs yet to be done. Who can say, for instance, what completely adequate medical care for all our people might mean a generation hence?

2. If this discussion has merit, there lies the possibility of providing experiences for people that will make adequate perception possible. We have tried to do this in our schools, but have not always accomplished it. We have succeeded very well in gathering information and in making it available to students. We have not succeeded too well in making such information meaningful. Can it be that the decreases in school success with advance through the school years is more a function of lack of meaning for students than lack of intelligence? Is it enough to assume that experience provided by us to the student is truly provided when he is free to experience it? Has the child in school, who is so worried about his relationship with his peers that he cannot perceive what his book is saying, truly been provided opportunity to perceive?

In our training of children of "low intelligence," we often provide situations wherein they are carefully taught to perform repeatedly a simple act. Is it possible that in so doing we may be further narrowing their fields of perception and building self-concepts that produce even narrower perceptive fields?

What kinds of environments could we construct that might more effectively result in increased perception? Such experiments as Lippitt and White have carried on with democratic and autocratic environments suggest some possibilities, but we need to know much more. Perhaps we could learn to build such environments from observing with greater care and understanding the methods of good teachers.

3. Who can say what possible effects might occur from a systematic release of the individual's perceptions by the satisfaction of his most pressing needs or goals? We college professors insist we can produce more, which is another way of saying perceive more, when we have the leisure time to do so, when we are freed from the necessity of spending our time satisfying our needs for sheer existence. Can this be less true of others? It is possible that the child with needs of love, affection, status, prestige, or a girl friend might also be freed to perceive more widely and richly, if we could but find ways of helping him satisfy his needs. Ordinarily, we pay a good deal of attention to the physical needs of a child, understanding that with these needs unfulfilled, he makes a poor student. Is there any good reason to suppose his psychological needs are less pressing or less important in freeing him to perceive widely and accurately? We spend much time and energy trying to find ways of "motivating" people or blaming them for not being motivated to do what we need them to do. We assume that if permitted to seek their own needs, people will not satisfy ours. Perhaps we should get further by helping them satisfy their needs; they might then be free to satisfy ours.

4. Most of our educational methods are directed at the provision of perceptions for the student. He is lectured, required, shown, exhorted, and coerced to perceive what someone thinks he should. It seems possible that with equal energy devoted to the matter of creating needs, goals, and values in students, rich and varied perceptions might be more efficiently produced.

What effects might we be able to produce by providing experiences that build adequate concepts of self in children and adults? What differences in the richness and variety of perception might result from a generation of people with "I can" rather than "I can't" conceptions of themselves? What possibilities of increased perceptions and hence of increased intelligence might accrue to such a program? Clinical experience has demonstrated frequently how a changed perception of self as a more adequate personality can free children for improved school performance, for example.

What would happen if we were consciously and carefully to set about the task of providing experiences that would lead people to conceptions of themselves as adequate, worthy, self-respecting people? If freedom to perceive is a function of adequate perceptions of self, it should not surprise us that the child who perceives himself as unwanted, unacceptable, unable, or unliked behaves in rigid fashion. It should be possible, too, to reverse this process and produce more adequate perceptions by systematic efforts at producing more adequate definitions of self. The possibilities seem tremendous but we have scarcely scratched the surface of this problem.

Finally, if threat to the individual has as important effects as seem indicated in this discussion, the removal of threat would seem a most important factor to consider in the release of the individual to perceive more adequately. The work of Rogers and his students in client centered therapy has already illustrated to some degree what possibilities freeing the individual to perceive more adequately may accomplish through the provision of a permissive nonthreatening relationship between counselor and client. We have already mentioned the effects Axline has reported following a permissive, nonthreatening form of play therapy.

Such effects do not seem limited to the therapeutic situation, however. A number of workers have applied this principle of permissiveness to the classroom situation with equally gratifying results. Experiments in student centered teaching at Syracuse have led many of us to believe in the tremendous educational possibilities in the removal of threat.

This paper has asked many questions. Indeed, it has asked far more questions than it has presumed to answer. That, it seems to me, is the function of theory. The picture of intelligence presented here as it seems from a phenomenological viewpoint may be accurate or false or, more likely, partly true and partly false. Only time and the industry of many observers can check its adequacy or inadequacy. It seems to me to pose problems that are both exciting and challenging. If it proves as stimulating to the reader as it has to the author, I shall rest content that a theory has achieved its purpose.

21 *Some implications for school practice of the Chicago studies of cultural bias in intelligence tests*

Related selections: 20, 34

The classic "nature versus nurture" debate of several decades ago failed to settle to everyone's satisfaction the question of the relative importance of heredity and environment in determining human intelligence. Recent years have seen an approach aimed at discovering

KENNETH EELLS, "Some Implications for School Practice of the Chicago Studies of Cultural Bias in Intelligence Tests," *Harvard Educational Review,* XXIII (Fall, 1953), 284–97. Reprinted by permission of the author and the publisher.

DR. EELLS (1913–   ) is Institute Psychologist, California Institute of Technology. He was formerly Head, Criterion Development Center, U. S. Naval Personnel Research Unit, San Diego, California. Prior to that he was at the University of Chicago.

whether the differences in intelligence between children from homes of unlike socioeconomic status are true differences or whether the measuring instruments used are biased in favor of a particular group. In this article Dr. Eells discusses the meaning of the work which he and others did at the University of Chicago on the cultural bias in intelligence tests.

Let us suppose for a moment that you have a friend in Australia and that you have gone to visit him in his home country. He has told you that he is to take an intelligence test that afternoon and suggests that you take it too, just for the fun of it. You agree to do so. When you first open the test booklet you say to yourself, "Well, I'm in a foreign country, but since they speak English, I shouldn't have any special difficulty with this." But soon you are in trouble. Some of the items deal with Australian history and local social conditions about which you know almost nothing. Then you come to some questions that have to do with mutton. You know something about mutton, but suddenly it occurs to you that your friend probably knows more about it than you do. A little further on in the test you wish you'd paid more attention to the kangaroo when you visited a zoo several years ago. The questions are all in English, of course, but you find that some of the words seem to have a little different significance, and occasionally you come across a word which is completely strange to you. You wonder whether this is a word you just happen not to know or whether it is a local term that you could not be expected to know.

However, it is an interesting experience—until your friend, half in fun, says, "Well, that was one of our best intelligence tests. How did you do?" As you think back over the test you are glad that the papers have not yet been scored. You realize that because of the mutton and the kangaroo, the strange words, the local information, and the variations in word connotations your friend had an advantage over you. If he thinks this is a good measure of your intelligence you are glad that he cannot compare your score with his.

Before leaving this somewhat informal introduction to the problem of cultural bias in intelligence tests, it would perhaps be well to point out that if your Australian friend had not called the test an "intelligence" test but had said instead that it was a test designed to measure your ability to read Australian newspapers and to converse with educated Australian persons effectively, you would have had no quarrel with the presence in the test of materials peculiar to the Australian culture, or with the test's use of words and grammatical construction which were strange to you. As a measure of your ability to get along in a certain portion of the Australian culture the test might be excellent, and you might willingly accept your low score as an accurate reflection of your "current ability." It is the labelling of the test as an "intelligence" test, with its accompanying implication that this is somehow a measure of some basic ability or potentiality of yours, that disturbs you. You have the feeling that if your friend could see your score he might decide you aren't very "intelligent" and that by this he might really mean that you aren't going to be able to solve effectively many of the major problems that you are faced with in living a full and successful life. You wouldn't object to being told you couldn't understand Australian newspapers very well; but to be told you're not very "intelligent" implies something more serious, doesn't it?

The comparison is not as farfetched as it may seem at first. The child who has been brought up on the "wrong side of the tracks" in an American community goes to a school presided over by administrators and teachers who are practically all drawn from a life different from the one he knows. They have grown up in different kinds of families, with different kinds of friends, and with different kinds of experiences. Now they ask the child to take a test to determine how intelligent he is, so that the school can plan properly a school program for him. He finds that the test is written in English, fortunately, but he also finds that it is a kind of English which is quite different from that which he has learned at home and which he hears in is own neigborhood. He is probably not asked for information about Australian history and mutton, but he *is* asked to answer test items dealing with symphony orchestra instruments, with typewriters, with fireplaces, with animals which he might have seen in a zoo if he had been brought up in another part of the city. He is asked about all sorts of things which he may or may not have ever seen and with which he almost certainly has had no chance to be really familiar. It all seems a little strange to him— perhaps even silly—since it has no very obvious importance for the kind of problems that are important to him. So he doesn't try very hard. Perhaps he marks the items rather quickly to end the painful process. Later his test paper is scored, and he is found to be somewhat below average in intelligence. His school program is arranged accordingly and the teachers are warned not to expect too much from him. This, in brief, is the problem of cultural bias in intelligence tests.

THE APPROACH

Most of what has been published thus far has dealt with problems of intelligence-test methodology. How much cultural bias is there in intelligence tests currently in use? If undesirable, how can the amount of it be reduced? Such questions have been investigated and discussed more fully than questions dealing with the implications for educational practice of the existence of such cultural bias. Assuming there is *some* cultural bias in present intelligence tests, what implications does this have for the actions of school administrators? What implications does it have for the classroom teacher? What does it mean for the guidance counselor? Such questions have received comparatively little attention thus far.

In the present article, some of these questions of practical implication are discussed. In this analysis, it is not assumed that all the methodological problems have been solved. Nor is it assumed that there is any way of measuring, at present, just how much cultural bias there is in intelligence tests. It is not even assumed that *all* of the differences which are known to exist between the scores of high-status children and of low-status children on intelligence tests are due to cultural bias in the tests. This may be true, and there are those who firmly believe it to be so. At present, however, there are no conclusive data to prove that it is so—nor, for that matter, to prove that it is not so.

One assumption, however, is made: that sufficient evidence is available to justify the conclusion that *at least a substantial part* of the known group differences in I. Q.'s of children from different sub-cultural groups may be accounted for by cultural bias in the intelligence tests. The writer believes that the evidence for this somewhat conservative statement is convincing enough to make an analysis of its implications for practical school purposes a worthwhile undertaking.

It would be comparatively simple to outline some of the specific implications— to provide a sort of list of cookbook rules for an administrator, teacher, or counselor to follow if he wished to make allowances for cultural bias in intelligence tests. However, this kind of approach would be likely to be misleading. It would leave many specific applications untouched, and it would be an insult to the intelligence of those responsible for different phases of the educational process. What will be attempted, instead, is to clarify the basic nature of cultural bias in intelligence tests and its relation to the school's objectives, and to leave to the reader the important task of making the necessary specific applications to a wider variety of specific school situations than would be possible to discuss by the first approach.

Once the essential nature of cultural bias in tests is seen clearly—along with its effect on scores, or I. Q.'s—school administrators, teachers, and guidance counselors will have little trouble in seeing a multitude of specific applications. Administrators will see the implications for establishing school objectives in terms of the abilities and needs of pupils, and for curriculum revision and teaching-method development based on the measurement of student ability. They will recognize a need for setting up in-service training activities for teachers and counselors. They will see implications for the assignment of teachers to schools, or to school-rooms, where children from low-status homes predominate. Teachers will see the need for looking at the "low I. Q. pupil" in a different light; they will see more clearly that some of the pupil's apparent lack of capacity is only a challenge for teacher exploration of new areas and new methods. Teachers will rcognize even more vividly than before a need for greater individualization of instruction—and for every teacher to prepare himself to understand sympathetically and intelligently the many differences which separate his "way of life" from that of many of his pupils. Guidance counselors will see important implications for interpreting the I. Q. scores of pupils who are seeking their help on academic, vocational, or personal matters.

Most of the specific applications to school practice will probably fall into three general categories: (a) the need for considerable caution in arriving at judgments of individuals or groups based on traditional intelligence-test scores, or I. Q.'s—especially in the case of children coming from sub-cultures other than the "middle-class" one from which most teachers and school administrators come, (b) the need for a new type of intelligence test, along lines suggested later in this article, in order to have a basis for sounder and more defensible decisions in those school areas where tests of basic mental ability are helpful, and (c) implications, for basic school reorganization, of previously unidentified abilities in pupils.

The first application is largely an individual matter, and one where little difficulty will be encountered in making the necessary allowances and interpretations when the nature of culture bias is better understood. The second kind of application—the development of a new type of intelligence test—involves technical problems which would not be appropriately discussed here. The balance of this article is concerned almost entirely with the last of these three types of applications—with the broad area of basic school organization. What are the implications for curriculum development, for teaching methods, for guidance practices, of the fact that our present intelligence tests probably underestimate, to a substantial degree, the abilities of a large proportion of our school children?

Let us consider first a few basic ideas related to what is meant, and what is not meant, by cultural bias in tests. Discussion in this general area has sometimes been somewhat beside the point when the discussants have failed to make clear precisely what they mean by the terms "cultural bias" or "intelligence." Several straw men have been set up and knocked down.

WHAT IS MEANT BY "CULTURAL BIAS" IN INTELLIGENCE TESTS?

Current controversy and doubts regarding possible cultural bias in intelligence tests have arisen in a number of places, and from different sources. For many years individual teachers, principals, and superintendents have had serious doubts as to the adequacy of the intelligence tests they were using. More recently an increasing body of research knowledge has become available which suggests the possibility that the scores on most intelligence tests are influenced substantially by the nature of the cultural material contained in the test. Much of this research has been carried on by Dr. Allison Davis, of the University of Chicago, and his colleagues and students. It is probably natural, therefore, that the point of view underlying such studies has come to be known in some quarters as "the Chicago point of view." This labelling is, however, an oversimplification and may be misleading.

In the first place, there is no single "Chicago point of view." While those most closely associated with Davis' research probably have certain basic points of view in common, they differ among themselves in the degree of emphasis which they attach to the factor of cultural bias in intelligence tests and to some extent in their interpretation of it. In the second place, much research in this area has been and is being carried on at other places than the University of Chicago.

BASIC DEFINITION.   The general thesis underlying the Chicago studies of cultural bias in intelligence tests may be stated very briefly: most presently used intelligence tests (both individual and group) are so constructed and so administered that scores on them are influenced by the cultural backgrounds of the children taking the test, in such a way that children from certain kinds of cultural backgrounds receive scores that are not accurate reflections of their basic "intelligence." "Intelligence" is defined, for the present purpose, in terms of problem-solving ability. The more "intelligent" child is one who can, when operating under conditions of maximum motivation, solve problems which seem (and which actually are) real and important to him more effectively and more expeditiously than can the less "intelligent" child.

The meaning of the concept of "cultural bias in intelligence tests" may be clarified by (a) placing it in the larger context of the heredity-environment controversy which has plagued psychological and educational literature for many decades, (b) noting the effect of cultural bias on group and on individual differences in intelligence, (c) differentiating the idea of a "culturally fair" intelligence test from the idea of a "culture free" intelligence test, and (d) differentiating an "intelligence" test from a "scholastic aptitude" test.

RELATIONSHIP TO THE HEREDITY-ENVIRONMENT CONTROVERSY.   The problem under consideration has an important relationship to the time-worn heredity-environment controversy regarding the causes of differences in intelligence, but the exact nature of that relationship is easily misunderstood. The relationship may be most clearly seen in the context of differences known to exist on traditional intelligence tests between children from high-status homes and those from low-status homes.

Alfred Binet made the first known study in this area, in 1910. He found that children of physicians, university professors, lawyers, etc., in a private school in Belgium did systematically better on his new intelligence-test items than did children from public schools in working-class neighborhoods of Paris. The superiority amounted to about a year and a half on the Binet Scale.

More than eighty similar studies have since been carried out, always with the same kind of results. In these studies a wide variety of intelligence tests, both individual and group, have been examined. Many different methods of measuring social status—occupational level of the parents, income level of the family, dwelling areas within cities, and specially devised scales—have been used. A variety of statistical techniques has been utilized. Without a single exception, these studies have shown that, on the average, children from high-status homes do better on standard intelligence tests than do children from low-status homes, When average I. Q.'s for children from professional and managerial homes are compared with average I. Q.'s for children from unskilled labor backgrounds, the I. Q. difference is usually in the neighborhood of 15 to 25 I. Q. points. When the relationship between social status and I. Q. is studied by correlational techniques, the correlations are typically in the neighborhood of .35, with half of the studies yielding correlations between .25 and .48. A comprehensive summary of the findings of these studies is available elsewhere.

While the existence of this social-status difference in average I. Q. is a well-established fact, the interpretation of its possible significance has led to much controversy. For many years this controversy was largely bipolar. Some psychologists and educators inclined to the view that the difference was due largely to hereditary factors. Their argument, in somewhat oversimplified form, claimed that the more intelligent parents gravitated to the occupational fields carrying higher status (professional, managerial, and to a lesser extent, skilled labor) while the less able parents gravitated to the lower status occupations, especially semi-skilled and unskilled labor. These superior parents then passed on their superior intelligence to their children through genetic processes. The findings of the research studies were taken as support of the hypothesis that intelligence is inherited genetically.

Other psychologists and educators inclined to the view that the difference in average I. Q. for children from high-status and from low-status homes was due largely to environmental factors. Their argument—again in somewhat over-simplified form—claimed that the parents in the higher-status occupations were able to provide more favorable and more stimulating environments for their children than were the parents in the lower-status occupations. Since the environments were more stimulating for the children from high-status homes these children developed more nearly to their full capacities, whereas children from low-status homes were stunted and did not develop fully. The findings of the research studies, it was pointed out, were consistent with this hypothesis and therefore supported it.

During the early years of the 20th century this controversy flourished some-what vigorously, with ardent advocates of each point of view claiming research support for their view, and with only an occasional voice pointing out that the nature of the research evidence available made it impossible to arrive at any definitive answer to the controversy. Since the homes in which the hereditary intelligence of the parents was supposed to be highest were also the same homes that were supposed to be environmentally the most stimulating, it was impossible to use the higher I. Q.'s of the children in these homes as evidence for either one of these two hypotheses.

As the years passed, the line of demarcation between these two extreme positions softened somewhat, with people on both sides conceding that the intelligence of children is probably a result of the dynamic interaction of both hereditary and environmental factors. While probably few today would claim that either hereditary or environmental factors are *totally* responsible for all I. Q. differences, there is still wide variation in the degree of emphasis assigned to the different kinds of factors by different psychologists, sociologists and educators.

While these two traditional points of view differ markedly in their assignment of causes to the observed I. Q. differences, they have in common an acceptance of the fact that there *are* genuine differences in basic intelligence between children from high-status backgrounds and children from low-status backgrounds. They differ only in the kinds of reasons which they believe explain these differences.

More recently, a third point of view has been expressed with increasing frequency. This point of view side-steps the heredity-environment controversy and questions, instead, whether the differences in average I. Q. found for high-status and for low-status children represent the real differences in intelligence that they have been assumed to represent. The persons taking this point of view point out that children from high-status homes have substantially different kinds of cultural experiences from children in low-status homes. These experiences are different in the kinds of things with which the children deal, in the vocabulary and language with which the children will be familiar, and in the attitudes and values which determine what problems seem important and what problems seem unimportant to the children. These people then point out that the usual intelligence tests draw more heavily from the content, the language, and the attitudes and values of the high-status culture than they do from the low-status culture. From this point of view, the differences in I. Q.'s, or scores, on the tests may be a reflection merely of this bias in the test materials, and not of basic differences in the real abilities of children from the different backgrounds.

In brief, while the discussion during the earlier part of the century revolved largely around the question of *why* children from high-status homes were more consistently found to be higher in mental ability (intelligence) than children from low-status homes, the present controversy deals more with the question of *whether* this apparent difference is a real one or whether it reflects merely a bias in the construction of tests.

This cultural-bias interpretation of intelligence-test results has long been generally accepted in the field of rural-urban differences. It has been recognized widely that when a test draws largely on experiences peculiar to urban life, it will penalize rural children and that lower scores of the rural children on such a test should be taken as indicating a deficiency in the test and not as indicating a genuine deficiency in mental ability of rural children. It seems strange that this same line of reasoning was not applied earlier to the I. Q. differences found between children of different sub-cultural levels within the urban culture. Perhaps this application had to await the development of more definitive research information on the extent of the difference in the cultural patterns to which children in different parts of the urban community are exposed. Warner and his colleagues, in particular, have contributed much to a clearer understanding of the extent of these differences.

GROUP AND INDIVIDUAL DIFFERENCES IN I. Q. Some misunderstanding has arisen through failure to differentiate between the effect of cultural bias on individual differences in I. Q.'s and its effect on the average performance of groups of children.

Although there are substantial differences in the average I. Q. of high-status children and the average I. Q. of low-status children, wide variation of I. Q. is always found among the individuals in any one status group. Even on the traditional intelligence tests not all the "brighter" children will be found in the high-status group, nor all the duller children in the low-status group. In one study, for example, it was found that eight percent of the low-status children were *above* the average of the high-status children and that seven percent of the high-status children were *below* the average of the low-status children. The implications of this wide variation of ability within each status group are frequently overlooked.

The cultural-bias argument, outlined above, is applicable only to systematic group differences. It is true that any individual child's performance on an intelligence test will doubtless be affected also by whether the items happen to sample particular experiences with which he has come in contact. However, the presence in the tests of a fairly large number of items probably assures a fair amount of averaging out of such discrepancies, *so long as the nature of the items is not systematically biased against a particular child.*

If, however, whole groups of children have certain kinds of experiences more frequently than do other groups of children, and the test items are drawn mostly from the kind of material with which one group is familiar, group differences in intelligence-test scores would be expected.

Suppose that it could be conclusively demonstrated (which it cannot at present) that *all* the difference in average I. Q., as between high-status and low-status children, is due to cultural bias in the test. A wide variety of individual scores would still occur even if the systematic bias were somehow eliminated. In this area of *individual* variation of I. Q.'s, the old controversy of hereditary and environmental causes—and a dynamic interaction of the two —is still applicable.

IS A "CULTURE FAIR" TEST A "CULTURE FREE" TEST? It is not surprising that some confusion has arisen between these two terms which sounds as though they might be synonymous or at least closely related. However, these two terms presumably are intended to refer to two quite different ideas. If by a "culture free" intelligence test is meant one in which the "intelligence" of a child is somehow measured entirely apart from the impact of any cultural experiences on the child, the term is practically a nonsense term. Psychologists and sociologists have long pointed out that all human beings are the product of an interaction between certain inner genetic characteristics and the forces which come from outside, usually called "cultural" or "environmental." From the moment of conception the development of any living organism is inescapably influenced by its environment—by "cultural" factors, in short. To attempt to devise test items to which a child can respond without being in any way influenced by the environment or culture in which he has been brought up is a task at least as hopeless as separating a baked pudding. Some test authors have apparently tried to construct "culture free" tests—at least they have so labelled them—by using arbitrary geometric figures which would be new to all children. Unless, however, the lines and elements which make up such designs, and the instructions which accompany them, are in some way tied in closely to the past experiences of the child, he will not be able to do anything with them. Furthermore, the very fact of requesting the children to work with material that looks meaningless to them introduces problems of culturally-determined work habits and attitudes.

Those who have proposed "culture fair" intelligence tests are not trying to eliminate all cultural material from the intelligence test. They are interested only in having tests which measure fairly the basic problem-solving ability of children from different kinds of cultural background. They are attempting to construct and administer tests so that children from each sub-group in the culture will have equal opportunity for being familiar with the materials and methods required for successful answering of the test items.

In summary, if an intelligence test is to be freed of "cultural bias," if it is to be fair measure of genuine problem-solving ability of children from different sub-cultural groups, three criteria must be met: (a) the tests must be composed of items which deal with materials common to the various sub-cultures in which it is to be used, (b) the test must be expressed in language and other symbols which are equally familiar to the children growing up in the different sub-cultures, and (c) the test must be so organized and administered as to stimulate equal degrees of interest and motivation for the children from the different sub-cultures. To the extent that an intelligence test does not meet these three qualifications, it cannot be said to be a culturally "fair" test. If it contains items which require familiarity with symphony orchestra instruments, with strange animals observable only in zoos and museums—or if it is expressed in academic, bookish words which are strange to children from the "wrong side of the tracks"—or if it is so uninteresting to children that the only children that will work hard at it will be those (mostly middle and higher status) who have been taught by their parents to do their best on anything the teacher asks—in any of these cases the test is characterized by "cultural bias."

WHAT IS THE PURPOSE OF MEASURING "INTELLIGENCE"?   A serious problem arises in the measurement of intelligence because of the lack of any generally accepted definition of "intelligence." The term has been defined by some as the ability to adapt to one's environment, by some as the ability to think abstractly, and in a great variety of other phrases. Some of these definitions differ from each other only in their verbal expression, but others represent more basically different concepts.

One problem of definition has a particularly direct and significant bearing on the proper use of the intelligence test in the school situation. There are those who say that the main purpose of an intelligence test is to predict which pupils are going to do well in school—or in particular school curricula. For practical purposes, "intelligence" is defined as the ability to do school work.

According to this view, since the primary purpose of the test is to predict success in performing school work, the test should be judged empirically on the basis of how well it predicts such success. The question of whether the test is culturally biased or not is irrelevant, so long as the test actually does predict school success reasonably well. It is possible that a culturally biased test will give a better prediction of school success in most schools, since most schools are based on curricular materials and teaching methods that are heavily loaded with concepts, language, materials, and values and attitudes that are characteristic of the middle-class or high-status culture. It is, in this view, quite appropriate for low-status children to be penalized on the "intelligence" test, since they will also be handicapped in their attempts to master the school program.

With this basic point of view, the writer is in substantial agreement. If what is wanted is as good a predictor as possible of success in the school program *as it is now organized,* the test should be constructed and validated empirically, with those items being selected for the test which discriminate most sharply between pupils who succeed in the school as now organized and those who do not succeed, without any regard for *why* any pupil does poorly on the test—or in the school. The question of cultural bias is then irrelevant. This is true even though the present tests are not very efficient predictors of school success (An intelligence test is considered as rather good which accounts for only about a quarter of the actual variance which occurs in school grades).

Acceptance of this view of an intelligence test as having as its chief purpose the prediction of success in the school as now organized requires a form of thinking, however, that is difficult to maintain. The term "intelligence" has been used by so many people to mean so many different things that it is difficult to keep in mind while using a test developed in accordance with the definition of intelligence described in the preceding paragraph that the logic applies only if predicting school grades is the sole purpose for which the test is being used.

If the term "intelligence" had no prior connotations to trouble those who use it, one could define it as the ability to do school work in schools as now organized, just as one could invent any new word and arbitrarily define it in this way. Probably it would be safe to say, however, that most persons not specifically trained in the field of intelligence testing and school-prediction problems will bring to the term a host of fairly vague connotations quite apart from the empirical definition just outlined. To many, "intelligence" will automatically evoke thoughts of a generalized "mental power," probably "native" or "innate," although this is quite irrelevant, and potentially misleading, if intelligence is being defined empirically as scholastic aptitude.

When a test is designed to predict success in a particular occupation—stenography, for example—it is usually *labelled* as a stenographic aptitude test. A test designed to predict successful performance in an algebra class is usually labelled as an algebra aptitude test. If a test is to be used to predict success in school work generally, why is it not more consistent, more descriptive, and less open to misunderstanding, to label the test as a test of scholastic aptitude rather than to refer to it as an "intelligence" test? This distinction is usually made at the college level. This may be because the cultural content of these tests at the higher levels has been more generally recognized than is the cultural content of "intelligence" tests at the elementary-school level.

If a test has been constructed according to the usual empirical procedures for constructing aptitude tests, it can be used to predict which pupil will probably do well and which will not do well in the school, so long as the school's program is similar to those of the schools where the test-construction and test-validation work was carried out. It is important to note, however—and this is frequently overlooked—that such a test cannot be used as a basis for planning school modifications or for evaluating school effectiveness.

One cannot legitimately say, "The intelligence test shows that certain of our pupils are bright and certain of them are dull. The bright ones succeed well in our school so our school is doing a good job with bright pupils. The dull ones are doing poorly, but the tests indicate they could not be expected to do any better, so we need not worry about them." Such an evaluative use of intelligence test results is utterly fallacious. One cannot justify securing poor educational results from "poor" students by saying the tests show them to be "poor" students; the tests were specifically constructed to do just this—to label as "poor" those students who do not do well in our schools as now organized.

Some may be willing to accept the present American schools as having the right kinds of school programs in all basic respects, and desire merely to identify those pupils who will fit into the existing school pattern successfully. In this case, the present "scholastic aptitude" tests, constructed empirically and without regard for cultural bias, can be quite useful. This is a legitimate use—and probably the only one—for these tests. It is a use whose limitations would be more clearly understood and less easily overlooked if the tests were labelled by a term like "scholastic aptitude" which describes their actual function rather than by a term like "intelligence" which suggests a variety of irrelevant thoughts to many users of the term.

Suppose, however, a school administrator and his teachers are interested in identifying the abilities and potentialities of all the children which the school is supposed to be serving, and wish to use these abilities and potentialities as a basis for planning school programs which will develop to the fullest possible extent all these abilities and potentialities. Tests of "scholastic aptitude" are almost worthless for this purpose. When "intelligence" tests are used in this way the problem of cultural bias becomes particularly crucial. If whole groups of children are labelled by the tests as possessing less "brightness" or "problem-solving ability" than they really have, the real abilities of those pupils will be underestimated, and the importance of developing special programs for developing such abilities overlooked.

The writer has seen a number of school systems—probably many readers of this article have had the same experience—where certain schools are regarded as "poor" schools; it is assumed that there isn't really much point in trying to educate the children attending these schools. In some systems new teachers and new administrators are assigned to these schools, with the understanding that they will be "promoted" to more promising schools after they have served their "term" in the less desirable schools. Such schools become, essentially, custodial institutions. In some cases these children from whom little is expected and to whom little is offered constitute only particular rooms rather than whole schools. In some cases the distinction is made on an individual basis. In any case, however, the child, or the group of children, with low I. Q.'s on tests which are at least to some extent biased against them because of the particular cultural background from which they come—are labelled as relatively uneducable, and little is offered them.

There is no virtue in useless sentimentality. If these children really are uneducable, or if the educational achievement of which they are capable is really considerably below an "acceptable" level, an attempt to educate them would be silly—a waste of time and a waste of human resources. The same resources could better be utilized in improving the educational opportunities for children who are more capable of profiting from educational advantages.

But suppose that many children are shunted off to the side of the mainstream of education through a fallacy, through failure to realize that the school program is not geared to their particular abilities. The resultant loss to thousands upon thousands of individuals is tragic.

If good tests of basic problem-solving ability could be developed that would measure the ability of children to solve real life problems of the kind that are important to them, school authorities could use such tests as a basis for curriculum planning and as a basis for teaching-method evaluation. If certain students still turn out to have very little "intelligence" (or problem-solving ability), the school might as well face the fact that such children are relatively uneducable and that the most it can do is to provide some sort of custodial care for them. If, however, children now labelled as of low intelligence should be shown by such culture-fair tests actually to have a higher degree of problem-solving ability than formerly suspected, would not that be a great impetus and stimulation for the development of new kinds of curricula, new educational objectives. new teaching methods to capitalize on these previously undiscovered talents?

It will not be easy for most of us, whose whole personal orientation and background are in the "middle-class" tradition, to re-orient our thinking enough to devise ways of developing the problem-solving abilities of children whose cultural resources are of quite a different sort from our own. We will have to learn to understand children whose definition of what constitutes a "problem" is often quite different from our own use of the term, children whose interest in school work is already strongly negative because of the child's discovery that the school now has little to offer him. But that is the challenge of education in a democracy that is as heterogeneous as the United States. If we are to provide education for all children, must it not be education geared to the cultural backgrounds, the cultural needs, and the cultural motivations of each child? Can we be content much longer to attempt to fit children from the "wrong side of the tracks" into a school program not designed in terms of their interests or abilities or needs? Certainly we cannot justify our attempt to do so by using so-called "intelligence" tests to indicate that these children really aren't up to educational standard anyway. We cannot justifiably do so while we use tests which are really tests of scholastic aptitude and which were specifically constructed to identify as "poor" the child who will not do well in the present program.

On the basis of scores from tests designed only to predict success in schools as they are now organized, with their heavy emphasis upon curriculum materials, teaching methods, and values and attitudes drawn almost entirely from the middle-class culture, we are helping to shape children's lives. What human resources are we squandering? How many individual potentialities are we failing to develop? Dare we take the responsibility, as administrators, as teachers, or as counselors, for guiding children into educational dead-ends on the theory that they are not capable of better educational opportunities when the only evidence we have for this condemnation is the kind of intelligence tests at present available?

This is the question raised by the problem of cultural bias in intelligence tests.

22 *Factors in mental retardation*

There is a growing recognition in our society of the need to help everybody, including the mentally retarded, to perform as near to capacity as possible. In this selection Dr. Jervis presents some basic information concerning the known and suspected causes of mental retardation. Although this information is of particular importance to those who will work with the mentally handicapped, it has meaning for prospective teachers who wish to have an understanding of the broad spectrum of mental ability.

Various sciences have contributed to our present concept of mental deficiency. For a long time sociologists have observed that there are individuals who, since childhood, have been socially incompetent and incapable of adequate self-support. Psychologists, coming later, have noted that this social incompetence is often associated with defective intellectual development. They have discovered ways of measuring the degree of intellectual deficit and of establishing certain correlations between intellectual endowment and social attainments. Then as medical science advanced, physicians became increasingly aware that some diseases occurring during fetal life or in infancy may result in lesions of the brain with consequent mental defect. Finally, with the advent of the science of human genetics the relevance of genetic factors in determining deviations of intelligence emerged.

Mental deficiency may be defined as a condition of arrest or incomplete mental development existing before adolescence, caused by disease or genetic constitution and resulting in social incompetence. This definition includes both the sociological concept which stresses the social inadequacy of the defective, and the psychological concept which is considered in the term "arrested" or "incomplete" mental development. The biological viewpoint is embodied in the mention of genetic factors and diseases.

Intellectual impairment developing after adolescence is not usually known as mental deficiency but as dementia, a customary differentiation for more than a century in both legal and medical thinking, in spite of its dubious validity.

GEORGE A. JERVIS, "Factors in Mental Retardation," *Children,* I (November–December, 1954), 207–11. Reprinted by permission of the Department of Health, Education, and Welfare, Social Security Administration, Children's Bureau.

DR. JERVIS (1903–   ) is Director of Clinical Laboratories, Letchworth Village, New York State Department of Mental Hygiene.

Thus defined, mental deficiency is not a single condition, but a symptom common to diverse conditions of disparate etiologies and of various manifestations.

In the recognition of mental deficiency, the results of psychological examination play the leading role. The mental age (MA) is determined by psychometric tests and the intelligence quotient (IQ) calculated as the rapport of the mental age to the chronological age (CA): $IQ = MA/CA \times 100$. Other factors besides intelligence quotient are taken into consideration, such as educational attainment, emotional reactions, general behavior, and social adjustment. The information from both familial and personal history is carefully evaluated. Finally, a complete medical examination is performed, using modern techniques of clinical and laboratory medicine. It is upon the evidence thus collected that the diagnosis is made.

Considerable difficulty is often experienced in diagnosing the borderline cases between "subnormality" and mental deficiency. The criterion of social adjustment is decisive in these instances.

INCIDENCE AND CLASSIFICATION

In estimating the incidence of mental deficiency, a great deal depends upon the criteria of diagnosis used in the assessment of defective individuals. For instance, if the criterion of social incompetence is adhered to, the incidence will be higher in a strongly competitive urban environment than in rural communities. If a purely psychological criterion is adopted, the test used and the arbitrary point of demarcation between the defective and the nondefective individual will determine to a large extent percentage figures. If one accepts an IQ of 75 instead of one of 70 as the lower limit for the nondefective, the percentage of defective population will be over twice as large. Estimates based on institutional censuses are obviously inadequate and always too low, since only a fraction of the mentally defective population is institutionalized. Those based on large-group testing of school children have their limitations and are perhaps too high. Accurate surveys using modern techniques of securing data and uniform criteria of evaluating intellectual and social development have been few in number and limited in extension.

On the basis of scattered and incomplete data collected from many sources, it may be assumed that the incidence of mental deficiency in the general population is around 1 percent, using IQ below 70 as the criterion. This figure yields a total of 1,500,000 mental defectives in the United States.

Defectives are usually classified into three groups—idiots, imbeciles, and morons, but the corresponding terms of low-grade, medium-grade, and high-grade defective are to be preferred. Defined in sociological terms and in the language of the English Mental Deficiency Act (1927), idiots are persons whose mental defectiveness is of such degree that they are unable to guard themselves against ordinary physical danger. Imbeciles are persons whose mental defectiveness, though less extreme than in idiots, still prevents them from managing themselves or their affairs, or, in the case of children, of being taught to do so. Morons are persons whose mental defectiveness, though not amounting to imbecility, is yet so pronounced that they require care, supervision, and control for their own protection or for the protection of others, or, in the case of children, appear to be permanently incapable of receiving proper benefit from instruction in ordinary schools.

In more precise psychological terms, an idiot is a person having a mental age of less than 3 years, or, if a child, an intelligence quotient of less than 20. An imbecile is a person having a mental age of 3 to 7 years, inclusive, or, if a child, an intelligence quotient from 20 to 49, inclusive. A moron is a person having a mental age of 8 to 11 or 12 years, or, if a child, an intelligence quotient from 50 to 70 (or 75).

Although of considerable value in dealing with practical problems of defectives, both sociological and psychological classifications present limitations, being purely descriptive in character. More comprehensive are medical classifications which follow mainly etiological criteria, grouping patients according to the cause of the defect. While this type of classification may offer considerable difficulty in individual cases, because of scanty and contradictory etiological data or the fact that more than one etiological factor may be responsible for the defect, it does bring about a better understanding of the problem in relation to preventive measures.

Etiologically, mental defect can be divided into two large groups—endogenous or primary, and exogenous or secondary. In the exogenous group the defect comes chiefly from environmental factors. This group can be subdivided into types according to the causative agent—infectious, traumatic, toxic, and endocrine. On the other hand, an endogenous defect is determined mainly by those hereditary factors known as genes. The group includes conditions due to the combined action of many genes each of which alone would have an insignificant effect, or to the action of a single dominant or recessive gene.

HEREDITARY DEFECTS

Multiple genes

Mental defects determined by multiple genes are "undifferentiated" in that they carry no specific physical distinction and are "aclinical" in that they show no clinical manifestations other than intellectual impairment. This group has also been designated by other terms: "residual" because it is composed of individuals who are left after a classification of specific forms; "subcultural" because so many of its members originate from low cultural environments; "familial" because of the high frequency of the condition in the patients' families. Since these cases can be diagnosed only by psychological and social adjustment criteria, differentiation between high-grade morons and dull-normal individuals may be difficult. While antisocial behavior and psychopathic traits occur in the group, they are far from universal.

Estimates of the incidence of undifferentiated mental defects run between 30 and 75 percent of all the mentally retarded, the lower figure probably running nearer to the facts. It includes defects of all grades, but high-grade morons predominate.

While the etiological factors determining the large number of undifferentiated cases of mental deficiency are still in dispute, it seems likely that they are similar to the factors responsible for general intelligence—in other words, genetic constitution. It seems reasonable to assume that most of these undifferentiated cases represent merely the lower part of the normal frequency-distribution curve of intelligence, known to statisticians as the Gaussian form. This means that a certain number of individuals are bound to appear in the range below the line indicating IQ 70. They are an integral part of the population as a whole, just as are individuals with superior intelligence with an IQ above 130. According to the curve, the majority of undifferentiated defectives are in the moron classification with IQ's between 50 and 70, and only a very few at the idiot level, with IQ's below 20—a picture which corresponds to observed fact.

Genetic constitution, however, is not the only source of all undifferentiated defectiveness, for environmental factors, such as subcultural milieu and poor hygienic conditions, undoubtedly play a causative role. The task of tracing the source of the defectiveness in individual cases is not easy, particularly when malnutrition and deprivation have been in the picture.

Single genes

Some differentiated defects are determined by the presence of a single dominant gene transmitted from parent to child. Such defects are always traceable in the family history unless of a type that prevents reproduction. Frequently they turn up in severe form in alternate generations occurring in the intermediate generation only in incomplete form. Sporadic occurrences in families with no history of the defect are probably caused by a new mutation in a parental germ cell.

Data collected at Letchworth Village indicate that dominant genes probably account for only about 1 or 2 percent of all mental defects. These are always characterized by some physiological changes which make them classifiable into specific or clinically recognizable diseases. Among them are tuberosclerosis, neurofibromatosis, and nevoid idiocy—diseases in which mental deficiency is accompanied by skin lesions—and several forms of mental defect characterized by changes of bone structures.

There are also clinically recognizable defects caused by the presence of two similar genes, known as recessive genes, one from each parent. Since persons of blood relationship are more likely to carry similar genes, such defects occur more frequently among the offspring of consanguineous marriages than in the general population.

In the great majority of the recessive cases the parents themselves are normal, being merely carriers of the gene, or, in genetic terms, heterozygous for the gene. The defect is characteristically distributed among 25 percent of the sibs, and is sharply distinguishable. While such defects are on the whole rare, they include a number of specific diseases: amaurotic family idiocy, a progressive and fatal disease accompanied by blindness which, according to type, may show up in infancy, childhood, or adolescence; gargoylism, a disease characterized by mental deficiency and grotesque bone changes; phenylpyruvic idiocy, the result of an inborn error in metabolism of an amino acid; hepatolenticular degeneration, a progressive form of mental deterioration caused by degeneration of nuclei at the base of the brain; and some forms of diffuse sclerosis, also a progressive disorder causing brain damage.

ENVIRONMENT-PRODUCED DEFECTS

A large but not yet clearly determined proportion of defectiveness comes from factors outside the hereditary constitution including infections, trauma, poison, glandular disorders, and physical or emotional deprivation. Rough estimates, based on unpublished data from a number of institutions, indicate that such factors may account for at least half of the mentally retarded population in the country.

Infection

Brain damage resulting from infection from the nervous system may occur in the womb or during infancy or childhood. The type of infectious agent, the severity of its attack, and the age of the child when attacked determine the degree of damage.

One of the most prevalent of such infections used to be syphilis, transmitted during gestation from an infected mother through the placenta to the fetus and resulting in brain damage to the fetus and later mental defect in the child. While syphilis still is responsible for a small percentage of all defectiveness, the proportion of infected children has already been reduced by venereal-disease control programs and undoubtedly will be further reduced in the future. Especially effective has been the increasing adoption of routine serological tests of pregnant women, prescribed by law in many States.

One form of severe mental deficiency comes from rubella infection (German measles) in the mother during the first 3 months of pregnancy. Besides the intellectual impairment resulting from fetal brain damage the rubella virus's attack on the fetus often produces congenital deafness, anomalies of the heart and eyes, and microcephaly (undersized head and brain).

Facts about the effects of other virus infections of the mother on the fetus are not so definitely established. It is possible that some other viruses may act in a manner similar to that of the rubella virus.

Brain fever is estimated to be responsible for the mental defects of 10 to 20 percent of all institutionalized defectives, according to Letchworth Village data. Caused by one of the encephalitis viruses or by a bacteria, such as the meningococcus of meningitis, it often strikes in infancy and childhood. While many children recover from it completely and others die, some recover with permanent impairments, the most common of which is mental defect. Measles, scarlet fever, chickenpox, whooping cough, influenza, and other communicable diseases common in childhood also occasionally leave brain damage.

Patients whose mental defectiveness has resulted from acute attacks of these diseases are usually referred to as post-encephalitics. The degree of mental defect among them varies considerably with the individuals. Many of them exhibit a peculiar behavior pattern marked by episodes of overactivity, restlessness, impulsiveness, assaultiveness, and wanton destruction.

Trauma

While accidents resulting in injury to the brain may sometimes occur in infancy or early childhood they are insignificant in comparison to injuries at birth or in the neonatal period as a cause of mental defect. Cerebral trauma during birth has been variously estimated to cause from 10 to 50 percent of all defectiveness. However, the incidence in institutionalized defectives does not seem to be above 20 percent. According to data gathered by the United Cerebral Palsy Fund, from one-half to two-thirds of the children in the general population showing evidence of birth injury are not mentally defective.

Difficult labor and prematurity are the most frequent causes of brain damage during birth, the former because of the risk of mechanical injury and the latter because of the immaturity of the brain. An immature brain is more prone to damage.

Brain damage at birth comes either by asphyxia or by hemorrhage. Asphyxia, which must be present for a relatively long period to produce irreversible damage, may result from premature separation of the placenta, cord complication, overdosage of the mother with analgesic drugs, or delayed breathing by the newborn. Hemorrhage, which may be within the brain or its envelopes, comes from direct injury during delivery—by forceps, or by a tearing of the tentorium, one of the membranes of the brain, in compression of the head during its passage through the pelvic canal.

Toxic causes

Little is known about the effects of toxic factors transmitted from mother to fetus during pregnancy, but evidence exists for suspicion that there are several ways in which fetal poisoning, resulting in malformation and mental defectiveness, may occur. Eclampsia, a severe intoxication of obscure origin suffered by some pregnant and delivering women, may affect the child detrimentally. Some toxic drugs taken by a pregnant woman may also damage the fetus but what these are and how great the dosage must be to be damaging are still mysteries.

X-rays, on the other hand, are definitely known to be damaging to the developing central nervous system. Several cases are on record of mothers who after receiving deep X-ray therapy to the abdominal region during pregnancy have produced microcephalic children or children with other congenital abnormalities, including mental defect. However, improved knowledge of the effects of X-rays has resulted in the routine testing of women of child-bearing age for pregnancy before radiation, and thus in the reduction of defects from this cause.

Blood incompatibility between mother and child also has a toxic effect upon the child. This comes about most frequently as a result of the Rh factor, an entity present in the blood of about 85 percent of the population, but absent in the other 15 percent. When an Rh-negative mother (whose blood possesses no Rh factor) carries an Rh-positive baby, toxic substances develop which may cause damage to the fetal blood, liver, and brain. However, this condition is responsible for less than 1 percent of low-grade spastic defectives, as fortunately only 5 percent of Rh-positive children of Rh-negative mothers develop the disease, while some who do develop it recover completely.

Mongolism, or mongoloid idiocy, a condition with a characteristic physical appearance, may also be toxic in origin, although little is definitely known about its etiology. Some authorities believe that the condition appears in the fetus before the third month of pregnancy as a consequence of a variety of toxic conditions inherent in the mother and associated with advanced age, endocrine disorders, or pathological lesions of the uterus. Mongoloids comprise about 5 to 10 percent of all defectives. Their IQ usually runs between 15 and 40. Because these children are prone to infection, they have a higher mortality rate than other defective children.

Endocrine disorders

While a certain percentage of mental defectives suffer from some glandular dysfunction, the proportion of defectiveness caused only by endocrine disorders is small. Cretinism is a form of mental defect definitely traceable to hypothyroidism or impaired function of the thyroid gland, either because of its lack of development or early destruction. This disease, which is also distinguishable by physical appearance, is endemic in areas where goiter is also prevalent, but it also occurs sporadically elsewhere. Dysfunction of the pituitary gland also causes mental defect, the most common type, Frölich's syndrome, being characterized by obesity, underdeveloped genitalia, and mild intellectual impairment.

Deprivation

Emotional deprivation, frustrations, and insecurity may not only bring about a condition among normal children resembling mental defect but may cause incorrect estimate of the intellectual abilities of high-grade defectives, especially those also physically handicapped. Pseudo-feeblemindedness is produced in normal children so deprived by an emotional blocking which responds to psychiatric treatment.

The most severe form of pseudo-feeblemindedness, infantile autism, is dramatic, if rare, evidence of the importance of emotional factors in the development of intelligence. Children so affected behave like idiots, do not talk, respond to stimuli, nor engage in any activity requiring intelligence, even though their intellectual capacity may be normal or better than average. Psychiatric examination shows that their apparent defect is a form of withdrawal.

The classical case of Kaspar Hauser exemplified the degree to which deprivation of the means of learning could impair intellectual development. Such extreme cases are not likely to occur today. Nevertheless, deprivation of cultural stimulation in some isolated communities still plays a role in producing the apparent low level of intelligence among the populace. More tragic are the effects of such deprivation on patients with disabilities interfering with academic learning. False diagnoses of feeblemindedness too often occur among children whose only impairments are in hearing, reading ability, word comprehension, minor motor handicaps, or other disabilities. In these children emotional factors are undoubtedly also contributing to the picture of apparent intellectual defeat.

THE INDIVIDUAL

In spite of the growing knowledge of the causes of mental defects few specifics are available for their treatment or prevention. As the foregoing shows, mental retardation is not an entity itself, but a characteristic of a variety of conditions, each with a different cause. Moreover, in each form there is a wide range of intellectual ability.

Prevention for some forms may lie only within the scope of eugenic measures, though more scientific knowledge in the field of human genetics would be required before such could be confidently prescribed.

Greater possibilities for preventing the exogenous forms through medical and public-health measures may be expected to be realized as knowledge of intrauterine life and development increases.

While treatment in the strict medical sense can be applied only to a small number of mentally defective individuals, in the broader sense of care and training it can be applied to all. But such a wide variation of conditions exists among children with mental defects that what kind of care and treatment each receives must be determined individually in line with a prognosis based on an accurate diagnosis of the case. While the goal can rarely be cure, it can almost always be improvement or the achievement of the maximum intellectual and social functioning of which the individual is capable.

23 *Conditions productive of superior children*

Related selections: 20, 21, 24, 34

*Is talent a rare natural resource simply to be discovered and uti-
lized, or is it a characteristic that may be developed through "social
engineering"? In this selection Havighurst suggests ways in which
our society, through its schools, can increase the supply of persons
of superior ability.*

Children become mentally superior through a combination of being born with
superior potential and being raised in a superior environment. Nobody knows
the relative importance of these two factors. Certainly, biological intelligence
is too low in some children to permit them to develop even average mental
ability. Probably a severe environmental handicap can prevent the potentially
most able child from showing more than average mental ability.

It seems probable that our society actually discovers and develops no more
than perhaps half its potential intellectual talent. Some evidence for this statement lies in the fact that former immigrant groups, which at one time did the
heavy labor of America, at first produced very few mentally superior children;
but after a sojourn in this country of two or three generations, they have produced large numbers of mentally superior people. They did this through better-
ing the environment in which they reared their children. The same process is
now going on in the underprivileged groups of today—the Negroes, the Puerto
Ricans, the rural southern whites—as they secure better economic conditions
and then create a more favorable environment for the mental development of
their children.

There is some validity to a view of the production of mentally superior people
as a *processing* of human material. Some of this material is of better biological
quality than other parts of it, but it all depends heavily on social processing for
the quality of the final product.

In this paper we shall deliberately ignore the biological element in the pro-

ROBERT J. HAVIGHURST, "Conditions Productive of Superior Children,"
Teachers College Record, 62 (April, 1961), 524–31. Reprinted by permission of the publisher and the author.

DR. HAVIGHURST (1900–   ) has been Professor of Education at the University of Chicago since 1941. In 1956–58 he was Co-director of the Brazilian
Government Center for Educational Research. His professional interests
include the fields of psychology, sociology, gerontology, juvenile delinquency, and child development.

TABLE 1

Efficiencies of the various social classes in producing
children in the top and bottom quarters of IQ distribution

Sixth Grade in River City

Social class	Percentage distribution of children	Efficiency ratio[1] in producing children in	
		Top quarter	Bottom quarter
Upper and upper middle	10	1.8	.4
Lower middle	27	1.5	.6
Upper lower	39	.8	1.1
Lower lower	24	.4	1.6

[1] These ratios indicate the relative efficiencies of the various social classes. If all classes were equally efficient in producing children of a given quartile in IQ, the ratios would all be 1.

duction of mentally superior children and consider only the cultivation of mental superiority through the family, the school, and the community. We shall try to answer the question: What kind of social environment produces mentally superior children most efficiently, and how can we expand this environment and make it more effective?

SOCIAL CLASS AND CITIES

Mentally superior children come in relatively high proportions from upper and upper-middle class families and in relatively lower proportions from lower working class families. This fact has been affirmed in dozens of studies of the relations between IQ and socio-economic status.

Some idea of the relative efficiencies of the various social classes in processing their children for mental ability is given in Table 1, which comes from a study of all the children in the sixth grade of the public schools of a medium-sized midwestern city. The upper and upper-middle classes, combined, produced 1.8 times as many children in the upper quarter of the IQ distribution as they would if all social classes had been equally efficient at this, and only .4 times as many children in the lowest quarter. The lower working class showed a reversal of these efficiency ratios.

If all four socio-economic groups had been as efficient as the upper and upper-middle class groups in providing children with IQ's in the top quarter (above about 110), there would have been 180 children with IQ's over 110 in this community for every 100 such children today. In other words, the numbers of mentally superior children would have been almost doubled, and the intelligence level of the child population would have been lifted enormously.

Similar conclusions arise from a study of high school seniors in a city of 500,000. Roughly 5 per cent of the seniors were selected by a systematic screening program as being "academically superior." As can be seen in Table 2, the various high schools contributed to this total in rough proportion to the socio-economic status of the parents. The school with highest socio-economic status contributed 19 per cent of its seniors to the select group. Within this group, 92 per cent of the fathers were high school graduates; 65 per cent were college graduates. The three schools with lowest socio-economic status contributed 1.5 per cent of their seniors to the select group. Less than 40 per cent of the fathers of the superior students in these three schools were high school graduates. If all schools had contributed as efficiently as School A to the production of superior students, there would have been 532 instead of 194, or almost three times as many. Probably the reason this proportion is higher than the proportion reported in Table 1 is that Table 1 refers to sixth graders, Table 2 to twelfth graders. The cultural advantages of the higher status children probably cumulated between the sixth and twelfth grades to give them even greater superiority over their less privileged age-mates.

Granted the assumption we are making in this paper—that mental superiority is largely a product of social environment—the mental level of the population would be raised very greatly if we could give all children the kinds of social environment which upper-middle class children have today.

Mentally superior children also tend to come from urban and suburban communities, rather than from rural communities. This is not as pronounced an effect as the social class effect, but it seems to indicate that the urban-suburban environment is more stimulating mentally than the rural environment.

Within the families lower on the socio-economic scale, there is enough production of mentally superior youth to indicate that socio-economic status alone

TABLE 2

Efficiencies of schools of various socio-economic levels in producing academically superior high school seniors

Data from an American city of 500,000 population

| | High School | | | | | | |
	A	B	C	D	E	FGH	Total
No. of graduates	412	392	325	71	400	1,203	2,803
No. of superior students in graduating class	77	45	30	5	17	20	194
Per cent of Per cent of superior students	19	12	9	7	4	1.5	5.1
Rank in socio-economic status	1	2	3	4	5	7	
No. of superior students if *A* ratio prevailed	77	74	62	14	76	229	532

is not what makes the difference between a good and poor environment for mental growth. It is probably certain cultural and motivational deprivations that often go with low socio-economic status that reduce the efficiency of lower status families. Whenever a very bright boy or girl is discovered in a family of low economic status, it turns out that this family has unusual characteristics which give the youth an advantage. These characteristics may consist of thrift and ambition or of an interest on the part of the mother or father in literature, art, or science.

Summing up the argument thus far, it seems that boys and girls who are mentally superior have become so because of (1) a home and school environment which stimulated them to learn and to enjoy learning; (2) parents and other significant persons who set examples of interest and attainment in education which the children unconsciously imitated, and (3) early family training which produced a desire for achievement in the child. When these influences act upon a child with average or better biological equipment for learning, the child will become mentally superior. They are sometimes found in unexpected places.

For instance, Paul is a very good student in high school. His mother has worked as a waitress for years, since her husband deserted her, to support herself and Paul. She placed Paul in a boys' home sponsored by a church, and he has lived there from the age of 8 until his present age of 18. He says, "My father and mother never went to college. I thought I'd like to do better in life than they did." At the boys' home, the superintendent and the teachers were demanding but warm. Under them, Paul performed well in the elementary school until time for senior high, when he went to the local public school. Here he had some difficulty at first. He says, "English was about my worst subject. The teacher helped me though, and I improved a lot. I consider her an important person in my life." A careers unit in civics helped him to decide on engineering or mathematics, and he will go to college with scholarship help. Two of his closest friends have college plans. The superintendent of the home has urged him to go. "He told me to go to college. He said I was a good student, and I ought to go to college."

DIVERGENT THINKERS

Among the mentally superior part of the population some people are creative and some are not. Much attention has been paid recently to the quality or qualities of creativity on the assumptions that our society needs not only intellectually facile people but, more especially, creative people, and that a high IQ does not guarantee creativity.

Guilford and others have made a distinction between "convergent thinking" and "divergent thinking." The person with "convergent" intellectual ability is retentive and docile. He tends to seek the single, predetermined "correct" answer to an intellectual problem. On the other hand, the "divergent" thinker is constructive and creative. He tends to seek the novel, experimental, and multiple answer to an intellectual problem.

Guilford has devised a number of tests of creative intelligence which have only a low positive correlation with the usual intelligence tests. Getzels and Jackson, using these tests, picked out a group of high school pupils who were high in IQ (average 150) but not especially high in creative thinking for comparison with a group high in creative thinking but lower in IQ (average 127). The two groups did equally well in achievement tests, but the high intelligence, non-creative group were preferred by their teachers as the kind of students they liked to have in their classes. The high creative group, in freely-written stories, showed more humor, more unexpected endings, more incongruities, and generally a freer play of fantasy. Similarly, Cattell and Drevdahl compared outstanding research scientists with outstanding teachers and administrators in the same fields on the 16 P.F. Personality Inventory. They found the researchers to be more self-sufficient and schizothymic (introverted), to have a greater drive for mastery, and to entertain more radical ideas.

We know relatively little, as yet, about creative people and even less about what makes them creative. If it proves to be true that some or all of the qualities of creativity can be taught, this will become another goal in the society's processing of mentally superior children.

THE UNDER-ACHIEVERS

In the study of the intellectually superior children, attention has been called to a substantial group whose educational performance falls below what might reasonably be expected from their performance on intelligence tests. These mentally superior under-achievers are people with biological or environmental superiority who have not put their superiority to use in school. They may be regarded as products of an inadequate processing in the home, the community, or the school. This conclusion emerges from a number of recent studies of bright under-achievers.

Thus, Terman and Oden, in their study of adults whom they had followed from childhood as gifted children, compared the 150 men in their sample who had been most successful in their occupations with the 150 least successful men. As children, these men had all had IQ's of 135 or higher. The more successful group had had an average IQ of 155 in 1922, while the less successful had had an average of 150. However, there were considerable differences in other respects between the two groups. Ninety per cent of the more successful had been graduated from college, compared with 37 per cent of the less successful. Fifty per cent of the fathers of the more successful group were college graduates, compared with only 16 per cent of the fathers of the less successful. In occupation, 38 per cent of the fathers of the more successful were professional men, compared with 19 per cent of the fathers of the less successful.

Terman concludes, "Where all are so intelligent, it follows necessarily that differences in success must be due largely to non-intellectual factors"; and "Everything considered, there is nothing in which the (more successful and less successful) groups present a greater contrast than in drive to achieve and in all-round social adjustment. . . . At any rate, we have seen that intellect and achievement are far from perfectly correlated."

Most of the studies of under-achievement have been made on boys rather than girls, because bright boys are under-achievers in school much more frequently than girls are. The many studies have produced substantially similar results and point to under-achievement as a form of personal and social maladjustment. In one or another of these studies, the following characteristics of under-achieving able students appear:

1. They see themselves as inadequate persons.
2. They have lower aspirations than achievers.
3. They do not like school as well as achievers do.
4. They do not enjoy learning from books.
5. They have lower popularity and leadership status in the eyes of their age-mates.
6. They tend to come from homes that are broken or emotionally inadequate in other ways.
7. They tend to come from homes of low socio-economic status.
8. Their vocational goals are not as clearly defined as those of achievers.
9. Their study habits are not as good as those of achievers.
10. They have narrower interests than those of achievers.
11. They have poorer personal adjustment than that of achievers.

Haggard, comparing high with low achieving high IQ children, found that the high achievers had better mental health. In particular, the high achievers in arithmetic "had by far the best-developed and healthiest egos, both in relation to their own emotions and mental processes and in their greater maturity in dealing with the outside world of people and things." Haggard concluded, "Our findings indicate that the best way to produce clear thinking is to help children develop into anxiety-free, emotionally healthy individuals who are also trained to master a variety of intellectual tasks."

Much the same conclusion is expressed by Gowan after reviewing a number of studies of under-achievement. He says, "To summarize, achievement is an indication that the individual has successfully transferred a large enough portion of his basic libidinal drives to areas of cultural accomplishment so that he derives a significant portion of his gratification from them."

Although the general proposition seems justified that high IQ under-achievers are people with inadequate socialization and poor personal-social adjustment, there are two major exceptions to this generalization. One exception refers to a group of high IQ boys with a limited horizon. They are well adjusted within a small world which does not require more than average school achievement and does not require a college education. Take Kenny, for example. With an IQ of

145, Kenny found school work easy and more or less coasted through his studies, doing enough work to get fairly good grades, but falling down somewhat in high school, where he graduated at about the middle of his class. Kenny's parents were earnest people, good church members, with little formal education. They did not read very much and had no intellectual interests. They were satisfied with Kenny's report cards and pleased that he was going further in school than they had gone. They were especially pleased with Kenny's interest in earning money. He always had several jobs waiting for him and showed great enterprise as a salesman. During his later years in high school, he worked in a shoe store where his employer was so pleased with his work that he offered Kenny a full-time job and a chance to buy into his business when he was graduated from high school. This seemed good to Kenny, and he is now getting along well as junior partner in the store.

The other exception refers to a rather large group of girls with high intelligence who achieve very well up to the end of high school, when their grades fall off and they show little or no interest in going to college. These girls either get married as soon as they finish high school or they take a job in an office or a shop for a few years until they marry. Girls do not generally show as under-achievers because their school grades are pretty well maintained until the end of high school. But they would be called under-achievers if under-achievement were defined as failure to go as far in education as one's abilities would justify.

With this broad definition of under-achievement, one can say that the gifted under-achievers have not been effectively processed by the society for maximal or optimal educational achievement for one or more of the following reasons:

> Inadequate home environment leaves them personally maladjusted and unable to use their intellectual ability.
>
> Inadequate home environment limits their horizon and fails to stimulate them to use education for vocational achievement, although they are personally well adjusted.
>
> Inadequate home environment fails to instill in them a deep drive or need for achievement.
>
> School and home together fail to instill in them an intrinsic love of learning.
>
> The social role of wife and mother is seen by some girls as more important than that of student; and the home, school, and community have caused them to see a conflict between marriage and a home, on the one hand, and continued educational achievement on the other.

INCREASING THE SUPPLY

Holding to our tentative assumption that production of mentally superior people is more a matter of social engineering than of discovery and exploitation of a rare natural resource, we may essay an answer to the question of how to in crease the supply of mentally superior children who are well motivated to achieve in school and college.

First, it must be remembered that our culturally deprived families, both in the big cities and in isolated rural areas, have always in the past improved themselves as producers of superior children when they had economic opportunity. The same process of improvement is evident today among working class Negroes, Puerto Ricans, and white emigrants from the rural South. It is to these groups that we may look for an increased supply of able youngsters, and the rate of increase is likely to be considerably facilitated by increasing their degree of economic opportunity and enriching their cultural environment. This point is a central one for those social policies related to our long-range needs for man-power and for school programs aimed at the underprivileged and academically impoverished. Within the schools, there is a grave need for greater attention to rewards for achievement within these groups, for a keener recognition of developing intellectual effort, and for a greater responsiveness to embryonic academic motives.

Second, counseling and guidance services could usefully focus on increasing educational motivation among superior pupils. The well adjusted child with limited horizons, like Kenny, represents a kind of national loss. If education is concerned with the actualizing of individual potentialities, then special attention to youngsters of this kind is more than warranted. A sound argument can be made for the school counselor's devoting more of his time to this sort of developmental enterprise than to the remediation of "problem cases" and to the support of the pathological, the delinquent, and the dull. Both kinds of service are desirable and necessary, of course; but we may have overemphasized the guidance worker's obligation to the educationally handicapped to the serious neglect, both in training and in on-the-job functioning, of his potentialities for working productively with the superior child with low academic motivation.

Third, studies of the unconscious drive for achievement, like those by McClelland and Rosen, indicate that the early training of boys in the home has a great deal to do with their motivation to use their mental ability for school achievement. Closer collaboration between school and home, especially with lower class parent groups, can be helpful here. Even more, an explicit and articulate concern with the development of intellectual motivations in the earliest school years could possibly harvest a more widespread drive for academic achievement and a deeper channeling of intellectual capacities into school work and the kinds of goals that our schools and colleges represent. It is not so much that boys lack a need to achieve, but they often find little reward in harnessing their motives to the activities of the conventional classroom or school.

Fourth, the demonstration that intellectually superior and "creative" abilities are not the same thing suggests that we could profitably expand our search for the gifted to include the "divergent thinker." More clarity and precision in our methods of identifying creative youngsters with above-average but not extremely high IQ's, and more imagination and effort in our attention to such children might yield a happy increment in the numbers of those able to think inventively about important problems. This approach requires, of course, that we reward the innovator, the person with new and deviant ways of dealing with the world; and while this requirement is one to which we all pay lip service, it is one that is likely to entail trouble and inconvenience if it is realistically met. That the trouble and inconvenience will be worth the result is highly probable, but the result hardly alters, although it may more than justify, the cost.

Finally, the most potent means of increasing the numbers of mentally superior children that lies at hand for teachers is to teach so that learning is made more attractive to children. This alone will cause children to increase their own mental abilities. For example, the experiment in Manhattanville Junior High School and the George Washington Senior High School in New York City is having this effect. Boys and girls from culturally deprived families are getting an enriched program, combined with guidance and attempts to improve the home environment. This program has kept pupils in school longer, and there has been a measurable increase in IQ points for these children as they have progressed from the sixth to the ninth grades.

24 Opportunities for creativity in education for exceptional children

Related selections: 20, 23, 25, 26, 59

In the past decade the schools of America have been under great pressures to "do something about" the gifted or superior student. In most cases the resultant actions taken by the schools may be classified as enrichment, acceleration, more rapid coverage of content, or increase in subject matter difficulty. As one person has stated, we have poured old wine into new bottles. More recently, we have begun to seriously examine the nature of creativity and the means by which it may be developed in the classroom. This selection and the two that follow cover substantially the same topic, but each has a different emphasis. They should be read as a group. In se-

HILDA TABA, "Opportunities for Creativity in Education for Exceptional Children," *Exceptional Children*, 29 (February, 1963), 247–56. Reprinted by permission of the author and the publisher.

DR. TABA (1902–), Professor of Education at San Francisco State College, has made many contributions to the field of curriculum development.

*lection 24, Taba examines the nature of creativity and the blocks
to its development; Torrance describes, in selection 25, his research
on the identification and development of creative thinking in the
early school years; and selection 26 by Eisner summarizes some of
the significant findings from the research on creativity.*

Creativity is a fashionable word today and its application to education is stressed
in many contexts. The adoption of a theme or word as a slogan is a phenomenon
of American education. Certain phrases will be repeated throughout the educational literature and convention speeches for a period of time, only to be replaced with new ones within about five years. This fate has overtaken many
slogans, such as Activity Programs, Experience Learning, and Project Method.

The dynamics of this phenomenon seem to be produced by the premature
conversion of an idea into a program without sufficient study of its meaning or
educational implications. This method usually produces crash programs, which
inevitably amount to pouring old wine into new bottles, merely giving existing
programs a new name.

The idea of creativity and the interest in programs for implementing it are in
this danger today. The danger is accentuated by the present trend in educational
thought and practice toward two opposite and perhaps even conflicting emphases.
On the one hand, we are concerned with autonomy of thinking, creativity, and
skills of productive inquiry. On the other, there is much enthusiasm for mechanization of learning and teaching, as illustrated by the spread of teaching machines, team teaching, and programmed learning. Both of these concerns represent a direct translation of social needs, pressures, and research into teaching
programs, without the necessary analysis of the exact nature of these needs,
pressures, and ideas and their proper place in educational planning.

Hersey summarizes the situation as follows: "School systems all over the
country, sensitive to fierce pressure from our society for technicians and experts
of every kind, are rushing headlong into programs to produce highly efficient,
useful, skilled, dependable, ready-made cogs for a scientific economy. . . . But
the job of freeing talent does not lend itself to this kind of attack. . . . The danger
is that a 'crash-program' approach to the problem of our country's needs for
talent may (a) not release talent, and (b) therefore produce disappointment
and revulsion which would cause the pendulum to swing away from special help
for the potentially talented."

UNDERSTANDING THE PROCESS

Translating what we know about creativity into educational practice requires a
clear analysis of what creativity is as a process and how it is or can be generated
and developed. It is, for example, impossible to develop a sound program for
creativity in general. One can do this only when the mental processes which

compose creativity are more or less understood. It is possible that today the definitions of creativity are not yet sufficiently clear to permit sound educational implementation.

Examination of the literature on education of the gifted suggests that old wine is being poured into new bottles. An exciting and promising description of creativity is presented, for example, in the opening chapters of recent books on programs for the gifted. But the goals and specific programs which follow do not fulfill this promise. The proposals simmer down to enrichment, often defined as offering a bit more on the same subjects, and acceleration, or covering the same curriculum more rapidly. As one proceeds from the statement of the potentialities of gifted students to statements on implementation of any sort, there appears a sort of reductionism toward the commonplace. The sharp edge of the new idea is somehow lost, and traditional curriculum and instructional practices are left intact. Essentially the same kind of mental processes are cultivated. The danger in such reductionism is that inevitably it leads to disillusionment and eventual discarding of the idea.

The meaning and implications of the idea of creativity must be examined before any actual program building takes place. Research findings must be translated into an educational approach which is adequate to developing creativity. Today such an approach is feasible, because research on creativity is being conducted on a rather wide scale and some findings have clear-cut implications for curriculum and instruction. A careful study of this research makes it possible to evolve programs for creativity which go beyond the sloganized crash versions.

In what follows, three questions regarding creativity will be discussed:

1. What does research in education and other areas say that might throw light on the nature of creativity or talent and how it can be kindled and developed?

2. What are the blocks that hinder the development of creativity, such as blocks inherent in our conception of the behavior of human beings or of the ways in which they learn?

3. What suggestions for educational programs for creativity do the answers to the above questions yield?

The discussion will also be focused largely on creativity in the cognitive realm, because artistic creativity still eludes analysis.

WHAT IS CREATIVITY?

We have been concerned with creativity for a long time, but have always conceived it to be a mysterious, spontaneous process which not only cannot be analyzed but is likely to be destroyed by analysis. This was the attitude expressed at a meeting at Lincoln School twenty-five years ago, when creativity was a very high-order business in education. The meeting was called by the evaluation staff of the Eight Year Study in an effort to analyze the objectives of creativity, in order to develop some instruments of evaluation. The school staff practically enacted a sit-down strike because they believed that taking apart the process of creativity would be a sure sign of destroying it. This attitude still prevails among a great many people engaged in teaching some form of the creative process.

Studies of creativity today, fortunately, are breaking through such barriers. Researchers in this field speak of creativity first as a potentiality which all people possess, but to different degrees. The educational task, then, is both to discover and to develop it. Second, creativity is more than a manifestation of unique talent, as that of a gifted musician or artist, who is creatively productive almost in spite of what or how he is taught. Third, it is possible to develop creativity by providing conditions which stimulate and nurture it. Fourth, there is fair evidence to the effect that creativity can be expressed in cognitive process and that, in turn, even so-called artistic creation presupposes cognitive acts.

These concepts open the way to planning educational strategies which are designed to cultivate the natural creative potentialities instead of depending on permissiveness alone to bring to fruition a natural inclination.

Psychological and anthropological literature suggest that not only have we failed to find the key to open the way for a richer actualization of creative potentiality in all human beings, but that also both our culture and our schools limit the manifestations of creativity by demanding conformity and rejecting deviations from the norm.

I was startled into a realization of the extent to which cultural setting circumscribes the realization of human potentiality at a recent conference on the Control of the Mind. In speaking of human potentialities Aldous Huxley asked the following question: "What would have happened to a child with an IQ equal to that of Isaac Newton if he had been born in a family of Upper Paleolithic cave dwellers 15 or 20 thousand years ago? The biologists assure us that there has been extremely little biological change in human beings since that time; the native equipment of such a child was probably just as good as it is today, but what possibilities would he have had for realizing his potentialities? The answer is that he would have had incredibly small possibilities, that in the very nature of things he would never have become more than a food gatherer or a hunter, which is what his whole culture was based upon. . . . He could have never gone beyond the narrow horizons which the cave dwellers were capable of seeing."

In a way every culture imposes a narrowing of horizon by its socializing processes and manner in which it conditions the ways of thinking. All of us are cave dwellers in the sense that our culture limits our vision. Yet we are also fortunate in that we can develop educational programs designed as a countervailing force to cultural conditioning. Through education we can open up a crack in the horizon set by the culture and cultivate the growing edge, whether of creativity or any other capacity. For education to have this power it is necessary to examine the studies of creativity to discover what there is in substance that could be translated into instructional strategy.

CHARACTERISTICS OF CREATIVE INDIVIDUALS

Creativity has been studied intensively only since about 1950. Generally speaking, the studies of creativity are of three kinds: (a) studies of the characteristics of creative persons, (b) studies of creative products, and (c) studies of the structure and dynamics of cognitive processes. Most extensive are the studies of the characteristics of successful creators who have produced something that their peers recognize as an outstanding achievement. These studies have yielded a long list of qualities that accompany successful creative production.

Creative individuals are supposed to have a high theoretical and aesthetic interest; they have an openness to inner experience; they don't reduce experience immediately into slogans, stereotyped symbols, and pat formulas; they respond to their own inner experience and create something with it. They have a high level of perception and an ability to play with elements and concepts. This approach to creativity provides us certain cues but, for educational purposes, it has definite limitations.

Most of these personality descriptions are too general to be helpful in building an educational program. These characteristics represent what some psychologists describe as psychological features of creativity. However, no matter what we know about the personality characteristics of creative individuals, educationally this knowledge leaves us in a wrong stance. It leaves us with an assumption that creativity is something that is given: one either has it or does not have it, and little can be done about developing it.

Correspondence between personality characteristics and creative achievement also leaves us in the dark about how individuals came by their characteristics or their creative capacity. Neither are these correspondences predictive. Many creative individuals are not aesthetically inclined. Superior intelligence does not inevitably lead to creative thinking. Openness to inner life, a high level of perception, and the ability to establish relationships are shared by many persons besides those who end up as successful creators.

However, the ability to play with concepts and elements of experience to form hypotheses, to translate ideas from one into another is more suggestive for educational strategy. A person can be taught to go beyond absorbing information, to break out of the mold, to discover new ideas, or to formulate novel hypotheses.

Furthermore, while adult creativity can be assessed in terms of the originality and social value of the product, such a yardstick cannot be applied to children, except perhaps to prodigies. Children can be creative even when their products are a repetition of what has already been thought or created.

STUDIES OF THE STRUCTURE OF COGNITION

Studies of the structure and development of cognitive processes are helpful in developing an understanding of creativity in the cognitive realm. Guilford, for example, suggests that thought and intelligence are not one unitary thing, but are composed of multiple abilities which can be grouped into what one might call styles of thinking or types of mental operations. Among the five main groups of abilities that he describes, two have particular bearing on understanding creativity.

One is convergent thinking, the tendency to seek known or predetermined answers by known or predetermined processes. Such thinking is encouraged when children are asked to name or to locate the important rivers of an area without revealing the criteria of importance. Inevitably, under school conditions, the importance is determined by the conventional criterion of length. The same effect prevails when instruction and testing concentrate on determining *the* cause of the Civil War or *the* classification of foods by their nutritional qualities, disregarding the fact that one can classify foods in several different ways depending on what differences and similarities are important or what the purpose for classification is. In our classrooms, children are not encouraged and often not even permitted to explore new ways of asking questions or of relating and interpreting facts.

Units are often developed in a convergent mode, such as proceeding from one form of transportation to another, and overlooking other dimensions of the topic of transportation, such as the relationship between the speed of transportation and the availability of goods.

This does not mean, of course, that there are not many problems and learning tasks which require convergent thinking. The danger lies in the dominance of this style of thinking in teaching and learning, because it cultivates an essentially non-creative approach to knowledge and a belief that all questions have specific predetermined answers.

The response by a group of sixth graders who were discussing why the Incas did not invent the wheel illustrates the consequences of an over-emphasis on convergent thinking. After an unsuccessful attempt to find an answer in the books the class asked the teacher. The teacher said that the reasons she knew were no better than "educated guesses," and that, furthermore, whatever they found in books was at best an "educated guess" also. The class, used to highly convergent thinking, was quite upset to discover that there are questions to which we have no sure answers. The imprint of conditioning to convergent thinking was already well enough established to make open-endedness an uncomfortable intellectual stance. This behavior is in sharp contrast to the behavior of younger children, who are curious, experimental, and a good deal more autonomous.

The contrasting mode of thinking is what Guilford calls divergent thinking. It involves reaching toward novelty, showing fluidity with association, words, and ideas, such as combining qualities and events that ordinarily do not occur together, showing flexibility in changing classes of objects, and probing new dimensions of problems.

Divergence may be simply a culturally unconditioned way of looking at the world, as illustrated in Getzels' story of a young child who, looking at a pool of oil spilled on wet pavement, says, "Oh, Mommy, see a rainbow in the gutter." In contrast, the mother's convergent answer is, "That's not a rainbow, that's a dirty oil slick."

Many aspects of divergent thinking, such as fluidity of ideas and unconventional solutions, are also aspects of creativity. For this reason, divergent thinking is often identified with creativity. This is misleading, for creativity transcends sheer inventiveness and originality to reach a new synthesis.

STUDIES OF THE DEVELOPMENT OF INTELLIGENCE

Studies of the development of intelligence by the Geneva School are another source of workable ideas about creativity in the cognitive realm. While Piaget has been writing since 1930, he was not widely recognized before the recent studies of cognitive processes began to quote him with reverence akin to that accorded Freud.

A few ideas from Piaget's rather complicated theoretical structure of mental development are relevant to thinking about creativity.

One is that the development of intelligence and of all cognitive operations is essentially an active transaction between the child and his environment. Essentially, the child keeps on "making" his mind or "creating" the conceptual structures with which his mind works. The child continually forms certain ways of organizing what he perceives into conceptual schemes, which in turn alter his way of perceiving at the next encounter with environment. Intelligence is not only what transpires in the child, nor is it exclusively experiential stimulus, but the transaction between the two. Each new experience is fitted into whatever organizing conceptual scheme is available. This is the process of assimilation. By the time children appear in school they have developed a whole repertoire of concepts which give meaning and organization to what they experience in school.

ASSIMILATION AND ACCOMMODATION

Whenever the child encounters phenomena which do not fit his existing schemata of concepts, an alteration or extension of the conceptual scheme takes place. This phenomenon Piaget calls "accommodation." Suchman's experiments in inquiry training illustrate the functioning of assimilation and accommodation. In one of these experiments a film shows what looks like a metal blade, but is actually a bi-metallic strip in which two metals of different expansion rates are welded together. When the blade is put over the flame, it bends. On seeing this, the children at first perceive the metal strip as a knife. The blade bends as a knife would when the metal softens from heat. The children organize and interpret what they see in the light of what they know about knives. In other words, they "assimilate" the phenomenon into their current conceptual framework and expect the blade to behave like a knife.

However, when the blade is turned around and heated again, it bends in the other direction. This phenomenon does not fit the conception of a knife. Therefore the children have to change their concepts to explain this new behavior of the blade. In other words, they must *accommodate* their conceptual structure to encompass the phenomenon which does not fit their current scheme.

These two mental operations, assimilation and accommodation, suggest several points for the development of creativity. One can help children to develop consciously a sequential order or hierarchy of concepts with which they can interpret experience and which organize the processing of what otherwise would be only fragments of knowledge. To enlarge the conceptual schemata, curriculum and teaching need to provide systematically experiences which force students to expand their concepts in order to accommodate new experience. This differs from "giving" children new concepts, principles, or names for classes.

The analysis of tapescripts of classroom proceedings, secured in connection with the study of thinking in elementary school children being conducted by the author, shows clearly the crippling effects of "giving" children what they should evolve themselves: a basis for classification and grouping, a generalization, a distinction between different aspects of an event, object, or a phenomenon.* In an effort to "promote" the right" answer, teachers tend to short-cut the processes of exploration which are the necessary prerequisite to making an accommodation and discovery, and thereby deprive students of an opportunity for autonomous or creative thinking.

There is also a sequence in the development of cognitive skills. Each step in this sequence should be a prelude to the next step, because it is a prerequisite to the next cognitive operation. For example, grouping or classifying requires discrimination among the properties or attributes of the phenomena being grouped, and a lack of precision in the lower level concepts prevents the possibility of forming more abstract concepts.

This problem of sequence in thought processes is illustrated in a sixth grade class attempting to classify a list of differences which they expected to find in Latin America. Among these were four items: weather, climate, altitude, and landscape. The class felt that these four items belonged together but they could not decide which way. Should weather be put under climate or vice-versa? How is landscape or altitude related either to climate or weather? Lack of precision in the concepts of climate, weather, and altitude created difficulty in grouping. Gradually the relationships, and therefore also the basis for grouping, began to emerge. Landscape could be described as altitude and altitude has something to do with climate, because the higher one goes the colder it is. This was followed by an observation that some places are high and warm, and others low and cold. The children were reaching greater precision in their concept of the relationship between altitude and climate.

---

* A Study of Thinking in Elementary School Children, supported by grant from the U.S. Office of Education, Department of Health, Education and Welfare. Hilda Taba, Director.

In developing teaching strategies to guide such a process, thinking must be regarded as a developmental process in which each new experience is a continuation of the preceding one and at the same time adds new possibilities. It is a continuous process, no matter what the content or level of the thought process may be.

Such skills as differentiating and abstracting elements of a concept and classifying information and ideas in several ways are powerful tools which are fundamental to productive and autonomous thought and at the same time transferable to new situations. In comparison, the knowledge of a scheme of classification is perishable and limited.

ELIMINATING BLOCKS TO CREATIVITY

There are also certain concepts and practices which hinder the development of creativity. Some recent writers have suggested that the concept of IQ as a static, unidimensional quality is one such barrier. In spite of a great deal of evidence regarding changes in the functioning of intelligence under changing experiential conditions, the concept persists of IQ as something which *is* and cannot be developed. Literature on culturally deprived children abounds in evidence regarding the effect of the amount and the nature of cultural stimulation on cognitive functioning. It is possible that many a student classified as mentally retarded is only culturally deprived.

The use of the IQ score as the chief basis for the identification of talent and giftedness has been criticized also. Several researchers have pointed out that intelligence tests are composed on the pattern of convergent thinking, do not accommodate divergence in cognitive functioning or cultural experience, and penalize the tendency to detect relationships other than commonplace or to follow an unconventional association pattern. Getzels and Jackson, for example, demonstrate that creativity and high IQ tend to correlate up to a certain point only. Torrance estimates this to be at about IQ 120. Evidently a certain level of intelligence is needed to be creative at all. Beyond that there is small correspondence between creativity and intelligence. Individuals who make the highest scores on IQ tests are not among the most creative, and those who are highest in creativity are not among the highest in intelligence, possibly because they tend to be too divergent. While Getzels and Jackson's study was confined to persons in the upper range of the IQ scale, the same conclusions were arrived at by Torrance, who replicated the study in the public schools.

Since intelligence tests require highly convergent thinking, it follows that by selecting students with high IQs for our programs for the gifted, we probably select only the highly convergent thinkers and eliminate the highly creative ones. This is disturbing and throws into question both the methods of identifying the gifted and the programs provided for them. In addition, it is possible that much talent goes undetected because the IQ tests are also non-functional for the culturally deviate.

Recent analysis postulates several sources of the functioning intelligence: (a) The native potential, which presumably exists in different measures in different individuals, but the upper limit of which is not known. According to Murphy, human potentialities are probably limitless. (b) The motivation. In whatever environment an individual functions, he is stimulated only by those elements which he selects to respond to. Different individuals respond to different things within the same environment. (c) The nature of the environmental stimulation. It is conceivable that some individuals with high capacity and a rich environment cannot make sufficient use of their environment because motivation and environment are mismatched. They cannot receive what they need from the environment.

These three factors of intelligence must be considered in combination in order to determine how the functioning of intelligence can be fostered.

OPPORTUNTIES FOR DEVELOPING CREATIVITY

The above ideas from research carry a number of implications for educational programs for creativity.

First, there is great danger in translating social needs or pressures directly into a program, without the intermediary step of a careful analysis of the processes of creative thinking. Without such analysis, which currently is only beginning, creativity is bound to be implemented by surface gadgets rather than integrated into a consistent and cumulative program that is different from the usual curriculum and is directly addressed to creativity. It seems something more is needed than enrichment, acceleration, sporadic exercises, and ability grouping.

Special exercises like brainstorming and asking questions such as, "What would happen in the United States if all the telephones suddenly went out of order?" may stimulate divergent thinking and surface originality, but can hardly contribute adequately to the development of creativity. Ability grouping is an administrative device, and may facilitate teaching in a uniform curriculum. The enrichment programs seem to be addressed more to rapid learning than to creativity, for usually they represent only an extension of the current curriculum. All these measures may even retard the development of an open-ended curriculum which is needed to develop creativity, by making it seemingly unnecessary to undertake the rather difficult job of basic curriculum revision.

To help children acquire the power of autonomous and creative thinking, we must analyze these processes, locate the elements that can be attained, and provide experiences for mastering them. Among the essential processes which underpin creativity is the ability to go beyond that which is given when interpreting data.

A still higher level of creativity is achieved when students learn to apply their knowledge in new situations. For example, students who have learned to explain light by the wave theory could be expected to explain sound by the same theory. This is achieved through the process of transfer, which puts at children's disposal a way of acquiring new knowledge or even creating it. Opportunities for acquiring these skills must be provided cumulatively throughout the curriculum; continuous stress is needed on stimulating hypothesizing, inference making, and applying knowledge to explain new phenomena. It is impossible to learn them from sporadic exercises.

Our current curriculum and teaching must be examined to discover the points which hinder the development of creativity. Many studies of elementary school programs indicate that creativity, which is manifest in the primary grades, is sharply reduced in the upper grades. This suggests that the school program somehow reduces the creative potential.

Two possibilities may be suggested as causes of this phenomenon. One is the fact that by far the greatest part of our curriculum and teaching is concerned with assimilation. We want people to cover a lot of ground now in order to prepare them for thinking later. This emphasis on assimilation may explain why creativity and the capacity for innovation shown in the primary grades somehow stops from the fourth grade on. The emphasis on content begins in the fourth grade. This emphasis on assimilation, on "covering the ground," not only prevents the possibility of training in productive thought. It also, inadvertently, cultivates a mental stance which is inimical to such thinking. The habit of reading for isolated points, which is a by-product of the ways of teaching reading, is one example. The expectation of firm answers to all questions creates an intolerance of ambiguity and of probabilistic thinking.

While a certain amount of assimilation is needed, assimilation alone is insufficient. We need also challenge for accommodation and stretching of the mind.

To balance accommodation and assimilation, we need also to select carefully the content we offer, in order to reduce the burden of assimilation. One way suggested in recent writing is that of focusing curriculum content on the essential ideas and principles of the subject matter, while practicing a judicious sampling of the detailed facts with which to achieve the understanding of these principles.

It is evident also that teaching strategies need to be revised because they employ methods which limit productive thought. Hughes seems to indicate that a large proportion of teaching acts are addressed to (a) finding very specific answers, (b) controlling both thoughts and behavior. Hughes' data suggest that up to 70 percent of teaching is devoted to control and only a bare 10 percent is designed to develop content or ideas. This means that the bulk of teaching represents training in conformity and only a small fraction even remotely encourages creativity. This stress on conformity occurs not necessarily because teachers prefer it. More likely it is caused by lack of familiarity with the skill necessary to create openness and to create an order within openness. Asking questions is one example. Classroom dialogues are full of questions like these: *who is? what is? how much is? when did? where?* There are relatively few *whys?*'s and very few *how comes?* and *what if?*'s. The same proportion is evident in questions that end in a closure in comparison to those that are open-ended, which focus a query but don't prescribe the answer or the way of getting at it. There is a scarcity of instructional techniques for challenging students' autonomy of thinking and for creating their own mental schemata.

One example of an open-ended yet focused procedure was provided by the classification process described above. If students are to learn to differentiate the common elements inherent in diverse objects or events, they need opportunity to compare and contrast, to find differences and similarities. A simple question of what similarities and differences there are in phenomena under consideration would accomplish this. This could be followed by asking students to describe why they thought the particular similarities or differences existed, and so on.

In place of correcting what might be considered the wrong classifications, teachers need to exploit such errors as guides in devising new tasks to help students overcome their errors. Not much is learned from being given a "right" classification. It is much more fruitful to invent a task or initiate a procedure which makes students re-think their basis for finding similarities and differences.

It seems then that planning curriculum for a systematic development of creativity involves a double agenda: (a) The sampling and organization of content in such a way that students are not so overwhelmed with assimilation that there is no room for thinking; (b) The organization of learning experiences to enhance the opportunities for creativity, divergence, and autonomy of thought. This is not an easy task. One must analyze the nature of the subjects to determine which ideas and concepts are basic and which details most economically provoke these ideas. It is necessary also to decide which instances of the general idea students must encounter in order to discover the general idea for themselves. Both the content ideas and the mental operations for dealing with them must be organized in a cumulative hierarchy of ascending abstractness and complexity in order to demand a greater range of association, more precise differentiation, a higher level of abstraction, and a wider scope of transfer and application. While there have been attempts to organize content around important ideas, little has been done to plan sequences of learning experiences.

Finally, we need to provide a greater range of materials which are shaped to open up thinking rather than effecting a closure, which generate questions instead of focusing only on recall, which push toward "accommodation" instead of sheer assimilation, and which offer invitation for open-ended interpretation in place of offering generalizations.

25 *Explorations in creative thinking*

Related selections: 23, 24, 26, 59

The preceding article by Taba with its accompanying headnote should be studied before this selection is read.

There are many reasons for school guidance workers to consider the identification and development of creative thinking important.

First, creativity is important from the standpoint of personality development and mental health. There is little question but that prolonged, enforced repression of the creative desire may lead to breakdown of the personality.

On tests of creative thinking, developed by the author and his associates, schizophrenics manifested amazingly impoverished imaginations, inflexibility and inadequacy of response, and similar characteristics. Their productions gave no evidence of the rich fantasy lives and wild imaginations popularly attributed to schizophrenics—only a tremendously impoverished and stifled creativity.

Second, creative thinking contributes importantly to the acquisition of information. Indeed, it ultimately may be demonstrated that creative thinking is as important in this respect as are memory and other intellectual functions.

Third, creative thinking is essential in the application of knowledge and in the achievement of vocational success. In almost every field of human achievement, creativity is usually the distinguishing characteristic of the truly eminent. The possession of high intelligence, special talent, and high technical skill is not enough to produce outstanding achievement.

Fourth, it is tremendously important to society for our creative talent to be identified, developed, and utilized. The future of our civilization depends upon the quality of the creative imagination of our next generation.

The author and his associates are engaged in a program of studies concerned with the identification and development of creative thinking from kindergarten through graduate school and into professional life. Thus far, most of our attention has been focused on explorations in the early school years.

The purpose of this paper is to describe a few of the results from these

E. PAUL TORRANCE, "Explorations in Creative Thinking," reprinted from *Education*, 81 (December, 1960), 216–20. Copyright 1960 by The Bobbs-Merrill Co., Inc., Indianapolis, Indiana.

DR. TORRANCE (1915–), of the Bureau of Educational Research, University of Minnesota, has been conducting extensive research into the nature and development of creative thinking.

studies, with their implications for school guidance. Problems of identifying creative talent and helping the highly creative individual adjust to his peer group without sacrificing his creativity will receive primary consideration.

IDENTIFYING CREATIVE TALENT

One of the first problems of interest to the guidance worker is that of identifying creative talent. Pioneering work in this field was done by Guilford (4), beginning in the late forties. He and his associates (5) identified the following kinds of thinking abilities involved in creative scientific thinking: sensitivity to problems, fluency of ideas, flexibility, originality, redefinition, ability to rearrange, abstracting ability, synthesis and closure, and coherence of organization.

Lowenfeld (6) identified essentially the same abilities in art. Other approaches have been reported by Barron (1), Getzels and Jackson (3), and others. The attempt to study the development of creative thinking from kindergarten through graduate school, however, has led the author and his colleagues in a number of new directions.

First, we introduced materials calculated to challenge the inventiveness of children (12). These materials consisted primarily of toys (nurse kit, fire truck, and dog), which the children were permitted to manipulate. Subjects were asked to think of ideas for improving each toy so that it would be "more fun to play with."

Responses provided quantifiable data for assessing several kinds of thinking ability which we believed were important in the creative individual. For example, flexibility of thinking was assessed reliably by analyzing the responses in terms of the number of different approaches used in modifying the toy. These approaches included the following well-known principles (8): addition, subtraction, multiplication, division, substitution, combination, magnification, minification, rearrangement, reversal, and sensory appeal (motion, sound, light, odor).

An inventivelevel score (13) was developed by adapting for our use some of the criteria used by the U. S. Patent Office (7) in making decisions about patent applications. A constructiveness score was devised by taking a cue from a finding by Rossman (9) that noninventors tend only to "cuss" the defects of their environment while inventors tend to say, "This is the way to do it."

A second direction in our innovations in the identification of creativity was stimulated by our definition of creativity as "the formation and testing of ideas and hypotheses" and by our desire to capitalize upon the child's curiosity. Our definition and desire gave birth to our "Ask-and-Guess Test" (14).

In this test, the subject was first shown a picture and asked to think of all the questions he would like to ask in order to understand what is happening in the picture. We asked subjects to pose only questions which could not be answered merely by looking at the picture. Next, we asked him to make as many guesses (formulate hypotheses) as he could about what caused the depicted event. Finally, we asked him to make guesses about all of the possible consequences of the action depicted.

Subjects of all ages found these materials interesting, and we established relatively simple principles for evaluating the quality of the responses. Scores also produced an extremely interesting set of growth curves. For example, we found that ability to formulate hypotheses concerning causation appears to develop slowly and gradually from first grade through the college years. In addition, we found that ability to formulate hypotheses concerning consequences develops much more rapidly in the early school years and is subject to a considerable amount of waxing and waning throughout this range.

The limits of this article do not permit a description and discussion of the other types of material developed to elicit creative ideation.

INTELLIGENCE AND CREATIVITY

Although the developmental patterns concerning the differentiation of intelligence and creativity are not yet clear, several consistent trends have emerged. The relationships between measures of intelligence and measures of creativity differ slightly from grade to grade and between the sexes. Most of the co-efficients of correlation are relatively low (around .30), but are higher among girls than among boys. Within the ranges of IQ (132 to 186, as measured by Stanford-Binet) in a class of gifted youngsters, we found a co-efficient of correlation of .03 between intelligence and a measure of creativity.

Following the pattern reported by Getzels and Jackson (3), in their study of high-school students, highly creative and highly intelligent groups were identified at each grade level from first through sixth grades. Members of the highly creative group ranked in the upper 20 per cent in their classes on measures of creativity, but not on traditional measures of intelligence. Members of the highly intelligent group ranked in the upper 20 per cent on measures of intelligence, but not on measures of creativity. Those in a third group ranked high on both measures.

Regardless of the measure of intelligence used (Stanford-Binet, Wechsler Intelligence Scale for Children, California Test of Mental Maturity, or Otis Quick-Scoring), about 70 per cent of the top 20 per cent on measure of creativity would have been excluded from gifted groups which were selected on the basis of intelligence only.

One of the most consistent findings, when the highly creative were compared with the highly intelligent, was that the latter were better known by their teachers and were considered as more desirable pupils than were the former. Even those pupils who were highly creative and highly intelligent were considered less desirable than the highly intelligent pupils who had lesser creative abilities. Students who were both highly creative and highly intelligent, in general, were considered by their teachers as more unruly, more dominant, more independent, more studious, and harder working than the students in other groups.

On the basis of peer nominations, those children who ranked highly on both measures were the "stars." They received the most nominations on talkativeness, good ideas, ideas for being naughty, and silly or wild ideas. Those who ranked high on intelligence, but lower on creativity, tended to have the most friends, while those who ranked high on creativity, but not on intelligence, tended to have the fewest friends.

On a measure of psychological accessibility, derived from the House-Tree-Person Test (2), those who rated high on creativity, but lower on intelligence, tended to be least accessible psychologically. This tendency should be of special importance to guidance workers, inasmuch as these youngsters have apparently estranged their teachers, as indicated by the author's studies and those of Getzels and Jackson (3).

PEER SANCTIONS AND CREATIVITY

It will be no news to guidance workers that peer groups exercise rather severe sanctions against their most creative members. In no group thus far studied has the author failed to find relatively clear evidence of the operation of these pressures. Both sociometric studies and small-group experiments have been used thus far. Both types of study have yielded many clues for helping youngsters avoid some of the severity of peer sanctions without sacrificing their creativity. Inasmuch as the results of the experimental study were simpler and more straightforward than the others, only this one study will be described here.

In this study (11), we formed groups of five children. In each, we placed one of the most creative children in the class, as identified by tests administered earlier. We then placed each group in a situation requiring creative thinking and involving competition among groups.

This situation permitted the group to experiment for twenty-five minutes, trying to discover all of the things which could be done with a box of science toys and to discover the principles whereby they worked. After a period of five minutes, used for planning, demonstrations, and explanations, each group was given twenty-five minutes in which to present their demonstrations. The focus of observation was upon the techniques used by the groups to control the most creative member and the strategies of the most creative member in coping with these pressures. Much of the behavior observed suggested that the highly creative individual was, in many cases, responsible for his own woes.

At the second-grade level, the most highly creative individuals were generally unpleasant, showing little consideration for the group; little or no goal orientation; little or no identification with the group; and little or no heed to the leadership attempts of their less creative peers.

In the third grade, the most creative subjects tended to work independently— and were ignored for the most part. This tendency persisted into the fourth grade, where the most creative members assumed little responsibility for leadership. Moreover, in the final ratings, these individuals were given little credit for important contributions which they actually made to the success of the group.

The highly creative subjects in the fifth grade manifested more leadership and were more dominant than those in the fourth grade, but they left themselves open to criticism and attack for "being too scientific" and for "being too greedy." These tendencies became more pronounced in the sixth-grade groups.

An examination of almost any of the many lists of personality characteristics of highly creative individuals suggests a number of valid answers to the question, "Why do highly creative individuals alienate their peers and elders?" Many of the highly creative individuals are disturbing elements in classroom groups in elementary schools. The problem of teachers and guidance workers resolves itself into one of helping highly creative individuals maintain those characteristics which seem essential to the development of creative talent and, at the same time, helping them acquire skills for avoiding, or reducing to a tolerable level, the peer sanctions.

Stein (10) has offered a set of interesting suggestions concerning the social role of the creative industrial reesarcher. If we apply Stein's principles to teachers and guidance workers, the objective in helping highly creative youngsters would run something like this: Help the highly creative child to maintain his assertiveness without being hostile and aggressive.

SUMMARY

The identification and development of creative thinking should be of concern to guidance workers. It is important from the standpoint of personality development and mental health, acquisition of information, vocational success, and social welfare.

A variety of materials have been devised and tested for identifying creative thinking at all educational levels. New developments have been in the direction of manipulative materials which yield measures of inventiveness, materials which permit exploration through questioning and formulating hypotheses concerning the causes and consequences of behavior.

Both measures of intelligence and creativity appear to be essential in identifying giftedness. Children who rate highly on measures of creativity appear to become alienated from their peers and teachers and tend to manifest behaviors which call forth sanctions by their peers. One of the problems of the guidance worker is to help the highly creative child cultivate those personality characteristics which apparently are essential to his creativity and to help him avoid or reduce the sanctions of his peers without sacrificing his creativity.

REFERENCES

1. Barron, F. "The Psychology of Imagination," *Scientific American*, Vol. 199 (September, 1958), pp. 150-166.
2. Buck, J. N. "The H-T-P Technique," Monograph Supplement to *Journal of Clinical Psychology*, Vol. 5 (1948), pp. 1-120.

3. Getzels, J. W., and Jackson, P. W. "The Meaning of 'Giftedness'—An Examination of an Expanding Concept," *Phi Delta Kappan*, Vol. 40 (1958), pp. 75-77.

4. Guilford, J. P. "Creativity," *American Psychologist*, Vol. 9 (1950), pp. 444-454.

5. Guilford, J. P., and Others. *A Factor-Analytic Study of Creative Thinking, Part I, Hypotheses and Description of Tests* (Los Angeles: University of Southern California, 1951).

6. Lowenfeld, V. "Current Research on Creativity," *NEA Journal*, Vol. 47 (1958), pp. 538-540.

7. McPherson, J. H. "A Proposal for Establishing Ultimate Criteria for Measuring Creative Output," in *The 1955 University of Utah Research Conference on the Identification of Creative and Scientific Talent*, ed. C. W. Taylor (Salt Lake City: University of Utah Press, 1956).

8. Osborn, A. F. *Applied Imagination* (rev. ed.; New York: Charles Scribner's Sons, 1957).

9. Rossman, J. *The Psychology of the Inventor* (Washington, D. C.: Inventors Publishing Co., 1931).

10. Stein, M. I. "A Transactional Approach to Creativity," in *The 1955 University of Utah Research Conference on the Identification of Creative and Scientific Talent*, ed. C. W. Taylor (Salt Lake City: University of Utah Press, 1956).

11. Torrance, E. P. *Explorations in Creative Thinking in the Early School Years, Part V, An Experimental Study of Peer Sanctions Against Highly Creative Children* (Minneapolis: Bureau of Educational Research, University of Minnesota, 1959).

12. Torrance, E. P., and Michie, H. W. *Explorations in Creative Thinking in the Early School Years, Part I, Scoring Manual for "How Good Is Your Imagination" (Form C)* (Minneapolis: Bureau of Educational Research, University of Minnesota, 1959).

13. Torrance, E. P., and Palm, H. *The Measurement of Inventivelevel and Constructiveness As Aspects of Creative Thinking* (Minneapolis: Bureau of Educational Research, University of Minnesota, 1959).

14. Torrance, E. P., and Radig, H. J. *The Ask-and-Guess Test: Rationale and Scoring Manual* (Minneapolis: Bureau of Educational Research, University of Minnesota, 1959).

26 *Research in creativity: some findings and conceptions*

Related selections: 23, 24, 25, 59

The two preceding articles by Taba and Torrance should be read before this selection.

Several important assumptions underlie the work of psychologists who study creativity. For one, creativity like most human characteristics is *not* viewed as a special gift possessed by a limited few but rather is conceived of as a capacity possessed in some degree by all human beings. Second, creativity is *not* considered a mystic or spiritual force that, when left unfettered, bursts into human action but rather is considered a product of both thinking on the part of the creator and judgment on the part of the viewer. That is to say, creativity exists in the transaction or relationship between the characteristics of a product and someone's judgment of it. Children, for example, may function in highly creative ways; but whenever these ways are private, they cannot be observed and hence fall outside the domain of human judgment. This means that, while a child may have all sorts of creative experiences, in order for him to be considered creative he must produce some product, some object or idea that meets at least two requirements. First, it must be public; second, it must be judged as novel, tenable, and useful or satisfying to some group at some point in time. A third assumption is that creativity can be elicited through certain test situations and that the responses to these test situations can be measured. Keeping these assumptions in mind—that creativity is a capacity possessed in some degree by everyone, that creativity *for the researcher* must be public and that creativity is measurable—I would like to examine some of the intriguing creativity research of the past twelve years.

Although the Progressive Education Association deserves the deepest bow for fostering interest in creativity, the person who probably has done the most to develop this interest along scientific lines is J. P. Guilford, a psychologist working at the University of Southern California. In 1950 he spoke of the appalling neglect of creativity by psychologists and outlined a research program that he was going to use to investigate it.

ELLIOT W. EISNER, "Research in Creativity: Some Findings and Conceptions," *Childhood Education*, 39 (April, 1963), 371–75. Reprinted by permission of the author and The Association for Childhood Education International, 3615 Wisconsin Avenue, N.W., Washington, D.C. 20016.

DR. EISNER is Assistant Professor of Education at the University of Chicago. His research interests include aesthetics and creativity.

DIVERGENT AND CONVERGENT THINKING

Subsequently Guilford developed two concepts which have been extremely useful in studying this behavior: divergent and convergent thinking. *Divergent* thinking is the type that most characterizes creativity. It is thinking that is speculative, that "takes off" from information already possessed. *Convergent* thinking, more conservative in character, uses information to converge upon an already existing answer. For example, in teaching about the Civil War, a question that would elicit divergent thinking might be, "What might be different today if the South had won the Civil War?" or "How differently would the South have been treated if Lincoln had not been assassinated?" A question eliciting convergent thinking might be, "How did Sherman enter the city of Atlanta?" or "How was the South divided after the Civil War?" In each subject area it is possible to devise questions which elicit these different types of thinking processes.

CREATIVITY AND INTELLIGENCE

Concepts of divergent and convergent thinking were then used by Guilford to construct some highly ingenious tests, some of which have proven to be useful in the study of creativity. It was these research tools and others that were used by my colleagues, Jacob Getzels and Philip Jackson, in their important study of creative adolescents.

Their study provided convincing evidence that the highly creative adolescent differed in many significant ways from his highly intelligent but not-so-highly creative peer. Getzels and Jackson found that the highly creative adolescent valued a sense of humor as a personal human trait more deeply than the high IQ student, that he had a much wider range of vocational aspirations, that he had a much richer phantasy life and that he considered his personal values and those of his teachers to be somewhat opposite.

Perhaps the most significant of the Getzels and Jackson findings has to do with the fact that they found that intelligence was far from a reliable predictor of creativity. Being highly intelligent does not insure high creativity and vice versa. As a matter of fact, if scores of tests of intelligence were used to identify creative youngsters, approximately 70 per cent of the most highly creative would be overlooked. Paul Torrance, who has also done much to further our knowledge of creativity, has some interesting findings.

LONGITUDINAL STUDIES

One of the most interesting of Torrance's findings is derived from his longitudinal studies of creative thinking. If you examine areas like reading, arithmetic or spelling and plot a curve describing achievement in these subjects over a time for a large group of children, what would the curve look like? You would expect that, on the average, achievement would rise as the age level increased. This is exactly what occurs. But what happens to this curve when it is drawn for creative performance? Torrance found that creative behavior increases from first grade through third but around fourth grade and again at seventh grade, creative performance sharply decreases. On the Ask and Guess Test (the student is shown a picture and asked to raise as many questions as he can that cannot be answered by the data in the picture) the number of questions third-grade boys asked was high and the fourth-grade dip was low. It took until the tenth grade for boys to raise as many questions as were raised at the third-grade level. The same general pattern holds for girls.

Torrance suggests that highly creative children who frequently meet pressures to conform tend to suffer greater emotional strain than children who are less creative. Psychopathology may be fostered by the child's struggle to harmonize conflicting internal and external demands.

CONDITIONS ENCOURAGING CREATIVE THINKING

There are some identifiable conditions that seem to encourage creative thinking on the part of students. *First,* there is some evidence to indicate that highly creative individuals can tolerate a great deal of ambiguity. They do not seem to have a pressing need to obtain immediate closure or immediate answers to problems. They can tolerate hypotheses of a highly speculative sort; it might be more accurate to say they enjoy such ambiguity. In the classroom this suggests that it might be useful to encourage children to deal with alternative solutions to problems, to put off formulating answers until they have explored a range of possibilities.

Second, children seem to need what Carl Rogers has called *psychological safety*. Osborn in his brainstorming technique has a standing rule that when idea sessions take place no one is allowed to evaluate them. At these sessions people are made to feel as comfortable as possible and criticism is not allowed. His reasons are simple: to remove the threat of embarrassment and to help the members of the group get their ideas out no matter how silly or "way out" they might seem. Providing this psychological safety in the classroom is extremely important if children are to feel free to venture new ideas.

Third, the individual needs to have experience and skill in the subject area itself if he is able to function in a highly creative way. In the past it was believed that if you just left the child alone, this would be sufficient. The energy of the libido left unhampered would rush forth in a splendorous burst of creativity. This is not only ethically irresponsible; it just does not work. For example, a child who has to worry about what color he will get by mixing yellow and blue to use in painting, or a child who has to struggle with spelling and grammar rules in writing is unlikely to have enough energy left to think in highly creative ways; in addition his attention will be focused elsewhere. This does not mean that spelling and grammar rules should not be taught. It means only that it is difficult to function in highly creative ways if these concerns are really problematic for the child. Those people who are the most highly creative in the disciplines are the ones who have so overlearned the basic tools and techniques that they are no longer problems. It is when they have done this that they can deal with other aspects of the problem. Nursery-school children often produce exquisite pieces of art work precisely because they pay little or no attention to technical precision or representational accuracy. When a child becomes primarily concerned with technique, and *at some point he must,* it often becomes difficult for him to capture the spontaneity that he displayed at a younger age.

Fourth, it follows from what has been said that to the extent that different subject areas make different sorts of demands on the child, to that extent they require different sorts of skills. Creative ability is, to a significant degree, specific to the subject matter. While some general traits such as flexibility and tolerance for ambiguity seem to be conducive to creative thinking, a person must be able to control the syntax and techniques of the discipline within which he is working if he is to be able to use the discipline in a highly creative way.

Fifth, creative behavior, like most other types of behavior, should be appreciated when it occurs. Perhaps one of the fundamental pieces of knowledge in the field of psychology is that behavior that is rewarded tends to persist. If recall is rewarded and divergent thinking unrewarded, it is not likely to flourish. Torrance has pointed out that not only is highly creative *behavior* unrewarded but *children* who are highly creative are not always looked upon favorably by their teachers or their peers. In the Getzels-Jackson study when the teachers were given a list of the highly creative and high-IQ students and asked to identify the ones they preferred to have in class, it was the high IQ's rather than the high creatives that they preferred.

TYPES OF CREATIVITY

Up to this point I have been discussing creativity as if it were one kind of behavior. I do not believe this is the case. In my own research I have formulated a conception of types of creativity. When I was teaching art in elementary and secondary schools it occurred to me that children were highly creative in quite different ways. For example, some students were highly creative in the original way they incorporated ideas into their art work. Their drawings and paintings were not always the most esthetic but frequently the most imaginative. I call these youngsters *boundary pushers* because they always seem to want to push the limits of ideas or objects. This group is creative because it used ideas or objects in novel ways like the man who first thought of installing electric shaver outlets in automobiles.

Another group of youngsters were quite creative in the way in which they used color, line and form. Their creativity was displayed in the highly esthetic way they organized visual qualities. I call this group *esthetic organizers.* They might never produce any really imaginative ideas but they have a marked sense for esthetic order. Their stories, poems and paintings are beautiful. These children are esthetically creative.

A third group of children who invent new objects by combining materials I call *inventors*. I recall one fifth-grade boy in the Laboratory School who spent a full two weeks of his art class trying to invent a new color for a crayon. He did this by making a plaster mold and by melting down an assortment of different colored crayons. The invention failed as a product—the wax would break when he tried to take it out of the mold—but his behavior was inventively creative just the same.

A fourth type of creativity, *boundary breaking,* is most rare. It rejects the assumptions that everyone else takes for granted and formulates new premises and proceeds to develop a radically new system of thought. Copernicus is one example. Because of him we now believe that the sun is the center of our planetary system. Would it not be revolutionary if someone were to prove that this was all wrong? Our whole conception of the universe would be shattered and we would have a new and perhaps a better one to take its place.

I have found through my own research that children who display one type of creativity in art do not always display another type. Even within the visual arts, children who are highly creative with one medium (like clay) may not be highly creative in another (like painting or drawing). If differences in creative performance exist even within one area, what should we expect about the carryover of creativity from subject to subject? If we look carefully enough we would find that almost every child is highly creative in one way or another *
—if not in some area of the curriculum, at least in some area of life. It is a mistake to look for *the* creative child. A person highly creative in all fields is rare indeed.

INTELLIGENCE WHICH INCLUDES CREATIVITY

One other issue concerning creativity has to do with the relationship between creativity and intelligence.

In previous years the tendency to link creativity to intelligence was quite common. The person thought to be highly creative was the person with the high IQ. The very concept of giftedness itself was most often conceived of in terms of IQ. With the Getzels-Jackson study and with work by other investigators this tendency has been sharply reduced—almost to the point where some conceive of these behaviors as being mutually exclusive. I have discussed creativity and intelligence, but this is mainly because I have followed terms used in the research. However, I reject a distinction between these concepts. If our conception of intelligence were more adequate, if we conceived intelligence not merely as what intelligence tests test but as the efficient and effective utilization of means to achieve desired ends, then the need for a separate concept of creativity disap-

* See *All Children Have Gifts* (Washington, D. C.: Association for Childhood Education International, 1958).

pears. In short, I am suggesting that the reason creativity and intelligence seem to be unrelated is that we have been using in our research a restricted conception and measure of intelligence.

In the adult world, such as in areas of literature or painting, a person is considered creative only after some group of people—usually experts or critics—compare the artist's work to the work of others and make a judgment about the creative quality of the work. The artist's age, country or amount of education are considered irrelevant. The work stands or falls on its merit as compared to others. As we move down the educational ladder we begin to take other considerations into account. For example, works by high school students are compared with works produced by other high school students to compete with adults. These considerations continue to expand until the primary grades where the first things we want to know before we make any judgment of the creative quality of a child's product are his age and many other things: the experience the child has had with the material, the amount of instruction he has received, his background and so forth. Similarly, in tests of creativity as in tests of intelligence, comparisons to groups are also made. Any individual's responses on a given test are compared with those of his peers. *Instead of comparing a student's product to the context of the group, why not compare his products to the context of his own work?* If it is true that novelty is one of the defining characteristics of creativity when an individual copes with a new problem, when he generates answers or solutions that were *personally* novel—in short, any time he uses his intelligence to create personally new answers to problematic situations —he is functioning creatively in some degree.

It does not seem to me that the only (or necessarily the best) context for creativity is the group, whether it is a group restricted to a particular age level or a group consisting of those over twenty-one. If the hallmark of a problem is a state of affairs for which no adequate response is available and if intelligence is the process through which an adequate response is formulated, then the exercise of intelligence in problematic situations is by its very nature creative. I hold that the distinction between creativity and intelligence is artificial; that the seeming separation between these concepts is due to a too narrowly conceived concept of intelligence. Indeed, without a conception of intelligence that includes "creative" thinking it would be difficult to understand how man could survive.

27 *Pupils psychologically absent from school*

Related selections: 29, 30, 56, 57

*The failure of some students to perform at the expected level indi-
cated by measures of their academic ability is a persistent problem
facing teachers. Often this seeming inability or reluctance to learn,
stemming from some emotional conflict, cannot be dealt with successfully by the classroom teacher. In this paper Dr. Talbot and
Mrs. Henson report the results of social work treatment provided
five students who were referred to them because of learning difficulties.*

Children who are present physically in school classrooms but absent psychologically have always presented a problem to educators and are now becoming the
concern of orthopsychiatrists as well.

In this paper we propose to discuss only one component of this complex problem: emotional conflict interfering with the continuous learning process. The
pupils herein represented had at least average intelligence and had experienced
no difficulty in mastering the rudiments of learning. There was no clinical evidence of either physical or neurological involvement, or of school phobia. The
problem, briefly stated, was that certain pupils continued to attend school but
did not continue to learn.

Conspicuously absent was any involvement of other areas of their lives on the
reality or conscious level. Outside of school, these children were able to function
and to gain some measure of satisfaction. This delimitation of the influence of
neurotic conflict was brought out by Ernst Kris, who quotes Hartmann: "He
points to the fact that not all of the child's achievements are related to his conflicts; that in physical and intellectual life, and in growth and development,
many steps are normally not affected by conflicts."

The level of our treatment, which was psychoanalytically oriented social casework in a school setting, revealed that these pupils were not otherwise handicapped. Our approach included not only the child, but also the home and the

MIRA TALBOT and ISABELLE HENSON, "Pupils Psychologically Absent from
School," *Journal of Orthopsychiatry*, XXIV (April, 1954), 381–90. Copyright, The American Orthopsychiatric Association, Inc. Reprinted by permission of the authors and the publisher.

At the time of publication of this article MISS TALBOT was Acting Supervisor of, and MRS. HENSON was Psychiatric Social Worker in, the Queens
(N.Y.) Center of the Bureau of Child Guidance.

school environment. Ackerman and Neubauer have stressed the necessity of considering the total environment in the treatment of a child. They emphasize the importance of the total approach: "To insure against failure, the therapist must have full knowledge of the child's environment as well as of the child. He must have working contact, therefore, with the parents, the school, and other aspects of the child's daily reality." Because our treatment was carried on in a clinic within an educational system, we had normal access to the child's life in the school as well as in the home. Consultations were held with a psychiatrist, psychologists, and school personnel.

A discussion of the role of the social worker in the treatment of children suffering from academic failures is of particular significance because this type of problem is usually considered the province of psychologists and guidance counselors unless sufficiently complicated to demand the technique of psychiatry.

To illustrate the *social work treatment* of certain pupils psychologically absent from school, five examples are given.

CASE 1.   In the case of Tim, treatment was not given at the onset of his difficulty. The community clinic to which the psychologist had referred Tim did not accept Tim for treatment. The worker made the common error of underestimating the possible seriousness of an isolated symptom of academic failure.

Initially, Tim was referred in 1950 when he was 13 years old and in the seventh grade. At that time the complaint from the school was: "Although he has very good ability, he has no interest in schoolwork and is failing in practically every subject. No other problem." He was again referred at 15, when he was in the second term of high school. The complaint was identical: he was failing in every subject.

Tim was living with his widowed mother and older sister, both office workers, in an apartment of upper middle-class status. His father had died in the summer of 1947. It was in the fall term of 1947 that his school marks first began to drop, and his general average was ten points lower. He admitted to the Bureau psychologist that his feeling of frustration and futility first engulfed him directly following his father's death. At that time, he had even left home for a few days. However, family, church and school personnel had considered this a normal reaction to a great loss. But Tim himself was worried because he found it impossible to complete his work. Intellectually, he was within the superior range, and his reading achievement was at least four years beyond his grade placement. His figures in the Person-Drawing Test were of a boy playing baseball and a girl diving.

Among his many interests enjoyed outside of school were swimming, football, photography, television, history and biography. He also was a member of a neighborhood social group consisting of both boys and girls. An outstanding characteristic was his deep concern for the underdog, and as a consequence he was consistently championing social causes. He could not pass by any wounded animal without giving it some care.

Physically, Tim was in excellent condition except for a slight visual defect and a slight tic of shoulder and head.

At the time of his second referral, the social worker offered him regular treatment sessions to be held in his school building. He responded: "I hope you can help me. There must be something wrong. I act as though I am stupid, but I know that I am not." Tim's own statement characterizes the description of a neurotic given by Dollard and Miller: "The neurotic, therefore, is, or appears to be, stupid because he is unable to use his mind in dealing with *certain* of his problems."

Tim took responsibility for keeping his weekly appointments—a total of 22 sessions—and also arranged for the therapist to see his mother several times. According to Tim, everyone thought his mother was perfect and therefore he felt ungrateful and disrespectful for not appreciating her. The reason he ran away after the father's death was that home was unbearable. The mother ran it like a business establishment: "Do for me, I'll do for you." Significantly, Tim did not mention the fact that his mother always called him "lover boy." Consciously, he perhaps was not aware of the intense emotional tie she admitted feeling for him, nor of his for her. He was aware of his hostility toward his mother. With bitterness, he told of his father's death. The morning he died, Tim was told by his mother that the father was sleeping; but later, while Tim was playing ball, he saw his father being carried out to a hearse and driven away. Somehow, he seemed to feel that his mother was accountable for his father's death.

Whenever schoolwork was mentioned, the boy repeated two episodes without any variation. First, he recounted his father's tragic life. In order to attain a college education, the father had studied nights and worked days. As soon as he had achieved his ambition, he became ill with cancer of the lungs, could hardly breathe for two years, and then suffered a painful death. Tim ended this story each time with "Look what happened to my father." Second, the boy described his mother's extreme perfectionistic standards, particularly in relation to schoolwork. When he was only in the first grade, she kept him up past midnight copying from a textbook. For the slightest error, he was made to recopy the entire page. He could not recall a single compliment, or word of praise or encouragement ever given him by his mother for his schoolwork.

Tim had concluded that his father's death was attributable to two causes: his mother and higher education. He was fearful of the same fate. On the other hand, his mother, who had practically no education, was determined that he should be as well educated as his father. To achieve this, she was willing to scrub floors if necessary, although she suffered from spinal arthritis. Unconsciously, the mother, by her negativism and persistence, was making it impossible for Tim to learn. As a result of social work interviews, the mother was able to relinquish her ambitions for academic achievement and to allow him freedom to follow his own motivations. Although he did no assigned schoolwork, he read selections from history and biography of his own choosing.

Despite the fact that the school personnel too discontinued all pressures, Tim still did absolutely nothing in the school setting. He even lost his notebook. There was no evidence of any resentment about his marks of zero in all major subjects. On the contrary, his complete failure seemed to be the justification he needed to enforce his own wishes to leave school. As soon as he became eligible, he obtained working papers. At the present time, he is employed as a mechanic in a garage, which he enjoys; he has an active social life with both boys and girls; he has many interests including sports and reading; and he acts as though he has been relieved of an overpowering burden.

Preceding the termination of treatment, information and preparation were given him regarding mental hygiene resources, in case he should ever be ready psychologically to undergo psychoanalytic therapy.

When Tim was taken on for treatment, he had internalized his problem to such an extent that direct treatment on the conscious or preconscious level was ineffective. In leaving school, he escaped from his neurotic involvement which was projected onto the school. This case illustrates the adjustment made when Tim was relieved of the expectation of learning in a school setting: a relatively good adjustment from his point of view and his mother's; a failure in treatment from the social worker's point of view.

CASE 2. In marked contrast to the preceding case, Edward was treated at the first indication of regression in academic attainments.

Edward, 14, was referred in May 1950, when he was in the second term of high school. He was failing in every subject and seemed to be "off in the clouds." Outside of school, his interests were music, photography, electricity, and Boy Scout activities. At the end of the first term, he was failing two subjects, although in elementary school Edward's achievement ratings had been well within the average range.

At home, there was no apparent difficulty except for fatigue, and he frequently went directly to bed after school. A possible explanation of his fatigue is given by Pearson, who quotes Fenichel: "Even in those cases of children where fatigue results from insoluble intrapsychic conflicts . . . the physiological basis for the feeling of fatigue and its associated symptomatology is the result of excessive muscular action. Anxiety, the sign of an insoluble intrapsychic conflict, produces tension in the muscles. . . ."

Edward lived with his parents, twin sister, and a brother, seven years old. The family were American middle-class and "agnostic." Although the mother doubted the father's claim to a junior college experience, she boasted of her own college education. The father was employed by a large corporation as an electrician.

No pathology was indicated in Edward's physical examination. Psychological examinations given at the school in June 1950 corroborated the opinion of his teacher that Edward had the innate capacity to do passing high school work. His reading achievement was at the ninth grade level. On the Wechsler-Bellevue Full Scale, he attained an IQ of 123. The Rorschach examination revealed feelings of insecurity and a compulsive drive for intellectualization and organized planning. The projection data also revealed that he harbored hostility and occasionally gave vent to uncontrolled emotional outbursts. He disregarded authority, particularly that centered around the father concept, and continued to cling to maternal protection excessively.

The treatment program included the mother, father, and school personnel, in addition to Edward. His twin sister was not included in the treatment program in order to help him gain the feelings of an individual in his own right. When the twins first started school, mother, believing that the girl twin was precocious, had arranged for separate class placements. The parental feelings expressed at the birth of the twins had persisted without change throughout the years. To quote the mother: "Edward is my very own. The girl is extra." On the other hand, the father wanted to keep the girl and give the boy away. Until recently, Edward had not only been whipped by the father, but had also been called "stupid" and "a fairy."

It became apparent that the father punished his son for the feelings of inadequacy he harbored about himself: his wife rejected his love-making as adolescent and excessive, and on the job, the father felt inadequate also. As the father was resistive to any treatment for himself, a few interviews only were held with him for the purpose of maintaining his cooperation in the therapy of Edward. However, the mother in her treatment sessions, totaling 28, was helped to understand and to modify the tense interrelationships within the home.

Social therapy, 44 sessions, with Edward was carried on by a male social worker. During an interview, Edward expressed the wish that his father were more like the social worker: he had previously told his mother that he hated his father and wished he were dead. The boy was given opportunity to express his negativism, and was reassured that he was a competent person in his own right, independent of his twin and his mother.

Concurrently with the boy's treatment, conferences were held with pertinent school personnel. As an outgrowth of these interdisciplinary sessions, the teachers gained an understanding of Edward's failures. One male teacher took a special interest in Edward and even continued his interest after termination of clinical treatment.

Within the year, Edward's movement in the learning process was evidenced by renewed energy, interest, and passing marks. He gained increased confidence in himself as a male, and when he showed interest in a girl classmate, he gained her response. His progress was attributable partly to his mother's changed handling. She relaxed in her high standards for him, and fostered his relationship with his father and maternal grandfather. As a consequence, a more harmonious family unit gradually evolved. Upon termination of treatment, the mother thanked the worker not only for the help to Edward, but also for strengthening her own sense of worth both to herself and her family.

CASE 3. The third boy's conflicts were on the threshold of consciousness and were treated before they were definitely internalized. Accordingly, the major focus in treatment was on the situation.

David, 14½ and in the second term of high school, was referred in 1952. The problem: "failing in schoolwork, and seems dazed." Following corporal punishment by his stepfather for failing, David, for one day only, truanted from school and stole a cigarette lighter.

David lived in a lower middle-class community with his mother, stepfather, brother and sister. The parents were American, Roman Catholic, of Italian descent. David's own father, of the same cultural orientation, died of tuberculosis of the spine when David was three years old. Within two years, the mother married a healthy, domineering man whose personality was the exact opposite of her first husband. The stepfather did not "spare the rod," which gave the mother the excuse she admittedly desired for overprotecting and indulging her favorite child. During her widowhood, the mother had been phenomenally successful in business, and had even been able to save money for David's college education.

David, small for his age, was susceptible to colds, and had the habit of biting his nails. On the psychological examination given in June 1952, David rated in the slightly above average group with an IQ of 111 on the Stanford-Binet Form L. He showed ability to reason with abstract material, to concentrate, and to persist. In contrast, his work on the Wechsler Performance Scale was inferior. Figure drawings indicated that he was acting out his conflict with reality, particularly in relation to heterosexuality.

In addition to direct therapy with him, one of the goals was to effect a change in the emotional climate of the home environment. As the mother was the only member of the family reaching out for help, she was the major focus in treatment. The social worker had 22 sessions with her and several with the father. David was seen several times in the school setting. Teachers, like all other adults, were responsive to him, and willingly made adaptations in his program.

It became evident that the mother's handling of David—the most appealing and vulnerable of their children—reflected not only the marital conflict, but also her own frustrated ambitions for a college education. She was envious of the stepfather's higher education, and determined that at least one of her sons would have the same advantage, and had selected David despite his own complete indifference.

Through her therapeutic sessions, the mother gained understanding of her part in David's problem. She came to appreciate that her overprotection of him started following her first husband's death. Since then, she had consciously thought that by her overindulgence she was protecting David from his stepfather's aggression. On the contrary, she learned that she was actually inciting her husband to be more punitive to her favorite son. When she gained insight into her repressed hostility toward her husband based on her competitive envy of him, the intense triangular conflictual situation began to disintegrate. At first the mother attributed the new serenity in the home to holidays and other external factors. In time, she faced the fact that she was more accepting of her marital status and her domestic role; this realization brought about a more harmonious family constellation.

Finally, the mother realized the impossibility of living her life over through David. The parents began to share recreational experiences with him and allowed him more freedom on his own. When the stepfather ceased tutoring David, he was able to learn.

David himself showed renewed interest in learning, his grades improved, and there was not a single recurrence of any delinquent trends, such as his one experience of truanting and taking a lighter. Now he is permitted to assist the stepfather in his store. His own comment was, "There's no problem now because everything is better at home."

CASE 4. Neither Jack nor his mother was treated directly. Owing to an unfortunate earlier experience with a psychiatrist, the mother objected to any treatment allied with psychiatry. As a consequence, an understanding of the problem was obtained from one interview with the mother and a few with Jack, including a psychological examination; and the clinical insights gained were transmitted to the school personnel for their use in the normal education process.

Although Jack, a 14-year-old boy in the second term of high school, seems to have superior ability, his scholastic record was only mediocre. He seemed to lack interest.

On the psychological examination, Wechsler Intelligence Scale, given in February 1952, he rated well within the superior group in handling the more abstract, verbal material. He showed good social comprehension and also reasoning ability. His reading was well above high school level. Projective techniques showed him to be an aggressive and dependent person; his hostility was directed largely to the mother figure. It was felt that his deep feelings of hostility would undoubtedly make it difficult for him to make and maintain good human relationships.

The mother, a woman of limited education and background, was separated from her husband, a highly educated, successful scientist. She attacked and belittled the advanced education of her husband. She expressed the fear that if her son should become better educated than she, he would desert her also. She was fearful of rejection by the man who was partially supporting her. Her extreme guilt over her own extramarital affairs seemed to color all aspects of her life and to make her extremely defensive.

Many conferences were held with school personnel. Jack was changed to a class for intellectually gifted pupils, which gave him increased appreciation of himself and the motivation he needed to study. Confidence in his ability to learn was restored gradually through the understanding of his teachers and guidance personnel. A teacher and an administrative assistant—both males—gave him individual attention focused on his scientific interests. Jack became very much upset when his mother objected both to these contacts and to his renewed interest in schoolwork. It was pointed out to him that he might reassure his mother that he would not talk about her or be ashamed of her. His face lighted up. "That's what's been worrying her! I couldn't understand." There have been no objections on her part since his reassurance. Through modifications of the curriculum and special attention by school personnel, Jack's interest in school has been sustained, his marks have skyrocketed, and he has easier relationships on a limited basis with other pupils.

CASE 5.   Roy, who was taken on for direct treatment at a crucial point in his school life, has made phenomenally rapid progress.

At 14, in the second term of high school, he was brought to the social worker's office, crying. He was apprehensive about a test in science which he expected later that day. In the preceding term, he had been allowed to make up his failure in this subject. His other marks were average.

He is the fourth of five children. In the first session with the social worker, Roy compulsively gave dynamic understanding of his dilemma. All of the other children are bright and tall: he is short and dull. His brother calls him "numb-skull," and his younger sister is taller than he and might get ahead of him in school. His father had trouble with his brains too, a brain lesion, and died the preceding summer after a long illness. His father's symptom was dizziness and Roy feels dizzy too at times. But his mother takes care of him, putting him to bed, bringing him food and comic books. His only real pleasures are swimming, playing baseball, and associating with his girl friend and his dog.

Weekly treatment sessions were held with Roy as well as conferences with his teachers and his mother. At his request, the content of the science course, including reproduction, was discussed with him. He was able to recognize his apprehension about his intellectual inadequacies and his short stature, but his apprehension about his identification with his father's ailment was less readily understood. In the beginning, he sat on the edge of his chair and frequently cried. All concerned agreed to the plan that he remain in school and attend the science class regularly. He did fail his first science test and his understanding teacher commented, "Not so bad to fail, is it?"

In subsequent sessions he became more relaxed and even whistled. He admitted that his concerns were less overpowering. He wanted to continue coming even though he was no longer afraid of science. In fact, he was passing all tests and had received several marks of 100. The fact that his father's condition was the result of an accident and not hereditary was discussed with him by both the social worker and the mother.

After only a few months of treatment, Roy acts like a different boy. According to him, "Science does not worry me any more." In English class, he wrote a composition about his girl friend, labeling it, "The First Chapter of My Life." He no longer complains of dizzy spells or asks to go home. However, treatment is being continued because his underlying anxiety has not been completely allayed.

SUMMARY

This paper presents social work treatment of five boys whose emotional conflicts interfered with the continuous learning process. The total situation, including the boy, the home and the school, was considered in the social diagnostic formulation in every case. However, the focus in treatment varied from a total approach to a segmented one in which the school personnel carried the responsibility.

The social findings revealed that each boy was protecting himself against an anticipated impending disaster by the defensive mechanism of ceasing to learn. The particular disaster feared on the conscious level was characterized by illness, death, divorce, passivity or femininity. Had therapy on the deeper level been given, these dreaded disasters might have been revealed as anxieties relating to castration and unresolved oedipal complex. Anna Freud has differentiated between the psychoanalytic and the psychiatric social work approach: "It [psychiatric social work] presents a picture of the psychoanalytic theory and practice shorn of their genetic content and approach." Genetic, here, means the exploration of the questions when, why, and how this particular form of behavior was *first* established. Our treatment did not aim to uncover *earliest* memories or experiences, but did aim to discover the forces in the child's preconsciousness and his particular social environment which were making continued learning impossible. These forces proved to be:

1. All of the boys had experienced loss of their fathers. Three fathers had died of serious illnesses: cancer of the lungs, tuberculosis of the spine, and injury of the brain. One father, divorced, was living out of the home; and another, although living at home, was completely dominated by his wife.

2. All of the boys had been "pressured" by their mothers for academic success and, concomitantly, had been prevented from achieving. The boys reflected the conflicts of their mothers, which were not fully described in this paper, however.

3. As an outgrowth of the first two experiences, all of the boys were afraid that academic success would bring upon them the fate suffered by their fathers. As a defense against this disaster, they found it impossible to continue learning, yet they were expected to learn and at the same time prevented from doing so by their mothers. Inevitably, they were in conflict.

We do not say that as a consequence of social work treatment the conflicts of these five boys were completely resolved. We do say, however, that the internal conflicts of four boys were minimized. This lessening of internal pressures was evidenced by movement on the reality level in the total growth process, including academic learning. The degree of success in treatment was determined by the timing of therapy, preferably at the first manifestation of the learning block; an understanding early in the treatment process of the reality depth and breadth of the conflict; and utilization of the total forces influencing the learning process.

In conclusion, this paper shows how social findings revealed an explanation of the conflicting forces interfering with the continuous learning process; and how social work treatment diminished the power of these conflicting forces. Of significance to the authors is the fact that internal conflicts were affected by external and environmental treatment of relatively short duration.

28 The lonely road of unreality

Related selections: 49, 50, 55, 57

What is the teacher's role in recognizing and treating the behavior problems of children? Evelyn I. Banning feels that, of the various adjustments the child makes in solving his problems, adjustment by withdrawal presents teachers with the greatest challenge. She describes some of the noticeable symptoms of prepsychotic behavior in children and mentions several things the teacher may do to help the preschizophrenic child.

Of the varied processes of adjustment in response to the child's inner needs, the natural events of his life, and the presence and activities of those about him, adjustment by withdrawal presents the greatest challenge to the teacher, not only because withdrawal responses often escape notice, but mainly because such avoidant modes, more insidious than others, may become habitual and pathological before recognition. According to Louttit, the boundaries between psycho-

EVELYN I. BANNING, "The Lonely Road of Unreality." Reprinted from *School and Society*, 72 (August 26, 1950), 132–33, by permission of the editors. At the time of publication of this article DR. BANNING (1903–   ) was a Professor at Wheaton College, Norton, Massachusetts. She was formerly a research associate at the Center for Field Studies, Harvard University Graduate School of Education.

neuroses and psychoses are no clearer than those between personality difficulties and psychoneuroses. In other words, between the child's seclusiveness and timidity, resulting from the withdrawing mode of behavior, and the borderlands of the functional psychosis of schizophrenia, there are no clearcut demarcations, no signposts that unquestionably indicate to the teacher that ahead lies the Lonely Road of Unreality. Nevertheless, the withdrawing, recessive personality, subjected to unbearable stresses and strains of his personal and social environment, may become the severely distorted and shattered personality of the psychotic.

Ten years ago Teresa, a slight, silent, and inactive child of seven completed grade one with a satisfactory record. The teacher's only comment at the time was, "Teresa is unsocial and shows no interest in playing with the other children." Today Teresa is institutionalized in a mental hospital, classified: schizophrenia, hebephrenic. And yet Teresa's behavior all through her eight years of public school received scarcely more than passing attention; indeed, no teacher considered her withdrawn manner or her extreme seclusiveness a matter of concern since she caused no disturbance in the classroom and showed great solicitation for teacher approval in the early grades.

Two questions immediately present themselves for our consideration of the teacher's role in recognizing and in treating behavior anomalies.

1. What are the symptoms of prepsychotic behavior observable in school children?

2. What help can the teacher actually give the child after recognizing these early symptoms?

The predisposing causative factors of schizophrenia are not definitely known; on the other hand, the precipitating factors, whether organic illness, physical discomfort, emotional trauma, psychic conflicts, or the developmental crisis of childhood or adolescence, merely evoke and exaggerate the schizophrenic response when the pattern has already been established. Bleuler states "There is nothing to be gained by listing the factors that have been implicated in the precipitation of the functional psychosis; obviously any incident toward which an individual may have become sensitized can tip the balance." For the teacher, therefore, the important consideration lies not in the etiology of the psychosis, either generally or in any specific case such as that of Teresa, nor in the therapy possible after the onset of mental deterioration, but rather in the recognition of the early symptoms of behavior disorders for the purpose of planning the best methods of improving the child's adjustment to reality. Likewise the full social significance of the value of early recognition is clear in view of the fact that schizophrenia is usually found among adolescents and young adults and that it accounts for approximately one fourth of all mental disorders.

Although sufficient data regarding prepsychotic behavior of more serious disorders are unfortunately lacking, the preschizophrenic symptoms, in a broad sense, do resemble the introverted type of personality described by Jung and others. The most distinctive feature, according to Young, is the gradual and insidious development of inattention and emotional indifference to the world outside of the individual. Extreme seclusiveness, excessive daydreaming, regression of personal interests, and odd behavior are primary symptoms. The teacher needs to observe carefully the behavior of the shy, timid, and quiet pupil who may be overlooked, since he does not disturb class routine. Inasmuch as it is not always easy to determine whether the child's behavior is a normal striving for a satisfactory adjustment or an abnormal inability to meet regular daily experiences, the teacher should have a sound understanding of the psychology of adjustment and of human behavior.

The secondary symptoms are many and varied, depending upon the developmental stage, all symptoms that give evidence of a disordered contact with the environment. Out of the specific experiences, the individual comes to develop certain standard or habitual forms of reaction, substitute responses that in psychotics tend to involve the entire organization. Secondary symptoms include temper displays, a diminished breadth of general interest, emotional expressions, negativisms, psychomotor agitation, a variety of speech disorders, and overt sex practices. In these more severe cases, the teacher should not consider herself qualified for therapy, but should instead refer the child to a clinical specialist or psychiatrist. Such use of available resources for the treatment of severe behavior disorders is distinctly a credit to the professional alertness of the teacher.

The school and the teacher, however, do play a significant part in treating behavior problems before the developing personality of the child begins to deviate conspicuously from a normal path. Both through modifying the environmental factors of the school and through working directly with the child, the individual may be taught to meet social and cultural frustrations successfully and may be shielded from unattainable ideals of success. Work that is within the capacity of the child, that is meaningful, and that provides him with some sense of accomplishment is essential. Mental balance can also be aided by additional ambivalent activities that are approved outlets for deep and unsatisfied wishes: art, avocations, and hobbies. Most important of all, however, is the therapeutic attitude of the teacher, that teacher who, by her real understanding and knowledge of behavior anomalies, her resourcefulness, and encouragement, offers affectional security to the quiet, insecure child in a social setting not unduly exciting. Thus the teacher may be of help to the preschizophrenic child who is giving evidence of difficulty in making a reasonably adequate adjustment to the world of reality.

29   *When are children ready to learn?*

Related selections: 11, 15, 16, 27, 34

*There is ample evidence that all children of the same age or grade
are not equally ready and able to learn the materials frequently expected of them. Yet thousands of classrooms are managed as if it
were axiomatic that children of a particular grade or group have
the same degree of readiness for certain experiences. This practice
takes its toll in wasted effort on the part of teachers and in misery
and maladjustment among children. Insight into how to evaluate or
appraise children's readiness for learning may be gained from Professor Trow's discussion.*

There is a tendency to think that children are "ready" to learn whatever happens
to be in the course of study for the grade they are in. The result is that fruitless
efforts are often made to teach children what they are not yet mature enough
to learn.

When, then, *are* children ready to learn?

WHEN THEY ARE HEALTHY

While most classroom teachers know that the greatest possible freedom from
physical defects is a sensible prerequisite for learning, the correction is not
always complete. For example, parents who have been told their children need
glasses, sometimes do nothing about it. But in spite of difficulties, physical examinations are important, and one has to follow through as best he can.

Sometimes children need sleep more than they need instruction, and the child
who does not pay attention, who is underactive or overactive, fidgety, cross, or
tired, probably needs a physical examination more than a reprimand. Such
children are not ready to learn anything; so, until something can be done about
their physical condition, there is not much use trying to teach them.

WHEN THEY ARE WELL ADJUSTED

Everyone seems to be satisfied that the harsh punishments of a century and more
ago have disappeared, but some self-appointed critics of modern education are

WILLIAM CLARK TROW, "When Are Children Ready to Learn?" *NEA Journal*,
XLIV (February, 1955), 78–79. Reprinted by permission of the author
and the publisher.

DR. TROW (1894–   ) is Professor of Educational Psychology, University of
Michigan, and the author of widely used texts in this field.

dubious about the practices of better schools where children are not given failing marks and are promoted to the next grade whether they can "do the work" or not. Such critics say life is competitive, that children should get used to the idea that they have to work for what they get and should not be coddled.

People who talk this way overlook the fact that children are compelled by law to go to school. Also, these critics do not realize that when children—or older people—are forced to work at things they cannot do, and are then humiliated (with failing marks) for not doing it, they don't like it. They become resentful or aggressive, or perhaps they give up or escape (play truant). In any case, they don't learn—or at least they are not learning what they were sent to school to learn.

But bad school practices are not the only conditions that frustrate children unduly and produce undesirable attitudes and maladjustments of one kind or another. They may be the result of unsatisfactory home conditions, of constant quarreling and fighting between parents, of feeling unwanted, of shame for what their parents or other relatives have done, and of their own misfortunes either fancied or real. Children tend to carry over into school the anxieties and the aggressive or retiring behavior they have developed at home.

Children have difficulties and need to be carried along for a while until they begin to get straightened around. There is no need to expect much of them for a few days, or even a few weeks or months. When they find that they are "accepted" at school, they will begin to learn again.

WHEN THEY ARE MATURE ENOUGH

The familiar term, *reading readiness*, applies to physiological and psychological maturing. We know that it is very inefficient to try to teach children to read before their mental age gets up around 6.5. By that time most of them are ready to begin; before that, they are not.

So various kinds of prereading experiences are provided—listening to stories, looking at pictures, telling about things that happened, and the like. Experienced teachers can tell when a child is ready to read, though tests may help, especially when classes are large.

But some children do not seem to be ready even when their mental ages hit the magic 6.5. Sometimes emotional maladjustments are involved. Sometimes children prefer to be read to, and seem to be afraid to lose this sign of interest and affection, as they think they will if they learn to read themselves. Or they may be uninterested in the simple reading they have to begin with as compared with the more mature stories that have been read to them.

Having rejected reading while the other children were learning, they may feel inferior because of their mistakes when they do try. Or it may be that, although the mental-test score is high enough, other basic maturing has not taken place.

In any case, there is one thing we do know: that, while opportunity and encouragement are desirable, any form of pressuring works in the opposite direction.

But what of readiness for arithmetic, for geography, or history, or poetry? The same principles apply to them. Pupils mature gradually, each at his own rate. Even those in the same grade are not equally ready to learn the same things.

A grade is a group of children of about the same age who are maturing at widely different rates and who are being provided with the kinds of experiences which it is believed will help them in the maturing process. Thus, it is not something children are promoted to if they have good marks, but instead it is a group in which the children who compose it can develop best.

They sometimes learn best if they drop back with the next younger group; i.e., by "repeating a grade." However, many pupils who repeat a grade do no better the second time than they did the first. More often they can learn more if they go along with their group. Some would, no doubt, do better if they were placed in the grade ahead.

The point is, of course, that there is a wide range of ability in any one grade, whatever the promotion policy of the school—usually about a six-year range.

While attention should be given to the needs of the slow learner, it should also be given to the superior child, who is ready for something before it appears in the school program and is quite bored when the class discussion is on material with which he has long been familiar. Such a child is likely to think up interesting ways to amuse himself that may cause some trouble for the teacher. There should be opportunities for more advanced work for some, as well as for easier work for others.

But pressure on pupils to do what they are not ready for, not mature enough to do, does more harm than good, while encouragement and help when they *are* mature enough is often quite effective.

How can one tell whether a child is too immature, or whether he is "just lazy" and "doesn't work up to capacity"?

WHEN THEY ARE INTERESTED

These are difficult questions. The answer seems to be a little complicated. In the first place, we are not too sure of just what a child's capacity is. Test scores are useful, but they are suggestive only.

And, besides, should children be expected to work up to capacity all the time when adults don't? We work up pretty close to capacity on some things, but on others—say our knowledge of the theater, sports, modern music, or even politics —we are content to ride along, picking up a little here and there as we go.

In the second place, pupils who do not apply themselves as we would like to have them are not necessarily lazy. They may not be healthy. They may have a low basal metabolic rate, or they may be disturbed and not well adjusted, so they don't feel like putting forth much effort.

As we have seen, these matters need separate attention. But if children are healthy and well adjusted, they are not lazy, even tho they seem to be.

One teacher was persuaded to abandon traditional methods of assign, test, mark. She tried a newer method the others were talking about—teacher-pupil planning, individual and group projects, and so on. Suddenly the class became alive, the pupils began asking *her* questions, and she didn't know the answers. It was terrible! Things couldn't go on that way. So pretty soon she got everything back in order again—assign, test, mark. And after that, some of the children were "lazy." They didn't work up to capacity!

The moral of this story, of course, is that, when children can work individually or in groups to find out something, they are more than likely to show unexpected enthusiasm, initiative, and perseverance. But when the object is only to get a mark—well, that's something else again.

Of course, miracles do not always happen. Pupil-teacher planning and setting up of projects (they don't necessarily go together) usually require wise guidance. Otherwise children may attempt the impossible and then be disappointed. Or they may prefer to let the teacher do the planning, the way some school faculties prefer to let the principal give the orders. They feel secure that way because all they have to do is do what they are told, and it leaves them free to gripe if things don't come out right.

The well-prepared classroom teacher, who knows more of his subject-matter than is in the pupil's textbooks, can often suggest phases of work that are of interest to certain pupils who are not motivated to learn according to the routine procedure.

For example, a girl uninterested in the usual political history may be thrilled by the history of art or dress design, especially if there are illustrated books in the school library. Or a boy not enamored of the regular science work may spend hours hunting and classifying sea or land shells.

A well-trained school librarian can be of tremendous help in suggesting books that interest and motivate pupils for further reading. The materials of all sorts that are available throw the burden of proof on the teacher who says the children are not interested in school work.

30 *Psychological health and classroom functioning*

Related selections: 27, 47, 49, 50

The subtitle of this research report is "A Study of Dissatisfaction with School among Adolescents." It is a commonly held belief that boredom experienced by gifted children and frustration experienced by low-ability students make members of these two groups far more dissatisfied with their school experiences than are more average students. In this selection Jackson and Getzels report some research that seems to disprove this belief and at the same time provide some suggestions for better understanding students' dissatisfaction with school.

The problem of dissatisfaction with school among children is of theoretical and practical significance to both psychologists and educators. At the theoretical level dissatisfaction with school becomes part of a broader area of inquiry which aims at an understanding of the individual's functioning in an institutional setting and which includes studies of staff morale, role conflict, productivity, and the like. At a practical level the question of why children like or dislike school is directly related to the immediate problems of school dropouts, grouping procedures, planning for the gifted child, and the like.

As might be expected, a social phenomenon as important as dissatisfaction with school is not without its explanatory hypothesis. Some of these spring from empirical findings, while others appear to be part of our cultural ethos. Educational studies that point to an empirical linkage between school failure and school dropouts, and industrial studies that demonstrate a relationship between low morale and decreased output, lead one to suspect that reduced effectiveness in school (i.e., low scholastic achievement) would be a natural concomitant of dissatisfaction with the institution. Thus one would expect to find heightened dissatisfaction among students who have low ability or who are unable for one reason or another to deal adequately with scholastic material.

PHILIP W. JACKSON and JACOB W. GETZELS, "Psychological Health and Classroom Functioning," *Journal of Educational Psychology*, L, 6 (1959), 295–300. Reprinted by permission of the authors and the American Psychological Association.

DR. JACKSON (1928–) is Associate Professor of Educational Psychology at the University of Chicago and DR. GETZELS (1912–) is Professor of Educational Psychology and Human Development at the same institution. They have collaborated in many research endeavors.

More recently it has been suggested (although never adequately demonstrated) that many successful students with high ability are dissatisfied with their school experiences; the term "boredom" is often linked with the term "gifted child" in current expositions by educators. The boredom problem among "gifted" combined with the failure experiences of the low ability child suggests that the greatest number of dissatisfied students is to be found among extreme ability groups. Those who are low in ability and achievement would be expected to show dissatisfaction because of the numerous frustrations they experience in the classroom. Those who are high in ability and achievement would be expected to show dissatisfaction because of the relative lack of stimulation which they experience in the classroom.

Both of these explanations (or, more accurately, hypotheses) contain the implication that dissatisfaction with an institution arises out of the individual's interaction with that institution. An alternative explanation might be that the individual brings a set toward satisfaction or disastisfaction *to* the institution— that it is a reflection of a more pervasive personal orientation and that success or failure experiences within the institution have a limited influence upon it. This hypothesis obviously places more emphasis than do the earlier ones upon psychological variables, as opposed to environmental variables, in understanding dissatisfaction with school. The research described here was designed to test the relative merit of these alternative views.

PROBLEM

The purpose of this investigation is to examine the differences in psychological functioning and classroom effectiveness between two groups of adolescents—those who are satisfied with their recent school experiences and those who are dissatisfied.

SUBJECTS AND PROCEDURE

The Ss of this investigation were two groups of adolescents identified from among 531 students enrolled in a Midwestern private school. These students were divided into five class groups ranging from the prefreshmen to the senior year of high school. In this institution a single grade, the prefreshmen, is substituted for the usual seventh and eighth grades. The instrument used to select the experimental groups, called the Student Opinion Poll, was a 60-item opinionnaire designed to elicit responses concerning general satisfaction or dissatisfaction with various aspects of school—viz., the teachers, the curriculum, the student body, and classroom procedures. The following are sample items, one in each of the four areas.

> 3. While there are some differences among them, most teachers in this school are:
>   *a.* Very inspiring
>   *b.* Quite inspiring

    c. Somewhat inspiring

    d. Not inspiring

16. Most of the subjects taught in the school are:

    a. Interesting and challenging

    b. Somewhat above average in interest

    c. Somewhat below average in interest

    d. Dull and routine

14. From the standpoint of intellectual ability, students in this school are:

    a. Too bright—it is difficult to keep up with them

    b. Just bright enough

    c. Not bright enough—they do not provide enough intellectual stimulation

5. The freedom to contribute something in class without being called upon by the teacher is:

    a. Discouraged more than it should be—students do not have enough opportunity to have their say

    b. Encouraged more than it should be—students seem to be rewarded just for speaking even when they have little to say

    c. Handled about right

The instrument was scored by giving one point each time the S chose the "most satisfied" response to a multiple-choice item. Thus, the possible range of scores was from 0 to 60. For the total school population the mean score on the Student Opinion Poll was 37.30; the standard deviation was 9.57. The experimental groups were chosen as follows:

> Group I—the "dissatisfied" group—consisted of all students whose score on the opinionnaire was at least one and a half standard deviations *below* the mean of the entire student body. This group contained 27 boys and 20 girls.

> Group II—the "satisfied" group—consisted of all students whose score on the opinionnaire was at least one and a half standard deviations *above* the mean of the entire student body. This group contained 25 boys and 20 girls.

The experimental groups were compared on the following variables:

1. *Individual intelligence tests.* In most cases this was the Binet. A small number of children were given the Henmon-Nelson, the scores of which were converted by regression equation into equivalent Binet scores.

2. *Standardized verbal achievement test.* The Cooperative Reading Test was used. Prefreshmen and freshmen were given Test C_1, Form Y; older students were given C_2, Form T.

3. *Standardized numerical achievement tests.* Because of differences in the curricula of the various grade groups it was not possible to administer the same test of numerical achievement to all *S*s. The following tests were given according to grade placement:

Prefreshman—Iowa Everypupil Arithmetic Test, Advanced Form O.

Freshmen—Snader General Mathematics Test.

Sophomores—Cooperative Elementary Algebra Test, Form T.

Juniors—Cooperative Intermediate Algebra Test.

Seniors—Cooperative Geometry Test, Form 2.

4. *California Personality Test.* Two forms of this instrument were used. The intermediate form was given to prefreshman; the secondary form was given to all of the older groups. Two subscores were obtained, "personal adjustment" and "social adjustment."

5. *Direct Sentence Completion Test.* *S*s were asked to complete 27 sentences of the type: "When I saw I was going to fail I ————," or, "I think my father is ————." Each sentence was given a plus or minus score depending upon the presence or absence of morbid fantasy, defeatism, overt aggression, and the like. The total score was the summation of the individual sentence scores.

6. *Indirect Sentence Completion Test.* This instrument was identical with the Direct Sentence Completion Test except that proper names were inserted for the pronoun "I," thus changing it from a "self-report" to a "projective" instrument. Boys' names were used in the male form of the instrument and girls' names in the female form. The instrument was presented as a "thinking speed" test. To reinforce this notion *S*s were asked to raise their hands when they were finished and the elapsed time was written on their test booklet. This instrument was administered approximately two weeks prior to the administration of the Direct Sentence Completion Test.

7. *Group Rorschach.* Cards III, IV, IX, and X were projected on a screen. For each picture the *S* was presented with 10 responses and was asked to choose the three which he thought to be most appropriate. Each list of 10 contained four "pathological" responses. The *S*'s score was the number of nonpathologic responses among his 12 choices. This group technique follows that described by Harrower-Erikson and Steiner (1945).

8. *Teacher ratings.* Each student was given three ratings by his present teachers. These ratings included: (*a*) his general desirability as a student; (*b*) his ability to become involved in learning activities; and (*c*) his possession of leadership qualities. Teachers were required to place all of their students on a five-point scale so that Categories 1 and 5 each contained one-twelfth of the students; Categories 2 and 4 each contained one-fourth of the students; and

Category 3 contained one-third of the students. The values 5, 8, 10, 12, and 15 were assigned to the categories and were used in quantifying the ratings.

9. *Adjective Check List.* From a list of 24 adjectives each student was asked to choose the 6 which best described his characteristic feelings while attending classes in particular school subjects. The list contained 12 "positive" (e.g., confident, happy, eager, relaxed) and 12 "negative" adjectives (e.g., bored, restless, misunderstood, angry). The use of the negative adjectives by the experimental groups was analyzed both quantitatively and qualitatively.

RESULTS

With the exception of the adjective check list the results of all comparisons are shown in Table 1. Contrary to popular expectations the "satisfied" and "dissatisfied" students did *not* differ from each other in either general intellectual ability or in scholastic achievement. Those differences which did appear were linked to psychological rather than scholastic variables. More specifically, each of the test instruments designed to assess psychological health or "adjustment" was effective in distinguishing "satisfied" from "dissatisfied" students within one or both sex groups.

For both sexes the experimental groups were differentiated by their scores on

TABLE 1

Mean scores, standard deviations, and t *statistics for satisfied and dissatisfied adolescents on dependent variables* a

	Boys					Girls				
	Dissatisfied (N = 27)		Satisfied (N = 25)			Dissatisfied (N = 20)		Satisfied (N = 20)		
	x	s	x	s	t	x	s	x	s	t
IQ	134.85	14.58	136.44	14.59	ns	128.45	15.06	128.00	11.45	ns
Verbal Achievement	49.96	8.69	50.68	7.87	ns	50.63	9.11	52.28	6.76	ns
Numerical Achievement	50.35	9.75	52.17	10.52	ns	47.78	8.61	48.50	10.26	ns
Calf. Personal Adjust.	45.58	9.82	53.40	7.63	3.18**	47.90	13.03	54.76	9.25	1.86*
Calf. Social Adjust.	44.85	11.37	51.84	8.93	2.45**	47.00	13.15	55.76	7.89	2.50**
Direct Sentence Comp.	46.93	10.58	49.25	10.02	ns	46.65	12.01	54.00	5.73	2.53**
Indirect Sentence Comp.	47.19	9.61	51.29	6.95	1.75*	49.60	10.35	53.47	7.97	ns
Group Rorschach	48.35	10.66	47.44	10.30	ns	47.35	11.35	54.16	8.32	2.15**
Teacher Rating I: Desirabilty as a student	8.94	1.83	10.35	1.70	2.85**	9.84	1.91	10.05	1.59	ns
Teacher Rating II: Leadership qualities	9.01	2.08	10.13	1.96	2.00*	9.91	2.37	10.04	1.24	ns
Teacher Rating III: Involvement in learning	9.09	2.14	10.23	1.69	2.14**	9.67	2.32	10.33	2.11	ns

* Significant at the .05 level.
** Significant at the .01 level.
a With the exception of IQ, all scores were based upon parameters of the total student body from which the experimental groups were drawn. The scores of all tests were transformed to T scores with a mean of 50 and a standard deviation of 10. For the total population the teacher ratings have a mean of 10 and a standard deviation of 2. The mean IQs for the total school population are: boys, 132, and girls, 128.

TABLE 2

Number of subjects choosing negative adjectives
when asked to describe typical classroom feelings

	Boys			Girls		
Adjective	Dis-satisfied ($N=27$)	Satisfied ($N=25$)	Chi Square	Dis-satisfied ($N=20$)	Satisfied ($N=20$)	Chi Square
Inadequate	19	16	ns	17	7	10.42**
Ignorant	19	13	ns	15	3	14.54**
Dull	25	16	6.36*	16	9	5.60*
Bored	24	13	8.61**	20	13	8.48**
Restless	20	15	ns	19	9	11.90**
Uncertain	20	21	ns	17	13	ns
Angry	15	4	8.76**	13	4	8.29**
Unnoticed	19	5	13.25**	7	4	ns
Unhelped	18	8	6.24*	9	6	ns
Misunderstood	16	5	8.31**	5	2	ns
Rejected	12	3	6.66**	4	0	ns
Restrained	17	2	16.91**	9	3	4.29*

* Significant at the .05 level.
** Significant at the .01 level.

the California Test of Personality. The experimental groups of boys were further differentiated by their responses to the Indirect Sentence Completion Test. For girls additional differences appeared in their responses to the Direct Sentence Completion Test and the Group Rorschach.

On all of these test variables the "satisfied" group attained the "better" score —i.e., the score signifying a more adequate level of psychological functioning. It is also worthy of note that whenever a significant difference appeared, the mean score of the total student population fell between the mean scores of the experimental groups. Thus, the variables that differentiate the experimental groups tend also to distinguish them from the total population of students.

In addition to showing differences on psychological health variables, "satisfied" and "dissatisfied" boys were perceived differently by their teachers. On all three of the teachers' ratings the "satisfied" boys received more favorable judgments than did "dissatisfied" boys. The fact that this result does not appear to be true for girls lends support to the popular expectation that boys are more likely to express their negative feelings publicly than are girls. This hypothesis receives some confirmation from the results of the adjective check list which are described below.

In Table 2 are shown the number of Ss who chose negative adjectives when asked to describe their typical classroom feelings. As they are arranged in Table 2 the adjectives reflect the rankings of four judges who were asked to rank the words on the degree to which they involved an implicit or explicit criticism of others. The 12 adjectives were typed on separate cards and were accompanied by the following directions:

On the following cards are a number of negative adjectives which a person might use to describe himself. Rank these adjectives on the degree to which they involve an implicit or explicit criticism of others. For each adjective ask the question: If a person used this adjective *to describe himself* would he also be implicitly or explicitly criticizing others? Give a rank of 1 to the adjective which would be *least* critical of others and a rank of 12 to the adjective which would be *most* critical of others.

Four psychologists served as judges. The average rank order correlation among the four sets of judgments was .84. The adjectives are presented in Table 2 according to the ranked sum-of-ranks of the judges. The adjective "inadequate" was judged as being most free of criticism of others, while the adjective "restrained" was judged as involving the greatest amount of criticism of others.

As might be expected, the use of negative adjectives was far more frequent among dissatisfied students than among satisfied students. Four adjectives seemed to discriminate equally well between the experimental groups for both sexes; these were: "bored," "angry," "restrained," and "dull."

An examination of Table 2 also suggests the existence of sex differences in the students' description of their typical classroom feelings. Remembering the classificatory scheme by which the adjectives are ranked in Table 2, it appears that dissatisfied girls are somewhat less likely than dissatisfied boys to use negative adjectives involving implicit criticism of others. Dissatisfied boys, on the other hand, are less likely than dissatisfied girls to be distinguished from their satisfied counterparts by the use of adjectives *not* involving implicit criticism of others. If one thinks of criticism directed towards others within Rosenzweig's schema of "intropunitiveness" and "extrapunitiveness" (Murray, 1945), then the observed sex differences may be conceptualized by saying that dissatisfied girls are more *intropunitive* than satisfied girls; dissatisfied boys are more *extrapunitive* than satisfied boys.

This difference in the direction of aggression may provide a context for the obtained differences in teacher ratings discussed earlier. If the dissatisfied boy is more likely than his female counterpart to lay the blame for his dissatisfaction upon others in his environment, particularly school authorities, it is reasonable to expect that he would be viewed as somewhat less than completely desirable by the classroom teacher. The dissatisfied girl, on the other hand, seems more willing to direct her negative feelings inward, thus avoiding the additional risk of counter-aggression by school authorities or by other adults.

DISCUSSION

Two major conclusions are suggested by the findings of this study. First, dissatisfaction with school appears to be part of a larger picture of psychological discontent rather than a direct reflection of inefficient functioning in the classroom. It is almost as if dissatisfaction were a product of a pervasive perceptual set that colors the student's view of himself and his world. Second, it appears that the "dynamics" of dissatisfaction operate differently for boys and girls. Boys seem to project the causes of their discontent upon the world around them so that adults are seen as rejecting and lacking in understanding. This tendency to blame adults may be one reason why these boys are seen as less attractive by teachers than are satisfied boys. Girls, on the other hand, are more likely to be self-critical, turning blame for their dissatisfaction inward. Feelings of inadequacy, ignorance, and restlessness more sharply differentiate satisfied and dissatisfied girls than is the case with boys. This tendency to be intropunitive may partially explain why teacher ratings fail to distinguish between our two experimental groups of girls.

The atypicality of the sample population used in this research places a number of limitations upon the inferential statements which can be made on the basis of these findings. Fortunately, however, the major portion of the investigation has recently been replicated using seventh and eighth grade lower-class Negro adolescents as Ss. The findings of the latter study are essentially the same as those reported here. Again the psychological rather than the intellectual or scholastic variables discriminated between satisfied and dissatisfied students. The findings with respect to the use of negative adjectives were not as clear-cut but, again, every intropunitive adjective was used more frequently by dissatisfied girls as compared with dissatisfied boys, while the latter exceeded the girls in their use of extrapunitive adjectives.

It should be noted that even the most satisfied students made some use of negative adjectives when asked to describe their typical feelings in the classroom. Also, the average member of the satisfied group expressed some dissatisfaction on one-sixth of the questions in the Student Opinion Poll. These two observations should serve as ample cautions against the danger of interpreting any sign of dissatisfaction with school as symptomatic of deeper psychological difficulties. Apparently, some degree of dissatisfaction is the rule rather than the exception. Nonetheless, the responses of the extremely disgruntled group of students leaves little doubt that dissatisfaction with school, like beauty, is frequently in the eye of the beholder.

SUMMARY

This investigation examines the differences in psychological functioning and classroom effectiveness between two groups of adolescents—those who are satisfied with their recent school experiences and those who are dissatisfied. The major findings point to: (a) the relevance of psychological health data rather than scholastic achievement data in understanding dissatisfaction with school; (b) the importance of differentiating the attitudes of dissatisfied girls from those of dissatisfied boys, the former being characterized by feelings of personal inadequacy, the latter by feelings critical of school authorities. Rosenzweig's concepts of intropunitiveness and extrapunitiveness are applied to these findings and a relevant theoretical framework is proposed.

EMOTIONAL AND
SOCIAL DEVELOPMENT

31 *Emotional development in early infancy*

Related selections: 17, 39

Inextricably interwoven with all problems of personality and adjustment are problems of emotional development. In fact, the problems of one are essentially the problems of the other. All human adjustments and behaviors are permeated in varying degrees by feelings and emotions. How do we get our feelings and emotions, our affective processes? Are they present in any degree at birth? If not, what is their genesis and how do they develop? Dr. Bridges draws her conclusions from findings of one of the early studies of emotional development.

The emotional behavior of 62 infants in the Montreal Foundling and Baby Hospital was carefully observed and recorded daily over a period of three or four months. The circumstances attendant upon these reactions were noted, and the whole data was studied from the point of view of development from age to age. A summary of the findings will be presented in the following paragraphs. They will be seen to lend support to the writer's theory of the genesis of the emotions and to add further illuminating detail.

The babies under observation were in separate wards more or less according to age. In different rooms were infants under one month, one to three months, three to six months, six to nine months, nine to twelve months, and twelve to fifteen months. An older group of children between fifteen and twenty-four months of age played together in the nursery.

KATHERINE M. BANHAM BRIDGES, "Emotional Development in Early Infancy," *Child Development*, III (December, 1932), 324–41. Reprinted by permission of the Society for Research in Child Development.

DR. BRIDGES (1897–) is an Associate Professor in the Department of Psychology, Duke University. Her research in emotional development was some of the pioneer work in this field. She is a Diplomate in Clinical Psychology.

The table below shows the number of children at the different ages whose behavior was observed for this study.

Age in Months	Number of Children
Under 1	3
1–3	16
3–6	23
6–9	18
9–12	11
12–15	20
15–18	8
18–21	5
21–24	6
Over 24	2

Development in the emotional behavior of the young child comprises three main classes of change. From birth onward there is a gradual evolution of the emotions taking place. The earliest emotional reactions are very general and poorly organized responses to one or two general types of situation. As weeks and months go by the responses take on more definite form in relation to more specific situations. It seems to the writer, as already mentioned elsewhere, that in the course of genesis of the emotions there occurs a process of differentiation. Coincident with the partial isolation of certain responses is a combining of the simpler reactions within the unit responses and the formation of bonds of association between these emotional syndromes and detailed aspects of the provoking situations. In this manner slowly appear the well known emotions of anger, disgust, joy, love, and so forth. They are not present at birth in their mature form.

In addition to the progressive evolution of the emotions, there is, going on at the same time, a gradual change in the mode of response of each specific emotion. Muscles are developing, new skills are being learned. So that the anger, for instance, expressed by the eighteen-month-old differs in detail of form from the anger manifested by the ten-month-old baby. Fresh bonds of association are being made between emotional behavior and the always slightly varying attendant circumstances. Different situations come to have emotional significance for the growing child and subsequently provoke emotional responses. Thus a gradual substitution takes place of the situations which prompt the emotions. In the language of the behaviorists, emotional responses become conditioned to fresh stimuli.

EXCITEMENT, THE ORIGINAL EMOTION

After observing the behavior of babies *under one month* of age, the writer felt more than ever convinced that the infant does not start life with three fully matured pattern reactions, such as have been mentioned by behaviorists and named fear, rage and love. Unfortunately the writer was not able to observe the infants within a few hours of birth, but this fact in no way invalidates observations made on children two or three weeks old. Moreover, if the above named emotional responses are really the three great primary emotions from which all our adult emotions are derived, surely they may still be observed a month or more after birth. And, even if the process of conditioning begins before or immediately upon birth, one may expect the original emotion-producing stimuli to elicit their natural responses at least for two or three weeks after birth.

It was observed in the hospital that, on presentation of certain strong stimuli, the infants became agitated, their arm and hand muscles tensed, their breath quickened, and their legs made jerky kicking movements. Their eyes opened, the upper lid arched, and they gazed into the distance. The stimuli producing such agitation or excitement were: bright sun directly in the infant's eyes, sudden picking up and putting down on the bed, pulling the child's arm through his dress sleeve, holding the arms tight to the sides, rapping the baby's knuckles, pressing the bottle nipple into the child's mouth, and the noisy clatter of a small tin basin thrown on to a metal table whence it fell to the radiator and the floor.

The loud sound startled only four of the one- and two-months-old babies, while six others lay practically undisturbed. None of the infants cried after hearing the noise. The same experiment was tried upon children of successive ages up to fifteen months. Under two or three months the reaction was one of sudden but rather mild general excitement as described above. Children of three or four months and older gave more of a jump and looked definitely in the direction of the sound. Afterwards they remained still with eyes and mouth open, and started towards the source of the commotion. One baby of eight months stiffened and turned away on the second trial. The corners of his mouth turned down, his eyes moistened and he looked to the adult for sympathy and comfort. Another child of eleven months sat wide-eyed and still, the corners of his mouth drooping as if he were ready to burst into tears. The older children merely stood, or sat, alert and attentive without further sign of distress.

Lowering the babies suddenly into their cribs, and in some cases lifting them quickly, also startled and excited them. Sometimes they would cry following upon such a surprise. Rocking a quiet child would cause him to open his eyes attentively. But gently rocking a crying infant would often, though not always, cause him to reduce his activity, stop crying, and eventually become tranquil. Gentle handling, slow patting, wrapping in warm blankets, and nursing easily soothed an agitated or crying infant, making him relax and yawn and become sleepy.

Light pinching of the arm left the three- or four-week-old baby unmoved. Deeper pressure caused him to kick slightly, breathe faster and move his arms. A sharp flick on the hand produced similar agitation, but a second rap resulted in a sudden check to breathing followed by a prolonged cry and other signs of distress. The first exciting experience had been found disagreeable and the second rap produced unmistakable distress.

Time after time on waking suddenly from sleep the infants were observed to wave their arms jerkily, kick, open and close their eyes, flush slightly, and breathe quickly and irregularly. Some grunted, some cried spasmodically for a moment or two, while others cried loudly for several minutes. The combined sitmulation of light, of sounds, of damp or restricting bed clothes, and the change from sleeping to waking breathing-rate seemed to produce a temporary agitation and often distress. Waking apparently requires emotional adjustment.

The hungry child before feeding would often show restless activity, waving, squirming, mouthing and crying at intervals. The infant who had been lying in one position for a long time and the tired child before falling asleep would also show emotional agitation. Their breath would come jerkily, uttering staccato cries of "cu-cu-cu-ah," and they would thrust out their arms and legs in irregular movements. At the moment the nipple was put into the hungry baby's mouth he again breathed quickly, occasionally cried, waved the free arm, and kicked in excited agitation.

The emotional reactions of the tiny infant are certainly not highly differentiated. The most common response to highly stimulating situations seems to be one of general agitation or excitement. It is a question which word most aptly describes the behavior. The former perhaps conveys more the idea of general disturbance, although the two words are often used synonymously. This vague emotional response to a large variety of circumstances must surely be one of the original emotions, if not the only one.

A kind of general excitement over new and startling or other highly stimulating circumstances may be seen at any age. The behavior manifestations vary from time to time, but the main characteristics of accelerated response, alertness, slight tension or restlessness remain as constant attributes. In the babies, excitement is frequently manifested in kicking movements. The month-old infants kick jerkily with both feet at random. In another month or so, the kicking becomes more regular, the legs being thrust out alternately. By five or six months the babies express their emotions in combined leg thrust, kicking with one foot, and in swinging the legs from the hips. At fourteen months when the children can stand they will hold on to a support and "mark time" with their feet or stamp. Stamping, jumping and running express excited agitation at a still later age.

Two- and three-month-old babies may be seen to suck their thumbs or fingers rapidly in moments of stress. At seven months and over, children bite, pull and suck their garments, as well as their fingers. This behavior seems to produce a gradual subsidence of the emotion. Body-rocking accompanied in many instances by rhythmic vocalizations is another expression of mixed emotion. Hungry, annoyed, excited or restless children will sit and rock for minutes on end. The five-month-old baby lies prone and pushes with his knees, or sways when lying dorsally. Seven-month-old infants support themselves on their arms and rock back and forth murmuring "m̄m-ŭm, m̄m-ŭm." After nine months they sit up and rock to and fro, or they kneel and bounce up and down holding on to the crib bars. Sometimes they sit and bump their backs against the side of the crib. This kind of behavior was observed in the nursery up to eighteen months of age.

Rhythmical movements were observed not only to be the outcome of emotional excitement or tension, but they were seen to have a soothing and pacifying effect. These must be attempts at adjustment on the part of the organism to reduce tension and restore emotional equilibrium or tranquility. In the light of these observations, it can be easily understood how long walks, games, field sports, singing, dancing, and sea-voyages are found to be so universally health-giving and positively curative for "nervous wrecks."

DISTRESS AND ITS DERIVATIVES

It is a moot question whether "distress" is an original emotion or whether it is a very early differentiated reaction to disagreeably painful and unsatisfying experiences. It may be that it is a part of the general emotional response of excitement which copes more satisfactorily with obnoxious stimuli. Tense muscles resist or remove pressure; activity warms a chilled body and reduces tension; and cries, at first reflex due to the rush of air in and out of the lungs, bring comfort and aid. These responses become differentiated from excitement, associated together and conditioned to the disagreeable stimuli as a result of experience. If such differentiation actually takes place, it must begin immediately after birth. For the two emotions of excitement and distress are already distinguishable in a three-weeks-old infant.

On the other hand, it is possible that there is a native emotional response to pain, particularly muscle pain. The sympathetic branch of the autonomic nervous system is predominantly active and the overt behavior is definitely that of distress. Other stimuli, such as loud sounds and sudden falling, merely produce startled excitement. Blanton observed that the infant's cry of colic had a specially shrill character accompanied by rigidity of the abdominal walls. She also noted that infants during the first days of life cried from "(1) hunger; (2) in response to noxious stimuli (including rough handling, circumcision, lancing and care of boils, sores, etc.) ; and (3) possibly fatigue or lack of exercise." The writer has observed the same phenomena in three-weeks-old babies. But, hunger, rough handling, and fatigue were also noticed on many occasions to produce a restless excitement rather than specific distress.

It is not easy, in the case of the very young infant, to distinguish distress from general agitation. Perhaps the most characteristic marks of the former are greater muscle tension, interference with movement and with breathing, closing of the eyes, and loud rather high-pitched crying. In children of two months and over, the eyes become moist and tears may flow. The crying of the infant *under a month* or even six weeks often seems to be part of the general activity in excitement. Breath comes more or less regularly, the cry emerging on both intake and expiration of air. There are no tears, and the skin does not flush. Movement is free though rather jerky; and the mouth is held open in an elliptic, round, or square shape.

The cry of distress, recognizable in the *month-old* baby, is irregular. There are short intakes of breath and long cries on expiration. The eyes are "screwed up" tight, the face flushed, the fists often clenched, the arms tense, and the legs still or kicking spasmodically. The mouth is open and square in shape or, more usually, kidney-shaped with the corners pulled down. The pitch of the cry is high and somewhat discordant, and sounds something like "ah, cu-ah, cu-ah, cu-æh."

Cries of distress were heard from month-old babies in the hospital on the following occasions: on waking suddenly from sleep, struggling to breathe through nostrils blocked with mucous, when the ears were discharging, when lying awake before feeding time, after staying long in the same position, lying on a wet diaper, when the child's buttocks were chafed, and when the fingers were rapped. The three main causes of distress at this age, therefore, seemed to be discomfort, pain, and hunger.

Crying from discomfort and on awakening usually developed slowly, and sounded like "cu-cu-cu-cah-ah—." The cry of pain came suddenly, often after a holding of the breath. The sound was a loud shrill prolonged "ă-ă-ă," and lowered in pitch slightly from the first emission. The cries of hunger were rather like those of discomfort. The former came perhaps more in intermittent waves; the intervening moments being taken up with mouthing or suckling movements. Occasionally the hungry child would utter a sharp loud cry, as if in pain, and then whine or moan for a time.

Two-month-old babies cry less of the total waking time; but slighter discomforting stimuli seem to cause distress more frequently than in the case of the younger infants. They are more disturbed by a wet diaper, by flatulence, and by tight clothing which restricts movement and makes breathing difficult. Their movements are freer and they tend to move their heads from side to side when they are distressed. While one-month-old babies kick irregularly with jerky movements, the two-month-old kicks his legs alternately and more regularly. He waves his arms up and down when agitated or distressed, as well as in spontaneous play. The sound or sight of an approaching person will not quiet his distress; but being picked up will do so, or being fed if he is hungry.

By *three months* of age a child will cry and show other signs of distress when placed in an unusual position or moved to a strange place; as, for instance, when lain temporarily at the foot of another child's bed. He will wave his arms laterally as well as up and down, and will kick more vigorously. The hospital baby has learned to associate feeding time with the presence of an adult; for, when he is hungry he shows some excitement at the close approach of a person. He stares at the person's face, waves, kicks, breathes faster, and opens his mouth. If no food is forthcoming, he becomes more tense and jerky in his movements and begins to cry. He is distressed at the delay in normal proceedings.

Should the adult remain tantalizingly near for some minutes without either picking up the child or feeding him, his cry increases in intensity, his eyes become moist with tears, he holds his breath longer, and utters prolonged flat "ă-ă-ă" sound reminiscent of an older child's "paddy" or temper cry. The infant's motor responses were all set for being picked up and fed, and then he was thwarted and disappointed. His excitement changed into bitter distress with a semblance of angry vexation.

The slight change in vowel sound of the cry, the long holding of breath combined with more than usually vigorous leg thrusts and arm movements, seemed to suggest that the emotion of anger is beginning to evolve from general distress at about this age. Although for the most part the distress shown at discomfort differs almost imperceptibly from distress in response to disappointment, occasionally the latter includes, to a marked degree, those behavior elements peculiar to the emotion of anger. The situations which evoke these demonstrations of temper in the tiny infant are a stop or check in the progressive satisfaction of a physical need. In the above instance the child's appetite was aroused but not satisfied. Lack of even the first sign of a need being satisfied merely produces vague distress.

A *four-month-old* baby shows distress at the same general sort of situation that troubles the younger child. He is, however, less frequently disturbed by bodily discomfort. He moves about sufficiently to relieve tired muscles and local pressures, and to eliminate gas from his stomach. He cries vigorously at delay in the feeding process and may show decided temper on such occasions. His arms then stiffen and tremble; he screws up his eyes, flushes, holds his breath and utters prolonged and irregular cries on expiration of breath; he kicks violently, pushes with his feet and looks at any adult, presumably to see the effect. He is getting very fond of attention at this age, and will show distress and often anger when a person leaves the room or ceases to pay attention and play with him.

At *five months,* the baby's interest in small objects, such as rattles, stuffed animals, and, of course, his milk bottle, causes him to be distressed when these objects are removed. He may express his displeasure as formerly by crying, squirming, waving and kicking, but he may also be heard merely to call out in a protesting tone of voice, "ah aye," without the half-closing of the eyes and the accompanying tensions of crying.

By this age the child may show slight revulsion for certain foods, coughing, spluttering, frowning and crying while he is being fed. Chopped vegetables and soup too thick in consistency were specially disliked by some babies in the hospital. Cereals, milk, and sweetish foods were almost always taken readily. It was noted that babies under three months often refused to drink sterile water. They just let it run out of their mouths without swallowing. There was no emotion involved in this reaction. Similarly, three- and four-month-old babies sometimes rejected their thin vegetable soup, but were not very disturbed about it. A genuine emotional revulsion did not appear till five months or later. Perhaps this is the beginning of the emotion of disgust. Revulsion at nauseating sights and smells,

the adult form of disgust, apparently does not develop until two or more years
of age.

Several of the babies in the hospital *between six and eighteen months* were
observed to splutter and choke, and refuse to swallow spinach more than other
vegetables. The mouthfuls that were rejected were usually, though not always,
those containing large or stringy pieces of spinach. When the latter was chopped
fine it was swallowed a little more easily; but only when it was mixed with
other vegetables was it eaten without any protest. There must be factors other
than consistency and size of morsel to account for this objection to spinach.

It seemed to the writer that some cans of spinach tasted more bitter than
others and were less palatable on that account. In order to find how the children
would react to a bitter taste, two teaspoonsful each of unsweetened grape-fruit
juice were given to nine children in the nursery. Four of them pursed or curled
their lips, one turned his head away, and one frowned. The others sat still and
solemn, and kept tasting their lips attentively for some time. There were certainly individually different reactions to this bitter-sour, astringent taste. Several
of the children definitely disliked it and none of them seemed to like it. It is
possible then that there is a bitter taste to spinach which may in part account
for children's aversion to it. Another factor, that of the dark green color of
spinach, may influence older children's and adults' feeling reaction towards
it. One two-year-old in the hospital on turning away and refusing to eat the
vegetable was seen to point to it and say "dirty."

The *six-month-old* baby's attention is usually arrested by the presence of
a stranger. His movements are inhibited and he watches the newcomer intently.
He is not pleased and one could hardly say he is afraid. But he seems diffident
and uncertain what to do, or utterly unable to move for a few moments. At
seven months he reacts in the same way to the approach of a stranger, though
the general inhibition of movement is greater and lasts longer. After a few
moments or several seconds of tension he may begin to cry slowly, or burst
suddenly into tears. The whole body is usually rigid and inactive. The eyes,
previously wide open, close tight and the head bends. Should the stranger touch
the child he will probably turn or draw away. Here is the emotion of fear already differentiated. Frightened distress results when the child through inhibition,
ignorance, or inability finds himself unable to respond at all adequately to the
situation.

At *seven months* of age an infant calls out protestingly when a familiar
person ceases to attend to him, instead of crying distressfully like a four-month-
old. He still cries and kicks angrily if some object in which he was deeply
engrossed is taken from him. He does so also after being highly excited by a
playful adult when the latter goes away or stops playing with him. He now
makes prolonged attempts to get at objects out of reach. If he fails to attain his
objective he may give up and cry in helpless distress, or he may just grunt in
protestation.

A *nine-month-old* child will struggle longer and make more varied attempts to reach the object of his desire. Should he fail to do so after putting forth considerable effort he may become tense and red in the face with anger. He will kick and scream and look for assistance, while tears flow copiously. The cry at this age is becoming exceedingly loud, and tears flow more readily than at the earlier ages. Prolonged crying at four or five months is accompanied by slight lacrimal secretion, but after six months of age tears often flow down the child's cheeks as he cries, especially after an adult's attention has been attracted.

Strangers are still quite terrifying to the nine-month-old baby. His movements are more completely arrested by the unfamiliar presence than those of the six-month-old. He will remain immovable for several minutes unless the newcomer approaches very close to him. In that case he will lie face down or bend his head and probably begin to cry. At ten months of age he may even be so frightened as to flop down suddenly on the bed and scream loudly. Then follows prolonged and tearful crying.

When children of *ten months* and over are hungry, uncomfortable, tired, or fretful and unwell, they will set up a whine or cry as the result of suggestion when another child cries. They do not, however, ordinarily imitate crying when they are occupied and happy. Under these circumstances they may call or babble in a pitch similar to that of the other child's cry. Small objects which can be manipulated interest them so intensely that they can be distracted from a distressing trouble fairly easily at this age. These objects need not necessarily be new so long as they are freshly presented.

Year-old babies often cry suddenly when they feel themselves falling, or when they lose their grip while climbing. If they miss the assistance of a helping hand they will also sit down and cry loudly. Sometimes their emotion is anger at the thwarting or failure of their endeavors. They scream, flush, and tremble in rage. At other times they sit motionless in fright and look for aid or comforting sympathy. When strangers approach the *twelve- or thirteen-month-old* baby he may hold his hand behind his ear in a withdrawing motion and stare apprehensively. He may actually hide his eyes behind his hands or look away so as not to see the awe-inspiring or annoying intruder.

At *fourteen months* or thereabouts we may see the real temper tantrum. At least, that is the age when it became noticeable in the hospital. If a child is not given his food or a coveted toy exactly when he wants it he may respond by throwing himself suddenly on the bed or floor. He then screams, holds his breath, trembles, turns red, kicks or thrusts his feet out together. Tears flow and he will wave away anything that is not the desired object. These outbursts may occur frequently for a few weeks, or only spasmodically for another year or eighteen months. The children under observation seemed to have their "off-days" when they were fretful and easily distressed or roused to anger. Such days were usually when they were incubating or recovering from colds, when the hospital routine was disturbed, or after the children had been excited by parents' visits.

Distressful crying becomes less common as the months go by. Extreme hunger and weariness after a long day or great activity may be accompanied by whining and intermittent outbursts of tears. Anger is expressed more in protesting shouts, pushing and kicking, but less in tearful screaming. So long as adults are present, however, the interference and rough handling of another child may bring forth cries and tears. A *fifteen-month-old* may show his annoyance by hitting a child who has taken his toy or who is holding on to the thing he most wants. He may even bite him or pull his hair without a preliminary scream or shout.

The attention of familiar and interested adults is much sought by children of *fifteen to eighteen months.* If such attention is given to another child there may be signs of deep distress. The neglected one may stiffen, stand motionless, bend his head and burst into tears. Here is perhaps the beginning of jealousy, distress at the loss of, or failure to receive, expected attention and affection. Some children will show aggressive annoyance when another receives the attention they covet. They do this usually by hitting the envied child.

A *twenty-one-month-old* child will show less mistrust of strangers than will a younger infant. He may, however, run away and watch the newcomer for a time at a safe distance. After eighteen months he shows anger at adult interference by obstinate refusal to comply with their requests. He may shake his head and refuse either to be fed or to feed himself. At two he will play with his food, throwing it about instead of eating it, as a spite against some offending or scolding adult. Distress is shown chiefly at pain and acute discomfort, though the child will cry miserably at much less discomfort if a sympathetic adult is close at hand.

The children in the nursery group, *between fifteen and twenty-four months,* were more or less unconcerned when being undressed for the annual physical examination. This part of the procedure was familiar and not unpleasant. Several of the children cried and stiffened somewhat when placed on the table in the examining room. One or two continued to show distress throughout the examination. Others smiled cheerily at the attendant nurse or the doctor, until they felt sudden and unexpected local pressure. All of the children cried at some time during the procedure. The most distressing events were when a flashlight was thrown into the eyes, and when the throat and ears were examined with the aid of the usual tongue-depressor and otoscope. The children had to be held firmly and their movements curbed during these operations.

It was patent to the observer that the children were undergoing rather different emotions according to their fast-developing individual idiosyncrasies. Some were mainly startled and afraid, their movements were paralyzed. Some seemed to be just generally distressed at the unusual proceeding and the discomfort; while others were chiefly annoyed at the interference with their freedom. Several children showed signs of all three emotions. These individual differences probably have their foundation in variants in the physical constitutions of the children, both hereditary and acquired. They are certainly very much determined by the particular experiences the infants have gone through since their birth. A continuous study of behavior week by week reveals the actual differentiation and consolidation of individual traits of temperament.

Two or three of the nursery children over fourteen months developed fears for specific objects or persons. Toy animals that squeaked frightened one or two, causing them to draw away, stare wide-eyed and perhaps cry. This squeak could hardly be called a "loud low sound" such as Watson describes as one of the original fear-producing stimuli. The sound is, however, rather unusual and comes at first as a surprise to the babies. One child was afraid of a particular aggressive little boy. No doubt he had gone up and hit her unexpectedly some time when the nurses were not watching. One youngster showed fear of a dark grey dog with a rough fur, rather different from the soft teddy-bears and other stuffed animals in the nursery.

Parents often remark how their children may suddenly show fear of some surprisingly trivial and inoffensive object. The answer to this may be found in certain partial associations with disturbing events of the past. It may also be found in the particular mental set of the child's mind and body when he came in contact with the object. He may have become suddenly aware of its presence and perceived it as an unwelcome intruder upon an entirely different line of thought or action. Still another phenomenon may account for the peculiar fears and objections of children. Timid behavior may be actually learned and preserved as a social asset, one of the numerous means of drawing attention.

The nursery child who cried and crawled away after touching the rough-haired, stuffed animal was flattered with the attention of all the adults in the room. A nurse brought the dog up to the child, smiling and saying "nice doggie." He looked up at her face, saw her kindly smile, then bent his head and began to whimper again. Another nurse laughed appreciatively as he put his hand to his eye, and tried to coax him with a toy cat. He turned away quickly, cried out again, then looked up to see the effect on the adults. He was having a delightful time out of his apparent fear.

DELIGHT AND ITS DERIVATIVES

Delight is much later in becoming differentiated from general excitement than distress. The baby under a month old is either excited or quiescent. Gentle stroking, swaying and patting soothe him and make him sleepy. When satisfied after a meal he is no longer excited nor even distressed by hunger. And yet he is not positively delighted. He is just unemotionally content, and either tranquil or busy mouthing and staring at distant objects. When he is *over two weeks old* he will sometimes give a faint reflex smile upon light tapping at the corners of his mouth. This is hardly an emotional response.

One- and two-month-old babies cry and kick from hunger before they are fed, rather than show delight on presentation of the much desired food. They become calm, however, immediately when given their milk, but not at the mere approach of the adult who brings it. At two months infants will give fleeting smiles upon being nursed, patted, wrapped warmly, spoken to, tickled, or gently rocked. Perhaps this is the beginning of the emotion of delight.

By *three months* of age the emotion of delight is becoming more clearly differentiated from agitated excitement on the one hand and non-emotional quiescence or passivity on the other. The child kicks, opens his mouth, breathes faster, and tries to raise his head upon sight of his bottle. He gives little crooning sounds when being fed, nursed or rocked. He smiles when an adult comes near and talks to him; and he will even stop crying momentarily at the sound of a person's voice. He may also show delight in distant moving objects. One baby in the hospital, for instance, lay and watched the moving leaves of the creeper on the window for a minute or two at a time. Her eyes were wide and her mouth rounded and open. At times she would breathe fast, or inspire deeply, and utter murmurings of "uh-uh-uh." Her arms would wave up and down and her legs kick alternately.

The chief characteristics of delight are: free as against restrained movement; open eyes and expansion of the face in a smile as contrasted with the puckering of the forehead and closing of the eyes in distress; body movements or muscle tension of incipient approach rather than withdrawal; audible inspirations and quickened breathing; soft, lower pitched vocalizations than those of distress or excitement; more or less rhythmic arm and leg movements; prolonged attention to the object of interest; and cessation of crying. Although behavior varies in detail from child to child at successive ages, delight is always recognizable from certain general types of response. Free and rhythmic movements, welcoming and approaching gestures, smiles and vocalizations of middle pitch are most common features.

A *four-month-old* baby laughs aloud when some person smiles and frolics with him. He smiles in response to another's smile and even when anyone approaches his crib, whether they be strangers or not. He spreads out his arms, lifts his chin, and tries to raise his body in approach to the attentive person. He takes active delight in his bath, kicking and splashing the water. Food, though sometimes welcomed eagerly, is often neglected for the more interesting attendant who talks and smiles at him.

At *five months* a child vocalizes his delight in sounds of "uh-uh-ing" in addition to waving, laughing, kicking and wriggling around. He shows special interest in small objects that he can handle and explore. Musical or noisy rattles are popular at this age. When hungry he kicks, breathes fast, and calls out eagerly at the first sign of the person who brings his food. His smiles are more transient, however, and his movements less vigorous on approach of a stranger.

By *six months* of age a child will reach towards a familiar person but will lie still and observe a stranger dubiously. He crows and coos frequently, taking pleasure in his own movements and sounds. In the hospital the babies of this age would watch each other through the bars of their cribs, sometimes laughing and kicking in response to the sight of the other's movements. They would swing their legs rhythmically when lying on their backs, or sway sideways when lying prone.

A *seven-month-old* baby is becoming increasingly interested in small objects and in the act of reaching and grasping those close at hand. He will even struggle to attain things somewhat out of his reach. When his efforts meet with success he often smiles, takes a deep breath and expresses his satisfaction in a sort of grunt. After a moment or two spent in examination and manipulation of the object, he goes exploring again with fresh vigor. Possibly this is the beginning of the emotion of elation, exhilarating pleasure in personal accomplishments. Resting periods, after the delightful satisfaction of feeding or explorative activity, are often taken up with a rhythmical rocking back and forth, the child supporting himself on his hands and knees.

At *eight months* of age the child seems to take more delight than ever in self-initiated purposeful activity. He babbles and splutters and laughs to himself. Especially does he seem delighted with the noise he makes by banging spoons or other playthings on the table. Throwing things out of his crib is another favorite pastime. He waves, pats, and coos, drawing in long breaths, when familiar adults swing him or talk to him. He will watch the person who nurses him attentively, exploring her, patting gently, and often smiling. Here are perhaps the earliest demonstrations of affection. The child will also pat and smile at his own mirror image. But his behavior is rather more aggressive and inquisitive than really affectionate.

A *nine-month-old* baby is very popular with adults. He laughs frequently, bounces up and down and tries to mimic their playful actions. He pats other babies exploratively but does not show particular affection for them. Strange adults may frighten him at first. But, after studying them for some time in the distance, he will smile responsively and join in play with them. By *ten months* of age the child is taking more interest in other babies. He will mimic their calls and even their laughter. The hospital babies of this age would pat and bang and laugh in imitation of each other.

An *eleven-month-old* baby takes great delight in laughter, not only his own but that of another. He will laugh in order to make another child laugh, then jump and vocalize and laugh again in response. At *twelve months* of age he will repeat any little action that causes laughter. He is becoming increasingly affectionate. He puts his arms around the familiar adult's neck, and strokes and pats her face. Sometimes he will actually bring his lips close to her face in an incipient kissing movement. He looks eagerly for attention; and may stand holding a support and changing weight from one foot to the other in rhythmic motion, as a solace when neglected.

Between *twelve and fifteen months* a child usually learns to walk with a little help. This performance, though often accompanied by panting and tense effort, causes great delight and even elation when a few steps have been accomplished.

The child calls out, smiles and waves ecstatically (i.e., rapidly and jerkily). Without further encouragement from adults, he will then set out again with renewed fervor. When attentive adults are too enthusiastic in their appreciation, the little one may become positively tense with excitement. His efforts may consequently meet with less success, and then he cries in vexatious disappointment.

There is already a noticeable difference between the responsiveness of different *fifteen-month-old* children to demonstrated affection. Some children come readily to be nursed and petted, others require a little coaxing. One or two will kiss back when kissed, while others merely cling closely to the adult caressing them. At this age the children begin to show definite affection for each other. They take hands, sit close to one another, put their arms about one another's neck or shoulders, pat and smile at each other. *Eighteen-month-olds* will also jabber nonsense amicably together. Again, with regard to playmates as well as adults some children are more affectionate than others.

These variations in affection no doubt have a number of causal factors. They depend upon the child's physical constitution and his condition of health at the moment. Sick children may be very clinging and affectionate with adults, or, in some instances, refractory and irritable. They may be both by turns. Whether a child is affectionate or not also depends upon the nature of his dominant interest at the moment. Affection for a grown person depends upon the child's attitude towards adults in general; and that again is largely a matter of the amount of fondling or scolding the child has received. Affection for other children is considerably determined by the agreeable or exasperating nature of chance contacts.

Between *fifteen and twenty-one months* the children find increasing enjoyment in walking and running about. They chase each other laughingly and enjoy snatching one another's toys. They come back again and again to adults to be lifted high or swung around. The nursery slide is very popular at this age. One or two of the hospital children pulled away and watched apprehensively in the distance after the first slide. A little encouragement from the nurses and the eager shouts of the other children soon overcame their fear, and they joined the sliding group again.

Gramophone music was listened to intently by almost all the nursery children. Some of them responded by swaying or nodding motions to time. The children at this age were beginning to find individual interests in things and to express their enjoyment each in their own peculiar way. Absorbed preoccupation, tight clasping, biting, and varied manipulation of the attractive object were common expressions of interest. Some children would knock one object against another in play, some would collect things, and others would find pleasure in throwing and scattering toys about. These variations in appreciative interest in things and activities may be the precursors of the more mature emotion of joy.

Most of the eighteen-month-olds in the hospital were anxious to attract attention. They called out or came running to greet an adult. They would smile and hold out their arms to a familiar nurse in expectation of being lifted. A stranger they would watch solemnly for a while. Then they would approach slowly, touch and explore her clothes, or hit and watch for the effect. The children seemed to recognize their nurses at this age, whether the latter appeared in uniform or not. Babies of seven to twelve months, however, would sometimes turn away in fear or hostility when the nurses approached them wearing outdoor clothes.

Slight preferences for certain nurses were noticed as early as six months, but definitely affectionate attachments were observed chiefly between the ages of twelve and twenty-four months. One or two youngsters of eighteen months showed preferences for certain playmates. A twin boy and girl seemed especially fond of each other. The children would be more responsive and playful with those they liked, more delighted at their approach and very anxious to keep them close. Some children were friendly with almost everybody including strange visitors. Others showed more specific and decided likes and dislikes. When a terrifying stranger was present, sometimes a child would show more than usual affection for his familiar nurse, but at other times he would be restrained and aloof from everybody. Similarly when a beloved parent was nursing a child on visiting day he might be hostile to anyone else; but more often he would smile agreeably at everybody including awe-inspiring strangers.

A specific "like" does not necessarily enhance a specific "dislike" by force of contrast, though this does sometimes happen. If the disliked object threatens the satisfaction or enjoyment of the object preferred then the dislike becomes stronger. Similarly a preferred object may be enjoyed with greater intensity in the presence of, or following upon, something disliked. It is a comforting relief from distress. This effect of contrast is perhaps what Freud terms "ambivalence." There are situations, however, where it has no noticeable effect. For instance, as cited above, a child made happy by one person may like everybody for the moment, regardless of previous attitudes towards them. A troubled child may be annoyed with everybody, even his favorite playmates. Strong emotions may thus have a decided "halo" effect.

Although children between *eighteen months and two years* of age tease and hit each other frequently, they show more affection for one another than younger infants. They not only pat and stroke fondly, but they will kiss and hug each other on occasion. The older children in the nursery group were seen to direct the younger ones' activities and point out their errors by gesture and exclamation. There was no evidence, however, of the parental affection and almost self-sacrificing care shown by four-year-olds for their much younger playmates.

Noisy activities delighted the *eighteen-to-twenty-four-month-old* youngsters. They took pleasure in tearing and pulling things to pieces and in lifting large but portable objects, such as their own chairs. They jabbered happily to each other at table. One child would repeatedly make strange noises to arouse the attention and laughter of another. With adults they would practice newly learned words and would seek to share their enjoyments. When the children received new toys in the hospital they would cling to them and guard them jealously from the other children. But they would hold them out for the nurses to share in their appreciation. Here is a mark of trusting friendship for their kindly guardians such as the children had not yet developed for one another. They would always rather share the other child's plaything than give up or share their own.

Affection, thus, begins as delight in being fondled and comforted by an elder. It becomes differentiated from general delight and manifested in tender caressing responses at about eight months of age. This earliest affection is essentially reciprocal in nature. Spontaneous affection for adults may be seen, however, by eleven or twelve months of age. Both reciprocal and spontaneous affection for other children make their appearance around fifteen months, but they are not as strong as affection for adults.

Specific affection for the grown-ups who give special attention may be manifested as early as demonstrative affection itself, i.e., eight or nine months. These preferences persist as long as the care and attention continue. Attachments between two children were not observed in the hospital till after fifteen months of age. They were usually very temporary, lasting only for a few hours or days. The behavior of a child-friend is so much more erratic and less dependable than that of an adult. Friendships between eighteen-to-twenty-four-month-old children would sometimes last, however, for several weeks. There seemed to be no preference in these attachments either for the same or the opposite sex. Little girls would become friends together, or little boys, or a boy and girl would show mutual affection for one another.

SUMMARY AND CONCLUSION

The emotional behavior of young infants as observed in the Montreal Foundling and Baby Hospital seemed to lend support to the writer's theory of the genesis of the emotions. Emotional development was found to take place in three ways. The different emotions gradually evolved from the vague and undifferentiated emotion of excitement. The form of behavior response in each specific emotion changed slowly with developing skills and habits. Different particular situations would arouse emotional response at succeeding age-levels, although these situations would always be of the same general type for the same emotions.

The one-month-old baby showed excitement in accelerated movement and breathing, upon any excessive stimulation. He exhibited distress by crying, reddening of the face and tense jerky movements at painful and other disagreeable stimulations. But he was more or less passive and quiescent when agreeably stimulated.

By three months of age the child was seen to exhibit delight in smiles, deep inspirations and somewhat rhythmic movements when his bodily needs were being satisfied. Between three and four months angry screaming and vigorous leg-thrusts, in response to delay in anticipated feeding, were observed. A few weeks later anger was aroused when an adult's playful attention was withdrawn.

Distress and delight came to be expressed more in specific vocalizations with increasing age. General body movements gave place to precise responses to details of a situation. A four-month-old baby would laugh aloud with delight and cry tearfully when distressed. A child of five months was seen to cough and reject foods of a certain taste and consistency in incipient disgust. He would reach towards objects that caused him delight. By six months of age he showed definite fear when a stranger approached. He remained motionless and rigid, his eyes wide and staring. It is possible that "non-institutional" children might show fear in response to other unusual or unexpected events a little earlier than this. There was little variation in the daily routine of the children under observation, and fear was a rare occurrence.

By seven months of age the child showed positive elation, and renewed his activity as a result of success in his own endeavors. At eight months he began to show reciprocal affection for adults, and by twelve months spontaneous affection. Delight was manifested in much laughter, bouncing up and down, and banging with the hand.

Between nine and twelve months of age the hospital babies would hide their heads, like ostriches, upon the approach of a relatively unfamiliar person. They would scream and become flushed with anger when their efforts or desires were thwarted; and they would cry out in fear and sit motionless after perceiving themselves falling.

It was observed that a child learns to kiss soon after twelve months of age, and by fifteen months he expresses his affection for other children. Anger over disappointment becomes more dramatic in its manifestation. The true temper-tantrum makes it appearance roughly about fourteen months of age. By eighteen months anger at adults is expressed in obstinate behavior; and annoyance at interfering children is manifested in hitting, pulling and squealing.

Eighteen-month-olds would constantly seek the attention of adults, and take great delight in running about and making noises. One or two children of this age showed depressed, and others angry, jealousy when another child received the coveted attention. A few specific fears were noticed; and several children developed particular affectionate attachments.

Thus it seems that in the course of development, emotional behavior becomes more and more specific, both as regards arousing stimuli and form of response. Distress, though more readily aroused, comes to find adequate expression in a variety of actions, and delight becomes sensitive appreciation and joy in numerous pursuits. The emotions evolve slowly, and the exact age of differentiation is difficult to determine.

A diagram showing the approximate ages of the appearance of the different emotions, as observed in the Montreal Foundling Hospital, is given in Figure 1. Study of a number of children in private homes might suggest a somewhat

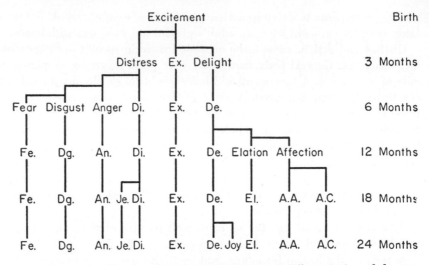

Figure 1   Showing the approximate ages of differentiation of the various emotions during the first two years of life. Key: A.A. = Affection for adults, A.C. = Affection for children, An. = Anger, De. = Delight, Dg. = Disgust, El. = Elation, Ex. = Excitement, Fe = Fear, Je. = Jealousy.

different age arrangement. Readers of the *Journal of Genetic Psychology* will note that a greater number of different emotions are attributed to the two year level than were suggested in a previously published diagram, based on a study of nursery school children.

Emotional behavior and development are very much determined by particular events and experiences and the routine of living. It is, therefore, to be expected that "institution babies" will show some deviations in their reactions from those of children at home. The former will probably exhibit fear of a larger number of things than other children, due to their very limited experience. On the other hand, they may show greater tolerance of interference, as a result of much practice in self-control in the nursery. They may also be more affectionate with other children, in consequence of the many happy play-hours spent together.

The daily round of feeding, washing, dressing and sleeping, however, has so many factors in common for all babies, that the observations made on the emotional development of a few hospital children, and the suggested inferences presented above, may have at least some general significance for infants brought up under other circumstances.

32 *Building secure children in our schools*

Related selections: 18, 49, 50, 53, 55

Some mental hygienists estimate that from ten to twelve of one hundred children in school will spend part of their lives in jail and mental institutions and that perhaps fifty will be somewhat maladjusted. What part does the school contribute to this maladjustment? Certainly we are aware that classroom practice is not keeping pace with theories and facts in child development. Celia Burns Stendler questions certain current notions about how children develop and suggests positive ways in which teachers may contribute to the adjustment of children.

In 1942, a study was published which had important bearings for classroom teachers in America. This was a study of the emotional adjustment of children in three large public schools of a midwestern city. On the basis of the evidence which Rogers presents, the average classroom teacher can expect that twelve per cent of the pupils in her classroom will have seriously maladjusted personalities and that as high as thirty per cent will show evidence of being poorly adjusted to some degree.

Those who are raising eyebrows at these figures and questioning whether the situation with regard to mental health is as serious as Rogers pictures it may be interested to know that the judgment of other experts supports Rogers' estimates. Indeed, one mental hygienist has estimated that out of one hundred children in school, one or two will spend part of their lives in jail, eight or ten will be committed to mental institutions, and thirty to fifty will be maladjusted to a lesser degree.

Sociologists, too, are pointing out that the kind of social order in which we live is creating serious personality disturbances. James West argues that " 'rugged individualism' exacts a heavy toll in the security of the individual by compelling him to maintain defensive hostilities to all around him outside the family unit

CELIA BURNS STENDLER, "Building Secure Children in Our Schools, *Childhood Education*, XXV (January, 1949), 216–20. Reprinted by permission of the author and The Association for Childhood Education International, 3615 Wisconsin Avenue, N.W., Washington, D.C. 20016.

DR. STENDLER (1911–) is Professor of Education, University of Illinois, and associate of the Bureau of Educational Research. She is author of *Children of Brasstown* and of texts in child development.

and even within it." A social order which fosters extreme competitiveness, hostility, and envy is not conducive to the best mental health.

Many teachers will support Mr. Rogers and the other authors quoted who share his point of view. Indeed, some teachers feel that the number of maladjusted children may be increasing. There are primary teachers who report that they are dealing with more children in their classes who are emotionally disturbed than ever before. There are junior high and senior high school teachers who are disturbed by the increasing number of difficult pupils with whom they come in contact.

Even if many teachers feel that predictions of the number of individuals who will have personality disturbances are exaggerated and that the situation is not as dark as has been pictured, nevertheless most of us will probably agree that many of the pupils with whom we are dealing have some peculiar quirks which keep them from functioning as efficiently as they might otherwise. Unfortunately, we teachers frequently adopt a procedure for dealing with these quirks which only serves to make them worse. Yet schools *can* promote better adjustment, can help to build secure children. It will be the task of this article to point out first steps in the process.

One of the first steps we shall need to take in building secure children in our classrooms is to examine our theories of child development. Whether we are a teacher of forty first graders or a science teacher in a junior high, whether we are a graduate of a two-year normal school or have a master's degree from a college of education, whether we have ever taken any work in the field of child development or not, we teach and treat children according to our ideas of how children grow and develop.

Most of these ideas are part of our culture and we learn them just as we learn habits of speech and attitudes toward other people. Perhaps because these ideas are learned so painlessly, we rarely question their origin or their validity. We may be surprised when we do so to find that recent research has proved some of our theories wrong and that we may be operating on a principle which stands in the way of doing an effective job in promoting the good adjustment of pupils. Indeed, some of us may actually be adding to the burden of troubled youngsters.

Let us examine some of our notions of how children develop to see which ones are based upon poor mental hygiene and which ones contribute positively to the adjustment of children.

IF HE DOES IT ONCE

One of the most common misconceptions of how children grow and develop is the notion that if a child does a thing once, chances are he'll be doing it that way for the rest of his life. Therefore, in order to build correct habits, we must correct a child the first time he does something wrong. We don't want him to build up wrong ways of behaving or develop the notion that he can get away with something. Here are a few examples of how this principle looks in operation:

> If a five-year-old has trouble with the letter "r" we must correct him every time he mispronounces a word so he won't be doing it that way forever.
> If we find a thirteen-year-old smoking cigarettes, we should punish him severely so he won't learn the habit at that age.
> If we tell John to remain at three o'clock to finish his work and he slips out to play baseball, we should call his home and have him return to school so he won't learn the habit of evading responsibility.

This notion undoubtedly represents a popularization of Watsonian behaviorism in its attempts to explain all actions in terms of the conditioned reflex. John would learn he could slip out after school if he did it once because the connection would have been made in his nervous system between (a) neglecting work and (b) having a good time after school. Similarly, the more a pupil says the "r" sound wrong, the stronger the improper connection becomes and the less likelihood is there of changing to the correct sound. But what John B. Watson left out of the picture were the two following principles:

> As the child moves from one phase of development to another, he will revise many of the habits which have prevailed for a time. The nine-year-old who delights in blood-and-thunder radio serials may completely reject these same programs when he is thirteen. The preschool child who says "I don't got any" will slough off such speech patterns of his own accord as he takes on the speech patterns of his social group. The dirty, unkempt preadolescent roughneck changes into a dandified gentleman when he first sees a girl as a girl. In other words, some of the traits which we see in children may be attributed to a particular phase of development and will disappear with age.
> All behavior is caused, and in many cases the explanation may lie deep in the emotions. Bill may continue to be dirty and rough and unkempt even when the rest of his gang has dolled up and is dating the girls. But the reason he continues in his preadolescent behavior may not be because he was not corrected when he first began but because he may have grown up with the idea that he doesn't amount to much. He may feel so inadequate, have such a poor opinion of himself that he can't bring himself to revise his old habits. An overly-simple, superficial explanation of Bill's behavior in terms of habit-formation may stand in the way of planning a program for the boy which will really help him.

IF HE TRIES HARD ENOUGH

A second misconception which bears examination is the belief that if a child will simply try hard enough, he can do anything. "He could be an A student if he'd only try hard enough." "Johnny can do his arithmetic when he puts his mind to it." "If he'd make more of an effort, he could learn to read."

Many of us make statements similar to these about some of our students. Such notions about how children grow and develop undoubtedly had their origins in theories of the will—that man can, by the use of his will-power, develop his capacities to the fullest extent. But let us see how this works out with children.

In the first place, we grossly misjudge the intelligence of children in our classrooms. One writer shows that teachers may err in estimating intelligence quotients of pupils even to the extent of classifying as geniuses some children with intelligence quotients well below 90.

In Lewis Terman's famous *Genetic Studies of Genius* he reports that if one is allowed only one method of locating the highest IQ in a classroom, the chances of getting the right child are better if one picks the youngest child in the room rather than if one trusts a teacher's judgment. In other words, unless we have some objective evidence, we may be wrong when we assume that a child *has* the ability to do better work.

In the second place, a child may not be able to produce to the best of his ability not because he doesn't want to hard enough but because of an emotional barrier. A third grade pupil may not be able to learn to read because he's been told in not too subtle a fashion that reading is something he's no good at; he may have repeated the first grade because he couldn't learn to read and so he may look upon it as something he can't do.

A sounder approach to child growth would include recognition of the fact that feelings sometimes get in the way of a child's doing his best work academically. Notice the word *academically*. This means that a student may actually be doing his best in other fields. A high school English pupil may not be doing well in class but it may be because he is putting so much time and energy into learning how to get along with the other sex. This latter job, and very important one, he does very well but receives no credit for it on his report card. Indeed, as Havighurst has pointed out, unless the high school student sees the relationship between the academic task and his developmental task, the academic task will have to be policed.

IF HE KNOWS HE'S GOOD

Another misconception of child behavior which many teachers harbor is that we must never let the child know how good he is; we must always hold up higher standards than he can possibly meet. Too many of us operate on the notion that once a child knows he's good, he will immediately stop trying to learn. Therefore, a child is never good; he is only better than he was and on his way to becoming still better.

> John has written a number of excellent compositions in the Fall but when report card time comes we give him a B so that he'll have the higher goal of A to shoot at in the next report. Giving him an A may keep him from trying to improve.
>
> Mary comes up to show her booklet. "It's nice," we say unenthusiastically, "but let's see what we can suggest to make it better."

There is no quarrel with the notion that most of us may be capable of doing better work more efficiently than we are now doing, but there is argument against the theory that the way to get a child to raise his level of aspiration is to tell him continually he isn't good enough the way he is. Actually the task of helping a child choose a goal of a higher degree of difficulty is not so simple.

However, we do know that praise facilitates the rise of the level of aspiration. An experiment with young children shows that when they are praised for what they have done, they tend to choose a task of a relatively higher degree of difficulty the next time. We also know that it may be necessary for a child to feel that he *can* lower his level of aspiration.

Experiments by C. Anderson would seem to indicate that if the choice of a goal with a lesser degree of difficulty is made impossible, regression of the maturity of aspiration can be observed. In other words, if a child is made to feel he *cannot* lower his level of aspiration, he may act in a manner characteristic of a younger age level.

Not only do we block progress by withholding praise but we are frequently unrealistic in setting goals in terms of a child's ability. As has been pointed out above, we frequently misjudge an individual pupil's ability. Furthermore, we are inclined to encourage children to overshoot the mark rather than to choose a level of aspiration they are capable of attaining.

IF HE IS HAVING FUN

A fourth fallacy in our thinking about how children grow and develop is the notion that if a child is having fun, he isn't learning; learning is a painful experience.

> Witness the kindergarten teacher who stops her class after fifteen minutes of "work period" where the children have been busy learning social skills in the doll corner, with the blocks, at the easel, at the workbench—the teacher who stops all this and calls her class together to start on a directed activity so that the children may begin to learn to work together.
>
> Or the high school English teacher whose class is engaged in a gripe session on certain school regulations before the period offi-

cially begins. When the bell rings, the teacher briskly calls the class to order and orgainzes a group discussion so that the class may have practice in discussion skills.

The plain fact of the matter is that we don't always recognize learning when we see it; we are too prone to think children can only learn when they are working directly with the teacher at tasks which are either tedious or difficult. While we may enjoy seeing children have fun, there is a bit of the Puritan in many of us and we feel rather strongly that children must not enjoy themselves too much when they are supposed to be working.

HE'S GOING TO FAIL SOMETIME

Closely related to the fallacy discussed above is a fifth one: children must experience hardship, frustration, and failure. It is good for them not only because it prepares them for failure later on in life but also because it teaches them to take the consequences of their behavior. A child who doesn't learn to read in the first grade must repeat the grade so that he won't learn "he can get away with anything," and since he is going to fail at something later in life he might as well learn now.

Aside from the obvious criticisms of such a position in the light of what we know about how and when children learn to read, there is also the question one might raise regarding the advisability of experiencing failure. Does experiencing continual failure or failure in an area deemed very important really teach a child a constructive lesson? Does it inspire a teacher to do better work to have a superintendent tell her she is a poor teacher and that she compares most unfavorably with other teachers? Is a housewife a better housewife because her husband continually reminds her that the house is untidy, that his shirts are not properly ironed, that she is too extravagant, and that she is also a failure as a mother?

The process of growing up inevitably brings many frustrations. Rather than deliberately setting the same standards for all children which automatically condemns some to failure, the teacher who is interested in building secure children helps them to set a goal which they can attain and gives them a pat on the back on their way to attaining it. Having many opportunities to achieve success builds up in a child the feeling of power, that he can do things, that he amounts to something. When he feels good about himself, he is better able to take the inevitable frustrations he will meet in life.

There are doubtlessly many other stereotyped notions which we have about how children grow and develop. The list presented here is not meant to be exhaustive. It is hoped that it may be a starting point for us to examine our ideas about children, to accept those that stand up under critical examination, and to reject those that stand in the way of building secure children.

33 *Values and our youth*

Related selections: 34, 35

The questions clustering around values and value instruction or development are becoming more and more important for our society. Our schools and colleges are becoming aware of the shortcomings of schooling that fails to take into consideration this aspect of development. Gordon Allport has been a student in this field for some time and is widely recognized and highly regarded. In this selection, prepared originally for delivery to an audience composed largely of teachers, the author raises important questions about the development of value orientations and discusses them in light of his experiences and research.

One aim of education is to make available the wisdom of the past and present so that youth may be equipped to solve the problems of the future. If this is so, then we have good grounds for a feeling of consternation concerning the adequacy of our present educational procedures. The reason is that in the immediate future, the youth of today will have to live in a world very unlike the world of the past from which our store of wisdom has been drawn.

SOME PROSPECTS

Think of the vastly changed nature of life in the future, for which we have little relevant wisdom from the past to call upon:

1. The new generation of students will have to face an ever increasing domination of life by science, by technology, and by automation. (One thinks of the story of two cows grazing along the roadside. An immense milk truck passes with the painted legend: Pasteurized, Homogenized, Vitamin B Added. One cow turns to the other and says, "Makes you feel inadequate, doesn't it?")

2. The new generation will have to recognize the impossibility of living any longer in a state of condescension toward the colored peoples

GORDON W. ALLPORT, "Values and Our Youth," *Teachers College Record*, 63 (December, 1961), 211–19. Reprinted by permission of the publisher and the author.

DR. ALLPORT (1897–) has been at Harvard University since 1942 where he is Professor of Psychology. He is a past-president of the American Psychological Association and the author of many volumes in his field.

of the world (about three-quarters of the world's population). Centuries of comfortable caste discrimination and segregation are from here on impossible to maintain.

3. The coming generation will have to deal with a population explosion whose predicted magnitude staggers our imagination.

4. It will need a completer understanding of world societies and their marked differences in values. In the past, we could be politely ignorant of such places as Africa, Latin America, and Asia in a way that is no longer possible.

5. It will have to create a world government or, at least, an effective confederation to forestall the threat of thermonuclear war.

6. As if a planetary world view were not difficult enough to achieve, the coming generation may have to develop an interplanetary point of view. (I find this prospect especially alarming because we seem to be solving the problems of outer space before those of the inner space of mind, character, and values.)

It is no wonder that this preview of problems confronting our youth throws us educators into a state of self-scrutiny bordering sometimes on panic. Where can youth find the needed equipment? Are they sound enough in mind and morale?

Sometimes our dismay finds an outlet in gallows humor. They tell of the benevolent lady who saw a depressing specimen of the very young generation sprawled on the curb of a city street, swilling down cans of beer. Greatly shocked, she asked, "Little boy, why aren't you in school?" "Cripes, lady," he replied, "I'm only four years old."

And they tell the story of the London bobby. London police, we know, are well trained for social work, even for psychotherapy. This bobby's beat was Waterloo Bridge. He spotted a man about to jump over and intercepted him. "Come now," he said. "Tell me what is the matter. Is it money?" The man shook his head. "Your wife perhaps?" Another shake of the head. "Well, what is it then?" The would-be suicide replied, "I'm worried about the state of the world." "Oh, come now," said the bobby. "It can't be so bad. Let's walk up and down the bridge here and talk it over." Whereupon they strolled for about an hour discussing the state of the world, and then they *both* jumped over.

Humor helps us put our dilemma into sane perspective, but it does not solve the problem. The vague apprehension we feel has led to certain empirical studies of the values of today's youth, with results, alas, that are not reassuring.

ASSESSING VALUES

Not long ago, Professor Phillip Jacob undertook to survey all available studies concerning the values held by college students. He found a marked uniformity among them. Fully three-quarters of the students were "gloriously contented, both in regard to their present day-to-day activity and their outlook for the future." Their aspirations were primarily for material gratifications for themselves and their families. They "fully accepted the conventions of the contemporary business society as the context within which they will realize their personal desires." While they will not crusade against segregation and racial injustice, they will accept non-discrimination when it comes as a "necessary convention in a homogenized culture." They subscribe to the traditional virtues of sincerity, honesty, and loyalty, but are indulgent concerning laxity in moral standards. They normally express a need for religion, but there is a hollow quality in their beliefs. They do not desire to have an influential voice in public policy or government. Their sense of civic duty stops at the elementary obligation of voting. They predict another major war within a dozen years, but they say that international problems give them little concern and that they spend no time on them. Only a minority value their college education primarily in terms of its intellectual gains. They regard it as good because it gives them vocational preparation, social status, and a good time. Such is the flabby value-fibre that Jacob discovers among college students of today.

The picture becomes more vivid when viewed in cross-national perspective. James Gillespie and I, in a comparative study of the values of college youth in 10 nations, asked students to write their autobiographies of the future ("My life from now until the year 2000") and also gave them an extensive questionnaire. The instrument was translated into nine different languages.

In comparison with youth of other nations, young Americans are delightfully frank and open, unsuspicious and cooperative. Their documents had no literary affectation (and, I may add, little literary quality). But the most important finding was that within these 10 nations, American students were the most self-centered, the most "privatistic" in values. They desired above all else a rich, full life for themselves, and showed little concern for national welfare or for the fate of mankind at large. The context of their outlook was private rather than public, passive rather than pioneer. The essential point is made clear by two excerpts, the first drawn from the autobiography of a Mexican girl, 18 years of age, and the second from a Radcliffe student of the same age:

> Since I like psychology very much, I wish on leaving this school, to study it, specializing in it and exercising it as a profession. I shouldn't like to get married right away, although like any woman I am desirous of getting married before realizing all my aspirations. In addition, I should like to do something for my country—as a teacher, as a psychologist, or as a mother. As a teacher, to guide my pupils in the best path, for at the present time they need solid bases in childhood in order in their future lives not to have so many frustrations as the youth of the present. As a psychologist, to

> make studies which in some way will serve humanity and my be-
> loved country. As a mother, to make my children creatures who are
> useful to both their country and all humanity.

Now follows the Radcliffe document. Its flavor of privatism is unmistakable:

> Our summers will be spent lobster fishing on the Cape. Later
> we'll take a look at the rest of the country—California, the South-
> west, and the Chicago Stockyards. I want the children, when they
> get past the age of ten, to spend part of the summer away from
> home, either at camp or as apprentices to whatever profession they
> may show an interest in. Finally, I hope we will all be able to take
> a trip to Europe, especially to Russia, to see what can be done about
> Communism.

Many critics have called attention to the same American value predicament. Our current social pattern, they say, is almost completely geared to one objective alone, namely, a profitable, expanding production. To insure expanding production, there must be more and more consumption. Hence comes the expensive glamor of our advertising and its control of our mass media. The sole objective seems to be to stimulate the accretion of goods. Self-respect and status, as well as comfort, are acquired in this way. Someone has called our national disease "galloping consumption." Half a century ago, William James saw the peril and was much worried by what he called "the American terror of poverty." He saw there was truth in the jibes that other countries direct at our "materialism."

HOPE IN UNEASINESS

Now a high standard of living is not in itself an evil thing. All the world wants what we already have. But the single-minded pursuit of production and consumption has brought a dulling of other values. One consequence is symbolized by the scandal of rigged quiz programs. These were in the service of advertising, which in turn was in the service of a profitable expanding economy. Another consequence is the accumulated froth of our TV, radio, and movies. Another is the widely discussed conformity of the organization man, as well as the futile rebellion of the beats. An especially peppery critic, Paul Goodman, has shown that the starved lives of juvenile delinquents and of young people caught in the organizational grind are at bottom much alike. Both are attracted to the cult of easiness and aspire to nothing more than amiable mediocrity. Both styles of living fail to prepare youth for the problems that lie ahead for themselves and for the nation.

A somewhat vulgar story seems to me to summarize all this mordant criticism. Moses, a stalwart leader of the old school, said to the Israelites in Egypt, "Load up your camels, bring along your asses, and I'll lead you to the promised land."

By contrast, the modern American prophet seems to urge, "Light up your Camels, sit on your asses, and I'll bring you the promised land."

All this familiar criticism is irritating; yet the fact that it flourishes is a hopeful sign. We suspect it may be too harsh. I am inclined to think so. It is rash indeed to indict a whole generation. At worst, Jacob's gloomy picture held for three-quarters of the college students studied, but not at all for a vital and far from negligible minority. And even though the gloomy generalizations have some truth in them, are the assets given fair attention? I myself have some favorable impressions, although one man's view is not reliable. But youth today appears to enjoy a certain freedom and flexibility that was not common in the more rigid days of our parents and grandparents. I even have the impression that there is less neuroticism among students now than among those of a generation ago. What is more, young people, I find, are not blind to the world changes that are occurring. Their apparent repression of the challenge is due largely to their bewilderment concerning proper paths to take. (And one has the feeling that our own statesmen in Washington are no less bewildered.) All in all, these are hopeful signs that should not be overlooked.

VALUES AND THE SCHOOL

Another hopeful sign is the fact that many teachers are asking, "What can we do to be helpful?" They know, and we all know, that the ability of the school to give training in values is limited. For one thing, the home is vastly more important. A home that infects the child with galloping consumption, that encourages only canned recreation and has no creative outlets, can only with difficulty be offset by the school. Another limitation lies in the fact that the school is ordinarily expected to mirror current social values and to prepare the child to live within the existing frame. It is an unusual school system and an unusual teacher who even *wish* to transcend the current fashions of value.

But assuming that we have an unusual school system and an unusual teacher, what values shall they elect to teach? If they do not choose to follow the prevailing fashions, what standards shall they follow? The ancient Romans were fond of asking, "Who will judge the judges?" and "Who will guard the guardians?" Can the guardians turn perhaps to standard discussions of "the aims of education"? Such discussions are numerous, abstract, and often dull. Their weakness, I feel, is their effort to formulate absolute goals, vistas of abstract perfection. The result is often a series of platitudes or generalizations so broad as to be unhelpful. Of course we want to develop "good citizenship"; we certainly want to "free the child's intellect." These and all other absolutes need to be reduced to concrete, stepwise processes before they can guide us in the strategy of teaching values.

The teacher must start with the situation as he or she finds it and in concrete instances sharpen the value-attributes of the lesson being taught. To a considerable extent, these value-attributes can be drawn from the codified wisdom of our nation. We cannot neglect the value of profitable production and high living standards, for all our vocational and professional education contribute to this end. But the codified wisdom of our unique society extends far beyond the obsession of today. Our values include also such matters as respect for civil liberties. Does the school accent this value? They include approval for individual initiative, for philanthropy, for compassion. And they imply much concerning civic duties that are the reciprocal of civic rights. What must we do to deserve our precious cornucopia of freedom? Vote? Yes. But voting does no good unless the voter is informed above the stereotyped level of the mass media. He must also pay taxes willingly. Do schools and colleges teach the young to pay a glad tax? I wonder. To me the most disturbing finding in *Youth's Outlook on the Future* lay in the elaborate talk about one's right to a rich, full life and in the almost total silence regarding one's duties.

I am saying that in the first instance teachers should choose the values they teach from the whole (not from a part) of our American ethos. Deep in our hearts we know, and most of the world knows, that our national values, derived, of course, from Judeo-Christian ethics, are about the finest mankind has yet formulated. In no sense are these values out of date, nor will they go out of date in the world of tomorrow. Yet many of them are badly rusted. Unless they are revitalized, however, our youth may not have the personal fortitude and moral implements that the future will require.

THE LARGER ANCHOR

Excellent as the American Creed is as a fountainhead of values, it does not contain them all. It says nothing explicitly, for example, about intellectual curiosity. And yet surely schools exist to augment this value. The most severe indictment of our educational procedures I have ever encountered is the discovery that a sizeable percentage of graduates of our colleges after completing their formal education never afterward read a single book.

There are other important values that are not spelled out in our American Creed. I am thinking of those details of human relationships that make all the difference between boorishness and brotherhood in the human family. As our population increases, it becomes more and more important to teach the elements of the new science of human relations which go far toward smoothing the roughness of common life by leading us to respect effectively the integrity of the other fellow. I recall a teacher of English whose class was studying *The Merchant of Venice*. She turned a wave of incipient anti-Semitism in her class to a sound lesson in values. Shylock, she explained, was like the resentful, self-seeking portion of every person's nature. We are all potential Shylocks. But while self-love is prominent in all of us, we are so constructed that it need not be sovereign in our natures.

To return for a moment to the relation between home and school—the former, as I have said, is far more important. Recognizing this fact, some people say,

"Well, let's leave the teaching of values to the home and to the church. Schools can't do much of anything about the matter."

This position is untenable. If the school does not teach values, it will have the effect of denying them. If the child at school never hears a mention of honesty, modesty, charity, or reverence, he will be persuaded that, like many of his parents' ideas, they are simply old hat. As they grow toward adolescence, children become critical of the teaching of both parents and the church. They are in a questioning stage. If the school, which to the child represents the larger outside world, is silent on values, the child will repudiate more quickly the lessons learned at home. He will also be thrown onto peer values more completely, with their emphasis on the hedonism of teen-age parties or on the destructiveness of gangs. He will also be more at the mercy of the sensate values peddled by movies, TV, and disk jockeys. What is more, some homes, as we have said, give no fundamental value training. In such a case, it is *only* in the school that the child has any chance at all of finding ethical anchorage.

This brings us to the hardest question: How does the teacher, the instructor, the professor, handle his assignment in the classroom? How is it possible to teach values, including the value of intellectual curiosity?

THE MEANING OF VALUE

Before tackling this question, we must pause to define what we mean by value. You will recognize that I am using the term psychologically, not in its objective philosophical sense. Values, as I use the term, are simply *meanings perceived as related to self*. The child experiences value whenever he knows that a meaning is warm and central to himself. Values, to borrow Whitehead's term, are "matters of importance" as distinct from mere matters of fact.

So much for definition. Now the hard-pressed teacher is given a solid substantive curriculum to teach. The curriculum in its original state consists of mere matters of fact. And on the number of facts absorbed the pupil's standing depends. It takes virtually all of a teacher's time to convey factual information and grade the pupil on his achievement. There is little time left to transmute these matters of fact into matters of importance, let alone teach all of the moral and social values we have thus far been discussing.

The curriculum itself is not, and should not be, a direct aid. Prescribed instruction in values would be laughed out of court. We have recently been bumped by Sputnik headforemost into core subjects. Get on with science, mathematics, language! Away with courses in folk-dancing, personal adjustment, and fudgemaking! I agree that value-study has no place in curriculum planning, but not because it is a frivolous subject—rather, because it is a subject too hard and too subtle for curriculum makers.

Education for values occurs only when teachers teach what they themselves stand for, no matter what their subject is. If I were to write a treatise on the teaching of values, I would give most of my emphasis to the moral pedagogy that lies in a teacher's incidental comments, to the *obiter dicta*. The hard core is central, but the hard core has a penumbra of moral significance. I mentioned the teacher of English who made a value-lesson out of Shylock. I recall also my college professor of geology who paused in his lecture on diatom ooze to say to us, "Others would not agree with me, but I confess that whenever I study diatoms, I don't see how anyone can doubt the existence of God because the design and behavior of these protozoa are so marvelous." Is it not interesting how we all recall the *obiter dicta* of our teachers, the penumbra of value they point out to us, surrounding the hard-core data? We remember them better than the subject matter itself.

Why does the student remember them so well? No current theory of learning seems able to tell us. I suspect it is because values, being matters of importance to the self, are always warm and central and ego-involved and therefore claim priority on our attention. The child, being value-ripe, cannot help being impressed when the teacher betrays excitement and enthusiasm for a mode of thought or for the content of the subject being studied. True, the youngster does not, and should not, adopt the teacher's values ready-made; but the teacher's self-disclosure leads the student to self-discovery.

What wouldn't we give if we could develop intellectual ardor in every child for hard-core subjects? Why is it that for most pupils arithmetic, spelling, physics, remain forever dull matters of fact and never become a meaning perceived as related to the self? One reason, I think, is that the weary teacher fails to convey his own sense of the importance of the subject to the student. If he did so, he would, as I have said, at least fix attention upon the value-potentiality of the subject.

Another reason perhaps is that not all of a teacher's *obiter dicta* are wholesome. Some, indeed, may be deeply damaging, though the teacher may be innocent of any such intent. Sometimes we hear incidental (but still attitude-forming) remarks like this one: "All right now, children. You have had a good time playing at recess; now settle down to your English lesson." Play is recognized as a matter of joyful importance. English, the teacher is saying in effect, is a mere routine matter of fact.

VALUES AND LEARNING

I think our educational psychology has been mostly wrong about the process of learning—or perhaps not so much wrong as woefully incomplete. At the beginning of his learning career, a young child cannot, of course, be expected to feel adult enthusiasm for the intellectual content of his studies. He does his work in the first instance to avoid a scolding or because he has a habit of obeying instructions. Soon he finds added incentive. The teacher—really in the role of mother—gives praise and love ("Susan, I am proud of you"). There is a great deal of such dependency in the learning situation. Love and social reward (as well as some fear of punishment) sustain the processes of attention and retention. When the child puts forth intellectual effort, he does so in order to obtain a gold star, commendation, or other symbols of love.

All these incentives are extraneous to the subject matter. The youngster does not learn it because it is a matter of importance. When he leaves school or college, he loses these extraneous supports. He finds his love relations directly; they are no longer a reward for intellectual effort. Hence, intellectual apathy sets in, and, distressing to say, no further books are read.

In such a case as this, intellectual curiosity was never tied to independence, only to extraneous supports. At some point in the schooling—and the earlier the better—intellectual activity should become not a second-hand but a first-hand fitting to the sense of self. At the beginning, all learning must be tied, perhaps, to specific reinforcements; but if the dependency is long continued, authentic curiosity fails to develop.

It would be going too far to put the blame for intellectual apathy onto our current teaching of educational psychology. Yet I am inclined to feel somewhat punitive about this matter. Psychology has not yet settled down to the problem of transforming matters of fact—whose acquisition current learning theories explain fairly well—into autonomous matters of importance—which they do not explain at all.

Our emphasis has been on learning by drill and by reinforcement. Such "habit acquisition" receives all the emphasis. But the learning theory involved postulates a continuing dependency relation (extraneous reinforcement). When the relation terminates, the habits of study simply extinguish themselves. I am surprised, therefore, that stimulus-response psychologists do not see this consequence of their own theory. Insofar as teachers employ an educational psychology of this order, they are not likely to break the dependency relation, which belongs properly only to the earlier stages of schooling.

Matters of importance, I strongly believe, are not acquired by drill or by reinforcement. They are transformations of habits and skills from the "opportunistic" layer of personality into the ego-system itself. Once inside the ego-system, these habits and skills turn into true interests and utilize the basic energy, the basic spontaneity, that the organism itself possesses. They are no longer sustained as "operant conditionings" by outside rewards. The interest, now being the very stuff of life itself, needs no outer supports.

FUNCTIONAL AUTONOMY

I have called this process of transforming means into ends, of changing extrinsic values into intrinsic values, *functional autonomy*. Concerning this concept, I am often asked two questions: "How do you define 'functional autonomy'?" and "How does functional autonomy come about?"

For a definition, I offer the following: Functional autonomy refers to any acquired system of motivation in which the tensions involved are no longer of the

298   GORDON W. ALLPORT

same kind as the antecedent tensions from which the acquired system developed.[1] To answer the question of how functional autonomy comes about requires a more extended and technical discussion. I can only hint at the direction of my answer. Neurologists are gradually discovering a basis for what I would call "perseverative functional autonomy." I refer to the "self-sustaining circuits," "feedback mechanisms," and "central motive states" that are now commonly recognized to exist in the nervous system. This line of discovery, I find, provides a partial answer to the question. But I believe we have to go further and call on the concept of self. Values, we have said, are meanings perceived as related to the self. Functional autonomy is not a mere preservative phenomenon; it is, above all, an ego-involved phenomenon. Besides admitting an opportunistic layer to personality, which is the exclusive concern of most current theories of learning, we have no choice but to admit also a "propriate" layer. It is in this layer that all matters of importance reside.

The goal of the educator, then, is to shift the content of the subject he teaches from the opportunistic (matter of fact) layer to the propriate. But there is no sure-fire, mechanical strategy to use. The best general rule, one that John Dewey saw clearly, is to strive ceaselessly to integrate routine matters of fact into the growing experience system of the child himself. It would take a long treatise to specify various detailed strategies of teaching that help achieve this goal.

Let me focus on only one aspect of this topic, upon a common mistake that teachers make. I myself am a continual offender. It is to present students with our own carefully thought out conclusions when they themselves lack the raw experience from which these conclusions are fashioned.

This particular error is inherent, for example, in the lecture system. Instead of lecturing on comparative religion, for instance, it would be much better to require all students to attend services of worship that are unfamiliar to them. If raw experience is present, then perhaps a lecture may be effective. Much of the intellectual apathy we complain about is due to our fault of presenting conclusions in lieu of first-hand experience. To us, our well-chiseled conclusion, summing up a long intellectual struggle with a problem of knowledge or of value, seems like a beautiful sonnet. To the student, it may be gibberish.

The fallacy of giving conclusions holds both for subject matter and for values. A lad of 15 cannot profit from the fully fashioned philosophy of life of a man of 50. To register at all, a statement about values must fall precisely on his present growing edge.

Teaching, then, is not the art of offering conclusions, however hard won and valid they may be. No teacher can forcibly enter the students' proprium and plant a functionally autonomous motive. He can at best open channels of ex-

[1] If this definition seems too technical to be immediately helpful, see Ch. 10 of *Pattern and Growth in Personality* for a more extended treatment of functional autonomy.

perience and, by his *obiter dicta,* sometimes lead the student to see the value-potential in the experience.

The theory of personality that we need to guide a more fully developed educational psychology will teach us something important about our basic verb "to educate." It will show us that only at the outset of learning is it a transitive verb. By drill, by reward, by reinforcement, the teacher does indeed educate the child —in matters of fact. But true maturity comes only when the verb is reflexive. For in matters of importance, where values lie, the growing individual alone can educate himself.

34 The structures of rewards and punishments in the middle and lower classes

Related selections: 20, 21, 23, 29, 35

The growing amount of research on social-class structure in America indicates that not only does this structure operate in the schools but that it operates to the detriment of lower-class children. Most public school teachers are from the middle class and need more understanding of the motivational structure of lower-class children and adolescents. What are the differences in basic drives of the lower and middle classes? What are the differences in their rewards and punishments? These are questions to which Dr. Davis has given much study. The student will profit from reading the entire Inglis Lecture, Social-Class Influences upon Learning, *of which the following selection is a part.*

Any attempt to trace the processes by which human beings in our society learn their social drives and social goals must face the problem of social-class differ-

Reprinted by permission of the publishers from ALLISON DAVIS, *Social-Class Influences upon Learning* (Cambridge, Mass.: Harvard University Press), pp. 23–37. Copyright, 1948, by The President and Fellows of Harvard College.

DR. DAVIS (1902–   ) is Professor of Education at the University of Chicago and was a staff member in the division of child development, Commission on Teacher Education, American Council on Education. He is a student of the class and caste structure of American society and its effects on human development.

ences in motivation. These differences occur in most of the basic areas of human psychology: in mental problem-solving, and in the motivational areas of hunger, sex, and aggression. The most urgent problem for the public schools is to learn the motivational structure of lower-class children and adolescents. About two thirds of our elementary school pupils have been trained in lower-class families and neighborhoods; at least one third of our school population comes from the bottom group within the lower class, the slum culture.

The fate of our nation, industrially, politically, and in case of war, depends primarily upon the ability of the public schools to help large numbers of children from these slum and farm-tenant groups to learn the basic skills of our society. The schools have not learned how to do this. Our public schools for the lowest third of our population, the schools in slums, are almost a complete failure. The staffs of these schools generally are aware of their basic failure, and are demoralized. Little serious effort has been made by our teachers, colleges, and universities to investigate this major problem in public education. Our effort here will be directed primarily, therefore, toward examining the motivational structure as learned by the lower-class child from his family and other cultural groups.

To understand the socialization of slum children, one must first view the slum adult-world, and trace the motivational system which slum adults exhibit, as a group. What are the basic social drives of slum adults? To put this question more carefully, what experiences does the slum individual learn from his group to define as "pleasant," and what experiences does he learn to define as "painful" among the available experiences in his world?

This approach seems to be the quickest route to an understanding of the social motivation of any group. For we know from cultural anthropologists that the primary function of all human cultures is to teach the members of the group to regard certain experiences as pleasant and others as painful. That is to say, nearly all rewards and punishments, so-called, vary with regard to their particular form, intensity, and effect from culture to culture. We wish to know, therefore, (1) what experiences seem, to the slum group, to be most attainable, pleasant, and free from anxiety, and (2) what experiences seem most unpleasant, or seem most dangerous to the physical survival or social acceptance of the individual. Anyone who has tried to increase the motivation of slum individuals to work or study regularly knows that these are not simple questions.

One of the most basic differences in motivation between lower-class and middle-class people is their attitude toward eating. Owing to the greater security of their food supply, middle-class people eat more regularly. They therefore have learned to eat more sparingly at any given time, because they know they are certain of their next meal. They have also developed a conscientious taboo upon "overeating"; they feel some guilt about getting fat and about what they call "raiding the icebox."

Slum people, however, have a very uncertain food supply. Their fear that they will not get enough to eat develops soon after the nursing period. Therefore, when the supply is plentiful, they eat as much as they can hold. They "pack food away" in themselves as a protection against the shortage which will develop before tht next payday. They wish to get fat for they regard fat as a protection against tuberculosis and physical weakness. Basically, the origin of this attitude toward eating is their deep fear of starvation.

Just as food-anxiety is far more urgent in lower-class than it is in middle-class society, so is the anxiety which is aroused by the danger of eviction from shelter, the danger of having too little sleep, the danger of being cold, and the danger of being in the dark. The middle-class individual is relatively certain that he will have enough coal or light; he buys his coal by the ton or the five tons; he burns five or ten electric lights. But the lower-class person's hold upon fire for heating is on a day-to-day or week-to-week basis. He buys coal by the bushel, or by the five bushels, or by one-ton loads. Every week or so, therefore, he has to face the fear of being cold, and of having his children cold.

Similarly with light, his anxiety is far more chronic and realistic. His evenings are spent in a gray light; if more than one or two bulbs are used, and those are not of the lowest candle power, he will not be able to pay the light bill. Therefore, the fear of not having so basic a necessity as light—a fear which middle-class people escape after childhood—is recurrent with the slum individual. Walk into any real slum housing at night. People are crowded together in a dingy, twilight world. Their streets and alleys likewise are full of darkness, so that their chronic expectation of assault or rape is increased.

Just as slum people have painful, anxiety-ridden associations with food, so they have with shelter, sleep, and darkness. To this list must be added the fear of being inadequately clothed in winter. Most slum men, Negroes and whites, have no overcoat in normal times. Most sharecroppers' children have no woolen clothes in cold winter weather.

Now, when these same people get relatively large increases in income—as they did during the late war—they spend their money "extravagantly," as middle-class people judge their behavior. What is the meaning of this "splurging" for fur coats, for expensive clothes for children, for new furniture, and so forth? Part of the motivation is a drive for prestige-symbols, an attempt to acquire some of the signs of middle-class status. Equally important, certainly, is its function as a defense against anxiety, which is similar to the function of their Gargantuan eating after payday. When one has money, he buys things which he will be able to buy only once or twice in his lifetime—such things as expensive, respectable, or warm clothes, and a "decent" bed. He burns all the lights he wants; he eats great quantities of meat.

Thus, lower-class people look upon life as a recurrent series of depressions and peaks, with regard to the gratification of their basic needs. In their lives, it is all or nothing, or next-to-nothing. When they have fire, their homes are stifling hot, and everyone sits as close to the fire as possible. For they remember anxiously what it was to be cold; to be too cold to sit in the house; so cold that the whole family must go to bed to keep warm. Just as their deep anxiety about starvation leads them even in good times to glut themselves, as middle-class people view their eating, so does the learned fear of deprivation drive lower-class people to get all they can of the other physical gratifications, "while the getting is good."

It would be more rational if they saved and budgeted their money, but human beings are not rational. They are what their culture teaches them to be. "Man is a reasoning, but not a reasonable animal." Lower-class people cannot learn middle-class foresight and moderation unless they can participate socially with middle-class people, whom they may then learn to imitate. So far, the public school is our only chance to teach lower-class people the middle-class motivational pattern. But the schools do not yet understand how to reward lower-class pupils. Furthermore, our economic system does not offer any prospect of a regular income to slum people; therefore, they lack the relative security which must underlie habits of saving, buying insurance, home buying, and so forth. As the average slum worker says, "Why should I try to save? The little bit I could put aside will be gone six months after the next depression starts."

Turning now to those experiences which are defined as painful chiefly by the social, as contrasted to the physical, environment, we find that the socially aroused anxieties are still more numerous. The middle-class view that slum people have no sense of respectability, feel no pressure for social conformity, is simply ignorance of the facts. Lower-class culture includes a vast number of social taboos, and therefore stimulates a great number of social anxieties. First— to return to the so-called "physical" area of food, shelter, heat, and so on— slum culture has its own "decent" or "respectable" standards for food and housing. Lower-class people learn their own group's cultural standard of "enough to eat," or "a good house," or "good furniture." It is probably only when the culture goals for subsistence (as "subsistence" is defined by slum culture) are threatened, therefore, that the person experiences marked anxiety. Lower-class people consider the same house or job as "good" which middle-class people regard as humiliating. The same standard of living that raises the anxiety of middle-class people will greatly allay the anxiety of slum people in our present social system.

The socially defined dangers of slum life originate in the threat of disapproval, ridicule, or rejection of the individual by his family, play-group, gang, church, club, and so on. All these lower-class groups make cultural demands of the child and adolescent, just as do the middle-class family, play-group, and so on. But the demands are generally different than those of the middle-class group. In other words, the lower-class individual is taught by his culture to be anxious about different social dangers. Whereas the middle-class child learns a socially adaptive fear of receiving poor grades in school, of being aggressive toward the teacher, of fighting, of cursing, and of having early sex relations, the slum child learns to fear quite different social acts. His gang teaches him to fear being taken in by the teacher, of being a softie with her. To study homework seriously is literally a disgrace. Instead of boasting of good marks in school, one conceals them, if he receives any. The lower-class individual fears *not* to be thought a street-fighter; it is a suspicious and dangerous social trait. He fears *not to curse.* If he cannot claim early sex relations, his virility is seriously questioned.

Thus society raises many anxieties in slum people also, but with regard to the attainment of what seem to middle-class people to be strange goals. For those who must live in a slum community, however, these goals are realistic and adaptive.

There is space here to consider only two areas of experience which are patterned by slum culture as chiefly pleasant. I do not believe that there is any evidence that these two areas, sex relations and physical aggression, are more basic physiologically than the food area or the heat-cold area of experience. But psychologically, the areas of sex and agression are the most formative of middle-class personality, because middle-class culture teaches the individual, from childhood, that sexual responses and physical aggression, more than any other behaviors, must be either inhibited or very carefully controlled. The result of this middle-class training of children to fear their own sex impulses and their own rage is usually to make sex and aggression the chief problem-areas of the middle-class personality. The manifestations of these two types of problems are usually highly disguised, but the source is very simple. Sex and aggression (including stealing) become, if not "properly" controlled and guided according to the middle-class cultural standard, the most dangerous forms of behavior to a person of middle-class status. The middle-class child is taught this lesson by precept and example. For a large portion of middle-class people, therefore, sex has been stamped as "dirty," or "unimportant," and filled with anxiety, because in both their childhood and adolescence their own sexual responses were made to appear too dangerous socially by their parents and teachers.

In slum groups, on the other hand, both children and adults are permitted far more gratification of their sexual responses and of their rage responses. This "permissiveness," as it seems to middle-class people, extends into most of the basic areas of adolescent behavior in the lower class.

Before comparing middle-class and lower-class adolescents, however, a warning must be injected here. We recall that the long, indulgent nursing period of lower-class infants does not prevent their developing marked fear of starvation in later childhood and adulthood. This fact means that new situations, if strongly organized physically or socially, make new behavior. This is a cardinal principle of the new integrated science of social psychology. Basic learning can and does appear at any age level, provided that society or the physical environment changes the organization of its basic rewards and punishments for the individual.

Secondly, we should not be so naive as to think that lower-class life is a happy hunting ground given over to complete impulse expression. Slum people must accept in some form all of the basic sexual controls on incest, homosexuality, and marital irresponsibility. In fact, there is evidence to indicate that they are more observant of the taboos upon incest and homosexuality than is the upper class. Furthermore, the same pattern which holds in their food-intake—of deprivation, relieved by peaks of great indulgence—is typical of lower-class sexual life. Lack of housing, lack of beds, frequent separations of mates and lovers, the hard daily work of mothers with six to fourteen children, the itinerant life of the men, all make sexual life less regular, secure, and routine than in middle class. In the slum, one certainly does not have a sexual partner for as many days each month as do middle-class married people, but one gets and gives more satisfaction, over longer periods, when he does have a sexual partner. With this reservation in mind, one may proceed to examine adolescent behavior in the two classes.

The aggressive behavior of adolescents is a crucial case in point. In the middle class, aggression is clothed in the conventional forms of initiative, or ambition, or even of progressiveness, but in the lower class it more often appears unabashed as physical attack, or as threats of and encouragement for physical attack. In general, middle-class aggression is taught to adolescents in the form of social and economic skills which will enable them to compete effectively at that level. The lower classes not uncommonly teach their children and adolescents to strike out with fist or knife and to be certain to hit first. Both girls and boys at adolescence may curse their father to his face or even attack him with fists, sticks, or axes in free-for-all family encounters. Husbands and wives sometimes stage pitched battles in the home; wives have their husbands arrested; and husbands try to break in or burn down their own homes when locked out. Such fights with fists or weapons, and the whipping of wives, occur sooner or later in most lower-class families. They may not appear today, nor tomorrow, but they will appear if the observer remains long enough.

The important consideration with regard to physical aggression in lower-class adolescents is, therefore, that it is learned as an approved and socially rewarded form of behavior in their culture. An interviewer of ours recently observed two nursery-school boys from lower-class families; they were boasting about the length of their fathers' clasp knives! The parents themselves have taught their children to fight not only children of either sex but also adults who "make trouble" for them. If the child or adolescent cannot whip a grown opponent, the mother or father will join the fight. In such lower-class groups, an adolescent boy who does not try to be a good fighter will not receive the approval of the father, nor will he be acceptable to any play-group or gang. The result of these cultural sanctions is that he learns to fight and to admire fighters. The conception that aggression and hostility are neurotic or maladaptive symptoms of a chronically frustrated adolescent is an ethnocentric view of middle-class psychiatrists. In lower-class families, physical aggression is as much a normal, socially approved and socially inculcated type of behavior as it is in frontier communities.

There are many forms of aggression, of course, which are disapproved by lower-class as well as by middle-class adolescents. These include, among others, attack by magic or poison, rape, and cutting a woman in the face. Yet all of these forms of aggression are fairly common in some lower-class areas. Stealing is another form of aggression which lower-class parents verbally forbid, but which many of them in fact allow—so long as their child does not steal from his family or its close friends. The example of the adolescent's play-group and of his own kin, however, is the crucial determinant of his behavior. Even where the efforts of the parent to instill middle-class mores in the child are more than half-hearted, the power of the street culture in which the child and adolescent are trained overwhelms the parental verbal instruction. The rewards of gang social prestige, of freedom of movement, and of property-gain all seem to be on the side of the street culture.

Like physical aggression, sexual relationships and motivation are more direct and uninhibited in lower-class adolescents. The most striking departure from the usual middle-class motivation is that, in much lower-class life, sexual drives and behavior in children are not regarded as inherently taboo and dangerous.

There are many parents in low-status culture, of course, who taboo these behaviors for their girls. Mothers try to prevent daughters from having children before they are married, but the example of the girl's own family is often to the contrary. At an early age the child learns of common-law marriages and extramarital relationships by men and women in his own family. He sees his father disappear to live with other women, or he sees other men visit his mother or married sisters. Although none of his siblings may be illegitimate, the chances are very high that sooner or later his father and mother will accuse each other of having illegitimate children, or that at least one of his brothers or sisters will have a child outside of marriage. His play-group, girls and boys, discuss sexual relations frankly at the age of eleven or twelve, and he gains status with them by beginning intercourse early.

With sex, as with aggression, therefore, the social instigations and reinforcements of adolescents who live in these different cultures are opposites. The middle-class adolescent finds the roads to sex and aggression blocked by painful and intimidating experiences; the lower-class adolescent is frequently rewarded, both socially and organically, for these same behaviors. The degree of anxiety, guilt, or frustration attached to the behaviors, therefore, is entirely different in the two cases. One might go so far as to say that, in the case of middle-class adolescents, such anxiety and guilt, with regard to physical aggression and sexual intercourse, are proof of their normal socialization in their culture. In lower-class adolescents in certain environments, they are evidence of revolt against their own class culture, and therefore of incipient personality difficulties.

35 Gang and narcotic problems of teen-age youth

Related selections: 19, 34, 45, 49, 50

Children and youth of today encounter more frustrations and anxieties, more uncertainties and confusions than youth have ever before experienced. In such a milieu it is not at all surprising that gang warfare and drug use and addiction, as well as other forms of social and emotional maladjustment, seem to be on the increase. Those who are interested in understanding the needs of youth and in working with their problems will find Dr. Dumpson's discourse a valuable source of information concerning the etiology of such problems.

INTRODUCTION

Within one decade we have experienced in urban areas of this country two crisis situations among adolescent youth. During the period immediately following World War II, many communities were concerned about teen-age gang warfare. Early in 1950, we became aware of the increased use of narcotic drugs by teen-age youth. Probably more public concern has been expressed about these two behavior manifestations among adolescents than any other adolescent activities with which we are familiar in recent years.

In organizing my thinking and my experience in planning community programs to meet the needs of youth engaging in deviant behavior, it became clear to me that there are outstanding similarities in the description of the phenomena of gang boy and youthful addict and in the causative factors that precipitate their deviant behavior. Antisocial gang activity and drug addiction are types of behavior symptomatic of social and emotional maladjustment in the individual. Each of these two behavior patterns serves a function in the psychic economy of the teen-ager who is involved. In each, the etiology is deeply rooted in a multiplicity of interacting physical, social, and psychological forces.

For the gang boy and the teen-age addict, the frustrations and anxieties created by a world that has experienced a prolonged and seemingly unending state

JAMES R. DUMPSON, "Gang and Narcotic Problems of Teen-Age Youth," *American Journal of Psychotherapy*, VI (April, 1952), 312–28. Reprinted by permission of the author and the publisher.

DR. DUMPSON (1909–   ) is Commissioner of Welfare, New York City. At the time of publication of this article he was Director, Bureau of Child Welfare, New York City.

of war; the uncertainties of the future in terms of marriage, family, and productive living; the changing function of the family resulting in basic changes in child-parent relationship; the confusion that develops as a result of what is taught in the rearing process, in contrast to the practices they observe in meaningful adults in day-to-day living; the damage to self-esteem flowering from the practices of segregation and discrimination to minority groups—all of these characteristics of our present day world are important factors in the production of damaged and disturbed youth. These social factors become forces for antisocial behavior and set in motion a number of psychological processes. The extent to which these processes are activated depends on the individual's personality structure, the strengths and weaknesses of that personality. This backdrop of social psychological pathology reaps its toll with individuals as they accommodate to it. The behavior of the addict and of the gang boy is each's response to the pressures of his environment accompanied by resultant intermediary psychological processes.

Notwithstanding the commonality of precipitating causative factors, certain adolescents respond differently to them. Antisocial gang activity represents one response; drug use and addiction represents another. It is hoped that the discussion of these factors, as I have observed their interaction in the gang boy and the addict, will contribute eventually to the development by this and similar groups of a theory of therapy that will be practical and effective.

In considering the antisocial teen-age gang, it is my purpose to suggest certain factors in gang structure and activity that were seen in the work of the Central Harlem Street Clubs Project of the Welfare Council of New York City during the three year period ending in March 1950, and to point up implications of gang membership and activity that may be pertinent to your interests as therapists. The material present here is based on the experiences reported by the Project as published in the book, *Working with Teen-Age Gangs* by Crawford, Malamud and your speaker. Major emphasis in my statement will be placed on administrative aspects of the problem and those treatment techniques that are within the function and skill of the casework process.

The gang is recognized as a specific type of structural division in associative life. Sociologically speaking, it is a primary group characterized by face-to-face contacts and direct inter-action, set up by common locality. In its genesis, the gang arises out of play groups from which it spontaneously develops. It is the next rung, after the family, in the social structure where the individual receives training in meeting his equal, in learning cooperation, and in struggling to express his own wishes. It is important to point out, however, that irrespective of its complex organization, in its full development, the gang is organized by the members themselves and not by adults interested in providing recreation or education for youth. In the course of contact with other play groups or gangs, and with the expression of adult authority, parents and police, the gang becomes formalized and structuralized. The impingement of certain social, physical and psychological pressures acting upon the individuals and the group produce antisocial behavior as one distinguishing characteristic of the gang.

The so-called "street gang" in its activity, may be classified as one of three types:

1. A group whose principal activities are antisocial. This is the criminal gang whose sole function and activities are antisocial in nature.

2. A group which occasionally engages in antisocial activities. This group is primarily a social unit engaging in activities common to all adolescents. In response to appropriate environmental pressures, it may engage in antisocial or delinquent behavior.

3. A group which does not engage in antisocial activity, although individual members of the group may follow confirmed patterns of delinquent behavior.

The first type is a common form of organization in social life among adults. The other two types are usual among teen-age youth and are characteristic phenomena of modern urban life.

Only brief allusion needs to be made to the history of hostile, aggressive behavior that began among teen-age gangs in various sections of New York City during the early 1940's, that reached its height in 1947, and recently has flared up again in Brooklyn and the Bronx. The activities of these gangs were not just boyish escapades; they were carried on in dead seriousness. Instead of sticks and stones as weapons, gang boys used home-made guns, knives, and other lethal instruments. Instead of ending up with a few bruised shins, scratched faces or black eyes, these fights frequently resulted in serious casualties, including death to the participants and innocent non-participants. Instead of the typical corner fight between two adolescent boys, street gang fighters have involved as many as 100 or more boys in each opposing group. Stealing is a commonly accepted practice, ranging from petty thievery to more serious offenses such as purse snatching, breaking into stores, and armed robberies. While sex offenses, as commonly defined, occurred very rarely, some of the older boys engaged in "line-ups" and committed rape. Truancy, drinking, gambling, and narcotics use were all part of the pattern.

The boys involved in the project lived in a community of inadequate health, education and recreation facilities; overcrowding, poor housing, and low economic status. The people reacted to segregation and discrimination with hostile and tense feelings which underlay many of their attitudes toward the value system of the community at large. The ambivalence of the adults toward the values and patterns of the larger community should be seen as a dynamic environmental factor in the development of teen-age antisocial gangs.

A partial understanding of the motivation of the behavior of these boys was identified when we attempted to discern how they defined their own situation. Some boys stated that they joined gangs out of their felt need for protection. Others indicated that the gang provided avenues through which satisfying recreational experiences were obtained. They all indicated that engaging in activities, considered antisocial by the community, was considered by them to be a normal way of relating to their environment. The boys tended to see adults as "authorities," "hoodlums," or "suckers." "Authorities" pushed them around, told them what to do and what not to do, moralized, made demands, threatened, condemned, and meted out punishment. "Hoodlums" were smart guys who got along in the world by exploiting, cheating, and outwitting the other fellow. "Suckers" were "softies" who worked for a living, never stepped out of line, and always did what was right. For these boys, most adults belonged to one of these groups. The boys hated and feared "authorities"; had wary respect for "hoodlums," and expressed contempt for the "suckers"! Many boys felt that their fellow club members were the only persons in the world for whom they cared and on whom they could count.

The four gangs with which the Project worked were well organized on both a formal and informal level. The broad base for the pyramidal structure of the club was the special interest club group, the social clubs, the baseball, basketball and football teams. Practically all of the boys identified with a club were participating members of one of these subgroups or teams. Their concept of the democratic process was built around a handful of powerful personalities that did the deciding. They had their cliques, power blocs, and boards of strategy, which were powerful groups with high status rank in the gang structure. One person, the gang leader, by virtue of his position, did most to determine the gang's structure, atmosphere, ideology, and activities. He might even determine its goals, have the central role in coordinating the activities, exert discipline and the means of reaching the group's goals. One gang leader was larger in physical stature than his followers and the only one to use his size and prowess to maintain control over the gang. The other three retained control by establishing themselves as ideals for the boys. Through their dash and daring, their cleverness and cunning, the impetuousness to act and to dominate, their drive to command and conquer, they maintained control over the group. While one leader was appointed, the others "topsied" into power. None was chosen by the democratic process, nor did any gain his position through the coup d'état. All were respected; all were feared. For the most part they were little men in quest of adventure and power!

Many workers with gang boys agree that these boys are psychologically sick, that their membership in and use of the gang, and the behavior that follows has its roots in seriously distorted personality structures and neurotic needs. We have been able to identify three basic forces that contribute materially to the emotional maladjustment of the gang boy: (1) damage to the boy's security feeling; (2) damage to the socialization process; and (3) damage to the self-esteem of the child. Cultural factors such as group prejudice, poverty, authoritarian family structure, and social disorganization are also identified as contributing to the individual's unhealthy ego development. Further, we identified factors in early childhood, such as parental rejection, family tension and disorganization, social isolation, and traumatic experiences as potent negative forces in the individual's development. Most workers with gangs also recognize the impact of current situational factors, such as chronic conflict in the environment, organic inferiorities, over-severe ideals, feelings of difference, and inability to meet cultural demands for masculinity or femininity. This formulation highlights, again, the bio-psycho-social aspect of delinquent gang behavior and suggests the need to discover whether there is a generic principle for treatment and preventing of such behavior.

As has been suggested, boys within the gang "interchangeably occupied the role of the persistent delinquent, occasional delinquent, and non-delinquent," reflecting frequently the alternative value systems virtually contained in each mode of conduct and reflecting, too, the duality of conduct norms of the area. The two-scale value orientation and its implications in the areas in which such gangs thrive need to be recognized and taken into consideration by therapists and caseworkers alike. Shifting adherence to the conventional value system and conduct norms and a deep motivation to change represent, frequently, the points at which the caseworker or the therapist may relate his role, his skills, and his function in treatment.

Out of our three year experience, we finally developed a conceptual scheme as a guide for working with antisocial street gangs. Basic to this conceptual scheme, I believe, is the need to recognize that the major determining factor in behavior is the need of the behavior. Only if we know the gang boy's needs and goals can we hope to affect change in his behavior. It is the need of behavior which gives it meaning, direction, and consistency. We have failed in our work with the "gang boy" and in handling similar deviant behavior to the extent that we have failed to find the answer to the question of what the boys need and why they misbehave. Behavior, delinquent or non-delinquent, is need satisfaction. Surely we find clues for treatment in recognizing that the gang boy, in his attempt to gain mastery over things and people, and his identification with the gang and the power inherent in such a group, is using mechanisms to defend his ego and to achieve a sense of self-esteem. The approach we developed recognized the technical limitations as well as the function of the casework process. While this theoretical framework is still provisional, I am certain that future efforts with teen-age gangs require staff persons who are psychiatrically oriented and should include the services of a psychiatrist to serve as a diagnostic consultant to the staff.

Three stages of relationship can be distinguished during the course of the worker's relationship with the boys. In the first, his primary emphasis was on overcoming the boys' distrust and gaining their acceptance. In the second, the worker focused on stimulating change in their attitudes and behavior. In the third, he aimed for a successful closing of relations. The stages overlapped and were interrelated; each presented its own opportunities and hazards, developed at different times for different boys or subgroups, and determined, at least partly, the kind of procedures that the worker followed. The following stages in relationships are suggested:

1. *Gaining acceptance:* It is axiomatic that the worker needed to gain the boys' acceptance before he could hope to effect constructive change. As their trust, respect, and affection for him grew, their amenability to his influence increased. They gave more careful consideration to his reasoning, interpretations, suggestions, insight-giving, and example-setting. They behaved in ways which they felt would please him and gain his approval, or they followed his example because they wanted to be like him. Techniques used successfully by the workers in establishing this first stage of relationship varied. For example, in order to "win" the boys, the workers attempted to satisfy their needs for affection, understanding and guidance. They did not condemn them for their behavior but showed confidence in the boys' capacity to work out their own problems constructively. They demonstrated their positive attitudes toward the boys not by words alone, but by spending time with them and sharing in their play, discussions, and planning. During this first stage, the workers learned all they could about the club's structure, its ideology, its activities, and its needs as well as evaluating the personality patterns of the individual members. They coped with such problems as gaining initial contact with a hostile, distrustful group, structuring their role with the boy and the group, and passing the boys' various "tests" of the worker. Obviously, the degree of success in this first stage of developing relationship influenced considerably the worker's effectiveness in subsequent stages.

2. *Stimulating change:* By the time the worker entered this stage, he had achieved at least an approximate understanding of the dynamics underlying the boys' attitudes and behavior. Based on this understanding, he developed a systematic conception of the conditions under which specific changes can be expected. He acquainted himself with the range of possible methods for stimulating change and developed skill in the use of those which appeared most appropriate. In this stage he had to meet such problems as resistance, pseudo-change, anxiety following change, and relapses.

3. *Closing relations:* In contrast to most therapy situations, because we were on a time limited project, the termination of the workers' relations with the boys depended on a predetermined closing date rather than the degree of progress shown by the group. Therefore, unusually careful preparation of the boys for the workers' separation was required. Such preparation, initiated at the very outset of the relationship, was given special attention in the closing months

of the project. During the final stage the worker, by tapering off his contacts and playing a progressively less prominent role in the affairs of the club, enabled the boys to test and gain confidence in their own capacity for responsible self-direction. In most instances, he encouraged the group to establish relations with other community adults or agencies, and referred for psychiatric or other specialized services those boys who needed it and were ready to use it.

This closing stage, too, presented a number of problems. Boys relapsed into antisocial behavior, some because they interpreted the worker's departure as betrayal or rejection, others because they had established a dependency on the worker and attempted to use their behavior to have him stay on. Members whose emotional ties to the worker were very deep frequently manifested their disturbance in the form of neurotic symptoms. Obviously, unless this stage is handled skillfully, the worker may nullify much of his previous accomplishment.

Working on this level of treatment with a group of 125 hostile, aggressive gang boys assigned to four male workers, none of whom were psychiatrically trained or oriented, after three years we assessed our results. What did we accomplish?

1. Each of the workers was able to establish a working relationship with a gang. While these relationships varied in quality and intensity, they placed the workers in a position to exert a constructive influence.

2. We did have a definite impact on the boys' aggressive behavior, but exerted much less influence on their escapist activities. From the time we established contact with the boys until the end of the project, there was no gang warfare in the project area. A decline in stealing was reported for three of the gangs, in sex offenses for one, and in truancy for another. There was, however, no significant change in the practice of narcotics use, drinking, or gambling.

3. The boys engaged in more organized recreational programs and won unprecedented opportunities for achievement and neighborhood recognition. Successful participation in planning, decision-making, and carrying out responsibilities gave the boys a new sense of confidence and self-esteem.

4. New services were made available to these boys. Individual counselling helped a few achieve a better personal and social adjustment. A few were referred for intensive psychiatric help.

Finally, however, without in any way detracting from the accomplishments listed above, I must point out what we failed to achieve: With the possible exception of two or three members, we did not effect basic changes in the boys' ideology. True, their hostility and aggression seemed to have diminished, their antagonistic attitudes toward the adult world softened, and they began to view the future more constructively and more hopefully. Despite these changes, we believe that their basic attitudes towards themselves and others, although dormant perhaps, still exist. To these boys the world is still a dangerous jungle. Yes, they may grant the presence of sympathetic allies in this jungle, but a jungle it is nonetheless. It is still important to them to be tough. Fearfulness and weakness are still despised traits. The exaggerated need for status, the contempt for the law, exploitative attitudes towards girls—these and other trends still operate virtually unmodified in most of the boys.

The second atypical group to be discussed in this paper is the teen-age narcotic drug user and addict. Actually, teen-age addicts do not organize themselves into any social group with a structure and dynamic of its own. We may refer to teen-age drug users and addicts as a group only in the sense that they present a common course of development as far as their addiction is concerned, and according to some studies, a common set of characteristics including certain common personality traits. My discussion of the teen-age addict here will be limited to a consideration of the two aspects of the problem which most youthful addicts seem to have in common—the course of development of drug use, and the characteristics of the youth group involved in the problem. We have had too little experience locally to discuss the effectiveness of treatment efforts of adolescent users and addicts and their results. To this effort we hope that many disciplines will contribute their thinking and experience.

It was in the spring and early summer of 1950 that we recognized the existence of drug use and drug addiction to an alarming degree in New York City. Actually, of course, the use of narcotic drugs by teen-age youth preceded the year 1950. Pescor, in his statistical analysis of hospitalized drug addicts in 1943, found "that while no age is exempt from drug addiction, there is a heavy concentration of cases in the decade 20 to 29 years, more than half being victimized during this period"; 16.5 per cent of those studied, he found, were 19 years of age or less at the onset of their addiction. Dr. Perry Lichtenstein reported in the New York Medical Journal of November, 1913, that "the number of young people addicted is enormous. I have come in contact with individuals sixteen and eighteen years of age, whose history was that they had taken a habit-forming drug for at least two years." In our contact with 125 teen-age gang boys we found that 79 or 42 per cent admitted to the use of narcotic drugs.

The startling fact about our current situation is the lowered age level and the increasing number of youth who are involved. In the past we were prone to identify drug use with individuals in particular social and economic strata of the community. Our experience clearly indicates that today, drug use among teen-agers cuts across all economic, social, racial, religious, and educational lines. Youth from all sections of the city are represented in the group of narcotic drug users or addicts.

The course of drug use and addiction among adolescents and the adaptation process involved are set forth in a preliminary study by Stanley K. Bigman, of the Bureau of Applied Research at Columbia University. Bigman describes the process by which adolescent addicts are made as having these phases:

1. *The phase of orientation:* The young person first goes through a process of learning which predisposes him favorably or unfavorably to the use of drugs. This orientation, we are told, comes from those who constitute the person's social world. There is substantial evidence that large numbers of boys and girls know about drugs in many sections of the city, and the ease with which it can be secured. The duality of conduct norms in many of these areas, previously discussed in connection with teen-age gangs, very likely condition the kind of orientation the youth receive.

2. *The phase of experimentation:* During this period, when narcotics are available for the first time, some youngsters will refuse to use drugs at all, some try their use intermittently, and some begin regular use culminating in addiction. The orientation to drugs of the key people in the lives of youth is an important factor in their orientation and the choice they will make concerning drug use.

3. *The phase of addiction:* With the experiencing of the symptoms of drug withdrawal, their interpretation as due to the absence of the drugs, and the resumption of drug use to alleviate them, addiction usually follows.

While Bigman's completed study of the adaptation of individuals to drug use leading to addiction, when considered in the light of psychiatric understanding, will be valuable to all of us, we already know that the youngster who plays with narcotics may be "hooked" before he is aware of it. For certain personality types, two or three experimentations with a potent drug, within a relatively short period of time may produce a mild physical dependency on the drug.

In addition to Bigman's sociological formulations concerning the adaptive process involved in adolescent drug addiction, other influential social and psychological factors must be considered. Any theory of therapy must recognize the search for status by many of these teen-age addicts (and a potent factor in motivating gang activity) who have had denied to them by institutions in the community the normal outlets for prestige and a sense of personal worth. Cognizance must be taken, too, of the fact that there is a concentration of teen-age addicts and users in the economically and socially deprived areas of our community. The socio-economic conditions of these areas represent important causative factors in the situation. They contribute to emotional instability and maladjustment and increase the addiction-prone characteristic of many of the youth in these areas. Zimmering, Toolan, Safrin, and Wortis, in a study of 22 consecutive adolescent boys admitted to Bellevue Hospital Psychiatric Division for heroin addiction in January and February, 1951, state that "all but one of our

22 patients have been Negroes or of Puerto Rican descent." They indicated that these boys all suffered psychologically from the discriminatory practices and attitudes directed against their racial groups. Their racial characteristics were considered to be a stamp of inferiority and they suffered injuries to their self-esteem. These authors state that "crime in its varied form flourished there (Harlem) and now the illegal drug traffic has become a major underworld activity." Bigman, not unlike other qualified observers, alleges that the orientation to drug use is unfavorable in the Negro community of Harlem. These two conflicting points of view about Harlem each contains a modicum of truth. They are illustrative of the dual value orientation and dual conduct norm of the area and have great importance to a full understanding of antisocial behavior in communities like Harlem.

How does addiction develop among teen-age youth? The Zimmering, Toolan, Safrin and Wortis study presents a composite picture of the development among the 22 boys studied. This picture is characteristic of the course followed among a majority in the adolescent group. The youth are initiated to drug use either by peddlers or addicted boys. Curiosity, experimentation, and group pressure facilitate the introduction of drug use by the youth. Reefer smoking, during the early stages of the current problem, preceded the use of other drugs. However, in a study of 151 youthful cases brought before the courts in New York City during March, 1951, we found that 66.4 per cent began their drug use with injections of heroin, indicating that reefer smoking and "snorting" the powder through the nose were by-passed for the subcutaneous ("skin-popping") and the intravenous method ("mainlining"). The intravenous method, widely popular among youth today, involves several rather simple steps. Heroin, the chief drug of choice, and a small amount of water are mixed in a spoon. This solution is heated over a flame and then drawn up in an eye-dropper. A hypodermic needle is fitted to the eye-dropper and the contents injected directly into the vein.

The Bellevue study and workers who have been in direct contact with the boys report that immediately after taking the drug, the user becomes a bit anxious followed by a feeling of complete well-being. This is described by the boys as a "charge" or "floating on a cloud." Interest in object relationships decreases; the sex drive is reduced; school, sports, and friends no longer hold interest for the young addict. The focus of their interest is obtaining and using the drug. The boys usually withdraw to a quiet dark room or go to a movie house and enjoy the effect as long as possible. They are irritable if disturbed, and are given to daydreaming and mild hallucinations. These youth do not participate in group activities and under the influence of heroin are not aggressive. The physical reactions that follow abstinence from the drug together with the depressed feeling produce the "yen" for larger and more frequent doses. They begin to sell and "push" the drug to other youth in order to secure funds to support the habit. Serious delinquent behavior is pursued in order to secure money with which to buy drugs. Physical and psychological dependency and tolerance to the drug establish the individual as a narcotic addict.

Planning for management of the problem is complicated by the conflicting evaluation of psychiatrists who have studied the addict. Dr. Herbert Wieder and others who have been associated with the U.S. Public Health Service Hospital at Lexington, as well as reports of psychiatric examinations in our local courts, state that the individuals who move into the addiction cycle may be classified as either psychoneurotics, psychopathic personalities, or as psychotics. On the other hand, the Bellevue study states "As a group they are not psychoneurotic. They do not suffer from crippling symptoms or character traits. Their condition can be described as Personality Disorders and under ordinary circumstances they make adequate adjustments." * In planning a local community program, we have moved on the theses set forth by the findings at Lexington. We recognize, however, that not all teen-agers exposed to drugs and those who are users of drugs will necessarily become addicts. We have proceeded on the theory that addicts either have constitutional make-ups that are conducive to addiction or their psychological problems precipitate addiction as a tool in their total psychic economy. For those who are addiction-prone, those with basic psychological problems, drugs solve internal conflict and put the individual in a state free of tensions. Our experience indicates that those youth who turn to drugs for the purpose of gaining status with the peer group, or for other "non-psychiatric" reasons, usually find it possible to give up drugs with little or no difficulty. The pleasure they receive is external, coming as it does from being like the group.

Of further significance are the findings of Zimmering, Toolan, Safrin and Wortis, concerning the common features of adolescent addicts. These authors describe them as soft spoken, and verbally adept. They are not the typical gang boy whom we have discussed earlier. "These boys are pleasant, likeable, and sociable, with a strong affinity for each other and seek each other out as friends." They lack aggression and the struggle for power and domination observed in the street gang boy. Again, unlike the gang boy, their friends are casual and they have no strong ties or buddies. While the gang boy is usually overtly rejecting of parental control, with a somewhat tenuous and loose relationship with his mother, the teen-age addict has a warm, close relationship with the mother. The father is described as a shadowy figure who has little meaning to the boy. It was interesting to note, again unlike the gang boy, that none of the boys studied at Bellevue as addicts had ever run away from home nor had the impulse to do so. The intellectual level of the addicts at Bellevue, as was true with the gang boy, ranged from borderline to high average I.Q. scores. Neither group can apply themselves successfully to intellectual tasks and both have difficulty in learning.

* *Note:* While the study presents many interesting facts, the inadequacy of the sample studied requires that generalizations based on the findings not be made concerning teen-age addicts and users.

In summary, the Bellevue authors state that the 22 teen-age addicts seen at the hospital were characterized by a "lack of aggression, strong attachment to the mother, poor object relationships, omnipotent striving, and a tendency to regress." Wisely, they caution, however, that not all adolescents with these personality patterns will become addicts, nor has the experience of others established that these or any particular personality pattern is unique for all young addicts.

This paper, I believe, would not be complete if it did not indicate the proposals for treatment as proposed by the Welfare Council of New York City. In setting up a treatment and preventive program, one must know not only the nature of the problem but also the extent of it. Notwithstanding the wide publicity given to the subject in New York City and the numerous plans formulated to cope with it, no one knows, as yet, with any degree of reliability, the extent of the problem in New York. No systematic reasonably unduplicated count of teen-age users and addicts has been made. Indications from the records of police arrests, from the dockets of the courts, from the experiences of the public schools and social agencies, established without any doubt that there has been and continues to be an alarming increase in the use of narcotics by teen-age youth. It is known, for example, that the number of teen-age users or addicts committed to city correctional institutions in 1950 represent a 700 per cent increase over 1946. If the rate of admissions for individuals under 21 for the first quarter of 1951 is continued, by the end of 1951 the increase will be some 900 per cent over 1949. In the period 1947 through 1949, two minors secured voluntary commitment to city correctional institutions as addicts. In 1950, 45 minors were admitted on voluntary commitment. In the first quarter of 1951, 42 were admitted. In 1950, 10 of the 56 deaths due to narcotics and reported to the Chief Medical Examiner of the City of New York were of youths under the age of 21. Of the 22 deaths so reported for the first six months of 1951, 7 were 21 years of age or under.

In 102 narcotic cases of minors brought before the Courts for any reason in New York during the month of March, 1951, we found that 64 per cent were charged with offenses involving narcotics. An additional 42 cases were reported by the Children's Court for possession, sale, use or suspected use of narcotic drugs: 66.4 per cent of all the cases studied began their practice with heroin; and more than half had used narcotics for less than six months. Three hundred and forty admissions of teen-agers, of whom 298 were users of heroin, were made to Bellevue and Kings County Hospitals for the period January 1, 1951 and October 15, 1951.

These statistics, while indicating the trend of increase, are inconclusive. No systematic research on the teen-age user and addict has been done. We have recommended, therefore, as a first step, that an adequate registration and reporting system be set up by having the Health Department of the City define narcotics use and addictions as a reportable disease. We believe that this will give some reliable measure of the problem and, in addition, provide the controls normally exercised by health departments in such situations.

In considering a treatment program, as previously stated, we identified narcotics addiction as a symptom of personality disorder usually described as psychoneuroses or character disorder. The narcotic user, as distinguished from the addict, is an emotionally immature, unstable individual succumbing to strong social and environmental pressures. We recognize that any user can become an addict. We accept that therapy for these teen-age addicts or identifiable potential addicts can best be carried out in a custodial setting under the control of staff trained in various phases of treatment. Such a facility should provide a program of good medical care, of occupational therapy, and where indicated, psychotherapy adapted to the needs and accessibility of the individual. The decision to employ psychotherapy we consider a medical problem and determined, in the main, by the personality characteristics of the individual and the level of emotional maturity he had reached prior to addiction. The unavailability of psychiatrists to carry out psychotherapy for those who need it and can accept it suggests the further exploration of group therapy techniques.

Within this formulation for treatment, we wholeheartedly support the announced plans of the Department of Hospitals to establish on North Brother Island a 150-bed school-hospital for teen-age youth. This facility will operate as a "receiving, screening, and intermediate to long-term treatment center," designed to provide a long-term rehabilitation for those teen-agers who can profitably use it, and to provide a valuable opportunity for study and research on the teen-age narcotic problem.

CONCLUSION

An attempt has been made to have this statement point up that the gang boy and the teen-age narcotic user and addict are manifesting varying degrees of emotional disturbances and social maladjustment. Neither the gang boy nor the teen-age addict represents a typical personality type. The gamut of psychiatric illnesses may be found in each group. I have attempted to point up the bio-social-psychological aspects of the behavior of each and have suggested the multidimensional treatment approaches that are demanded if these problems are to be corrected. Whether we focus on the pathology in the social milieu—bad housing, economic deprivations, faulty ethical and moral values; or whether we focus on the psychological factors of faulty ego development, emotional frustration, rejection and broken family life—we find conditions for the addict and the gang boy that precipitate feelings of insecurity, anxiety and inability to find need satisfactions. For the gang boy it may be relief sought in aggressive reactions, guilt, anxiety and more aggression. For the addict relief may be sought in escape from the internal and external pressures. The aim of therapy for both is the rediscovery of inner security. How to provide the kind of experience that will release the pressures whether they be internal or external, resolve the conflict, and fulfillment of need satisfactions, is the challenge that the gang boy and the teen-age addict present to all who are engaged in the helping process.

PERSONALITY
ORGANIZATION

36 The self-other process: how self and other emerge simultaneously to consciousness

Related selections: 7, 37, 39

How one acts or behaves in any given situation depends in large measure on his concept of self. How the child feels about himself determines what his problems are and how he will attack them. One of the functions of the teacher is to assist the child in the enhancement of self and, when necessary, to help him change his self-concept. This introductory chapter to Professor Kilpatrick's book will contribute to one's understanding of the early beginnings of the self-concept.

The intent of the early chapters of this book is to defend the thesis that human personality, in any desirable sense, is inherently a social product; that only by the self-other process substantially as herein discussed has historic man been able to achieve his distinctly human attributes of language, critical thinking, sense of responsibility, conscience, and the use of standards. And only by the same process can the growing child of today build these invaluable cultural achievements into his own character. In brief, the operation of the self-other process was essential alike to selfhood and civilization as historically achieved and is still essential in each individual case.

To make more explicit the general thesis just stated, the following specific theses are here set out, to be elaborated and argued later:

WILLIAM HEARD KILPATRICK, *Selfhood and Civilization* (New York: The Macmillan Company, 1941), pp. 1–10. Reprinted by permission of the author.
PROFESSOR KILPATRICK (1871–) is Professor Emeritus of Education, Teachers College, Columbia University, and is a renowned teacher and scholar.

No one is born a self, nor is selfhood merely a matter of internal maturation (as this is now frequently used). Selfhood has to be achieved.

Man alone of all living organisms has been able to achieve selfhood. No brute can.

The process of achieving selfhood is an extended one, involving various stages and degrees.

This selfhood can be achieved only and necessarily in a social milieu, and the surrounding culture enters essentially into the process of achieving as well as into the resulting character achieved.

Consciousness of self and consciousness of others emerge simultaneously to the individual, each growing and contributing during the rest of life mutually to round out and implement the other.

At any one time after the process has been well begun, each, the self and the other, is inextricably composed of both self and other.

The selfhood thus achieved becomes a highly significant factor in and for the further life of the individual and for society. Personality as such and civilization alike depend on it.

THE MEANING OF THE TERM "SELF":
A FIRST DEFINITION

. . . We can here set down a first working definition [of self] in terms of the distinctions the child learns to make in ordinary social situations. It will be clear, as asserted, that man alone learns to make these distinctions.

We say that a child has achieved selfhood, at least in working degree, when:

(1) he distinguishes himself clearly from others by the appropriate use of such pronouns as *I, me, my, mine; you, yours; he or she, him or her, his or hers;*

(2) he recognizes himself as an agent, one who can effect, bring to pass, and for this purpose uses such sentences as: "I didn't do it. Mary did." "I can do it. Let me do it all by myself";

(3) he has achieved a sense of time, past and present, including a notion of the continuity of his self, and for this will use such sentences as: "I am going to Grandmother's tomorrow. I was there last summer. Grandfather showed me the calf, but Mother says it is bigger now"; and

(4) he has built a sense of conscious intent and of accompanying accountability and responsibility, as shown by using such a sentence as: "I hurt John's hand, but I didn't mean to do it."

It will be noted that the definition as given is an instance of operational procedure: the defining procedure has to work in life in order to be accepted for thought. The test as to whether selfhood has been achieved is that the pertinent words shall be used in an ordinary social situation to the satisfaction of competent observers. The child is not only to use these words and sentences of his own motion; but he must also intend them in their ordinary meaning, and the other person must be able to see (within reason) from the life context that they are so understood and so intended. All of which is to say that the words must function properly in ordinary communication.

. . . .

THE PROCESS OF THING-MAKING

As a preliminary to the actual process of self-building, consider how the normal child comes to build a group of related experiences into a "thing." Such "thing-making" is so inevitable and is accomplished so early and easily that most have never thought of it as the personal achievement it is. The child's experience with his milk bottle will serve as an illustration.

A child ordinarily learns in time to suck from a bottle. From the use of the bottle and how it answers to felt want, the normal child learns to recognize how the bottle feels in his hand; he learns to shift it for more successful use; he associates pleasure with using it. Thereafter the sight of the bottle coming when he is hungry makes him expect handling and sucking and enjoyment. Now all these experiences, actual and potential, with more not here named, get somehow very closely associated in the baby's "mind"; he learns to recognize the bottle when he sees it or feels it and to expect the other experiences that are a usual accompaniment. These recurrent, associated experiences now constitute for the child a "thing"; the bottle has become differentiated from the "big, buzzing, blooming confusion"—to quote William James—of the environment around him, has become something more or less well defined in itself, something having a kind of existence of its own, suggesting certain meanings and arousing certain expectations.

This process of thing-making is, in its simpler and more concrete instances, inevitable with normal humans. However, names help with the process; frequent hearing of the words *bottle, milk* help to crystallize the situation. Helpful, too, is the fact that life in the family or group turns upon the common recognition of the thing under consideration. The child seeks to share in the common life process and so will in high degree accept from the others their practice, including specifically whatever of conception or distinction their practice may turn upon. It is under such circumstances that conceptions of things are built, each with its reliable unified abidingness. The milk bottle, for example, along with its name becomes for the child a means of entering into effective relationship with the family life going on about him.

Along with the milk bottle go also many other analogous "things," such as crib, carriage, cap, foot, finger. But chief of all the "things" that make up the child's world are certain moving objects which you and I, farther along life's road, call persons. Mother early comes to be of strategic significance, especially if she herself nurses the child. She is, to use our language, source and guarantee of security and protection, the reliable ever-present source and help in time of trouble. When life appears darkest and the child is at the last gasp of pain and despair, she (or another of these mysterious things) suddenly appears out of the chaos and all is set right. It happens not once, but every day and regularly. Its very occurrence defines reliability and regularity. Happy the child whose mother does so love him as to let him feel from the first thus secure in her sympathetic care!

In this way Mother comes to be the first object of call when the child learns to cry not simply as a reflex, but as a dawning means to his dawning ends. No mother but knows this difference between cries. Meanwhile other persons share also in this process. In time several such moving objects come to have for the now growing child each its defined place and type of expectation. The child is getting ready for a great advance.

ACHIEVING INTERNAL UNITY

While the "outside" world of things is thus taking on objective character, the child's internal life begins, so we believe, also to take on a certain interrelated unity. Although this internal process is not open to the same observation as is the external thing-making, still its actuality seems probable. The external process is subject to fairly definite observation; the internal remains more a matter of inference in the light of further developments. Certainly, however, the child has a succession of wants, pains, wishes, and efforts. Some of these recur sufficiently often to be recognizable even to the child—external movements seem to show this. As already indicated, the child begins in time to cry in order to attract attention. He will even get angry when attention is withheld. Any observant person learns the signs. This fact of agency, of using means to attain ends, grows as a defined part of the child's life and begins to be a "willed" affair.

It is easy then to believe, but not essential to the succeeding argument, that the normal child does in various ways build at this stage a preliminary conception of himself, of his internal life as some sort of abiding unity parallel with the abiding unity we call external things. The full internal process can go on, it seems certain, only by contrast with other processes. This fuller process comes in the next stage, but it seems probable that in this first stage some dawning unity begins, growing perhaps out of the feelings that accompany efforts. The child continually meets obstacles. Efforts follow. Some external things seem friendly, others unfriendly. The feelings connected with the mutually opposed external things stay with the child, favorable feelings with the friendly things, unfavorable feelings with the unfriendly, but all together forming an interrelated system. It is in the abidingness of this system and especially in the feelings of effort involved that William James (*Principles* I, 298ff.) found the sense of abiding personal identity. It is easy to believe that some of this starts early.

THE SIMULTANEOUS COMING
OF SELF AND OTHER

As the process of thing-making just discussed continues there comes a time when interaction begins more definitely between what may, with a certain exaggeration, be called the child's two worlds, the world of observed things, on the one hand, and the world of more immediately felt wants, pains, efforts, on the other. What he knows "externally" (as we say) begins to be so related with what he knows "internally" that a new kind of growth takes place: what he knows in one way begins to throw light on what he knows the other way.

What others call his hands and feet, he can move. Sister Mary also has hands and feet. They look like his; and hers, too, move. His and hers are small. Father's and Mother's are large. But they are all hands and feet.

He has a name, and Mary has a name.

He has his toys, and Mary has her toys. Mother will make Mary yield his toys to him and make him yield Mary's toys to her. It is an abiding distinction; Mother is herein again reliable and invariable. He hears Mary say, "It is mine, not yours." Eventually he says of his, "It is mine, not yours."

Mary falls, bumps her head, cries. Mother soothes her. Not long ago he, too, fell, bumped his head, cried. Mother soothed him. Now Mother says to him, "Poor Mary, she bumped her head. It hurts her, just as yours hurt you when you fell."

From such incidents consistently repeated, it gradually begins to dawn on this child that he (his body) is one among those other moving things and then that they feel pains like his. Enlightenment enters upon a higher stage. He now sees himself "from the outside": he has hands, feet, fingers, toes, head, just as Mary has. He now sees also that she, "on the inside," feels pains and cries, just as he does. Also she eats and he eats. She has little clothes, as he has little clothes. She and he are small editions of the same things that older people are.

In all of this a new self is in process of becoming, and these moving objects, persons, begin to emerge as other selves. His new compound self (composed in part of what he first saw in himself, in part of what he first saw in others) begins gradually to take over the conscious direction of his organism. He begins to act out of a self that knows itself. The factor of gradualness in the coming of this process must be emphasized. It is easy, but wrong, for us to read into the child's meager beginning the fullness of thought and distinction that we have achieved.

But once begun, the process grows continually throughout life. Until one has lived, any literature, even the simplest, is a closed book. Until one has felt love, one cannot understand it in others. Until one has suffered bereavement, one cannot in any full sense sympathize with the bereaved. Self and other thus continue to grow, each by what it learns from the other. The two emerge, for conscious consideration, simultaneously. The self is thus, as said before, a compound from both sources. One part has come directly from one's own immediate "internal" experiencing; the other part has come from observing the lives of others. After the first beginning, the two parts are inextricably interwoven. And a like compoundedness holds of my conception of others. Each other is for me composed of things that I have seen first or peculiarly in others but also of things that I attribute to the other because I know them in myself. As will be emphasized later, each human old enough and advanced enough to be a self has achieved a selfhood inherently and inextricably social in origin.

It may be well at this point to call attention to certain other features of self-other making that at times manifest themselves in even early life—some ugly, others good. All who know children have remarked upon a negativism often prominent in the early years, apparently the result of the first clear recognition of the fact of conscious consent or refusal. Gordon Allport tells of a child, not yet three, who made a daily visit to his grandmother simply to announce, apropos of nothing in particular, "Grandma, I won't."

The exaggeration of an emerging trait is frequent. This self-insistent negativism appears to be simply an instance in point. Having got far enough along to refuse and negate, the child simply does so in excessive and exaggerated degree. Disagreeable as this may be to others, it probably serves to augment his nascent sense of selfhood through an aggressive exercise of self-determination where it seems, at that time, to count for most. Similarly some children build a pathological self-centeredness. They simply must, for the duration of this interest, hold the spotlight, occupy the center of the stage. Few things are more annoying, or more hurtful to healthy growth, than this maladjustment in its worst forms.

A more pleasing and more serviceable early development growing out of the self-other process and helping it along is imaginative play. In this the child takes on now this character and now that in such fashion as to call for the study and use of the characteristics assumed.

In all these varied ways, and in many more besides, is the individual advancing to a new and higher level of being. Henceforth, in the degree that selfhood has been achieved, will the child be able to see himself as others see him, so that he can (and in some measure does and will) consider his acts as he thinks others will judge them. So achieved, this attainment will enter as a positive factor in all conscious life thereafter. Thenceforth all that he consciously does is affected by the fact and existence of this new compounded self. It is not simply that he is conscious of himself in a new light. More than that, this consciousness itself enters with its compoundedness into the very constitution of the self to affect inherently all that is done. It is most literally true that the individual henceforth lives on a new and higher level, a level to which none other of the animal world can aspire. This higher level is at least an essential part or aspect of, if not scene and foundation for, all that we value most in human experience.

37 *Some observations on the organization of personality*

Related selections: 7, 20, 36, 39, 56

Teachers everywhere are concerned with changing behavior, be-
havior that has to do with the whole gamut of children's experi-
ences, feelings and relationships—their work habits, their efforts,
their desires, the way they act and feel toward other people and
things. Clinical evidence indicates that efforts to change behavior
should be directly concerned with changing perception of self. As
Dr. Rogers points out, changes in behavior occur as changes take
place in perception of self and perception of reality. His discussion
of the conditions under which change occurs in perception of self
holds significant implications for educational practice.

THE RELATION OF THE ORGANIZED PERCEPTUAL FIELD TO BEHAVIOR

One simple observation, which is repeated over and over again in each successful therapeutic case, seems to have rather deep theoretical implications. It is that as changes occur in the perception of self and in the perception of reality, changes occur in behavior. In therapy, these perceptual changes are more often concerned with the self than with the external world. Hence we find in therapy that as the perception of self alters, behavior alters. Perhaps an illustration will indicate the type of observation upon which this statement is based.

A young woman, a graduate student whom we shall call Miss Vib, came in for nine interviews. If we compare the first interview with the last, striking changes are evident. Perhaps some features of this change may be conveyed by taking from the first and last interviews all the major statements regarding self, and all the major statements regarding current behavior. In the first interview, for example, her perception of herself may be crudely indicated by taking all her own statements about herself, grouping those which seem similar, but otherwise doing a minimum of editing, and retaining so far as possible, her own

CARL R. ROGERS, "Some Observations on the Organization of Personality," *The American Psychologist*, II (September, 1947), 359–68. Reprinted by permission of the author and the American Psychological Association.

DR. ROGERS (1902–) is Professor of Psychology and Psychiatry at the University of Wisconsin. He was formerly Professor of Psychology and head of the Counseling Center, University of Chicago. He is a past-president of the American Psychological Association.

words. We then come out with this as the conscious perception of self which was hers at the outset of counseling.

> "I feel disorganized, muddled; I've lost all direction; my personal life has disintegrated.
>
> "I sorta experience things from the forefront of my consciousness, but nothing sinks in very deep; things don't seem real to me; I feel nothing matters; I don't have any emotional response to situations; I'm worried about myself.
>
> "I haven't been acting like myself; it doesn't seem like me; I'm a different person altogether from what I used to be in the past.
>
> "I don't understand myself; I haven't known what was happening to me.
>
> "I have withdrawn from everything, and feel all right only when I'm all alone and no one can expect me to do things.
>
> "I don't care about my personal appearance.
>
> "I don't know *anything* any more.
>
> "I feel guilty about the things I have left undone.
>
> "I don't think I could ever assume responsibility for anything."

If we attempt to evaluate this picture of self from an external frame of reference various diagnostic labels may come to mind. Trying to perceive it solely from the client's frame of reference we observe that to the young woman herself she appears disorganized, and not herself. She is perplexed and almost unacquainted with what is going on in herself. She feels unable and unwilling to function in any responsible or social way. This is at least a sampling of the way she experiences or perceives her self.

Her behavior is entirely consistent with this picture of self. If we abstract all her statements describing her behavior, in the same fashion as we abstracted her statements about self, the following pattern emerges—a pattern which in this case was corroborated by outside observation.

> "I couldn't get up nerve to come in before; I haven't availed myself of help.
>
> "Everything I should do or want to do, I don't do.
>
> "I haven't kept in touch with friends; I avoid making the effort to go with them; I stopped writing letters home; I don't answer letters or telephone calls; I avoid contacts that would be professionally helpful; I didn't go home though I said I would.
>
> "I failed to hand in my work in a course though I had it all done; I didn't even buy clothing that I needed; I haven't even kept my nails manicured.
>
> "I didn't listen to material we were studying; I waste hours reading the funny papers; I can spend the whole afternoon doing absolutely nothing."

The picture of behavior is very much in keeping with the picture of self, and is summed up in the statement that "Everything I should do or want to do, I don't do." The behavior goes on, in ways that seem to the individual beyond understanding and beyond control.

If we contrast this picture of self and behavior with the picture as it exists in the ninth interview, thirty-eight days later, we find both the perception of self and the ways of behaving deeply altered. Her statements about self are as follows:

> "I'm feeling much better; I'm taking more interest in myself.
> "I do have some individuality, some interests.
> "I seem to be getting a newer understanding of myself. I can look at myself a little better.
> "I realize I'm just one person, with so much ability, but I'm not worried about it; I can accept the fact that I'm not always right.
> "I feel more motivation, have more of a desire to go ahead.
> "I still occasionally regret the past, though I feel less unhappy about it; I still have a long ways to go; I don't know whether I can keep the picture of myself I'm beginning to evolve.
> "I can go on learning—in school or out.
> "I do feel more like a normal person now; I feel more I can handle my life myself; I think I'm at the point where I can go along on my own."

Outstanding in this perception of herself are three things—that she knows herself, that she can view with comfort her assets and liabilities, and finally that she has drive and control of that drive.

In this ninth interview the behavioral picture is again consistent with the perception of self. It may be abstracted in these terms.

> "I've been making plans about school and about a job; I've been working hard on a term paper; I've been going to the library to trace down a topic of special interest and finding it exciting.
> "I've cleaned out my closets; washed my clothes.
> "I finally wrote my parents; I'm going home for the holidays.
> "I'm getting out and mixing with people; I am reacting sensibly to a fellow who is interested in me—seeing both his good and bad points.
> "I will work toward my degree; I'll start looking for a job this week."

Her behavior, in contrast to the first interview, is now organized, forward-moving, effective, realistic and planful. It is in accord with the realistic and organized view she has achieved of her self.

It is this type of observation, in case after case, that leads us to say with some assurance that as perceptions of self and reality change, behavior changes. Likewise, in cases we might term failures, there appears to be no appreciable change in perceptual organization or in behavior.

What type of explanation might account for these concomitant changes in the perceptual field and the behavioral pattern? Let us examine some of the logical possibilities.

In the first place, it is possible that factors unrelated to therapy may have brought about the altered perception and behavior. There may have been physiological processes occurring which produced the change. There may have been alterations in the family relationships, or in the social forces, or in the educational picture or in some other area of cultural influence, which might account for the rather drastic shift in the concept of self and in the behavior.

There are difficulties in this type of explanation. Not only were there no known gross changes in the physical or cultural situation as far as Miss Vib was concerned, but the explanation gradually becomes inadequate when one tries to apply it to the many cases in which such change occurs. To postulate that some external factor brings the change and that only by chance does this period of change coincide with the period of therapy, becomes an untenable hypothesis.

Let us then look at another explanation, namely that the therapist exerted, during the nine hours of contact, a peculiarly potent cultural influence which brought about the change. Here again we are faced with several problems. It seems that nine hours scattered over five and one-half weeks are a very minute portion of time in which to bring about alteration of patterns which have been building for thirty years. We would have to postulate an influence so potent as to be classed as traumatic. This theory is particularly difficult to maintain when we find, on examining the recorded interviews, that not once in the nine hours did the therapist express any evaluation, positive or negative, of the client's initial or final perception of self, or her initial or final mode of behavior. There was not only no evaluation, but no standards expressed by which evaluation might be inferred.

There was, on the part of the therapist, evidence of warm interest in the individual, and thorough-going acceptance of the self and of the behavior as they existed initially, in the intermediate stages, and at the conclusion of therapy. It appears reasonable to say that the therapist established certain definite conditions of interpersonal relations, but since the very essence of this relationship is respect for the person as he is at that moment, the therapist can hardly be regarded as a cultural force making for change.

We find ourselves forced to a third type of explanation, a type of explanation which is not new to psychology, but which has had only partial acceptance. Briefly it may be put that the observed phenomena of change seem most adequately explained by the hypothesis that *given certain psychological conditions, the individual has the capacity to reorganize his field of perception, including the way he perceives himself, and that a concomitant or a resultant of this per-*

ceptual reorganization is an appropriate alteration of behavior. This puts into formal and objective terminology a clinical hypothesis which experience forces upon the therapist using a client-centered approach. One is compelled through clinical observation to develop a high degree of respect for the ego-integrative forces residing within each individual. One comes to recognize that under proper conditions the self is a basic factor in the formation of personality and in the determination of behavior. Clinical experience would strongly suggest that the self is, to some extent, an architect of self, and the above hypothesis simply puts this observation into psychological terms.

In support of this hypothesis it is noted in some cases that one of the concomitants of success in therapy is the realization on the part of the client that the self has the capacity for reorganization. Thus a student says:

> "You know I spoke of the fact that a person's background retards one. Like the fact that my family life wasn't good for me, and my mother certainly didn't give me any of the kind of bringing up that I should have had. Well, I've been thinking that over. It's true up to a point. But when you get so that you can see the situation, then it's really up to you."

Following this statement of the relation of the self to experience many changes occurred in this young man's behavior. In this, as in other cases, it appears that when the person comes to see himself as the perceiving, organizing agent, then reorganization of perception and consequent change in patterns of reaction take place.

On the other side of the picture we have frequently observed that when the individual has been authoritatively told that he is governed by certain factors or conditions beyond his control, it makes therapy more difficult, and it is only when the individual discovers for himself that he can organize his perceptions that change is possible. In veterans who have been given their own psychiatric diagnosis, the effect is often that of making the individual feel that he is under an unalterable doom, that he is unable to control the organization of his life. When, however, the self sees itself as capable of reorganizing its own perceptual field, a marked change in basic confidence occurs. Miss Nam, a student, illustrates this phenomenon when she says, after having made progress in therapy:

> "I think I do feel better about the future, too, because it's as if I won't be acting in darkness. It's sort of, well, knowing somewhat why I act the way I do . . . and at least it isn't the feeling that you're simply out of your own control and the fates are driving you to act that way. If you realize it, I think you can do something more about it."

A veteran at the conclusion of counseling puts it more briefly and more positively: "My attitude toward myself is changed now to where I feel I *can* do something with my self and life." He has come to view himself as the instrument by which some reorganization can take place.

There is another clinical observation which may be cited in support of the general hypothesis that there is a close relationship between behavior and the way in which reality is viewed by the individual. It has been noted in many cases that behavior changes come about for the most part imperceptibly and almost automatically, once the perceptual reorganization has taken place. A young wife who has been reacting violently to her maid, and has been quite disorganized in her behavior as a result of this antipathy, says "After I . . . discovered it was nothing more than that she resembled my mother, she didn't bother me any more. Isn't that interesting? She's still the same." Here is a clear statement indicating that though the basic perceptions have not changed, they have been differently organized, have acquired a new meaning, and that behavior changes then occur. Similar evidence is given by a client, a trained psychologist, who after completing a brief series of client-centered interviews, writes:

> "Another interesting aspect of the situation was in connection with the changes in some of my attitudes. When the change occurred, it was as if earlier attitudes were wiped out as completely as if erased from a blackboard. . . . When a situation which would formerly have provoked a given type of response occurred, it was not as if I was tempted to act in the way I formerly had but in some way found it easier to control my behavior. Rather the new type of behavior came quite spontaneously, and it was only through a deliberate analysis that I became aware that I was acting in a new and different way."

Here again it is of interest that the imagery is put in terms of visual perception and that as attitudes are "erased from the blackboard" behavioral changes take place automatically and without conscious effort.

Thus we have observed that appropriate changes in behavior occur when the individual acquires a different view of his world of experience, including himself; that this changed perception does not need to be dependent upon a change in the "reality," but may be a product of internal reorganization; that in some instances the awareness of the capacity for reperceiving experience accompanies this process of reorganization; that the altered behavioral responses occur automatically and without conscious effort as soon as the perceptual reorganization has taken place, apparently as a result of this.

In view of these observations a second hypothesis may be stated, which is closely related to the first. It is that *behavior is not directly influenced or deter-mined by organic or cultural factors, but primarily* (and perhaps only), *by the perception of these elements.* In other words the crucial element in the deter-mination of behavior is the perceptual field of the individual. While this percep-tual field is, to be sure, deeply influenced and largely shaped by cultural and physiological forces, it is nevertheless important that it appears to be only the field as it is *perceived*, which exercises a specific determining influence upon behavior. This is not a new idea in psychology, but its implications have not always been fully recognized.

It might mean, first of all, that if it is the perceptual field which determines behavior, then the primary object of study for psychologists would be the person and his world *as viewed by the person himself*. It could mean that the internal frame of reference of the person might well constitute the field of psychology, an idea set forth persuasively by Snygg and Combs in a significant manuscript. . . . It might mean that the laws which govern behavior would be discovered more deeply by turning our attention to the laws which govern perception.

Now if our speculations contain a measure of truth, if the *specific* determinant of behavior is the perceptual field, and if the self can reorganize that perceptual field, then what are the limits of this process? Is the reorganization of perception capricious, or does it follow certain laws? Are there limits to the degree of reorganization? If so, what are they? In this connection we have observed with some care the perception of one portion of the field of experience, the portion we call the self.

THE RELATION OF THE PERCEPTION
OF THE SELF TO ADJUSTMENT

Initially we were oriented by the background of both lay and psychological thinking to regard the outcome of successful therapy as the solution of problems. If a person had a marital problem, a vocational problem, a problem of educational adjustment, the obvious purpose of counseling or therapy was to solve that problem. But as we observe and study the recorded accounts of the conclusion of therapy, it is clear that the most characteristic outcome is not necessarily solution of problems, but a freedom from tension, a different feeling about, and perception of, self. Perhaps something of this outcome may be conveyed by some illustrations.

Several statements taken from the final interview with a twenty year old young woman, Miss Mir, give indications of the characteristic attitude toward self, and the sense of freedom which appears to accompany it.

> "I've always tried to be what the others thought I should be, but now I am wondering whether I shouldn't just see that I am what I am."

> "Well, I've just noticed such a difference. I find that when I feel things, even when I feel hate, I don't care. I don't mind. I feel more free somehow. I don't feel guilty about things."

> "You know it's suddenly as though a big cloud has been lifted off. I feel so much more content."

Note in these statements the willingness to perceive herself as she is, to accept herself "realistically," to perceive and accept her "bad" attitudes as well as "good" ones. This realism seems to be accompanied by a sense of freedom and contentment.

Miss Vib, whose attitudes were quoted earlier, wrote out her own feelings about counseling some six weeks after the interviews were over, and gave the statement to her counselor. She begins:

> "The happiest outcome of therapy has been a new feeling about myself. As I think of it, it might be the only outcome. Certainly it is basic to all the changes in my behavior that have resulted." In discussing her experience in therapy she states, "I was coming to see myself as a whole. I began to realize that I am *one* person. This was an important insight to me. I saw that the former good academic achievement, job success, ease in social situations, and the present withdrawal, dejection, apathy and failure were all adaptive behavior, performed by *me*. This meant that I had to reorganize my feelings about myself, no longer holding to the unrealistic notion that the very good adjustment was the expression of the real 'me' and this neurotic behavior was not. I came to feel that I am the same person, sometimes functioning maturely, and sometimes assuming a neurotic role in the face of what I had conceived as insurmountable problems. The acceptance of myself as one person gave me strength in the process of reorganization. Now I had a substratum, a core of unity on which to work." As she continues her discussion there are such statements as "I am getting more happiness in being myself." "I approve of myself more, and I have so much less anxiety."

As in the previous example, the outstanding aspects appear to be the realization that all of her behavior "belonged" to her, that she could accept both the good and bad features about herself and that doing so gave her a release from anxiety and a feeling of solid happiness. In both instances there is only incidental reference to the serious "problems" which had been initially discussed.

Since Miss Mir is undoubtedly above average intelligence and Miss Vib is a person with some psychological training, it may appear that such results are found only with the sophisticated individual. To counteract this opinion a quotation may be given from a statement written by a veteran of limited ability and education who had just completed counseling, and was asked to write whatever reactions he had to the experience. He says:

> "As for the consoleing I have had I can say this, It realy makes a man strip his own mind bare, and when he does he knows then what he realy is and what he can do. Or at least thinks he knows himself party well. As for myself, I know that my ideas were a

little too big for what I realy am, but now I realize one must try
start out at his own level.

"Now after four visits, I have a much clearer picture of myself
and my future. It makes me feel a little depressed and disappointed,
but on the other hand, it has taken me out of the dark, the load
seems a lot lighter now, that is I can see my way now, I know what I
want to do, I know about what I can do, so now that I can see my
goal, I will be able to work a whole lot easyer, at my own level."

Although the expression is much simpler one notes again the same two elements—the acceptance of self as it is, and the feeling of easiness, of lightened
burden, which accompanies it.

As we examine many individual case records and case recordings, it appears
to be possible to bring together the findings in regard to successful therapy by
stating another hypothesis in regard to that portion of the perceptual field which
we call the self. It would appear that *when all of the ways in which the individual
perceives himself—all perceptions of the qualities, abilities, impulses, and attitudes of the person, and all perceptions of himself in relation to others—are accepted into the organized conscious concept of the self, then this achievement is
accompanied by feelings of comfort and freedom from tension which are experienced as psychological adjustment.*

This hypothesis would seem to account for the observed fact that the comfortable perception of self which is achieved is sometimes more positive than
before, sometimes more negative. When the individual permits all his perceptions
of himself to be organized into one pattern, the picture is sometimes more flattering than he has held in the past, sometimes less flattering. It is always more
comfortable.

It may be pointed out also that this tentative hypothesis supplies an operational type of definition, based on the client's internal frame of reference, for
such hitherto vague terms as "adjustment," "integration," and "acceptance of
self." They are defined in terms of perception, in a way which it should be
possible to prove or disprove. When all of the organic perceptual experiences—
the experiencing of attitudes, impulses, abilities and disabilities, the experiencing
of others and of "reality"—when all of these perceptions are freely assimilated
into an organized and consistent system, available to consciousness, then psychological adjustment or integration might be said to exist. The definition of adjustment is thus made an internal affair, rather than dependent upon an external
"reality."

Something of what is meant by this acceptance and assimilation of perceptions about the self may be illustrated from the case of Miss Nam, a student.
Like many other clients she gives evidence of having experienced attitudes and
feelings which are defensively denied because they are not consistent with the

concept or picture she holds of herself. The way in which they are first fully admitted into consciousness, and then organized into a unified system may be shown by excerpts from the recorded interviews. She has spoken of the difficulty she has had in bringing herself to write papers for her university courses.

> "I just thought of something else which perhaps hinders me, and that is that again it's two different feelings. When I have to sit down and do (a paper), though I have a lot of ideas, underneath I think I always have the feeling that I just can't do it. . . . I have this feeling of being terrifically confident that I can do something, without being willing to put the work into it. At other times I'm practically afraid of what I have to do. . . ."

Note that the conscious self has been organized in "having a lot of ideas," being "terrifically confident" but that "underneath," in other words not freely admitted into consciousness, has been the experience of feeling "I just can't do it." She continues:

> "I'm trying to work through this funny relationship between this terrific confidence and then this almost fear of doing anything . . . and I think the kind of feeling that I can really do things is part of an illusion I have about myself of being, in my imagination, sure that it will be something good and very good and all that but whenever I get down to the actual task of getting started, it's a terrible feeling of—well, incapacity that I won't get it done either the way I want to do it, or even not being sure how I want to do it."

Again the picture of herself which is present to consciousness is that of a person who is "very good," but this picture is entirely out of line with the actual organic experience in the situation.

Later in the same interview she expresses very well the fact that her perceptions are not all organized into one consistent conscious self.

> "I'm not sure about what kind of a person I am—well, I realize that all of these are a part of me, but I'm not quite sure of how to make all of these things fall in line."

In the next interview we have an excellent opportunity to observe the organization of both of these conflicting perceptions into one pattern, with the resultant sense of freedom from tension which has been described above.

> "It's very funny, even as I sit here I realize that I have more confidence in myself, in the sense that when I used to approach new situations I would have two very funny things operating at the same time. I had a fantasy that I could do anything, which was a fantasy which covered over all these other feelings that I really couldn't do it, or couldn't do it as well as I wanted to, and it's as if

now those two things have merged together, and it is more real, that a situation isn't either testing myself or proving something to myself or anyone else. It's just in terms of doing it. And I think I have done away both with that fantasy and that fear. . . . So I think I can go ahead and approach things—well, just sensibly."

No longer is it necessary for this client to "cover over" her real experiences. Instead the picture of herself as very able, and the experienced feeling of complete inability, have now been brought together into one integrated pattern of self as a person with real, but imperfect abilities. Once the self is thus accepted the inner energies making for self-actualization are released and she attacks her life problems more efficiently.

Observing this type of material frequently in counseling experience would lead to a tentative hypothesis of maladjustment, which like the other hypothesis suggested, focuses on the perception of self. It might be proposed that the tensions called psychological maladjustment exist when the organized concept of self (conscious or available to conscious awareness) is not in accord with the perceptions actually experienced.

This discrepancy between the concept of self and the actual perceptions seems to be explicable only in terms of the fact that the self-concept resists assimilating into itself any percept which is inconsistent with its present organization. The feeling that she may not have the ability to do a paper is inconsistent with Miss Nam's conscious picture of herself as a very able and confident person, and hence, though fleetingly perceived, is denied organization as a part of her self, until this comes about in therapy.

THE CONDITIONS OF CHANGE OF SELF-PERCEPTION

If the way in which the self is perceived has as close and significant a relationship to behavior as has been suggested, then the manner in which this perception may be altered becomes a question of importance. If a reorganization of self-perceptions brings a change in behavior; if adjustment and maladjustment depend on the congruence between perceptions as experienced and the self as perceived, then the factors which permit a reorganization of the perception of self are significant.

Our observations of psychotherapeutic experience would seem to indicate that absence of any threat to the self-concept is an important item in the problem. Normally the self resists incorporating into self those experiences which are inconsistent with the functioning of self. But a point overlooked by Lecky and others is that when the self is free from any threat of attack or likelihood of attack, then it is possible for the self to consider these hitherto rejected perceptions, to make new differentiations, and to reintegrate the self in such a way as to include them.

An illustration from the case of Miss Vib may serve to clarify this point. In her statement written six weeks after the conclusion of counseling Miss Vib thus describes the way in which unacceptable percepts become incorporated into the self. She writes:

> "In the earlier interviews I kept saying such things as, 'I am not acting like myself,' 'I never acted this way before.' What I meant was that this withdrawn, untidy, and apathetic person was not myself. Then I began to realize that I was the same person, seriously withdrawn, etc. now, as I had been before. That did not happen until after I had talked out my self-rejection, shame, despair, and doubt, in the accepting situation of the interview. The counselor was not startled or shocked. I was telling him all these things about myself which did not fit into my picture of a graduate student, a teacher, a sound person. He responded with complete acceptance and warm interest without heavy emotional overtones. Here was a sane, intelligent person wholeheartedly accepting this behavior that seemed so shameful to me. I can remember an organic feeling of relaxation. I did not have to keep up the struggle to cover up and hide this shameful person."

Note how clearly one can see here the whole range of denied perceptions of self, and the fact that they could be considered as a part of self only in a social situation which involved no threat to the self, in which another person, the counselor, becomes almost an alternate self and looks with understanding and acceptance upon these same perceptions. She continues:

> "Retrospectively, it seems to me that what I felt as 'warm acceptance without emotional overtones' was what I needed to work through my difficulties. . . . The counselor's impersonality with interest allowed me to talk out my feelings. The clarification in the interview situation presented the attitude to me as a 'ding an sich' which I could look at, manipulate, and put in place. In organizing my attitudes, I was beginning to organize me."

Here the nature of the exploration of experience of seeing it as experience and not as a threat to self, enables the client to reorganize her perceptions of self, which as she says was also "reorganizing me."

If we attempt to describe in more conventional psychological terms the nature of the process which culminates in an altered organization and integration of self in the process of therapy it might run as follows. The individual is continually endeavoring to meet his needs by reacting to the field of experience as he perceives it, and to do that more efficiently by differentiating elements of the field and reintegrating them into new patterns. Reorganization of the field may involve the reorganization of the self as well as of other parts of the field. The self, however, resists reorganization and change. In everyday life individual adjustment by means of reorganization of the field exclusive of the self is more common and is less threatening to the individual. Consequently, the individual's first mode of adjustment is the reorganization of that part of the field which does not include the self.

Client-centered therapy is different from other life situations inasmuch as the therapist tends to remove from the individual's immediate world all those aspects of the field which the individual can reorganize except the self. The therapist, by reacting to the client's feelings and attitudes rather than to the objects of his feelings and attitudes, assists the client in bringing from background into focus his own self, making it easier than ever before for the client to perceive and react to the self. By offering only understanding and no trace of evaluation, the therapist removes himself as an object of attitudes, becoming only an alternate expression of the client's self. The therapist by providing a consistent atmosphere of permissiveness and understanding removes whatever threat existed to prevent all perceptions of the self from emerging into figure. Hence in this situation all the ways in which the self has been experienced can be viewed openly, and organized into a complex unity.

It is then this complete absence of any factor which would attack the concept of self, and second, the assistance in focusing upon the perception of self, which seems to permit a more differentiated view of self and finally the reorganization of self.

RELATIONSHIP TO CURRENT PSYCHOLOGICAL THINKING

Up to this point, these remarks have been presented as clinical observations and tentative hypotheses, quite apart from any relationship to past or present thinking in the field of psychology. This has been intentional. It is felt that it is the function of the clinician to try to observe, with an open-minded attitude, the complexity of material which comes to him, to report his observations, and in the light of this to formulate hypotheses and problems which both the clinic and the laboratory may utilize as a basis for study and research.

Yet, though these are clinical observations and hypotheses, they have, as has doubtless been recognized, a relationship to some of the currents of theoretical and laboratory thinking in psychology. Some of the observations about the self bear a relationship to the thinking of G. H. Mead about the "I" and the "me." The outcome of these might be described in Mead's terms as the increased awareness of the "I," and the organization of the "me's" by the "I." The importance which has been given in this paper to the self as an organized experience and to some extent as an architect of self, bears a relationship to the thinking of Allport and others concerning the increased place which we must give to the integrative function of the ego. In the stress which has been given to the present field of experience as the determinant of behavior, the relationship to Gestalt psychology, and to the work of Lewin and his students is obvious. The theories of

Angyal find some parallel in our observations. His view that the self represents only a small part of the biological organism which has reached symbolic elaboration, and that it often attempts the direction of the organism on the basis of unreliable and insufficient information, seems to be particularly related to the observations we have made. Lecky's posthumous book, small in size but large in the significance of its contribution, has brought a new light on the way in which the self operates, and the principle of consistency by which new experience is included in or excluded from the self. Much of his thinking runs parallel to our observations. Snygg and Combs have recently attempted a more radical and more complete emphasis upon the internal world of perception as the basis for all psychology, a statement which has helped to formulate a theory in which our observations fit.

It is not only from the realm of theory but also from the experimental laboratory that one finds confirmation of the line of thinking which has been proposed. Tolman has stressed the need of thinking as a rat if fruitful experimental work is to be done. The work of Snygg indicates that rat behavior may be better predicted by inferring the rat's field of perception than by viewing him as an object. Krech (Krechevsky) showed in a brilliant study some years ago that rat learning can only be understood if we realize that the rat is consistently acting upon one hypothesis after another. Leeper has summarized the evidence from a number of experimental investigations, showing that animal behavior cannot be explained by simple S-R mechanisms, but only by recognizing that complex internal processes of perceptual organization intervene between the stimulus and the behavioral response. Thus there are parallel streams of clinical observation, theoretical thinking, and laboratory experiment, which all point up the fact that for an effective psychology we need a much more complete understanding of the private world of the individual, and need to learn ways of entering and studying that world from within.

IMPLICATIONS

It would be misleading, however, if I left you with the impression that the hypotheses I have formulated in this paper, or those springing from the parallel psychological studies I have mentioned, are simply extensions of the main stream of psychological thinking, additional bricks in the edifice of psychological thought. We have discovered with some surprise that our clinical observations, and the tentative hypotheses which seem to grow out of them, raise disturbing questions which appear to cast doubt on the very foundations of many of our psychological endeavors, particularly in the fields of clinical psychology and personality study. To clarify what is meant, I should like to restate in more logical order the formulations I have given, and to leave with you certain questions and problems which each one seems to raise.

If we take first the tentative proposition that the specific determinant of behavior is the perceptual field of the individual, would this not lead, if regarded as a working hypothesis, to a radically different approach in clinical psychology and personality research? It would seem to mean that instead of elaborate case histories full of information about the person as an object, we would endeavor to develop ways of seeing his situation, his past, and himself, as these objects appear to him. We would try to see with him, rather than to evaluate him. It might mean the minimizing of the elaborate psychometric procedures by which we have endeavored to measure or value the individual from our own frame of reference. It might mean the minimizing or discarding of all the vast series of labels which we have painstakingly built up over the years. Paranoid, pre-schizophrenic, compulsive, constricted—terms such as these might become irrelevant because they are all based in thinking which takes an external frame of reference. They are not the ways in which the individual experiences himself. If we consistently studied each individual from the internal frame of reference of that individual, from within his own perceptual field, it seems probable that we should find generalizations which could be made, and principles which were operative, but we may be very sure that they would be of a different order from these externally based judgments *about* individuals.

Let us look at another of the suggested propositions. If we took seriously the hypothesis that integration and adjustment are internal conditions related to the degree of acceptance or nonacceptance of all perceptions, and the degree of organization of these perceptions into one consistent system, this would decidedly affect our clinical procedures. It would seem to imply the abandonment of the notion that adjustment is dependent upon the pleasantness or unpleasantness of the environment, and would demand concentration upon those processes which bring about self-integration within the person. It would mean a minimizing or an abandoning of those clinical procedures which utilize the alteration of environmental forces as a method of treatment. It would rely instead upon the fact that the person who is internally unified has the greatest likelihood of meeting environmental problems constructively, either as an individual or in cooperation with others.

If we take the remaining proposition that the self, under proper conditions, is capable of reorganizing, to some extent, its own perceptual field, and of thus altering behavior, this too seems to raise disturbing questions. Following the path of this hypothesis would appear to mean a shift in emphasis in psychology from focusing upon the fixity of personality attributes and psychological abilities, to the alterability of these same characteristics. It would concentrate attention upon process rather than upon fixed status. Whereas psychology has, in personality study, been concerned primarily with the measurement of the fixed qualities of the individual, and with his past in order to explain his present, the hypothesis here suggested would seem to concern itself much more with the personal world of the present in order to understand the future, and in predicting that future would be concerned with the principles by which personality and behavior are altered, as well as the extent to which they remain fixed.

Thus we find that a clinical approach, client-centered therapy, has led us to try to adopt the client's perceptual field as the basis for genuine understanding. In trying to enter this internal world of perception, not by introspection, but by observation and direct inference, we find ourselves in a new vantage point for understanding personality dynamics, a vantage point which opens up some disturbing vistas. We find that behavior seems to be better understood as a reaction to this reality-as-perceived. We discover that the way in which the person sees himself, and the perceptions he dares not take as belonging to himself, seem to have an important relationship to the inner peace which constitutes adjustment. We discover within the person, under certain conditions, a capacity for the restructuring and the reorganization of self, and consequently the reorganization of behavior, which has profound social implications. We see these observations, and the theoretical formulations which they inspire, as a fruitful new approach for study and research in various fields of psychology.

38 New vistas in personality research

Related selections: 17, 20, 27, 37, 40

One of the most exciting fields of endeavor in psychology is research leading to more and better insights into the formation of personality and concepts concerning the transformation of human behavior. Gardner Murphy describes five vistas in personality research, and highlights recent promising research in each. Some pertinent suggestions for research methodology are also given.

As he guided his little sailboat along the Maine coast, my most beloved college teacher said quietly but firmly, "The most important thing in the world is human personality." Though I loved him much, I was a little taken aback, a little alarmed, for he was a teacher of English literature, and I, unscrubbed behind the ears, was pushing into experimental psychology. I hoped that we could transcend and make more scientific those principles of experience and of individuality

GARDNER MURPHY, "New Vistas in Personality Research," *Personnel and Guidance Journal*, 40 (October, 1961), 114–22. Reprinted by permission of the publisher and the author.

DR. MURPHY (1895–   ) is Director of Research, The Menninger Foundation, Topeka, Kansas. For many years he was Professor of Psychology at Columbia University and at the College of the City of New York.

which ancient India and ancient Greece had defined for us in their philosophies, their dramas and their budding, new, inductive sciences. It took me a long time to see how the path through literature and history and the path through evolutionary science and the experimental laboratory could converge honestly and without giving up their specific messages, could converge at points of new vistas, new outlooks, for the study of man. As we look out from the peaks where such paths meet, we see in the mist other paths coming in to either side and above us, new intersections, and the top of the mountain is as yet nowhere in sight. We are proud of the new vistas of today, but sure that they are not final; sure that other men are tramping on paths as rich and promising as our own and destined to converge upon us higher up. And perhaps in moments, when the sky clears, we may even catch ridges and high bluffs beyond which, as Goethe says, "there is rest," because in fact through our climbing, we have earned it.

Indeed, when new perspectives—ravishingly beautiful though they are today—are offered to us only because of the enormous labor of those who have gone before, it is not the easy and casual glimpses only, indeed it is mainly the patiently built and patiently tested modes of looking at reality that are likely to be fruitful. I would like to say something that might interest or even perhaps in a fortunate moment inspire a few of my hearers, but if I had to choose, I would far more willingly act as reminder, instigator, critic, gadfly, and general troublemaker who might enable you to see how hard the new vistas are to achieve, how much work goes into science in all its forms, how hard the sifting of reality will have to be if we are to get to higher levels and wider perspectives. I shall, for this reason, not hesitate to be technical when I think the technical emphasis is necessary.

I shall try to lead you from our little laboratories to the doors which open out upon five great new regions of personality research. I shall name them (1) the biosocial conception of human individuality; (2) the path to the unknown depths of our inner resources; (3) the discovery of the control of the simpler processes by those more complex; (4) the determination of the counseling process from above downwards; (5) the transformation of all reality with the discovery of identity.

I

My first task is to remind you of the convergence in recent years of major lines of information about human individuality which have come, on the one hand, from biological laboratories, and from cross-cultural labor on the other, in the derivation of the basic facts about human life in different cultural settings, primitive and advanced, agricultural and technological. We have come to see that man's creative nature, as it cuts its way into the future, is neither a simple expression of his biological evolution, nor a simple impress upon him from the ways of living which our scientific and economic order has imposed upon him, but a delicate interaction of the biological and the cultural at the intersection point which we may call biosocial reality. Most of the work of showing just *how* the biological interacts with the social is just today beginning to be done.

We saw that nothing in the personality structure of man is fully inherited in the classical Mendelian sense. The genes are enormously important, but they do not call the shots. They do not punch the IBM cards; they do not sort us out and throw us into bins, where we can be counted or measured. Neither do the environmental contexts about us predetermine the slots, the grooves, through which we must glide. Rather, there is a strange, delicate process, hardly understood at all, by which certain latent potentialities within the genes are drawn out, molded, shaped as glass is shaped by the individual glassblower, and in the same way, though we less frequently think of it this way, that the social forces at work are drawn upon, channeled and funneled into the living system in such a way as to accelerate or retard, magnify or minimize what the genes are trying to say. We go on talking about the biosocial, but what research do we have on the nature of this interaction, this process by which one is potentiated by the other, this process by which a new individual, biosocially rich and unique, is created! Kurt Lewin lived and died with this potentiality latent and at times explicit in his own half-formed thoughts. H. J. Muller, L. C. Dunn, Edmund Sinnott, on the biological side, Margaret Mead, L. K. Frank and others on the cultural science side, have been pointing to possibilities; but as yet clear, verifiable laws, sharply delimiting the area of study, permitting the comparison of research groups and control groups, and giving us quantitative before-and-after data, are still largely a matter of a scientist's dream. The technical research problem waits to be solved.

And yet, such problems as these have to be solved in one way or another every time we mold a little child's way of feeling about brothers and sisters, pets, toys, colors, tones, and the patterns and symphonic orchestrations which make up his little world of reality. Every one of us teaching in the grades or in college, every one of us counseling or guiding, is working with a potential which expresses an interaction between a hidden force and an instigator. We are all working with the nature-nurture problem in one form or another. We are all gathering data which involve "testing the limits," to see how far people with built-in limitations or built-in potentialities can be lured, enticed, stimulated, into richer or stronger, healthier or more happy patterns of life; we are concerned always with the question of the relativity of human limits and the discovery of that which, though ordinarily impossible, may under certain conditions become possible; the exploitation, not only of known limits and known potentials, but of the unknown limits and the unknown potentials which somehow we grab for in the dark, somehow we subconsciously or intuitively guess *must* be present. If we are honest in recording our observations and honest in our follow-ups, we can use even such intuitive materials to sharpen our hypotheses and gradually lift ourselves beyond the guesswork level into the realm of checkable and sharable science, for there are literally unnameable and unknowable resources in collective humanity and in the individual. It is a question of knowing the key, the Open Sesame, the word which will swing back the great door, or even at times the word unspoken, the breathing-rate change, the postural, gestural language of caution or support, mature impulse control or wide fling of new daring posture.

Since so much happens so fast, it is of special importance for people in your profession to do three things: first, to keep up with your biology, know what is meant by the new investigations of genetic potentials as they come to us in the recent work of the laboratories and the recent studies of population genetics; secondly, to note the amazing new breakthroughs by which environment may change personal and social patterns, as, for example, in the India, the Israel, the Hawaii, of recent years; and third, and above all, to keep these precious daily records of your work in a form which permits you to make predictions of what can reasonably be expected and then later obtain uncontaminated observations by independent judges, finding how the data fall into the three great classes; first, those things which were expected; second, those things which were unexpected but dreamed about as possibilities; and third, those that were not even dreamed about. The idea has confused us in recent years that the verification of sober and obvious hypotheses is all that there is in science. Often it is the verification of the long, long shot, the fact that a remote possibility exists and will occasionally appear, just as these long shots have been of such central importance in the physics of the last 20 or 30 years.

And finally note the capacity to *observe* that which was not even dreamed about. I have in mind the discoveries in nuclear physics in which new elements have suddenly jumped into observation or even perhaps jumped into existence, and the Nobel Prize had to go to him who could recognize the reality when it appeared, rather than simply verify a hypothesis. Curious new phenomena, like those produced by penicillin, smote the attention of the investigator when he had no specific hypothesis at all, but had a capacity to keep his mind and his eyes wide open and, as William James had it, "let the universe be itself."

Now how in the world can the laboratory scientist, or the field investigator, or the guidance research man, or the everyday, ordinary counselor or guide or therapist develop the capacity to function in these ways and make the most of his own latent potentialities to develop this kind of research insight? I think something depends here upon what Theodor Reik has called "Listening with the Third Ear," or what we think of in Freud's terms as suspended attention, a sort of pivoting or pirouetting like a top which spins, slips, and skids, but if closely watched tells us something about the surface upon which it is moving, and catches the little gusts of wind which nobody would have suspected. If we are in suspense like the spinning and slipping top, we can be moved by gentle gusts of evidence, so to speak, which the heavy equipment of your weather vane would fail to catch. There is in such a special state of suspense a moment perhaps of empathy, new resonance to your client or friend, a moment of new perceptiveness or of explicit discovery, or indeed a moment which Rollo May would call *encounter*, a sudden confrontation, assimilation, acceptance, internalization, of the other person's world of reality and his own hidden capacity to reach out to you and to the world. Or occasionally what Maslow would call a "peak experience," an experience in which you are lifted to a new observation point by your own special helicopter. In such moments of encounter or ecstasy much may be lost if our interest is solely in the momentary excitement of a discovery. But we know that two further things are possible: first, learning to recognize such experiences or at least the little fingers and toes which they show us from beneath the curtain, so that we can more and more consistently recognize their presence; and secondly, learning actually to create the special conditions of encounter, that is, learning to set up that atmosphere of interchange with another human being which makes possible that the other should be himself.

Of course, it is partly among those who have been skilled in the interpretation of small signs that one should expect this, but it is also in large measure those who have learned to accept *themselves* and to note the little indications that they themselves are likely to change, are likely to lose their tempers, or to become sour, or to become sentimental, or to begin to miss the point. There are times when it is wise to retreat, times when it is necessary to crash ahead and utilize the rare and special moments in which discovery of the other person and how to give him genuine counsel may come. I should like to summarize these special conditions which we learn to recognize and to use under two heads: (1) those rare, benign moments when a wisdom which we did not know we had suddenly finds itself expressed through our own lips, when somehow we say and do the right thing; (2) to recognize the likely onset of those special states, those special experiences, which we may learn to encourage and constrain to our own purposes, in order that we may make unique adaptations to the special problems of each individual person. Because counseling involves the intimate interplay of two individualities, it is dyadic or reciprocal, and necessarily entails our being guided by our client in the same sense in which he is being guided by us; and this means that, just as we learn to recognize the little skills molded together into the unity by which we offer something of value to him, we begin to observe the little skills by which he manages to teach us, to guide and counsel us in the effective execution of our own specialized task. We learn, in other words, how to create the interpersonal atmospheres in which guidance is possible.

My first point, you see, dealt with the light which the concept of interaction and interdependence between the biological and social has brought to us, indicating the intimate union or fusion of concepts from the biological and from the social, and emphasizing the fact that those who actually work in interpersonal relations, like counselors, can, if their eyes are open to the possibilities, contribute substantially to the advancement of our understanding of their basic issues.

II

I turn now to another large area of contemporary personality research, which I believe is fraught with implications for those who give counsel. I am referring to the area known as stimulus deprivation or isolation research, the investigation of what it means to the human being to lose contact with his fellows. The spectrum of realities to be investigated reaches here all the way from isolation chamber research, stimulus impoverishment, to the study of lonely, out-of-touch human beings, whether they man radar sets in the far Arctic North or sit in Wright Field aviation laboratories at Dayton, Ohio, or whether they just drift as members of the Lonely Crowd in and through the masses without really making contact with anyone, whether they come to our colleges, or our clinics, or our guidance centers, stung or numbed by failures which they do not understand, reaching and yet not knowing how to reach for a contact which they would reject if they could begin to feel it moving their way. In this highly extroverted industrial society of ours, Riesman has offered something fundamental in suggesting that this avid extroversion is a cover-up for a loneliness, and Theodore Newcomb may be right in the suggestion that in mental illness it is the communication process itself which is sick, rather than the individual. I hardly need remind you that the study of artistic and scientific creativeness and of the social and political creativeness to which we turn in a period of such agonized fears may be the obverse of the same process by which, after rejecting social reality, so many of us set up barriers to prevent our getting back into such reality again. It has often been suggested that modern psychopathology—and indeed modern social psychology, too—arose from the great clinics of France three-quarters of a century ago in which it was discovered how different the isolated mind, the mind of dissociated and hypnotized persons, is from the every-day, socially-versatile mind of the normal person, with withdrawal into schizophrenic isolation as one pole and the mad flight into reality and the madness of crowds and mobs as the polarized expression of the same thing. There supervened a period of excitement about dreaming and individual creativeness which has been one of the richest periods in the history of psychology, largely because Freud and his contemporaries began to realize how deeply the individual craves the isolation of sleep and of the dream, permitting the upwelling, the subliminal uprush or creative fantasy, which often is lacking in the waking state, but through the artist can command a social audience because the loneliness of the dreamer or inventor makes contact with the comparable loneliness of his audience.

Perhaps the biosocial problem of heredity and environment to which I first draw attention is the identical twin brother of this problem of stimulus deprivation. Isolation, failure of communication, underscores the need for a strong parent or parent surrogate, a strong prophet, priest, and friend all rolled into one, who can be leaned upon and yet can enable one to find one's own feet, who can give advice and yet enable one to seek counsel within the depths of his own individuality, discovering in the group setting an educational process which is never complete when one lacks feedback, lacks communion with those who seek the same realities, those who can mirror back one's own craving for closeness.

I think we have here a part of the meaning which has come from the insights of David Rapaport and Lawrence Kubie, who have reminded us that in the creative process we are for the moment free both of the overwhelming pressures of an external environment which tells us to adjust to it, and likewise free of the imperious controls of our inner life, whether arising from instinct or the tension level of our body musculature or the unforgettable core of memories which connect us with the past, or the ruminative bewildering quest for meaning which is always deeper than words and more unquenchable than recurring appetites. In the little narrow band between peremptory pressures of the outer and the peremptory pressures of the inner world, there is a balancing act which, as you may recall from Nietzsche's *Thus Spake Zarathustra,* gives us the tightrope walker caught in the enormous danger of that which lies before and that which lies behind. Learning all that can be learned regarding ego control within the perspective of outer and inner worlds to be conquered, each of us may use the resources of these two worlds and share them with others caught in the same great predicament of life. We may do more than capture these moments for a supreme creative effort. We may learn to use these favorable states, just as the poet and the composer may through the years learn how to express through words and through tones the imperious language from within and the enticing or threatening commands from without.

If this applies to the creativeness of the musician and the poet, it applies likewise to the creativeness of the teacher, and to the creativeness of the counselor, mentor, and guide who transcends them, fuses them at high temperature with feeling for life and for persons and creates something new. Ultimately, the psychology of the learning process will include the study of this orchestration of feelings in the interpersonal situation. We need to know how to use what we know, and we need also to be honest and explicit about what we do not know, in order that more may be achieved and communicated from one to another in this field of interpersonal experience.

My second point is then that the modern excitement about isolation research and the excitement about creativeness are in large measure related to one another or even at times identical, and that without fully knowing why or how, the research psychologists have been mustering their strength not just to shoot people in capsules through the vast interplanetary spaces, but to understand a little more the enormous stress which loneliness entails, the enormous disorganization of human personality by deep and prolonged loneliness, the enormous challenge which comes to the door of anyone with a method for coming closer to his fellow, combining professional services with familial warmth, wisdom, and perspective.

III

I turn now to a third and still closely related type of modern personality research, which I shall call the control of the simpler processes by those more complex. A few years ago it was still seriously believed that human behavior, whether motor, emotional, or verbal, was mainly derived from very simple Pavlovian types of conditioned responses. Now I believe that those who have followed the Soviet experiments of recent years are in accord on two very fundamental points regarding the meaning of this approach and view in a new and different light the principles relating to the origins of personality. Mrs. Murphy and I had the opportunity last summer to make some brief observations in three Soviet cities and to visit a number of institutes in which research on human learning and personality formation is going on. Not that what we have to say is so very different from what many others have observed, but that it is now more real to us, because we were able to see some of the people and some of the laboratories which represent contemporary Soviet trends and can point out how these are related to comparable American research trends that have to do with the conditioning and learning processes.

From the modern viewpoint the classical conditioning process in which, for example, the dog encounters meat powder just after he hears a buzzer, and through conditioning soon gives us a salivary response to the buzzer alone, exemplifies what is known as the primary signal system. It is real and the concept applies both to adults and to children, even to infants, but there are two enormous changes of perspective to be noted here in recent years. In the first place, before the conditioning process starts in, there occurs the orienting reflex, the what-is-it response, the response of adjusting the sense organs and the head or the whole body to the fact that something new is happening. Life calls for a new adjustment or adaptation. Highly creative and original Soviet scientists, like E. N. Sokolov at Moscow, are making fine measurements of both adult and child orienting responses and showing how very fundamental it is in all life to map out that which is stable and that which is changing, and to make a corresponding orienting response. The first thing an organism has to do is to know whether the environment is constant or whether it is undergoing change. This has immediate implications for schooling which are not being overlooked. Often you have to work with the orienting reflex, with the readiness responses, before you can start with the conditioning program. You have to consider whether the thing that you have to offer is really new, because if it is not, there will be rapid adaptation to it; and if what you offer has only small details that are new, they are likely to be the ones that make their decisive effect, even before you know it. Beyond the orienting response stands the Pavlovian system of conditioning, of which we have long had word; it is known as conditioning through the *primary signal systems*. But above and beyond this, there is *another* vast system, the *secondary signal system*, consisting of the higher responses to the more elementary responses expressing an architecture in which the simple primary signal system leads on and up through the formation of words into the formation of verbally designated concepts. Having once acquired some skill in the use of language, the individual is ever thereafter a cultural entity living in a verbal cultural world, no longer behaving like Pavlov's dogs, as a matter of fact generalizing, extinguishing, and showing the other aspects of learning in a manner very different from those which obtain with the primary signal system.

There are immediate and profound implications here for all the human sciences. Elkonin, for example, put to us very clearly the fact that the aim of Soviet education is to make everything as conscious, as rational, as possible; never teach anything robotwise if you can teach it at a higher level. Leontiev explained to us that in any skill, intellectual or motor, the first thing is to understand the aim and the process. You use the simple primary signal system and the Pavlovian dog types of learning only at your peril, and only when you have made sure that there is a high-level comprehension of the task and of its place in the social scheme. Or to choose a third example of contemporary Soviet psychology, Mrs. Yarmolenko of Leningrad, emphasizing the higher or secondary system, explains that the need to understand is as fundamental as the need to eat.

Now all of this means that we are beginning to understand that personality is really an architectural system, not a series of jackstraws or pebbles lying all at the same level on the floor, but that meaningful structures develop in which often the higher have a downward and forcible effect upon the lower structures. I believe that every one of our educational arts, including college teaching and very much including counseling, are beginning to be affected by this trend toward the achievement of maximal intelligibility. Thus in the contemporary work of Lee Cronbach and of Jean Piaget, the interest is in fitting our procedures to the actual structure of the understanding mind, rather than to the simple mechanics of an association psychology on the model of the low-level conditioned reflex. It is indeed likely that Piaget and Cronbach are underplaying the importance of the emotional and impulsive components in the functioning of the secondary signal system. However that may be, the answers to some questions will come not at the level of piling up more knowledge of *simple* learning acts through elementary reinforcements and repetitions, but through a study of the architecture of the system.

IV

And I would emphasize a principle that you use all the time: the principle that the simpler processes which make up our little habits and skills express our total individuality. The experimental movement in psychology toward studying the way in which feelings, needs, wishes, and drives influence the way in which we perceive, recall, remember, and think, which we might broadly call the "new look" psychology, expresses this recognition of complex, high-level functions in which cognitive processes become genuine samples of total personality functioning. If this be correct, the counselor will need to keep constantly in touch with the contemporary evidence about the specific ways in which the knowledge and skills of one's client expresses his fears, hopes, and wishes, indeed guide the ways in which we all perceive and understand one another. Indeed, the counselor, being human, is as much caught in this interplay of feeling and cognition, this meshing or interpenetration of desires and processes of remembering and knowing, as he finds himself caught in the interplay between himself and his client. There is no hiding place for pure preception or memory or thought, freed of all contact with emotional tugs and distortions, just as there is no real freedom for him to hide behind his notes and his verbiage and to keep out of the world of the person who sits there before him.

A few examples:

In such a situation I am tempted to say, regarding a boy who came to me for help: "*I made it perfectly plain to him; why can't he see it?*" You would be right in replying to me: "Maybe while you were saying something as clear as crystal with your *words*, your gestures and facial expression, your breathing and posture were saying the opposite (leaving him in a double bind). Or maybe he can't see it because you have made it too self-evident; that is, self-evident from *your* viewpoint, not from *his;* to him it is still ego-alien. Yet in a sense it is too obvious *even* to *him;* he has no chance to work with it, make it his own; it offers no challenge. He does not want more and more of his tiresome and frustrated self. He does not come to you to be told what he already deeply knows; he wants not plain English, but electricity. But at times it is also true that he cannot understand you because he *fears* to understand you; or fears that if he follows your counsel he will have to give up part of his image of himself, and perhaps that is all he has. The rag doll that he continues to hug after he has to move to a new house." And you would be right. But can we take all this for granted without being lured into a chess game with our young friend, or to tease or to lecture him?

V

Finally this leads into a fifth vast area of rapid and vivid development of new concepts, the area to which Erikson's term *identity* applies, the area defined in earlier years by William James and G. H. Mead in terms of consciousness of self, or self-image. More recently we encounter areas of research defined by Victor Raimy and others from a more clinical and a more quantitative viewpoint in which the self is regarded as a central psychological reality which influences the perception and the action going on at any given time. There is almost nothing left from the psychology of 50 years ago regarding sensation, affect, intelligence, learning, memory, which does not look profoundly different when we ask: how is all this assimilated to the existing concept of the self? What is the person doing with his own self-concept as he assimilates or rejects each new self that you try to make real to him, or which he feels you are trying to belittle or mutilate, or which slips protean-fashion through your hands as you and he both undergo self-transformations? From Rogerian therapy to classical analytic concepts of ego weakness and strength to the concepts of sex, class, age, and cultural differences in self-definition, we have found ourselves dealing with a self-psychology even broader than that of William James. I suspect that this, too, is connected with the scientific technological revolution, with the loneliness which I described in terms of Riesman, with the bizarre universe of isolation research, or what we might call capsule and rocket research.

This emphasis on the self, however, does something very radical to all the familiar concepts which I have suggested this evening. Indeed it tends to turn them inside out, as a coat is turned inside out. The self that is looked at in this way is indeed the self we have known through anthropology and through litera-ture, especially through the dream and through the world of creativeness. It has, however, a number of new dimensions, because we find that here in the depths of the self there is paradoxically a great deal that was never known to be a part of the self and which we can see, as it were, aborning, in *statu nascendi*. A good many biological realities of the human organism, which never previously related to the self as such, but which under conditions of great stress, are forced up near the level of recognizability. The person finds urges within him even deeper than the drives, and even more powerful than the phenomena of conflict or of impulse control. I refer, for example, to such studies as those of photic driving in which one discovers that the basic organic rhythms differ from person to person and that by various artificial devices, physical and chemical, you can bring out, almost as by a histologic stain, attributes of his individuality which no one could ever have guessed before. The isolation research is putting stress likewise on future astronauts, and the creativeness studies are tending to show that what is most vulnerable, what is very profoundly at the root of one's own struggle to maintain one's inner integrity against the stresses of this world, may be that which stands out, in idiosyncratic form, in the moment of the highest creation. Hughlings Jackson suggested in the early days of Darwinism that the most re-cently arrived evolutionary functions, those of the most recently developed brain function, are those which are most vulnerable to disease. There is a great deal to suggest that the apex of human individuality lies in this region of the most sensitive, most vulnerable, most stress-prone, that which is most easily thrown out of kilter. If this be true, personality research will not look so much for the modal or the average, but for the heights and depths, the things which, though they occur rarely, throw light upon the hidden propensities which bespeak the individuality of man or woman or child. Beware of normal distribution curves! Beware of linear relations of x's and y's! They all have their place as reference points. There is also that which is special, that which is off the distribution curve.

And so we come full circle. We began with the unknown potentialities, which first we tried to see through the language of biosocial interaction. We went on to the study of isolation and of the creativeness related to such isolation. We found ourselves dealing with the effect of strain and with the problem of vulnerability, and now we have concluded that, along with one's regular, daily bread-and-butter tasks of probabilistic suiting of everyday needs and capacities to everyday demands and tasks, there may be an important place to keep one's weather eye out for the exceptional, the rare, the once-in-a-lifetime, the highest and the lowest of which the individual is capable.

Incidentally, if one does this, one may find a strange change of perspective regarding one's own individuality. As one wakes up in the morning, one may not simply greet the good old familiar face in the mirror and feel the muscles jog into their familiar weight-bearing and body-carrying habits; one may discover, if one listens, that this third ear will hear some things that are inside as well as outside. One may discover in one's own individuality much that had no business being there, but much which, when seen in a new perspective, one might be grateful to acknowledge. You know it might really turn out that it is actually true that each person makes up some chords which have never been played before.

39   *The relation between psychoanalysis and pedagogy*

Related selections: 7, 31, 36, 37, 56

In this selection Anna Freud, daughter of the great Sigmund Freud, points out to a group of teachers in Vienna how Freudian psychoanalysis can aid pedagogy. She reviews its theory of personality and accuses education of "shooting at sparrows with cannon balls" in forcing children to repress instinctual behavior. On the other hand, she points out how the gratification of all instinctual sexual desire can arrest development and cause the individual to fail to develop enough inner restraint to allow the diversion of energy from sexual activity to other more socially approved activities.

We must not demand too much from one another. You must not expect that in four short lectures I shall succeed in presenting to you more than the most important

From ANNA FREUD, *Psychoanalysis for Teachers and Parents* (New York: Emerson Books, Inc., 1947), pp. 92–114. Reprinted by permission of the publisher.

DR. FREUD (1895–   ), a psychoanalyst now living in London, has done extensive work in the area of child analysis and has contributed greatly to the solution of many of its technical problems.

principles of a science the study of which would require many years. I, on the other hand, cannot expect you to remember all the details which I have put before you. Out of my summary, condensed from a great abundance of data and thereby probably often confusing, perhaps you will be able to retain for your guidance only three of the characteristic viewpoints of psychoanalysis.

The first of these ideas is concerned with the division of time. Psychoanalysis distinguishes, as you have already learned, three different periods in the life of the child: early childhood up to about the end of the fifth year; the latency period to the beginning of the prepuberty stage, about the eleventh, twelfth, or thirteenth year; and puberty, which leads into adult life. In each period there is a different emotional reaction of the child to those around him, and a different stage of instinctual development, each of which is normal and characteristic. A special attribute of the child, or his method of reaction, cannot therefore be judged without reference to the specific period of his life. An act of instinctive cruelty or shamelessness, for example, which belongs to the early period and to puberty, will cause anxiety to the observer if it occurs in the latency period, and if found in adult life will have, perhaps, to be judged as a perversity. The strong link with the parents, which is natural and desirable in the first period and in the latency period, is a sign of retarded development if it still exists at the end of puberty. The strong urge to rebel and to have inner freedom which in puberty facilitates the emergence into normal adult life may be regarded as an obstacle to the right development of the ego in earliest childhood or in the latency period.

The second aspect is connected with the inner growth of the childish personality. You have probably up till now pictured to yourself the child with whom you have to deal as a homogeneous being, and consequently have not been able to explain the difference between what he wants to do and what he is able to do, the clash between his intentions and his actions. The psychoanalytic conception shows you the personality of the child as of a three-fold nature, consisting of the instinctual life, the ego, and the superego, which is derived from the relationship with his parents. The contradictions in his behavior are to be explained, therefore, when you learn to recognize behind his different reactions that part of his being which at this particular moment predominates.

The third principle is concerned with the interaction between these divisions of the childish personality; we must not imagine this to be a peaceful process, but rather a conflict. The issue of such a duel, for example, between the ego of the child and an instinctive wish he knows to be undesirable, depends upon the relative strength of the libido at the disposal of the instinctive impulses compared with the energy of the repressing force derived from the superego.

But I fear, indeed, that these three principles for practical application which I have put briefly before you do not give you all that you hoped to get from psychoanalysis in the way of help for your work. Probably you seek practical advice which will be a guidance to you rather than an extension of your theoretical knowledge. You want to know for certain which methods of education are the most to be recommended; which must be absolutely avoided if you do not want to imperil the child's whole development. Above all, you want to know whether we shall continue with more education, or give less than we have in the past.

In answer to the last question it should be said that psychoanalysis, whenever it has come into contact with pedagogy, has always expressed the wish to limit education. Psychoanalysis has brought before us the quite definite danger arising from education. You have learned how the child is forced to fulfill the demands of the adult world around him. You know that he conquers his first great emotional attachments by identification with the beloved and feared adults. He escapes from their external influence, but meanwhile establishes a court of judgment within, modeled on the authority of those beings, which continues to maintain this influence within him. This incorporation of the parent-figures is the dangerous step. When this takes place the prohibitions and demands become fixed and unchangeable. In place of living beings they become an historical background which is incapable of adapting itself to progressive external changes. In reality the parent-figures would be influenced by reason in their conduct and would be accessible to the claims of a new situation. Naturally they would be prepared to concede to the thirty-year-old man what was forbidden to the three-year-old child. But that part of the ego which has been formed from the demands and standards of the parents remains inexorable.

The following examples are given to elucidate these points. I know a boy who was extremely fond of dainties in his earliest years. As his passion for dainties was too great to be satisfied by legitimate means, he hit upon all kinds of unlawful expedients and dodges in order to procure sweets, spent all the money he possessed upon them and was not too particular as to how he procured more. Education was called upon to act; the boy was forbidden sweets, and his passionate devotion to his mother, who had interfered with his pleasure, gave special emphasis to the prohibition. His extreme fondness for dainties disappeared, to the great satisfaction of his elders. Yet today this lad, now an adolescent who has plenty of money at his disposal and the freedom to buy up all the sweetmeats of the Viennese confectionery shops, is not able to eat a piece of chocolate without blushing furiously. Everybody who observes him is at once certain that he is doing something forbidden—that he is eating things bought with stolen money. You notice that the restrictions imposed upon him earlier have not automatically yielded to the changed situation.

Listen again to another example, this time not so harmless. A boy loves his mother with special tenderness; all his desires are directed toward filling the place which actually belongs to his father, and toward being her confidant and protector and her best-beloved. The child now suffers repeatedly the devastating experience that his father is the rightful owner of the position for which he is striving. It is his father who has the power to send him away from his mother at

any time and to show him his own childish helplessness and impotence. The prohibition to aspire to his father's place is strengthened by his own fear of the
father's great potency. Later, when he is an adolescent, this boy evinces a
tormenting timidity and uncertainty which he feels as an unbearable obstacle
when he finds himself in the same house as the girl he loves. This basis of his
fear is that somebody may come and declare that the place he is occupying
belongs to another and he has no right to it. To avoid this extremely painful
situation he employs a great deal of his energy in preparing excuses which could
plausibly explain to this other person his presence there.

Or take another case. A tiny little girl develops an extreme pleasure in her
naked body, shows herself naked to her brothers and sisters, and delights in
running through the rooms stark naked before she goes to bed. Education steps
in and again with success. The little girl now makes a very great effort to suppress
this desire. The result is an intense feeling of modesty that continues in later life.
When the question of choosing a career arises somebody suggests an occupation
which would necessitate sharing a room with companions. She unhesitatingly
states that this career is not for her. Behind the rational motive the fear is
ultimately revealed that she will have to undress before the others. The question
of qualification or preference for the career is of no consequence compared with
the strength of the prohibition carried over from childhood.

The psychoanalyst who is engaged in his therapeutic work of "resolving"
such inhibitions and disturbances in development certainly learns to know education from its worst side. Here, he feels, they have been shooting at sparrows
with cannon balls! Would it not have been better perhaps to have given somewhat
less value to decorum and convention in these various nurseries, and to have let
the first child be greedy and the second imagine himself in the role of the
father; to have permitted the third child to run about naked and a fourth to play
with his genitals? Would these childish gratifications really have had any important adverse effect as compared with the damage wrought by a so-called "good
education"? Compare them with the division which is thus introduced into the
childish personality; the way in which one part of him is incited against another;
soo how the capacity to love is diminished and the child grows up incapable,
perhaps, of enjoyment and of accomplishing his life-work. The analyst to whom
all this is apparent resolves, so far as he is concerned, not to aid such an education, but to leave his own children free rather than to educate in this way. He
would rather risk the chance of their being somewhat uncontrolled in the end instead of forcing on them from the outset such a crippling of their individuality.

But you are, I feel sure, shocked at the onesidedness of my views. It is high
time to change the standpoint. Education appears to us in another light when
we have another aim in view—for example, when it is concerned with the
neglected child, such as August Aichhorn deals with in his book *Neglected Youth*.

The neglected child, says Aichhorn, refuses to take his place in society. He
cannot succeed in controlling his instinctive impulses; he cannot divert enough
energy from his sexual instincts to employ them for purposes more highly

esteemed by society. He refuses, therefore, to submit to the restrictions which are binding on the society in which he lives, and equally withdraws from any participation in its life and work. No one who has had to do with this type of child in an educational or psychoanalytical connection can fail to regret that in his childhood there had been no force from without which succeeded in restricting his instinctual life, so that these external checks would have been gradually transformed into inner restrictions.

Take as an example a child who for a little while occupied the attention of the Vienna Children's Court. This eight-year-old girl was equally impossible both at home and at school. From every educational institute or convalescent home she was unhestitatingly sent back to her parents after three days at the most. She refused to learn anything or to share in the activities of the other children. She pretended to be stupid, and so cleverly that in several places she was diagnosed as mentally defective. During the lessons she lay down on a bench and played with her sexual parts. Any interruption of this occupation resulted in a wild howling horrifying the grownups. At home she was ill-treated—this was the only idea the parents had of dealing with her. An analytic investigation showed two things. The external circumstances were peculiarly unfavorable to the development of any kind of emotional relations between the child and her environment. No one could offer a love that would have in any way compensated the child for giving up the gratification obtained from her own body. It also showed that the severe punishments from which the parents had obviously expected a restraining influence could not fulfill this purpose. Either owing to her own disposition or on account of significant early experience the little girl had developed such strong masochistic tendencies that each beating could only become once more a stimulus to sex excitement and sex activity. Compare this case of neglect with the one of repression which I described to you earlier. You can see that a free and self-reliant human being does not evolve from this child either. She is nothing but a cowed little animal whose further moral development has stopped simultaneously with her mental growth.

Aichhorn mentions in his book *Neglected Youth* another severe case of maldevelopment—that of a boy who from about his sixth year onward had found every kind of sexual gratification in his mother, and finally, after reaching sexual maturity, lived with her in actual sexual intercourse. He had thus actually accomplished what the other children had enjoyed only in fantasy. Neither has this boy developed into a self-reliant, harmonious, vigorous human being, as we might have expected, considering the evil effects of education described above.

A kind of "short-circuiting" had occurred in his development. By the actual fulfillment of his childhood's wishes he had saved himself the necessity of traversing the whole circle of "becoming grown-up." The wish to become like his father in order to attain all the possibilities of the gratifications permitted to his father was now superfluous. He had indeed escaped the "splitting" of his personality, but in return for that he had given up any further development.

But you will find that the problem is not so difficult as I have represented it to you, and that disturbances in development and delinquency may be merely extreme results, showing, on the one hand, the injurious effect of too great repression, on the other the lack of all restraint. The task of a pedagogy based upon analytic data is to find a *via media* between these extremes—that is to say, to allow to each stage in the child's life the right proportion of instinct-gratification and instinct-restriction.

Possibly a detailed description of this new analytical pedagogy should have been the content of my lectures to you. But for the present no analytical pedagogy exists. We have only as yet individual educators who are interested in this work, and having been analyzed themselves they now seek to apply to the education of children the understanding that psychoanalysis has brought to them of their own instinctual life. It will be a long time before theory and practice are complete and can be recommended for general use.

But in spite of this you ought not to say that psychoanalysis has done nothing beyond giving indications as to the future; that it certainly does not profit teachers engaged in practical work to study psychoanalysis, and that probably it would be better to dissuade them from having anything to do with it. Nor should you say that they had better make enquiries in ten or twenty years' time as to what has been accomplished meanwhile in the application of psychoanalysis to pedagogics.

I maintain that even today psychoanalysis does three things for pedagogy. In the first place, it is well qualified to offer a criticism of existing educational methods. In the second place, the teacher's knowledge of human beings is extended, and his understanding of the complicated relations between the child and the educator is sharpened by psychoanalysis, which gives us a scientific theory of the instincts, of the unconscious and of the libido. Finally, as a method of practical treatment, in the analysis of children, it endeavors to repair the injuries which are inflicted upon the child during the processes of education.

The following example illustrates the second point, i.e., it explains the pedagogical situation by means of the unconscious background of the conscious behavior.

An excellent woman teacher began her career in her eighteenth year when, in consequence of unhappy family circumstances, she left home to take a post as governess to three boys. The second boy presented a serious educational problem. He was backward in his lessons and appeared very timid, reserved, and dull; he played a subordinate part in the family, and in contrast to his two gifted and attractive brothers was constantly pushed into the background. The teacher devoted all her efforts and interest to this boy, and in a comparatively short time had obtained a wonderful success.

The boy got very fond of her, was more devoted to her than he had ever been to anybody before, and became frank and friendly in his ways. His interest in lessons increased, and by her efforts she succeeded in teaching him in one year the subjects laid down for two years, so that he was no longer behind in his work. The parents were now proud of this child, whom until then they treated with but slight affection; they took much more trouble about him, and his relations to them and also to his brothers improved, until the little boy was finally accepted as a most valued member of the family circle. Thereupon an unexpected difficulty arose. The teacher to whom the success was entirely due began now on her side to have trouble with the boy. She no longer gave him any love, and could not get on with him. Finally, she left the house, where she was greatly appreciated, on account of the very child who had been in the beginning the center of attraction to her.

The psychonanalytic treatment which she underwent nearly fifteen years later for pedagogic reasons revealed to her the true facts of the case. In her own home, as a child, she had, with more or less justification, imagined herself the unloved child—the same position in which she had actually found the second boy when she began to work with him. On the ground of similar slighting treatment she had seen herself in this boy, and had identified herself with him. All the love and care which she had lavished upon him meant that she was really saying to herself: "That is the way I ought to have been treated to make something out of me." Success, when it came, destroyed this identification. It made the pupil an independent being who could no longer be identified with her own life. The hostile feelings toward him arose from envy; she could not help grudging him the success which she herself had never attained.

You will say, perhaps, it was a good thing that this teacher, when she dealt with her pupil, had not yet been analyzed; otherwise we should have lost a fine educational success. But I feel that these educational successes are too dearly bought. They are paid for by the failures with those children who are not fortunate enough to reveal symptoms of suffering which remind the teacher of her own childhood and so make sympathy with them possible for her. I hold we are right in demanding that the teacher or educator should have learned to know and to control his own conflicts before he begins his educational work. If this is not so, the pupils merely serve as more or less suitable material on which to abreact his own unconscious and unsolved difficulties.

But in addition, the manifest behavior of the child is very seldom sufficient ground for a correct judgment. I will now give you the following notes which a boy dictated as the first chapter of an extensive book. As is so often the case with children, it remained a fragment.

CHAPTER ONE

The wrong things
grown-up people do

Here, you grown-up people, listen to me, if you want to know something! Don't be too cocky and imagine that children can't do everything that grown-up people do. But they can do most of what you do. But children will never obey if you order them about like this, for example: "Now, go and undress, quick's the word, get along." Then they will never undress, don't you believe it. But when you speak nicely, then they will do it at once. You think you can do all you want to do, but don't imagine any such thing. And don't ever say: "You must do this, you 'must' do that!" No one "must" do things, neither therefore "must" children do things. You think children "must" wash themselves. Certainly not. Then you say, "But if you don't wash everybody will say, 'Oh fie, how dirty he is!' and so you 'must' wash yourself." No, he "mustn't," but he does wash, so that people won't call him dirty.

When you tell children what they are to do that's enough, and don't tell them so much about how they are to do it, for they do what they think right, just as you do. And don't always say to them, "You 'mustn't' buy such and such a thing," for if they pay for it themselves they can buy what they like. Don't always say to children, "You can't do that!" For they can do many things better than you, and you won't ever believe it, and afterwards you are astonished. Don't always talk so much; let the children sometimes get a word in!

Now, suppose these written remarks were found in a school and taken to the head master. He would say to himself that this was a dangerous boy on whom one must keep one's eye. From further inquiry he would find out still more serious things about him. The boy was in the habit of making blasphemous remarks about God; he described the priests in language that can scarcely be repeated; he strongly urged his companions not to put up with any interference, and indeed he even planned to go into the zoological gardens and set free the animals whom he regarded as wrongfully imprisoned there. Now a conservative teacher of the old school would say: The rebellious spirit of this boy must be broken by some means or other before it is too late and he has become a serious menace to society. A modern educator, on the contrary, would have the highest hopes of this child's future, and would expect to see in him a future leader and liberator of the masses.

I must tell you that both teachers would be wrong, and all methods of training which they might base upon their knowledge of the manifest situation would be harmful and false. The eight-year-old boy is a harmless little coward, who is in terror when a dog barks at him, who is frightened to go along the dark passage in the evening, and certainly would not be capable of injuring a fly. His rebellious sayings come about in the following way. His early passionate emotional relations, accompanied by an intense preoccupation with his penis, were destroyed as the result of education and of medical treatment from which he experienced severe shock. As a safeguard against new temptations there remained an immense fear, that of being punished on the guilty part of his body, the fear which psychoanalysis names *castration-fear*. This fear caused him now to deny any kind of authority. When anybody has power, he says to himself, then he has the power to punish me. Consequently every possibility of a heavenly or earthly ruler must be removed from the world. The greater his fear of temptation the more he seeks to drown it by his quite harmless attacks on those in authority. This noisy method of protecting himself is, moreover, not his only one. Although he acts the part of an atheist, he kneels down in the evening and prays, secretly impelled by fear. He thinks: "There is indeed no God. But perhaps after all there might be one, and then it would be a good thing, in any case, to behave properly to Him." Now I take it this boy will become neither a menace to society nor a liberator of the masses. What he needs is, indeed, neither admiration of his efforts nor harshness and restrictions, but only—by some means or other—an abatement of his fear which will enable him, released now from his neurotic way of living, to obtain later on the capacity for enjoyment and work.

The psychoanalytic method of treatment which can achieve this is, then, the third service that psychoanalysis has rendered to education. But the description of this method, namely, child analysis, would go far beyond the limits of this course.

40 *Cognition of being in the peak experiences*

Related selections: 12, 33, 37, 38, 53

Are we normally sick? In this selection Maslow states his belief that most people most of the time are ill if they are compared to fully functioning and healthy individuals. His studies have previously led him to the identification and description of self-actualizing persons. In this selection he asserts that the characteristics of such persons are not limited to a relatively few people in our society but are exemplified by many in relatively rare "peak experiences." He presents the characteristics of such experiences and supports his

A. H. MASLOW, "Cognition of Being in the Peak Experiences," *The Journal of Genetic Psychology*, 94 (1959), 43–66. Reprinted by permission of The Journal Press and the author.

DR. MASLOW (1908–   ) is Professor and Chairman of the Psychology Department at Brandeis University. He is past-president of several divisions of the American Psychological Association. His most recent book is *Toward a Psychology of Being*.

position from philosophy, religion, art, and psychoanalysis as well as from his own research and clinical experience.

A. INTRODUCTION

Self-actualizing people, those who have come to a high level of maturation, health, and self-fulfillment, have so much to teach us that sometimes they seem almost like a different breed of human beings. But, because it is so new, the study of the exploration of the highest reaches of human nature and of its ultimate possibilities and aspirations is a difficult and tortuous task. It has involved for me the continuous destruction of cherished axioms, the perpetual coping with seeming paradoxes, contradictions, and vaguenesses and the occasional collapse around my ears of long established, firmly believed in, and seemingly unassailable laws of psychology. Often these have turned out to be no laws at all but only rules for living in a state of mild and chronic psychopathology, and fearfulness, of stunting and crippling, and immaturity which we don't notice because most others have this same disease that we have.

Most frequently, as is typical in the history of scientific theorizing, this probing into the unknown first takes the form of a felt dissatisfaction, an uneasiness with what is missing long before any scientific solution becomes available. For instance, one of the first problems presented to me in my studies of self-actualizing people was the vague perception that their motivational life was in some important way different from all that I had learned. I first described it as being expressive rather than coping, but this wasn't *quite* right as a total statement. Then I pointed out that it was unmotivated rather than motivated, but this statement rests so heavily on which theory of motivation you accept, that it made as much trouble as help. In a more recent paper, I have contrasted growth-motivation with deficiency-need motivations which helps, I think, but isn't definitive enough yet, because it doesn't differentiate Becoming from Being. In this address, I shall propose a new tack (into a psychology of Being) which should include and generalize the three attempts already made to put into words somehow, the observed differences between the motivational and cognitive life of fully developed people and of most others.

This analysis of states of Being (temporary, non-striving, purposeless, self-validating, end-experiences and states) emerged first from a study of the love-relations and sexual experiences of self-actualizing people, and then of other people as well, and finally from dipping into the theological and philosophical literatures. It became necessary to differentiate two types of love. The one is love that comes from ordinary love-need, what Fenichel calls love as the need for narcissistic supplies, for gratification of a deficiency of love. It can therefore be conveniently called deficiency-love (D-love). It is typically and normally found in children and adolescents (of whatever age) in our culture.

But this creates a paradox. Self-actualizing people, by definition gratified in their basic needs, including the love-need, should cease loving and wanting love, if the only determinant of love were the basic love-need. But the finding is that they are *more* loving people than the average, rather than *less* loving, especially from the point of view of being able to give love as well as to receive it. The attempt to understand this led to the formulation of another form or type of love, closely akin to what the theologians have called Agapean love, or Godly love, and which the psychonanalysts have named object-love and never described further. It is a love for the essence of or Being of the other person, in the style that Scheler has described, quite apart from what he can give the lover, a love for the person in himself rather than for what we can get from him, detached, altruistic, admiring, unneeded, unselfish. It is love for another person because he is what he is, rather than because he is a need-gratifier.

In this state of love for the Being of the other person or object, I found a particular kind of cognition for which my knowledge of psychology had not prepared me but which I have since seen well described by certain writers on aesthetics, religion, and philosophy. This I shall call Cognition of Being, or for short, B-Cognition. This is in contrast to cognition organized by the deficiency needs of the individual, which I shall call D-Cognition. The B-lover is able to perceive realities in the beloved to which others are blind, i.e., he is more acutely and penetratingly perceptive.

This paper is an attempt to generalize in a single description some of these basic cognitive happenings in the B-love experience, the parental experience, the mystic or oceanic, or nature experience, the aesthetic perception, the creative moment, the therapeutic or intellectual insight, the orgasmic experience, certain forms of athletic fulfillment. These and other moments of highest happiness and fulfillment I shall call the peak-experiences.

This is then a chapter in the Positive or Ortho-Psychology of the future in that it deals with fully functioning and healthy human beings, and not alone with normally sick ones. It is therefore not in contradiction to Psychology as a Psychopathology of the Average; it transcends it and can in theory incorporate all its findings in a more inclusive and comprehensive structure which includes both the sick and the healthy, both deficiency, Becoming and Being.

B. B-COGNITION IN PEAK EXPERIENCES

I shall present one by one now in a condensed summary, each of the characteristics of the cognition found in the generalized peak-experience, using the term cognition in an extremely broad sense.

1. *In B-Cognition the experience or the object tends to be seen as a whole, as a complete unit, detached from relations, from possible usefulness, from expediency, and from purpose.* It is seen as if it were all there was in the universe, as if it were all of Being, synonymous with the universe.

This contrasts with D-Cognition, which includes most human cognitive experiences. These experiences are partial and incomplete in ways that will be described below.

We are reminded here of the absolute idealism of the 19th century, in which all of the universe was conceived to be a unit. Since this unity could never be encompassed or perceived or cognized in any other fashion by a limited human being, all actual human cognitions were perceived as necessarily part of Being, and never conceivably the whole of it.

2. *When there is a B-Cognition, the percept is exclusively and fully attended to.* This may be called "total attention," or as Schachtel has called it, "focal attention." What I am trying to describe here is very akin to fascination or complete absorption. In such attention the figure becomes *all* figure and the ground, in effect, disappears, or at least is not importantly perceived. It is as if the figure were isolated for the time being from all else, as if the world were forgotten, as if the percept had become for the moment the whole of Being.

Since the whole of Being is being perceived, then all those laws obtain which would obtain if the whole of the cosmos could be encompassed at once. I shall discuss this further below.

This kind of perception is in sharp contrast to normal perception. Here the object is attended to simultaneously with attention to all else that is relevant. It is seen imbedded in its relationships with everything else in the world, and as *part* of the world. Normal figure ground relationships hold, i.e., both the ground and the figure are attended to, although in different ways. Furthermore in ordinary cognition, the object is seen not so much per se but as a member of a class, as an instance in a larger category. This kind of perception I have described as "rubricizing," and again would point out that this is not so much a full perception of all aspects of the objects or person being perceived, as it is a kind of taxonomy, a classifying, a ticketing off into one file cabinet or another.

To a far greater degree than we ordinarily realize, cognition involves also placing on a continuum. It involves a kind of automatic comparing or judging or evaluating. It implies higher than, less than, better than, taller than, etc.

B-Cognition is quite different. It may be called non-comparing cognition or non-evaluating or judging cognition. I mean this in the sense in which Dorothy Lee has described the way in which certain primitive peoples differ from us in their perceptions.

A person can be seen per se, in himself and by himself. He can be seen uniquely and idiosyncratically, as if he were the sole member of his class. This is what we mean by perception of the unique individual, and this is, of course, what all clinicians try to achieve. But it is a very difficult task, far more difficult than we are ordinarily willing to admit. However, it can happen, if only transiently, and it does happen characteristically in the peak experience. The healthy mother, perceiving her infant in love, approaches to this kind of perception of the uniqueness of the person. Her baby is not quite like anybody else in the world. It is marvelous, perfect, and fascinating (at least to the extent that she is able to detach herself from Gesell's norms and comparisons with neighbors' children).

Concrete perceiving of the whole of the object implies, also, that it is seen with "care." Contrariwise, "caring" for the object will produce the sustained attention, the repeated examination that is so necessary for perception of all aspects of the object. The caring minuteness with which a mother will gaze upon her infant again and again, or the lover at his beloved, or the connoisseur at his painting will surely produce a more complete perception than the usual casual rubricizing which passes illegitimately for perception. We may expect richness of detail and a many sided awareness of the object from this kind of absorbed, fascinated, fully attending cognition. This contrasts with the product of casual observation which gives only the bare bones of the experience, an object which is seen in only some of its aspects in a selective way and from a point of view.

3. While it is true that all human perception is a product of the human being and is his creation to an extent, still we can make some differentiation between the perception of *external objects as relevant to human concerns and as irrelevant to human concerns.* Self-actualizing people are more able to perceive the world as if it were independent not only of them but also of human beings in general. This also tends to be true of the average human being in his highest moments, i.e., in his peak experiences. He can then more readily look upon nature as if it were there in itself and for itself, and not simply as if it were a human playground put there for human purposes. He can more easily refrain from projecting human purposes upon it. In a word, he can see it in its own Being rather than as something to be used, or something to be afraid of, or to be reacted to in some other human way.

As one example, let us take the microscope which can reveal to us as we look at histological slides either a world of per se beauty or else a world of threat, danger, and pathology. A section of cancer seen through a microscope, if only we can forget that it is a cancer, can be seen as a beautiful and intricate and awe-inspiring organization. A mosquito is a wondrous object. Viruses under the electron miscroscope are fascinating objects (or, at least, they *can* be if we can only forget their human relevance).

B-Cognition, beacuse it makes human-irrelevance more possible, enables us thereby to see more truly the nature of the object in itself.

4. One difference between B-Cognition and average cognition which is now emerging in my studies, but of which I am as yet uncertain, is that repeated *B-cognizing seems to make the perception richer.* The repeated experiencing of a face that we love or a painting that we admire makes us like it more, and permits us to see more and more of it in various senses. This we may call intra-object richness.

But this so far contrasts rather sharply with the more usual effects of repeated experiencing, i.e., boredom, familiarization effects, loss of attention and the like. I have found to my own satisfaction—although I cannot prove it to anyone else— that repeated exposures to what I consider a good painting will make the paint-ing look more beautiful to people preselected as perceptive and sensitive, while repeated exposures to what I consider a bad painting will make it look less beautiful.

In this more usual kind of perception, where so frequently the initial perception is simply a classification into useful or not useful, dangerous or not dangerous, repeated looking makes it become more and more empty. The task of normal perception which is so frequently anxiety-based or motivation-determined, is fulfilled in the first viewing and thereafter the object or person, now that it has been catalogued, is simply no longer perceived. Poverty shows up in repeated experiencing; so, also, does richness. Furthermore not only does poverty of the percept show up in repeated looking, but also the poverty of the beholder.

I am becoming more convinced that one of the main mechanisms by which love produces a profounder perception of the intrinsic qualities of the love-object than does non-love, is that love involves fascination with the love-object, and therefore repeated and intent and searching looking, seeing with "care." Lovers can see potentialities in each other that other people are blind to. Customarily we snicker and say "Love is blind," but we must now make room for the possibility that love may be under certain circumstances more perceptive than non-love. Of course this implies that it is possible in some sense to perceive potentialities which are not yet actual. I do not think that this is as difficult a research problem as it sounds. The Rorschach test in the hands of an expert is also a perception of potentialities which are not yet actualized. I think this is a testable hypothesis in principle.

5. American psychology, or more broadly, Western psychology, in what I consider to be an ethnocentric way, assumes that human needs, fears, and interests must always be determinants of perception. The "New Look" in perception is based upon the assumption that cognition must always be motivated. The further assumption is implied that cognition is a coping, instrumental mechanism, and that it must to some extent be egocentric. It assumes that the world can be seen *only* from the vantage point of the interests of the perceiver and that the experience must be organized around the ego as a centering and determining point.

I consider this point of view ethnocentric not only because it arises so clearly as an unconscious expression of the Western world outlook, but also because it involves a persistent and assiduous neglect of the writings of philosophers, theologians, and psychologists of the Eastern world, particularly of the Chinese, Japanese, and Hindus, not to mention Western writers like Goldstein and Angyal.

My findings indicate that in the normal perceptions of self-actualizing people and in the more occasional peak experiences of average people, *perception can be relatively ego-transcending, self-forgetful, egoless.* It can be unmotivated, impersonal, desireless, unselfish, not needed, detached. It can be object-centered rather than ego-centered. That is to say, that the perceptual experience can be organized around the object as a centering point rather than being based upon the ego. It is as if they were perceiving something that had independent reality of its own, and was not dependent upon the beholder. It is possible in the aesthetic experience or the love experience to become so absorbed and "poured into" the object that the self, in a very real sense, disappears. Some writers on aesthetics, mysticism, on motherhood, and on love have gone so far as to say that in the peak experience we may even speak of identification of the perceiver and the perceived, a fusion of what was two into a new and larger whole, a super-ordinate unit. This could remind us of some of the definitions of empathy and of identification, and, of course, at once opens up the possibilities of research in this direction.

6. *The peak experience is felt as a self-validating, self-justifying moment which carries its own intrinsic value with it.* That is to say it is an end in itself, what we may call an end-experience rather than a means-experience. It is felt to be so valuable an experience, so great a revelation, that even to attempt to justify it takes away from its dignity and worth. This is universally attested to by my subjects as they report their love experiences, their mystic experiences, their aesthetic experiences, their creative experiences, and their bursts of insight. Particularly with the moment of insight in the therapeutic situation does this become obvious. By virtue of the very fact that the person defends himself against the insight, it is therefore by definition painful to accept. Its breaking through into consciousness is customarily crushing to the person. And yet, in spite of this fact, it is universally reported to be worthwhile, desirable and wanted. Seeing is better than being blind, even when seeing hurts. It is a case in which the intrinsic self-justifying, self-validating worth of the experience makes the pain worthwhile. Not only do my subjects attest to this finding but so, also, do the numerous writers on aesthetics, religion, creativeness, and love. Uniformly they describe these experiences not only as valuable intrinsically, but as *so* valuable that they make life worthwhile by their occasional occurrence. The mystics have always affirmed this great value of the great mystic experience which may come only two or three times in a lifetime.

The contrast is very sharp with the ordinary experiences of life, especially in the West, and, most especially, for American psychologists. Behavior is so identified with means to ends that by many writers the words "behavior" and "instrumental behavior" are taken as synonymous. Everything is done for the sake of some further goal, *in order to* achieve something else. The apotheosis of this attitude is reached by John Dewey in his theory of value, in which he finds no ends at all but only means to ends. Even this statement is not quite accurate because it implies the existence of ends. Rather, to be quite accurate the implies that means are means to other means, which in turn are means, and so on ad infinitum.

The peak experiences are for my subjects ultimate goals of living and the ultimate validations and justifications for it. That the psychologist should by-pass them or even be officially unaware of their existence, or what is even worse, in the objectivistic psychologies, deny a priori the possibility of their existence as objects for scientific study, is incomprehensible.

7. *In all the common peak experiences, or at least in those which I have stud-*

ied, there is a very characteristic disorientation in time and space. This goes so far that it would be more accurate to say that in these moments the person is outside of time and space subjectively. For instance, in the creative furor, the poet or artist becomes oblivious of his surroundings, and of the passage of time. It is impossible for him when he wakes up to judge how much time has passed. Frequently he has to shake his head as if emerging from a daze to rediscover where he is.

But more than this is the frequent report especially by lovers of the complete loss of extension in time. Not only does time pass in their ecstasies with a frightening rapidity so that a day may pass as if it were a minute but also a minute so intensely lived may feel like a day or a year. It is as if they had, in a way, some place in another world in which time simultaneously stood still and moved with great rapidity. For our ordinary categories, this is of course a paradox and a contradiction. And yet this is what is reported and it is therefore a fact that we must take account of. I see no reason why this kind of experiencing of time should not be amenable to experimental research. The judgment of the passing of time in peak-experience must be very inaccurate. So, also, for consciousness of surroundings. This, too, must be much less accurate than in normal living and, therefore, can be researched with.

8. I have been much impressed with the implications of my findings for a psychology of values. I find them very puzzling and yet so uniform that it is necessary not only to report them but also to try somehow to understand them. To start at the end first, *the peak experience is only good and desirable, and is never evil or painful or undesirable.* The experience is intrinsically valid and the experience is perfect, complete, and needs nothing else. It is sufficient to itself. It is felt as being intrinsically necessary and inevitable. It is just as good as it *should* be. It is reacted to with awe, wonder, amazement, humility, and even reverence, exaltation, and piety. The word sacred is occasionally used to describe the person's reaction to it.

The philosophical implications here are tremendous. If, for the sake of argument, we accept the thesis that in the peak experience the nature of reality *may* be seen more clearly and its essence penetrated more profoundly, then this is almost the same as saying what so many philosophers and theologians have affirmed, that the whole of Being is only neutral or good, and that evil or pain or threat is only a partial phenomenon, a product of not seeing the world whole and unified.

Another way of saying this is to compare it with one aspect of the concept of God which is very widespread in many religions. Those gods who can contemplate and encompass the whole of Being and who therefore understand it, must see it as good, just, inevitable, and must see "evil" as a product of limited vision and understanding. If we could be god-like in this sense then we, too, out of universal understanding would never blame or condemn or be disappointed or shocked. Our only possible emotions would be pity, charity, kindliness, and perhaps sadness for the shortcomings of the other. But this is precisely the way in which self-actualizing people react to the world, and in which *all* of us react in our peak moments. I remind you that this is precisely the way in which all psychotherapists *try* to react to their patients. We must grant, of course, that this god-like, universally tolerant and accepting attitude is extremely difficult to attain, probably even impossible in a pure form, and yet we know that this is a relative matter. We can approximate it more closely or less closely and it would be foolish to deny the phenomenon simply because it comes rarely and impurely. Though we can never be gods in this sense, we can be more god-like or less god-like.

In any case the contrast with our ordinary cognitions and reactions is very sharp. Ordinarily we proceed under the aegis of means-values, i.e., of usefulness, desirability, badness or goodness, of suitability for a purpose. We evaluate, judge, condemn, or approve. We react to the experience in personal terms and perceive the world in reference to ourselves and our ends, thereby making the world no more than means to our ends. This is the opposite of being detached from the world, which means in turn that we are not really perceiving *it*, but perceiving ourselves in it. We perceive then in a deficiency-motivated way and can therefore perceive only D-values. This is different from perceiving the whole world, or that portion of it which in the peak experience we take as surrogate for the world. Then and only then can we perceive *its* values rather than our own. These I call the values of Being, or for short, the B-values. These are the same as Robert Hartman's "intrinsic values."

These B-values are so far as I can make out at this point, (*a*) wholeness, integration, unity and interconnectedness (*b*) necessity, perfection, completeness and inevitability (*c*) aliveness, good functioning, spontaneity and process (*d*) richness, intricacy, and complexity (*e*) beauty, awe-fulness (*f*) goodness, rightness, desirability (*g*) uniqueness, idiosyncrasy and expressiveness (*h*) effortlessness, ease of achievement, lack of strain or striving, and finally (*i*) occasionally, but not always an element of humor or playfulness.

Not only is this, then, a demonstration of fusion and unity of the old trinity of the true, the good, and the beautiful, but it is more than that. I have elsewhere reported my finding that truth, goodness, and beauty are in the normal person only fairly well correlated with each other, and in the neurotic even less so. It is only in the healthy and mature human being, in the self-actualizing, fully functioning person that they are so highly correlated that for all practical purposes they may be said to fuse into a unity. I would now add that this is also true for other people in their highest moments, i.e., in their peak experiences of love, of sex, of creativity, of aesthetic perception, of religious or mystic experience, and of insight and understanding.

This finding, if it turns out to be correct, is in direct and flat contradiction to one of the basic axioms that guides all scientific thought, namely, that the more objective and impersonal perception becomes, the more detached it becomes from value. Fact and value have almost always (by intellectuals) been considered to be antonyms and mutually exclusive. But perhaps the opposite is true, for when we examine the most ego-detached, objective, motivationless, passive cognition, we find that it claims to perceive values directly, that values cannot be shorn away from reality and that the most profound perceptions of "facts" are tinged with wonder, admiration, awe and approval, i.e., with value.

9. Normal experience is imbedded in history and in culture as well as in the shifting and relative needs of man. It is organized in time and in space. That is to say it is part of larger wholes and therefore is relative to these larger wholes and frames of reference. Since it is felt to depend upon man for whatever reality it has, then if man were to disappear, *it,* also, would disappear. Its organizing frames of reference shift from the interests of the person to the demands of the situation, from the immediate in time to the past and the future and from the here to the there. In these senses experience and behavior are relative.

Peak experiences are from this point of view more absolute and less relative. Not only are they timeless and spaceless in the senses which I have indicated above, not only are they detached from the ground and perceived more in themselves, not only are they relatively unmotivated and detached from the interests of man, but they are also perceived and reacted to as if they were in themselves, "out there," as if they were perceptions of a reality independent of man and persisting beyond his life. It is certainly very difficult and also very dangerous scientifically to speak of relative and absolute and I am quite aware that I am walking into a semantic swamp. And yet I am compelled by the many introspective reports of my subjects to report this differentiation as a finding with which we psychologists will ultimately have to make our peace. These are the words that the subjects themselves use in trying to describe experiences which are essentially ineffable. *They* speak of "absolute," *they* speak of "relative," and it is my duty to report it.

Again and again we ourselves are tempted to this kind of vocabulary, for instance, in the realm of art. A Chinese vase may be perfect in itself, may be simultaneously 2000 years old and yet fresh in this moment, universal rather than Chinese. In these senses at least it is absolute, even though also simultaneously relative to time, to the culture of its origin, and to the aesthetic standards of the beholder. Is it not meaningful also that the mystic experience has been dscribed in almost identical words by people in every religion, every era, and in every culture? No wonder Aldous Huxley has called it "The Perennial Philosophy." The great creators, let us say as anthologized by Brewster Ghiselin, have described their creative moments in almost identical terms, even though they were variously poets, chemists, sculptors, philosophers, and mathematicians.

The concept of absolute has made difficulty partly because it has almost always been permeated with a static taint. It is now clear from the experience of my subjects that this is not necessary or inevitable. Perception of an aesthetic object or a beloved face or a beautiful theory is a fluctuating, shifting process but this fluctuation of attention is strictly *within* the perception. Its richness can be infinite and the continued gaze can go from one aspect of the perfection to another, now concentrating on one side of it, now on another. A fine painting has many organizations, not just one, so that the aesthetic experience can be a continuous though fluctuating delight as it is seen, in itself, now in one way, now in another. Also it can be seen relatively in one moment, absolutely in the next. We needn't struggle over whether it is *either* relative *or* absolute. It can be both.

10. Ordinary cognition is a very active process. It is characteristically a kind of shaping and selection by the beholder. *He* chooses what to perceive and what not to perceive, he relates it to his needs and fears and interests, he gives it organization, arranging and re-arranging it. In a word, he works at it. Cognition is an energy consuming process. It involves alertness, vigilance, and tension and is, therefore, fatiguing.

B-Cognition is much more passive and receptive than active although, of course, it never can be completely so. The best descriptions that I have found of this "passive" kind of cognizing comes from Eastern philosophers, especially from Lao-Tse and the Taoistic philosophers. Krishnamurti has an excellent phrase to describe my data. He calls it "choiceless awareness." We could also name it "desireless awareness." The Taoistic conception of "let be" also says what I am trying to say, namely, that perception may be undemanding rather than demanding, contemplative, rather than forceful. It can be humble before the experience, non-interfering, receiving rather than taking, it can let the percept be itself. I am reminded here, also, of Freud's description of "free-floating attention." This, too, is passive rather than active, selfless rather than egocentric, dreamy rather than vigilant, patient rather than impatient. It is gazing rather than looking, surrendering and submitting to the experience.

I have also found useful a recent memorandum by John Shlien on the difference between passive listening and active, forceful listening. The good therapist must be able to listen in the receiving rather than the taking sense in order to be able to hear what is actually said rather than what he expects to hear or demands to hear. He must not impose himself but rather let the words flow in upon him. Only so can their own shape and pattern be assimilated. Otherwise one hears only one's own theories and expectations.

As a matter of fact we may say that it is this criterion, of being able to be receiving and passive, that marks off the good therapist from the poor one of whatever school. The good therapist is able to perceive each person in his own right, freshly and without the urge to taxonomize, to rubricize, to classify and pigeon hole. The poor therapist through a hundred years of clinical experience may find only repeated corroborations of the theories which he learned at the beginning of his career. It is in this sense that it has been pointed out that a therapist can repeat the same mistakes for 40 years and then call it "rich clinical experience."

An entirely different, though equally unfashionable, way of communicating the feeling of this characteristic of B-cognition, is to call it, with D. H. Lawrence and other Romantics, non-voluntary rather than volitional. Ordinary cognition is highly volitional and therefore demanding, prearranged, and preconceived. In the cognition of the peak experience, the will does not interfere. It is held in abeyance. It receives and doesn't demand. We cannot command the peak experience. It happens *to* us.

11. *The emotional reaction in the peak experience has a special flavor of wonder, of awe, of humility before the experience.* This sometimes has a touch of fear (although pleasant fear) of being overwhelmed. My subjects report this in such phrases as "This is too much for me." "It is more than I can bear." "It is too wonderful." The experience may have a certain poignancy and piercing quality which may bring either tears or laughter and which may be paradoxically akin to pain, although this is a desirable pain which is often described as "sweet." This may go so far as to involve thoughts of death in a peculiar way. Not only my subjects but many writers on the various peak experiences have made the parallel with the experience of dying, that is, an eager dying. A typical phrase might be: "This is too wonderful. I don't know how I can bear it. I could die now and it would be all right." Perhaps this is in part a hanging on to the experience and a reluctance to go down from this peak into the valley of ordinary existence. Perhaps it is in part, also, an aspect of the profound sense of humility, smallness, unworthiness before the enormity of the experience.

12. Another paradox with which we must deal, difficult though it is, is found in the conflicting reports of perception of the world. *In some reports, particularly of the mystic experience or the religious experience or philosophical experience, the whole of the world is seen as a unity, as a single rich entity. In other of the peak experiences, most particularly the love experience and the aesthetic experience, one small part of the world is perceived as if it were for the moment all of the world.* In both cases the perception is of unity. Probably the fact that the B-cognition of a painting or a person or a theory retains all the attributes of the whole of Being, i.e., the B-values, derives from this fact of perceiving it as if it were all that existed at the moment.

13. In another paper I have tried to demonstrate the substantial difference between the cognition that abstracts and categorizes (rubricizing) and the fresh cognition of the concrete, the raw, and the particular. This is the sense in which I shall use the terms abstract and concrete. They are not very different from Goldstein's terms. There I pointed out also that most of our cognitions (attendings, perceivings, rememberings, thinkings, and learnings) were abstract rather than concrete. That is, we mostly categorize, schematize, classify, and abstract in our cognitive life. We do not so much cognize the nature of the world as it actually is, so much as we do the organization of our own inner world outlook. Most of experience is filtered through our system of categories and rubrics, as Schachtel has also pointed out in his classical paper on "Childhood Amnesia and the Problem of Memory." I was led to this differentiation by my studies of

self-actualizing people, *finding in them simultaneously the ability to abstract without giving up concreteness and the ability to be concrete without giving up abstractness.* This adds a little to Goldstein's description because I found not only a reduction to the concrete but also what we might call a reduction to the abstract, i.e., a loss of ability to cognize the concrete. Since then I have found this same exceptional ability to perceive the concrete in good artists as well, even though not self-actualizing. More recently I find this same ability in ordinary people in their peak moments. They are then more able to grasp the percept in its own concrete idiosyncratic nature.

Since this kind of idiographic perceiving has customarily been described as the core of aesthetic perceiving, as for instance by Northrop, they have almost been made synonymous. For most philosophers and artists, to perceive a person concretely, in his intrinsic uniqueness is to perceive him aesthetically. I prefer the broader usage and think that I have already demonstrated that this kind of perception of the unique nature of the object is characteristic of *all* peak experiences, not only the aesthetic one.

I find it useful to understand the concrete perceiving which takes places in B-cognition as a perception of all aspects and attributes of the object simultaneously or in quick succession. Abstracting is in essence a selection out of certain aspects only of the object, those which are of use to us, those which threaten us, those with which we are familiar, or those which fit our language categories. Both Whitehead and Bergson have made this sufficiently clear, as have many other philosophers since. Vivanti has phrased it well when he pointed out that abstractions to the extent that they are useful, are also false. In a word, to perceive an object abstractly means *not* to perceive some aspects of it. It clearly implies selection of some attributes, rejection of other attributes, creation or distortion of still others. We make of it what we wish. We create it. We manufacture it. Furthermore, extremely important is the strong tendency in abstracting to relate the aspects of the object to our linguistic system. This makes special troubles because language is a secondary rather than a primary process in the Freudian sense, because it deals with external reality rather than psychic reality, with the conscious rather than the unconscious. It is true that this lack can be corrected to some extent by poetic language but in the last analysis much of experience is ineffable and can be put into no language at all.

Let us take for example the perception of a painting or of a person. In order to perceive them fully we must fight our tendency to classify, to compare, to evaluate, to need, to use. The moment that we say this man is, e.g., a foreigner, in that moment we have classified him, performed an abstracting act and, to some extent, cut ourselves off from the possibility of seeing him as a unique and whole human being, different from any other one in the whole world. In the moment that we approach the painting on the wall to read the name of the artist, we have cut ourselves off from the possibility of seeing it with complete freshness in its own uniqueness. To a certain extent then what we call *knowing*, i.e., the placing of an experience in a system of concepts or words or relations, cuts off the possibility of full cognizing. Herbert Read has pointed out that the child has the "innocent eye," the ability to see something as if he were seeing it for the first time (frequently he *is* seeing it for the first time). He can then stare at it in wonder, examining all aspects of it, taking in all its attributes, since for the child in this situation, no attribute of a strange object is any more important than any other attribute. He does not organize it; he simply stares at it. In the similar situation for the adult, to the extent that we can prevent ourselves from only abstracting, naming, placing, comparing, relating, to that extent will we be able to see more and more aspects of the many sidedness of the person or of the painting. Particularly I must underline the ability to perceive the ineffable, that which cannot be put into words. Trying to force it into words changes it, and makes it something other than it is, something else *like* it, something similar, and yet something different than *it* itself.

It is this ability to perceive the whole and to rise above parts which characterizes cognition in the various peak experiences. Since only thus can one know a person in the fullest sense of the words, it is not surprising that self-actualizing people are so much more astute in their perception of people, in their penetration to the core or essence of another person. This is also why I feel convinced that the ideal therapist, who presumably should be able as a professional necessity, to understand another person in his uniqueness and in his wholeness, without presupposition, ought to be at least a fairly healthy human being. I maintain this even though willing to grant unexplained individual differences in this kind of perceptiveness, and that also therapeutic experience can itself be a kind of training in the cognition of the Being of another human being. This also explains why I feel that a training in aesthetic perceiving and creating could be a very desirable aspect of clinical training.

14. *At the higher levels of human maturation, many dichotomies, polarities, and conflicts are fused and resolved.* Self-actualizing people are simultaneously selfish and unselfish, Dionysian and Appolonian, individual and social, rational and irrational, fused with others and detached from others, and so on. What I had thought to be straight line continua, whose extremes were polar to each other and as far apart as possible, turned out to be rather like circles or spirals, in which the polar extremes came together into a fused unity. So also do I find this as a strong tendency in the full cognition of the object. The more we understand the whole of Being, the more we can tolerate the simultaneous existence and perception of inconsistencies, of oppositions, and of flat contradictions. These seem to be products of partial cognition, and fade away with cognition of the whole. The neurotic person, seen from a god-like vantage point, can then be seen as a wonderful, intricate, even beautiful unity of process. What we normally see as conflict and contradiction and dissociation can then be perceived as inevitable, necessary, even fated. That is to say if he can be fully understood, then everything falls into its necessary place and he can be aesthetically per-

ceived and appreciated. All his conflicts and splits turn out to have a kind of sense or wisdom. Even the concepts of sickness and of health may fuse and blur when we see the symptom as a pressure toward health, or see the neurosis as the healthiest possible solution at the moment to the problems of the individual.

15. *The person at the peak is god-like not only in senses that I have touched upon already but in certain other ways as well, particularly in the complete and loving and uncondemning acceptance of the world and of the person,* however bad he may look at more normal moments. The theologians have long struggled with the terrible task of reconciling sin and evil and pain in the world with the concept of an all-powerful, all-loving, all-knowing God. A subsidiary difficulty has been presented by the task of reconciling the necessity of rewards and punishments for good and evil with this concept of all-loving, all-forgiving God. He must somehow both punish and not punish, both forgive and condemn.

I think we can learn something about the resolution of this dilemma from the study of self-actualizing people and from the comparison of the two broadly different types of perception discussed so far, i.e., B-perception and D-perception. B-perception is a momentary thing ordinarily. It is a peak, a high spot, an occasional achievement. It looks as if all human beings perceive most of the time in a deficiency way. That is, they compare, they judge, they approve, they relate, they use. This means that it is possible for us to perceive another human being alternately in two different ways, sometimes in his Being, as if he were the whole of the universe for the time being. Much more often, however, we perceive him as a part of the universe and related to the rest of it in many complex ways. When we B-perceive him, *then* we can be all-loving, all-forgiving, all-accepting, all-admiring, all-understanding. But these are precisely the attributes assigned to most conceptions of God. In such moments we can then be god-like in these attributes. For instance, in the therapeutic situation we can relate ourselves in this loving, understanding, accepting, forgiving way to all sorts of people whom we normally fear and condemn and even hate—murderers, pederasts, rapists, exploiters, cowards.

It is extremely interesting to me that all people behave at times as if they wanted to be B-cognized. They resent being classified, categorized, rubricized. Ticketing off a person as a waiter or a policeman or a dame instead of as an individual often offends. We all want to be recognized and accepted for what we are in our fullnes, richness, and complexity. If such an acceptor cannot be found among human beings, then the very strong tendency appears to project and create a god-like figure.

Another kind of answer to the "problem of evil" is suggested by the way in which our subjects "accept reality" as being-in-itself, in its own right. It is neither *for* man nor is it *against* him. It just is impersonally what it is. An earthquake which kills poses a problem of reconciliation only for the man who needs a personal God who is simultaneously all-loving and omnipotent and who created the world. For the man who can perceive and accept it impersonally and uncreated it presents no ethical or axiological problem, since it wasn't done "on purpose," to annoy him. He shrugs his shoulders and if evil is defined anthropocentrically, he simply accepts evil as he does the seasons and the storms. Of course it is much harder to achieve this attitude with human actions which are hurtful to him, but it is occasionally possible, and the more matured the man is, the more possible it is.

16. *Perception in the peak moment tends very strongly to be idiographic.* The percept, whether a person or the world or a tree or work of art, tends to be seen as a unique instance, and as the only member of its class. This is in contrast to our normal nomothetic way of handling the world which rests essentially on generalization and on an Aristotelian division of the world into classes of various sorts, of which the object is an example. The whole concept of classification rests upon general classes. If there were no classes the concepts of resemblance, of equality, of similarity and of difference would become totally useless. One cannot compare two objects which have nothing in common. Furthermore for two objects to have something in common means necessarily abstraction, e.g., such qualities as redness, roundness, heaviness, etc. But if we perceive a person without abstracting, if we insist upon perceiving all his attributes simultaneously and as necessary to each other, then we no longer can classify. Every whole person from this point of view or every painting or every bird or flower becomes the sole member of a class and must therefore be perceived idiographically.

17. *One aspect of the peak experience is a complete, though momentary, loss of fear, anxiety, inhibition, defense and control, a giving up or renunciation, delay, and restraint.* The fear of disintegration and dissolution, the fear of being overwhelmed by the "instincts," the fear of death and of insanity, the fear of giving in to unbridled pleasure and emotion, all tend to disappear or go into abeyance for the time being.

It may be thought of as pure gratification, pure expression, pure elation. But since it is "in the world," it represents a kind of fusion of the Freudian "pleasure principle" and "reality principle." It is therefore still another instance of the resolution of normally dichotomous concepts at higher levels of psychological functioning.

We may therefore expect to find a certain "permeability" in people who have such experiences commonly, a closeness and openness to the unconscious, and a relative lack of fear of it.

C. OTHER CHANGES IN THE PERSON

In addition to all these changes in the cognition of the world (including attitudes toward it), all sorts of other changes occur in the person in the peak experience and afterward.

For one thing, not only the world but also he himself becomes more a unity, more integrated, and self-consistent. This is another way of saying that he becomes more completely himself, idiosyncratic, unique. And since he is so, he can be more easily expressive and spontaneous without effort. All his powers then come together in their most efficient integration and coördination, organized and coördinated much more perfectly than usual. Everything then can be done with unusual ease and lack of effort. Inhibition, doubt, control, self-criticism, diminish toward a zero point and he becomes the spontaneous, coördinated, efficient organism, functioning like an animal without conflict or split, without hesitation or doubt, in a great flow of power that is so peculiarly effortless, that it may become like play, masterful, virtuoso-like. In such a moment, his powers are at their height and he may be startled (afterwards) by his unsuspected skill, confidence, creativeness, perceptiveness, and virtuosity of performance. It is all so easy that it can be enjoyed and laughed with. Things can be dared that would be impossible at other times.

To put it simply, he becomes more whole and unified, more unique and idiosyncratic, more alive and spontaneous, more perfectly expressive and uninhibited, more effortless and powerful, more daring and courageous (leaving fears and doubts behind), more ego-transcending and self-forgetful.

But these are almost the same as the list of B-values already described above. Which is to say that as the essential Being of the world is felt by the perceiver to be cognized, so also does he concurrently come closer to his own Being, or to being himself, or to self-actualization, or to perfection in his own kind, etc. As the experience becomes more unified, so does he also become more unified, as it becomes richer, so does he, as it becomes more itself, so does he as well, and so on. He and the world become more like each other as they both move toward perfection. Perhaps this is what is meant by the well-known fusion of lovers, the becoming one with the world in the mystic experience, the feeling of absorbed fusion and unity with the work of art in the aesthetic experience, the feeling so often reported by our great creators that their words take hold of them and practically write themselves as if they were being dictated, the great philosophical insights in which one becomes *part* of the unity one experiences and merged into it. This is what Angyal is talking about in part, when he speaks of the trend to homonomy. Also relevant here is my conclusion that just those qualities which describe a good painting (Wilson's criteria) also describe the good human being, i.e., the B-values of wholeness, uniqueness, aliveness, richness, etc.

May I now attempt briefly to put all of this in another frame of reference which is more familiar to you, the psychoanalytic. Secondary processes deal with the real world outside the unconscious. Logic, science, common sense, good adjustment, enculturation, responsibility, planning, rationalism are all secondary process techniques. The primary processes were first discovered in neurotics and psychotics and then in children, and only recently in healthy people. The rules by which the unconscious works can be seen most clearly in dreams. Wishes and fears are the primary movers, the Freudian mechanisms, the primary techniques. The well adjusted, responsible, common sense man who gets along well in the real world must usually do this in part by turning his back on his unconscious and denying and repressing it.

For me, this realization came most keenly when I had to face the fact about 15 years ago that my self-actualizing subjects, picked because they were very mature, were, at the same time, also childish. I called it "healthy childishness," a "second naivete." It has since been recognized by Kris and the ego-psychologists as "regression in the service of the ego," not only found in healthy people, but finally conceded to be a *sine qua non* of psychological health. Balint has recognized love to be a regression (i.e., the person who can't regress can't love). And, finally, the analysts agree that inspiration and great (primary) creativeness comes partly out of the unconscious, i.e., is a healthy regression, a temporary turning away from the real world.

Now what I have been describing here may be seen as a fusion of ego, id, super-ego, and ego-ideal, of conscious and unconscious, of primary and secondary processes, a synthesizing of pleasure principle with reality principle, a regression without fear in the service of the greatest maturity, a true integration of the person at *all* levels.

D.   REDEFINITION OF SELF-ACTUALIZATION

In other words, any person in any of the peak experiences, takes on temporarily many of the characteristics which I found in self-actualizing individuals. That is, for the time they become self-actualizers. We may think of it as a passing characterological change if we wish, and not just as an emotional-cognitive-expressive state. Not only are these his happiest and most thrilling moments, but they are also moments of greatest maturity, individuation, fulfillment—in a word his healthiest moments.

This makes it possible for us to redefine self-actualization in such a way as to purge it of all its static and typological shortcomings, and to make it less a kind of all-or-none pantheon into which some rare people enter at the age of 60. We may define it as an episode, or a spurt in which the powers of the organism come together in a particularly efficient and intensely enjoyable way, and in which he is more integrated and less split, more open for experience, more idiosyncratic, more perfectly expressive or spontaneous, or fully functioning, more creative, more humorous, more ego-transcending, more independent of his lower needs, etc. He becomes in these episodes more truly himself, more perfectly actualizing his potentialities, closer to the core of his Being.

Such states or episodes can, in theory, come at any time in life to any person. What seems to distinguish those individuals I have called self-actualizing people, is that in them these episodes seem to come far more frequently, and intensely and perfectly than in average people. This makes self-actualization a matter of degree and of frequency rather than an all-or-none affair, and thereby makes it more amenable to available research procedures. We need no longer be limited to searching for those rare subjects who may be said to be fulfilling themselves most of the time. In theory at least we may also search *any* life history for episodes of self-actualization, especially those of artists, intellectuals and other especially creative people, of profoundly religious people, and of people experiencing great insights in psychotherapy, or in other important growth experiences.

E. THE QUESTION OF EXTERNAL VALIDITY

So far I have described a subjective experience in a phenomenological fashion. Its relationship to the external world is another matter altogether. Just because the perceiver *believes* that he perceives more truly and more wholly is no proof that he actually does so. The criteria for judging the validity of this belief ordinarily lie in the objects or persons perceived or in the products created. They are therefore, in principle, simple problems for correlational research.

But in what sense can art be said to be knowledge? The aesthetic perception certainly has its intrinsic self-validation. It is felt as a valuable and wonderful experience. But so also are some illusions and hallucinations. And furthermore you may be aroused to an aesthetic experience by a painting which leaves me untouched. If we are to go at all beyond the private, the problem of external criteria of validity remains, just as it does with all other perceptions.

The same can be said for loving perception, for the mystic experience, for the creative moment, and for the flash of insight.

The lover perceives in the beloved what no one else can, and again, there is no question about the intrinsic value of his inner experience and of the many good consequences for him, for his beloved, and for the world. If we take as an example, the mother loving her baby, the case is even more obvious. Not only does love perceive potentialities but it also actualizes them. The absence of love certainly stifles potentialities and even kills them. Personal growth demands courage, self-confidence, even daring, and non-love from the parent or the mate produces the opposite, self-doubt, anxiety, feelings of worthlessness and expectations of ridicule, all inhibitors of growth and of self-actualization.

All personological and psychotherapeutic experience is testimonial to this fact that love actualizes and non-love stultifies, whether deserved or not.

The complex and circular question then arises here "To what extent is this phenomenon a self-fulfilling prophecy" as Merton has called it. A husband's conviction that his wife is beautiful, or a wife's firm belief that her husband is courageous, to some extent *creates* the beauty or the courage. This is not so much a perception of something that already exists as a bringing into existence by belief. Shall we perhaps consider this an example of perception of a potentiality, since *every* person has the possibility of being beautiful and courageous? If so, then this is different from perceiving the real possibility that someone may become a great violinist, which is *not* a universal possibility.

And yet, even beyond all this complexity, the lurking doubts remain to those who hope ultimately to drag all these problems into the domain of public science. Frequently enough, love for another brings illusions, the perceptions of qualities and potentialities that don't exist, that are not therefore truly perceived but created in the mind of the beholder and which then rest on a system of needs, repressions, denials, projections, and rationalizations. If love can be more perceptive than non-love, it can also be blinder. And the research problem remains to nag us, when is which? How can we select out those instances in which perception of the real world is more acute? I have already reported my observations at the personological level, that one answer to this question lies in the variable of the psychological health of the perceiver, in or out of the love relationship. The greater the health, the more acute and penetrating the perception of the world, all other things being equal. Since this conclusion was the product of uncontrolled observation, it must be presented only as a hypothesis awaiting controlled research.

In general, similar problems confront us in aesthetic and intellectual bursts of creativeness, and also in the insight experiences. In both instances, the external validation of the experience is not perfectly correlated with phenomenological self-validation. It is possible for the great insight to be mistaken, the great love to disappear. The poem that creates itself in a peak experience may have to be thrown away later as unsatisfactory. Creation of a product that will stand up feels subjectively the same as the creation of a product that folds up later under cold, objective critical scrutiny. The habitually creative person knows this well, expecting half of his great moments of insight not to work out. All peak experiences feel like Being-experience but not all are truly so. And yet, we dare not neglect the clear hints that, sometimes at least, greater perspicuity and greater efficiency of cognition can be found in healthier people and in healthier moments, i.e., some peak experiences *are* B-experiences. I once suggested the principle that if self-actualizing people can and do perceive reality more efficiently, fully and with less motivational contamination than we others do, then we may possibly use them as biological assays. Through *their* greater sensitivity and perception, we may get a better report of what reality is like, than through our own eyes, just as canaries can be used to detect gas in mines before less sensitive creatures can.

As a second string to this same bow, we may use ourselves in our most perceptive moments, in our peak experiences, when, for the moment, *we* are self-actualizing, to give us a report of the nature of reality that is truer than we can ordinarily manage.

F.   THE AFTER-EFFECTS OF PEAK EXPERIENCES

Completely separable from the question of the external validity of cognition in the various peak experiences, is that of the after-effects upon the person of these experiences which in still another sense, may be said to validate the experience. I have no controlled research data to present to you. I have only the unanimous agreement of my subjects that there *were* such effects, my own con-

viction that there were, and the complete agreement of all the writers on creativeness, love, insight, mystic experience, and aesthetic experience. On these
grounds I feel justified in making at least the following affirmations or propositions, all of which are testable.

1. Peak experiences have some therapeutic effects, in the strict sense of removing symptoms. I have at least two reports—one from a psychologist, one
from an anthropologist—of mystic or oceanic experiences so profound as to
remove neurotic symptoms forever after. Such conversion experiences are of
course plentifully recorded in human history but so far as I know have never
received the attention of psychologists or psychiatrists.

2. They change the person's view of himself in a healthy direction.

3. They change his view of other people and his relation to them in many
ways.

4. They change more or less permanently his view of the world, or of aspects
or parts of it.

5. They release him for greater creativity, spontaneity, expressiveness, idiosyncrasy.

6. He remembers the experience as a very important and desirable happening and seeks to repeat it.

7. The person is more apt to feel that life in general is worth while, even
if it is usually drab, pedestrian, painful or ungratifying, since beauty and
goodness and excitement and honesty and truth and meaningfulness have been
demonstrated to him to exist.

Many other effects could be reported that are ad hoc and idiosyncratic, depending on the particular person, and his particular problems which he considers to be solved or seen in a new light as the result of his experience.

I think that these after-effects can *all* be generalized and a feeling for them
communicated if the peak experience could be likened to a visit to a personally
defined Heaven from which the person then returns to earth. Desirable after-
effects of such an experience, some universal and some individual, are then
seen to be practically inevitable.

And may I also emphasize that such after-effects of aesthetic experience, creative experience, love experience, mystic experience, insight experience, and
other peak experiences are taken for granted and commonly expected by artists
and art educators, by creative teachers, by religious and philosophical theorists,
by loving husbands, mothers, and therapists. As a matter of fact, they are a
commonplace to all but psychologists.

CONCEPT FORMATION
AND CRITICAL THINKING

41 *Implications of research on children's concepts*

Related selection: 42

In the selection below, Dr. McCullough lists and draws briefly upon a sample of the research findings related to children's concept formation and what teachers can do to foster this phase of learning. The reader may wish to study selection 42, which deals in part with the same topic.

One has only to look at the more than 2500 references in Dale and Reichert's revised *Bibliography of Vocabulary Studies* (7) to be properly awed by the interest which investigators have shown in the vocabulary and concepts of children. Inflated egos may require an additional look at Russell's 900 references in *Children's Thinking* (22) to realize that a quick answer to the problem of children's ideas—the ways they are formed, and children's experiences with the symbols which represent them—is farther from our grasp than the moon today. The purpose of this article is to give the reader something of the knowledge that is available to teachers about the most basic ingredients in the reading program: the ideas which the child brings to the page and the ideas which he attaches to the words in their relationships.

WHAT A CONCEPT IS

Mr. Webster attempts to settle what we are talking about by describing a concept as "a mental image of a thing formed by generalization from particulars

CONSTANCE M. MCCULLOUGH, "Implications of Research on Children's Concepts," *The Reading Teacher*, 13 (December, 1959), 100–7. Reprinted by permission of the publisher.

DR. MC CULLOUGH (1912–) has been at San Francisco State College since 1947 and holds the rank of Professor of Education. She has made many contributions in reading and language arts research.

. . . an idea of what a thing in general should be" (36). Russell (22) helps by speaking of concepts as dealing with objects (chair, fish), qualities (honest, clean), and relationships (under, when, because). Jarolimek and Foster (16) refer to concepts as definite (one-half teaspoon of salt) and indefinite (a generous helping of salt). (Generous for what, generous in whose opinion?)

Facets of a concept can be numerous. Take the word *paws*. As a spoken word, of course, it must first be untangled from *pause*. Position makes a difference (front or back), kind (raccoon or dog), shape (long, broad), size (big, little), composition (three-toed, bare, furry), feeling (cold, rough), sound (thumping, stealthy), time (old, young), number (many, few). You can probably think of others.

The facets of a concept can sometimes be illuminated by pairs of words and their relationships to each other: ceramic—dish (general—specific), father—child (numerous facets), fish—fowl (flip versus flap), in—on (position), peace—war (complex opposites), glory—prize (state and symbol).

Russell (22, p. 162) reminds us that a concept may be known thoroughly (toothbrush?), partially (parents?), inaccurately (mother-in-law?), or not at all (income tax regulations?). He attempts to explore children's grasp of concepts by resorting to questions requiring classification, function, definition, appearance or description, characteristics, association with other words, and varied meanings of the same word (23).

How do concepts affect reading? Chall, in *Readability* (5), points out that the more different words there are on a page, the more ideas, the more involved the sentence structure, the more abstract the words, the more remote the words from fundamental life experience—the greater the difficulty of the material for the reader. Authors can throw roadblocks before the concept builder. Since all types of reading matter do not require the same quantity or quality of comprehension, the varied reading activities in and out of school demand a readiness of the child for many degrees of challenge.

HOW CONCEPTS ARE FORMED

Some insight into the teaching of concepts may be gained by consideration of the manner in which concepts are formed. Russell points out that concepts are often developed slowly "out of percepts, memories, and images, and their development is aided greatly by language or other symbols." Some concepts help explain other concepts: "Concepts of time help explain concepts of social custom . . . aesthetic and humorous concepts grow in relation to social concepts" (22, p. 162). (Slipping on a banana peel is funny because it violates the social idea of the dignity of man.) He further remarks that concepts "seem to move along a continuum from simple to complex, from concrete to abstract, from undifferentiated to differentiated, from discreet to organized, from egocentric to more social" (22, p. 249). The parenthetical remarks throughout this article are concrete examples offered to ease the shock of the abstractions which are being discussed. (I am reminded of the child skating along on one roller skate, his other foot occasionally on the "concrete" to push the "abstract" along.)

In developing his concepts "the child employs naming, counting, measuring, discriminating, abstracting, and generalizing." He must recognize the common elements in objects or situations, setting aside unrelated items in the process. (If he has known only short-haired dogs, he must mentally give a shaggy dog a haircut before he can see the generalization "dog"; but, at the same time, he must be ready to add shagginess to his original concept of what a dog can be.) The child gains concepts by an active process, during "sensory impression, muscular activity, motor manipulation, questioning, reading, and problem solving." The process "involves inductive thinking and, at least sometimes, deductive and creative thinking" (22, p. 249).

In books, concepts can be built by pictures which accompany the text, and by the way the words are used in the verbal context. Capitalization and punctuation may hint at the relationship of a strange word to those surrounding it. ("The Keeper of the Privy Seal" is clearly—to experienced readers—a compact title because of the capitalization.)

FACTORS INFLUENCING CONCEPT DEVELOPMENT

What factors influence the development of a concept? Clearly, a concept is based upon experiences, and the more direct these are, the better (28). There may be experiences with objects, processes, and lower-level concepts upon which the needed concept is built, or experiences with the world itself in hearing, speaking, reading, and writing situations. Of course, the mere use of a word by a child is no assurance of his grasp of its meaning. This goes for college students as well as others (18). That the teacher must have a part in book experiences is shown by the fact that many of the common words of multiple meanings used in primary readers are not accurately comprehended by primary grade children (12). If this is true of a controlled vocabulary, how much more true it must be of children's literature in general.

Children of higher socio-economic status tend to score higher on vocabulary tests than children of lower socio-economic status (32). The opportunities which accompany the status partially account for this difference.

Age, probably a reflection of experience, also has been found to be a factor in concept development. Durkin (10), in investigating children's ideas of justice, found that older children (junior-senior high school) tended to be aware of many more factors to be considered in meting out justice. (He swatted me. I'll swat him back . . . but he didn't mean it. Somebody pushed him. His arm just flew back. He thought I was that other guy.) Kruglov (17) found that, in Grades 3 through 8, younger children chose concrete definitions for words they were given, while older children chose more often the abstract definitions or synonyms of the words.

Intelligence, which makes it possible for a child to benefit from experience, to observe, to remember, to generalize, to deduce, to discriminate, and to hold images in mind, is also a factor in concept development (22, p. 25). While Durkin found no relationship between children's concepts of justice and their levels of intelligence, it is sensible to suppose that this lack reflects variations in education and opportunity rather than the unimportance of native ability to one's grasp of the environment. Similarly, McCullough (19), finding children of varied intelligence rather uniformly poor in getting meaning from context clues, supposed this finding to reflect the uniform lack of attention to this skill. So direct teaching as well as intelligence can be a factor.

Sex, with its cultural overtones, shows some influence in concept building. In Russell's study of the dimensions of children's vocabulary (23), boys showed some superiority to girls in their knowledge of vocabulary in science, sports, hobbies, and recreation. (He didn't examine the groups on the properties of Vel, Genie, and Mr. Clean.) Templin (32), studying children aged three through eight, found that the older boys had achieved greater average word knowledge than the older girls, while the latter had better average articulation. (The girls can say it better but the boys know what it means!)

Well-meaning attempts to generalize about factors influencing concept building are defied by the presence of individual differences. Differences are extensive in the same age group and become greater with the age of the children concerned (22). Fennema (11) reported different degrees of imagery among children, which would affect not only the development of concepts, but the ability to hold in mind the symbols representing them. Davis (8) stated that speech maturity had a direct bearing on meaning-getting in early reading activities; and the variations among children in speech at early ages is well known. Russell cites the importance of emotional factors, tensions, needs, and the presence of problems to be solved.

Written material itself contributes to the ease or difficulty with which a child develops understandings. Concepts explained by an author through difficult vocabulary and involved sentence structure may never filter through to the reader (30). Too much to learn on a page, and too frequent use of indefinite terms may result in inaccurate or incomplete concepts, or in none at all (27). On the positive side, Traxler reminds us that wide reading offers the opportunity for a reader to infer meanings from context (34); and Werner (37), that a word may lose its lexical meaning and gain new facets through context. On the negative side, Sachs (24) and others report that meanings are not always gained from context, whether the fault be with the difficulty of the passage, the absence of context clues, the lack of reading ability, or the lack of experience or effort on the part of the reader.

WHAT TEACHERS CAN DO

Materials

The literature on the development of concepts suggests a number of guide lines for teachers. Some of these relate to material. Clyse (6), studying occupational ideas in eight third-grade readers, found over a thousand incidents which could be used to teach attitudes, skills, and appreciations essential for vocational success. Through discussion and other experiences teachers can capitalize on what is offered and round out partially-developed concepts.

In choosing materials for children we should realize that the presence of modifiers means enriched meanings, perhaps more complicated ideas, and, in either case, something to be asked about and noticed by the children. Books containing technical words, common words used in a technical sense, uncommon words used in the general vocabulary of the author, and different words used interchangeably for the same meaning, mean a job of concept building and some direct teaching.

If a choice is possible between interestingly written material and material of the same content written in a less interesting way, the former selection means better understanding on the part of the child (2).

Understandings

Understandings can be built in a classroom which provides materials to be seen, handled, operated, discussed. An actual object, short of an elephant, is preferable to a movie (39), but films are indeed helpful in clarifying book meanings (21, 38). Our ears are tired of the cliché, "providing rich experiences for the child," and probably should be. We need to put a point on this weapon, giving experiences with pointed questions for the development of specific meanings for the child's current reading. First hand experiences should be used as much as possible (22).

If we are dealing with children of lower socio-economic level, we should expect to have to engage in more concept building (22). This, of course, does not mean that we should assume that children of higher socio-economic status have fully-developed concepts. We should, rather, ask them for meanings to see whether the grasp exists.

It is important that we ourselves speak clearly in naming the concept, and that we require clear speech by the children (8). *Goad* and *goat* are not the same, though they both provide propulsion from the rear.

Motivation

Since basic needs and favorable feelings grease the wheels of learning, we should as much as possible use the "hot moment," the time of keen interest, for providing the learning. (However, we should not be above starting a few fires ourselves.) The study of concepts which children's current text and recreational reading utilize, with the children fully aware that these are the needed concepts, means more efficient learning.

Group learning

In working with groups we must expect a wide range of concept-grasp. We should use the children who do know, to explain, dramatize, demonstrate, experiment, and illustrate for those who do not know. ("Who can tell us about ——? Willy, didn't I see you watching that bulldozer yesterday?")

Sometimes in dealing with the meaning of a word, we can write down on the chalkboard the different definitions the children in the group offer (21), then help them seek verification (studying the actual object, rerunning the film, going to the dictionary, etc.), and choose or compose a proper definition.

Since brighter pupils seem to grasp prefix, root, and suffix meanings more readily than average or dull children (20), we might use the brighter pupils to lead in the group study of these aspects of word structure and meaning.

Group approaches to concept building are particularly valuable. Even we, "the omniscient," cannot with our one-life experience compensate for the facets other minds might bring to group discussion.

Exploration of a concept

Children need guidance with multiple meanings. In dealing with multiple meanings of words (9), such as *up*, we can say, "Who can show us what up means in this sentence? (He went up the street.) In this one?" (He reached up to the high shelf). The presence of a word of many meanings is an opportunity for introducing the other common meanings of it. Younger children may have to demonstrate meanings rather than express them in words, but gradually they should be given the defining words to use, and be encouraged to use them.

In probing for the meaning of an abstraction like *justice* (10), we should probably ask questions which make children aware of the factors which affect it. "Why did he do it? What had just happened to him? What would this make him think?" Discussions of many situations involving justice gradually build the complex meaning.

To help children generalize (22), we must give them a number of examples to study for their common characteristics. ("What is true about all of these Fidos, Neros, Rovers, etc.?"—in getting at "dogness.") In the process of deduction we can help by saying, "If this is what a dog is, do you think this (showing another example) is a dog? Why or why not?" Measuring how many pints of water can be poured into a quart jar gives concrete evidence of the relationship between pints and quarts. Counting the number of eggs (Watch out there!) in a dozen builds the idea of dozen. Naming the parts of an object observed requires more thorough observation than a child might ordinarily give.

We must remember that we build more easily from the concrete to the abstract. In so doing we must be sure that we start with what is concrete to the child, not just to us. *Prize* may be to us a concrete aspect of *achievement;* but to the child prize *may* be the as-yet unrealized abstraction referring to the doughnut he won yesterday and the marble he won the day before.

Acquisition of concepts

The concepts we get from reading may not automatically become the property of the children who read this same material (16). Jarolimek and Foster report that comparison, problem-solving, contrast, and interpretation of sentence meanings are useful techniques in word study. Sutton's study (31) suggests that we base word exercises on words the children encounter in their texts, have the children find the meanings in the dictionary, and build sentences using the words with these various meanings. Werner (37) proposes that we let children know that the meaning of a word changes with use through the years, introducing them to such books as Epstein's *First Book of Words* (Watts, 1954), Lambert's *Our Language* (Lothrop, 1955), and Laird's *Tree of Language* (World, 1957). Bloomer's study (3) leads to the conclusion that we should pay attention to modifiers: "What does the word *hungry* do to your idea of the lion?" Children can engage in creative activity with modifiers—changing the wording to other possibilities (the well-fed lion) and discussing what happens to the meaning.

We can hope that wide reading will build concepts, but cannot expect that all will be achieved by this means (34). Setting a standard of understanding clearly what is read, we can encourage children to bring puzzling words and expressions in context to the class for discussion. Many studies, including those by Vineyard and Massey (35), Gray and Holmes (13), show the effectiveness of direct systematic study of word meanings. Taking cue from several studies, we can require the classification of words (4), an expression of the function of an object, a definition or description of it, the enumeration of its characteristics, a discussion of its relationship to other concepts (23). Other suggestions are that children study words in context (28), the meanings of roots (1), prefixes (29), suffixes (33), stems, and the parts of a compound (15).

Application

Children should be urged to use a concept as a word and as knowledge which can be applied. We often permit children to use words loosely, vaguely, and even inaccurately (14), when we might be offering more exact words for the situations (a funny day, a funny accident, a funny look, a funny feeling, act funny). Since mastery and retention of new learnings are based upon frequent and proper use, we may deliberately set up situations calling for thinking about the new concept, using it in speech, listening to it, reading it, and writing it.

These are only samplings of the ideas research offers the teacher in this very important work. They may provoke us into further reading of such studies as well as inspire us to creative application of the practices they support.

REFERENCES

1. Barry, Robert F., and Smith, Paul E. "An Experiment in Ninth-Grade Reading Improvement," *Journal of Educational Psychology,* XLV (Nov., 1954), 407-414.
2. Bernstein, Margery R. "Relationship Between Interest and Reading Comprehension," *Journal of Educational Research,* XLIX (Dec., 1955), 283-288.
3. Bloomer, Richard H. "Level of Abstraction as a Function of Modifier Load," *Journal of Educational Research,* LII (Mar., 1959), 269-272.
4. Bradley, Martha, Cahill, Loretta A., Tate, Harry L. "Acquisition of a Reading Vocabulary," *Elementary English Review,* XVIII (Jan., 1941), 19-21, 32.
5. Chall, Jeanne S. *Readability: An Appraisal of Research and Application.* Bureau of Educational Research Monograph No. 34. Columbus, Ohio: Ohio State University, 1958. Pp. 202.
6. Clyse, Juanita. "What Do Basic Readers Teach About Jobs?" *Elementary School Journal,* LIX (May, 1959), 456-460.
7. Dale, Edgar, and Reichert, Donald. *Bibliography of Vocabulary Studies,* Revised Ed. Columbus, Ohio: Ohio State University, Bureau of Educational Research, 1957. Pp. 174.
8. Davis, Irene Poole. "The Speech Aspects of Reading Readiness," *National Elementary School Principal,* 17th Yearbook, 1938. Pages 282-289.
9. Dolch, Edward, and Leeds, Donald. "Vocabulary Tests and Depth of Meaning," *Journal of Educational Research,* XLVII (Nov., 1953), 181-189.
10. Durkin, Dolores. "Children's Concept of Justice: A Further Comparison With the Piaget Data," *Journal of Educational Research* (March, 1959), 252-257.
11. Fennema, Elizabeth H. "Mental Imagery and the Reading Process," *Elementary School Journal,* LIX (Feb., 1959), 286-289.
12. Gammon, Agnes L. "Comprehension of Words With Multiple Meanings," *California Journal of Educational Research,* III (Nov., 1952), 228-232.
13. Gray, William S., and Holmes, Eleanor. *The Development of Meaning Vocabularies in Reading: An Experimental Study.* Publication No. 6 of the laboratory schools of the University of Chicago. Chicago: Department of Education, University of Chicago, 1938. Pp. 140.
14. Gunderson, Agnes G. "What Seven-Year-Olds Like in Books," *Journal of Educational Research,* L (March, 1957), 509-520.
15. Hunt, Jacob Tate. "The Relation Among Vocabulary, Structural Analysis and Reading," *Journal of Educational Psychology,* XLIV (April, 1953), 193-202.
16. Jarolimek, John, and Foster, Clifford D. "Quantitative Concepts in Fifth-Grade Social-Studies Textbooks," *Elementary School Journal,* LIX (May, 1959), 437-442.
17. Kruglov, Lorraine P. "Quantitative Differences in the Vocabulary Choices of Children as Revealed in a Multiple-Choice Test," *Journal of Educational Psychology,* XLIV (April, 1953), 229-242.
18. Lange, Philip C. "Study of Concepts Developed by Students in an Undergraduate Course in the Psychology and Practice of Teaching," *Journal of Educational Research* (May, 1943), 641-661.
19. McCullough, C. M. "Learning to Use Context Clues," *Elementary English Review,* XX (April, 1943), 140-143.
20. Otterman, Lois M. "The Value of Teaching Prefixes and Root-Words," *Journal of Educational Research,* XLVIII (April, 1955), 611-616.
21. Reid, Florence. "Films Provide a Rich Source of Vocabulary Study," *Journal of Educational Research,* LI (April, 1958), 617-23.

22. Russell, David H. *Children's Thinking*. Boston: Ginn and Co., 1956. Pp. 449.

23. Russell, David H. *The Dimensions of Children's Meaning Vocabularies in Grades Four through Twelve*. Publications in Education, Vol. 11, No. 5. Berkeley: University of California Press, 1954. Pages 315-414.

24. Sachs, H. J. "The Reading Method of Acquiring Vocabulary," *Journal of Educational Research*, XXXVI (Feb., 1943), 457-464.

25. Serra, M. C. "A Study of Fourth Grade Children's Comprehension of Certain Verbal Abstractions," *Journal of Experimental Education*, XXII (Dec., 1953), 103-118.

26. Serra, M. C. "Amplifying and Simplifying Instructional Materials: Effects on Comprehension," *Elementary School Journal*, LV (Oct., 1954), 77-81.

27. Serra, M. C. "The Concept Burden of Instructional Materials," *Elementary School Journal*, LIII (May, 1953), 508-512.

28. Serra, M. C. "How to Develop Concepts and Their Verbal Representations," *Elementary School Journal*, LIII (Jan., 1953), 275-285.

29. Stauffer, Russell G. "A Study of Prefixes in the Thorndike List to Establish a List of Prefixes That Should Be Taught in the Elementary School," *Journal of Educational Research*, XXXV (Feb., 1942), 453-458.

30. Stolurow, Lawrence, and Newman, J. Robert. "A Factorial Analysis of Objective Features of Printed Language Presumably Related to Reading Difficulty," *Journal of Educational Research*, LII (March, 1959), 243-251.

31. Sutton, Rachel S. "The Effect of Vocabulary Building on Reading Skills," *Elementary School Journal*, LIV (Oct., 1953), 94-97.

32. Templin, Mildred. *Certain Language Skills in Children*. Minneapolis: University of Minnesota Press, 1957. Pp. 183.

33. Thorndike, Edward L. *The Teaching of English Suffixes*. Teachers College Contributions to Education, No. 847. New York: Teachers College, Columbia University, 1941.

34. Traxler, Arthur E. "What Does Research Suggest About Ways to Improve Reading Instruction?" In Arno Jewett, Ed., *Improving Reading in the Junior High School*, pages 5-15. Bulletin No. 10, U.S. Department of Health, Education, and Welfare. Washington: U.S. Government Printing Office, 1957. Pp. 165.

35. Vineyard, Edwin E., and Massey, Harold W. "The Interrelationship of Certain Linguistic Skills and Their Relationship With Scholastic Achievement When Intelligence Is Ruled Constant," *Journal of Educational Psychology*, XLVIII (May, 1957), 279-286.

36. *Webster's New Collegiate Dictionary*. Springfield, Mass.: G. and C. Merriam Co., 1953.

37. Werner, Heinz. "Change of Meaning: A Study of Semantic Processes Through the Experimental Method," *Journal of General Psychology*, L (April, 1954), 181-208.

38. Witty, Paul A., and Fitzwater, James P. "An Experiment With Films, Film-Readers, and the Magnetic Sound Track Projector," *Elementary English*, XXX (April, 1953), 232-241.

39. Yock, Douglas H., and Erlandson, Forrest L. "The Effectiveness of Visual Aids in Dental Teaching," *Journal of Educational Research*, LII (Sept., 1958), 11-15.

42   *Wishful thinking about children's thinking?*

Related selection: 41

The assumption that a child's thinking process closely resembles that of the adult, differing chiefly in a quantitative rather than in a qualitative way, is but one of the illustrations of wishful adult thinking pointed out by Dr. Almy in her discussion below. She draws upon the writings of Piaget and augments his views with some insightful observations from her own studies of children's modes of thought.

"So little for the mind," say the critics. Some react against school programs where "doing" seems to supersede learning; others against situations where memorization and repetition seem ascendant over problem solving and critical or creative thinking. So educators, ever mindful of the pressure of public opinion and not insensitive to the criticism from within their own ranks, turn their attention more and more to the mind and to the processes of thinking.

Support for their interest comes from the psychologists, who, following some years of preoccupation with more directly observable aspects of human behavior, are now increasingly interested in the ways man acquires knowledge of himself and of his environment. As their research in the cognitive processes grows, some of them extend their concerns beyond the laboratory and into the classroom. This territory was once off limits to all but the educational psychologist, and even he was seldom completely at home there.

But the psychologist does not share his interest in thinking with the educator alone. The scientist, the mathematician, and the linguist have also begun to inquire into the nature of children's thinking, looking for evidence that children can think effectively. They are concerned that the school equip its graduates to deal more adequately with the complexities of a changing world.

DIFFERENT VIEWS

Representing different disciplines and different professions, each of these individuals has a characteristic way of looking at thinking. The educator, perhaps, is most aware of what the teacher does or says in attempting to influence think-

MILLIE ALMY, "Wishful Thinking About Children's Thinking?" *Teachers College Record*, 62 (February, 1961), 396–406. Reprinted by permission of the author and the publisher.

DR. ALMY (1915–) is on the faculty of Teachers College, Columbia University. Her research and writings are in the field of child development.

ing; the psychologist centers his attention on the responses of the individual children, whereas the other specialists are concerned with the logical structure of their particular subjects. Eventually, if the children are to be taught to think effectively and to the satisfaction of all concerned, these differing viewpoints need to be reconciled.

Perhaps, when specialists with differing outlooks view the intellectual life of the classroom simultaneously, they can avoid the inclination to think wishfully, rather than realistically, about the ways that children think. Many adults reveal this wishful tendency when they assume that the thinking of the five- or ten-year-old basically resembles their own, and again when they take whatever he says to mean what they would mean if they were saying the same things.

The process of education would be considerably simplified if children, once having acquired speaking vocabularies resembling those of adults, also shared with them similar ways of explaining and viewing the world. If youngsters of seven and seventeen did indeed think alike, the second grade teacher and the high-school teacher could use similar methods, and the presentation of subject matter could be determined by its own particular logic.

CHILDHOOD LIMITATIONS

Much of the literature related to the curriculum is replete with statements implying that the processes of concept formation differ little, if at all, from the kindergarten or even the nursery-school years to adulthood. Similarly, many of the principles cited in educational methods courses rest on the assumption that children and adults arrive at and understand new concepts in basically similar ways. Such principles, unfortunately, gloss over what appear to be important limitations in the thinking abilities of children as compared to adults.

These limitations are not such as to necessitate a curriculum of intellectual pablum in the elementary school. The problem is not that children are unable to cope with ideas, but rather that they apprehend them in ways that are characteristic of their level of development. To postpone opportunities to deal in their own fashion with certain aspects of science, mathematics, art, or literature until they have reached the age of high school or even college may be to offer them only the bare bones of abstraction stripped of real significance. The danger in current attempts to erase the idea that the "public schools are easy schools," generating mediocrity in thinking, appears to lie less in the attempt to inject more content into the curriculum than in failure to recognize that each level of development contributes its own special understandings of that content.

Like many other educators interested in the kindergarten and primary grades, the writer long believed that the only important difference between the reasoning abilities of younger and older children lay in the greater experience of the older youngsters. Qualitatively, the thinking of five-year-olds and six-year-olds should be similar to that of older children. If this were the case, the kinds of experience provided in the early childhood curriculum should importantly influence children's thinking, both immediately and later. To test this notion, a study of children's thinking about natural phenomena was undertaken. For many years the curriculum for young children in kindergarten and in elementry school has included attention to this area. But the kinds of understanding that may be possible at this level of development have not been much investigated.

The exploratory phases of the study were designed to examine the efficacy of the demonstration-interview as a technique for revealing children's conceptions about such presumably familiar aspects of their world as air, water, objects that float and those that sink, living and non-living things. Two groups of kindergarten children were interviewed at the mid-year and end of kindergarten and again at the end of first grade. Eighty interviews with children ranging in age from three-and-a-half to seven years were conducted by students in developmental psychology. The results suggested explanations for some of the many discrepancies to be found among studies of children's thinking using the interview as a method, and between those studies and others based on observations of children at work and play. But the most significant result of the exploratory study lay in its assault on the writer's own wishful belief that the child's words had the same meaning to him as they did to her and that his logic was basically no different from her own.

ADULT DIFFICULTIES

Some consolation for finding herself in this position has come from the realization that other educators and psychologists, as well as scholars from various other disciplines, are also prone to indulge in wishful thinking about children's thinking. When one reads the literature on concept formation, begins to examine the thought processes lying behind the verbal facade children present in the classroom, and then listens to what educators say the children are thinking and what scholars assert the children should be thinking, the difficulties of maintaining a realistic view of children's thinking are obvious.

Mistaken assumptions about the nature of a young person's thinking are perhaps most likely to occur in relation to early childhood. Most of the illustrative material for this article is drawn from this stage of development. But there is little reason to believe that those who are concerned with learning in the high school as well as in the middle and upper elementary school years (and perhaps even in college and graduate school) are not also sometimes inclined to be influenced by their desires.

Wishful thinking on the part of teachers is readily demonstrable. They are easily misled by a glib response, an expected answer, or even an eager look, forgetting that a facile memory and a sensitivity to adult expectation may mask meanings and understandings that are quite different from those the teacher expects. But those who build the curriculum, who are concerned with either the earliest or the most strategic moments for teaching particular concepts, are also not immune to wishfulness. They reveal it when they imply that first and second graders can readily become miniature physicists and mathematicians. They and others reveal their own predilections when they assign priorities to either concrete or abstract thinking. That children do indeed learn by doing is surely not debatable, but that activity must *dominate* the curriculum from kindergarten to college is open to question.

It also appears that some scholars, perhaps a few psychologists, and at least an occasional educator would like to center all attention on a kind of pure thought, analytic thinking undefiled by emotion or fantasy. Granted that logical thinking is essential, the important contribution of intuition, insight, and imagination to effective thought ought not be overlooked.

Similarly, recent attempts to plan the curriculum of the school around the logical structure underlying the various disciplines are promising in many respects. But here again, one must question whether some scholars are not prone to assume that whatever approach leads to effective thinking in their own discipline will probably apply to others as well. Undoubtedly, the underlying logical structure has been made considerably more explicit in certain disciplines than in others. This is perhaps reflected in the fact that the most comprehensive research in the nature of children's thinking has been in the area of physical science and mathematics. The bulk of it has been contributed by Piaget and is best represented in English by his work with Inhelder, *The Growth of Logical Thinking from Childhood to Adolescence.*

In studying thinking processes, Piaget has played the dual role of logician and psychologist. This approach has alienated him from many of his American colleagues. Yet, what appears to be his basic idea has considerable potential appeal for those who plan the content of children's schooling. Essentially, he uses symbolic logic as an instrument for describing the thinking processes necessary to the understanding of the structure of a given discipline. Confronting children of successive ages with representative problems, he has been able to demonstrate the sequence of appearance of increasingly complex reasoning abilities.

Nevertheless, the author's study of kindergarten children's thinking about natural phenomena was based partially on a conviction that Piaget's assertion of limited reasoning abilities in young children failed to take into sufficient account the possibility that experience of a kind that could be provided in a classroom could readily modify their thinking. She was unprepared to have the children, almost as though they had read and comprehended Piaget, demonstrate so many of the limitations in reasoning that he describes as characteristic of early levels of development. On the other hand, the children also revealed that they were accumulating, classifying, and organizing a great deal of information about their world. These findings raised many provocative questions and led to what now appears to be a more intelligent grappling with ideas about cognitive development, of which Piaget's remain most fruitful.

PIAGET'S VIEWS

Piaget's unique contribution lies in his use of "operations." Operations are actions or ways of getting information from the world of reality into the world of thought. During infancy, the child capable only of direct action on his world. Later, he internalizes his actions and is able to carry them out symbolically. But it is not until he is also able to cancel or "reverse" them mentally (i.e., to be aware of a previous thought) that he can comprehend the world in the way the adult does. Not until this point can the adult hope to teach him the most elementary concepts of physics or mathematics. Similarly, it is not until he can mentally handle potentiality or possibility as effectively as reality that he can comprehend mathematics or physics in abstract terms. At this point, he is no longer limited to considering what "is" but can deal with "might be." He can theorize that under certain conditions, certain variables may behave in a variety of ways. He does not need to create the conditions or actually to manipulate the variables in order to predict the outcome.

During the period ordinarily encompassed by the elementary and high school years, the child, according to Piaget, moves from the stage of *intuitive thought*, in which his experience is predominantly perceptual, into a stage of *concrete operations*. At this level, he can reason similarly to an adult, but not until he reaches the stage of *formal operations* does genuine abstract thinking become possible. The shift from intuitive thinking to concrete operations appears to take place by age seven, while progress from concrete toward formal operations begins around eleven. Age is used here, of course, only as an indication of general maturity level. Piaget's studies are not normative, and considerable variability among children can be assumed.

Thinking remains on the intuitive level so long as the child confronting the world is dominated by his immediate perception. It appears, for example, when he believes that a given amount of liquid placed in a tall slender vessel is not the same when it is spread out in a shallow wide vessel. This notion persists even when he seems to understand that the point at issue is not the appearance of the liquid but the amount "to drink." Or he may think that a friend has more clay than he has when, after having receiving an identical amount, the friend breaks his into small bits, distributing them over a large area.

In this stage, the child cannot hold on mentally to the before and after aspects of a particular phenomenon. He cannot coordinate relationships. His comments, for example, may indicate that he deals first with the height of the tall vessel and then with the width of the shallow one. He is not yet able to think of the height of the one as related to the width of the other. Nor will it occur to him, as it will later, to test the relationships by pouring the liquid from one vessel to another.

At this intuitive level, the child does not yet understand "conservation," the fact that the substance or material of an object remains constant even while it undergoes changes in appearance or that a given number of objects remains the same regardless of how they may be arranged. He also lacks what Piaget terms "reversibility," the ability to cancel mentally a transformation that he has seen occur. It is as though, for example, having thought about the size of an object, he cannot go back to a previous thought about its weight. Once these ideas are attained, the child can begin to handle logical relationships, although he does so through direct actions rather than abstractly. He has reached a stage of *concrete operations.*

With these operations, the child can in an orderly fashion handle the equivalences among a group of objects—say, a collection of toy soldiers—and also deal systematically with their differences. Thus, he recognizes that the "soldiers" include both all the plastic soldiers and all the metal soldiers, and that there are more "soldiers" than either plastic or metal soldiers. But he can also sort them into classes of "privates" and "sergeants" and include in those classes both those that are metal and those that are plastic. He can also create a series, arranging them in order of size or, perhaps, even according to their authority (who gives orders to whom).

The ability to form classes and series considerably enhances the child's ability to manipulate and to understand number, space, and time. Various aspects of his physical world take on additional meaning.

Up to this point, however, the child cannot deal with sheer possibilities except experimentally, by actual trial and error. Not until he moves into the stage of *formal operations* can he examine the consequences of various combinations of factors in a systematic and orderly fashion. His thinking is then no longer bound to the immediate task. Rather, he is able to devise theories, state them verbally, and then test them in actual experience. He can reason in the same way as the logician, even though he has not been taught logic.

SUPPORTING VIEWS

The sequence of intellectual development described by Piaget corresponds with the findings in other studies of concept formation, although it is doubtful whether any other single investigator has covered so many concepts over so wide an age range.

Studies like those by Welch, for example, have indicated that conceptualization proceeds from simple levels (men and women are all people) to more complex levels (such as the understanding that potatoes are vegetables, apples are fruit, and that both vegetables and fruit are food). Piaget notes, however, that a child may learn these ideas without being able to manipulate them effectively. By the age of 8, according to Welch, children can conceptualize on these levels but cannot deal with more remotely abstract classifications. Such inclusive classes as "living substance" or, still more abstractly, "substance" are too difficult.

Reichard, Schneider, and Rapaport, using sorting tests, found three levels of development. At the concretistic level up to 5 or 6 years, children classified objects on the basis of nonessential incidental features. A functional level, where classification was made on the basis of use, extended to the age of 8, and the abstract level was not much used before the age of 10.

Studies summarized by Heinz Werner similarly indicate a sequence in concept formation from a "naming" or describing level to later concrete and abstract levels. Werner, however, holds to a theory of mental development that suggests a spiral evolution rather than a series of stages. He appears to agree with Piaget when he indicates that a task can be achieved by genetically different analogous processes, but he also notes that at any stage of development, the level of performance depends on the relative novelty of the task.

The challenge put to the educator by such studies of the development of thinking processes is that of ascertaining, on the one hand, the level at which children can think and, on the other, the level of thinking the material presented demands if it is to be understood. Can adults, who have put away (or believe that they have put away) their own childish ways of thinking, readily recapture them to understand what is going on in the minds of children? Some of the resistance to the observations made by Piaget, and also evidence from other studies of concept formation, suggests that such a return is difficult. Yet Piaget seems to say that unless the adult can enter into the thinking of the child, he can have very little influence over it.

The problem the adult faces is perhaps most acute when the children he wishes to teach are still at an intuitive level of thought, still too caught up in the perceptions of the moment to be able to deal logically with the relationships between various aspects of their experience. To what extent are children in kindergarten, first, and, perhaps, even second grade thinking in these ways, and how is their ability to learn affected?

THINKING IN THE CLASSROOM

The unexpected results of the exploratory study prompted a further examination of assumptions about young children's thinking in both the practice of early childhood education and the literature related to it. Instances of wishful thinking about what might be going on in the minds of children were easy to find. But, there were also some realistic efforts to get behind the verbal facade. On the whole, it seems that neither the limitations the child has in his thinking, nor the special contribution this level of development may make to eventual adult thinking, are fully appreciated. One suspects that an inquiry related to the period of transition between "concrete" and "formal" thinking would yield similar results.

Few would deny that many five-year-olds come to kindergarten with a background of experience broader than that brought by their fathers and mothers twenty years ago. Undoubtedly, they have traveled more miles, whether by car or plane. They have had the stimulation of television and probably of children's records and books. It is likely that their vocabularies are larger. Certainly, the information they have available concerns a somewhat different variety of things from those their parents knew about. Does this mean that the beginning school child of the 1960's has reached a level where he is able to think more logically, to deal with more complex relationships than his parents were? Can he cope more readily with the abstract symbols involved in reading? Will he move more directly to computation in arithmetic? Are space rockets and dinosaurs more appropriate for his science curriculum than the geography of his neighborhood and the care of rabbits and turtles? Must his social studies center around the "community helpers," or can he begin to understand the structure of laws, taxation, and administration that supports the fireman and the policeman?

One has only to eavesdrop for awhile on the spontaneous conversations of any group of five or six-year-olds to recognize that many if not all of them are keenly alert to pictures and their captions, whether in books, magazines, or TV commercials. They recognize a variety of signs. They handle nickels and dimes and quarters as they buy lollipops and Good Humors. They talk about planets and satellites, and they refer to historic and even pre-historic events. They know something about income taxes and sales taxes. Their teachers say that they are forming concepts. But what kinds of concepts? What kinds of understandings lie behind their glibness? Are their "concepts" stable enough so that they can be related to one another, classified, compared? Or are the responses the teacher labels "concepts" still pretty much names or labels for personal experience?

Recently, several kindergarten teachers, who had been introduced to Piaget's theory that children of five or six are likely to be in a transitional state between intuitive and operational thought, attempted to gather evidence about the kinds of thinking their children revealed. Coming from privileged homes, these youngsters were verbally facile, competent in managing most of their own affairs, and generally alert to their environment.

At the beginning of the kindergarten year, all of one group of eighteen children were able to count, some of them to one thousand. Yet, the teacher discovered none of them had any stable notion of number beyond three. Asked to select four pebbles to match those held by the teacher, they scooped up as many as twelve. Only one child was ingenious enough to count off the number the teacher had with her own four fingers, and then apply the same four fingers to her pile of pebbles.

In the same group, a highly verbal youngster demonstrated how extensively his thinking was dominated by his perception when he attempted an explanation of the reason certain objects stayed on the flannel board when others did not. He volunteered the notion that the material on the board was rough and that the material on the back of the pictured objects was also rough. Not misled by its apparent logic, the teacher picked up a piece of paper and inquired as to whether he thought it would stick to the board. The child replied that it would not because it was "round," whereas the other objects were not.

In another group, almost at the end of the year, the children were confronted with the problem of building a larger enclosure for some chickens they had received at Easter. Using blocks, they constructed a building almost as tall as they were. Gradually, the realization that they could not get the chickens out of the enclosure dawned on them. But for some time none of them were able to fathom the relationship between their height and the depth of the enclosure. They summoned their teacher, and when she could not reach into it either, advised her to get a stool to stand on. She did so, but, of course, to no avail. Still unsatisfied, they ask her to get a stepladder and remained baffled by the results.

CONCEPTS AS CONCEPTIONS

Clearly, all of these children were still thinking largely on a perceptual level. Although their teachers might say that they were developing concepts of number, of causality, and of height, none of them had really gone (at least in these examples) beyond a stage of naming certain aspects of their own experience. They had labels for experiences such as "four," "rough," "round," "deep," "tall," "high"; but they were unable to relate or compare the properties they could describe.

One reason for confusion here lies in the fact that the term "concept" is used in quite different ways by the teacher, the psychologist, and the person representing a particular discipline such as mathematics or physics. The teacher thinks of a concept as something that she wants children to learn. The psychologist often regards a concept as a system of related meanings held by an individual. In contrast, the mathematician or the physicist views concepts as integral parts of the logical structure of a particular discipline. He is not concerned about *personal* meanings; his attention is concentrated on those common or agreed-upon meanings which make possible scientific communication.

Failure to distinguish adequately between *concepts* as "abstractable, public, essential forms" and *conceptions* as "individual mental images and symbols" leads to inevitable confusion. In recent years, psychologists and others have tried to show teachers how importantly the array of meanings a child brings to a particular problem influences his solutions of it. Accordingly, curriculum has emphasized the provision of "meaningful experience." Sometimes, however, educators lose sight of the fact that for the solution of certain problems, the application of meanings other than those that are public and abstract is a hindrance to efficient solution. There comes a time when the concrete is no longer enriching. In mathematics, for example, the child cannot indefinitely perform calculations with counters, beads, and so on. Numbers and their relationships must eventually be dealt with abstractly. In physics, the notions that some objects float and others sink, followed by the awareness that objects of equivalent size may have different weights, must eventually be replaced with the abstract idea of specific gravity as a quantifiable relationship.

If teachers at all levels of education could understand the kinds of thinking demanded by the material they present to their students and recognize whether or not the students are coping with it as anticipated, much time and effort might be saved. The kindergarten teacher, for example, would not be satisfied that the children had arrived at any particular generalizations about transportation merely because they had all looked and talked about pictures of trains and airplanes. The elementary school teacher would rely more on the children's demonstration of their understandings than on their comments. Teachers of algebra and geometry would check for evidence of ability to deal with abstraction before proceeding to teach further abstractions.

TEACHING CONCEPTS

Inhelder has suggested that,

> . . . it might . . . be interesting to devote the first two years of school to a series of exercises in manipulating, classifying, and ordering objects in ways that highlight basic operations of logical addition, multiplication, inclusion, serial ordering, and the like. For surely these logical operations are the basis of more specific operations and concepts of all mathematics and science. It may indeed be the case that such an early science and mathematics "pre-curriculum" might go a long way toward building up in the child the kind of intuitive and more inductive understanding that could be given embodiment later in formal courses in mathematics and science. The effect of such an approach would be, we think, to put more continuity into science and mathematics and also to give the child a much better and firmer comprehension of the concepts which, unless he has this early foundation, he will mouth later without being able to use them in any effective way.

The crucial question, perhaps, is whether it is possible to provide experiences for young children that involve more than memorization, or the automatic repetition of the correct response. Inhelder's use of the term "exercise" does not do justice to the active inquiry the child has to bring to problems like those represented in Piaget's demonstrations, nor does it adequately represent the opportunities available to the child for learning from his own mistakes.

Inhelder's proposal also implies a formality of approach that seems incompatible with active, energetic American first and second graders. However, the experience she envisions could be made an inherent part of any program concerned with the adequacy of children's thinking. Isaacs has suggested, for example, that the planning, constructing, and building, and the opportunities for learning by error that typify the modern infant school offer numerous possibilities for the intuitive child to develop toward an operational mode of thinking.

In the long run, the important contributions of the kindergarten and possibly even the first grade to later intellectual development may lie as much in the nurture of the normal child's curiosity and zest for learning as in the early exercise of incipient logical thinking. The encouragement of keen observation, furtherance of the awareness of the properties and the actions of the objects that make up his world, and the development of a vocabulary adequate to describing them, all appear to be appropriate educational goals. Indeed, if the children in the exploratory study, particularly those coming from lower socio-economic backgrounds, provide a good example, such goals may sometimes take priority over the early promotion of "concrete operations."

THINKING AND EMOTION

Surely the present, possibly belated, swing of the educational pendulum towards a re-emphasis on the school's responsibility for intellectual development carries with it all that is currently known about children. But some individuals who are concerned with schools are prone to overlook much that is known. They think that strict concentration on the intellectual or the academic aspects of education will obviate most, if not all, of the problems that have beset the schools in recent years. They are either unconcerned with or ignore the emotional aspects of children's thinking. In contrast, another group of individuals are alarmed at the present emphasis on the intellectual. They assume that such emphasis *necessarily* implies a rejection of the emotional. Both groups seem to be thinking more wishfully than realistically.

It is of course possible to look at the outcomes of cognitive processes, the materials mastered, or the problems solved, as something apart from the motives involved in the individual's thinking. Piaget takes note of this when he says that cognitive "structures" are unaffected by affect; but he notes at the same time that there is no cognitive mechanism without its emotional element and, conversely, no state of pure emotion without its cognitive element. Feelings of success or failure may influence a child's solution of a mathematical problem, but his addition can still be viewed as either right or wrong.

Despite Piaget's insistence on the constant interaction between emotions and intellect, his studies, with the possible exception of his investigations of the thinking of the very young child, do not seem to have exploited the relationship very fruitfully. He indicates, for example, that under conditions of stress a child regresses to an earlier level of thinking. But he gives little attention to the implications of optimal motivation either for a given level of development or for the facilitation of transition from one level to another.

Work with children with learning difficulties indicates how emotion can distort thinking. Underachieving ten- and eleven-year-olds, who, according to Piaget's theory, should be able to function logically, are often unable to understand the problems, much less cope with them in the way that other youngsters of their age do. Like preschool children, they are too bound to their immediate perceptions to deal effectively with any complex relationships. Their perceptions, in turn, seem dominated by fears and anxieties, preventing their attainment of a more mature level of cognitive development.

If unresolved emotional conflict at one level of development may permeate thinking at a later level, what are the more usual contributions of one level to the next? Piaget's theory accounts for the emergence, stage by stage, of the ability to use logical abstractions. But this represents only one area of cognitive functioning. It does not account, for instance, for critical and creative thinking. Drawing on imagination and intuition, these may be as firmly rooted in the early childhood period as the ability to think operationally seems to be in the years from seven or eight onward.

It is perhaps more than coincidence that the developmental stage labeled "intuitive" by Piaget is seen as a period of developing initiative and "power testing" by psychoanalytic ego psychologists. Not yet understanding which aspects of his environment are likely to remain constant and which will change momentarily, the young child lives, at least for the time, in a world of many possibilities. Thus, he is often much more inclined to experiment and try than is the older youngster, who knows, for example, that water does not stay in a sieve or that a cake of sand inevitably falls apart. However limited they may be in handling complex relationships, children in the "intuitive" stage are probably as apt in perceiving analogies as they will ever be. If such ability could be nurtured, it should contribute importantly to later insight and cognitive inventiveness.

Similarly, Piaget's period of concrete operational thought is paralleled in psychoanalytic theory by a period of achievement and mastery. Provided the preceding period has been resolved in such a way that the child is emotionally free to tackle new learnings with zest, he relishes acquiring new skills and knowledge. His thinking at this stage may be less ebullient than at the earlier level, but he is acquiring better ability to direct it and to check its outcomes. Thus, he is building an important resource for adolescence, a period that will confront him with new kinds of problems, both emotional and intellectual.

THOUGHT AND PERSONHOOD

When thinking, whether logical or intuitive, is thus viewed as an aspect of the developing personality, motivated in the same ways as other kinds of behavior, the fallacy of a belief that concentration on the outcomes of thinking can free the school from concern with personality development seems clear. The mind has its entity in the person. To comprehend a child's mind adequately is to know him and those who are like him. It is to know how he views the world and what is meaningful to him; and good teaching requires that he then be offered the means and the challenge to build further meanings. As more is known about the nature of thinking and the processes of cognitive development, it is clear that the teacher can aid and abet the student's thinking more effectively. But it is still possible to overestimate, perhaps wishfully, the extent of his influence.

The Prophet may yet be sustained. Speaking of children he says, "They have their own thoughts." When the teacher is indeed wise he does not bid his students enter the house of his wisdom but, rather, leads them to the "threshold of their own minds."

43 *Problem solving as teaching method*

Related selections: 8, 10

How does an individual learn to think? Is problem solving the one method by which this fundamental human process is learned? Professor Hermanowicz explores the origins of problem solving as a teaching method, points out its limitations, and speaks for the utilization of a wide variety of instructional procedures lest problem solving become the new orthodoxy in teaching method in our schools.

Many curriculum theories for elementary as well as secondary education exemplify a primacy of method within the proposed school program. This method usually consists of some form of problem solving procedure as the basis for most, if not all, teaching-learning activities.

The purpose of this article is threefold: (a) to describe the source of problem solving as a teaching method; (b) to explore some of the significant contributions of this teaching method to education; and (c) to raise some questions concerning the applications or limitations of this method in organizing learning activities throughout the curriculum.

DEWEY'S ANALYSIS

In the famous book, *How We Think*, Dewey wrote that learning is learning to think. Although Dewey recognized the existence of many ways of thinking, he

HENRY J. HERMANOWICZ, "Problem Solving as Teaching Method," *Educational Leadership*, 18 (February, 1961), 299–306. Reprinted by permission of the author and the publisher. Copyright 1961 by the Association for Supervision and Curriculum Development.

DR. HERMANOWICZ is Associate Professor of Education at Illinois State Normal University.

402 HENRY J. HERMANOWICZ

insisted, "The better way of thinking is reflective thinking." [1] This reflective thinking, according to Dewey, involved a process of translation "from a situation in which there is experienced obscurity, doubt, conflict, disturbance of some sort into a situation that is clear, coherent, settled, harmonious."

Dewey made a logical analysis of this concept of reflective thought by describing five phases that he considered essential functions of this particular mental process. However, he drew cautions about interpreting these phases as discrete steps following each other in a set order. Furthermore, contrary to some popular journalistic interpretations of Dewey, he considered intellectual curiosity and perseverance the most important attitudes to be formed by learners. Along with reflective thought, "the desire to go on learning" was central to Dewey's concept of an educational experience. [2]

It is difficult to understand whether Dewey intended his logical analysis of reflective thought to become the Titan of method that exists in many curriculum proposals today. However, six years after the original edition of *How We Think*, the classic *Democracy and Education* was published in which Dewey stated:

> While we may speak, without error, of the method of thought, the important thing is that thinking is the method of an educational experience. The essentials of method are therefore identical with the essentials of reflection. [3]

Furthermore, Dewey translated his five phases of reflective thought into more pedagogical language, making them sound like a prescription for educational method. These essentials of method were described as follows:

1. That the pupil have a genuine situation of experience—that there be continuous activity in which he is interested for its own sake.
2. That a genuine problem develop within the situation as a stimulus to thought.
3. That he (the learner) possess the information and make the observations needed to deal with it.
4. That suggested solutions occur to him which he shall be responsible for developing in an orderly way.
5. That he have opportunity and occasion to test his ideas by application, to make their meaning clear and to discover for himself their validity.

INTERPRETATIONS

Thus, Dewey's writings opened the door to a variety of interpretations related to problem solving as a teaching method. Subsequent developments in cognitive learning theory seemed to add support to the refinement and application of this teaching method. Perhaps it was inevitable that educators would try to derive

[1] John Dewey, *How We Think*. Revised edition. Boston: D. C. Heath & Company, 1933, p. 3.
[2] John Dewey, *Experience and Education*. New York: The Macmillan Company, 1938, p. 49.
[3] John Dewey, *Democracy and Education*. New York: The Macmillan Company, 1916, p. 192.

new teaching techniques by their inferences from Dewey's philosophy and from gestalt psychology.

Dewey had many middlemen who interpreted or spelled out his ideas for practical application in education. Among the more distinguished and influential interpreters of Dewey was William H. Kilpatrick. With combined intellectual and emotive appeal, Kilpatrick's ideas concerning "The Good Life" and "The Project Method" excited the imagination of many educators. In a sense, Kilpatrick was providing a do-it-yourself kit for teachers ready to react against stagnant teaching methods that existed in the schools. It is interesting to note the similarity between Dewey's problem solving and a teaching unit outline suggested by Kilpatrick. This unit, according to Kilpatrick, is an "instance of child living" which includes the following five phases:

1. The individual (or group) faces a situation. He has no satisfactory way of responding to it and is hence perplexed both as to what aspect of it he should respond and how he should respond.
2. He continues to face the situation; begins to analyze it so as to locate details that might be of help in deciding what to do and how to do it.
3. Out of his past experiences and his present analysis of the situation he makes plans for resolving his difficulty and chooses, on the basis of careful thought, the plan he prefers to try out.
4. He tries out the plan selected, revising it whenever it seems desirable to do so.
5. If the plan works, the perplexity is resolved. If the plan does not work, he may go back through the various activities again and again until some solution has been reached or else the individual abandons the situation.[4]

In addition to Kilpatrick's project method and "instance of child living," Dewey's phases of reflective thought have manifested themselves in many other educational proposals. For example, Alberty has transformed these phases of reflective thought into a type of group problem solving which he considers "the emerging concept of general method" in education. Klausmeier, Dresden, Davis and Wittich outline a general pattern of teacher-pupil planning for the elementary school which is similar to Dewey's concept of reflection. The implication behind these proposals appears to be that all learning evolves from the method of problem solving.

Not confined to teaching method

Thorpe and Schmuller write that Dewey's insistence upon the identity of reflection and educative experience eventually altered the very concept of learn-

[4] William H. Kilpatrick, *Remaking the Curriculum.* New York: Newson and Company, 1936, p. 1-47,

ing. Taking a somewhat eclectic view in formulating some tentative principles of learning, Thorpe and Schmuller point out the significant impression that Dewey's problem solving has stamped upon these principles.

Sometimes Dewey's problem solving has been equated with "the" method of science. Many elementary and high school science textbooks contain descriptions of "the scientific method" which bear a remarkable resemblance to Dewey's phases of reflective thought. In addition, Dewey's problem solving steps have been cited as representing the elements of design for all applied research in education.

Dewey's problem solving is the general teaching method in education. It is a significant part of learning theory. It is the design of applied research in education. It is the scientific method. This makes one wonder what other claims could be made in its name.

QUESTIONS SHOULD BE RAISED

Undoubtedly the applications of Dewey's problem solving method did much to revitalize the nation's classrooms. Problem solving as a teaching method even in its most stylized form was a procedure for improving upon the cut-and-dried classroom techniques that largely involved an assign-study-recite sequence. The new methodology also gave educators some hope for helping children learn to deal with a variety of problems and situations as an important part of their education in a rapidly changing culture. Interdisciplinary experience in dealing with significant problems is an important educational function that often gets lost in the present debate regarding curriculum improvement.

Without attempting to negate these important contributions to education, perhaps some questions should be raised concerning the omnipotence of the problem solving method. Should all learning depend upon a student's exposure to problematic situations? Does all learning involve conscious inquiry? Even if it is assumed that the better kind of thought process involves elements found in Dewey's concept of reflective thought, should these elements be translated into a general teaching method? What limitations would the use of a general problem solving method as "the" teaching procedure impose upon learners? Does a general scientific method exist?

A GENERAL SCIENTIFIC METHOD?

It is conceivable that a collection of scientists might debate both pro and con the question, "Does a general method of science exist?" However, as an area of knowledge and as a human enterprise, describing "the method of science" in terms of problem solving steps must be viewed as a rather naive interpretation of the nature of science. Representing these steps (i.e., recognizing that a problem exists, stating the problem in specific terms, formulating hypotheses, and so on) as the method of science at best offers misleading information to students of science. Writing as a scientist, James Bryant Conant states:

The usual descriptions of "the scientific method" are descriptions actually of the very limited procedure by which a person can improve a particular practical art.[5]

Other scientists have criticized the concept of a general method of science. The following is a summary of criticisms directed at this doctrine:

First, there is not one scientific method, but several, differing certainly from field to field, and even, in many cases, from problem to problem.

Second, . . . a single doctrine is misleading or meaningless unless taken in conjunction with a number and variety of examples—this can indicate limitations of the doctrine by exhibiting exceptions to it.

Third, no one doctrine on the nature of scientific method, known to us, is sufficiently complete and multidimensional so as to include all others.[6]

Cautions from psychology

In discussing the importance of problem solving in learning, Lee J. Cronbach states that it is usually not possible to teach a definite procedure for dealing with a problem. While Cronbach does not minimize the significance of having learners deal with problems, he also describes a procedure for teaching concepts which does not involve a problem solving approach. This procedure is:

1. Adequate realistic experience to provide a basis for understanding. Such understanding can come only if the experience is reflected upon.
2. Formulation of generalizations in explicit terms.
3. Application of the generalization by the student to a variety of concrete or visualized situations.
4. Consideration by the student of systematic relations between concepts.[7]

There is some experimental evidence which seems to indicate that it is possible for negative learnings to result when students learn to follow one procedure to solve a variety of problems. This possibility represents a serious indictment against transforming Dewey's phases of reflective thought into a form of teaching method even on a general level. Of course, other experimental studies have been supportive of the application of a problem solving teaching methodology.

[5] James Bryant Conant, *Modern Science and Modern Man.* New York: Columbia University Press, 1952, p. 21.
[6] Earl McGrath, Editor, *Science in General Education.* Dubuque, Iowa: William C. Brown, 1948, pp. 74-75.
[7] Lee J. Cronbach, Editor, *Text Materials in Modern Education.* Urbana, Illinois: University of Illinois Press, 1955, p. 80.

Curriculum literature often displays this supportive evidence creating unequivocally positive impressions of a problem solving teaching procedure. It is desirable for those interested in curriculum to be cognizant of the negative aspects of this teaching method.

A study by A. S. Luchins indicated that students taught to follow a particular method or procedure were actually being taught not to think in their problem solving. The students in the experiment usually applied the same procedure when given a different type of problem. Furthermore, giving these students instructions to generalize a method of solution had a tendency to increase their "set" or inflexibility toward attacking and solving problems.

An experiment by Schroeder and Rotter demonstrated that students who worked on a variety of problems where no single attack was successful learned to be flexible. On the other hand, those students who had continued success with one method used it rigidly even where it was incorrect.

To think of problem solving as a general method may be a mistake insofar as the learners themselves are concerned. In an article summarizing recent research on problem solving as classroom teaching method, Gross and McDonald state:

> When the focus of interest in investigation has been on the general methodology of the problem solver, it has been consistently found that the subjects tend to use a variety of general methodologies.[8]

SOME CURRICULUM IMPLICATIONS

The rationale behind "the problem solving method" as a classroom procedure usually is given in the form of cognitive learning theory, democratic principles, and Dewey's philosophy of instrumentalism. You might say that the teaching method of problem solving has been derived or synthesized from three or more different sources. Derivation of any specific or general classroom technique from a learning theory, philosophy, and democratic principles is a hazardous process. While the rationale behind the final educational product (in this case the problem solving teaching method) may give it connotations of intellectual respectability, neither the rationale nor the sources of derivation can make the final product reliable or valid.

Perhaps those of us in education interested in improving teaching methods should use the field of teaching itself as the basis for developing more promising teaching procedures. There is a fundamental distinction between a psychologist viewing all learning as problem solving and an educator organizing content and teaching technique in the form of problems-to-be-solved in the classroom. However, just as a psychologist develops theoretical constructs to help analyze and explain learned behavior, the educator can develop theories to help explain and gain knowledge about teaching. It is rather strange that we continue to "derive"

[8] R. E. Gross and F. J. McDonald, "Classroom Methods: The Problem-Solving Approach." *Phi Delta Kappan* 39:259-65, March 1958, p. 261.

teaching methods from a variety of sources other than teaching itself. This seems to be part of the dilemma inherent in an analysis of the problem solving method as teaching technique.

In view of the foregoing information, it may be unwise to consider all learnings as a form of problem solving in organizing content or potential learning experiences in the curriculum. This writer's professional prejudices are such that he believes that a significant function or emphasis of a school program should be to help students learn to deal with a wide variety of important problems. However, it is questionable to assume that the total curriculum should be organized around problematic situations or as problems-to-be-solved.

In addition, the function of problem solving in the school program might not best be implemented in terms of "a" general teaching method. Despite the apparent built-in flexibility of "the problem solving method" as classroom technique, it has dangers of being an orthodox procedure in itself. A wide variety of teaching methods should be employed to help students develop their own abilities in decision making. The teacher's role is to help students seek relevant knowledge, understand important values, analyze possible alternatives, and project probable consequences involved in dealing with different problems. This will foster the type of critical thinking that was Dewey's original goal in emphasizing the development of reflective thought.

The trouble with using Dewey's problem solving as a step-by-step teaching method is that the application of the method can defeat the purpose for having students deal with problems. The gradual passing of the recitation as "the" method in educational practice should not result in another orthodoxy to act as a replacement. The mechanized application of problem solving as teaching method can become a thought inhibiting rather than a thought provoking device; whereas, problem solving should help develop originality and diversity in student thinking.

44 Computer simulation of thinking

The high-speed computer has become an important research tool in the behavioral sciences as described in the following article on the adaptation of high-speed computer techniques to the simulation of human thought processes. This selection by Dr. Hovland will be beyond the understanding of the student who is unfamiliar with present developments in computer technology, but the qualified student will peruse it with interest.

It is commonplace in the history of science for developments in one field of knowledge to have profound effects on other related areas. The dramatic influence of advances in atomic physics on biology, genetics, and medicine is a good case in point. We are currently witnessing a similar phenomenon in the repercussions of high speed computer technology on reesarch in the behavioral sciences. The initial impact came from the computational efficiency of these devices which permitted calculations formerly prohibitive in terms of time and effort. A more recent and less direct effect has been in stimulating machine-like methods of analysis of human thought and behavior through simulation on high speed computers. It is these newer techniques and their applicability to psychological problems that is the topic of the present paper.

The analogy between the high speed computer and human thinking has long been noted. We frequently see the Univacs, Johniacs, Illiacs referred to in the popular press as "giant brains" or "thinking machines." In most uses of high speed computers, however, there is an attempt to attain objectives beyond the scope of human capabilities, either because of their speed or their extensive storage capacity (called, interestingly enough, their "memory"). But in the investigations I shall be describing, the utilization is quite different. Here we are primarily concerned with the use of computing machines to stimulate in exact fashion the way a human solves a problem. Both human weaknesses, such as limited and fallible memory, and strengths, such as the ability to choose an efficient solution out of innumerable alternatives, must be represented. We say that we can simulate human problem solving when we are able to specify both the prior information a human possesses and the sequence of steps by which

CARL I. HOVLAND, "Computer Simulation of Thinking," *American Psychologist*, 15 (November, 1960), 687–93. Reprinted by permission of the publisher.
DR. HOVLAND (1912–1961) was Sterling Professor and Director of Graduate Studies in Psychology at Yale University. He was a member of the Social Science Research Council Committee on Simulation of Cognitive Processes.

he utilizes this information in the solution of the problem. We are then able to set up a computing machine to carry out this same sequence of operation.

Those familiar with the operation of high speed computers will readily understand the way in which simulation proceeds. Just as in ordinary operations of a computer, one gives the machine a set of "instructions" to execute. These constitute a "program." In arithmetical operations these are sentences like the following: "square the product of the first and second number," "store the product in memory," "compare the first and second number," "select the larger of the two numbers compared." Or such instructions as: "find the number of dollars paid to the individual last month," "add to this amount the number of dollars earned this month," and so forth. The machine then executes each of these instructions through an intricate electronic system, printing out its answers on an electric typewriter. Sequences of instructions can then solve the most complicated numerical problems, such as making out a payroll with each individual working different numbers of hours, at different wage rates, with advance payments to some workers, with different deductions for subscriptions to health and accident insurance, different income tax credits, and so forth. The nub of the simulation problem involves the use of similar types of "programs" of "instructions" to the machine in order to reproduce the steps an individual goes through in thinking out the solution to a difficult problem. One specifies the steps the individual uses by stating them in an unambiguous way so that a computing machine is able to carry them out. These may be instructions like: "store the answer to the last problem," "determine whether you have stored in memory any similar problems," "if so, what are the differences between the past problem and the present problem," "see if applying Rule a will convert the old problem into the new one," and "apply Rule b" to convert the answer to the former problem into the solution to the present one. Thus the computer can be given information which is exactly equivalent to that of the human problem solver, as well as a specification of the way the human goes about processing that information to reach a solution.

The obvious point is that if we can be precise enough about a process to describe it in terms which can be programed and executed by a machine, we indeed know quite a bit about that process. And if we can specify singly each of the subprocesses involved, we can determine the effects of combinations of them and of variations in order of execution of the steps. The outcomes are almost impossible to foresee without actually carrying out the combinations and variations.

Let me begin by giving a concrete example of the new techniques, namely, simulation of the solving of geometry problems. We certainly think of the solving of theorems in Euclidian geometry by a high school sophomore as constituting a clearcut example of intelligent human behavior. But Gelernter and Rochester (1958) of the International Business Machines Company have now successfully developed a program whereby a high speed computer is able to solve many of the theorems in Euclid's geometry, for example, that the diagonals of a parallelogram bisect one another. A human learner who tries to solve such a problem has usually been taught a series of fundamental principles, or axioms, together with a set of rules for inferring relationships by which the basic symbols in the system may be manipulated. He is then asked to prove a new theorem. He tries to find a way of transforming and combining previous axioms through the set of rules until he achieves the proof of the new theorem. Typically he starts out in rather routine fashion, then has a flash of insight as to a possible means of solution, and then methodically tests the adequacy of the solution. The geometry computing machine is set up to operate in an analogous fashion. It is given a set of basic formulas and axioms, together with rules as to possible ways of manipulating them in order to form new theorems. The new theorem is then presented to the machine to prove. The machine is equipped with a number of rules of thumb for possible ways of solving problems. For example, it is instructed that if the proposition to be proved involves parallel lines and equality of angles, there is a good chance that it may be useful to try the theorem: "If two parallel lines are intersected by a third line, the opposite interior angles are equal." This instruction constitutes a short-cut which often works well but is by no means sure to be of value. Successful solution typically involves setting up a series of subgoals which are then worked on in succession. For example, in the problem cited earlier the machine ascertains that it can solve the theorem if it can establish the fact that the distance from one corner of the base of the parallelogram to the point of intersection must equal the distance from the intersection to the opposite corner of the parallelogram. This is then a subgoal, which in turn can be proved if the triangle formed by the bisecting lines and one of the sides of the parallelogram is equal to the triangle formed by the opposite side and the corresponding bisects. A device is incorporated into the computer which makes constructions and measures lines and angles. This operates by means of coordinate geometry. Once the sequence of subgoals leads from the initial axioms to the theorem to be proved, the machine routinely tests the accuracy of the proof. This it can do in an exhaustive manner, since once one has a possible proof, checking it is largely clerical. The chief problem is to find a possible method of proceeding, out of the almost infinite number of alternatives. It is here that the short-cut methods operate. They permit the use of likely and plausible methods of solution, just the way a clever high school student would proceed. Once the proof has been verified, the machine prints QED. Throughout the entire operation the machine prints out on paper a complete tracing of the steps it tries—this is analogous to an individual's account of the way he solves a problem in geometry. Some of the machine's failures in finding proofs closely resemble those made by beginning geometry students.

It will be noted that the methods of solution built into the computer closely resemble those used by humans solving similar problems. Let me again call attention to the fact that in this way they differ from the usual uses of high speed computers which methodically go through every possible solution in a deliberate way. The complete methods guarantee that if there is a solution it will be found, although an extraordinary number of trials may be required. Solutions of this type are referred to as "algorithms." These are used here to check proofs. In contrast, finding a possible solution is facilitated by short-cuts and rules of thumb following each move. In addition this machine has some capacity to generalize on the basis of past experience and to store the generalizations themselves. With these learning mechanisms it appears possible for the computer to learn in a short period of time to play a better game of checkers than can be played by the person who wrote the program.

Many of the formulations of learning are made without any special assumptions that learning processes are consistent with known neurophysiological mechanisms. A number of students are attempting to close this gap by simulation studies of the way in which nerve networks become organized into systems and are then modified through use. There is quite extensive investigation along these lines, some of it instigated by the speculations of Hebb about the nature of nervous organization. Suffice it to say that a number of researchers have been able to program computers to simulate the changing of neural organization patterns as a result of repeated stimulation of nerve fibers and further work of a similar type is in progress (cf. Clark and Farley, 1955, and Rochester, Holland, Haibt, and Duda, 1956).

In the work in our laboratory the emphasis is on understanding and simulating the processes involved in acquiring complex concepts through experience (Hovland and Hunt, 1960). The learner acquires a particular concept when he is told which of a series of specific instances presented to him belong in the concept class and which do not. This is similar to the way in which a child learns the concept of "animate" through some experiences in which parents and teachers label a given stimulus as "animate" and others in which they label it as "inanimate" (Hovland, 1952).

Our type of problem is illustrated by a situation in which there are a large number of slides of cancer cells, some of which are known to be malignant and others nonmalignant. The task of the individual (or the machine) is one of inducing the base of difference between the two types and subsequently labeling correctly new slides previously unidentified. Medical pathologists have just such a task and have achieved considerable success, although not 100% accuracy, in making such distinctions. It is of interest in passing that there is a machine available which can make such a distinction on the basis of slides presented to it, but here the combination of characteristics (the "concept") was formulated by the scientist who developed the instrument. The machine's task is to see whether the new specimen conforms to certain specifications, that is, whether on the basis of density and structure the cell belongs in the "malignant" or "normal" category. Thus it has the "concept" built into it, obviating the need to start from the beginning in order to induce it.

The input to the type of concept learning in which we are interested is a series of pictures, say flower designs, some of which are labeled "positive" instances (examples of the concept) and some "negative" instances (examples of what the concept *is not*). The characteristics of the instances are represented as symbols for processing by the machine. It is hoped later to have this transformation automatic through the use of techniques developed at the Bell Telephone Laboratories which employ a television camera to convert the visual representation into electrical impulses as input to the computer. Thus the picture would become converted into one set of symbols representing the characteristics which constitute the instances of the concept (like A1B2C1D1E2F1G1H2), while another string of symbols will represent instances of what the concept *is not* (like A2B1C1D2E1F1G1H2).

Potentially, a machine can then consider combinations of all of these characteristics as possible ways of categorizing and distinguishing between the class of "A" and of "not A." Typically, human learners only attend to part of the potential set of characteristics because of perceptual limitations. We have devoted considerable research effort toward determining just how attention and perception vary during the course of learning. We have incorporated in the machine simulation a selective scanning of possible aspects of the complex stimuli with provision for the fact that some individuals see only some of the characteristics while other individuals pay attention to different aspects.

Human subjects, at least at the adult level, operate on material of this type by developing strategies involving some generalization as to what concepts are like. Some details of these strategies have been investigated by Bruner, Goodnow, and Austin (1956). The strategies may be different for different types of concepts. Logicians describe some concepts as being of the *conjunctive* type, where all the members of the class share certain common characteristics. For example, rubies share the characteristics of hardness, translucence, and redness. A second type of concept is called *disjunctive*, in which possession of either one characteristic or possession of a different characteristic makes the instance subsumable under the general class. This is illustrated by the concept of "strike" in American baseball which is either a pitched ball across the plate and between the batter's knees and shoulders *or*, alternatively, any pitch at which the batter strikes but fails to send into the field. A third type of concept is *relational*, where the instances of the concept share no common fixed characteristics but do have certain relationships in common. A sample would be the concept of "isosceles triangles." All instances of this concept involve triangles with two equal sides. But any fixed characteristics, such as lengths of the equal sides, lengths of the third side, or sizes of angles, are not an adequate basis for inclusion or exclusion in the concept class.

In preparation for later simulation, we have carried out extensive experimentation to determine the order in which these various types of concepts are considered by human learners. We find that for our type of stimulus materials, conjunctive and relational concepts are considered much more commonly than disjunctive ones (Hunt & Hovland, 1960). So our present machine will have built into it a hierarchy of responses in which the first attempts to organize the material will be in terms of shares characteristics—conjunctive type concepts. Alternatively the machine will consider concepts which are based on relationships between the stimuli. Only when these have been extensively and unsuccessfully explored will the machine try disjunctive concept patterns.

At present, then, we have the program for a machine which is able to receive drawings having a number of different dimensions. It is then able to try a number of possible ways of organizing into a concept the prior information it has received regarding confirming and nonconfirming instances. First it considers possibilities of concepts which have various combinations of features. When none of these suffice, it considers relational concepts. When these are not successful, it considers various disjunctive concepts where one set of features or another alternative set define the concept. When a solution is reached the description of what constitutes a concept is printed out on tape and subsequent unlabeled instances are classified A's or non-A's. A scanning device is built into the machine to take into account only certain of the characteristics available for consideration. The present machine remembers all that has been presented to it. We are currently considering various devices to simulate the gradual loss of information, or forgetting, which is all too human a characteristic. Our experimental studies have indicated the overall mathematical form which the loss should take, but there are alternative means of producing such a loss (Cahill and Hovland, 1960). Each alternative represents a different theory of the way in which forgetting occurs and investigation of the different theories is of fundamental importance. Simulation again provides a powerful tool for specifying the operation of the process of forgetting.

A high proportion of our research effort goes into new experimentation with human learners to determine their methods of handling various aspects of the problem, as compared to other efforts which stress programing the actual simulation. It is expected that this type of imbalance in effort will continue, but we are perennially hopeful that as more and more information becomes available an increasing amount of our effort will go into the simulation itself.

Work has now progressed to the point where I think we can see more clearly both the opportunities provided by these methods and some of the difficulties involved. I hope that the foregoing discussion has suggested some of the advantages of these new techniques. Let me briefly summarize the potentialities. First, simulation methods have a tremendous role in sharpening our formulations concerning mental processes and phenomena. It is one thing to say, as earlier students have said, that problem solving involves a number of different stages, for example, those of preparation, incubation, illumination, and verification, and quite another thing for one to specify exactly what is involved in each stage. The pioneering studies by Newell, Shaw, and Simon (1958) on the

General Problem Solver indicate the great forward strides which result from specifying the nature of these processes in such complete detail that a computer is able to solve problems by following the sequence of steps programed into the machine.

Closely related is the second advantage of the computer, the emphasis which it places on developing theories that have both descriptive and predictive power. Many of the theories which exist in psychology and sociology are so general and vague that they have little real predictive power. The program written for the computer to describe a particular process constitutes a theory which, if successful in carrying out the process in the same way as the human, is highly efficient in predicting the effects of changes in conditions and in specifying what other individuals will do under particular conditions.

Lastly, the simulation of human responses has the same overwhelming advantages for our understanding of behavioral phenomena as similar methods in other sciences. For example, the use of the wind tunnel represents a complex set of interacting conditions in actuality which could not be duplicated and whose effects could not be predicted from theory alone. Analogously in the present case, for single factors one can analyze effects without simulation, but when one seeks to understand the combined action of a number of factors interacting in complex ways, no satisfactory way of predicting the exact outcome may be possible. Those working on the geometry simulator, the General Problem Solver, and the chess and checker-playing machines, all testify to the fact that many of the moves made by the computer greatly surprised their inventors.

I hope that my remarks on the importance of simulation methods do not give rise to the feeling that these methods automatically lead to quick success in areas which have been investigated for decades using other techniques. Two examples of the difficulties confronting us may be mentioned. The first is the complexity of the process to be simulated. At present we consider ourselves fortunate if we can simulate on a machine the typical performance of a single individual in solving a particular problem. This is indeed a great step forward. But for simulation to be maximally effective we would like to be able to predict machine solutions which simulate not only a single individual under some specified condition, but also the effects for different individuals under different environmental conditions, and after various amounts of experience. To date, most simulation has been of the performance of one individual, either real or an imaginary average individual. It may prove to be extremely difficult to carry out the next step, that of specifying which characteristics must be known about each individual to be able to simulate the way he varies from the typical pattern. In addition, the effects of environmental variables, such as the effects of drugs on performance, or of pressure to complete a task, should then be simulated. Finally, the effects of experience should be specified, so that the way in which a problem is attacked is appropriately changed as a result of the machine's ability to learn. This leaves for the future such a complex problem as analysis of the interactions between type of individual and amount of learning under different environmental conditions. It is apparent that a long and difficult road lies ahead before we can accomplish successful simulation of a single type of task which has all of these variables programed. But when they can be successfully specified we will know a great deal about the problem. Most research generalizations in the social sciences are only true for a group of people, not for each individual. Computer methodology may make possible a broadening of our understanding of behavior by emphasizing the simulation of single individuals and then studying variations between them. The integration of these complementary approaches in new computer work will help us to reduce the gap between group averages and individual processes.

A second example of the difficulties of machine simulation is attributable to the nature of the process with which we are concerned. Simulation methods have most successfully been employed where it is possible to define the final performance of a task as an outcome of a succession of single steps. Thus where the mental process involves steps in a sequence one can synthesize the process by having the computing machine work first on stage one, then stage two, etc. Much more difficult are those processes where a number of stages are going on simultaneously, in parallel fashion. It certainly appears that much of our perceptual and thought process operates in this way. Under these conditions it is much more difficult to untangle the processes at work prior to simulation. In addition, present machines are not as suitable for these purposes as they are for sequential operation. New and radically different machines may ultimately be required to cope with this problem. Most of our present work is being carried out with computers which were built for quite other purposes, namely, high speed arithmetical computation. It would be possible to design machines more closely simulating thought processes and more flexible in their operation, but they would be expensive to construct and would not have the large number of potential purchasers who ordinarily help defray the costs of development.

Despite the difficulties mentioned, work on simulation of complex psychological processes is yielding results of increasing importance. Processes which were thought to be understood turn out to require much more explicit statement. But along with the increased explicitness comes new understanding and precision. At present most computer programs grapple with only one phase of complex processes, but we are beginning to see common features in a number of different programs, permitting the construction of comprehensive programs from simpler subprograms. Work on simulation has also had a stimulating effect on research on the higher thought processes themselves. Attempts to program computers have repeatedly revealed that we lacked much information as to how humans carry out seemingly simple thought operations. This has led to the return of workers to the laboratory which in turn has further enriched our knowledge of the human thought process.

Let not this enthusiastic report on the scientific potentialities of simulation research arouse anxieties of the sort raised by Norbert Wiener (1960) and other writers that machines will take over our civilization and supplant man in the near future. Rather, I think, there is great hope that detailed knowledge of how humans learn, think, and organize will redound to human welfare in removing much of the mystery which surrounds these processes and in leading to better understanding of the limitations of current ways of solving problems. It may, of course, become possible for us to then build machines which will work out solutions to many problems which we now consider distinctively human and to do so in a manner surpassing present human performance. But that this will lead to the machine becoming master and the designer, slave, seems to me most unlikely. Rather it will free man for novel creative tasks which are progressively beyond the capability of machines designed by man.

PART THREE

The learning situation

ORGANIZATION
AND ATMOSPHERE

45 *Psychology of group behavior: the class as a group*

Related selections: 6, 35, 46, 48, 56

Many teachers view their classes as aggregations of individuals and not as functioning groups. Others recognize that the human inter-relationships existing within classroom walls have a significant effect upon the learning of the individual child. This article by Trow and his colleagues reviews some of the earlier research findings in group dynamics and describes how teachers may utilize the dynamics of the group to further the learning process.

Social psychology has been experiencing a marked development in recent years; and because of the many implications for learning situations, those tilling the educational fields should be alert to the new points of view and new findings which are emerging. This statement does not imply that individual educational psychology is to be discarded, but rather that it is now directly complemented by the basic socio-psychological concept of the group and the consideration of intra-group relationships. As long as sociologists confined their attention largely to such social groupings as crowds and mobs, criminals and delinquents, the family, and to census groups with racial and nationality characteristics, the help they could furnish to the classroom teacher was relatively slight. But with the

WILLIAM CLARK TROW, ALVIN ZANDER, WILLIAM MORSE, and DAVID JENKINS, "Psychology of Group Behavior: The Class as a Group," *Journal of Educational Psychology*, XLI (October, 1950), 322–37. Reprinted by permission of the publisher.

For a biographical note on PROFESSOR TROW, see the footnote for selection 29. PROFESSOR ZANDER (1913–) is at the Research Center for Group Dynamics, University of Michigan; PROFESSOR MORSE (1915–) is Professor of Educational Psychology, University of Michigan; PROFESSOR JENKINS (1916–) is Associate Professor and Director, Group Dynamics Center, Temple University.

419

development of field theory and the study of interaction of individuals in a face-to-face group, and more specifically with the coming of the Iowa studies of democratic, autocratic and *laissez-faire* leadership, followed by the energetic labors of those in the field of group dynamics, the picture has changed. To this has been added the later Freudian influence in the mental hygiene movement, its expansion in the area of inter-personal relationships, and the exploitation of such treatment techniques as those of group work and play therapy. We are forced to ask ourselves whether the school class is a group, and, if it is, what this should mean to educational psychologists whose task it is to introduce teachers to the principles which should aid them in developing the best possible environment for learning in their classrooms.

DEVELOPMENTAL BACKGROUND

It should be recognized at the outset that educational psychology has from the beginning devoted itself almost exclusively to modifying the responses of individuals to more or less separate stimuli. The principles of learning, derived from the performances of laboratory animals and sometimes of children, though the results were brought together statistically, have been applied to the individual learner; and his performance has been tested by presenting him with a series of tasks to perform, and measuring his success in performing them. To describe the educational psychology of the past and the present in this way is not to belittle it. Tremendous improvements have been made in instructional materials and methods as a consequence of this view. We can well feel proud of the contributions of our colleagues and wish for their continuance, for there is much more to be done. After all, individuals are individuals, and they are probably here to stay!

The single-line, teacher-pupil relationship, however, has other sources than the psychological laboratory. There seem to have been changing patterns in our educational assumptions as to the most effective and desirable learning situations for the pupil. At one time the tutorial arrangement, the scholar and the single student in a face-to-face relationship, was felt to be most nearly ideal. And it may be for certain kinds of learning. But the practical situation in our public schools has not, of course, permitted this kind of teacher-pupil ratio; so we tried to make our classes of twenty-five or more pupils into twenty-five simultaneous one-to-one relationships. At any rate we followed this pattern, in our classwork, of teacher control, assignment, and class discussion, all dependent on the teacher-pupil-teacher-pupil kind of interaction. In this tradition we not only have emphasized the importance of the individual pupil of the subject-centered curriculum, but also of individualized instruction, and the child-centered school.

This arrangement tended to be strengthened by virtue of the fact that it provided a more direct system of control. Any break in the line, with consequent spontaneous interaction among pupils might well mean that the teacher had lost that control which he felt it necessary to maintain. If the class were allowed to become an interacting group, the behavior of the pupils would presumably not be contributing to the learning goals which the teacher had in mind. Thus, "groupiness" implied "bad discipline."

Two factors have probably contributed to the movement away from this tutorial conception of our classrooms: the increasing interest and attention being given to social learning, and the awareness that the classrooms are, potentially at least, social situations. With the acceptance of the broader social goals of learning, no longer restricted to scholarly and intellectual activities alone, dependence on the tutorial tradition began to lessen, and the potentialities of the class as a medium for instruction in social learning became clearer.

The point where modern social psychology can offer desirable additions to the individualized approach lies in a recognition of the complex nature of what has in the past been rather loosely referred to as the stimulus situation when this situation is largely made up of other persons. The exploration of this phenomenon, and of the function of perceptual and conceptual processes in relation to it, is the chief contribution of the gestalt psychologists, whose point of view the late Kurt Lewin was largely responsible for bringing over into the interaction field of social psychology. Teachers have long known that pupils responded to other stimuli than the words of wisdom emanating from behind the teacher's desk. But the teacher's task was to eliminate such distraction so far as possible. And while this is still often desirable, we are now interested in these other stimuli also, in the interactions of the pupils among themselves and with the teacher. We are asking, what are the implications of viewing the class not merely as a number of individuals in the same room, but as a group?

The exposition of this point of view in education did not have to wait for the recent developments in social psychology. Although the tone is definitely authoritarian, beginnings are found for example in a volume entitled *School Discipline*, by William C. Bagley, published in 1917. In this volume Bagley discussed in some detail the problem of what he called the "unruly school." He pointed out twin antithetical causes: "harsh and unsympathetic treatment," and "indulgence and weakness of control," conditions not too far removed from frustrating autocracy and *laissez-faire*, respectively. He went on to indicate some of the "difficulties of reconciling the opposing ideals of individualism and collectivism." For transforming the unruly school he included among other conditions, "the importance of the objective attitude, and stimulating group responsibility."

Likewise many school practices, particularly in the extra-curricular field, have laid a foundation for group interaction. For a number of years group games and sports provided for coöperative as well as for individual effort, and teacher-sponsored "activities" of the hobby-club variety tended to promote more informed teacher-pupil relationships. The project method, while it chiefly emphasized individual performance, also had a place for group activities. With the activity program came the educational heyday of group participation involving the imitation of adult activities in stores, post offices and the like, but largely employed as a means for motivating learning and providing practice in the traditional subjects.

However, in nearly if not all of these situations, the teacher is set off against the class. His view of the class as a kind of unit is exemplified when the teacher asks a question and then says "Class," calling for all to respond more or less in unison. The teacher is boss, though at times he would tolerate some freedom of action on the part of the children that would permit some release of tensions. Even when an "audience situation" is provided for pupils to read or recite passages they had learned, the same condition maintains. Similarly in matters of student deportment, now usually referred to as citizenship, the teacher is the interpreter of the mores of the culture for the pupils, and serves as judge, jury, and lord high executioner, all bundled into one.

In some schools, the system of student government, with a student council, ideally shifts some of the responsibility to the pupils and permits pupil interaction and group decisions. Similarly, in what is referred to as teacher-pupil planning the teacher forsakes his antithetical position and becomes an actual group member in the rôle of a resource person. It becomes clear that there has been a long period of gradual change in theory which has been followed by practice in some schools, the majority however probably trailing far behind. At any rate, it may be concluded that education is ready for a systematic overhauling of its theory and practice in dealing with the class as a group, and that it is the proper task of educational psychologists to lead the way.

CONCLUSIONS FROM RESEARCH IN GROUP DYNAMICS

First, in order to explore some of the possible directions that our inquiry might take, let us review briefly a few of the research findings that deal with group functioning and group interrelations in a wide variety of social settings. Although teachers work with groups and are daily troubled or aided by group phenomena in their classrooms, there has been strikingly little research on the dynamics of classroom groups. It is often difficult to identify and study the many forces at work in a classroom situation, but recent research in group dynamics indicates that it is possible to develop the necessary theoretical formulations, hypotheses, and measuring methods for testing these hypotheses. The task remains to identify those areas in which we feel the presence of group phenomena is most relevant to the classroom setting. We have much to learn about the forces involved in the relationships among students, and between students and teacher. Since the relationship between teacher and class-groups, for example, is by its very nature changing and flexible, it is important that the concepts employed be adequate to deal with the dynamics of relationships involving changing relationships among persons, and changing perceptions of the teacher and the class, as the members acquire new insights and learnings.

A number of assertions from recent research in group dynamics have both theoretical and practical value for the field of educational psychology and teaching methods. This list is not exhaustive and there will be no attempt to describe the nature of the studies from which these data are derived. Many of these findings are from laboratory investigations with groups, but a sufficient number of them were obtained in field-experiment settings to indicate that work of this nature can readily be done in the actual classroom setting, as well as in the laboratory. Some of these assertions are well-tested and validated. Others are less well proven. All of them have relevance and promise for educational psychology.

1. The attitudes of an individual have their anchorage in the groups to which he belongs. Present evidence makes it apparent that many attitudes can be changed more easily by making changes in certain properties of the group than by directly teaching the individuals, as individuals, even in a classroom audience situation.

2. The conduct and beliefs of pupils is regulated in large measure by the small groups within a classroom, such as friendship cliques, and the cohesive groups of students within a school. These groups demand conformity from their members to certain group standards, and the more cohesive the group, the greater is its power over the member.

3. In some instances failure to learn may be advantageously conceptualized as resistance to change, using resistance here in the same sense as the therapist uses it in his relationships with a patient.* For example, the group standards developed by persons who were learning a motor task quite similar to a previously perfected one, and who were simply told what they were to do, were entirely different from the group standards developed in a group in which the learners participated in a discussion and made group decisions about the necessity for, and the nature of, the new task to be learned. Those who participated in the discussion learned much more, more rapidly, and with much less aggression and resentment toward the persons inducing them to make this change.

4. When frustrations are met, highly cohesive groups maintain their effort in movement toward the group goal much more vigorously and effectively than do groups of low cohesiveness.

5. Groups, especially those similar to classroom groups, can be disrupted into separate cliques; or this threat of disruption can be eliminated, by the alteration of forces which determine the attractiveness of the group for the members. (For example, helping them to become aware of the strength of attraction they have for each other, or the degree to which membership in the group provides a way to achieve things they value highly.) This condition can be brought about most easily when the members become aware of the forces influencing them, but it can

---

* It should be noted, however, that failure to change may be due to such "resistance." There may be an inadequate set, unsatisfactory motivation, inability to comply with the demands of the goal or a rational non-acceptance of a new position.

also be effected by an outsider, such as a teacher, who adroitly helps the group to change the impact and strength of these forces surrounding and within their group.

6. The training of persons for effective social action such as performance in school or civic service, can lead to greater effectiveness of effort by the trainees if they are members of a group which is being trained to work as a group, than will result if they are merely individuals in an audience situation.

7. The amount of interaction among students in a class is determined in part by group factors. For example, in highly cohesive groups arriving at a decision that has general approval, the person whose viewpoint is too different from that of the rest will be rejected—that is, ignored. In a less well knit group, in which the discussion is not directed to a group decision, the deviate member is likely to get more comments directed to him than the person whose ideas are quite similar to those of the rest of the group.

8. When the members see themselves competing for their own individual goals which make coöperative effort impossible, there is disruption of the ready communication of ideas, the coördination of efforts and the friendliness and pride in one's group which are basic to class harmony and effectiveness. The competitive grading system commonly used today is an illustration in that it creates mutually exclusive goals among the members of a class group.

9. The group climate or style of group life can have an important influence on the members' personalities. One such style of group life can develop hostile, obedient, uncreative, 'goldbrickers'; another can produce confused, purposeless, competitive, drifters; and still another can mould coöperative, flexible, purposeful, turn-taking, we-spirited persons. The group climate that produces such effects is created by the resultant of a number of group properties which can be combined in various ways, among which are the leadership style of the teacher or that of those who function most as group leaders, the degree of cohesiveness, which has already been mentioned, the group-member-skills, the suitability of the group process for the task in hand, the techniques employed by the teacher to satisfy his ego and other needs, and the tension-release patterns used by the group.

10. The reasons for the occasional failure of project methods, and other teaching procedures which depend upon effectively functioning groups often lie in the ineffective use of group problem-solving methods, or in the unskillful handling of group procedures. Groups can help themselves to mature and improve their ability as a learning or producing team by diagnosing their own failures and planning ways of repairing their own deficiencies. Students of group development have devoted much attention to methods of group diagnosis, ways of presenting the findings to a group, and methods for alleviating a group's procedural difficulties.

11. Certain forms of classroom behavior may be recognized as mechanisms developed for relieving tensions somewhat similar to those employed by an individual in relieving his tensions. For example, they employ patterns of group

behavior which help avoid difficult tasks or unpleasant situations. These mechanisms are often difficult to identify since they may either be wrongly perceived by the teacher as signs that the group is keeping busy, or they may be accepted as the usual troubles one gets into by the use of committee methods.

12. Difficulties in the transfer of verbal learning to social behavior can often be overcome by the use of that form of rôle-playing referred to as reality practice, in which the participants try-out the behavior they are expected to use in a situation from which all threat has been removed. Inhibition blindnesses, or fears of 'learning' certain content, or behaving in unaccustomed ways can be removed by the use of a 'cultural-island,' a situation where new group standards are generated while away from the source of the inhibitions. This procedure is effectively used in excursions, conferences, summer camps, and other group activities in which the person is under the pressure of group standards that are different from those at home, and so he dares to adopt forms of behavior which might be quite desirable for him, but which he might hesitate to try out in his accustomed environment for fear of adverse criticism.

Thus we can safely accept the view that group phenomena definitely affect the progress of learning, as well as the kind of learning that takes place. The educational significance of this view derives from the fact that the pupil's attitudes as well as his behavior patterns are modifiable. Increased motivation in participating in the classroom activities, and consequently in learning, derives from several different potential sources in a group atmosphere where good mental hygiene prevails.

Three such potential sources of increased motivation will be considered. The first of these sources lies in method of *goal determination*—the extent to which the goals of the class are determined by the entire group including both pupils and teachers, in a truly co-participant sense. When this procedure is followed, the child will feel that he has some control over his own destiny and, therefore, is able to accept the group goals which he helped select as being his own personal goals. They are things which he himself wants to do and, therefore, he is more likely to follow through on them. The absence of such codetermined objectives does not mean the absence of group standards, but some of these standards are not likely to be the ones which the teacher would choose, or the ones which best promote learning. Such group standards as the 'gentlemen's mark' of C, and the group rejection of the student who is too 'eager,' are familiar to all. Thus group standards in a classroom may inhibit good learning as well as accelerate it.

The second source of increased motivation lies in the extent to which the teachers and the pupils build a *supportive atmosphere* in the classroom, one which helps each child to realize that he is an accepted group member. When this condition maintains, each child has his own 'area of freedom,' within which he is free to make his own decisions. This area can often be much wider than is ordinarily supposed by teachers who are constantly making pupils' decisions for them. Although the group may not approve of everything a pupil does, it still accepts him as a person. In this kind of an atmosphere the child is able to develop a greater feeling of security with his fellows. In addition—and this is the important contribution to learning—he is likely to feel freed from personal threat and criticism and, therefore, more willing to go ahead and try new things without fear, realizing that if he fails he will not be rejected either by the class or by the teacher. Thus failure can be a very positive learning experience because, once the emotional threat is removed, the child can look at his abilities and limitations far more objectively and with greater awareness of what next steps are required for his learning. It would seem that little learning can occur if the child is denied positive opportunities to make errors.

A third potential source of increased motivation lies in the extent to which the various members of the class are accepted as *participating members*. When they are so accepted, each can benefit from the knowledge, skills, and abilities of all the other members. They are no longer dependent primarily or solely on the teacher for all information and guidance. Besides offering the possibility of the development of broader understandings, this gives to each pupil the opportunity to be a contributor to the group, and the classroom becomes, then, a situation for mutual exchange, for mutual sharing. Research is beginning to show the increased productivity of groups which have this coöperative pattern of relationship. Goal determining by the group, a supportive atmosphere, and a participating membership, then constitute three conditions of group organization of great effectiveness in developing motivation which contribute to the promotion of effective learning.

THE RÔLES OF A TEACHER

What can the teacher do to develop and maintain these conditions conducive to learning? There are three fundamental rôles which cover the things a teacher does. Actually these are not discrete parts of the teacher's job, but they do carry quite different implications. The rôles that will be discussed are the following: (1) the instructional rôle, (2) the rôle of the democratic strategist, and (3) the rôle of the therapist. Following this, we will ask how the teacher selects the proper rôle, and how the actual operation of this rôle can be evaluated.

First, the *instruction rôle*. It is obvious that the concept of what a teacher should do has changed over the years. To the Hoosier schoolmaster the matter was quite simple. He was the drill sergeant. The cadence of recitation was akin to the sound of marching feet. As master of the drill, he called the steps. This teacher also held the rôle of academic authority; not only did he choose the school experiences, but he was also revered for his great storehouse of information. His very person was the embodiment of learning, and he was categorically right. This fundamental instructional rôle has mellowed with the years. Now the teacher does not always have to know. He operates as an adult with superior learning to be sure, but serves more as a resource person explaining, telling, and demonstrating. His drill-master's uniform has been exchanged for the

Socratic garb, for his instruction is more concerned with fostering the students' power to think and reason. This major 'informational rôle' of the teacher is often discussed and is perhaps quite well understood. But it should be clear that this rôle itself is not exclusively the property of the teacher. At times, especially as the content of the course falls within the experience of the students, the class members share or take over the instructional rôle. As we come to understand more about the dynamics of the classroom, we realize that the way in which this rôle is handled by the teacher has important effects on the total learning situation.

A second major rôle which the teacher must play is that of democratic strategist. This has been discussed by other writers under the heading of "group formation." With the goal of pupil participation the teacher must provide the occasion for the introduction of processes to facilitate teacher-pupil planning. To play this rôle successfully two things are required: a high regard for democratic values, and their implications, and a high level of psychological insight into group factors and individual personality. In the rôle of a democratic strategist, the teacher helps the group utilize various methods of progress evaluation, and the information about their progress which they secure. He further helps them see and clarify their accomplishments, blocks, and failures, as well as the values in democratic group action. Thus the task is more than that of being merely an exponent of democratic education. This rôle becomes one of activating democratic processes by helping the class to experience democratic goals and relationships in the design of their everyday classroom experiences.

Understanding the dynamic forces which are affecting the class as a group and those which the techniques bring into play makes possible a contribution to democratic learning because our democratic ethics have established the educational goals and values. Techniques are selected in terms of their potentiality for contributing to the democratic goals of the group at the particular time. It should be pointed out that on the basis of a different set of ethics for the same conditions in a group, different techniques would be selected in order to achieve the goals determined by these differing ethics. However, since it is a contribution toward democratic learning that is desired, it is essential that teachers become as skilled as possible in understanding and working with their classroom groups. For a lack of such skill is likely to result in conditions which are quite the opposite of democratic, even though democratic techniques were supposedly being used. Democratic techniques do not exist *per se;* a technique is democratic only to the extent that it serves as a means to help the group achieve its democratic goals at a particular time. For example, the democratic technique of voting has been used as a very effective method of imposing some small minority opinion on the group.

A third important rôle of the teacher can be subsumed under the title of therapist—a combination of clinician and group worker. Lest someone remonstrate at this obligation, let him be reminded that, willingly or not, every teacher plays this rôle. Sometimes it is somewhat separate from other functions, but

more often it is embedded in the classroom life while other functions predominate. No teacher avoids being a group worker, although some are more successful
than others and some do crude jobs to be sure. The rôle of therapist implies
group management to the end of helping all of the children toward individual
and social adjustment. This means a degree of permissiveness, the establishment
of rapport with each child, and the conduct of the work without the teacher's
ego becoming involved. Such masterful, objective, 'impersonal' human relationships are hard to come by. No one person is able to meet the differential needs
of thirty-five or more children and serve as a cushion to soften the blows of
harsh reality dealt out by the child's peer culture. But one tries. To do this the
teacher must so act as to be the implicit embodiment of an acceptable code of
behavior. Time and time again the mores of mental hygiene are illustrated as
the teacher relates to the children, to their feelings and to their problems.

It is through the supportive atmosphere previously discussed that the teachers' therapeutic work is carried on. In a conflict situation pupils may come to
the teacher as a judge or decision maker. The case need not be handled arbitrarily, but it must be handled. Teachers can never be neutrals but are continually interpreting 'the law' as it applies in individual cases. In the therapist
rôle, the teacher shares insights concerning human behavior, helps to get at
causes of conflict and to find methods of resolving it. Sometimes the teacher
serves this end by just being a friend, or he may provide, or himself be, an
example with whom the child can identify in the Freudian sense. At any rate,
the teacher must be an expert in human relations, understanding both the group
and the individual.

In general teachers play this rôle least adequately of all. They tend toward
being moralists, policemen, or punitive agents expecting good character to be
developed by decree. While we have much to learn in applying the therapist
rôle to the teacher, we already understand enough to know that such a playing
of the rôle spells failure. The reason for such failure may often be that the
teacher, having personal needs, tends to exploit the situation to satisfy these
needs. We have in mind the need to be loved, the desire to avoid conflict, or
pressures from latent hostility as examples. A very common attitude is the desire
for dependency, where the teacher is happy if the students remain attached
and dependent. Redl has written a very interesting paper approaching this from
a slightly different angle in which he shows how teachers tend to orient the
whole atmosphere so that it plays into a masochistic or sadistic syndrome, to
take only two examples. This is a complicated study in depth psychology,
fraught with controversy. But it is not without point to us.

SITUATION AND CHOICE OF RÔLE

From the point of view we have been discussing, it will be seen that there is no
single complex of rôles a teacher plays. The different legitimate objectives of a
classroom demand different emphases. Certainly groups of children differ in

their leadership qualities, and other individual and group factors need to be studied and understood. The question the teacher would then ask is: "What technique will contribute most effectively, in terms of the dynamics of my class at this time, to the goals and values which are held by the class (or myself, depending on who determines the goals)?" Two things are needed in selecting the techniques: (1) a knowledge of the dynamics of the technique itself, and (2) a knowledge of the goals and values of the group.

Knowledge about groups will help materially in gaining an understanding of the dynamics of a particular technique, and of the kinds of forces in the group which it brings into play in a positive (or negative) manner under speci- fied conditions. To know these dynamics is important. Otherwise the teacher may fall into the trap of thinking that certain techniques are 'good' *per se*, for- getting that a technique will contribute to the group only as it is able to draw on the positive forces present in the group at the time. If the condition of the group is different at a particular time, the 'good' technique may bring out all that is 'bad' in the group, causing him to wonder why it didn't work, or to blame the group for 'not coöperating.'

SOME TYPICAL CUES
FOR RÔLE CHANGES

How is it possible to determine which rôle to play at a particular time? What are the characteristics of a group which will serve as cues for shifting rôles? One such cue is group 'apathy.' If the group is lethargic and passive, one must start searching for reasons. Is it the course content? The teaching methods? A general atmosphere of repression? Children who do not become boisterous at times are living under the control of teachers who are misers of freedom.

Another cue is to be found in the rapidity of 'spread of disorder.' In a group with adequate morale and goal involvement, disturbances do not spread easily. If one child upsets the room, individual work with that child is, of course, in- dicated. But more important is the signal it gives about the group condition. If a 'bad actor' is a source of rapid contagion, the bond of common purpose must be weak indeed. This condition may be caused by such a simple thing as the need for a change of activity due to a requirement for overlong attention to a specific task. It may be a tension for muscle discharge, or it may go far beyond this to a fundamental dissatisfaction with the teacher behavior.

Other cues for further diagnosis and rôle modification include the presence of isolates, cliques, scapegoating, exclusiveness, extreme competitiveness, and the like. How much do teachers know about diagnosing these things? Indeed, how much help can educational psychologists give? Once the teacher really under- stands the situation and appreciates its deeper aspects, the rôle complex to meet the situation can usually be found. The task of the educational psychologist is to see that teachers are so trained that they will understand the dynamics of that situation.

Understanding more about the dynamics of groups helps the teacher in a variety of ways toward increasing his effectiveness in the rôles that are appropriate in different situations. As more is learned about the theory and research on groups, new ways of thinking about the classroom situation will at first be gained, ways which may have been overlooked before. The importance of effective communications will come to be recognized in giving instructions and in expressing ideas. The relationships between the various pupils in the class will be studied, how they feel about each other, and the leader-group relationships, and gradually the teacher will become aware of his own behavior in the class and the kinds of effect it has on the pupils.

Of course, it is not easy to take one's knowledge into the classroom and become immediately aware of these complex interrelationships. Often it takes considerable training in observation and experience to be able to see, espcially at the time it is happening, what is occurring in the group and what its causal relationships and potential effects are. The transition from 'book learning' to 'observation skill' is a difficult one to make, but it must be made if knowledge about groups is to contribute to teaching effectiveness.

EVALUATION

How does one know one has effectively employed the correct rôle? Were the results in the true psychological sense, those which were described? Was there progress by the individual or the class in the direction of the goals which had been established, and was this progress as great as it might have been if some other teacher rôle had been used, or if this present rôle had been carried through more effectively? And were the dynamics of group relationships improved as a result of this particular rôle? Is the class in the 'healthier' condition and more ready to take forward steps toward whatever new goals may be established, or have they achieved some of their important goals at great cost to themselves and to their interrelations in the group?

Information about these questions can come from different sources. The teacher, by employing the same sensitivity and observational skill used in individual diagnosis of pupil difficulties will become accustomed to diagnosing the group. An examination of the condition of the group will be an examination, at least in part, of the way in which the rôle previously employed affected the group and their response to it. Diagnosis and evaluation, then, go hand-in-hand as a continuing process for the teacher. Evaluation of a previous step, in a large measure, provides the cues for the next step, and for the choice of the rôle to be employed.

Of course, the teacher is not the only source of evaluation data in the classroom. To overlook the students' contributions is to disregard not only a most important source of information, but it is to deny the students the opportunity of evaluating their experience in the class which is the basis for making decisions to improve themselves as individuals and as class members for future work. It is not an easy task, obviously, to carry through an effective evaluation as a group, but the process may be a most valuable educational experience for all.

A third source of evaluation data depends on the availability of outside persons who could be called into the classroom as observers. Someone who is not himself involved in the group is often able to note many important situations which the person who is trying to carry through an effective teaching job almost necessarily overlooks. The outside observer—whether he be a supervisor, principal, fellow teacher, or trained clinician—can note these situations. And to the extent that he has the personal skill in his relationships with those individuals to discuss his observations with the teacher freely and acceptingly, he can be of service in increasing the teacher's own skill in the classroom. He may also take the next step and open his insights to the group as a whole, helping them to see and comprehend more fully the processes of group interaction.

46 The organization of the elementary school and the development of personality

Related selections: 45, 47, 53

Organizational structure, established to facilitate the administrative function, has a way of assuming a sanctity and vested position that tend to obscure the very process that is being administered. In the public schools many illustrations of this phenomenon may be found; for example, the influence of the Carnegie unit on the high school program. In the elementary school certain organizational practices do not seem to agree with what we know about personality development and learning. In the article below, Dr. Heffernan and her colleagues critically examine the elementary school structure in the light of the educational goal—"for every child a healthy personality." Although this article was written more than a decade ago, the organizational questions raised are the very ones for which answers are being sought today.

HELEN HEFFERNAN et al., "The Organization of the Elementary School and the Development of Personality," *California Journal of Elementary Education*, XX (February, 1952), 129–53. Reprinted by permission of the publisher.

MISS HEFFERNAN (1896–) is Chief, Bureau of Elementary Education, California State Department of Education.

"For every child a healthy personality," the theme of the Mid-Century White House Conference on Children and Youth, emphasized an important goal of education. One session of the 1951 California Conference of Elementary School Principals and District Superintendents of Schools was devoted to evaluating elementary school practices in relation to this goal. The practices evaluated were presented by the elementary education staff of the State Department of Education. The staff, basing its judgment on research and experience, chose for presentation the elementary school practices indicated by the following questions:

1. Does the practice of grade placement assure pupils opportunities to develop healthy personalities?
2. Does the departmental teaching in the elementary school offer opportunities for pupils to develop healthy personalities?
3. Do current practices in reporting pupil progress to parents tend to give pupils good opportunities to develop healthy personalities?
4. Does the maintenance of grade standards assure opportunities for pupils to develop healthy personalities?
5. Does an articulated program of instruction provide superior opportunities for pupils to develop healthy personalities?

No brief was held for the selection of these questions in preference to others, but the staff believed that the questions cover areas that are of concern to every principal and teacher who sees in healthy personality development the major purpose of modern child-rearing.

A HEALTHY PERSONALITY

Before approaching the problems set by the questions, common ground was sought for the meaning of the term "healthy personality." The concept of personality that was expressed during the White House Conference gave significant emphasis to the qualitative aspects of human relations and indicated that everyone who works in the service of children must take *children's feelings* into account. This way of looking at children leads inevitably to the conclusion that demeaning poverty, inadequate school and health services, and racial or ethnical discrimination not only are in and of themselves handicapping to children but also constitute a denial of the democratic ideal that every person is of precious and equal worth. As Allison Davis pointed out, these are serious considerations in a country which at this moment urgently needs all the skilled people it can get. More than 60 out of every 100 children in the United States live in families of low socioeconomic status. The ability represented in this large group of children is largely undiscovered and unused.

To be sure, emotional ill health may have many causes. Inadequate food and housing, racial discrimination, physiological malfunctioning, lack of guidance toward sound life values, and lack of love and affection of parents are all part of the pattern which may disturb or obstruct well-balanced development in children. The problem in the elementary school is to determine ways to be sure that none of its practices constitute hazards to sound development.

The origin of the word "personality" is interesting. The word comes from the Greek *persona* or "mask," something which an actor puts on to conceal his true identity. Many advertisers seem to use the word in somewhat the same sense—the "man of distinction" becomes associated with a commodity available in bottles; an irresistible epidermis can be attained by liberal applications of a gooey substance in a tube or jar; social acceptability is somehow connected with the advertiser's toothpaste or deodorant.

But these were not the meanings of "personality" basic to the White House Conference. Rather, the philosopher, the psychologist, the physiologist, the sociologist, the psychiatrist pooled their ideas and came out with another meaning of personality. They said, "By personality we mean the thinking, feeling, acting human being, who conceives of himself as an individual separate from other individuals. The human being does not have a personality; he is a personality."

What then are the components of a healthy personality? These components, said Erikson, are the sense of trust, the sense of autonomy, the sense of initiative, the sense of accomplishment, the sense of identity, the sense of intimacy, the parental sense, and the sense of integrity. These components will bear elaboration as bases for consideration of the organization of the elementary school.

The sense of trust

The first component of the healthy personality is the sense of trust. Trust can exist only in relation to something. The baby begins at an early age to develop the sense of trust as he learns that there are adults in this world who will relieve his hunger, provide for his physical comfort, and give him the affection he needs. Infants that are brought up in institutions in which the environments are unfavorable to their emotional stability show by listlessness, emaciation, pallor, immobility, unresponsiveness, poor appetite, poor digestion, and a wide variety of evidences of unhappiness that their experiences have not led them to develop a sense of trust. Fortunately most infants in our society find the comfort and affection that are essential to a developing sense of trust. Both nature and culture are conducive toward making mothers motherly at the very time the child's personality is in need of the nurture which develops this basic component of the healthy personality.

The sense of autonomy

Next in chronological order of development is the sense of independence or autonomy. The second and third years of life are roughly the beginning of the individual's struggle to establish himself as a human being with a mind and will of his own. The young child must experience over and over that he is a person who is permitted to make choices. Personal autonomy is an outstanding feature of the American way of life. Every red-blooded American resents being bossed, being pushed around; he maintains vigorously that everyone has a right to express himself, has a right to control his own affairs. The American people want each child to grow up to be the upstanding, look-you-in-the-eye kind of individual. That is the type of person Americans admire.

Although the beginnings of this sense of autonomy are important in the early years of life, independence is not established once and for all time any more than is the sense of trust. The period during which these components of personality first emerge is crucial, but if we want youngsters to emerge into adulthood with healthy personalities, we must continue to nurture their sense of trust, respect their desire to assert themselves, help them learn to hold their desire for independence within bounds, and avoid treating them in ways to arouse any doubts in themselves or feelings of shame in connection with their accomplishments.

A sense of initiative

At four or five years of age, the young child wants to find out what kind of a person he can be. He watches the activities of adults about him; he recreates their activities in his play and yearns to share in their activities. It is important for the child's developing personality that much encouragement be given to the enterprise and imagination which characterize these years. The child is ready and avid to learn. This sense of initiative must be constantly fostered. If it is restricted, resentment and bitterness and a vindictive attitude toward the world may develop as a functioning part of the child's personality.

A sense of accomplishment

If during the early years of life a child has developed the sense of trust, the sense of autonomy, and the sense of initiative, we may expect when he is about six years of age to see the beginning of great development of the sense of accomplishment. While this sense is developing, a child wants to engage in real tasks that he can carry through to completion. After a period of time characterized by exuberant imagination, a child then wants to settle down to learning exactly how to do things and how to do them well. Much of this period of a child's life is spent in the elementary school. Under reasonably favorable circumstances, this is a period of calm, steady growth, especially if the problems of the previous stages have been well worked out. Although this is a rather unspectacular period in human growth, it is an important period, for during it there is laid the basis for responsible citizenship. And during this period children acquire knowledge and skills that make for good workmanship, the ability to coöperate and to play fair, and otherwise to follow the rules of the larger social game.

The chief danger a child may encounter during this period is the presence of conditions which may lead to a sense of inadequacy and inferiority. If in the home or school too much is expected of a child, or if a child is made to feel that achievement is beyond his ability, he may lapse into discouragement and lack of interest. It is important, therefore, that children have a feeling of successful accomplishment in connection with their school work. Studies of delinquent children frequently show that they hated school—hated it because they were marked as stupid, awkward, and not able to do so well as other children. Children who accept their inferiority passively are perhaps more damaged psychologically than those who react aggressively to frustrating experience.

A sense of identity

At the onset of adolescence an individual begins to seek clarification of his concept of who he is and what his role in society is to be. During this period a youth is preoccupied with his appearance in the eyes of others—particularly his peers. If the course of personality development has been healthy up to this period, the young person will have acquired a reasonable feeling of self-esteem which will carry him through the tensions and strains that are biologically or culturally imposed on adolescents.

A sense of intimacy

Only if the young person has acquired a sense of identity can he achieve the next component of a healthy personality in his relation to others—a sense of intimacy. The surer the young person is of himself, the more successfully can he enter into relations of friendship, love, and inspiration.

The parental sense

In its broadest meaning, the parental sense involves the qualities of creativity and productivity. As the individual advances into adulthood, this sense develops normally if the preceding steps have been achieved with reasonable success.

The sense of integrity

The final component of a healthy personality is the sense of integrity. Throughout the child's development, his home and school have been helping him to accept the dominant ideals of the culture—honor, courage, purity, grace, fairness, self-discipline. These are the core of integration of the healthy personality. The acquisition of these values and ideals is the ultimate goal of American culture.

With this abbreviation of the background concepts that the White House Conference used as a guide, present practices in elementary education may be examined to determine whether or not they contribute to healthy personality development.

THE EFFECT OF GRADE STANDARDS

Do grade standards contribute to the development of a healthy personality? Is the development of a healthy personality extended by a classification of pupils based on rigid grade standards? For those who accept the findings of research regarding individual differences, the answer is "No." Would healthy personality growth be furthered if the organization of the school provided a program of continuous learning and advancement in accordance with the growth patterns of individuals?

Research clearly indicates that the personality development of a child may be greatly affected by the maintenance of formal grade standards. Successful accomplishment gives the child confidence in himself, while retardation or assignment to slower groups tends to destroy the child's sense of personal worth and to cause him to have feelings of frustration. Rigid grade standards cannot be met by all members of any class. To the child with strong academic interest and ability, who succeeds almost effortlessly in school, the grade standard has no threatening consequences. To the child whose limitations are greater than average, the grade standard constantly threatens defeat and thereby prevents wholesome personality growth.

Grade standards originated as an administrative device and not as an answer to the question, What is best for the child? Can we justify the continuance of rigid grade standards as a basis for classifying pupils? Fixed grade standards are untenable in the light of what is now known about the best ways to meet the needs of children. A plan for continuous growth is widely recognized as more desirable than the experience of annual evaluation followed by promotion or nonpromotion. Learning is continuous and must progress according to individual rate and ability. Schools cannot, therefore, justify the continuance of annual promotion or retardation as sound practice.

An adult can never fully know how a child feels about failure unless the adult has experienced such failure. Were you ever failed? Who knew that you failed? Did you lose status with your mother or your father, with big brother or sister? Children have feelings about failure even though some teachers say that children do not mind failure. How would you cover it up if you failed in your job? The hurt is deep, it must be hidden. To carry on, one must appear indifferent. Children are courageous. They are helpless in the face of adult decisions—decisions which so irrevocably affect their personality growth.

Can each of thirty-five children, all nine years old, make the third-grade standard on May 26? Can each of the thirty-five youths, fourteen years old, be expected to pass the *same test* in United States history for graduation from the eighth grade? Can thirty-five children, six years old, each read all the same pre-primers, primers, and first readers? Roma Gans in her book, *Reading is Fun*, says that "perhaps no subject has been taught with greater disregard for child development than has reading." The eyes of all six-year-old children do not focus well; the children may not speak in complete sentences; their family may speak Spanish at home; Dad may have gone to Korea and Mother may be working. Are children in each of these circumstances equally ready to read?

Statistics show that teachers fail over one-seventh of the children in their classes. Are teachers aware that under such circumstances it is the school that has failed? Grade standards for subject and skill mastery do not promote the development of healthy personalities. Yet there appears to be something compulsive about the desire of teachers and school authorities to make all children alike even though they know that each child differs from all other children.

A basic democratic principle is violated when the school fails to recognize the worth of the individual. The educational principle of individual differences is widely accepted. Equally widely accepted is the knowledge that learning is an individual, not a mass, accomplishment. More than twenty-five years ago psychologists publicized information about individual rates of development, abilities, interests, and needs. For many years William Heard Kilpatrick has directed our attention to the fact that a child learns what he lives. If the child is to learn democracy, teachers and principals must make the school environment such that he lives democratically and successfully in accordance with his potentialities. Success motivates, failure frustrates children.

The child as a whole must be accepted. Intelligence, which is measurable to a degree, is but one of the factors which the child brings to the learning situation. To a high degree, ability to learn is conditioned by emotions, health, and past experiences as well as by native mental ability. Teachers must help children to grow, not attempt to force them nor to drive them down standardized roads to learning through slavish attention to the same book. Children must be helped to know themselves, and to build their destinies in terms of their strengths. No one ever had his personality developed by constant emphasis on his weaknesses. Since individuals are different, fixed standards are not conducive to healthy growth. In a flexible program, differentiated materials and opportunities permit each child to explore and experiment, to figure, to discuss, to share and collect, and to find answers at a rate that is commensurate with his ability and interest.

When individuals have purpose they can master arithmetic combinations, learn to write a business letter, and read for information material adapted to their level of achievement. They will move steadily ahead, even though they may move slowly. When the child knows his needs, knows the next steps to be undertaken, and has had a part in planning how to attain his objectives, he is ready to learn. Interest motivates the child to put forth effort. Opportunities for continuous growth are challenging and stimulating to him. Attempts to force learning are not only unnecessary, but they are also futile unless the child is responding to inner drives of interest which encourage him to put forth effort.

Education to meet the needs of all children includes education to help parents understand their children and their children's problems. Parents must be helped to understand that there are some things that the school cannot do for children. Leaders in education to whom parents rightfully turn for information and guidance must help parents to understand individual differences and to accept their child and to love him as he is, even if he is a slow learner. Parents must know that the school cannot teach the child to read before he is ready and that no amount of effort to do so will produce the results desired. And parents must know that attempting to force a child toward masery of a skill, before he is capable, produces frustration and delays learning. Schools must prevent frustrations, emphasize prevention, and do away with the need for remedying problems that they have created. Parents must realize that each child is unique; that his rate of learning, his ability, experiential background, health, and emotions strongly influence his learning. The individual's ability to learn differs from that of others as does his personal appearance or physical strength. Teachers must be honest and straightforward but kindly and understanding as they seek the help of parents. Parents and school people must become a team that believes in and supports each child.

Expediency should never be the basis for determining the treatment that a child shall be accorded. Democratic philosophy emphasizes the sanctity of individual personality. Change requires effort. When principals and teachers become dissatisfied with preesnt practices in education they will willingly put forth the effort necessary to find improved ways of helping children. If inflexible grade standards do not meet individual differences or provide for continuous learning, schools must find better ways to do these things. The task of schools is to build, not to destroy, personalities. Each child must be accepted as he is, where he is, and provided with opportunities for continuous growth. Democracy needs confident, healthy personalities. Schools must modify practices so that during each day each child has satisfying opportunities for growth toward the realization of his individual potentialities.

DEPARTMENTALIZATION AND PERSONALITY DEVELOPMENT

As part of the major topic—"Does the organization of the elementary school contribute to the development of a healthy personality?"—one subtopic to be considered is the following: "Does departmentalization of the elementary school or departmental teaching in the elementary school contribute to the development of a healthy personality?"

By departmentalization or departmental teaching we mean the type of organization in which a group of children has a different teacher for instruction in each subject or in a combination of subjects.

We will agree that any type of organization has advantages and disadvantages. Before a principal and a faculty adopt a program of departmentalization, they should weigh the advantages and disadvantages of such an organization in terms of the wholesome personality development of children.

Departmentalization has its roots in tradition. In the development of schools in our country there came into prominence, particularly in New England toward the close of the eighteenth century, the type of school organization known as the "departmental school." The chief characteristic of the departmental school was the vertical division of the course into a reading school and a writing school. Although the two departments were housed in the same building, each of them had its own master, its own room, its own set of studies. The pupils attended each department in turn, changing from one to the other at the end of each half-day session. This type of organization appeared to further the purposes for which schools were maintained at that time.

Another quick look at the organization of elementary schools in our country reveals that departmentalization passed out of the picture during the nineteenth century but was reintroduced in the New York City schools, particularly in the upper grades, in 1900. Various types of departmentalization were introduced into elementary schools during the next twenty years. During this period the "platoon school" reached full development.

The various types of organization in existence in the twenties and thirties gave rise to extensive research relative to the values of different types of organization. The chief claim of the advocates of departmentalization was in terms of better achievement in understanding subject matter. The advocates of the platoon school were the most ardent supporters of departmentalization. The studies which were made to evaluate the platoon school and various types of departmentalization failed to show unquestioned superiority of that form of organization in teaching subject matter. The research of such men as Stewart, Gerberich, Prall, Spain, Shepard, Courtis, and Bonser supports this statement.

It would appear from the research evidence this group made available that by the early thirties departmentalization had ceased to grow. But the tendency at the present time for certain elementary schools to reintroduce departmentalization, especially in the seventh and eighth grades, makes it appear that the facts pertaining to departmentalization have to be rediscovered by each generation of educators.

Let us look, then, at the advantages and disadvantages of departmentalization. As we consider the purposes of schools in a democratic society, the objectives of education, the needs of boys and girls, and the ways of learning that are psychologically sound and conducive to wholesome personality development as the basis for analyzing departmental organization, there appear the following disadvantages in departmental organization:

1. It organizes learning experiences in terms of areas of subject matter.
2. It distintegrates rather than integrates learning experiences.
3. It separates the tool subjects from the activities in which the tools are used.
4. It fails to utilize ways of learning that are psychologically sound.
5. It interrupts continuity and destroys the relatedness of learning experiences.

6. It requires a teacher to meet an exceedingly large number of children each day; thus no teacher knows each child well enough to perform important guidance functions.
7. It results in the situation where a number of teachers make demands upon one pupil.
8. It requires a rigid schedule, which interrupts activities and thus prevents purposes from being realized and interests satisfied.

The scales are heavily weighted against departmentalization. Except in a few instances, departmentalization appears to be unjustified in the first six grades of the elementary schools. Departmentalization might be justified in those rare instances in which certain teachers are unable to instruct pupils in such specialized areas as music and art.

In the seventh and eighth grades some departmentalization may be justified in the organization of learning experiences for young adolescents only if it permits these youth to satisfy their special interests and develop their abilities in such areas as art, music, physical education, and science. If a departmental organization making these provisions is used, it should permit the child to spend at least half his school time with one teacher. The social studies should constitute the core of his learning experiences. The social studies, language arts, science, and mathematics should be integrated in his learning experiences.

REPORTING PUPIL
PROGRESS TO PARENTS

The answers to the question: "Do current practices in reporting pupil progress to parents contribute to the development of a healthy personality?" is "No," if the practice involves sending home at regular intervals one of several varieties of what have been called "nasty little status cards" as the sole means of acquainting parents with the social and academic progress of their children.

Analyze a few of the cards used to report pupil progress. The fairly innocuous one sometimes given to children in the kindergarten asks the teacher to respond to two items: (1) "He does his best," and (2) "He could do better." Perhaps the child is marked: "Does his best." Why? Does the teacher like the child? Does the family see that his physical and emotional needs are being adequately met? Do the school and the home work well together? He may be marked: "Could do better." Why he could do better is left out. Could he do better if his tonsils were out, if his mother prepared more nourishing meals, if he felt better about the new baby, if his mother and father got along without quarreling, if his father were home from the army, if the teacher gave him more chances to succeed, if the experiences of the school were closer to his out-of-school experiences and made sense to him?

The unanswered questions that arise in the minds of many parents as they read such a report cause them to lose confidence in the school program and to develop a feeling of separation from activities of the classroom. Such reports make it difficult for attitudes of confidence to develop between home and school.

In discussing another type of report card, one that is marked S and U, a mother remarked that these report cards were "U" to her. In one case a child received a U in physical education although both the parents and the teacher knew that the child's flat feet prevented him from running and playing games as well as the other children. On being questioned about this mark, the teacher said: "I couldn't give Tommy an S because it is apparent that he can't play the same games other children play. It wouldn't be fair to the others or keep up the standards. Besides, the children know that he doesn't play as well as they do. You can't fool them." And so a child is marked down for having a physical defect and is made to feel even more inadequate.

Another type of marking employs a series of numbers or letters—1, 2, 3, 4, or A, B, C, D, and F. One of the arguments for this kind of marks on a report card is that they are "so definite." Great importance is often given to the value of retaining the "F." The argument for it is that failure occurs in life and, therefore, children must be habituated early to experiences of failure. People holding this position are saying in effect that lessons in failure must begin when one is young and must be continuous; otherwise—to carry out this thought —the strength of the human spirit might triumph and a nonreader might grow up to think he amounts to something.

"A" marks may be bad for a child, too. They may cause him to have feelings of smugness or an exaggerated sense of intellectual power when he is only being rewarded for natural ability, docility, or skill in pleasing the teacher.

Marks are meaningless and unreliable. Try a little experiment to prove this fact to yourself. Mark a set of papers as efficiently as you know how. Put them away for three months. Mark them again. Compare the two sets of marks. The testimony in your own handwriting will be convincing.

Unreliable measures of achievement encourage destructive competition. Yet the evidence is clear that competitive systems are not effective in stimulating effort toward the attainment of desirable goals. A child who has done well feels that he has failed because someone else has surpassed him. Another child may be proud of mediocre achievement if he is ahead of others, and thus the levels of aspiration are lowered for both children.

Report cards on which a marking system is used do not contribute to the development of healthy personality. Their evil effect may be minimized by many factors; teachers who realize the harm which competitive and comparative marks do may mark accordingly, or strong feelings of friendliness and confidence between home and school may exist in spite of report cards only because both discount the importance of the report card.

Reporting to parents can be a positive factor in building mental health if parents are informed of their child's growth through frequent conferences with the child's teacher. In order to make these conferences successful, teachers should be given time within the school day for conducting them.

The 1950 yearbook of the Association for Supervision and Curriculum Development, *Fostering Mental Health in Our Schools,* will prove helpful to teachers conducting conferences with parents. The section on developmental tasks is especially useful. Clerical assistance in the typing of anecdotal records, in the preparation of cumulative records, and in preparing reports of conferences should also be available to teachers.

An important part of any parent-teacher conference should be the development of a plan of action outlining the next step in learning. A parent and teacher sit down together to consider the total development of the child, his strength, his weaknesses, and how home and school can best help him. A record should be made of the simple steps which parents and teacher plan to take to help the child. A part of such a record might read as follows:

THE PARENT'S PLAN

Mr. Jones will play ball with Jerry after school so that he will learn to catch better and will be willing to play with the other children. Mrs. Jones will invite small groups of children to play with Jerry after school so that he will not be alone so much. Billy was suggested as a good child to be included in this group.

Now that Mrs. Jones is busy with the new baby, she realizes that Jerry may be feeling rejected and left out; so she is planning to have her mother give him some special attention by taking him on trips and entertaining him. She also realizes that he needs to have some responsibility for the care of his little brother.

THE TEACHER'S PLAN

I will see that Jerry gets some playground success. I will also give him some special attention in the room. He might have charge of the hall exhibit box for the rest of the term.

What does this tell a teacher who may have the child the following year? This program for action indicates to the discerning teacher that Jerry has been feeling insecure because of a new baby brother in the family, that he needs more attention from adults, that he should develop playground skill, and that home and school share responsibility for helping him.

This child might have had a report card that would have read: "Deportment, U, Physical Education, U." What would either the child, the parent, or a new teacher have known about the child under these circumstances? It is possible that the new teacher would have pushed Jerry further from the attention he needed, that the mother would have felt that his bad behavior in school added one more burden to her problems at the time that she was much concerned with the new baby. Jerry's father may have looked at the U in physical education and wondered how in the world he could have a son who couldn't catch a ball.

Jerry's new teacher would take a look at the report card and say with a sigh: "Another child who doesn't know how to behave and who can't do anything on the playground!" Clues to the underlying causes of behavior do not appear in the traditional report card, and no provision is made for suggestions as to remedial action.

Parent-teacher conferences can be supplemented by having the children prepare and take home statements of their own progress, by frequent classroom evaluations, by informal notes or phone calls, and by planned programs which acquaint parents with the purposes of education in a democracy and the specific ways in which the school is working to fulfill those purposes.

Parents have a right to know the facts about the progress of their children in school. The cumulative record tells more than any report card. The major purpose of reporting to parents is to provide the information necessary for a sound working relation between them and school, and many avenues of communication should be opened to make this relation operate successfully.

GRADE PLACEMENT OF PUPILS

Does the grade placement of pupils contribute to healthy personalities? In answering this question regarding the effect of grade placement on personality, children who have been retained in a grade should be considered. Should judgment regarding the placement of a child be left to a teacher who may not be familiar with the research in the field or who may be operating on the basis of personal opinion and limited experience? To answer these questions let us consider the problem of Larry.

Larry, a 13-year-old, is in the sixth grade. Larry is of average size for his age, which means he is one of the larger boys in the class. He was retained in the first grade because he seemed immature and did not learn to read. He was retained again in the third grade because of poor progress and because he was not ready for fourth-grade work.

Larry's ability is low average as measured by standardized tests. His achievement is about two years below the norm for the class he is in and three years below his potential. Larry wastes his time, fools around, and shows little interest in school activities.

Larry's father is a sheet-metal worker in the railroads yards. He is disgusted with Larry. "What that kid needs," he says, "is a job and the sooner the better. He is wasting his time in school." His father is disgusted with the school, too. "It's this modern education," he says, "it's too soft. They don't make the boy work. The discipline is poor. Too much time is spent on frills and not enough on the three R's."

Larry says, "I don't like school. It's not much fun. I'd like to learn a trade if I ever get to high school, but I doubt if I'll ever make it."

The teacher asks the following questions: "Should I promote Larry this year? Promotion would reward lack of effort. Would that destroy the morale of the others who worked hard? Would Larry believe that he could always get by without working? Wouldn't promotion for Larry mean lowering standards—a soft education?"

The teacher says, "Larry is not ready for seventh-grade work. To promote him would mean too wide a range of achievement for the seventh-grade teacher to handle. He would surely fail in the seventh grade. Shouldn't Larry understand that he has to work if he is going to get anywhere in this tough world?"

What does educational research show about Larry? Research shows that to dislike school, to waste time, to make little effort, to achieve below capacity is the behavior expected of a child who has experienced nonpromotion. Larry is running true to form.

The threat of nonpromotion, or nonpromotion itself, does not increase motivation but lowers the level of aspiration for most children. So it is with Larry. Larry has no fun in school because he is not well accepted by the others. The findings of research show that this is what usually happens to children who have experienced nonpromotion. The other children in Larry's grade either overtly state or tacitly think that he is stupid, which colors all their attitudes toward him.

Has Larry's nonpromotion reduced the range of achievement in Larry's class and thus provided a more homogeneous group? No, Larry is still at the tag end in achievement but he is the most mature boy in interests and physiological development. This heterogeneity in development and interests of the pupils is more of a problem to the teacher than the wide range of materials she must provide.

Will Larry straighten out when he gets to high school and learns a trade? The probability is that he will not get through high school. One research study showed that of 643 pupils who dropped out of high school, 638 had repeated the first grade. Research also shows that the most common characteristic of "drop outs" from high school is overageness.

How will Larry get along socially and emotionally as an adolescent? This is problematical. The correlation of school failure to delinquency is high. The effect of failure on personality is to develop either withdrawing behavior or compensating mechanisms which are usually unwholesome in their effect on social adjustment. Grade retardation has not been profitable for Larry nor has it eased the instructional problem in school.

Larry's problems have not all arisen from nonpromotion in school. A meager home background, limited ability, lack of understanding and encouragement by parents, and too little home guidance have been the roots of his problem. When it allowed Larry to fail in school work, the school relinquished its opportunity to guide, inspire, and help him, and to compensate for the inadequacies in his home. He has lost his trust in the school and in himself. His initiative, if he has any left, will never be directed toward improving himself through education. . . .

Would Larry have had a better chance of promotion had his name been

Loretta? Yes, the facts show that among girls and boys of equal ability and achievement, girls are promoted more frequently. Why is this true? Research regarding the causes has not been completed but a good guess is that a Loretta would have been more submissive and less annoying to her teachers than Larry was and thus her failure to meet standards might have been overlooked.

How many childern in California schools raise similar questions in the minds of teachers? The age-grade status of 234,000 children in 28 counties was studied in 1950. In this study it was found that 51 per cent of the boys and 37 per cent of the girls were over the expected age by the time they had reached the eighth grade. No doubt some of these children had entered school late, but it can be presumed that most of them had been retarded one or more years in grade placement. The range in age in each grade was from five to ten years, and 19,528 of the children were more than one year overage. Many youths 15, 16, 17, and 18 years old were found in the eighth grade. Eighth-grade enrollment was significantly lower than other grades even when differences in birth rate were considered, showing that drop-outs occur in elementary as well as in high school.

Certainly individual cases exist in which nonpromotion is desirable. No truth is universal; there are exceptions to every rule. There may even be individuals for whom grade failure could be a salvation. But the mountains of research evidence against nonpromotion are so high that the burden of proof that a child should be failed rests with the school that fails him. Only a psychologist qualified to evaluate the physical development of a child, to measure his maturity, to diagnose his personality needs, and to understand his home should say, "*This* child should not be promoted." The psychologists should be able to say with certainty: "All the bad effects of nonpromotion which we know happen to most children will not happen to this child because he is so different." Only then is a school justified in running counter to well-established research evidence by insisting upon nonpromotion of any pupil. And even in these circumstances, careful follow-up studies should be made to detect the onset of possible bad effects and to prevent permanent harm to any pupil through nonpromotion.

ARTICULATION OF UNITS
OF THE SCHOOL SYSTEM

Does an articulated program of education contribute to the development of a healthy personality? Recently an elementary school teacher who is unusually adept in establishing friendly rapport with her pupils and who is teaching children in a large elementary school from which pupils enter a departmentalized junior high school was reviewing certain of her observations during the past three years. She said:

> I have been teaching children in the sixth grade in this school for the past three years. The children who were with me during my first year in this position are now in the eighth grade of a highly

departmentalized junior high school. Last year when they were in the seventh grade, and this year, too, they have invited me to their social gatherings which are usually held in a home of one of the group. Sometime before each evening is over they discuss their school activities. They tell one another and me, too, what they like about school. They also tell the things in elementary school that they miss, and one thing comes up over and over. It seems that in their junior high school the pupils not only have different teachers every hour on the hour but find themselves with different members of their group in the different classes. They miss most the opportunity to become acquainted with one another and with their teachers. They speak of one teacher as a home-room teacher but discern little difference between their home-room teacher and other teachers except that she appears to have more records to keep. They miss particularly a close association with one another. They enjoy and keep alive the social gatherings that were begun three years ago because they can meet with boys and girls they know well and with people who know them. They seek a sense of intimacy, friendship, love, and inspiration.

An eighth-grade teacher was talking about a boy who completed the eighth grade last June. She said:

I teach in a rural school. After students finish the eighth grade, they are picked up by a school bus provided by the high school district and ride many miles to the high school. I don't see them often after they start to high school because they leave early and get home late. Last week, however, one of the boys who finished the eighth grade last June came to talk with me. He was a good pupil in my class. I thought he was an unusually promising boy. While in the eighth grade, he had talked about taking courses in high school that would prepare him to work with the 'business part of getting fruit ready for the market,' to use his words. But now, after we had talked for a while, he said he was thinking about quitting school and getting a job. When I asked him why he was thinking about quitting he said, 'My grades aren't very good. We have a lot more homework to do now than we had last year and I don't get mine done. Last year we didn't have much homework and I got along fine. Whenever we did have homework last year, I didn't get mine done at home. You know there are three of us kids at home and we still live in the trailer. When I try to do my homework I'm in everybody's way and I don't get it done. I've thought about it for a long time now and believe the thing for me to do is to earn some money. Maybe after I have earned some money to help at home I will be able to go to school again. Then, too, I'll have enough money to buy clothes and go places like the others do.' I felt depressed after he left and began to wonder what I could do to familiarize his high school teacher with the problems confronting him.

This statement by the eighth-grade teacher raises several questions. If feelings of discouragement persist in this once promising boy, can he have a healthy personality? Will such feelings give him the help he needs to develop a sense of accomplishment, a willingness to settle down to learning how to do things and do them well? Will they permit him to select desirable social goals and to feel reasonable security with his peers?

The two incidents mentioned are not isolated. They are typical of statements by teachers regarding young adolescents in many elementary schools.

A program of education contributes to the development of a healthy personality if each administrative unit is articulated in a total, continuous program. More specifically, schools which contribute to the development of a healthy personality are those in which the following statements describe school goals, planning, and procedures:

1. Twelve years of education are regarded as minimum preparation for citizenship in today's complex society.
2. School activities are guided by a unified philosophy of education which combines the guidance concept with intellectual education.
3. The objectives or goals for each administrative unit are arrived at with joint representation and mutual understanding of all administrative units which constitute the school system.
4. The curriculum is planned jointly by elementary and secondary teachers, particularly for grades 6-7 and 9-10 in the 6-3-3 systems and for grades 8 and 9 in the 8-4 systems.

Educators today are accepting the idea of separate elementary and secondary schools only as convenient administrative units in a continuous, total program of public education. Educators today recognize that problems peculiar to elementary or secondary schools derive from the maturity levels of young people, not from any special institutional function or purpose. The elementary, junior high, and senior high schools joined end-to-end should provide an articulated program for the child from the time he enters school until he is prepared for adult citizenship in our modern society.

A principal in an elementary school enrolling young adolescents in grades seven and eight reported the following incident which led to improved articulation in his school system.

One boy in the school was frequently referred to the principal because he did not always conform to the pattern of conduct expected of pupils. The principal said that he had long ago become convinced of the value of looking at the cumulative record of individuals before talking about their personal problems. He recalled that this youth was nearing his seventeenth birthday, was in the eighth grade, and was rated as average in ability by most of his teachers but below average by certain teachers. The boy was tall, well-developed physically, and would pass for a youth older than his actual age. The principal judged that the youth had a wide background of experience, responsibility, and association with older people. He had come to school by transfer from another state and seemed to get along satisfactorily most of the time.

The principal listened with interest whenever he succeeded in getting the boy to talk about himself, for then his hostility would diminish and before the end of the conversation he could analyze his present situation and his problems.

During one of these meetings, the boy said, "I like my home-room teacher very much. If it weren't for my home-room teacher I would quit school. It is lucky for me that I am in her room a half day every day and longer on some days. I could quit school, you know. I am old enough to quit."

The principal said, "Yes, you are old enough to stop coming to this school and go to continuation school, providing it is necessary for you to work and providing you find a job. But you haven't done that and there are reasons why. Would you mind telling me what they are?"

This is a part of the boy's reply: "No one in our family [and the principal remembered that there were two brothers and a sister] has finished the eighth grade. Where we lived before coming to California we did not have to stay in school until we were sixteen, so my brothers and sisters dropped out to work as soon as they could. My parents wish they had gone to school longer. They are getting along, but I see the need to get more schooling. I want to graduate. The thing that bothers me most is getting mixed up with the rules around the school. I'm careful about some things. I know that I shouldn't smoke around the school so I don't. All my after-school friends are in high school or out of high school. We are mostly interested in cars and ways to earn money. I'd sure like to be in that auto mechanics shop in the high school."

The principal concluded the discussion with this statement: "This boy and others like him caused us to examine our promotion policy in kindergarten through grade twelve. As a result we now have provision for steady progression through the twelve grades. The high school accepts children from the elementary school after they have gone through our school. They pass from grade eight to grade nine on the same basis as they go from grade three to four or five or six.

"Our high school recognizes the principles of human growth and development. The faculty knows that we have done our best to help each child achieve his fullest potentiality as he moved through our school. The high school teachers accept their guidance function and think of their great task as that of meeting the physical, social, and emotional needs of young people as well as their intellectual needs. We are working to provide educational experiences that will keep all or nearly all of the young people of our community in school for twelve years. We want children and youth to stay in their normal social group and not acquire feelings of inferiority by being classified with younger and smaller children. The problem of adjusting instruction to the needs of individuals must be met in every group. We are gradually getting away from artificial grade standards as we understand children better."

Healthy personality will be promoted as the elementary and secondary schools of a community put themselves through the process of developing and employing an educational philosophy that will make education a continuous, developmental experience for boys and girls.

47 Classroom social structure as a mental health problem

Related selections: 46, 48

Does there exist in the elementary school classroom a socioemotional environment marked by stratification of the children involved? If such a stratified environment exists, does it have any relationship to the mental health problems of children? The report below explores these questions, drawing upon research findings obtained from a sample of 39 elementary school classrooms.

RONALD LIPPITT and MARTIN GOLD, "Classroom Social Structure as a Mental Health Problem," *Journal of Social Issues,* XV, 1 (1959), 40–49. Reprinted by permission of the publisher.

DR. LIPPITT (1921–) is Professor of Psychology and Director of the Research Center for Group Dynamics at the University of Michigan.

DR. GOLD (1931–) holds the position of Assistant Program Director at the Research Center.

One of the two most important and influential environments for the child is the classroom in which he lives during a part of each day. His relations with his teacher and with his peers are two major aspects of his school environment. These relations have a variety of important meanings for the child: "What is expected of me?" "What can I do and what can't I do?" "What will happen if . . . ?" "Who do I like?" "Who don't I like?" "Who likes me?" "Who doesn't?" "Who does the teacher like?" "Who's the strongest?" As clarification emerges about the meaning of such important questions, relations in the classroom develop a stable pattern or structure, which we are calling the classroom socio-emotional structure. Stratification becomes clear about those who are looked up to and down on in various ways. Each child finds he has a position, or several positions, in this socio-emotional structure. This social structure becomes a dominant aspect of his school environment and of his total life situation. His position in this structure becomes a very important determinant of his personal mental health situation, and of his motivation and ability to participate in classroom interaction.

This paper reports a research exploration of the development and maintenance of the classroom socio-emotional structure in a sample of 39 elementary classrooms. The paper also explores some of the mental health correlates of the child's position in this socio-emotional structure, which in turn suggest focal points for diagnosis of socio-emotional problems in the classroom situation and formulation of the therapeutic strategy in working toward the improvement of classroom mental health.

THE DEVELOPMENT OF THE
SOCIO-EMOTIONAL STRUCTURE
OF THE CLASSROOM

To what degree can we really talk about a social structure in the classroom? How much consensus is there among classmates about who belongs where in the structure? How stable is the structure over time?

All of the children in all of the 39 elementary school classrooms rated all their classmates on a four point scale, indicating the degree to which the ratee was perceived as able to get the others to do what he wanted them to do. The resulting stratification is called the social power structure of the classroom. If we look at the consensus among the group members in making these ratings, we find that in the average primary grade the children in the top third of the power structure received 47 per cent of the high power (number 1) ratings from peers while the bottom third received 18 per cent high ratings and 46 per cent lowest ratings. Consensus is even higher among 4th, 5th, and 6th grades with 58 per cent of the highest ratings going to the top third and only 11 per cent to the bottom third. The agreement on who is liked most and who least is comparable. The most disliked third of the average class received over half of the strong dislike ratings.

Not only is there high consensus about who belongs where in the social structure, but there is high stability of the structure from early in the school year to the middle of the school year and to the end of the school year. Looking first at the social power structure we find that for the first, second, and third graders there is an average classroom correlation (Pearson r) of .73 between the social structure in early October and in the middle of January; between January and May the average correlation is .72; and from early fall until the end of the school year, the correlation in the primary grades is .63. All of the individual correlations are highly significant. For the fourth, fifth, and sixth grades the average correlation between October and January is .77; between January and May it is .78; and between early October and May, .75. The structures concerning who is liked and disliked and who is regarded as expert and inexpert in classroom activities have an even higher stability, with most of the correlations being above .80. The evidence is clear that the interpersonal social structure of the classroom forms rapidly and maintains a high degree of stability throughout the school year. The same children remain in positions of low power and isolation or dislike throughout the year, and the same children stay at the top of the totem pole.

But are the same children at the top and the bottom of all the totem poles? A partial correlation program was carried out for four different social structures in each classroom; the social power structure, the affective (like and dislike) structure, the expertness structure, and the coerceability (ability to use physical coercion) structure. These analyses were summarized separately for younger and older classrooms in the elementary grades, and also for the beginning and end of the year. We find that with the other variables controlled there is still a high relationship between the power structure and the affect structure, a correlation of .57 at the beginning of the school year and .65 at the end of the year. The correlation is significantly higher for older than for younger boys (.44 as compared to .69). There is a smaller but significant relationship between the power structure and the expertness structure (.21 in October and .29 in May). The relationship of the coercion structure to the power structure increases from a zero relationship in the fall to an average correlation of .27 in the spring, although there is a great variability between groups in this relationship, and the relationship is accounted for to a great extent by the boys in each classroom rather than the girls. There is a significant relationship (.40) between the affect structure and the expertness structure in the fall which drops somewhat during the school year (.21 in May). There is a scattering of insignificant positive and negative correlations between the coerceability structure and affect structure and between the coerceability structure and the expertness structure. It is clear then that the children are making differentiations in their judgments of one another, and that being highly liked or being perceived as expert are both significant paths to social influence in the socio-emotional structure of the group.

But how do the children really think about each other when they have a chance to freely apply their own descriptive and evaluative labels? Are these dimensions we have been measuring really the central dimensions of the interpersonal structure as far as the children are concerned, or have they been somewhat imposed by measurement procedures? Gold (1958) has explored this question in a substudy of 152 children in kindergarten through the sixth grade. In a preliminary study he had fairly lengthy interviews with 21 children representing all the grade levels exploring with open ended questions their perceptions of their peers. From these interviews emerged seventeen characteristics or properties of children which seem to be matters of some concern as peers describe each other. These items fell into four areas; expertness characteristics (e.g. smart, has good ideas, good at making things); physical characteristics (e.g. fighting ability, strength, appearance); socio-emotional characteristics (e.g. friendliness, fun to be with, doesn't tease); and "associational" characteristics (e.g. likes to do same things I do). These open ended interviews clearly confirmed the previous researches in camp settings (Polansky, Lippitt and Redl, 1950) concerning the salience of the dimensions of socio-emotional structuring studied in the classroom groups. In a second part of the study specific low power and high power children were compared as to their possession of the valued characteristics. Gold found that the children gave the highest value to socio-emotional characteristics, but also placed a high value on expertness and the lowest value on physical prowess. It was also found that highly valued characteristics were attributed significantly more often to children who were high in the power structure of the classroom group. It seems clear that children do perceive each other in terms of these characteristics, and that these characteristics are evaluated in such a way that they become resources relevant to the acquiring of high or low position in the social structure of the group.

MENTAL HEALTH CORRELATES OF POSITION IN THE CLASSROOM SOCIAL STRUCTURE

Let's turn from the perceptions of peers to the judgments and assessments of adults. Adults in the school environment who have an interest in mental health tend to perceive children in terms of adjustment and deviancy along similar socio-emotional dimensions. We might expect, therefore, that there would be some relationship between perceptions and evaluations by peers and mental health assessments by adults. Two explorations of this question have been carried out as part of a larger study. Douglas (1958) conducted a study of the responses of 115 children to frustration in a series of story completion situations where a child is frustrated by a loved adult. In these situations children use various types of psychological defenses against the expression of their feelings of aggression toward powerful loved adults. Working within a theoretical framework developed by Miller (Miller and Swanson, 1959), Douglas coded the primitivity or maturity of the defenses used by the children in coping with frustrating situations. Partialing out the effects of intelligence and age, Douglas found that the children who are lowest in the socio-emotional structure of the classroom more often used the most primitive defense of denial in the face of conflict than those children high in being liked and influential, who were more apt to use more mature defenses showing relatively minor distortions of the reality situation. In terms of clinical judgments, the use of the more primitive defenses is a symptom of poorer mental health in coping with conflict situations.

In a study of seven elementary classrooms, Echelberger (1959) analyzed cumulative teacher ratings of children on the Haggerty-Olson-Wickman Behavior Rating Schedule (1930). This schedule yields five scores: behavior problem symptoms, problems in intellectual functioning, problems of physical characteristics, social adjustment problems, and problems of emotional temperament. Echelberger correlated the position of the child in the socio-emotional structure in the classroom with the behavior problems scale (e.g. cheating, temper outbursts, truancy), the social adjustment scales (e.g. shyness, relation to authority, assertiveness), and the emotional adjustment scales (e.g. cheerfulness, excitability, suspiciousness). The tabulation below reports some relevant correlations (those .26 and greater are significant at the .05 level or better).

In every case it can be noted that the more influential and more popular children impress their teachers with a significantly more favorable mental health picture. They show fewer behavior problem symptoms, greater social adjustment, and more stable emotionality.

Jennings (1943) has proposed that an important dimension of personality health is the ability to make and maintain social connections, to have the capacity for friendships with others. In this context we might expect that the amount of positive affection, as compared to negative affect, which a child feels toward his peers might be considered a mental health criterion. In our classrooms each child indicated how much he liked or disliked other children in the class on a four point scale, with ratings 1 and 2 indicating two degrees of liking the other, and points 3 and 4 indicating two degrees of intensity of dislike. The tabulation below indicates that in the older grades the children in high status positions express more positive affect in their ratings of peers than do low status children.

TABLE 1

Correlations (Pearson r) or sociometric ratings with selected H.O.W. ratings, by grade

Grades	N	Behavior problems	Social adjustment	Emotional adjustment
1–3	64			
Power x		—.28	.26	.21
Popularity x		—.46	.36	.27
4–6	72			
Power x		—.31	.36	.41
Popularity x		—.29	.35	.38

TABLE 2

Comparison of mean-percentages of liking choices (spring)
made by high and low power children, by grade and sex

	High Status		Low Status	
	Mean	N	Mean	N
Kindergarten to grade 3				
Boys	60%	(79)	62%	(83)
Girls	60	(82)	61	(67)
Grades 4 to 6				
Boys	72	(103)	64	(77)
Girls	70	(73)	62	(78)

(The differences of 8 per cent are significant beyond the .02 level.) Through the course of the school year, this difference becomes greater, the low status children increasing the proportion of negative feelings toward their fellow classmates.

Direct observation of the children interacting in the classroom supports this conclusion about negative and positive affect. We recorded on quantitative behavior schedules an hour of classroom interaction in a standardized situation a few weeks after the school year began. The children participated in four activities designed to maximize the need for cooperation and coordination with others. Each child interacted with every other child in the classroom in at least one of the activities. The data from these observations permit typing each child in terms of a behavioral output pattern. In the tabulation below we can see that those behavior patterns which indicate aggressive-assertive or passive-hostile activity output are more frequently characteristic of the low power children in the classroom social structure. Low status children tend to behave in ways that are likely to disrupt interpersonal friendships and also classroom functioning. (Differences of 5 per cent are significant beyond the .05 level.)

To summarize, then, we can say that children in low positions in the socio-emotional structure of the classroom tend to have mental health difficulties which

TABLE 3

Comparisons of percentages of low power with other children
in behavior output type categories

Behavior output type categories	Low Power (N = 311)	Other (N = 654)
1 Active-assertive, friendly	14%	25%
2 Active-assertive, unfriendly	27	22
3 Neutral or mixed	27	28
4 Passive, friendly	22	21
5 Passive, unfriendly	10	4
	100%	100%

are reflected both in inner psychological processes, in interpersonal relationship difficulties, and in behavior patterns which disrupt the life of the classroom group.

THE IMPACT OF CLASSROOM MILIEU
ON THE CHILD'S MENTAL HEALTH SITUATION

It becomes very important to consider the question: do the on-going processes of the classroom tend to aggravate or to alleviate the mental health problems of children low in the socio-emotional structure of the classroom? Looking first at the meaning of the on-going relationship with peers, we find that children who are low in the social structure have a continuing experience of social failure and rejection. For example, the success of each child's attempts to influence his peers during the standardized activity situation proved to be significantly correlated with his position in the social structure. Those low in the social structure experienced more failure of their own attempts and were more dominated by the behavior of others. This correlation increased during the course of the school year. Some of the low status children reacted to these behaviors from their peers by more withdrawal, and others reacted by more aggressive-assertive efforts to improve their position, which only resulted in still more failure.

That the children are sensitive to this incoming feedback from their peers is revealed by the self-evaluation index, which is a combination of self ratings on the social power and liking scales. The tabulation below indicates that children's self evaluations tend to correspond to the feelings expressed by peers. (Differences between high and low power means are significant by T-test beyond the .05 level, except among the younger boys.) The younger boys seem to be less sensitive to the feelings of others about them, although their ratings also indicate some awareness of their status. It may be that they are more prone to make defensive self ratings to help them cope with their unhappy position in the group.

It is quite apparent to the children's teachers that high and low status pupils are treated differentially by their peers. We asked the teachers in the experi-

TABLE 4

Comparisons of mean self-evaluation score (fall) of high and low power children, by grade and sex

	High power		Low power	
	Mean	N	Mean	N
Kindergarten to grade 3				
Boys	3.47	(79)	3.86	(83)
Girls	3.23	(82)	3.91	(67)
Grades 4 to 6				
Boys	3.76	(103)	4.53	(77)
Girls	3.74	(73)	4.35	(78)

TABLE 5

*Comparison of percentages of teacher interaction
with high and low power children, by sex*

	N	Social behavior evaluation	Performance evaluation	Total content tallies	Supportive remarks	Critical remarks	Total supportive-critical tallies
Girls:							
High	43	16%	84%	104	57%	43%	104
Low	44	24%	76%	116	73%	27%	116
Boys:							
High	37	22%	78%	102	62%	38%	103
Low	35	30%	70%	176	42%	58%	176

mental classrooms to rate each child on the relative amount of warmth he received from others. These ratings were significantly correlated with the peer ratings of social power and likeability. The correlations were considerably higher in the spring than in the fall.

But peers are only part of the classroom milieu. The teacher is an important part of the environment. What about her contribution?

Part of our study included observations of a sample of classroom activities by a team of graduate student observers. Each observer watched an individual elementary school child for an hour at a time, recording (1) with whom the child interacted and who initiated the interaction; (2) the affective quality of the interaction, whether friendly, neutral or unfriendly; (3) whether the content of the interaction was primarily social or was concerned with the performance of a learning activity. None of the observers had any knowledge of the pupils' social status in the classroom. Each child was observed by two different observers. There are 318 child hours of observation in the sample of classrooms.

TABLE 6

*Comparison of affective quality of teachers' interactions
with high and low power pupils, by sex*

	N	Teachers' approaches to pupils			Total teachers' approaches
		Friendly	Neutral	Unfriendly	
Girls:					
High	43	32%	48%	19%	99
Low	44	36%	51%	14%	111
Boys:					
High	37	36%	47%	18%	118
Low	35	28%	52%	20%	167

Part of the analysis deals with pupil-teacher interactions which can be summarized only briefly here.

It will be noted from Table 5 above that teachers pay attention to the social behavior, rather than the performance behavior, of low status pupils more often than of high status pupils. Evidently this aspect of their behavior leads to social evaluation and response more frequently on the teacher's part, just as it does for classmates. How the teacher responds depends on whether she is interacting with a low status girl or boy. Low status boys tend to receive more criticism than their high status boy classmates; but low status girls receive more support. In Table 6 we see that teachers were friendly slightly more often toward low status girls than other girls, but more often neutral or unfriendly toward low status boys. Differences in children's behavior probably evoke these different responses from teachers. Looking at the data on the children's approaches to their teachers, we note that low status girls are actively affectionate in their approaches while low status boys do not show such positive affect. From other data we can infer that low status girls are not only more warm in their relations with the teachers, but are relatively passive and withdrawing, while low status boys are more aggressive and troublesome than their higher status classmates.

This brief discussion of teachers' behavior should not be construed to mean that the teachers involved in the study were "playing favorites." Rather, we think that teachers, faced with the task of teaching youngsters in classroom groups and necessarily having to maintain order to do so, must respond critically to disruptive behavior, and respond quite naturally with affection to little girls who seem to be asking for it and apparently getting little from their peers. But, we must ask, what are the implications of these findings for evaluating the classroom as a mental health milieu? What solutions to mental health problems do low status boys find from the generally critical and rejecting classroom relationships; or low status girls, who depend upon their relationships to teachers in the absence of satisfying give and take with their peers?

		Pupils' approaches to teachers			Total pupils' approaches
	N	Friendly	Neutral	Unfriendly	
Girls:					
High	43	29%	66%	5%	111
Low	44	49%	49%	2%	100
Boys:					
High	37	20%	66%	14%	64
Low	35	17%	74%	9%	118

IMPLICATIONS FOR DIAGNOSTIC
FOCUS AND THERAPEUTIC STRATEGY

When we try to close in on the locus of pathology which maintains and aggravates the unhealthy situation of certain children in the classroom group, it is apparent that the difficulties are created and maintained by a circular social process contributed to by the individual child, by his classmates, and by the teacher. If we focus on the individual child who is in difficulty we see that he contributes to the unhealthy situation by (1) his negative self evaluation and his response to this; (2) his hostility toward others; (3) his unskilled and unrealistic behavior output of assertive aggressiveness or withdrawing noncontribution; (4) his insensitive and defensive reception of feedback from others which might potentially give him more guidance for his own behavior.

If we look at the rest of the group as a source of difficulty for the individual child we see that there is (1) a very rapid evaluative labelling of a child and a strong tendency to maintain this evaluative consensus in spite of further information about the individual child as stimulus; (2) very inadequate skills of the group in providing the member with feedback which communicates sympathetic guidance rather than rejection or ignoration; and (3) a lack of group standards concerning the acceptance and support of deviancy.

If we look at the role of a teacher and her contribution to the situation we note (1) a lack of teaching effort focussed on developing personal attitude and group standards about good human relations; (2) a lack of interpersonal grouping practices and other procedures guided by mental health goals; (3) a lack of clear presentation of constructive behavior patterns toward low status children which could be imitated by her other pupils.

The conversion of these diagnostic insights into a mental health strategy is a challenging task. How much can one do by working directly outside the classroom group with the children in need of help, to assist them to initiate changes in the social process? How much can be done by working directly with the high power children who have the most influence on the socio-emotional structure of the classroom? What can be done by helping teachers to initiate curriculum content and training procedures which will have a direct influence on the socio-emotional structure of the class? These are the questions we are exploring with our collaborating classrooms.

48   *Experiments on autocratic and democratic atmospheres*

Related selections: 45, 46, 53, 58

The work of Lewin and his associates in studying the effects of social climate on the behavior of individuals has made a strong impact on the thinking of teachers, administrators, and others who work in our schools. His work has focused attention on the human relations within the group as a determinant of behavior.

Are group actions against scapegoats always organized, or can such a situation arise as spontaneous group action? What are the conditions of such action and who is predestined to become the scapegoat? How does a democratic or an autocratic atmosphere influence the stability of group structure? What difference does it make whether intensive work is the outcome of strict order or spontaneous interest? The answer to questions such as these is approached experimentally in a study on democracy and autocracy carried on by R. Lippitt at the Iowa Child Welfare Research Station with clubs of ten- to eleven-year-old boys. At present he and R. White are repeating the experiment with other individuals and different leaders, and have extended their scope of "social climates" to include "laissez faire."

To attack experimentally such problems as democracy and autocracy may seem hopeless or even absurd for a number of reasons. Democracy, for instance, as a cultural and political pattern in the United States is something which has been built up gradually through hundreds of years, created a multitude of institutions, and formed political procedures. It has deeply influenced business as well as hospitality; family life as well as education. In short, *it has affected all and every interrelation between persons.*

Is democracy then not much too large a subject for an experimental approach? Would such an experiment not presuppose having the control of a full country with cities, streets, and factories and a hundred years to learn the outcome of the experiment?

Furthermore, is the question of democracy not much too "complicated" for a direct experimental attack? Does not a scientific analytical study of such a

KURT LEWIN, "Experiments on Autocratic and Democratic Atmospheres," *Social Frontier*, IV (July, 1938), 316–19. Reprinted by permission.

PROFESSOR LEWIN (1890–1947), late Director of the Research Center for Group Dynamics, Massachusetts Institute of Technology, was the inventor of "topological" and "vectorial" psychology. His extensive writings touched upon many aspects of intragroup relationships.

phenomenon imply the necessity of breaking the problem up into smaller units to be approached one by one?

METHODOLOGY OF "FIELD" INQUIRIES

These questions remind me of some arguments the group of psychologists had to face who, around 1920, endeavored to study problems of will and emotion in a more serious manner than just measuring reaction time. They were told by their colleagues, by philosophers, and by practitioners, that it was foolish to study, for example, the problem of decision as long one could not create some "real events of life," such as telling the mother of the subject to study his reaction. The issue of complexity too was raised: "real" emotions such as anger were said to be too complicated for direct experimental approach. One should split them into emotional "elements" and study those.

Today these arguments are dead. The experimental studies on will and emotion, although proceeding slowly, are definitely under way. Psychology sees somewhat more clearly the general methodological issues involved. In particular:

(1) Science has to be *analytical* in determining and measuring the factors influencing behavior. However, that does not mean that the experiments have to split up objects and events into smaller parts. An isolated ion behaves very differently than in its setting within an atom. You cannot study the behavior of molecules by studying only the atoms in isolation, or more generally, you cannot study wholes without keeping them intact. Similarly, one cannot study group life or draw conclusions for group life by making experiments on isolated individuals.

(2) The absolute *size* and *intensity* of a psychological event or "object," like a group, is of course important in psychology. More important, however, are the *type* of event and the *pattern* of the setting. If an experiment is able to create the *constellation* it wishes to study, even though on a smaller scheme, it will go quite a way toward understanding the laws of this constellation.

(3) Psychology will have to get hold of such factors as "atmosphere" or "social climate" of a situation if it wishes to understand behavior. The concept "atmosphere" seems to be rather vague and not very scientific. On the other hand, every teacher knows that he will have no disciplinary difficulties if he can create the right atmosphere. If he is unable to create the proper atmosphere he might never overcome these difficulties, whatever single measure he might apply. Experiments on emotions (Dembo, Prescott), on regression and frustration (Baker, Dembo), on the effect of the pedagogical-cultural atmosphere in orphanages, foster homes, and nursery schools (Wellman and Skeels), and the findings of cultural anthropology in regard to so-called primitive societies (Mead) all show increasingly the importance of the social atmosphere.

As a rule, the general atmosphere of the situation can be said to be in the long run more important for behavior and for development than even a rather crucial single experience.

No one would attempt to understand the movements of a physical body without taking into consideration the character of the field of gravity (to speak in terms of classical mechanics) in which it is located. *Similarly, psychology will have to find a way of conceptually characterizing and quantitatively measuring the properties of the general field in which a person is located.* Doubtless the social atmosphere is one of the outstanding characteristics of that field: the group to which a person belongs, its culture and social climate. It is the *ground* on which the person stands. The character of the group and of the person's position within the group determines whether this ground is firm or shaky, whether the situation is clear or unclear, and therefore whether the person feels secure or insecure. Moreover, the ideology of the group determines to a very high degree the goals of the individual, his values, and his style of living.

EXPERIMENTING WITH MINIATURE SOCIAL "SYSTEMS"

The set-up in Lippitt's and White's experiments is about the following:

The personal interrelations between the children of two different classes were studied by means of the Moreno Sociometric tests, by observations, and with the help of the teacher. From the children who volunteered to be members of a club, the purpose of which would be to make theatrical masks, two groups were chosen which were matched according to leadership qualities, friendship-rejection, interpersonal relationships, etc. In Lippitt's experiment a democratic and an autocratic group under the same student leader were compared; in the experiment of Lippitt and White four different groups were chosen under four different student leaders, the atmosphere being democratic, autocratic, or "laissez faire." Also the variety of club activities was extended greatly but equated within the different atmospheres as much as possible. Group loyalty to the club was built up by permitting the children to choose the name of the club and to decorate and equip their own club rooms. In this experiment, after a number of weeks a new leader came in and at the same time the atmosphere was shifted, for instance, from democracy to autocracy, or to laissez faire (or vice versa). Thus the same group of children could be studied in all three atmospheres and in different orders of change.

It should be mentioned that no attempt was made to copy an extreme autocratic regime such as Nazism. The autocrat always tried to be friendly and did not purposely suppress free expression. He merely told the children what to do, with whom to work, and how to do it. As a whole, this was an atmosphere not too different from that created by a friendly teacher who believes in strict discipline. In the democratic group all problems of policy were put up to the children to decide. The leader acted as fully as possible as a regular member of the group. In laissez faire, no encouragement was given to cooperative decision. The leader stood entirely apart from the group, but ready to give technical information when approached.

WHAT DIFFERENT LOCAL
STRUCTURES DO TO THEIR MEMBERS

Lippitt's comparison of autocratic and democratic groups gave the following quantitative results:

(a) Probably the greatest quantitative difference is the amount of *hostility* expressed among the members of the group. It is about thirty times as high in the autocratic group as in the democratic group.

(b) This is probably due partly to the greater *tension* which seems to prevail in the autocratic group. This tension shows itself in the fact that the *total volume of social interaction* is 55 per cent greater in the autocratic group, in spite of the fact that objectively there is less need of communication in regard to the ongoing activity because it is directed by the autocratic leader.

(c) The autocratic group shows a *less stable group structure*. In 38 per cent of the time the members of the autocratic group work each by himself (group structure 1—1—1—1—1), or only one of the children works with another (2—1—1—1), whereas, in the democratic group such structure occurs only in 18 per cent of the time. The more cooperative group structures in which all or at least four of the five children worked together (5, 4—1) occurred in the democratic group much more frequently: 56 per cent, against only 12 per cent in the autocratic group. In the autocratic group the more cooperative group structures had to be built up by the experimenter and had a tendency to break down rather quickly, whereas in the democratic group this cooperation developed spontaneously.

(d) The autocratic group shows *more dominating behavior* and *less objective behavior*. This difference was particularly great in relation to out-groups where the autocratic group showed 102 per cent more ascendent behavior than the democratic group.

(e) The democratic group showed 47 per cent more feeling of *"we'ness"* as expressed in language and in test situations; the autocratic group 27 per cent more feeling of *"I'ness."*

(f) It is in line with this that the democratic group showed *more cooperative* endeavor: more often cooperation was offered and asked for, and there were many more occurrences of praise and expression of friendliness.

(g) There was more expression of an objective, *matter-of-fact attitude* in the democratic group, as against more *personal feelings* in the autocratic one; many more constructive suggestions were offered in democracy and there was more give-and-take of objective criticism without personal involvement.

(h) The *constructiveness* was higher in the democratic group as shown in the superiority of the group products. Certain test periods where the experimenter left the room for a short while were introduced. In such periods, typically, the constructiveness of work in the autocratic group fell down very quickly, whereas in the democratic situation work went on with very little change.

(i) Feeling for *group property and group goals* was much better developed in the democratic group. The records show that the children at the close of the club had the tendency to destroy the masks or take them for themselves individually in the autocratic group, whereas in the democratic group they presented them to their leader and teacher.

(j) During the twelve meetings of the club twice the situation of a *scapegoat* arose, where the whole group ganged together against one of the members. At the fourth meeting most of the hostility was directed against one member. The next day he was still the center of hostility. As a matter of fact, he was treated so badly that he ceased to come to the club. A few weeks later another member was made the scapegoat. He too quit, saying that he had bad eyes and that he could not come because his physician said his eyes needed the fresh air.

As a whole one might say then that the autocratic situation was characterized by what one might call a state of higher "basic tension," less objectivity, and more hostile aggressiveness. This aggressiveness was not directed openly against the autocrat (towards whom the children generally were rather submissive) but tended to find an outlet in the easy and less dangerous way of attacking a scapegoat.

ASSOCIATED PHENOMENA

Here is not the place to go into the specific dynamics behind the individual and social "mechanism," more than to say that it obviously has to do with the combination of the narrowing down of the space of free movement, the loss of status, and the resultant of forces in this constellation.

Sometimes the behavior in the autocratic group is such that overtly everything seems to go along smoothly, and that the children even seem to like the situation. It was quite a revelation when the interviews with these children (which were conducted by a person not connected with the experiment) brought out a most intensive dislike of the autocrat. Not infrequently the dominant note in autocracy is not so much an atmosphere of hostility as one of primitivation, lack of initiative, and listlessness.

This is shown, I think, rather effectively by one of our films which recorded the change of the same group of children from democracy to autocracy. The last day of democracy showed the children lively and intensely working (independent of presence or absence of the leader), an atmosphere of friendly cooperation, and considerable conversation among the children. It is striking to see how quickly, during the first hour of autocracy, the conversation between the children dies down. Only the leader is approached if a question arises; the faces of the children become definitely less alive, more apathetic. On the fifth day of autocracy the films show these trends firmly established. When the autocratic leader leaves the room the intensive work going on in his presence quickly fades out, and that with the same children who have shown in democracy independent productive work in full swing.

The rapidity with which a shift in social atmosphere affects ideology and conduct is as impressive in some of the other transitions. The last day of "laissez faire," for instance, as shown by the film, reveals the typical characteristics of that atmosphere: cooperative work between a few children might arise, but it usually disintegrates very quickly into individual undertakings, and ends generally in horse-play. The difference between a democratic atmosphere and that of laissez faire is rather striking and speaks for the necessity of strictly distinguishing both social climates: namely, the one where decisions are made cooperatively and then carried out individually or collectively according to the nature of the project (democracy), from the climate of "total freedom" (laissez faire) where goals are set individually. The quantitative analysis of that situation is not yet available; however, the children often give the impression of feeling bored. *The actual space of free movement in our situation of laissez faire seems not to be greater but smaller than in democracy and insofar similar to that of autocracy.* The lack of time perspective of worthwhile goals for long-range actions seems definitely to narrow down the children's space of free movement, although the limitations are in this case not set by the ruling of an autocrat.

DEMOCRACY IN LEARNING
AND TEACHING FUNCTIONS

When the new democratic leader enters the group a quieting down of the chaotic behavior is clearly visible even in the first hour. By unobtrusively listening-in and cooperating in the work of the children, without bossing them, the leader is able to build up a spirit of democratic cooperation more quickly than one might expect.

Naturally, it seems to take somewhat more time to establish democracy than to establish autocracy. *The democratic style of life presupposes active participation on the part of every member.* The members therefore have to experience this style and acquire a feeling for handling it before it will be well established. Besides, democracy depends much more upon every one of its members: one person out of line is apt to do more harm to the total atmosphere than in autocracy where the individuality of the members matters less.

One might think that the quickness with which conduct and outlook changes with the change in social atmosphere might be characteristic only for children and for experimental situations. However, reports on historical events, such as the recent shift to Nazism in Austria, seem to indicate that the conduct of an entire population can be changed over night rather deeply if the change in its social situation is sufficiently great. (In some respects, by the way, the shift to Nazism seems to have produced results similar to those which come up in the experiments of Lippitt and White.)

I do not like to conclude without cautioning the reader against a too quick generalization. It was not the purpose of these experiments to test "the" democracy, the "ideal" autocracy, and "the" situation of laissez faire. Obviously, a great variety of each of these climates is possible. The purpose of the experiments is to study the dynamics of the factors involved rather than to copy historically-given examples. Nevertheless, certain conclusions as to the value of the different climates for education might readily be made. In addition, one general outcome might be stressed:

These experiments point anew to the great possibilities vested in education, and to the responsibility given to moulders of young lives which are so sensitive to the present social climate and are so dependent upon it.

49 *Children's behavior and teachers' attitudes*

Related selections: 28, 32, 35, 50

Today's teacher realizes that an important aspect of the classroom behavior exhibited by the child is its significance in revealing what is happening in his development. In an earlier day, behavior was judged "good" or "bad" according to the accepted adult standard for conduct in the classroom. In the mid-1920's, Wickman conducted a famous study comparing the attitudes and evaluations of teachers and of mental hygienists in respect to pupil behavior. He found some striking differences. A quarter of a century later, Stouffer repeated the earlier study and compared the results. The two selections that follow should be read in sequence. The reader may wish to consider if the teacher of the 1960's holds attitudes that differ greatly from his earlier counterparts.

What identifies the problem child? How do we determine that a child is well adjusted, or maladjusted? What kinds of behavior are undesirable in any child? How "normal" is misbehavior in children?

The answers that teachers make to these questions are the subject of this experimental study.

However perplexing the questions may be to the modern parent or teacher, the immediate requirements of child rearing and training necessitate definite answers.

E. K. WICKMAN, *Children's Behavior and Teachers' Attitudes* (The Commonwealth Fund, 1928), pp. 1–5, 129–30. Reprinted by permission of the publisher.

DR. WICKMAN (1895–   ) was formerly Director of the Division of International Fellowships of The Commonwealth Fund, New York City. He is a co-developer of the H.O.W. Behavior Rating Schedules.

Such answers are to be found in the direct responses of adults to the distressing behavior of their children. Some customary responses to child behavior have lately been called in question, subjected to careful examination, and are being modified according to our growing knowledge of child life and child needs. But many everyday habits of regarding and treating problems in child behavior are so taken for granted that they are rarely formulated into words or held up to intellectual scrutiny. This study is an effort to analyze prevailing attitudes toward behavior problems of children.

The subject of child behavior has recently taken on a new significance. The relationship of behavior disorders of children to social-pathological problems of the adult is inviting careful attention. The importance of the social and emotional development of children is becoming recognized along with the need for their intellectual and physical training. Education is turning serious attention to preparing the child for life. With our concepts of child needs and child problems in a state of reorganization, it is appropriate to inquire at what point we have arrived in defining the issues of child behavior in our everyday practices.

That our study is concerned with teachers' viewpoints on these questions is the result of fortuitous circumstances. Facilities were offered in representative public schools of two cities for making experimental studies on the behavior problems of elementary school children. In carrying on these investigations it was necessary to appreciate the teachers' points of view toward the behavior disorders of their pupils. Though the original purpose of the investigations was to secure factual data on behavior-problem children, it seemed as the study progressed that the attitudes of teachers were fundamental to any study of the behavior disorders of their pupils. The experiments were forthwith turned in this direction. Later on it became desirable to extend the studies to a measurement of the attitudes of many groups of teachers.

Personal and social attitudes are important factors in the solution of any human problem. When physical ailments were considered the affliction of evil spirits, medical science was precluded. So long as insanity was regarded as demoniacal possession or punishment from God, those suffering from mental derangements were banished or abused. If behavior problems of children are defined in terms of "bad," "evil," "wrong" behavior, their natural causation cannot be appreciated. Fortunately, we are beginning to think more objectively about conduct disorders and to evaluate child behavior in terms of child welfare; unfortunately, the welfare of the child seems not infrequently to be confused with the convenience of the adult.

Whereas the influence of attitudes toward physical and mental disorders affects chiefly the treatment of those diseases, attitudes toward behavior are an integral part of behavior disorders. Behavior, in the social sense in which it is here employed,* is a socially evaluated and socially regularized product; and

---

* Webster's definition: "Behavior applies to our mode of behaving in the presence of others or toward them."

behavior problems represent conflicts between individual behavior and social requirements for behavior.

It is to be noted that the very existence of a behavior problem is designated by personal or social attitude. There can be no problems in behavior, in the active social sense, unless someone reacts to them as such. Moreover, any form of conduct in a child or adult may become a problem if it is regarded and treated as undesirable behavior by the social group in which the individual happens to live.

This definition of behavior problems in terms of personal and social attitudes is forced upon us as soon as we undertake a systematic study of social maladjustments in children. Here we find ourselves so lacking in consistent standards of behavior evaluation that it is impossible to establish any criteria which will be serviceable in all social situations. What is acceptable behavior to one parent, teacher, or school system may become unacceptable when the child passes into the control of another parent, teacher, or school. No two families maintain exactly the same requirements for the behavior of their children. The school may revoke the standards of conduct set up for a child in the home. The parent in turn often criticizes the teacher's requirements for the child's behavior. Racial, religious, educational customs and practices contribute heavily to differences in attitudes toward individual behavior. In so far as parents and teachers have different nervous constitutions and different experiential backgrounds there will be differences in the requirements they impose for, the responses they make to, the behavior of their children.

What constitutes a behavior disorder and why certain forms of behavior are "problems" are thus questions of personal and social attitudes.

However wisely or unwisely a parent or teacher may designate a behavior problem in a child, that designation must be the starting point of any study of the child's behavior disorder. The problem is the maladjustment between the child and those who seek to regularize his behavior. The very designation of undesirable conduct, and the attitudes toward the child in consequence of this, become stimuli for the child and determinants of his behavior.

In ordinary practice the factor of attitudes is often forgotten in the behavior equation. When parent or teacher is distressed by the behavior of a child, the usual assumption is that the difficulty is with the child. From an objective point of view the issue becomes: (1) why is the adult distressed by the child's behavior, and (2) why does the child behave in a fashion that distresses the adult? The first question is obviously one of adult or social attitude, and our interest is directed to the factors that determine the designation of unacceptable behavior. The second question also involves the consideration of attitudes, for its answer is to be found in the child's behavior responses to the requirements of behavior which parent, teacher, school, or social order impose. Any attempt to study and treat behavior problems of children, then, involves an analysis, first, of the child whose behavior is distressing, second, of the social order that declares the behavior unacceptable or unwholesome, and, third, of the interactions between them. It is impossible to consider a child's behavior apart from the attitudes that are taken toward his conduct. The two are intimately related and bound up in the same issue.

The dictionary defines the term "attitude," in the sense in which it is here employed, as "any habitual mode of regarding anything; any settled behavior or conduct, as indicating opinion or purpose regarding anything." * In examining teachers' attitudes toward behavior problems of children we shall need to inquire into (1) their habitual mode of regarding child behavior with reference to the kinds of behavior which they consider undesirable or unwholesome, (2) their customary responses to these problems, (3) their opinions and purposes that lead them so to evaluate and respond to the behavior of their pupils.

The factual evidence secured in our investigation of teachers' attitudes relates chiefly to the first and partially to the second of these three items. An analysis of data secured with reference to the manner of the teachers' reactions to behavior problems in children affords some basis for an interpretation of the opinions and purposes that underlie these reactions.

In interpreting teachers' responses to child behavior as indicated in these studies, it will be necessary to bear in mind the particular nature of their teaching responsibilities and their special interests in child training. The professional responsibilities of teachers are in a large measure laid upon them by the school system and by the established aims of modern, public school education. In so far as the functions of the school coincide with the concepts of child training held by parents, we may surmise that teacher and parental attitudes toward child behavior are in agreement; in so far as the school stresses special aspects of child training, we may expect teachers' attitudes to be peculiar to their profession. In a sense, the measurement of teachers' responses to child behavior constitutes a measurement of the attitudes of the public school.

The conclusions that will be drawn from our study relate only to the most general, though possibly very fundamental, characteristics of prevailing attitudes toward child behavior. It may be that this report contains nothing fundamentally new beyond bringing to conscious recognition some facts that reveal *how we behave* toward the misbehavior of our children.

. . . . . .

The differences in attitudes toward behavior problems represented in the ratings obtained from mental hygienists and teachers should be interpreted as differences in stress laid upon the seriousness of the various problems. Teachers stress the importance of problems relating to sex, dishonesty, disobedience, disorderliness and failure to learn. For them, the problems that indicate withdrawing, recessive characteristics in children are of comparatively little significance.

---

* This is the definition of the Standard Dictionary. Webster defines the term "Position or bearing as indicating action, feeling or mood."

Mental hygienists, on the other hand, consider these unsocial forms of behavior most serious and discount the stress which teachers lay on anti-social conduct. Such differences in attitudes imply essential differences in methods of treatment and discipline.

In interpreting these findings it is essential to bear in mind that the clinicians, unlike teachers, were not laboring under pressure for educating children according to prevailing curricula and thus were not especially sensitized to those problems in behavior which disturb or frustrate the teachers' interests in the educational achievement of pupils. Moreover, in making their ratings, the clinicians were influenced, both by their particular professional interests and by specific instructions, to consider (1) the effect produced on the future development and on the social, emotional adjustment of the child by the possession of any behavior problem which is allowed to run its usual course; and (2) the need for remedial work, and the nature of remedial efforts, in treating the behavior disorders in question.

. . . . . .

[The following chart shows how teachers in the Wickman study regarded the seriousness of certain related types of behavior problems in children.]

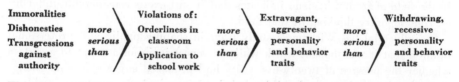

The ratings made by the mental hygienists are not quite as well arranged according to types of problems; but we may formulate the direction of their reaction to the importance of behavior disorders in contrast to the teachers' reactions, as follows:

Withdrawing, recessive personality and behavior traits	*more serious than*	Dishonesties Cruelty Temper tantrums Truancy	*more serious than*	Immoralities Violations of school work requirements Extravagant behavior traits	*more serious than*	Transgressions against authority Violations of orderliness in class

50 Behavior problems of children as viewed by teachers and mental hygienists

A study of present attitudes as compared with those studied by E. K. Wickman

The preceding selection by Wickman, with its accompanying head-note, should be read before this article.

In 1928 a study was published which has been described both as "a classic investigation" and as "one of the most illuminating and interesting studies in the field." This was E. W. Wickman's *Children's Behavior and Teachers' Attitudes*. The study has been widely quoted and, as the author of this paper discovered, it is also very often misquoted, or variously interpreted. Even though it was conducted twenty-five years ago, the inclusion of data from it in recent books in the field of mental hygiene indicates that it still exerts considerable influence on contemporary thinking in that field.

So influential has Wickman's study been in shaping public and professional opinion that it was thought worth while to repeat it, in an attempt to ascertain whether the passage of twenty-five years had produced any measurable change in teachers' attitudes toward children's behavior, and whether any new problems of child behavior confronted to-day's teachers.

In the present study, which follows the pattern established by Wickman, rating scales were submitted to teachers in elementary schools and to mental hygienists—psychiatrists, psychologists, and psychiatric social workers—in child-guidance clinics. On these scales teachers and mental hygienists recorded their judgments as to the degree of seriousness of each of 50 behavior problems of children. The raters were directed to make their ratings at any point on a scale that was descriptively captioned to indicate an ascending degree of seriousness, from minimal concern on the part of the rater to judgment of the problem as a grave one. The calibrated rule contained twenty equal divisions, to facilitate statistical treatment of the data obtained.

One questionnaire—Form A—was administered to teachers, with a set of directions for completing it. This form duplicated in every respect the one

GEORGE A. W. STOUFFER, JR., "Behavior Problems of Children as Viewed by Teachers and Mental Hygienists," *Mental Hygiene*, XXXVI (April, 1952), 271–85. Reprinted by permission of the publisher.

DR. STOUFFER (1911–) is Dean, Department of Undergraduate Studies, Indiana State College, Indiana, Pennsylvania.

completed by the teachers in Wickman's original study. A second questionnaire—Form C—was rated by the mental hygienists who coöperated in the study, duplicating the one submitted by Wickman to his group of mental-hygiene experts. The mental hygienists were furnished with their own set of directions and conditions under which they were to rate the various problems. These were different from those given the teachers. A third questionnaire—Form B—was administered to the same teachers who had completed Form A. In this form the directions and conditions for rating were the same as those under which the mental hygienists had made their ratings on the 50 problems.

A brief explanation may be in order as to how the directions and conditions for rating differed for the various forms. The conditions for rating the behavior problems on Form A included a time limit, and the directions were worded with the aim of obtaining the rater's immediate impression and, perhaps, emotional reaction to a current situation. On Forms B and C, which were identical, there was no time limit for completing the ratings and the wording of the directions was aimed at getting the raters' intellectualized attitude toward a problem, not as to its effect at the moment, but as to how they thought it would affect a child's future development. This modification of Wickman's procedure was made to meet criticisms of his findings growing out of the lack of uniformity in the directions and conditions for the rating of the scale by teachers and by mental hygienists. In brief, an attempt was made to find out whether the teachers' ratings differed when they used the two different sets of directions and conditions.

The 481 male and female elementary-school teachers who coöperated in the study were chosen as a representative sample of teachers from all parts of the country, teaching pupils of various racial extraction and socio-economic status, in rural and urban schools, with a variety of educational philosophies. The 70 mental hygienists participating included psychiatrists, psychologists, and psychiatric social workers on the staffs of thirteen child-guidance clinics throughout the country. The over-all sampling closely approximated the one used by Wickman.

When the data were collected and evaluated, the relationship between the rating of the 50 problems of child behavior by the teachers of Form A and by the mental hygienists on Form C was recorded as shown in Table I. Table II shows a rank-order comparison of to-day's teachers' ratings (Form B) and those of the mental hygienists when both groups were using identical questionnaires.

The results both of inspection and of statistical treatment showed that to-day's teachers, psychologists, psychiatrists, and psychiatric social workers were in much closer agreement as to the seriousness of certain problems of children's behavior than they were twenty-five years ago. This appears in our first comparison, Table I, in which we used Wickman's procedure of furnishing the teachers and the mental hygienists each with their own set of directions and conditions for rating the behavior problems; and an even greater similarity in attitude is found when both groups were given the same directions and conditions for rating.

The data on the ratings by teachers and by mental hygienists were organized

TABLE I

A rank-order comparison of the ratings by to-day's teachers
(Form A) and mental hygienists of the relative seriousness
of 50 behavior problems of children

Teachers (Form A)	Mental hygienists
1. Stealing	Unsocial, withdrawing
2. Cruelty, bullying	Unhappy, depressed
3. Heterosexual activity	Fearfulness
4. Truancy	Suspiciousness
5. Unhappy, depressed	Cruelty, bullying
6. Impertinence, defiance	Shyness
7. Destroying school material	Enuresis
8. Unreliableness	Resentfulness
9. Untruthfulness	Stealing
10. Disobedience	Sensitiveness
11. Resentfulness	Dreaminess
12. Temper tantrums	Nervousness
13. Unsocial, withdrawing	Suggestible
14. Obscene notes, talk	Overcritical of others
15. Nervousness	Easily discouraged
16. Cheating	Temper tantrums
17. Selfishness	Domineering
18. Quarrelsomeness	Truancy
19. Domineering	Physical coward
20. Lack of interest in work	Untruthfulness
21. Impudence, rudeness	Unreliableness
22. Easily discouraged	Destroying school materials
23. Suggestible	Sullenness
24. Fearfulness	Lack of interest in work
25. Enuresis	Cheating

to appraise the agreement of these two groups of people who are concerned with child behavior and mental hygiene. This was done by three methods of examination. First, we considered the relative position, in the rank-order arrangement as to seriousness, assigned respectively by the teachers and the mental hygienists of to-day to the various problems of children's behavior. Little in the way of agreement seems apparent in an examination of Table I. No item of behavior in the teachers' column is in juxtaposition with the same item in the mental hygienists' column. Of the ten problems rated the most serious by the teachers, and, therefore, appearing as the first ten in the rank-order arrangement, only two are found in the ten rated most serious by the mental hygienists. At the other end of the rank-order arrangement of the problems, of the ten rated least serious by the teachers, only four are found in the last ten positions in the rating by the mental hygienists.

Further examination of the problems ranked in order of seriousness by the teachers and the mental hygienists reveals that the most marked differences in the ratings are in the following behavior items:

Teachers (Form A)	Mental hygienists
26. Masturbation	Selfishness
27. Laziness	Quarrelsomeness
28. Inattention	Heterosexual activity
29. Disorderliness in class	Restlessness
30. Sullenness	Inattention
31. Physical coward	Impertinence, defiance
32. Overcritical of others	Slovenly in personal appearance
33. Sensitiveness	Tattling
34. Carelessness in work	Obscene notes, talk
35. Shyness	Laziness
36. Suspiciousness	Stubbornness
37. Smoking	Attracting attention
38. Stubbornness	Thoughtlessness
39. Dreaminess	Imaginative lying
40. Profanity	Disobedience
41. Attracting attention	Carelessness in work
42. Slovenly in personal appearance	Masturbation
43. Restlessness	Impudence, rudeness
44. Tardiness	Inquisitiveness
45. Thoughtlessness	Disorderliness in class
46. Tattling	Tardiness
47. Inquisitiveness	Interrupting
48. Interrupting	Profanity
49. Imaginative lying	Smoking
50. Whispering	Whispering

Disobedience	Smoking
Impudence, rudeness	Masturbation
Impertinence, defiance	Heterosexual activity
Disorderly in class	Obscene notes, talk
Profanity	Unsocial, withdrawing

It would appear that these problems, all of which seem to represent an objective type of behavior, might be thought of as problems that outrage the teachers' moral sensitivities and authority, or that frustrate their immediate teaching purposes. According to the ratings by the mental hygienists, however, only the "unsocial, withdrawing" behavior could, with reasonable certainty, be considered as representing a serious future threat to the school child's stability.

Since this first appraisal of the relative seriousness assigned to the behavior problems of children by the two groups did not seem to be too productve, an examination of the data in a more precise fashion was made.

An evaluation for agreement or disagreement between the teachers and the

TABLE II

A rank-order comparison of the ratings by to-day's teachers (Form B) and mental hygienists of the relative seriousness of 50 behavior problems of children

Teachers (Form B)	Mental hygienists
1. Unreliableness	Unsocial, withdrawing
2. Stealing	Unhappy, depressed
3. Unhappy, depressed	Fearfulness
4. Cruelty, bullying	Suspiciousness
5. Untruthfulness	Cruelty, bullying
6. Unsocial, withdrawing	Shyness
7. Truancy	Enuresis
8. Impertinence, defiance	Resentfulness
9. Cheating	Stealing
10. Easily discouraged	Sensitiveness
11. Resentfulness	Dreaminess
12. Destroying school material	Nervousness
13. Suggestible	Suggestible
14. Heterosexual activity	Overcritical of others
15. Domineering	Easily discouraged
16. Temper tantrums	Temper tantrums
17. Selfishness	Domineering
18. Nervousness	Truancy
19. Disobedience	Physical coward
20. Laziness	Untruthfulness
21. Impudence, rudeness	Unreliableness
22. Lack of interest in work	Destroying school material
23. Fearfulness	Sullenness
24. Sensitiveness	Lack of interest in work
25. Carelessness in work	Cheating

mental hygienists was made by examining the means of their ratings on the same items of problem behavior for statistically significant differences. This technique revealed that to-day's teachers and mental hygienists were in substantial agreement as to the importance of the following behavior problems of children:

Resentfulness	Physical coward
Nervousness	Restlessness
Domineering	Imaginative lying
Easily discouraged	Thoughtlessness
Suggestible	Lying
Sullenness	

In Wickman's original group of teachers and mental hygienists, only two problems, "cruelty" and "temper tantrums," were assigned about the same degree of seriousness by the clinicians and by the teachers. Of the eleven items about which the mental hygienists and teachers now find themselves in agreement, in Wickman's study there was complete disagreement as to the seriousness of

Teachers (Form B)	Mental hygienists
26. Masturbation	Selfishness
27. Overcritical of others	Quarrelsomeness
28. Quarrelsomeness	Heterosexual activity
29. Obscene notes, talk	Restlessness
30. Enuresis	Inattention
31. Slovenly in personal appearance	Impertinence, defiance
32. Sullenness	Tattling
33. Physical coward	Slovenly in personal appearance
34. Shyness	Obscene notes, talk
35. Suspiciousness	Laziness
36. Inattention	Stubbornness
37. Stubbornness	Attracting attention
38. Tardiness	Thoughtlessness
39. Disorderliness in class	Imaginative lying
40. Dreaminess	Disobedience
41. Thoughtlessness	Carelessness in work
42. Profanity	Masturbation
43. Attracting attention	Impudence, rudeness
44. Inquisitiveness	Inquisitiveness
45. Restlessness	Disorderliness in class
46. Imaginative lying	Tardiness
47. Tattling	Interrupting
48. Interrupting	Profanity
49. Smoking	Smoking
50. Whispering	Whispering

"resentfulness," "easily discouraged," "suggestible," "physical coward," "imaginative lying," and "domineering." All of these problems, with the exception of "lying" and "thoughtlessness," were characterized by Wickman as "problems describing the withdrawing, recessive personality and behavior traits" or as "extravagant, overdetermined personality and behavior traits."

The behavior problems that the clinicians rated as more serious than did the teachers include:

Unhappy, depressed	Overcritical of others
Unsocial, withdrawing	Sensitiveness
Fearfulness	Shyness
Enuresis	Suspiciousness
Dreaminess	

Again it would appear that overt, objective behavior is rated as more serious by the teachers, and a subjective type of behavior by the mental hygienists.

TABLE III

A comparison of the rank-order arrangement of 50 behavior problems of children as rated by 481 of to-day's teachers (Form A) and 511 teachers in E. K. Wickman's study

Wickman's study	Present study
1. Heterosexual activity	Stealing
2. Stealing	Cruelty, bullying
3. Masturbation	Heterosexual activity
4. Obscene notes, talk	Truancy
5. Untruthfulness	Unhappy, depressed
6. Truancy	Impertinence, defiance
7. Impertinence, defiance	Destroying school material
8. Cruelty, bullying	Unreliableness
9. Cheating	Untruthfulness
10. Destroying school material	Disobedience
11. Disobedience	Resentfulness
12. Unreliableness	Temper tantrums
13. Temper tantrums	Unsocial, withdrawing
14. Lack of interest in work	Obscene notes, talk
15. Profanity	Nervousness
16. Impudence, rudeness	Cheating
17. Laziness	Selfishness
18. Smoking	Quarrelsomeness
19. Enuresis	Domineering
20. Nervousness	Lack of interest in work
21. Disorderliness in class	Impudence, rudeness
22. Unhappy, depressed	Easily discouraged
23. Easily discouraged	Suggestible
24. Selfishness	Fearfulness
25. Carelessness in work	Enuresis

However, more agreement between the two groups than was found in Wickman's original inquiry seems clearly to emerge.

In a third method of evaluation correlations were obtained by arranging the means of the ratings by the mental hygienists of the respective behavior problems of children in order of seriousness from the highest to the lowest, and listing opposite the corresponding values for these behaviors as judged by the teachers. The matched means were then converted into ranks, which in turn were converted into per cent positions. The per cent positions were changed to "scores" by the use of Hull's table. In computing the coefficient of correlation between the above matched scores, Pearson's product-moment formula was employed.

Wickman reported a coefficient of correlation of minus .11 between the rank-order arrangements as to seriousness of the problems of child behavior as rated by the mental hygienists and by the teachers. In the present study a coefficient of correlation of plus .52 was secured when Wickman's original procedure was duplicated (teachers' Form A and mental hygienists' Form C), and a coefficient of correlation of plus .61 was obtained when Wickman's procedure was modified

Wickman's study	Present study
26. Inattention	Masturbation
27. Quarrelsomeness	Laziness
28. Suggestible	Inattention
29. Resentfulness	Disorderliness in class
30. Tardiness	Sullenness
31. Physical coward	Physical coward
32. Stubbornness	Overcritical of others
33. Domineering	Sensitiveness
34. Slovenly in personal appearance	Carelessness in work
35. Sullenness	Shyness
36. Fearfulness	Suspiciousness
37. Suspiciousness	Smoking
38. Thoughtlessness	Stubbornness
39. Attracting attention	Dreaminess
40. Unsocial, withdrawing	Profanity
41. Dreaminess	Attracting attention
42. Imaginative lying	Slovenly in personal appearance
43. Interrupting	Restlessness
44. Inquisitiveness	Tardiness
45. Overcritical of others	Thoughtlessness
46. Tattling	Tattling
47. Whispering	Inquisitiveness
48. Sensitiveness	Interrupting
49. Restlessness	Imaginative lying
50. Shyness	Whispering

to provide both groups with the same directions and conditions for rating the problems (teachers' Form B and mental hygienists' Form C).

In a comparison of the ratings by to-day's teachers and by the teachers of twenty-five years ago, shown in Table III, it was found that problems relating to honesty, sex, truancy, and to classroom order and application to school tasks are rated among the most serious of the 50 problems of behavior by to-day's teachers, as they were by the teachers of Wickman's study. However, several of the problems concerned with withdrawing, recessive personality traits—*i.e.*, un-happiness, depression, unsociability, and withdrawing—have moved toward the top of the list as rated by to-day's teachers. Masturbation has dropped sharply in the teachers' estimation as a serious behavior problem. Interesting changes in position downward as to seriousness are those of smoking and profanity, in which there were striking shifts in position.

On the ratings for obscene notes, masturbation, and heterosexual activity there were large standard deviations of the means, indicating considerable variance of opinion among to-day's teachers as to the seriousness or importance of these

TABLE IV

*A rank-order comparison of the ratings by the mental hygienists
of Wickman's study and those of the present study on the relative
seriousness of 50 behavior problems of children*

Wickman's study	Present study
1. Unsocial, withdrawing	Unsocial, withdrawing
2. Suspiciousness	Unhappy, depressed
3. Unhappy, depressed	Fearfulness
4. Resentfulness	Suspiciousness
5. Fearfulness	Cruelty, bullying
6. Cruelty, bullying	Shyness
7. Easily discouraged	Enuresis
8. Suggestible	Resentfulness
9. Overcritical of others	Stealing
10. Sensitiveness	Sensitiveness
11. Domineering	Dreaminess
12. Sullenness	Nervousness
13. Stealing	Suggestible
14. Shyness	Overcritical of others
15. Physical coward	Easily discouraged
16. Selfishness	Temper tantrums
17. Temper tantrums	Domineering
18. Dreaminess	Truancy
19. Nervousness	Physical coward
20. Stubbornness	Untruthfulness
21. Unreliableness	Unreliableness
22. Truancy	Destroying school materials
23. Untruthfulness	Sullenness
24. Cheating	Lack of interest in work
25. Heterosexual activity	Cheating

three problems. Wickman's teachers had disagreed most markedly on "smoking" and "nervousness," as judged by the size of the standard deviations.

A separate evaluation of the ratings of the male elementary-school teachers was made. When the ratings of the male teachers were matched against those of the entire group, including these male teachers, no item was rated by the male teachers as being more serious than by the entire group of teachers. However, the following behavior problems were rated as less serious or less undesirable:

Heterosexual activity	Impertinence, defiance
Masturbation	Unreliableness
Physical coward	Disobedience
Smoking	Temper tantrums

This may indicate that there are measurable sex differences between male and female teachers in attitude toward certain problems of behavior.

It was discovered that while teachers have changed their attitudes toward the

Wickman's study	Present study
26. Lack of interest in work	Selfishness
27. Enuresis	Quarrelsomeness
28. Obscene notes, talk	Heterosexual activity
29. Tattling	Restlessness
30. Attracting attention	Inattention
31. Quarrelsomeness	Impertinence, defiance
32. Imaginative lying	Slovenly in personal appearance
33. Impudence, rudeness	Tattling
34. Inattention	Obscene notes, talk
35. Slovenly in personal appearance	Laziness
36. Laziness	Stubbornness
37. Impertinence, defiance	Attracting attention
38. Carelessness in work	Thoughtlessness
39. Thoughtlessness	Imaginative lying
40. Restlessness	Disobedience
41. Masturbation	Carelessness in work
42. Disobedience	Masturbation
43. Tardiness	Impudence, rudeness
44. Inquisitiveness	Inquisitiveness
45. Destroying school materials	Disorderliness in class
46. Disorderliness in class	Tardiness
47. Profanity	Interrupting
48. Interrupting	Profanity
49. Smoking	Smoking
50. Whispering	Whispering

behavior problems of children in the past twenty-five years, there has been little change in the attitude of mental hygienists, as shown in Table IV. The change, however, can best be determined by examining the statistical significance of the difference of the means of the ratings of the two groups of clinicians. When this was done, it was found that the psychiatrists, psychologists, and psychiatric social workers of to-day's child-guidance clinics rated 37 of the 50 problems of child behavior exactly as had the mental hygienists of twenty-five years ago. On the remaining 13 items, there were few marked reversals of attitude or shifts in opinion, as measured by the evaluation of the seriousness or importance of certain problems. Of the 13 changes, Wickman's mental hygienists rated the following problems of more importance than did the mental hygienists of to-day:

Suspiciousness	Physical coward
Resentful	Sullenness
Overcritical of others	Selfishness
Easily discouraged	Stubbornness
Domineering	

Problems regarded as more serious by to-day's clinicians are:

Enuresis
Destroying school materials
Restlessness (overactivity)
Disorderliness in class

The increased importance of enuresis might possibly be explained upon the basis of the increased psychological significance attached to it as an evidence of underlying emotional maladjustment, rather than as a purely medical problem. It would seem that the problems that the mental hygienists of twenty-five years ago found more important than do those of to-day largely represent subjective behavior. Behavior that the present-day group thought more important than did the group of twenty-five years ago would seem to represent objective behavior. The coefficient of correlation between the rating by the mental hygienists in Wickman's study and those in the present study was found to be a plus .87.

To determine whether to-day's teachers were confronted with any new behavior problems of children, other than those reported by the teachers of twenty-five years ago, 232 of to-day's teachers, of all grades, were asked to report and rate the undesirable behavior of their pupils. The only new problems of behavior were "reading comic books" and "watching television." When teachers were asked to evaluate the problems they had listed as to seriousness or importance, it was found that their ratings of the problems were uniformly similar to the rating of the same problems supplied by the investigator.

The majority of the items listed by teachers as undesirable represented what children do rather than what they fail to do. In analyzing the lists of problems, it would seem that the behavior-problem child in school is still, as he was twenty-five years ago, identified chiefly by annoying, disorderly, irresponsible, aggressive, untruthful, and disobedient behavior. Teachers of to-day, however, are not so oblivious to behavior indicative of social and emotional maladjustment as were those reported in Wickman's inquiry.

All the evidence would seem clearly to indicate that the passage of years has brought changes in teachers' recognition, understanding, and practice in the area of the mental hygiene of the school child. The teachers' changed attitudes might be attributed to a change in the total social and, in particular, school situation as it exists to-day. If we accept the judgment of the psychologists, psychiatrists, and psychiatric social workers as an adequate criterion, we can authoritatively say that teachers have grown in their knowledge of how the school child develops and behaves.

While we may be gratified by the increased degree of similarity in attitude toward the behavior problems of children by the teachers and clinicians of to-day, we cannot ignore the fact that a difference still does exist. In comparing the attitudes of the mental hygienists and the teachers, one must recognize the differences in professional interests. The psychologist, the psychiatrist, and the psychiatric social worker are interested solely in the social and emotional adjustment of the individual child. Society has caused the chief interest of the teacher to be the educational achievement of the child. Does the public think that the teacher's job is that of a social engineer, engaged in promoting the all-round growth and development of pupils, or that of a filling-station attendant whose job it is to fill the tank in the child's mind with subject matter? All persons connected with schools know that children are sent to school to be "educated." Social pressures seem to operate to the disadvantage rather than the welfare of the child. The teacher cannot escape this pressure in determining his or her chief interest; and it is important to remember that no such pressure is brought to bear upon the psychologist, the psychiatrist, or the psychiatric social worker, who usually works in the seclusion of his office, isolated from the many potent and influential forces of the community.

In interpreting the comparative ratings in a study of this sort, it should be remembered that the teachers, in rating behavior items like "masturbation" and "truancy," were probably making their evaluations, particularly on our Form A of the rating scale, in terms of a larger perspective than the more restricted professional horizon of clinicians. Teachers are undoubtedly aware of the dire consequences for the child, the school, and the teacher if community opinion is outraged by a violation of conventional sexual taboos. Similarly, their concern about truancy is understandable. How can you reach the goals of education, largely community prescribed, if the pupils fail to attend classes?

In assessing the total picture of the attitudes of teachers and those of mental hygienists toward the behavior problems of children, one cannot but wonder if there are not in conventional school practices certain things that aggravate and promote the development of behavior problems. If would appear that our present tradition-bound school, with its regimentation and its regimented teachers, of necessity fosters behavior that is pathological from a mental-hygiene point of view. If this is true, who is to accept the responsibility for the teacher's attitude? The teachers in question make the natural mistake—owing, no doubt, to practical schoolroom conditions—of evaluating children's behavior in terms of good order and recognition of authority. On the other hand, the psychologist, the psychiatrist, and the psychiatric social worker think in terms of the effects of behavior in the long run. Teachers are expected to maintain reasonable order, and in doing this, at times make the mistake, from a mental-hygiene point of view, of favoring withdrawing behavior and ruthlessly suppressing overtly aggressive (symptomatic) behavior without thought of the consequences thereof.

Are the differences between the attitudes of teachers and mental hygienists toward certain problems of children due to social pressure rather than to a wide gulf between them in knowledge of the principles of mental hygiene and understanding of the child's welfare?

Considerable emphasis has been placed by Wickman and other investigators in similar areas upon the amount and significance of the disagreement between teachers and clinicians as to the importance of the symptoms of "shyness," "sensitiveness," "unsocial," and other withdrawing behavior in children, but the trend, the data would tend to indicate, is in the direction of eventual agreement or similarity of attitudes in the two professional groups. This, by the way, is not to imply that all shy, unsocial, sensitive, withdrawn children are of necessity headed for the neuropsychiatric hospital.

Certain implications for teacher-training institutions would seem to grow out of the findings of a study of this nature. The increased emphasis upon an understanding of child growth and development on the part of these institutions has undoubtedly been reflected in the changing attitudes of teachers. However, an increased fusion of the twin disciplines of education and psychology in the training courses of prospective teachers might conceivably increase their over-all knowledge and understanding of the physical, mental, social, and emotional life of the child.

There must be continued instruction of the teacher in the dynamics of child behavior. New knowledge must continuously be made a part of the teacher's understanding and approach to the child. Some teachers undoubtedly will need reëducation and eradication of fixed attitudes in regard to the emotional and experiential factors that produce behavior problems in children.

The public—and parents in particular—must be reoriented, where necessary, as to the rôle of the school and the teacher in the education of children and they must constantly be given information to assist them in understanding what could and should be accomplished in the best interests of the child.

Psychologists, psychiatrists, psychiatric social workers, and teachers need to exchange ideas and experiences in regard to the behavior problems of children. It would appear that these professional people have much to offer one another, and from their mutually increased knowledge would come marked advances toward the goal of complete understanding of the child. Continued and coöperative research in the multiple issues of child behavior is important. If education for life is to become a meaningful concept, we will need to know more about and constantly to investigate the social and emotional dynamics of behavior as well as the intellectual development of the child.

51 *An attempt to evaluate the threat of failure as a factor in achievement*

Related selections: 20, 32

Critics of present-day school practices often voice the opinion that rigid grade standards should be observed and that a greater number of students should fail or not be promoted. Many people believe that if the threat of failure is minimized, children and youth will lack an important motivation for learning. The experiment described below raises serious questions concerning the necessity of this threat as part of a teaching situation.

The problem of pupil failure or non-promotion in school has been a crucial issue in school administration throughout the history of elementary education in the United States. Numerous statistical studies and a few experimental investigations regarding pupil failure have been made. Administrators and teachers everywhere have struggled to reduce the amount of non-promotion, and in some school systems the percentage of failure has been reduced to less than two or three and in a few cases almost to zero. Many and varied methods have been used in efforts to lower the percentage of children required to repeat the grade at the end of the school term. One of the most disturbing elements in the general move to reduce failures has been the fear that the quality of school work would depreciate and that the standards of achievement of the schools would drop to scandalous depths if the failure rate should approach zero. School workers were perfectly willing that the percentage of failure should be lowered, but they were equally convinced that the practice of failing *some* pupils must be continued as an insurance against low standards of achievement. In other words, the threat of failure must be retained to guarantee that every child will keep his shoulder to the wheel and will work to capacity. The threat of failure is thus deemed essential as a motivating device in elementary education.

There are some educational workers, however, who believe that it is not neces-

HENRY J. OTTO and ERNEST O. MELBY, "An Attempt to Evaluate the Threat of Failure as a Factor in Achievement." Reprinted from *Elementary School Journal*, XXXV (April, 1935), 588–96, by permission of the University of Chicago Press.

DR. OTTO (1901–   ) is Professor and Chairman of the Department of Educational Administration, University of Texas. DR. MELBY (1891–   ) is Distinguished Professor of Education, Michigan State University. He was formerly Dean of the School of Education, New York University.

sary to hold over children's heads the whip hand of failure in order to bring pupils to achieve and to achieve willingly and to capacity. It is the contention of these workers that educational science has progressed far enough so that there are many ways of handling and motivating children which bring better results and which are more conducive to mental health of both teacher and pupil than is the threat of failure. The study reported in this article was an effort to discover whether pupils threatened with non-promotion throughout the semester if they did not attain desirable achievement levels would make greater, less, or the same academic progress, as measured by standardized achievement tests, as did pupils who were told at the beginning of the semester that they would all be in the next higher grade in the following semester. The study was conducted in four typical school systems of northern Illinois during the second semester of 1933–34 and involved 352 pupils and 18 classroom teachers. One hundred and ninety-two pupils in Grade II A and 160 in Grade V A remained in the same school and class throughout the semester so that beginning and end tests could be given to them. Eight sections or classes of pupils in Grade II A were taught by eight teachers, and ten sections of pupils in Grade V A were taught by ten teachers.

In organizing the experiment each superintendent selected two teachers of Grade II A and two teachers of Grade V A who in his judgment were among the most competent of his teachers and who were interested in participating in the investigation. In West Aurora Superintendent Smith found it opportune to include six sections of Grade V A which had been classified into X, Y, and Z divisions. The classes used in the study were taken just as they were found in the typical school situation; that is, the organization of classes and the classification of pupils normally found in a particular school were not disturbed. It was thought that similar groups of children in the same grade would not reveal a sufficient number of statistically significant differences to influence the study. The accuracy of this supposition is borne out in the data which follow. The entire study was conducted in such a way as not to disturb the routine of administration in the least. For this reason teachers were not rotated. It was thought that the factor of teacher variation would be largely overcome by having four control-group and four experimental-group teachers in each grade.

At the beginning of the second semester the Kuhlmann-Anderson Intelligence Tests and the New Stanford Achievement Test, Primary Examination, were given to all children in Grade II A who were to be included in the study. The same intelligence test and the Unit Scales of Attainment were given to all pupils in Grade V A. Different forms of the two achievement tests were given before the close of the semester. In each of the four school systems one second-grade class and one fifth-grade class were designated as experimental groups, and one class in each of the two grades was designated as a control group, except in West Aurora as already explained.

Each teacher of an experimental group told her pupils at the beginning of the semester and several times during the semester that they would all be in the next higher grade the following term. Teachers were instructed (in most cases orally and by written statement by the writers) to make these announcements, not as sudden thunderbolts, but as statements of encouragement, and to make them so clearly that no pupil would lack a full understanding of the fact that there were to be no failures in his class during the term.

Each teacher of a control group informed her pupils at the beginning of the semester and several times during the semester that anyone who did not work hard and do well would have to repeat the grade. As in the experimental groups, the announcements in the control groups were not given in such an abrupt way that all or some of the pupils would become frightened about a sudden change in the academic requirements of the school; yet the announcements were made with sufficient clarity that every pupil would understand the proposition put before him. Doubtless in many instances the situation in the control groups was no different from the situation during any other semester with a particular teacher nor different from the setting in the majority of the elementary-school classrooms in the country.

Except for these announcements in the experimental and the control groups, no changes were made in the teaching situation. Each teacher was urged to carry on her teaching exactly as she would have done if no experiment were under way. Control-group teachers kept before their pupils the possibility of failure if good work were not done, while experimental-group teachers kept pupils aware of the fact that in the following term they would all be in the next higher grade. Obviously, experimental-group teachers were denied the use of the threat of failure as a motivating device.

The data for the experimental and control groups are summarized in Table I. It will be noted that there are no statistically significant differences for Grade II A. In this grade the mean gain of the experimental group is 1.1 months greater than the gain of the control group. In Grade V A the initial and the final educational ages showed statistically significant differences in favor of the experimental group. However, the difference in the mean gain is only 0.7 a month, and this gain is in favor of the experimental group. In other words, in so far as these data show, there is no difference between the achievement of children (taken as groups) who have been threatened with failure and that of children who have been told at the beginning of the semester that they would all be promoted to the next higher grade at the end of the term.

In an effort to discover whether the threat of failure as a factor in pupil achievement might operate differently for children of different levels of intelligence, the children in Grade II A were divided into three groups: (1) pupils with intelligence quotients of less than 90, (2) pupils with intelligence quotients between 90 and 110, inclusive, and (3) pupils with intelligence quotients above 110. Within each intelligence group the data for the experimental and the control pupils were compared. In no instances were the differences statistically sig-

TABLE I

Comparison of pupils in Grades II A and V A in experimental group who worked with no threat of failure and control group with whom threat of failure was used

	Experimental group	Control group	Difference	Standard error of difference	Critical ratio
Grade II A:					
Number of pupils	93	99	—	—	—
Mean chronological age (in months)	92.5	91.4	1.1	0.7	1.57
Mean mental age (in months)	96.4	96.5	— .1	.8	.13
Mean intelligence quotient	104.4	105.9	−1.5	1.2	1.25
Mean initial educational age (in months)	99.0	100.3	−1.3	1.4	.93
Mean final educational age (in months)	107.0	107.2	— .2	1.1	.18
Mean gain	8.0	6.9	1.1	.8	1.38
Grade V A:					
Number of pupils	73	87	—	—	—
Mean chronological age (in months)	130.7	131.0	— .3	1.6	.19
Mean mental age (in months)	136.0	134.6	1.4	1.6	.88
Mean intelligence quotient	104.7	103.4	1.3	1.9	.68
Mean initial educational age (in months)	144.2	138.6	5.6	1.9	2.95*
Mean final educational age (in months)	150.4	144.1	6.3	2.1	3.00*
Mean gain	6.2	5.5	0.7	1.3	0.54

* Statistically significant differences.

nificant. As the number of second-grade children with intelligence quotients below 90 was small, the data for this group probably have little reliability, but the middle and the upper groups contained 140 and 46 pupils, respectively.

The children in Grade V A were similarly reclassified into three intelligence groups. The number of cases in the groups were as follows: intelligence quotients of less than 90, twenty-one pupils; intelligence quotients between 90 and 110, ninety-one pupils; intelligence quotients above 110, forty-eight pupils. Within each intelligence group the experimental and the control groups were compared, and no statistically significant differences were found in the final educational age and the mean gain of any of the intelligence groups. Such minor differences as existed were in favor of the experimental groups.

As a partial index to the way in which the two promotion policies represented in this study might operate under different teachers, the experimental and the control groups in each city were compared. There were eight teachers of

Grade II A and ten teachers of Grade V A for which such comparisons could be made, four comparisons in Grade II A and five comparisons in Grade V A thus being possible. There were no statistically significant differences in the mean gains in the four comparisons made for Grade II A; in three of the four comparisons the minor differences existing were in favor of the experimental groups. For Grade V A there were no statistically significant differences in the mean gains in any of the five pairs of groups which were compared; in three out of the five comparisons the small differences found were in favor of the experimental groups. One might reasonably conclude, therefore, that in the total experiment variations due to teachers were not of sufficient importance in any one or a few classrooms to distort the general findings of the study.

At the end of the semester a one-page questionnaire was submitted to the participating teachers, on which they were asked to give their reactions to certain aspects of the study. Six teachers in each grade returned the inquiry blank. The first question was: "Did you notice any changes in the reactions, attitudes, or application of pupils which you believe are due to the conditions imposed by the experiment? If so, explain fully." The following answers to this question were received.

EXPERIMENTAL-GROUP TEACHERS IN GRADE II A

1. No.
2. Perhaps the realization that they were working toward a higher goal made them put more conscious effort into their work. I think there was a normal desire to improve, taking the group as a whole.
3. Yes. There seemed to be a little slacking up on work by a few, but, when they were reminded that the work in Grade III would be easier if certain work were accomplished in Grade II A, there was a better spirit of cooperation. A happier and more satisfied attitude toward the work was noticed.

EXPERIMENTAL-GROUP TEACHERS IN GRADE V A

1. No.
2. Yes. There was a general slump in attitude and quality of work. It was difficult to arouse a feeling of pride in work well done. It was necessary to do a great deal of checking up to bring in completed assignments and neat papers.
3. I have in the past had the experience of an "I don't care, I'm not going to pass anyway" idea. I have encountered no such attitude at the end of this semester.

CONTROL-GROUP TEACHERS IN GRADE II A

1. I really did not notice any definite reaction except possibly the real dislike of work in some children.

2. No change was noticed because, being in the control group, the conditions before and during the experiment were practically the same.
3. The children at all times seemed fully aware of the fact that they must reach certain standards in order to be promoted.

CONTROL-GROUP TEACHERS IN GRADE V A

1. No.
2. There was a slightly greater application on the part of some pupils. There was an attempt to bring subjects in which they were weak up to a higher standard, but children are always trying to improve in those subjects for daily lessons.
3. In most cases I think the pupil worked harder as many asked for homework.

The second question asked the teachers read as follows: "Did pupils seem to work harder, about as hard, or less hard during the experiment than groups ordinarily do, according to your past experience?" The following replies were received to this question.

EXPERIMENTAL-GROUP TEACHERS IN GRADE II A

1. About as hard as usually.
2. I thought my pupils worked about as hard as they do ordinarily.
3. About as hard.

EXPERIMENTAL-GROUP TEACHERS IN GRADE V A

1. Just as hard.
2. Less hard unless it was a subject they liked.
3. I could see no difference.

CONTROL-GROUP TEACHERS IN GRADE II A

1. Children seemed to work harder.
2. I think they may have worked a trifle harder when spurred on by a threat of failure.
3. The pupils seemed to work about as hard as usual during the experiment.

CONTROL-GROUP TEACHERS IN GRADE V A

1. About the same in some cases, while in others much extra work was done at home and in the morning before school.
2. About as hard.
3. About as hard.

A third question asked teachers was: "After having spent the semester co-operating in this experiment, what is your opinion as to the desirability of conducting an experiment of this kind?" Typical answers to this question are as follows:

1. I think an experiment of this kind would have to extend over a period of years in order to be of value.
2. I liked the close follow-up work in testing which the experiment afforded, but I am not sure it stimulated the group to greater effort solely because of the emphasis on promotion.
3. It has been extremely interesting, and I feel that it will help in solving some of the problems about non-promotion which confront the elementary school.
4. Changing the control group in Grade II A to an experimental group next semester should give some interesting reactions, especially from four pupils who so far in their school life have been "jacked up" quite persistently by their teachers.
5. I don't see that it changed the work in the room.
6. I feel it is an excellent experiment.
7. Very desirable.
8. The child does not expect any drastic change from his past experience. If he has been allowed to go on before when he was not as good as the rest of the group, he thinks he may do so again.

Teachers were asked a fourth question: "Do you think the basic character of this experiment has sufficient significance for education and pupil welfare so that the study ought to be expanded and developed along several unexplored lines?" Nine of the twelve teachers answered in the affirmative, many of them giving excellent suggestions for steps which should be taken next in an effort to solve the many related problems suggested by the present study.

SUMMARY

This investigation represents a preliminary effort to evaluate the effect of the threat of failure as a factor in the achievement of children. Within the limited range of this study it seems fair to conclude that children who are told at the beginning of the semester that all will be in the following grade the next term do as well on a comprehensive achievement test as children who throughout the semester are reminded that they must do good work or suffer non-promotion. This generalization applies about equally well to the groups in Grade II A as to the groups in Grade V A. In general, the statements of experimental-group teachers are to the effect that the elimination of the threat of failure did not affect materially, either favorably or unfavorably, the quality of work, the attitudes, or the application of the pupils. These opinions of teachers are supported by the test results. Consequently, if the line of research represented here can be extended and expanded, there may be hope that within a short time the elementary school can be liberated from the undesirable aspects of non-promotion.

It should be clear to any reader that the study reported herein is only a preliminary step and that the experiment has many limitations. There are numerous questions raised by a project of this kind. What, for example, will be the ultimate effect on the attitudes of children toward success and failure if the policy of 100 per cent promotion is followed throughout a child's elementary-school career? Will six years in the absence of the threat of failure result in a total educational growth by the end of Grade VI as great as the growth attained under the constant pressure of the threat of failure? What differences will there be in the mental health, personality development, and social adjustment of children? How will children who have been permitted to go on regularly from grade to grade in spite of low attainment fit into the academic activities of typical achievers in the intermediate grades? Do teachers now have, or can they be taught, motivating devices other than the threat of failure which will cause each child to achieve to capacity? Is the threat of failure more useful and valuable in higher than in lower grades? What is the relation between promotion policies and report cards? These and many other questions must be investigated more fully before the policy of non-promotion can be generally eliminated in public-school practice.

52 *Attitudes about mental health*

> *In the selection below, Dr. Haun speculates on the causes for misunderstanding, apathy, and prejudice on the part of the general public and among many professional people in matters of mental health. He proposes a different approach to defining reality as a first step toward fostering changed attitudes.*

It would be a somewhat thankless task to add to the collection of statistics designed to show that the general public is skittish about mental illness, and that a distressingly large proportion of professional people share its views. If we are willing to accept this unpleasant fact as already demonstrated, we are free to speculate on why a few general practitioners of medicine display such alarming ignorance of mental disease, why little boys continue to scare each other by

PAUL HAUN, M.D., "Attitudes about Mental Health," *Mental Hygiene,* 43 (1959), 351–57. Reprinted by permission of the publisher.

DR. HAUN (1906–) is Director of Psychiatric Education for the New Jersey Department of Institutions and Agencies. He has been a visiting professor of psychiatry at a number of institutions.

peeking into the windows of psychiatric hospitals, why a Broadway comedy can scarcely hope for success unless it has a few jokes about psychiatry, and why our friends and neighbors grumble about going into the hospital for an appendectomy but sink into soul-wrenching terror at the thought of a mental illness.

There is, I fear, no documented explanation for these sorry facts—no certain answer to the questions that they raise. A conjectural inquiry may, nonetheless, serve a useful purpose if it helps us recognize a new dimension of reality, and assists us in channeling some of our efforts in more promising directions.

I was vacationing at a remote but in no way inaccessible region of the mountains when I met George Hicks. He was a slight, wiry man in his middle fifties who worked in a small furniture factory tucked away among the pine trees. His home was comfortable although it lacked what we nowadays tend to expect in the way of electricity, plumbing and central heating. He and his wife worked their acre or two of ground less as a farm than as a kitchen garden and were able by this means and the exercise of reasonable thrift to stay out of debt and to own a second-hand car and decent clothes. George liked to hunt and fish but was not interested in travel for its own sake and had visited the county seat, a town of some 12,000, only twice in his life. He and his wife, members of the same church attended by the majority of their acquaintances, liked to visit their neighbors and have friends drop in for an evening's sociability.

George had stopped school in the fourth grade to help his father clear a piece of land and had never found the time to go back. He knew all the arithmetic he needed for his work in the furniture factory and for his occasional purchases at the store. He could read, although he habitually formed each word with his lips and kept his place on the page with a forefinger. On the infrequent occasions when he was obliged to sign his name, he did not write it but would draw it clearly and carefully like a picture. He was a dependable, careful worker who got on well with most people. Now and then someone asked his advice, and his opinions were usually respected.

The thing about George, however, was that he believed the world was flat. He had never mentioned it to me and felt no compulsion to persuade others to his view. It came out only after I had known him and his fellow workers at the factory for some little time, and they had gradually discarded some of their company manners. A rather disagreeable young man who enjoyed needling George whenever an opportunity occurred came out with it abruptly one day. George shot a lightning glance at me, ready to run for cover, while the young man who had been his tormentor prepared for a loud guffaw at George's expense. I must have been able to react in much the fashion that would have been expected had I been told that George was fond of cucumbers, because when I asked him how he had come to this conclusion he answered me candidly and quite adequately.

Mountain crests were obviously higher than valleys. Up was up and down was down. If the world was a sort of glorified baseball, it had a top and a bottom. It had up and it had down. It simply went against a man's daily observation that water could be made to run uphill. Unless the world was flat, all the water in the streams and in the oceans would naturally follow the laws of up and down and drain away something in the fashion of the Sherwin-Williams trademark in which big globs of paint are pouring down the sides of the earth and dripping off the bottom. To George the horizon was not the point at which the curvature of the earth became manifest. It was simply the limit of human vision. However far he had walked on his hunting trips, he had seen nothing spherical about the ground beneath his feet and every stream had obviously run downhill.

How about circumnavigation though? Didn't that put his theory in question? George grinned at this, and it was clear that he was still on familiar territory.

Here he was open-minded and felt that there were two possible explanations. First of all, it was hearsay. No one of his acquaintance claimed to have sailed around the world, and George had heard enough fish stories in his life to know that men were not above pulling your leg with a tall tale. He leaned more, however, to the thought that these people were self-deceived and that they had actually mistaken a circular journey on a planar surface for circumnavigation. Those who affirmed that the world was a baseball were stuck with the conclusion that China was directly under foot and, as a consequence, that Chinamen walked upside down—a bit of nonsense which stirred George's risibilities.

It would have been easy to think of George as a fool or, at best, an eccentric. Yet there were certain uncomfortable consequences to this conclusion. In historical perspective a high percentage of humanity would have had to be lumped together as buffoons, including Sophocles and Alexander the Great, Mohammed and Julius Caesar. As late as the sixteenth century there were plenty of competent navigators who if they ventured too far from land were by no means sure that their vessel might not slip over the edge of the world into the measureless void beyond. In fact, I think we will have to give George credit for a greater measure of native intelligence than his tormentor. He came to an unfashionable conclusion based on a careful scrutiny of everything he was able to observe, of every fact he had at his disposal. His tormentor simply accepted the conclusions of other people without the vaguest understanding of how they had been reached. We'll return to George a little later.

I would now like to interpolate two pertinent passages from *The Witch's Hammer*, a book written by two Dominican inquisitors accredited by Pope Innocent VIII. It was first published in Cologne in 1489. Fourteen editions had been issued by 1520, and another 16 between 1574 and 1669. It was a sort of inquisitorial Blackstone, a handbook to which for some 200 years pontiff and king, bishop and judge made constant appeal in their struggle against witchcraft. How did Pope Innocent see the threat? In his Bull Summis Desiderates he says:

"It has indeed lately come to our ears, not without afflicting Us with bitter sorrow, that in some parts of Northern Germany, many persons of both sexes, unmindful of their own salvation and straying from the Catholic Faith, have abandoned themselves to devils, incubi and succubi, and by their incantations, spells, conjurations, and other accursed charms and crafts, enormities and horrid offences, have slain infants yet in the mother's womb, as also the off-spring of cattle, have blasted the produce of the earth, the grapes of the vine, the fruits of trees, nay, men and women, beasts of burthen, herd-beasts, as well as animals of other kinds, with terrible and piteous pains and sore diseases, both internal and external; they hinder men from performing the sexual act and women from conceiving, whence husbands cannot know their wives nor wives receive their husbands; over and above this, they blasphemously renounce that Faith which is theirs by the Sacrament of Baptism, and at the instigation of the Enemy of Mankind they do not shrink from committing and perpetrating the foulest abominations and filthiest excesses to the deadly peril of their own souls, whereby they outrage the Divine Majesty and are a cause of scandal and danger to very many."

The book deals exhaustively with every problem, with every difficulty that could be foreseen, discussing it, resolving it. Part One treats of the three necessary concomitants of witchcraft, which are the devil, a witch and the permission of Almighty God. Part Two treats of the methods by which the works of witchcraft are wrought and directed, and how they may be successfully annulled and dissolved. Part Three relates to the judicial proceedings in both the ecclesiastical and civil courts against witches and indeed all heretics.

In a chapter dealing with some of the more distressing examples of witchchaft we find the following case history. The authors write:

"A certain high-born Count, in the diocese of Strasburg, married a noble girl of equal birth; but after he had celebrated the wedding, he was for three years unable to know her carnally, on account, as the event proved, of a certain charm which prevented him. In great anxiety, and not knowing what to do, he called loudly on the Saints of God. It happened that he went to the State of Metz to negotiate some business; and while he was walking about the streets and squares of the city, attended by his servants and domestics, he met a certain woman who had formerly been his mistress. Seeing her, and not at all thinking of the spell that was on him, he spontaneously addressed her kindly for the sake of their old friendship, asking her how she did, and whether she was well. And she, seeing the Count's gentleness, in her turn asked very particularly after his health and affairs; and when he answered that he was well, and that everything prospered with him, she was astonished and was silent for a time. The Count, seeing her thus astonished, again spoke kindly to her, inviting her to converse with him. So she inquired after his wife, and received a similar reply, that she was in all respects well. Then she asked if he had any children; and the Count said he had three sons, one born in each year. At that she was more astonished, and was again silent for a while. And the Count asked her, 'Why, my dear, do you make such careful inquiries? I am sure that you congratulate me on my happiness.' Then she answered, 'Certainly I congratulate you; but curse that old woman who said she would bewitch your body so that you could not have connexion with your wife! And in proof of this, there is a pot in the well in the middle of your yard containing certain objects evilly bewitched, and this was placed there in order that, as long as its contents were preserved intact, for so long you would be unable to cohabit. But see! it is all in vain, and I am glad,' etc. On his return home the Count did not delay to have the well drained; and, finding the pot, burned its contents and all, whereupon he immediately recovered the virility which he had lost. Wherefore the Countess again invited all the nobility to a fresh wedding celebration, saying that she was now the Lady of that castle and estate, after having for so long remained a virgin. For the sake of the Count's reputation it is not expedient for us to name that castle and estate; but we have related this story in order that the truth of the matter may be known, to bring so great a crime into open detestation."

As with George, who believed the world was flat, it is easy for us to feel a shocked abhorrence at a society which believed in demonic possession and burned miserable old women at the stake because they had been declared to be witches. Yet suppose, for the sake of argument, that witches do exist, that they do cast evil spells upon the innocent and are the proximate cause not alone of a vast amount of human misery, but of the eternal damnation of countless souls who, throughout eternity, will be doomed to unspeakable punishment. Would we not feel a pressing need to combat this terrible threat and to eradicate it root and branch? Would not our humanitarian consciences compel us to be exquisitely cautious in all that we undertook so that no innocent person was mistakenly punished, no hysteria created, no venal motives countenanced? It will interest you to know that this is the consistently reiterated theme of *The Witch's Hammer*. The sober and consistent insistence of its authors—Do not be impulsive! Make no mistake! Destroy only that which is surely evil! Grant only the basic assumption that witches exist and all the rest becomes necessary for the preservation of humanity. We will return to *The Witch's Hammer* a little later.

Having jumped from a hillbilly who believed the world was flat to medieval witchcraft, our next speculative flight is to the comfortably rational year of 1898 and the publication of a novelette by Henry James. He came from a remarkable family and, through long association with his brother, William James, distinguished educator and psychologist, became interested early in his career in the quirks and oddities of personality. Dry facts uncovered in William's careful scientific investigations were seized upon and transmuted in the cold flame of Henry's artistic genius into quite remarkable works of art. The little book he published in 1898 called *The Turn of the Screw* is an exquisitely precise invocation of terror, a clinically exact anatomization of its specific qualities. I challenge anyone who is capable of having a nightmare to read it without experiencing a first-class attack of the creeps. Even to think of the children, Miles and Flora, of Miss Jessel and Mrs. Grose, or of red-haired Peter Quint is to feel our hearts begin to thump and our hair to prickle.

James' success in writing what to many of us is the one authentically terrifying book in the English language is reducible to a quite simple technical device. By his skill as an author he persuades us to believe in the reality of the people and the events he describes. He then whispers a hundred clues which might account for the whole affair and masterfully avoids weighting any of them in a fashion which would clarify the matter or cancel out all of the remaining hints. We are left to flounder helplessly from one speculation to another, each more horrifying than the last, and to find that none has sufficient solidity for us to feel that, bad as it is, we understand at last. For the time that we are under his spell, James compels us to face the unknown, the inexplicable, the incomprehensible, and it is this which is the essence of terror.

Each of us is born with a set of needs which must be met if we are to survive. Most of these we share with other forms of mammalian life: the need for air to breathe, for a degree of warmth, for food, for water, for sleep. None of these is peculiar to our species. Surprisingly enough, there is another need which is seldom mentioned, perhaps because it is so basic that it has escaped our attention. Although it is essential for human development, I would suspect that it is in or near awareness only among human beings. In this sense, it distinguishes the human organism from all other forms of life. Quite simply and quite obviously, it is the need for order, for a measure of predictability in ourselves, in our physical environment and in our relationships with other beings. In this frame of reference, man's entire existence from birth to death is an uninterrupted sequence of educational experiences. The initial lessons concern the difference between a leg which is attached to my body and a rattle which is interruptedly attached to my hand; between a noise and a mouthful of milk; between a mother and the odor of soap. Many years later the lessons may concern the difference between a proton and an electron, or between a note delivered through official diplomatic channels and an inspired editorial appearing in a government-controlled newspaper.

If the infant's hand became first a teddy bear and then a doorknob, and the next instance a noise of ringing bells all in a completely capricious and altogether unpredictable fashion; if all mothers were werewolves, now a bat, now a mote of dust, now the rustle of autumn leaves; if electrons obeyed no discoverable law and nations acted in a manner which could never be defined as probable or improbable, we would have arrived at chaos—and no human being can survive in chaos.

Although the examples I have used are extreme to the point of irrationality, they illustrate the essential nature of the principle. When the titre of uncertainty in existence rises too high, human life becomes impossible. We walk confidently in the daylight because our past experiences which began in infancy and the stream of visual stimuli impinging on our brain assure us that the sidewalk will be solid beneath our feet. We grope and shuffle in the dark because we cannot predict what lies ahead—a precipice, a wall, or a highwayman.

If I believe my friend when he tells me that I am in the center of the Bonneville salt flats and that the ground is entirely without irregularity beneath my feet for miles in all directions, I will consent to run, tightly blindfolded, at top speed for whatever distance my wind holds out. This is faith which, in our search for order and predictability, is quite as serviceable as any other kind of evidence.

We are ready now, I think, for the conclusion. George Hicks needed a picture of the world in which to orient himself. The threat of slipping off a terrestrial sphere into free-floating space flight seemed, according to his best judgment and the direct testimony of his senses, an imminent possibility if the world was not comfortably flat and correspondingly stable. He felt insecure and doubtful with the one theory, comfortable and content with the other. His need for order and for predictability was answered if he accepted what clearly appeared to be the fact. He was satisfied with the opinion held by countless generations of his forebearers.

Pope Innocent VIII believed unshakably in witches, as did his contemporaries. Their existence allowed him to remain convinced of God's mercy and goodness. Their evil works explained a large chunk of the otherwise inexplicable. They were the reason why upright men were visited by disaster; why virtue was not always rewarded; why strange sicknesses attacked, as he says, "infants when in the mother's womb, beasts of burthen, herd beasts, as well as animals of other kinds, vineyards, orchards, meadows, pastureland, corn, wheat, and all other cereals." Belief in witches spared him and all men from a conviction, which in that day appeared as the only alternative, that God had created a capricious, unpredictable and chaotic universe totally lacking in order.

Henry James in his vignette of terror reminds us that we share with George Hicks and with Pope Innocent the same fear of chaos, the same need to have all that touches our lives, categorized by experience, by reason or by faith as somehow, someway susceptible to law; obedient even though obscurely to the dictates of order.

This, I suggest, may explain to some degree our queasiness about madness; our difficulty in accepting the mentally ill as ordinary folk victimized by their genes, or their environment, or their metabolism. Until day before yesterday leprosy gave everybody an attack of supernatural shudders because we were quite unable to understand it. Until this morning epilepsy was the divine disease, quite unsatisfactorily explained by a mishmash of ideas involving possession by evil spirits, prophetic gifts and superhuman strength. Is it then so strange that many of our fellow citizens react with apprehension and anxiety when mentally ill people say unpredictable things, behave in erratic ways, are subject to inexplicable impulses, and make startling demands upon us which we often cannot understand and which appear to have no order about them whatsoever?

In the course of his correspondence with Ralph Waldo Emerson, Henry James, Sr., once wrote: "I am led, quite without any conscious willfulness either, to seek the *laws* of these appearances that swim round us in God's great museum

—to get hold of some central *facts* which may make all other facts properly circumferential, and *orderly."*

The bogeyman who lives in the attic above junior's bedroom is not exorcised by patient explanation and sweet reason. He is routed by father's reassuring presence and by switching on a great many 100-watt light bulbs. Of course, he moves to some other dark and mysterious abode, the hayloft perhaps, or the root cellar, but this is quite another matter. While the lights are on and while father's arm is around Junior's shoulder there are no mumbling phantoms crouched on the broken furniture or shuffling among the attic trunks.

The hospital volunteer and the new employee have a similar experience, I would expect, when they enter their first psychiatric ward. It is the light of understanding and the reassurance of experience which soon dispel the imagined terror and in time allow the willing observer to see more and more of the mentally ill, not as unpredictable monsters, but as lonely, suffering and unhappy human beings.

Some mental health education would appear doomed to failure because its naive exhortations are entirely dissociated from audience experience. It is, I think, akin in its ineffectiveness to a parent's insistence at the dinner table that there are no bogeymen in the attic. Junior simply asks for another dish of ice cream and keeps his own counsel with respect to goblins and their place of residence. Other educative efforts may be less than successful in spite of their unquestioned truth and logical coherence only because they are too fine-spun, too recondite. Their message has yet to be persuasively translated into language that the rest of us can lay hold of, into understanding that we can make our own.

If, as I believe, Henry James, Sr., was expressing a universal human need when he cried out to Emerson for an understandable order in God's great museum, then we whose vocations and interests are in the field of mental health may take comfort in our own insight into what remains about us of social prejudice, public apathy and legislative indifference. With a better understanding of the origin of these attitudes, and of the purposes they serve, we can reflect on the value of our dinner table exhortations about bogeymen, and wisely seek for ever better systems of illumination to push back the darkness.

53 Education for the development of personality

Related selections: 32, 46, 48, 55

Slowly but steadily over the past several decades the point of view that personality or character development must be placed high on the list of the school's objectives has been gaining acceptance. Some critics of the modern school have made this a central point of their criticism, alleging that attention to this phase of develop- ment has lessened the attention spent on enterprises that are more legitimately the function of the school, for example, learning se- lected subject matter. Other students of education feel that person- ality development and subject-matter learning are not rivals for time in the school day, but that the time and energy spent in creat- ing an environment and arranging experiences to enhance per- sonality development pay good dividends in increased subject- matter learning.

In a study of adolescent fantasy extensive case records were gathered on 40 nor- mal adolescent boys and girls. These records include not only the main data of the study—stories told in response to the pictures in the Symonds Picture-Story Test—but also the results of interviews with the pupils and their parents and teachers, autobiographies written by the pupils, personality questionnaires, and information available from the school records. It is believed that these data make it possible to form accurate impressions of this group of pupils—their backgrounds, present abilities, behavior and personalities, and their motivations and outlooks on life.

As each of these cases was reviewed the question was asked: What can the school do that will be of the greatest aid in furthering this pupil's personality development? Naturally, different pupils would apparently profit by different features of school life, so in planning a school program for personality develop- ment it should be recognized that no part of such a program would pertain equally to all pupils. Any school must be ready to relate its program to the individual needs of its pupils, but if a school provided each of the features sug-

PERCIVAL M. SYMONDS, "Education for the Development of Personality," *Teachers College Record*, L (December, 1948), 163–69. Reprinted by per- mission of the publisher.

DR. SYMONDS (1893–1960) was Professor of Education, Teachers College, Columbia University. He was a scholar and author in the fields of psy- chology and personality and developer of projective techniques in testing.

gested herein it would take care of the personality needs of most of its pupils insofar as this can be done in school.

SUGGESTIONS FOR A SCHOOL PROGRAM

The following is not a theoretical armchair program, but one that grew out of intimate acquaintance with 40 normal boys and girls as they were observed by teachers, parents, and fellow students, and as their own attitudes and inner tendencies were revealed by a projective technique, the Symonds Picture-Story Test.

SOCIAL PARTICIPATION. The greatest need among these adolescents was that of opportunity for social participation. Many of them seemed inhibited and withdrawn. This may seem strange in view of the democratic and social nature of schools and society today, but more intimate acquaintance with individuals shows that the greatest personality handicap still is social isolation. Boys need an opportunity to mingle in give-and-take with boys, girls with girls, and boys with girls. This opportunity would be provided in the classroom by a more democratic organization, by more occasions for free interchange of opinion in discussion, and by activities which call for sharing and joint participation. Too much of the work in the classroom is carried on in individual isolation. Classroom learning is too often thought of as an individual process rather than a group process. In addition, the school should provide opportunities for social participation outside the classroom. This can be done in passing from class to class and in the lunchroom, gymnasium, and assembly room, for example. Clubs and organizations should be democratically organized under pupil direction, with provision for group participation that will permit each individual to contribute according to his talents. Must schools relegate the clubroom to some building across the street, or would it be possible to provide something in the nature of a clubroom within the school itself?

Of special importance for some pupils—both boys and girls—is the opportunity to engage in the kind of competition provided by sports. Most boys would profit by participation in contact sports such as basketball, volley ball, soccer, or football. It is surprising how many boys there are of whom it is said, "spends all spare time at home," "fusses in kitchen, cooks," "hobby-photography," "unobtrusive, childish, immature, inattentive," "is now taking up tap and ballroom dancing." This problem is not solved merely by providing the opportunity for participation; these boys are the very ones who would not attend any social activities that the school might provide. Nor would assigning them arbitrarily to activities or trying to force them to participate be successful. They need patient, kindly encouragement to join a group, and should be led to feel that demands would not be made upon them that they could not meet.

ACCEPTANCE. The second plank in the school's platform for personality growth and development is emotional acceptance of these boys and girls by their teachers. Many come from homes in which they do not feel accepted. Some are living in homes as state wards, as foster children, or as stepchildren; some are competing with brothers or sisters and feel that they are not favored by their parents. Consequently, these cases especially need to feel that they are accepted by the school and by their teachers. They need to feel that they "belong" and are welcome.

This necessitates no elaborate machinery or organization. The only requirement is accepting teachers; teachers who like boys and girls of adolescent age, who understand them, who can accept them with all of their aggression, carelessness, irregularity, guilt, and need of punishment. It is not necessary to have long individual conferences with pupils to accomplish this. It can be done by a friendly smile, saying "Good morning," and by recognizing the child when his turn comes. It can be done by judicious praise and encouragement instead of by adverse criticism. Some children need positive expressions of affection which teachers should be willing to give. It increases a child's emotional security in school to know that he really belongs to the school, to his classes, and to organizations within the school.

FREEDOM.   At least 10 of the 40 cases of this study need greater freedom in school. They come from homes in which they are held under strict discipline. The parents take the responsibility for the children's school progress and the children sabotage their efforts by various kinds of passive resistance. What appears in many instances to be lack of ability or lack of interest is really part of an unconscious campaign of non-cooperation. These children need the opportunity to manage themselves, to make their own decisions, to plan and execute their own work. The transition period would be somewhat chaotic before the boy or girl accepted the challenge to assume responsibility for himself. Fear of this transition period is obvious in the anxiety of both parents and teachers with regard to a child's school progress.

FIRMNESS, STRICTNESS.   Not every child needs more freedom. At least 9 of the cases would profit by stricter discipline. These are the boys and girls who come from homes where too much freedom is allowed and there is not enough strictness in laying down requirements and adhering to them. These pupils would profit by being held more strictly accountable for requirements. This should be accomplished by means of frequent and careful checks, not in a repressive, faultfinding way but, after eliciting the pupil's cooperation, with firmness and tact. At least one boy definitely needs to be repressed. He should be required to wait his turn, to be courteous in class, and in general to tone down his smart-alecky attitude. All of this group would benefit by being helped to plan a regular schedule and live up to it.

OPPORTUNITY TO EXPRESS EMOTIONS.   At least 7 cases would benefit by an opportunity to express their emotions. These are children who have been overly repressed, with the result that their personalities are expressionless and colorless. The school should provide opportunity for expression in writing, speaking, drawing, painting, modeling, singing, playing a musical instrument, play-acting, building or making things, and in social activities. The choice of activity should be left pretty much to the pupil, so that he may follow lines of interest already partially developed. It is of particular importance that these children be given freedom to express their hostilities and their loves, the two types of feelings most often repressed in this culture.

For some of these pupils much of the school's program could be looked upon as the constructive expression of aggression. A boy who is described as quick-tempered, impatient, excitable, and having difficulty in personal relations has never learned to put his aggressive impulses to constructive use. The school's program should provide such a boy an opportunity to carry through his work successfully, to construct things, and to take responsibility, so that some of his awkward, aggressive energy will be directed into more satisfying channels. In the case of some girls, the school can help by encouriging them to express their feminine qualities, particularly if they wear severe clothes and tend to compete with boys. A girl should be accepted and admired as a girl, and not made to feel she must be "first," or the dominant person in the group.

SUCCESS.   Schools should provide every boy and girl an opportunity to be *successful* in something, both in the classroom and outside. In the classroom this consists, in large part, of adapting materials and methods to the ability of the individual; and in our big cosmopolitan schools this means more than anything else placing the boy or girl in the group where the work is adapted to his maturity. But success is more than being confronted with a possible task, neither too hard nor too easy: it depends largely on the encouragement of the teacher and her capacity to find something gratifying in the work of a boy or girl. The child who has had unfortunate school experiences, who has suffered by having to compete with a more successful brother or sister, who is spoiled and undisciplined, or whose parents are demanding and critical needs the taste of success in order to find satisfactions which can wean him from disappointment in other areas.

AVOIDANCE OF PUNISHMENT.   In the case of at least 4 children in this group it would be essential for the school to avoid punishment or anything that could be interpreted as punishment. These are in the group of pupils who would benefit from greater freedom—those who have been punished at home and held strictly to the parents' demands. In general, punishment is to be avoided in school, control being maintained by more positive methods. The boys mentioned above have been punished to make them conform to their parents' wishes, and in school they should receive encouragement, praise, and opportunities for self-expression.

PROVISION FOR RESPONSIBILITY.   Giving pupils responsibility, which has been mentioned before, now comes up for special discussion. Responsibility is hard for teachers to give; concern with getting the task done seems to take precedence over development of personal growth. But if pupils are to take responsibility they must be given it, even though the results are not always letter perfect. Giving responsibility means keeping hands off until the task is completed, but holding pupils strictly accountable for what is assigned to them. If the task is one which has meaning to the group as well as to the teacher, then there will be social pressure to see that it is completed: the child will be held accountable to the group as well as to the teacher. If the group's goals are likely not to be met, then the pupil in charge of a project may have to be relieved, but this signal of failure is to be avoided, if possible, and every effort made to help the pupil who has been given the responsibility to carry it through successfully. Much will depend on the insistence and enthusiasm of the teacher.

ENCOURAGEMENT.   Encouragement, which also has been mentioned previously, is needed particularly by those boys and girls who come from homes where they are rejected and feel that they are not loved. These pupils need not only acceptance but also the boost that comes from their being encouraged and urged to do their best. They need more than anything else the steady trust of a teacher who, believing in them, will encourage them to pick up after each discouragement and try again.

OPPORTUNITY FOR PLEASURE.   In the case of two individuals, both girls, who seemed to be somewhat moody and depressed, it was believed that their school life could be made to compensate for the drabness of their homes by providing opportunities for fun. For such boys and girls the school at its worst is a haven and every activity is pleasurable. But schools should strive to make each activity enjoyable for *all* children. The curriculum should be adapted to the interests of the different ages, and it should be organized so as to present a challenge the successful meeting of which brings a thrill. Probably pleasure in school comes as much from being a member of a happy family with important tasks to perform as from any mechanical or organizational arrangement.

FREEDOM FROM COMPETITION.   At least one of the group would derive benefit from a school program in which competition was reduced to a minimum. In the section on "Social Participation" it was pointed out that some boys and girls need the give-and-take of competition. But for others, particularly those already engaged in family rivalries, the competitive nature of many school activities only aggravates an unfortunate personality trend. If competition is introduced into school it should be in a spirit of play; competing for marks, awards, and promotion becomes too serious and threatening for many pupils and should be eliminated.

PROVISION FOR INSIGHT.   It was believed that several pupils in the group would be helped by insight into their personalities. The mirror might be held up to their personalities so that they could see themselves as they appear to others.

Each boy and girl could be helped to understand what purpose various personality trends serve and how each individual adjusts to circumstances in which he lives. This insight can be provided in two ways: in group guidance activities, through exercises of personality description and general discussions of mental hygiene and simple aspects of the psychology of adjustment; in personal counseling, through helping individual boys and girls to know themselves better and to understand the meaning of their adjustments.

PSYCHOLOGICAL HELP.   At least two boys in the group needed professional help. Their adjustments bordered on the psychotic; their fantasies were gravely distorted, and they needed special assistance to bring them back to normal ways of thinking and of meeting their problems. This could be accomplished only if the parents, too, were acquiring saner and more normal attitudes. While only two boys (5 per cent) in the group were definitely in need of professional help (and this is perhaps a fair portion to expect in any school), more than this number could profit from individual professional psychological counseling. And every pupil in school needs the advantage of an educational and vocational counseling program.

It is not suggested that all pupils need all aspects of the above program in the same degree. All aspects should, nevertheless, be provided by the school so that the needs of all individuals can be served. What the school program can contribute to each child must be determined for the individual separately by a detailed case study. Only by such a case study can it be determined whether a pupil needs more freedom or more strictness, more emphasis on social participation or on achieving success, more competition or less, more opportunity to express emotions, or more attention to fulfilling the obligations of a planned program.

It should be stated in all candidness that the suggestions which were blocked out for each pupil in this study came more from life material than from fantasy material. The life history material revealed lacks to be filled and trends to be corrected. The fantasy material did not show the nature of actual adjustments, but pointed out their meaning by revealing the wishes, hopes, desires, anxieties, and guilt feelings that lay beneath them. One boy needed more acceptance and more encouragement because (as revealed by the case material) he was rejected by his stepmother, an attitude which resulted in his continual backsliding in school. His aspirations and ambitions apparent in the fantasy material existed *only* in fantasy and needed the encouragement of his teacher to realize them. The fantasy material often indicated what was lacking, but seldom furnished a clue to how to supply the deficiency.

The school should reinforce the influence of the home in the case of well-adjusted pupils, and counteract and supplement its influence in the case of the poorly adjusted pupils. Actually, it would be difficult for a school to carry through such a program successfully. The parent who expends his aggression in overambition for and strictness with a boy expects the school to reinforce his efforts. For the school to give this boy more freedom would be a distinct threat to the goals of the parent, who would then criticize the school and bring pressure to bear on it to reinforce his own tactics with his boy. Any school, therefore, that genuinely proposes to institute a program of personality development must seek the cooperation of the parents of its pupils and, if necessary, arrange a program of guidance and counseling that will enable parents to adapt their attitudes to the needs of their children.

SUMMARY

After studying the needs of the 40 boys and girls and planning educational programs for them, the conclusion was reached that an understanding of the fantasy life has a secondary but nevertheless important role in determining the essential features of a program for personality development. It is of major importance to know the nature of the child's adjustments, as they can be observed, and something of his background. Knowledge of fantasy helps in discovering the meaning of a child's adjustments and the lacks in his personality development. Any teacher will achieve more sympathy with and understanding of a pupil through acquaintance with his fantasies. The program outlined provides for increased social participation, acceptance by teachers, freedom, firmness, opportunity to express emotions, opportunity to be successful, avoidance of punishment, pupil responsibility, encouragement, opportunity for pleasure, freedom from competition, personality insight, and psychological help. It is emphasized that no one pupil needs all aspects of such a program. Each pupil in a school should be studied intensively as an individual with a view to learning what the school can contribute to his optimum personality development.

THE TEACHER'S
ROLE

54

What psychology can we feel sure about?

Related selections: 1, 6

Is there substantial agreement among psychologists concerning the learning process, child development, instructional method, and other matters of importance to the classroom teacher? Or is it possible to find support in psychology for almost any educational practice and belief that a teacher may choose to utilize and hold? In this selection Watson identifies fifty propositions upon which, he maintains, almost all psychologists can agree, and which have significance for classroom instruction.

Educators and others who wish to apply psychology in their professional work have long been troubled by controversies among psychologists themselves. Behaviorism arose to challenge the introspective method; Thorndike's connectionism was controverted by Gestalt concepts; psychoanalysts talked an almost completely different language. It was natural for teachers to say, "Let's wait until the psychologists themselves straighten out their various systems!" It looked for a while as if one could support almost any educational practice by choosing which psychologist to cite.

Gradually, however, a body of pretty firm facts has accumulated. While it remains true that research findings will be somewhat differently expressed and explained within different theoretical frameworks, the findings themselves are fairly solid.

GOODWIN WATSON, "What Psychology Can We Feel Sure About?", *Teachers College Record*, 61 (February, 1960), 253–57. Reprinted as a separate pamphlet under the title *What Psychology Can We Trust?* (New York: Bureau of Publications, Teachers College, Columbia University, 1961).

DR. WATSON (1899–) is Professor Emeritus of Psychology, Teachers College, Columbia University, and a distinguished scholar and writer in his field.

A workshop of educators recently asked me to formulate for them some statements of what we really know today about children and learning. To my own surprise, the list of propositions with which few knowledgeable psychologists of any "school" would disagree, grew to fifty.

In no science are truths established beyond the possibility of revision. Einstein modified thinking about gravity, even though Newton's observations were essentially correct. Psychology is much younger and more malleable than physics. New facts are constantly accumulating in psychological research, and these will doubtless introduce some qualifications and modifications—conceivably even a basic contradiction. The educator who bases his program on these propositions, however, is entitled to feel that he is on solid psychological ground and not on shifting sands.

What follows is a listing of fifty propositions, important for education, upon which psychologists of all "schools" would consistently agree. These are presented in twelve classifications.

NATURE–NURTURE

1. Every trait in human behavior is a product of the interaction of heredity (as determined at conception by genes) and environmental influences. Some traits (preferences in food or clothing, for example) are easily influenced by nurture; others (height, rate of skeletal ossification) seem to be affected only by extreme differences in environment.

2. There are specific stages in individual development during which certain capacities for behavior appear. The manner in which these capacities are then utilized sets a pattern for later behavior which is highly resistant to change. If unutilized then, they are likely not to develop later (for example, visual perception, mother attachment, language pronunciation, sports skills, peer relations, independence from parents, heterosexuality).

3. The significance of the important biological transformations of pubescence (growth of primary sex organs, development of secondary sex characteristics, skeletal and muscular growth, glandular interaction) lies mainly in the *meaning* which cultural norms and personal history have given to these changes.

LEARNING PROCESS

4. Behaviors which are rewarded (reinforced) are more likely to recur.

5. Sheer repetition without indications of improvement or any kind of reinforcement is a poor way to attempt to learn.

6. Threat and punishment have variable and uncertain effects upon learning; they may make the punished response more likely or less likely to recur; they may set up avoidance tendencies which prevent further learning.

7. Reward (reinforcement), to be most effective in learning, must follow almost immediately after the desired behavior and be clearly connected with that behavior in the mind of the learner.

8. The type of reward (reinforcement) which has the greatest transfer value to other life-situations is the kind one gives oneself—the sense of satisfaction in achieving purposes.

9. Opportunity for fresh, novel, stimulating experience is a kind of reward which is quite effective in conditioning and learning.

10. The experience of learning by sudden insight into a previously confused or puzzling situation arises when: (*a*) there has been a sufficient background and preparation; (*b*) attention is given to the relationships operative in the whole situation; (*c*) the perceptual structure "frees" the key elements to be shifted into new patterns; (*d*) the task is meaningful and within the range of ability of the subject.

11. Learners progress in any area of learning only as far as they need to in order to achieve their purposes. Often they do only well enough to "get by"; with increased motivation they improve.

12. Forgetting proceeds rapidly at first—then more and more slowly; recall shortly after learning reduces the amount forgotten.

MATURATION: LIFE TASKS

13. The most rapid mental growth occurs during infancy and early childhood; the average child achieves about half of his total mental growth by the age of five.

14. Ability to learn increases with age up to adult years.

15. During the elementary school years (ages 6 to 12) most children enjoy energetic activity—running, chasing, jumping, shouting, and roughhouse. For most staid adults this is uncomfortable. Boys are generally more vigorous, active, rough, and noisy than girls.

16. Not until after eleven years of age do most children develop the sense of time which is required for historical perspective.

17. Readiness for any new learning is a complex product of interaction among physiological maturation, prerequisite learning, the pupil's sense of the importance of this lesson in his world, and his feeling about the teacher and the school situation.

INDIVIDUAL DIFFERENCES

18. No two children make the same response to any school situation. Differences of heredity, physical maturity, intelligence, motor skills, health, experiences with parents, siblings, playmates; consequent attitudes, motives, drives, tastes, fears—all these and more enter into production of each child's unique reaction. Children vary in their minds and personalities as much as in their appearance.

19. Pupils vary not only in their present performance but in their rate of growth and the "ceiling" which represents their potential level of achievement.

Some "late bloomers" may eventually surpass pupils who seem far ahead of them in grade school.

20. Gains in intelligence test scores by children are positively related to aggressiveness, competitiveness, initiative, and strength of felt need to achieve.

21. Pupils grouped by ability on any one kind of test (age, size, IQ, reading, arithmetic, science, art, music, physical fitness, and so forth) will vary over a range of several grades in other abilities and traits.

LEVEL OF CHALLENGE

22. The most effective effort is put forth by children when they attempt tasks which fall in the "range of challenge"—not too easy and not too hard—where success seems quite possible but not certain.

23. According to some studies, many pupils experience so much criticism, failure, and discouragement in school that their self-confidence, level of aspiration, and sense of worth are damaged.

TEACHING METHOD

24. Children are more apt to throw themselves wholeheartedly into any project if they themselves have participated in the selection and planning of the enterprise.

25. Reaction to excessive direction by the teacher may be: (a) apathetic conformity, (b) defiance, (c) scape-goating, (d) escape from the whole affair.

26. Learning from reading is facilitated more by time spent recalling what has been read than by rereading.

27. Pupils *think* when they encounter an obstacle, difficulty, puzzle or challenge in a course of action which interests them. The process of thinking involves designing and testing plausible solutions for the problem as understood by the thinker.

28. The best way to help pupils form a general concept is to present the concept in numerous and varied specific situations, contrasting experiences with and without the desired concept, then to encourage precise formulations of the general idea and its application in situations different from those in which the concept was learned.

"DISCIPLINE" AND LEARNING

29. Over-strict discipline is associated with more conformity, anxiety, shyness and acquiescence in children; greater permissiveness is associated with more initiative and creativity in children.

30. When children (or adults) experience too much frustration, their behavior ceases to be integrated, purposeful and rational. Blindly they act out their rage or discouragement or withdrawal. The threshold of what is "too much" varies; it is lowered by previous failures.

GROUP RELATIONS

31. Pupils learn much from one another; those who have been together for years learn new material more easily from one of their own group than they do from strangers.

32. When groups act for a common goal there is better cooperation and more friendliness than when individuals in the group are engaged in competitive rivalry with one another.

33. At age six, spontaneous groups seldom exceed three or four children; play groups all through childhood are smaller than school classes.

34. Children learn that peer consensus is an important criterion; they are uncomfortable when they disagree with their peers, and especially when they find themselves in a minority of one against all the others.

35. Groups which feel some need (internal coherence or external pressure) to work together try to influence deviates toward the group norm. If there is no felt need to stay together, the deviate may be ignored and thus excluded.

36. Leadership qualities vary with the demands of the particular situation. A good leader for a football team may or may not be a good leader for a discussion group, a research project, or an overnight hike; leadership is not a general trait.

37. In most school classes, one to three pupils remain unchosen by their classmates for friendship, for parties, or for working committees. These "isolates" are usually also unpopular with teachers.

SUBJECT MATTER

38. No school subjects are markedly superior to others for "strengthening mental powers." General improvement as a result of study of any subject depends on instruction designed to build up generalizations about principles, concept formation, and improvements of techniques of study, thinking, and communication.

39. What is learned is most likely to be available for use if it is learned in a situation much like that in which it is to be used and immediately preceding the time when it is needed. Learning in childhood, forgetting, and relearning when needed is not an efficient procedure.

40. Television is the most frequently reported activity of elementary school pupils, occupying about the same number of hours per week as are given to school—far more than would voluntarily be given to school attendance.

ATTITUDES AND LEARNING

41. Children (and adults even more) tend to select groups, reading matter, TV shows, and other influences which agree with their own opinions; they break off contact with contradictory views.

42. Children remember new information which confirms their previous attitudes better than they remember new information which runs counter to their previous attitudes.

SOCIAL STRATIFICATION

43. Attitudes toward members of "out-groups" are usually acquired from members of one's "in-group."

44. Children who differ in race, nationality, religion, or social class background, but who play together on a footing of equal status and acceptance, usually come to like one another.

45. Children who are looked down upon (or looked up to) because of their family, school marks, social class, race, nationality, religion, or sex tend to adopt and to internalize this evaluation of themselves.

46. Two thirds of the elementary school children of America come from lower-class homes; the one third who come from the lower-lower class usually find school very uncongenial.

47. Children choose most of their "best friends" from homes of the same socioeconomic class as their own.

48. More girls than boys wish, from time to time, that they could change their sex.

EVALUATION

49. If there is a discrepancy between the real *objectives* and the *tests* used to measure achievement, the latter become the main influence upon choice of subject matter and method.

50. The superiority of man over calculating machines is more evident in the formulation of questions than in the working out of answers.

55 The classroom teacher and the emotional problems of children

Related selections: 28, 32, 53, 57

We are often reminded that "the whole child comes to school." Many teachers, however, ask if it is possible for them to foster desirable emotional development of children and provide help for

C. H. PATTERSON, "The Classroom Teacher and the Emotional Problems of Children," *Understanding the Child*, XXI (June, 1952), 67–72. Reprinted by permission of the National Association for Mental Health.

DR. PATTERSON (1912–   ) is Professor of Education at the University of Illinois. He was formerly a counseling psychologist with the Veterans Administration.

those who have some degree of emotional disturbance. Dr. Patterson makes specific suggestions for the teacher who desires to maintain a classroom environment that embodies the conditions for good mental hygiene.

Increasingly it is being accepted that the classroom teacher is responsible for more than the academic development of the child. Education now tries to supply the physical needs of the pupil as well, since it has been recognized that a child handicapped by a temporary or permanent physical disability is also handicapped in academic learning. In comparison with the physically handicapped, relatively little has been done in the classroom for the emotionally disturbed or handicapped pupil. But it is just as true, perhaps even more true, that the academic progress of the child is affected by his emotions and feelings. As Dorothy Baruch and others point out, children bring their emotions, as well as their minds and bodies, to school with them.

It is true that much progress has been made since the study of Wickman, which revealed the disagreement between teachers' concepts of the seriousness of behavior characteristics and the opinions of mental hygienists. Since that time considerable effort has been made to help teachers recognize emotional disturbances when they exist. The well-behaved, overly quiet child may be covering up a serious emotional disturbance.

The emphasis, however, has been upon the recognition, or diagnosis, of emotional problems. Many teachers have become quite skilled in detecting signs of emotional disturbances in children who should be referred for special treatment. This is well and good, since early treatment is desirable. But emotional disturbance is a matter of degree, and there are many less serious problems, or beginning problems, which cannot be treated by the limited number of psychiatrists and psychologists available. And there are the more or less normal or temporary emotional disturbances of the so-called "average" child. The teacher has a responsibility in these cases, so that emotional development will continue normally. That is, the teacher should be able to maintain a healthy environment for the emotional development of all of her pupils.

Little has been done to help the teacher meet this responsibility and opportunity. There has been much discussion of the problem, but not of how to handle it, except through referral of serious cases. More than this is necessary. The teacher must acquire and be able to put into practice the attitudes and techniques of good mental hygiene. This is necessary because, as suggested above, not all maladjusted children can be treated in a clinic; because there are many borderline cases for which there are no treatment facilities; and because the principles of mental hygiene which are effective with maladjusted children are equally good for the normal child, who also has emotions.

CHARACTERISTICS OF
EMOTIONAL DISTURBANCE

As a background for dealing with emotional maladjustment, it is essential that the teacher understand what the emotionally disturbed child is like. There are several points which must be kept in mind.

1. *The emotionally maladjusted child is not a malingerer.* He is not faking, he is not pretending or feigning in order to gain something, inventing complaints for his own ends. He is not deliberately manufacturing excuses and alibis.

2. *Emotional maladjustment is not a willful or consciously developed condition.* It is not brought on by conscious design, but develops against the will of the child. It is not an indication of wickedness, stubbornness, laziness or perverseness. It is not true, as is sometimes thought, that an emotionally maladjusted child can cure himself if he only wants to, if he will only "buckle down," try to control himself, or "snap out of it." Of course, maladjusted behavior serves a purpose, but it is not consciously developed as a clever trick to avoid something unpleasant.

3. *The physical complaints so common in emotional maladjustment are not imaginary.* Another mistaken notion is that the aches and pains of the emotionally maladjusted individual are not real. But the fact that a symptom or pain is of functional or psychological origin rather than of physical origin does not make it any the less painful or annoying. The nervous child actually suffers from his physical symptoms. A functional pain or symptom is just as real and painful and disabling as one due to organic disease.

4. *An emotional disturbance is not a sign of weakness.* It is trite to say that everyone has his breaking point, but it is true. The stresses and strains of military life were severe enough to cause many individuals to become emotionally maladjusted who might never have become so if they had continued in civilian life. There are many emotionally disturbed—or neurotic—individuals who are very successful in business, the professions, and the arts. Many are hard-working, ambitious, conscientious individuals, who perhaps take things too seriously at times. Emotional maladjustment is not something to be ashamed of; it is a misfortune, not a disgrace. The emotionally disturbed child is therefore not to be considered inferior, worthless, or untrustworthy. He is not of tainted heredity. He is not a slacker or coward. During the war the proportion of medals was as great among those who broke down in combat as among those who did not.

5. *Emotional maladjustment takes many forms.* It has been called the great imitator. It may manifest itself in tremors, headaches, backaches, other pains, shortness of breath, palpitation of the heart, rapid pulse, high blood pressure, excessive perspiration, anorexia, vomiting, indigestion, stomach upset, constipation, diarrhea, irritability, fatigue, restlessness, inability to concentrate, fears and phobias, functional blindness, deafness or muteness, stuttering, functional paralyses, as well as hostility, over-aggressiveness, etc. Because of the physical symptoms, it is important that a physical examination be given to check for any

organic disease. However, if after thorough examination no physical basis for the complaint is found, an emotional disturbance is probably present. It has been estimated that from one-half to two-thirds of those individuals seen by the average doctor have a psychological, or emotional, basis for part or all of their complaints.

Many of these symptoms are present at times in all of us, without any physical basis. We are all familiar with the headache which develops—on a purely unconscious level—when we face an unpleasant engagement. A temporary emotional disturbance may be responsible for a variety of physical and psychological symptoms, without, however, warranting the classification of the individual as a neurotic.

WHAT CAN THE TEACHER DO?

With the general understanding of emotional disturbances just discussed, what can the teacher do for the emotional needs of the child? Without being a psychologist or a psychiatrist, how can she handle emotionally disturbed children, or the temporary emotional upsets of the average child? We shall discuss briefly some of the attitudes and techniques which are important in such situations. First, there are several "don'ts" which follow from the characteristics of the emotionally disturbed individual just presented.

1. Since the emotionally disturbed child is not a malingerer, or pretending, he should not be treated as such. He shouldn't be accused of faking, of making up or exaggerating his complaints. He is honest and sincere in his claims, and should be respected as such, with belief, not suspicion.

2. Since emotional maladjustment is not willful, but is beyond conscious control, no one should be blamed for it. Don't condemn the maladjusted child. It does no good to tell him to use his will power, to "snap out of it"—he would if he could. Lectures, sermons, exhortations are usually useless. Avoid such comments as "you should know better"; "you're old enough not to do that"; "what if your mother knew about this?"; "you should be ashamed of yourself."

3. Since the pains and physical complaints are real, not imaginary, don't deny them, or tell him to forget them, or try to argue him out of them. Accept his aches and pains, recognize them as unpleasant and disabling. Don't deny him medical attention—if he doesn't need it, the doctor will tell him so.

4. Since the emotionally disturbed child is not a weakling or coward, he should not be condemned as one, or blamed or censored as if he had committed a crime. Anger, reproval, "telling him off," are harmful to his attempts to adjust. His feelings of self-condemnation, guilt, and failure are so strong that reproach or condemnation by others may drive him deeper into despair and hopelessness.

5. Don't diagnose or label, or classify the emotionally maladjusted child as abnormal, neurotic, or "a mental case." It is not necessary to be familiar with psychiatric terminology; applying a psychiatric label to the child doesn't help him, but will probably hurt him. The psychiatrist is the only one qualified to make a psychiatric diagnosis.

6. Don't talk about the child in his presence, to his parents or to anyone else. Frequently teachers have been overheard talking about a child, in very uncomplimentary terms, while he is present but ignored, as if he weren't present, or didn't count—almost as if he weren't a person at all, but an inanimate object. Such treatment is damaging to the child and to his self-respect. He should be treated as a human being who has feelings.

The teacher should be able to do more than to avoid these mistaken attitudes, however. She should be able to do something positive to foster the adjustment of the child. Teachers frequently complain that they don't have training in mental hygiene, or that they don't have time to study each child as an individual. But it is not necessary to have extensive training in mental hygiene to be helpful. Nor is it necessary to have a detailed, complete case history, to know all the facts about the background, development, and home life of each child. There are certain basic, fundamental attitudes and techniques that are applicable in all situations involving emotional expression which teachers can cultivate, with no more background in mental hygiene than has been just discussed.

1. The most essential element in handling emotional disturbances is that there be a real understanding and acceptance of the child, as he is, with his negative attitudes, hostility and aggression, destructiveness, etc. These emotional reactions are just as natural as the more positive ones—they are not bizarre, "crazy," shameful, but natural expressions under the circumstances. Realizing this the teacher must avoid condemnation, criticism, and moralizing. It is not necessary that the exact cause of the behavior be known; it is enough to know that it is natural under certain conditions. These conditions almost always involve situations in which the child has been hurt, frightened, threatened. It is only natural that resentment, aggressiveness, anger, and other negative emotional behavior result. The test of the ability of a teacher to handle emotional disturbances constructively is whether or not she can accept such negative, hostile, emotions and resulting behavior as natural responses.

The most important need of the child is to be understood and accepted—to be able to share his thoughts, without fear, suspicion, or defensiveness. The maladjusted child feels aggressive because he feels threatened. He actually is threatened by others, usually the adults in his environment, when they criticize, condemn, exhort, or shame him. He needs to feel understood, to feel that someone accepts him as he is for what he is, with all his faults, to feel that someone knows how he feels.

To be able to put oneself in the place of another helps in understanding that other person. It is in this way that empathy develops, which leads to the ability to understand the other person.

2. If one really understands the emotionally disturbed child, and accepts his negative, hostile behavior as natural under the circumstances, the next step is to realize that emotions, once stirred up, need to be expressed or released. This may seem to be contrary to the attitude of many teachers, who feel that

negative behavior and emotions must be controlled. They believe that the child cannot be allowed to express hostility, anger, or hatred of others, including his parents and teacher. If he cannot control these emotions, the teacher attempts to suppress them. But such attempts to exert control result only in suppression, or perhaps gradually repression by the child himself—the emotions continue to exist, and to cause emotional maladjustment in the child. Contrary to general opinion, the freedom to express the emotions of hostility and hatred does not result in an increase of such negative emotions and behavior, after the initial period following such freedom. It rather allows the negative emotions to drain themselves off, so that the more positive, constructive emotions and behavior have a chance to show themselves. Discipline and punishment are thus not the answers to negative emotions and behavior. Expression rather than suppression or repression is necessary if the child is to reach a stage of better adjustment.

This does not mean that the child is allowed to be physically assaultive or destructive. There must be limits set to prevent injury to other children and adults, and damage to property. But while destructive behavior is prohibited when it injures others, there is no limit to the expression of destructive and aggressive thoughts and feelings, and if possible the expression of such behavior on substitute objects, such as rubber toys, especially dolls representing the individuals towards whom the child feels aggressive or resentful. Verbalization of feelings and emotions is to be encouraged, and accepted without surprise or shock. It is important that the teacher really be able to accept such feelings, without actually condemning or judging the child in her thoughts. Children are acutely aware of our feelings, and sense if they are really being understood and accepted, or if we are only pretending to do so. If it is the latter, the child will know it and be suspicious, afraid of being tricked into saying or doing something for which he will be punished. We must really prove to him that we are accepting and understanding. Being able to express in words those feelings which the child himself is unable to verbalize is often helpful in showing him that we do understand.

It is impossible here to go into the detailed methods and techniques of developing an understanding of the child, of encouraging the expression of his emotions, and of helping him handle them constructively. Rogers has developed this method as a means of therapy with adults. Baruch has applied the same principles to handling children in the home. They are just as applicable to dealing with children in the school. Student-centered teaching is the term used for applying the principles of client-centered therapy to teaching. Excellent discussions of this approach will be found in Axline, Rogers, and Snygg and Combs. The teacher who wishes to provide the best emotional environment for her pupils, and who feels that the emotional development of pupils is at least as important as their academic progress, will want to learn more about these new techniques and methods.

56 Education and psychotherapy

Related selections: 7, 27, 37, 39, 57

It is often said that teachers should help students to develop healthy personalities. This concern for the all-round development of children is evidenced by the reading and study that teachers are doing in the area of personality development and psychotherapy. Some see this as a desirable, constructive movement in present-day education. Others raise serious questions about the feasibility of relatively untrained persons' attempting to apply the principles of therapy. Professor Symonds points out the basic similarities and differences between education and psychotherapy and clarifies many of the issues involved.

At the beginning of the movement toward psychoanalytic education and the introduction of mental hygiene principles into education the aims and methods of education and psychotherapy were far apart. Psychotherapy was concerned with bringing mentally disturbed persons to normality; while education was concerned with imparting knowledge, helping in the formation of skill, and in general in assisting boys and girls to develop along lines that would help them to fit as responsible members into the society in which they were growing up. With the passage of years the function of psychotherapy is conceived to be that of assisting in belated personality development while education, too, has accepted greater responsibilty for the all-round development of the individual instead of for isolated segments of his personality. Methods of the two disciplines, too, have become more and more alike until some writers suggest that they are almost identical.

Axline, for instance, says: "The basic principles of non-directive therapy seem to have far-reaching implications for educators" . . . "the most important single factor in establishing sound mental health is the relationship that is built up between the teacher and his or her pupils." . . . "It is the permissiveness to be themselves, the understanding, the acceptance, the recognition of feelings, the clarification of what they think and feel that helps children retain their self-

PERCIVAL M. SYMONDS, "Education and Psychotherapy," *Journal of Educational Psychology*, XL (January, 1949), 5–20. Reprinted by permission of the publisher.

For a brief biographical sketch of DR. SYMONDS, see the footnote accompanying selection 53.

respect; and the possibilities of growth and change are forthcoming as they all develop insight. . . . It is in the establishment of this relationship that the basic principles of self-directive therapy loom up into an important position. . . . The teacher will accept each and every child exactly as he or she is. . . ." "The teacher will establish a feeling of permissiveness in the relationship so that the child feels free to express his feelings and to be himself. . . . The therapist-teacher is alert to recognize the feelings the child is expressing and reflects those feelings back to the child in such a manner that the child gains insight into his behavior. This can be done to a great extent in any classroom situation if the teacher has an understanding of her pupils and an insight into human behavior."

This lengthy quotation would imply that the distinction between psychotherapy and teaching has diminished so as to have reached the vanishing point. Perhaps the pendulum has swung too far and the time has come to point out in what way psychotherapy and education differ as well as how they are alike. One's attention is caught by the attitude expressed by Cantor who has suggested introducing progressive methods into college teaching. In discussing a conference with a student he says: "He [the student] wanted to talk about the backgrounds of his difficulty. It was a temptation to which I almost yielded since I felt that he would be immensely relieved if he could express what was troubling him. But talking about what led up to his poor work would have been another way of avoiding doing something about it.

I am not a therapist. My function is to deal with a student's difficulty only insofar as his work in the course is involved."

This raises the question: What psychotherapy and what education am I talking about? It is recognized that there are many differing points of view and shades of opinion about both education and psychotherapy. However, a recent symposium designed to ventilate possible differences in point of view concerning psychotherapy concluded that there was more general agreement than disagreement on many issues. Agreement among educators may not be so apparent. The point of view taken in the following pages to represent education corresponds closely to what is known as Progressive education and may have little correspondence to education as it is found in actual practice up and down the land. The following discussion, however, explicitly recognizes and attempts to clarify many of the unsolved issues in both disciplines.

SIMILARITY BETWEEN
PSYCHOTHERAPY AND EDUCATION

First let us review some of the points of similarity between psychotherapy and education.

1. *Both teachers and therapists should treat children as individuals with potentialities for progressively taking over direction of themselves.* This principle certainly has not always been followed by teachers in practice. Many teachers, sensing so strongly the immaturity of children, do not have faith in their poten-

tialities to take responsibility for themselves and hence exercise close restraint and control. And it must be admitted that it becomes difficult, if not impossible, to see the individual when he is one child in a class of forty. But this principle is being accepted more and more by progressive teachers for whom the conditions of teaching permit giving children greater responsibility.

2. *Both teachers and counselors should be warm, friendly, outgoing, pleasant and kindly.* The exact attitude and relationship here must be defined carefully. It does not mean effusiveness, a bubbling-over approach, lavishing affection or sympathy. It does not consist of giving praise, or flattery. It exercises itself in such qualities as genuine interest, sensitivity to the feelings of others, willingness to listen to the other person, and being unhurried, sincere and genuine. It may mean little more than the friendly nod, the cheery "good-morning" or the sympathetic smile. Snyder who has discussed the meaning of warmth in non-directive counseling seems to find the essence to lie in the correct use of standard therapeutic procedures, minimizing the emphasis on emotional outgoingness. Perhaps the essence of what is meant by warmth cannot be defined in terms of what the therapist does, the feelings he expresses, or the attitudes he assumes, but rather is a less tangible quality which emanates from a personality which is free from tension and anxiety.

3. *Both teachers and therapists are counseled to accept the child as he is— no matter how stupid, lazy, dirty, resistive, or disorderly.* One of the cornerstones of modern psychotherapy is the acceptance of the patient by the therapist. Accepting means more than tolerating. It means on the one hand avoiding negative feelings toward a child of dislike, contempt or disgust, and withholding criticism, censure, or blame; but it also means that there must be some genuine liking as might be shown when the teacher is glad when a boy comes to school and is sorry when he is absent. For the teacher this means accepting potentiality and promise in a child as well as the skills and habits actually present. A teacher may like a boy because he sees that he has potentialities for growth. Children are highly sensitive to minor indications of lack of interest, boredom, preoccupation with other matters and other attitudes of unconcern which the therapist or teacher may show.

Should the teacher accept negative behavior? Should the teacher accept breaking of the rules, destructiveness, hostile behavior? He may accept them no more than the therapist. A teacher is expected, as we have seen, to express what he as a person and as a representative of society does and does not stand for. But it is possible at the same time to accept the person who has broken these rules. It is possible to accept the person while at the same time rejecting what the person does. Many a child feels sure that his mother or teacher really loves him when the parent or teacher takes time to chide or reprimand him. A teacher may be disappointed in what a child accomplishes, to be sure, but faith and belief in his potentialities still persist. And both therapist and teacher must show tolerance, a willingness to overlook and be forgiving, with faith in the final triumph and emergence of the forces of good.

Acceptance, *per se*, does not mean approval, or disapproval; that is the valuation of behavior. But here is where teaching and therapy part company. Therapy, since it is not interested in directing change, does not evaluate. Education, since it is interested in directing change, adds to mere acceptance valuation through praise and criticism.

Should the teacher accept negative feelings? Yes, temporarily as a therapist for the purpose of helping the child to accept himself and eventually to reduce the need for negative feelings. But since teachers cannot work with negative feelings as teachers, these feelings must be discouraged so that positive feelings can operate in their place. Teachers may use the therapeutic method of dissipating negative feelings by recognizing them, sensing from whence they spring and recognizing the justification for them, and also helping the child to recognize them, but they can also be dissipated by disregarding them, or jollying and 'kidding' a person along about them.

But being accepting means a certain greater degree of emotional restraint by the therapist than the teacher, for the therapist avoids giving praise, rewards, gifts, advice and suggestions, in fact, any outgoing response that can be interpreted as a form of control.

4. *Teachers and therapists may also be expected to be permissive—but to a degree only.* Teachers and therapists not only should accept the child in spite of his past behavior, but give the child permission to be himself, in feeling particularly, in behavior as far as possible. Both teachers and therapists believe in the practice of restraining dangerous and destructive behavior, and both believe in giving freedom for the expression of feeling. But the teacher is not merely a permissive person; he also positively encourages, stimulates and directs. A good teacher finds a happy balance between being permissive on the one hand, and using his influence in directing, acting, thinking and feeling on the other.

5. *Both teachers and therapists have a responsibility to understand the child.* A therapist is expected to be particularly sensitive to unconscious motives and the mechanisms by which they are expressed. A teacher is expected to be particularly sensitive to conscious motives and interests, but the teacher who is also sensitive to unconscious motives may be better able to tolerate the bad in a child and hence to find opportunity for the release of negative feelings while at the same time he may appreciate untapped possibilities for constructive growth and be more courageous and patient in encouraging their expression.

6. *Both teachers and therapists should be sensitive to feelings expressed by the child and should help the child to be aware of them.* This is one of the therapist's principal tasks, but only one of many angles of the teacher's task. Many teachers, however, would not dare to let pupils express their feelings openly and freely—to do so would be too great a threat to the teacher's prestige and authority. But children should learn at school not only about the world around them, but also about the world within, and this *insight* can be best acquired by permitting pupils to express their feelings freely and then directing their attention toward them.

DIFFERENCES BETWEEN
PSYCHOTHERAPY AND EDUCATION

Having now pointed out six points which education and psychotherapy have in common, let us review the ways in which they differ.

1. *A teacher is principally concerned with the world of reality and his task is to help children to become effective in the real world.* A therapist, on the other hand, according to Rogers, *gives his attention primarily to the feelings expressed by a child* and neglects or overlooks as of less importance the content of what a child says. Instead of helping a child to adjust to the real world, a therapist helps a child to accept himself with all his immaturity, limitations and shortcomings. This distinction, however, need not be too sharply drawn. The teacher, too, must give attention to feelings when feelings interfere with attention to the task at hand. The wise teacher selects some activities such as dramatics, painting and drawing, music, story-telling or rhythms to promote and encourage the release of feelings. Constructive activities in shop and laboratory may provide outlets for aggressive tendencies. When a teacher, however, has to pause to pay attention to the feelings which his pupils are expressing he is, strictly speaking, stepping out of his rôle as a teacher and temporarily functioning as a therapist. If the child responds readily to recognition of his feelings and returns quickly to the task at hand instead of having further to defend himself, the teacher can well afford this brief excursion into the therapeutic realm. If, on the other hand, the child is slow to respond and needs to have his attention called repeatedly to the feelings he is expressing, or if he lacks control even after he has given his attention to them, then the teacher is stepping out of his rôle as teacher for therapeutic ends. If the child is his only pupil then that may be the best use of his services, but if he is the teacher of a class then this one child may be usurping time which the teacher should be devoting to the educational interests of other children who are ready to use it.

2. *A teacher feels and expresses love, but avoids hate; a therapist does not express either love or hate.* A teacher enters himself into the relationship emotionally—he gives of himself to his pupils. He cares for them, devotes himself to their needs and interests and uses his energies on their behalf. A teacher, to be successful, must like his pupils—like them well enough to work for them as well as for himself. He gives of himself freely and not only on condition that the child meets his expectations. It is in response to these expressions of love that a child learns; he learns in order to retain this love and to avoid anxiety lest love be withdrawn. The teacher cannot afford to hate, however, for hate stirs up antagonistic emotions in the child, which interfere with learning.

The therapist, on the other hand, neither loves nor hates but avoids becoming emotionally involved in the relationship. Hamilton says of this: "The 'love' of the therapist consists of warmth, concern, therapeutic understanding, interest in helping the person to get well. . . . The therapist does not give love in the ordinary sense, just as he must not disapprove of or dislike what the client is, says, or does." When the therapist enters actively into the therapeutic situation with tokens of love there is danger that the child will be encouraged to become more infantile and dependent than ever—just the opposite of the therapeutic aim. Ackerman has written at length on the problem of the therapist's "giving love." He says: "A large number of patients who seek the aid of psychotherapy are able initially neither to receive nor to give love. For them, the psychotherapist's aim must be not so much to 'give love' as to modify their characters in order to prepare them to accept love and then return it." And again: "Patients need love. They have suffered privations in their childhood and, especially, they have been denied love by their own parents. Nevertheless, certain important obstacles interfere with compensating for that original lack." Ackerman goes on to discuss at length mechanisms in the client that prevent him from being able to accept love and in the therapist from giving it.

With regard to the giving of gifts by the therapist to the child, Allen says: "Some therapists might feel like giving a child a present at the end, but I do not like the practice, as it seems false and confusing. At the end some children feel guilty about wanting to stop; giving a present can accentuate that feeling."

3. *The teacher expresses himself boldly and readily.* He not only imparts information and guides in the formation of skill, but also expresses his stand on issues. *The teacher is a dynamic, vigorous, outgoing individual.* Society expects a teacher to direct and lead the way. In controversial issues a teacher may be expected to present fairly both sides and in any case he ought to present the bases and arguments for each point of view. But a *therapist is expected to be a more passive individual.* Although he should be warm, friendly, interested, tolerant and sensitive, he avoids exposing or exerting his personality too directly or openly on the client. His principal task is to understand the client, to be sensitive to his feelings and hence to help the client to accept and become more tolerant of his own feelings and tendencies to action. *The therapist believes that his task is not directively to influence or control his client;* indeed, he believes he will defeat his purpose of encouraging his client to self-expression if he exercises too much control.

4. *The teacher uses praise and blame, reward and punishment to aid in the education process.* Teachers that I have observed who have been most successful in their work have been extravagantly lavish with praise. The praise has been given warmly and with enthusiasm; but it has been genuine praise for acts or work that has been deemed praiseworthy and children have been sensitive to its sincerity. Children respond to praise with increased effort and the use of praise helps to establish the positive relationship mentioned above.

The teacher also uses censure or blame judiciously. Mild criticism probably meets Estes' criterion of a punishment that is mild and which actually influences unlearning. A severe punishment inhibits behavior and hence removes an act from the influence of either positive or negative learning. Mild criticism or blame may permit an act to be repeated without satisfaction or reward or rein- forcement and, hence, satisfies the conditions for experimental extinction and unlearning. The wise teacher, however, does not criticize or blame without mak- ing sure that a positive love relationship has already been established, for it is only on the basis of a positive relationship that positive learning can take place to supplement the reaction that is being extinguished.

The therapist uses neither praise nor blame, reward nor punishment. The task of the therapist is to encourage response, to enable the subject to accept himself as he is, to reduce the necessity for continued use of defensive measures, to avoid encouraging a person to over-estimate himself, and to help a person to become self-directing. Praise certainly encourages a subject to follow the suggestion of the would-be therapist and may lead to over-self-valuation. Criticism would force the continued and increased use of defensive measures and would defeat tendencies toward self-acceptance.

5. *The teacher stimulates, encourages, directs, guides.* This is the teacher's recognized and established function. He has been employed by society to act as a leader and a guide. This does not mean that he need operate autocratically, or with use of coercion or force. His influence rather can be that of a kindly older person who can show the way that children want to go. And as he suggests or advises it is always with the child's interests in mind. As Rank points out, "The child will instinctively grasp the ideologies offered to him, because he needs them as props for the unfolding and justification of his individual ego." So the teacher uses influence without undue pressure. By stating his position and his likes and dislikes vigorously, the child who already loves, respects and trusts his teacher will want to go in the direction pointed out.

The therapist, on the other hand, consistently avoids using any influence in the form of suggestion, advice or encouragement. The therapist's task is to strengthen the ego of the child, to make the child more independent and more self-directing and self-supporting. To influence the child by suggestion or guid- ance is to interfere with the development of self-determination.

The teacher, too, is interested in helping children become more mature. Con- sequently he provides considerable genuine freedom, but the teacher is always there to offer suggestions or support, recognizing that the immature child may need guidance or support for his own emotional security.

These principles regarding the neutrality of the therapist are sometimes vio- lated in the interest of the reality of the situation. When a child threatens vio- lence and harm or damage either to persons (including the therapist himself) or to property, then the therapist may exert a restraining influence. A distinc- tion is made between verbal (or fantasy) expression and motor expression. Motor expression can become so violent and disorganized that it loses any growth value it might have, whereas verbal or fantasy expression would seem always to be closer to the influence of judgment and reason. It would seem then that there are occasions when the therapist must broaden his rôle and act more like a teacher until the child regains his emotional equilibrium. On the other hand, these controls must not be placed too high for there is sometimes therapeutic value in the cathartics of strong emotional release.

It is of interest that the therapist in deciding to wield no directing influence himself depends on a principle of self-realization in the client to take care of direction. He posits an innate tendency toward self-direction in the client which will lead him to make wise choices and decisions. Rogers, who has elucidated this principle at length in recent papers, says concerning it: "One is compelled through clinical observation to develop a high degree of respect for the ego-integrative forces residing in each individual. One comes to recognize that under proper conditions the self is a basic factor in the formation of personality and in the determination of behavior. Clinical experience would strongly suggest that the self is, to some extent, an architect of self, and the above hypothesis simply puts this observation into psychological terms" . . . And again: "the client has a strong drive to become mature, socially adjusted, independent, productive" . . . "In most if not in all individuals there exist growth forces, tendencies toward self-actualization. . . . The individual has the capacity and the strength to devise, quite unguided, the steps which will lead him to a more mature and more compatible relationship to his reality." Rogers implies here that the subject not only has innate forces within him that lead him to seek a better integrated adjustment toward reality but that these same forces direct him toward that reality.

The following incident from one of Axline's cases would indicate that the direction of the adjustment is a product of education rather than of some internal force. Ernest who visits his mother with traumatic results comes to his next play session expressing his aggressive feelings with profanity. " 'They are the God-damnest nails. Bitty baby nails. Mama and papa nails. Look at this old bitch! Son-of-a-bitch if I ever saw one.' Therapist: 'You've learned some new words that you want to show off.' [Beautiful handling of this situation by recognition of the attitude the child is expressing. Note again that the satisfactory classification of an attitude, in an accepting atmosphere, immediately dissolves the need for symbolic expression. It is this that accounts for the fact that accepted catharsis, that is, outgiving of feelings, alters behavior.] Ernest: 'Mrs. R. has a fit. She says I'll go to hell. They are bad words.' Teacher: 'Mrs. R. says they are bad words, but you still like to use them.' "

According to the report Ernest used no more profanity during the session. But can this be attributed to the result of an inner tendency of self-realization or ability to accept Mrs. R.'s judgment that these are bad words? It seems obvious that the direction of the behavior is determined in part culturally, that is, by the influence of education in the broad sense. Therapists believe that they defeat their own purposes if they themselves try to direct behavior, but it is obvious that they depend on society's offering very pronounced efforts to direct behavior. The task of psychotherapy is to assist in a reorganization of personality so that the individual is able to benefit by education.

6. *A teacher should on occasion be firm.* He should take a stand and express

himself with conviction with regard to many issues and stick to his stand with consistency. Firmness, however, need not involve the use of force and should not be confused with punishment. It would be of little use for a teacher to exert firmness if he had not already shown love and in turn won love from his pupils. If a positive relationship has been established, if pupils are sensitive and responsive to his expressions of approval and disapproval, then force is unnecessary, for the relationship will be sufficient to be effective.

A therapist, however, need not in general be firm, for he is actually not expected to take a stand on any issue, but to be neutral, accepting and permissive. However, to the extent that a therapist feels that he must enforce limitations in the subject's behavior in the interests of reality to prevent harm or damage to persons or to property, then a show of firmness would be appropriate. But the setting of limitations is not part of the therapeutic process—it sets conditions in the world of reality which permit therapy to take place. Setting limitations in therapy helps a child to control himself and reduces guilt. In setting practical limitations there is no intention on the one hand to restrict the expression of feeling or, on the other to coerce the child to follow a line of action which must come about eventually from his own inner choice and decision.

7. *A teacher should have a program and be directive. A therapist should be non-directive.* This principle is by no means universally accepted either by all educators or by all therapists. While it is generally believed that schools should have courses of study and that some, if not much, learning should be laid out in advance, there are advocates of the child-centered school in which children not only determine or have a hand in determining day-to-day goals but also the larger objectives. Many teachers believe that self-determination of goals is an essential ingredient in the educational process. Even the most extreme of the child-centered advocates, however, would expect the teacher to exercise some leadership or at least be available for friendly counsel in the process. But whether one gives the teacher or the children the principal responsibility in deciding upon the program, a program there must be so that at the end of the year one can point to tangible results in the form of growth and learning.

Whether the therapist should or should not be directive has been the focus of another controversy. There are some like Thorne who believe that there are occasions when the therapist, like any physician, must step in with positive suggestions to wield his influence through persuasion if necessary to help a person work out better adjustments. The weight of opinion, however, follows Rogers that such methods are palliative only and that real personality change takes place when the therapist by his non-direction forces the client to take responsibility for himself.

It is clear that the rôles sometimes become confused on this issue. There are some therapists who simply do not trust the subject to have the intelligence, judgment and control to select the reasonable way, and feel that they must exercise the teacher's function of guiding and directing. And there are some teachers who have such a profound belief in the child's capacity to learn through the opportunity of making his own decisions that they adopt the therapists' non-directive rôle. But somewhere, sometime children must learn the meaning of honesty, helpfulness, good sportsmanship, self-control, generosity and the like, and how will they ever learn these character traits unless someone in the rôle of the parent or teacher leads the way and directs them?

There are other less obvious and more subtle differences between the teacher and therapist.

8. *The teacher works only through the positive forces in the child and the good teacher calls out only these positive forces.* Everything the good teacher does throughout the school day is designed to call forth positive constructive attitudes and behavior from pupils. As Isaacs says, the teacher "must be a 'good' parent to the child, even though she be a strict one . . . I do not mean that educators have to be inhumanly perfect before they can educate at all. Children readily forgive occasional outbursts of anger and other real faults in an adult whose general attitude is reliable and friendly and understanding . . . But she must not, by her real qualities, attract to herself the negative explosive reactions of hatred and aggression."

It is not the teacher's task to have to deal with a child's hostile attitudes as such, for education cannot take place in an atmosphere of defiance, mistrust, or rebellion. Teachers are expected to put a child's aggression to work in constructive channels, and the successful teacher is able to harness children's aggressive energies to the activities and tasks at hand. When the child displays hostility in the classroom through no fault of the teacher, then the teacher must temporarily step out of his rôle of teacher to act as therapist possibly by verbalizing the child's feelings and attitude, thus bringing them to his attention and helping the child thus to reduce the strength of his feelings and control his attitudes. If simple measures do not work then the child is in need of more thoroughgoing therapy for he is at the moment uneducable. Punishment is seldom called for in the control and reduction of hostility, for it only represses feeling, inhibits behavior, and does not get at the root of the difficulty.

The therapist, on the other hand, must be ready to deal with negative attitudes of the child. Not that the therapist stimulates negative attitudes, but he must be ready to accept negative attitudes that will inevitably arise in the child who needs therapy. The therapist has to be able to tolerate the child's aggression without adopting punitive attitudes of counter-aggression.

9. The next point is one in which we are in a state of transition in our thinking. It is obvious that the teacher's main concern is with conscious processes as they express themselves openly in interests and activities. He is also concerned with motivation in terms of conscious wishes and desires. There is a question, however, of the extent to which the teacher needs to be aware of unconscious processes and motivation. Isaacs says the unconscious lies outside the teacher's sphere. "The teacher has no direct concern in her work as an educator with the

fact that the child's love and wish to make may be covering his fear and hate and wish to destroy. That is the analyst's concern, not the teacher's. . . . Unconscious wishes as such are not, and cannot be within the competence (of the teacher)—any more than the teaching and training of the child in skilful manipulation or understanding of the external world is within the competence of the analyst. . . . The educator [teacher] can only make use of unconscious trends in so far as they are available within the field of the conscious life, and in the form in which they are available in conscious life." Is it not possible that Isaacs has gone too far in this point of view? Might not the teacher of the 'goody-goody' child who harbors unconscious hostility be more successful as a teacher if he knows of the child's unconscious hostility and provides occasions for the expression of it? Might not the teacher of a delinquent be helped if he knew of the child's inner conflicts and struggles between the good and the bad, his potentialities for achievement so that the teacher could lend his strength to help the child choose the more socially approved ways and exercise control against the socially unapproved? Granted, however, that the teacher should use his knowledge of unconscious forces to assist him in the selection of educational devices and not in direct interpretation of them to the child.

There are some who believe that teachers are not able to understand and make use of unconscious material because they themselves have not been analyzed, and because the point of view in terms of unconscious motivation is too far removed from a common sense interpretation. This dogma has long gone unchallenged. There is reason to believe that these points of view can and are being assimilated by teachers in courses in psychology emphasizing the dynamic point of view and by projects such as are reported in the book, *Helping Teachers Understand Children,* which makes a start at interpretation on a very elementary basis.

Unconscious forces are generally recognized as being the special province of the therapist or child analyst. Just how these unconscious forces are to be handled is the subject of another unresolved controversy. Rogers believes that the therapist should not recognize them until they are verbally expressed by the subject (and hence have become to a degree conscious). Many successful child analysts (Blanchard, Gerard, Isaacs and others) believe in the value of more direct interpretation of wishes and motives that are not conscious. "At times, when the unconscious wish . . . comes near the surface, the anxiety of the child may mount up and take violent forms of defense by aggression, if it is not relieved by the analyst's immediate interpretation." Isaacs believes that the analyst can work best through the transference, that is, attitudes that the child expresses directly toward the analyst. "The analyst is at all times functioning also as an ego, since through all these character situations she makes clear to the child at each point what he, the child, is doing and why he is assigning this or that part to the analyst; and so assists the intelligence and judgment and sense of reality of the child himself to work upon the material of his own inner world." It is clear, however, regardless of how a therapist operates, that the teacher and child analyst make quite different uses of unconscious impulses. *The therapist tries to understand unconscious impulses, the teacher provides them opportunity for expression.*

57 Function and focus in the learning process

Related selections: 13, 27, 28, 55, 56

Can the teacher teach the "whole child"? Is the teacher directly concerned with the personal development of his students? Professor Cantor answers these questions in the negative and calls for schools to re-focus their efforts in the learning process. The reader may note a difference between the viewpoint expressed in this selection and the position taken by certain other contributors to this volume of readings, for example, C. H. Patterson (selection 55).

The aim of this essay is to clarify the function of the classroom teacher. The analysis of the teacher's function will apply, generally, to teachers on the primary and secondary levels and in the colleges of arts and sciences.

Much of the current thinking about the aims of primary and secondary education rests upon two related concepts, namely, "the whole child" and "life adjustment courses." Insufficient attention, however, has been given to the *process* by which these aims are to be realized.

It is impossible, I think, to teach "a whole child" or to teach "life adjustment." One always teaches a child *something specific,* or helps a child to adjust to a *specific* problem rather than to "life." The rejoinder may be made that the above concepts refer to over-all objectives and not to any specific content. If this be the case the problem is narrowed to discovering the most effective use of a teacher in furthering these over-all goals. To state objectives should not be confused with the process of realizing them. I submit that a professional teacher

NATHANIEL CANTOR, "Function and Focus in the Learning Process," *Journal of Educational Research,* XLV (November, 1951), 225–31. Reprinted by permission of the publisher.

PROFESSOR CANTOR (1898–1957) was a sociologist specializing in criminology and at the time of his death was department chairman at the University of Buffalo. He developed a strong interest in the classroom learning process and published several important volumes in this field.

is most effective when he operates within carefully defined limits. The skilled teacher becomes sharply aware of his function and the focus of his effort. This requires explanation.

No one lives in a vacuum. Each of us lives in a world of people, objects, and situations with which or against which we must contend. We have to learn to accept limitations of time, place, persons, opportunities, talents, health, and so on.

We are in a constant process of adjustment *to* something or someone. We do not adjust generally once and for all. We cope with specific problems, at specific times, under specific conditions. In order to adjust to a given situation we must take into account what can't be helped so that we can judge what can be. Adjustment and development always occur in a given context, part of which consists of limitations with ourselves and obstacles about ourselves.

Teaching takes place in a given context. The particular school has its own peculiar organization: staff, standards, goals, governing board, curriculum requirements, physical equipment, and supporting community. The teacher's function will be qualified and limited by any or all of these several factors.

The particular school, then, through its administrative personnel articulates, more or less clearly, what services it offers and selects the teachers who are to offer *those* services through *particular* skills. The particular services and the particular skills are the stable, given factors in the educational context. What instructors and students do, the direction in which they move, will be defined by the declared objectives of the school and the specific skills of the teacher. Were this not so, teaching would become a glorified, chaotic eight-room circus. The teacher, otherwise, would be willing to help the student in anything, at any time, since "the whole child" is involved.

The student exposed to this kind of limitless confusion would never discover what he wants nor how to go about getting it. He would not know what the teacher stood for, nor what was expected from him.

By this time most readers have replied that no school actually operates in this fashion. The individual teachers, you say, are prepared to teach a specific subject. There are history teachers, social study teachers, economic citizenship teachers, home economic teachers and band leaders. The state departments of education or local boards do set limits (so many pages of history, so many units of credit, so many courses to qualify teachers, etc.). This is so. What, then, happens to teaching "the whole child"? How is the child helped in "life adjustment" through conjugating irregular Latin verbs or by memorizing the dates and routes of early explorers of the North American continent or by charting the distribution of metals in the United States?

Recently I met a physical education instructor of a very reputable high school in Western New York. I asked him what he did in the gym. He replied, "I teach basketball." "Why do you teach basketball?" I politely inquired. He smiled patiently and said, "You see, I'm the gym teacher." "Yes, I understand, but

I'm interested in what you consider to be your function as a gym teacher. What do you really do for the kids in your gym classes?" "Oh, I see," he said. "I teach them the rules of the game and how to shoot baskets." "Oh, I see," I said, and I did.

The issue will be clarified, I think, if the double meaning of the term "function" is pointed out. A goal or function of education is to help students develop into competent citizens who understand the kind of world they live in and their relations to others. (The particular goals are unimportant in the present context. The above general goal merely illustrates the meaning of the function of education in reference to an ultimate purpose.)

The function of a particular instructor, however, is to help the student to learn a *particular* content.

The individual courses, however far apart in specific content, acquire integration, if they do, in light of the general purpose of education.

When we speak of life adjustment or educating the whole child the reference is to the overall purpose of education. To confuse the general function of education with the particular function of the teacher leads to a misunderstanding of both. I should like to give an example of how the teacher through his particular course tries to carry out the general purpose of education.

> Mr. Robin was called to a conference with me. He had failed to hand in several previous assignments. He came 45 minutes late for the appointment. Another time was arranged and he was 10 minutes late.

ROBIN: What did you want to see me about?

INSTRUCTOR: I thought we might discuss your work in relation to the class. (Robin remained silent.) How do you feel about the quality of work you are doing?

ROBIN: I'm very much interested in the course as you can tell by my discussions in class.

INSTRUCTOR: Apparently your interest doesn't extend to handing in the written assignments.

ROBIN: Oh, those. The reason for that is simple. I don't like to hand in papers written in my sloppy handwriting, I prefer typing them.

INSTRUCTOR: Yes, I find it much easier to read. But I've received no typewritten papers.

ROBIN: I want to do good papers and haven't got 'round to complete them.

INSTRUCTOR: I believe they were all due weeks ago.

ROBIN: Well, you wouldn't want me just to hand in a paper for the sake of being on time if I haven't anything to say?

INSTRUCTOR: It may be that if you have nothing to say, the course isn't giving you enough, and you should resign from it. That sometimes happens.

ROBIN: I don't want to do that, I'm getting lots out of the course.

INSTRUCTOR: What are you giving to it?

ROBIN: You mean the papers, again?

INSTRUCTOR: That is your responsibility.

ROBIN: I am interested in the course, but I carry three lab courses and am taking the course in flying. The trips to and from the flying field take an awful lot of time, and I can't get around to writing the papers.

INSTRUCTOR: You mean typewriting the papers.

ROBIN: Well, that was the original reason I gave.

INSTRUCTOR: If you are too busy with other matters, I suppose the wise thing to do is to select what interests you most. If you haven't time to carry the responsibility of this class, perhaps it's best that you drop it.

ROBIN: I don't want to drop out. (I said nothing during the next half minute of silence.) Suppose I accept whatever penalty goes with not handing in papers?

INSTRUCTOR: It isn't a matter of penalty which should interest us, but whether you are doing the best kind of work of which you are capable.

ROBIN: Well, what do you want me to do?

INSTRUCTOR: That's up to you. What do you want to do?

ROBIN: What's the point of going through the motions and just handing in black scribbling on white paper—just to hand something in?

INSTRUCTOR: There isn't much point to that.

ROBIN: Well, I could do that like others are doing.

INSTRUCTOR: Perhaps some of the others who just hand in anything also aren't meeting their responsibility, doing their best work? I suppose, too, that what they do is irrelevant to our problem. (There was silence for about a minute.)

ROBIN: Will you do something for me, Dr. Cantor?

INSTRUCTOR: If I can.

ROBIN: I've been in a jam in my other work, too. I don't know what's the matter. I'm having trouble with my girl and my parents. Can you understand what I mean? (Tears started to appear.)

INSTRUCTOR: I appreciate something of the difficulties which must be involved. And in addition you have the problem of doing something about your work in criminology.

ROBIN: You're the only professor I feel like talking to.

INSTRUCTOR: What would you like me to do about helping you in your work in criminology?

ROBIN: Will you give me a week's time to think the whole matter over?

INSTRUCTOR: What is there to think about?

ROBIN: I want to decide what to do about the course.

INSTRUCTOR: Very well, suppose we meet a week from today at the same hour.

The papers he failed to hand in were relatively unimportant. It was important that I try to help Mr. Robin assume responsibility for a decision and the consequences which flow from that decision. I was interested in Mr. Robin and not the student in criminology. The college wants to help him to develop into a responsible citizen (general goal of education). I try to help him through my particular skill and the specific limits of the courses (specific function of teacher). Change and growth occur only as by-products of meeting specific challenges.

A surgeon shows interest in the *general health* of his patient not by operating generally (that is an autopsy), but by a specific operation for which he has skill. If the specific source of infection is removed, the entire organism makes a recovery. The function of medicine is to maintain and preserve the health of individuals. Preventive and corrective medical service is always specific.

To function in a limited way, through specific problems and skills, as they relate to the needs of the students in a particular course, while at the same time keeping in the teacher's *background* the goal of general education, requires the highest kind of professional teaching skill.

Consider the problem of grade or high school teachers assuming responsibilities for "child guidance." An eighth grade history teacher, let us say, observes that Richard isn't paying attention (to her!). Furthermore, he disturbs the class. A few minutes with the boy lead to the discovery of a very bad home situation. What should the history teacher do? There are several answers. She can "talk" to the boy. How long and how many times? Suppose there are five such "difficult" students out of a class of 36? Has she the time and energy to teach history and counsel students? Furthermore, what qualifies a history teacher to undertake the extremely delicate role of therapist? Meat-cleavers, ordinarily, are not certified to perform neuro-surgery. The knowledge and skill required to mend a broken heart are, to say the least, as involved as the knowledge and techniques required to set a shattered home. Turn the situation around. Is the well-developed guidance counselor ordinarily prepared to teach solid geometry or intermediate Spanish?

I do not mean to imply that the history teacher requires special development to learn how to greet the children with a spontaneous and friendly smile, or to offer friendly help in minor matters. All teachers, during their professional development, should have acquired sufficient background in personality growth and mental hygiene to recognize serious student problems which they should not attempt to deal with. This is the job of the professional counselor or therapist. The teacher should have sufficient awareness to realize when the child should be referred to the counselor or the guidance clinic. It is extremely regrettable that too few of the large urban schools and almost none of the rural schools provide professional counselling service.* Regrets and practical difficulties, however, do not invalidate the logic of the case.

* This service, of course, has nothing to do with vocational guidance or testing services. The reference is to therapeutic help for students.

The teacher prepared to offer her services in a particular content-area is, I submit, not *directly* concerned with the whole student or with the student's personal development or with adjusting the life of the student. (How many of us are highly "successful" in adjusting our own lives?) Her limited function is to help to develop the meaning of the particular course. That is what she is in the class for. That is the particular service for which she was engaged. The interpretation of the data in light of its meaning to the student is the factor which the teacher can consciously control. Presumably she is competent in her limited, special field. In so far as the student shows interest in, or has his interest awakened by a special subject he can be helped to develop or modify his understanding and attitudes *with reference to that limited course.*

Attitudes and adjustments are not developed in a vacuum. They are acquired and made by facing and working through specific, limited problems which narrow confusion and define areas of challenge. There must be a focus which enables the student to decide what, if anything, he can do about his particular responsibilities. *The teacher focuses on her service to the student, not on the student.* Interestingly enough, this focus provides the most effective means for the student's development as a person.

To function in a limited way, through the specific course as it is related to the problem of the student *in that course,* while keeping in one's *background* the goal of general education requires the highest kind of professional teaching skill.

Such skill cannot be effectively exercised unless the teacher is continually and keenly aware of the general aims of education and of the way her limited specific function focuses on the realization of them. To discover and rediscover the way provides the challenge of a great profession and the opportunity for creative teaching.

58 *Explorations in classroom management*

Related selections: 48, 49, 50

The problem of "maintaining discipline" is a very real one in the mind of the beginning teacher. His requests for advice in matters of classroom management, however, seldom produce anything beyond some "gimmicks" that experienced teachers have found helpful in their situations or some vague principles that are little more than clichés. In the article below, Kounin and his colleagues report on a series of experiments that examine the human interactions and reactions resulting from classroom management practices. Their findings bring a new dimension to the term "discipline."

The origins of the researches to be summarized here lay in the authors' feeling of inadequacy in trying to help teachers, especially beginning ones, with problems of importance to them. Discipline is one problem frequently verbalized by teachers. Teachers' questions about "what to do when Johnny disturbs" have been shrugged off with impatience, or have been answered with slogans or "principles." Scientific research about the technology and theory of controlling misbehavior in a classroom is either lacking or inadequate.

Consequently, we turned our attention to a study of the practical problem of classroom management, from the standpoint of technology. We wanted to see whether there is not some lawfulness about discipline in classrooms or, on the other hand, whether the variety of variables involved is so great as to preclude the possibility of predicting pupils' reactions from the qualities of disciplinary techniques employed.

Since the teacher must work with groups or, at least, "aggregates" of pupils, we shifted the focus from the effects of disciplinary measures upon an individual child to that of the audience reactions, or the "ripple effects."

Specifically, how does a teacher's method of handling the misbehavior of one child (henceforth to be referred to as a *desist-technique*) influence *other* children who are audiences to the event but not themselves targets?

JACOB S. KOUNIN, PAUL V. GUMP, JAMES J. RYAN III, "Explorations in Classroom Management," *Journal of Teacher Education*, 12 (Number 2, 1961), 235–46. Reprinted by permission of the publisher.

DR. KOUNIN (1912–) is Professor of Educational Psychology, and DR. GUMP (1920–) is project director and research associate, Education Research Project, Wayne State University. DR. RYAN (1928–) is Assistant Professor of Psychology, University of Nevada.

The factors to be discussed can be grouped into two major classifications: (1) variables operating at the time of the desist-technique (e.g., the qualities of the desist-technique, the social position of the target) and (2) prevailing variables (e.g., the audience-pupils' intensity of motivation to learn and their liking for the teacher).

I. VARIABLES OPERATING AT THE TIME OF THE DESIST-TECHNIQUE

A.   *Threatening vs. supportive desist-techniques*

In a fashion characteristic of psychologists, we started with an experiment using college students (these are "captive subjects" that do not require administrative clearances and parental approvals). Four classes of students in a college of education were used as subjects. Two classes were taught by a young instructor of educational methods; two classes were taught by an older professor of psychology.

The experiment was conducted as follows:

1. At the second meeting of the class a researcher, posing as a graduate student, obtained questionnaire data on the attitudes of students regarding their instructors, the degree of seriousness of classroom misbehaviors (including "coming late to class") and causes of racial prejudice. The student reports were anonymous.

2. The two instructors of each of the four classes began the third class period with a lecture which gave "his own evidence" that the single most important cause of racial prejudice was repressed hostility toward punitive parents that is displaced upon minority groups.

3. A male student, previously informed about the experiment, arrived late to class—toward the end of the instructor's lecture.

4. The instructor directed either a threatening or a supportive desist-technique at the late-comer. Both desist-techniques stated that coming late interfered with the instructor's presentation and should cease. The supportive desist-technique went on to offer the late-comer help in acquiring the lecture material he had missed. The threatening one stated coldly that "this cannot help but affect my evaluation of you and your grade."

5. The "graduate student" readministered his attitude questionnaire.

Two conclusions emerged from this preliminary experiment:

1. Students who are not themselves targets of a desist-technique *are* affected by it.

2. The *two methods* of handling misbehavior in a classroom *produce* statistically significant *different results*. That is, there is a degree of predictability from some dimensions of desist-techniques to some effects upon audience students.

Threatening desist-techniques, for both instructors, resulted in significantly lowered judgments of the instructors' helpfulness, likeability, freedom from authoritarianism, and fairness; threatening techniques also raised ratings of the amount of classroom tension.

For the young instructor—but not for the professor—differences between the two desist-techniques produced significant changes in ratings of the instructor's competence in his subject-area and in the freedom of the students to communicate with the instructor.

Students in none of the groups changed their attitudes about the seriousness of the deviancy (coming late), and all groups shifted significantly towards the position of the instructors about the causes of racial prejudice.

It would seem, then, that differences in the effects of certain qualities of desist-techniques are more marked in some areas than in others; that the prestige of the emitter of the desist-technique makes some difference; and that some norms of classroom behavior are so well established in colleges as to be rather resistant to change by an instructor's stand on the issue. Influence attempts of instructors that are directly related to course content are not readily changed in relation to a single example of their desist-technique style.

However, another finding may well serve to limit the generalizability of the above results. Although 97 per cent of the students reported that they did *not* perceive that the event was contrived, the students who winessed either technique were surprised that a college instructor would take time out to correct a student for coming late, even though they rated coming late as a serious misbehavior. Most of them, especially those who witnessed the threatening desist-technique, felt that the behavior was *not* typical for the instructor. There were frequent comments on a post-incident questionnaire such as: "He must have had an argument with his wife," or "He probably got caught in a traffic-jam." This reaction to an unexpected behavior of an instructor, in a sense "excusing it away," may actually function to reduce the changes produced by differences in desist-techniques. From the viewpoint of research methodology and strategy these findings also point to the advisability of using teacher-style variables that are within expectations and that have some ecological prevalence.

B. Punishing vs. reprimanding vs. ignoring

In an experiment with eighth and ninth graders (for whom teachers' use of desist-orders is not unexpected) Ryan, Gump, and Kounin[1] investigated whether qualities of a desist-technique make any difference in audience-pupils' reactions.[2]

---

[1] James J. Ryan, Paul V. Gump, and Jacob S. Kounin, "An Experiment on the Effect of Motivation to Learn Upon Students' Reactions to Teachers' Desist-Techniques." (In preparation.)

[2] This experiment was actually started at a later time in the sequence of explorations in order to study the effects of pupil-motivation. (It will be referred to later as the "high-school experiment.") We are referring to it here because it does show that qualities of the desist-technique make some predictable differences in audience-pupils' reactions.

Volunteer paid subjects were recruited from three metropolitan junior high schools during the summer months to come to a university campus for the purpose of participating in a research studying different methods of teaching. Volunteers were randomly assigned to groups of about twenty-five each where they were asked to consider themselves as being in a regular classroom.

After each group assembled it experienced the following sequence of events: the experimenter introduced the activities of the day; a female teacher (the same for each group) introduced herself to the class; the subjects filled out a questionnaire containing mostly ratings of their first impression of the teacher; the teacher taught a lesson, using slides, about Turkey; a pretrained pupil (also the same person for all groups) misbehaved (got up and sharpened a pencil while the slides were being shown); the teacher issued a desist-technique; the subjects filled out another questionnaire about the activities, the teacher, and the deviancy-event.

Three desist-techniques were used: (1) punitive and intense (walked toward him, saying "Hey you, who do you think you are?" in a firm, irritated voice, put her arm on his shoulders in a gesture of pushing him into his seat, saying, "Now sit down! If you ever do that again, I'll really make trouble for you."); (2) simple reprimand (saying in a matter-of-fact tone: "Don't do that again. Please sit down in your seat now."); and (3) ignoring (indicated awareness of the behavior, but did nothing).

The "take" of the experimental manipulation was evidenced by the existence of a significant difference between all groups in the predicted direction regarding the subjects' ratings of the teacher's meanness, anger, and degree of determination to stop the misbehavior.

Compared to the others, the punitive technique resulted in the subjects' rating the *deviancy* as "most serious," the degree of *interference* with attention to the task as "greatest," the *teacher* as "making too much of an issue" over the event, the experience "most discomforting," and the *teacher* "best able to maintain order in a class of 'tough kids.'"

The simple reprimand produced the highest ratings for teacher fairness and also resulted in the subjects' reporting their paying more attention to the lesson following the event and to the teacher being judged as best able to maintain order in "most classes."

Subjects witnessing "ignoring" as the desist-technique thought the misbehavior most likely would recur, but rated the teacher highest in her degree of liking for pupils.

There were no differences between the groups in subjects' ratings of how much the teacher knew about the subject or how well she could explain it. When equivalent effects are considered (likeability, fairness, felt discomfort) it should be noted that the results of punitiveness in this experiment are quite similar to the results obtained from the threatening desist-technique in the college experiment.

C.   Clarity, firmness, and roughness

In one study by Kounin and Gump [3] fifty observers were trained to record critical incidents in Barker and Wright [4] specimen-record style. These were incidents in which an audience-child was aware of a teacher directing a desist-technique at another child. Twenty-six kindergarten classes were selected to represent the range of socio-economic and ethnic neighborhoods in a large city. All observations were made during the first four days of beginning kindergarten. The observers were instructed to record: (1) what the deviant and the audience-child were doing immediately before the teacher intervened, (2) the full content and manner of the desist-technique and the deviant's immediate reaction, and (3) the behavior of the audience-child during and for two minutes following the desist-technique.

When the resulting 406 incidents were analyzed, it was possible to reliably characterize both the teachers' desist-techniques and the behavior of the audience-children.

The qualities of the desist-technique were rated along dimensions of: (1) clarity (defining the deviancy and stating what to do to stop it) ; (2) firmness (this included items conveying an "I mean it" quality—walking closer to the deviant, or continuing to look at the deviant until he stopped) ; and (3) roughness (angry remarks and looks, or punishment).

The reactions of the audience-child were classified as (1) no reaction (no overt behavior which the coder could interpret as related to the desist-technique incident) ; (2) behavior disruption (overt signs of negative emotionality such as fear, anxiety, and restlessness or a shift away from an originally constructive direction) ; (3) conformance (stops a deviancy of his own or behaves even better, i.e., sitting more "correctly" himself) ; (4) nonconformance (engages in a misbehavior of his own) ; and (5) ambivalence (both conforms and misbehaves).

Statistically significant differences were obtained in the overt behavior of the audience-children as related to the desist-technique used by the teacher. Techniques increasing "clarity" resulted in increased "conformance," but had no effect upon "behavior disruption." Techniques increasing "roughness," on the other hand, had no effect on "conformance or nonconformance," but did increase "behavior disruption." The effects of "firmness" differed from both.

Some of the conclusions of this study are as follows:

1. What teachers *do* makes a difference. There is some lawfulness about the effects of techniques. It was not necessary to obtain personality ratings or IQ tests of the teachers as persons; it was only necessary to find out what they do

[3] Jacob S. Kounin and Paul V. Gump, "The Ripple Effect in Discipline," *Elementary School Journal* 158-62; Fall 1958.
[4] Roger C. Barker and Herbert F. Wright, *Midwest and Its Children* (Evanston, Illinois; Row, Peterson, and Company, 1954), 532 p.

and how they do it. (Whether teachers with personality factor-x can or cannot *do* things certain ways is another issue.)

2. There are contextual or prevailing variables that also effect how an audience-child will react to an event. Two such contextual variables stand out from the kindergarten study. One refers to the degree of familiarity the pupil has with the teacher and the situation. (Such familiarity, of course, relates to the amount of time one has spent in a particular experience. For example, there were more "no reactions" on the *last* three days than on the first day.) The other contextual variable is the audience-child's orientation at the time of the incident. Techniques high in "firmness," for example, produced increased "conformance," but *only* for audience-children who were themselves oriented toward, or interested in deviancy at the time of the event.

3. "Roughness" is not an increased degree of "firmness." In terms of their effects, it is evident that these are different dimensions.

Although it does not deal specifically with the ripple effect, we would like to summarize another study on the effects of "punitiveness" since it is closely related to the dimension of "roughness." In a study by Kounin and Gump [5] we attempted to determine the influence of teachers judged to be punitive upon children's attitudes toward misconduct. Three pairs of first-grade teachers, each pair from the same school, were *selected*. One of a pair was rated as "punitive" (anti-child, ready to threaten and inflict harm) by principals, assistant principals, the two investigators, and a supervisor of student teachers; the other member of the pair was rated as "nonpunitive." All teachers were rated as having good organization and as achieving the learning objectives for their grade. Children from these classes were interviewed individually during the third month of attendance at school. The interview consisted of the question: "What is the worst thing a child can do at school?" and, following the reply, "Why is that so bad?" The misconducts talked about were coded for content and for certain qualities. The following was found:

1. Children with teachers judged to be punitive showed more preoccupation with aggression—their misconducts were more serious, their targets suffered more harm; they more frequently cited physical assaults on others as misconduct, and their replies contained more gory—or "blood and guts"—phrases.

2. Children with punitive-rated teachers had more conflicts and were more unsettled about misbehavior in school. They selected misconducts to talk about for which they expressed abhorrence and yet which required premeditation, or "malice aforethought."

3. The children with nonpunitive teachers gave more "reflexive justifications" as explanations for why given misconducts were bad. This was coded when a child gave no consequence for either himself or others in his explanation of

[5] Jacob S. Kounin and Paul V. Gump, "The Comparative Influence of Punitive and Nonpunitive Teachers Upon Children's Concepts of School Misconduct," *Journal of Educational Psychology*. In press.

why the misconduct was bad—the reason given being "because it's not nice" or "because it's bad." We suggested two interpretations for this finding: (a) that children with nonpunitive teachers have less conflicts about misconduct than have children with punitive teachers—to say "you don't do x because it's not nice" reflects a settled issue; and (b) a sort of naive faith and trust in the teacher is reflected by children with nonpunitive teachers—a reflexive justification for a school misconduct is like, say, "x is bad because teacher says so."

4. Punitiveness of teachers detracts from children's concern with school-unique values and results in less internalized socialization. Children with punitive teachers talked more about physical attacks on peers—misconduct by no means unique to the classroom setting. Children with nonpunitive teachers talked more about learning, achievement losses, and violations of school-unique values and rules.

D.　Task-focus vs. approval-focus

Since discipline is centrally related to problems of power and influence and methods of exerting power and influence, another study was undertaken in which Alden [6] dealt with some variables pertaining to these factors. Following French,[7] she hypothesized the following bases for teacher power and influence: the coercive role (the teacher as one who can punish); the "legitimate" role (the teacher as an official leader); reward; and pupils' liking for a teacher and teacher expertness.

The base of a new teacher's power (specifically, "expertness" and "liking") was manipulated by varying the experimenter's introduction of the teacher. All classes were given a lesson in secret writing. A "high expert" was introduced as knowing all about codes and as having a high position in the military intelligence for coding and decoding secret codes; the "low expert" was introduced not as an expert but simply as a teacher who had agreed to teach the lesson. The "high liking" new teacher was introduced as being very fond of children and the "low liking" as not caring about children one way or another.

The desist-techniques used by the teacher were related to these concepts. Some desist-techniques focused upon liking and teacher approval ("I see a boy playing with some paper clips. I just don't like a boy who plays with things when he should be paying attention."). Other desist-techniques related to expertness and focused upon the task ("I see a boy playing with some paper clips. Because secret writing demands concentration, I don't see how he can learn much about it when he plays with things instead of paying attention.").

Fifth graders were divided randomly into eight classes in which a new teacher taught a lesson (in a pedantic, "academic" manner) about secret writing. In

---

[6] Elizabeth Alden, *The Effects on Non-Target Classmates of the Teacher's Use of Expert Power and Liking Power in Controlling Deviant Behavior.* Doctor's thesis, Wayne State University, 1959. 158 p.

[7] John R. P. French, Jr., "A Formal Theory of Social Power," *Psychological Review* 63: 181-95; May 1956.

this manner, both "high" and "low expert" and "high" and "low liking" teachers used both approval-focused and task-focused desist-techniques. In each group three desist-orders were directed at three children who had been trained to act the role of misbehaving pupils. In four of the groups, the desist-technique focused upon teacher liking and approval and in four groups the desist-technique focused upon the task.

One of Alden's most impressive findings was the following: in all cases, desist-techniques focusing upon the task were more effective in eliciting desirable student reactions than desist-techniques focusing upon the teacher's approval. (With the exception of scores on a test of how much was learned from the lesson, measurements of results were all based upon differences between measures given before the lesson and measures given after the lesson.) For some effects, the superiority of the task-focused desist-techniques held, regardless of whether the introduction of the teacher focused upon her expertness or her liking for children. Thus, in all groups, task-focused desist-techniques increased audience-children's ratings of the teacher's skill in handling children and increased their rated degree of interest in secret writing.

For some effects, the use of a task-focused desist-technique combined with the teacher's expertness to affect the pupils' reactions. Thus, when expert teacher used a task-focused technique it increased the children's judgment of how much she liked pupils and would be inclined to reward pupils; it resulted in the pupils' considering the deviances she corrected as being more serious and feeling less inclined to misbehave themselves; and it led to a greater amount of information recalled by the pupils from the lecture itself. The influence of being introduced as having high liking for children made a significant difference on one measurement: a teacher with high liking for children *and* high expertness using task-focused desist-techniques resulted in pupils' feeling more inclined toward discussing personal matters with her.

E.   The deviant's reaction and prestige

An experiment by Gnagey [8] was directed at two questions: (1) What is the effect of the deviant's reaction to a teacher's desist-technique upon audience-pupils? (Specifically, does whether the deviant submits to or defies the teacher's desist-order make any difference on how audience-children react to the event?) (2) Does the prestige of the deviant among his classmates influence audience-pupils' reactions to a desist-order event?

In this study, four intact classes of fifth graders were shown a science film during which a male classmate "misbehaved" (saying aloud, "Hey, is this film about over?"). This deviant boy then became the target of a desist-order exerted by the teacher. This teacher, who was new to the class, directed the deviant to

---

[8] William J. Gnagey, "Effects on Classmates of a Deviant Student's Power and Response to a Teacher-Exerted Control Technique," *Journal of Educational Psychology* 51: 1-9; February 1960.

leave the room and report to the principal. The deviants were pre-selected on the basis of sociometric scores. (Of course, their classmates didn't know that the deviancies were part of an act.) Two male deviants had high attributed influence among their classmates and two had low influence. Two (one high-influence and one low-influence) were trained to behave in a *submissive* manner (saying, "Yes ma'am, I'm sorry" (on leaving the room), and two were trained to react in a *defiant* manner (saying belligerently, "I'll leave the room, but I won't go to the principal's office. The heck with you!").

Gnagey found that the target's reaction did make a predictable difference in audience-pupils' reactions. Compared to pupils who saw the deviant defy the teacher, pupils who witnessed the deviant submit to the teacher rated the teacher as "more capable of handling kids" and as more expert in showing films; they rated the desist-technique as fairer; and they recalled more facts from the film. The magnitude of the differences between the effects of the two kinds of deviant reactions was greater for boys than for girls and was greater for boys who were audience to a high-influence deviant than boys who were audience to a low-influence deviant.

The Gnagey study also points up one reason for an audience-person to be affected by a desist-order directed at someone else, namely, some sort of linkage with the deviant. In this case it is a sociometric linkage—the linkage of an audience-pupil's motivation to identify with a same-sexed person in a high-prestige position. Hence, the finding, for boys only, of a greater effect of a high-influence male's reaction than that of a low-influence male's reaction. Another sort of linkage—to the deviancy event—was illustrated by the previously mentioned kindergarten study. Here, when the audience-child was either deviant himself or was watching the deviancy, he was more likely to react to the desist-technique than if he had no such relationship to the deviancy. In both the Gnagey study and the kindergarten study, then, linkages are shown to be important: linkages to the deviant person, and linkages to the deviancy event.

II. THE INFLUENCE OF PREVAILING VARIABLES

With the exception of the kindergarten study, all the studies previously referred to dealt with contrived conditions and with audience-pupils' reactions to qualities of desist-orders as these were emitted by teachers unknown to them except for that one time. As such, they may be loaded in favor of discovering a ripple effect. For a desist-order may have an effect on a nontarget classmate because something in it contains new information for him concerning the teacher or the rules of the setting. This is probably the reason for the finding in the kindergarten study that the degree of clarity of a desist-technique makes a difference in the conforming behavior of an audience-child, especially on the first day of school attendance when the situation is not completely structured. Except for the facts pertaining to learning scores in the Alden and in the Gnagey studies, most of the effects dealt with attitudes and judgments.

Research conducted in other contexts shows that judgments of others are sub-ject to selective perception and perceptual distortion on the basis of the receiver's motivations as well as on the basis of the receiver's relationship to the emitter of behavior (relative prestige, liking for, etc.).[9] Accordingly, it seemed pertinent to investigate audience-pupils' reactions to naturally occurring desist-techniques in actual classrooms with regular teachers. The design employed here was similar to that used in the kindergarten study but with two differences: older children were used as subjects and interviews were utilized in order to study judgments and attitudes. The research sought to determine the influence of variables "within" audience-pupils as such influences affected their reaction to desist-orders. These "within" variables were: (1) the degree of intensity of students' motivation to learn the subject-matter and (2) students' degree of liking for their teacher.

The subjects, randomly selected, included sixty-three boys and sixty-two girls who were just entering high school. They were interviewed between the fourth and tenth day of their attendance at the school and again three months later. One high school was located in a predominantly lower-class neighborhood, one in a lower-middle-class area, and the third in a middle-middle-class neighborhood.

The interview centered around students' descriptions of a most-recent incident when another student engaged in a misbehavior which the teacher did something about. A complete description of the deviance and of the teacher's method and manner of handling it was obtained. The students' open-ended evaluations of the incidents and how they were handled and their reports of how the incidents affected them also were obtained. Finally, students' responses to pre-structured, forced-choice items (relating to the teacher's fairness, his own inclination to behave better or worse afterwards, etc.) were secured. Reports of two such incidents were obtained from each student: one based on the academic class in which he said he was "most determined to learn" and one relating to the class in which he said he was least determined to learn the subject matter. (Gym, music, and shop were excluded.) For the first interview descriptions of, and reactions to, 250 desist-order incidents involving sixty-four different teachers were obtained. (The second interview included eight fewer subjects.)

The first focus of this study was upon audience-pupils' intensity of motivation to learn as it affected their reactions to desist-orders. Assuming that most high-school teachers concentrate on subject matter,[10] we hypothesized that pupils highly motivated to learn would see desist-orders as facilitating their goals,

---

[9] Some examples are: A. Pepitone, "Motivational Effects in Social Perception," *Human Relations* 3: 57-76; 1950; and Jacob I. Hurwitz, Alvin F. Zander, and Bernard Hymovitch, "Some Effects of Power on the Relations Among Group Members," in Dorwin Cartwright and Alvin Zander, *Group Dynamics* (Evanston, Illinois: Row, Peterson, and Company, 1953), 642 p.

[10] A study by Hilton indicates this is a tenable assumption. See Thomas L. Hilton, *Ego-Involvement in Teaching: Its Theory and Measurement by a Word Completion Technique.* Doctor's thesis, Harvard University, 1955. 192 p.

would be more inclined to perceive desist-orders in terms of task-salient dimensions, would see deviancies as more interfering and more serious, would react more favorably (in respect to teachers' intents) to desist-orders, would attribute more power and influence to teachers, and so on.

Ofschus [11] developed codes for various aspects of the reported incidents. He scored the responses of the pupils and compared the reactions of pupils reporting a desist-incident in the class in which they were "highest in determination to learn" with their reactions when reporting a desist-incident in a class in which they were lowest in motivation to learn.[12] He found that audience-pupils' intensity of motivation to learn the subject *did* predict reaction to a desist-event. In high-motivation classes deviancies were rated as more disturbing to the class and more serious, desist-techniques were rated as more fair, students tended to take more of the teacher's side as opposed to that of the deviant, and the students tended to report acting even better themselves after the incident. In low-motivation classes, students tended to report more teacher-punitiveness and anger and to judge more of the teachers as "making too much of an issue" of the incident. In evaluating the desist-technique, more of those in the high-motivation group evaluated it on the basis of its effectiveness in stopping the misbehavior, whereas more in the low-motivation group used teacher-manner (anger, fairness) as a basis for evaluating the incident.

In line with this finding, Osborne [13] coded pupils' responses to a request to describe the teacher. More of those in the high-motivation group talked about task-relevant attributes (competence in explaining, homework properties) while more in the low-motivation group talked about non-task teacher-attributes (fairness, personal qualities, etc.). It would appear, then, that "motivation to learn" may operate to select saliencies in what pupils perceive about teachers and to influence judgments about, and reactions to, teachers' desist-techniques. However, other findings show that such a viewpoint may be over-simplified. When talking about teachers in classes where pupils were highly motivated to learn, only a small number of pupils felt neutral to or disliked the teacher; in the low-motivation classes more than three times as many pupils felt neutral towards or disliked the teacher. Evidently intensity of motivation to learn is highly associated with liking for the teacher. Are these prevailing variables separable? And which gives rise to which?

By comparing the reaction of pupils in classes with both high-motivation and liking for the teacher with the same pupils' reaction in classes with low-motivation and high-liking and separately with classes with low-motivation and low-

[11] Leon T. Ofschus, *The Effects on Non-Target Classmates of Teachers' Efforts to Control Deviant Behavior.* Doctor's thesis, Wayne State University, 1960. 357 p.

[12] Most of these were found to be run-of-the-mill incidents—most of the deviancies were coded as quite mild (mainly talking or noise and laughter) and most of the desist-techniques seemed to involve either no harm, or only mild harm, to the deviant.

[13] Keith Osborne, *Saliencies in Students' Perceptions of Teachers.* Doctor's thesis, Wayne State University. In preparation.

liking Ryan [14] was able to separate the effects of motivation and liking for the teacher. In general, it was found that "motivation to learn" was associated with degree of attention paid to the task and tendency to behave even better after a desist-event. Judgments about the desist-technique, however, varied with liking for the teacher. Liking for the teacher predicted judgments of fairness and siding with the teacher; disliking the teacher was associated with seeing teacher anger, punitiveness, and overreacting to the deviancy. It appears, then, that knowledge of both motivation to learn and liking for the teacher help predict reactions to a desist-event, but they may relate to different facets: "motivation" predicts reactions regarding the task and behavior conformance; "liking" predicts evaluative judgments regarding the teacher's behavior in the event.

The above comparisons were made for the total population of desist-events. Do these findings hold for all types of desist-events or only for certain kinds? Is the predictability of a pupil's reaction improved by knowing the qualities of the desist-event in addition to knowing the pupil's motivation to learn and liking for the teacher?

In order to answer the above questions the pupils were divided into four categories: (1) high motivation to learn and high liking for the teacher (HiM HiL); (2) high motivation to learn and low liking for the teacher (HiM LoL— this group was not included in the statistical analysis for the first interview because of the small number of cases); (3) low motivation to learn and low liking for the teacher (LoM LoL); and (4) low motivation to learn and high liking for the teacher (LoM HiL).

Two questions may be asked regarding any of the above comparisons: (1) *Within* any one group, does it make any difference whether a desist-technique does or does not have a certain quality? For example, do the pupils in the HiM HiL group react differently to a desist-technique that contains punishment than to one that does not? (2) Are there differences *between* groups in how the pupils react to a desist-technique involving a certain quality? For example, do the pupils in the LoM HiL group react differently to a desist-technique containing punishment than do the pupils in the LoM LoL group?

One of the organizing concepts in this study focused on the concept of commitment. Pupils in the HiM HiL group may be thought of as committed in a positive direction to both the task and the teacher. Pupils in the LoM LoL are committed in a negative direction to both the task and the teacher. Pupils in the LoM HiL have a mixed commitment—they are committed in a negative direction to the task and in a positive direction to the teacher.

The audience-pupils' reactions in this research were categorized as follows: (1) reactions relating to the task (these relate to the inclination to pay more attention, or not to, and to behave better, or not to, following a desist-order); (2) reactions involving evaluations of the teacher (these have to do with

[14] James J. Ryan, "Factors Associated With Pupil-Audience Reaction to Teacher Management of Deviancy in the Classroom," *American Psychologist* 7; July 1959.

whether the teacher is judged as making too much of an issue of the deviancy or not, whether she was fair to the deviant or not, and whether the audience-pupil tended to take the teacher's or the deviant's side in the event) ; and (3) reactions in which an evaluation of the teacher is not involved. (The data here dealt with how *serious* the pupil rated the misbehavior.)

In general, the results of Ryan's study supported the following hypotheses regarding the task-related dimensions of attention and behavior conformance:

1a. Hypothesis: When there is a *clear prevailing commitment* to the task, *negative or positive,* variations in desist-techniques will not produce shifts in task-related reactions of an audience pupil to a desist-event. In *none* of the four within-group comparisons did the presence or absence of punishment, of anger, or of strong firmness make a difference in whether pupils reported an inclination to pay more attention to the task or to behave better themselves.

1b. Hypothesis: When there is a low or negative task-commitment, task-related reactions to desist-technique qualities that manifest the teacher's intent will be effected by whether the pupil likes the teacher or not. In the LoM groups only, pupils who witnessed desist-techniques involving strong firmness, anger, or punishment shifted in a direction of paying more attention and behaving better if they liked the teacher but not if they were neutral toward or disliked the teacher. When the desist-techniques did not contain anger, punishment, or firmness (when teacher-intent was not signalled) there were no differences between the LoM HiL and LoM LoL groups.

1c. Hypothesis: When there is high positive commitment to the task, task-related reactions to desist-technique qualities that manifest the teacher's intent will not be affected by difference in liking for the teacher. There were no significant differences between the HiM HiL and HiM LoL groups in attention and behavior-change reactions to desist-techniques containing punishment, anger, or firmness.

In order to account for the results involving judgments that evaluate the teacher's behavior, we have looked to Heider's [15] theory of balance. Briefly, Heider postulates forces to avoid imbalance and maintain balance between our perception of people and their acts. Thus, to perceive a liked person to do something "bad" is an unbalanced perception; an example of a balanced perception is to perceive a person who is liked as doing good things. Assuming "unfair" to be bad, we would expect pupils who like the teacher to judge her desist-techniques as fair. Accordingly, we proposed and tested several hypotheses (see 2a and 2b in the following paragraphs) regarding evaluations of the teacher.

2a. Hypothesis: When there is a clear prevailing commitment to the teacher, variations in desist-techniques or in motivation to learn will not produce shifts in those teacher evaluations that have clear good-bad connotations.

[15] Fritz Heider, *The Psychology of Interpersonal Relations* (New York: John Wiley and Sons, 1958) 322 p.

In none of the four *within*-group comparisons did the presence or absence of anger, punishment, or firmness make a difference in whether pupils rated a desist-technique as fair or unfair.

2b. Hypothesis: When there is a clear prevailing commitment to the teacher, judgments of a desist-technique having clear good-bad connotations will be in balance with this commitment irrespective of the quality of the technique or the commitment to the task.

HiL groups judged desist-techniques as more fair than LoL groups whether or not the desist-technique contained punishment, anger, or firmness, and this held true for both HiM and LoM groups.

Assuming that taking the teacher's side versus the deviant's side also tends to follow the balance theory, but perhaps not as closely, since this judgment does not have such clear good-bad connotations as does fairness, we further hypothesized that:

2c. Hypothesis: When desist-techniques contain some strong property, commitment to the teacher will influence how pupils evaluate the event in evaluations not having clear good-bad connotations.

When desist-techniques contained punishment, anger, or strong firmness, HiL groups differed significantly from LoL groups; HiL groups were more on the teacher's side and LoL groups were more on the deviant's side. When the desist-technique did not contain anger, punishment, or strong firmness the HiL groups did not react differently from the LoL groups.

Judgments which did not involve evaluations of the teacher were related to the nature of pupil commitment by hypotheses pertaining to the kinds of cues that influence a pupil when he judges the seriousness of a deviancy (see 3a and 3b which follow).

3a. Hypothesis: When there is a clear commitment to both the task and the teacher, judgments of deviancy-seriousness will not be dependent upon whether or not the desist-technique manifestly signals the teacher-value.

Within neither the HiM HiL nor LoM LoL groups did the teacher's using or not using punishment, anger, or firmness make any difference in how the pupils rated the degree of seriousness of the deviancy.

3b. Hypothesis: Where there is no commitment to the task, but where there is commitment to the teacher, pupils will utilize the teacher's manifest value to judge the seriousness of the deviancy.

Only within the LoM HiL group did the teacher's use of punishment, anger, or firmness relate to pupils' ratings of the seriousness of the deviancy. In this group, when the teachers signalled their value by anger, punishment, or firmness the pupils increased their ratings of the seriousness of the deviancy. Differences between LoM LoL and LoM HiL in judgments of the seriousness of the deviancy were significant when the desist-techniques contained anger, punishment, or firmness, but were not when the desist-techniques did not contain these teacher-message properties.

In summary, certain variables an audience-pupil carries "within" him do appear to influence how he reacts to a desist-event directed at a target other than himself. The pupil's intensity of motivation to learn is one. This commitment to the task, positive or negative, is mainly influential in affecting how much attention he focuses on the task and how much he is inclined to behave even better after witnessing a desist-event—both being task-related variables. The pupil's liking for the teacher is another relevant variable. This commitment to the teacher, positive or negative, is mainly influential in determining how the student arrives at evaluative judgments about the event. These judgments follow the laws of balance, i.e., a liked person tending to be perceived as doing good things and a disliked person tending to be perceived as doing bad things. Thus, the desist-techniques of liked teachers tend to be seen as more "fair," those of disliked teachers as more "unfair." In addition, when a teacher signals his intent or value in the desist-technique the pupil who likes him takes his cue about the deviancy from him.

One study mentioned earlier and one additional research may be referred to here to illustrate efforts that were made to determine whether motivation to learn effects liking for the teacher or whether liking for the teacher effects motivation to learn.

In the high-school experiment previously mentioned in 1b, we attempted to create experimentally conditions which would result in high and low motivation. Considerable difficulty was experienced in creating low motivation for the paid volunteers who came to a university campus to participate in research. After four experimental failures to create a low motivation condition, we finally produced comparatively lower motivation in one group than in another. Although there were significant differences in reactions to desist-technique qualities, the reactions of the "high" and "low" motivation groups did not differ. This failure to replicate some aspects of the "interview study" leaves the issue unsettled; the results may mean that motivation to learn follows liking of the teacher, or merely that only relatively lower motivation rather than actual low motivation was produced in the low motivation condition, or, still again, that there are differences in commitment in an experimental setting as compared to an actual classroom.

In another study we obtained, by use of questionnaires, estimates of pupils' "premotivation to learn world history" two weeks prior to their attendance in high school. About one to two weeks after their attendance in the high school we replicated the "interview study" with questionnaires in which classes of pupils described some desist-events and rated their reactions to it. While "premotivation to learn" did predict ($r = .49$) "post-motivation to learn," it did not predict students' reactions to the desist-event in the post situation. Both "post-motivation to learn" and "post-liking for the teacher" were significantly related (as were motivation and teacher-rated ability to explain and to make the subject interesting). Allowing for differences between questionnaire and interview methods (results from the questionnaire, as might be expected, contained much more sparse descriptions of the events and the teacher which were more difficult to code reliably), the results seem to indicate that motivation to learn is not solely determined by what a pupil brings to the class but is effected, even in one week, by what happens in the class and by whatever it is that teachers do that leads to their being rated as being liked and as being able to explain and make the subject interesting.

III.   WHAT ABOUT LIKING FOR A TEACHER?

While liking for the teacher stands out as an important variable, we must pause to ask what this means. Do the same behaviors that contribute to teachers' being liked account for persons in other roles being liked? Or does the teacher role carry its unique properties as far as "being liked" is concerned?

The questionnaire study showed a relationship between ratings of "explains well" and "makes interesting" and pupils' liking for the teacher. The Alden study showed a relationship between task-focus desist-techniques and rated liking for the teacher. When Osborne [16] compared the pupils' descriptions of teachers in "high-" and "low-liked" groups, the differences were about the same as the differences obtained when "high-" and "low-motivation" groups were compared. When describing "high-liked" teachers, task-property descriptions were predominant, e.g., "explains well," "assigns the right amount of home work," "helps you learn." (Seventy per cent of the pupils mentioned this dimension when talking about "high-liked" teachers.) Only 19 per cent of the pupils mentioned "friendliness" or "meanness" (more of the "low-liked" teachers being included when this non-task dimension was described). In contrast, in a study by Polansky and Kounin [17] in which adults and college students were asked to describe a professional helper (physician, social worker, college counselor) they had just seen for the first time, the majority talked about "friendliness," "helpfulness." "Understanding" was referred to by 49 per cent of the clients when talking about professional helpers, compared to 7 per cent of the high-school students who used this term when describing teachers.

In a study of the ripple effect in a camp milieu Gump and Kounin [18] also asked campers to describe camp counselors. The most frequently used dimension was that which we called "gratuitous giver": 63 per cent of the campers (ranging from seven to thirteen years of age) described their counselor with statements illustrated by "gives us candy" and the like. Only 2.3 per cent of the campers used terms that might be equivalent to "explaining well," e.g., "taught us how to play ball better." It also was found that concepts of misbehavior (obtained from the questions, "What's the worst thing to do?" and "Why is that

[16] *Op. cit.*

[17] Norman Polansky and Jacob S. Kounin, "Clients' Reactions to Initial Interviews," *Human Relations* 9: 237-64; 1956.

[18] Paul V. Gump and Jacob S. Kounin, "Issues Raised by Ecological and 'Classical' Research Efforts," *Merrill-Palmer Quarterly of Behavior and Development* 6: 145-53; 1959-1960.

so bad?") also differed, depending upon whether the camper was talking about camp, home, or school milieus. The role of the central adult (parent, teacher, counselor) as a sufferer from children's misbehaviors and as a retributor also differed as between milieus.

All the above leads us to believe that the salient dimensions used to analyze adult-child relationships probably differ for parents, camp counselors, teachers, and other adult-child role figures. Equivalences may be theoretically possible at a higher level of abstraction, but concrete techniques cannot be directly extrapolated from one adult-child role to another.

It would seem, further, that studies of the attributes of teachers as such, whether obtained from projective and inventory-type measures or from boy-scout-type lists of characteristics (trustworthy, loyal, helpful, friendly) are inadequate to the task of analyzing what constitutes teachership. We need to know what teachers *do* that makes a difference for the learning and behavior of *pupils* in *classrooms*. Not only do we need to know what teachers do to manage misbehavior, but we must know what they *do* to evolve and sustain motivation to learn and to become "liked." What *are* the really significant dimensions of what we call teaching? (We are inclined to believe that the "desist-style" dimension here discussed is not as important as some others.)

What is more, studies are needed to better inform us about what constitutes the nature of the classroom as a unique setting distinct from other kinds of settings for children's groups. For, television or not, the locus of necessity of educational practice and the point of application of learning theory or group dynamics theory or other psychological theories is the classroom with a teacher in charge of a group of children or adolescents. And what we know of teachers or students, separately or together, must be relevant to this basic context if it is to be of benefit to those doing the job.

Researchers should get into the classrooms; and teachers and administrators should let them in.

59 *A parent looks at teaching*

Related selections: 24, 25, 26

We have all observed that the freely expressed curiosity so evident in the young child and his constantly voiced "Why?" seem to disappear as he progresses up the educational ladder. Is this change a real one? If so, is it the result of maturation or has this desirable characteristic been stifled by the classroom practices to which the child has been exposed? In the selection below a parent challenges members of the teaching profession to re-examine their teaching methods and to find ways to preserve curiosity and creativity in children.

At the outset, I would like to say that I am most grateful for the opportunity to communicate with the teaching profession; and I would like to add that I do so with considerable humility. For your information, and perhaps disillusionment, I do not speak as an expert, or as an educator, or as a psychologist. I speak, essentially, as a concerned parent.

I do not intend to try to look at the entire subject of creativity. I would like, instead, to focus on one small aspect. In order to achieve this focus I may presume upon the reader's good nature, I may oversimplify, and I may select some non-typical examples that he may consider unfair. However, I hope to find a way to point up what I consider to be one of the most serious problems facing our schools today.

To state the problem simply and concisely, I believe that some of our teaching methods today, instead of developing and encouraging and nurturing creativity, are instead, in too many cases, effectively discouraging and stamping out much of the creativity with which our children are naturally endowed. Furthermore, I believe that these teaching methods, which we may recognize as destructive to the child's creativity while in school, also may have a very grave and damaging effect upon the adult's attitude toward education and learning after graduation, and perhaps for the rest of his life.

WILLIAM M. SIMPSON, "A Parent Looks at Teaching," *Journal of Secondary Education*, 38 (March, 1963), pp. 175–81. Reprinted by permission of the publisher.

MR. SIMPSON is consultant to the Chief Scientist, Pacific Missile Range, and a parent concerned with some of today's educational problems.

YOUTHFUL CURIOSITY AND THE ADULT

In order to illustrate the problem let us consider a young boy, an average young boy, of 6 or 7. He is curious and eager to learn. He is almost breathless in his ecstatic desire to know more about the world. He is uninhibited and unashamed in his desire to learn, and in the questions he asks.

Now let us consider this same boy, this average boy, when he becomes a senior in high school. Does he still have the same zest for learning, the same uninhibited desire to know more things, the same eagerness to try his hand at new skills? Or has he become disenchanted with learning and reluctant to face his homework assignments? This may be a good place to mention the large percentage of students who drop out of school before graduation. And perhaps we should face up to the findings that the majority of our high school graduates never read another book after the last book they were forced to read in school.

I would like to inquire, "What has happened to the divine spark of curiosity, what has quenched the burning desire for knowledge, and what has changed the venturesome, uninhibited young boy into a fugitive from learning?"

I believe that our young boy was forcibly drawn, naturally and irresistibly, to the wonderful fountain of knowledge, to the marvelous source of enlightenment. He wanted to approach in his own manner, at his own pace, and along a path of his own choosing. But every time he drew near to the fountain of knowledge, some adult laughed at him, or shamed him, or told him that he could not approach the sacred fountain unless he followed the procedures and the path specified by his teachers.

It has been amazing to me how just one teacher can damage or destroy a child's enthusiasm for a given subject. Here I am not talking about a course that occupies just one semester or one year. I am referring to the entire sequence of mathematics, or reading, or history, or science. It seems that just one teacher in an entire sequence, a teacher who does not know the subject material, or who gives an unfair grade, or who is unsympathetic, or who offends the student's pride—just one such teacher can seriously damage, or perhaps permanently destroy, a student's love for that particular subject. And each successive blow to the student's enthusiasm for a given subject often seems almost irreversible. Once he takes a dislike to the subject, he may not care to regard it in a rational or objective manner. He simply may not like it and he may not want to be bothered with it.

ENCOURAGING CONFORMITY

I am sure you realize that I am not talking about the obedient, docile, conformist students who always seem willing to approach the fountain of knowledge exactly as instructed, and who develop such skill in repeating and reproducing, for our delight and approval, the facts and logical procedures we have crammed into them. These slavish imitators, by acquiring more factual knowledge, and also more superior skill in its use, often surpass the other students in their classwork, and then they discover that their greatest applause comes when they listen to the little helpful hints and suggestions from their teachers. By doing extra study and outside projects they find themselves showered with rewards for their magnificent "creativity."

Some warped individuals might consider this to be a very humorous joke. Do we really have a school system that handicaps the individualistic, creative students and tries to relegate them to mediocrity, while pampering the submissive conformist students and proclaiming that they, the conformists, are the most creative? Additional evidence of this amazing inconsistency was provided by a psychological study that was made on creative children in the first six grades. It was observed that in the first and second grades the most creative and productive children liked to work by themselves. When those same children reached their third and fourth grades, they were being badly treated by the other children and also by the teachers; and when they reached the fifth and sixth grades it was found that they were effectively excluded from group activities. It is easy to understand why such students may fall further and further behind, and how they may become progressively more disenchanted with their teachers, with schools, and with learning.

Perhaps I should take time out here to apologize to those who are beyond the pale of my remarks. Some of you have learned that you must get acquainted with each student as an individual, and you have learned to work within the framework of each student's individual capabilities. You know that each student must be allowed to retain some self-respect, that the student's pride must not be wounded too deeply as he is led, or pushed, or perhaps tricked into exploring his own capabilities and limitations.

And now let me speak to those teachers who have the privilege of teaching about this wonderful physical universe. You do not enjoy the special privileges of the voice teacher or the track coach. Their students are essentially contemporary with all the other singers and sprinters throughout recorded history, and it is understood that those teachers must develop a personal relationship with each student. However, you dispensers of information and logic, you have fallen into the trap of mass production, or perhaps we could say mass dispensation. And each year adds to the tremendous body of knowledge that must be crammed into the reluctant students. And as we work harder and harder to stuff them with more and more information, and as we develop more efficient methods for doing the cramming, the chief result seems to be a destruction of motivation for many of the students.

I am sure that every one of you could describe exceptional cases to prove that I am wrong. But I am not talking about the brilliant students, or about those compliant tractable students who successfully flatter your egos by performing so well. I am speaking about the great majority of average and below average students, and also about those independent souls who are too proud to knuckle under to rules they consider to be unreasonable, or to assignments they consider to be foolish and unimportant.

THE POOR TEACHER AND CREATIVITY

I believe that some of the greatest blows against creativity are struck by those teachers who are primarily concerned with the making of assignments that are chosen for the teacher's comfort and convenience, and with simple, easy, objective methods of grading. Perhaps you would be interested in an example that I observed last year. The student was a boy who had been thinking seriously of becoming a chemist. The teacher of his first chemistry class did not know much chemistry, although he had been trained as a teacher, and he had a misconception about the true function of teaching methodology. He had developed a series of assignments that were very convenient for the teacher, and they were admirably suited to a simple objective grading system.

Night after night the boy who wanted to major in chemistry sat up memorizing the periodic table of elements, and after each memorizing exercise the class was given a quiz. First the boy had to memorize the atomic numbers of the elements, next the chemical names and symbols, then the atomic weights, and then the valences. This went on for several weeks. The boy's father knew something about chemistry and he was curious to know why the periodic table was being memorized, and what the information would be used for. The boy was not able to explain why. The boy never found out why. However, I can report that when the boy's sister came home and announced that she had enrolled in chemistry for the next year, the boy told her that she was crazy, that chemistry was just a junky course where she would not learn anything. He said it was just a bunch of silly memorizing.

It seems almost unbelievable that our modern enlightened school system could produce such a fiasco. You may protest that the chemistry teacher was not typical, and I will agree that there are many good chemistry teachers. But a student who encounters only one bad chemistry teacher may become sadly disillusioned with chemistry.

I know a girl who liked history and historical novels, but one bad history teacher, and countless nights spent in memorizing thousands of names and dates and places seem to have destroyed her eager desire to major in history. And she no longer gets pleasure from reading.

PATTERNS OF LEARNING AND TEACHING

I would like to differentiate very sharply between patterns of learning and patterns of teaching. Patterns of learning must be determined and applied by the students. The chemistry teacher and the history teacher had developed some very easy and convenient procedures for making assignments and for determining grades. It seems obvious that their patterns of teaching were adopted for the teachers' comfort, but not to promote student learning. Perhaps the greatest harm was done in the stifling of motivation, and in damage to the human spirit.

It is this preoccupation with teaching comfort, characteristic of some teachers, which leads me to question the profession's position on the merit system. Recently I heard a school superintendent tell a school board association meeting that a merit system for rewarding better teaching would be harmful to the educational profession. He warned that any school that tried to impose a merit system upon its teachers would not be able to recruit or keep good teachers. Is this what you want? Is this in consonance with your professional responsibilities as educators? I would be the first to agree that an objective merit system would be difficult to design and operate, but that does not seem to be sufficient justification for opposing the principle of the merit system.

It is unfortunate that there are so many ways to stifle the natural creativity that is inherent in the nature of the child. And we all do it, as parents, as teachers, as the enforcers of our civilized rules and regulations, and as adults who must maintain superiority over our children by pretending to know everything. If we look only at the child's motivating spark, at the eager desire to learn, we find that most of the influences on our children have a negative force. Almost everything a child tries is either harmful, or sinful, or ridiculed, or not permitted. And so we come to the inevitable question—what can we do that will have positive value? How can we teach in a manner that will stimulate the student to want to learn, for all the rest of his life? How can we inspire children to derive pleasure and excitement from the quest for knowledge, or from the discovery of a different and better way of doing a thing?

I believe the clue can be found in the words "different" and "better." Because each child believes that his way is different and better.

And so I must ask, how can the student appreciate the discoveries of yesterday when he is led, chained, through the magic forest? How can he thrill to the quest for new paths and undiscovered treasures when he is seldom allowed to walk upright, or permitted to see ahead? Perhaps I exaggerate, but how many students are privileged to follow a learning pattern that is based upon a realization of need comparable to that which prompted an original discovery? And for those few who may achieve some understanding of the motivations that led to an original discovery, how many are ever permitted, by following a path of their own choosing, to rediscover the marvelous treasure, a treasure which does not seem to mind being discovered over and over again?

We say that necessity is the mother of invention, but our children are supposed to develop initiative and creativity without any awareness of necessity, without any vision of the treasure being sought, without freedom to try their hands at discovery, and certainly without the opportunity to make some of the mistakes that were committed by the pioneers in the original quest.

But you say the children are not yet prepared for this joyous dance through the magic forest. And I ask, when can they be permitted this freedom? And you answer, only after they have learned all of the material that we prescribe, and in the manner we permit. And then I must answer, by that time it will be too late. Unless they taste the joys of discovery while their enthusiasm is still young, they may end up, as most of us, conformists who learn, too late, the frustrations and sorrows of a stunted creativity. Or they may rebel, against school, against learning, and perhaps against society.

And now, in conclusion, I would like to apologize for the harsh things I have said. If I did not feel the matter a crucial one, if I did not respect your special abilities and training, and if I did not honor your high motives and objectives, I would not have written these words.

TWIN CHALLENGES

I would like to leave you with two challenging assignments or tasks. First, I would like to challenge each individual teacher to try a little harder, day by day, to find the pleasant, natural patterns of learning that will motivate and inspire his students, instead of imposing upon them certain mechanized packaging procedures that often are selected for the teacher's individual convenience. I know that many of you feel overworked and underpaid, and I suppose that I may have felt the same way when I was a teacher, but the ineptitudes of an occasional administrator and the indifference of the public do not justify an irresponsible attitude toward your professional duties. As a matter of fact, I would suspect that the indifference of the public toward education may be, in part, attributed to the fact that some of your predecessors did precisely the things I am complaining about. When they, the public, were young and eager to learn, some of their teachers also would not let them approach the fountain of knowledge, except by unnatural procedures, and with subservient manner. You are paying the price for that disillusionment, and some of you seem willing to place a similar burden upon your successors.

As a second challenge I would like to suggest that the educational profession has a responsibility to re-examine the ideals and objectives that were used to establish the special legalized privileges that you now enjoy. I would suggest that your profession devote at least a small percentage of the time that is now spent on teaching methods, on efforts to rationalize grading techniques, and on the mechanization of many of the sensitive, personal teacher-student relationships, to research on optimum patterns of learning for individualistic, creative children, and also to techniques for inspiring and motivating students to want to learn, for all the rest of their lives.

We must decide what type of people we want in this world. Do we want our world citizens to be sterile repositories for so-called factual information that was packaged and sealed prior to their graduation? Do we want our world citizens merely to conform and agree with their political leaders? Or should we try to send forth competent citizens into the world of tomorrow who will regard graduation from school as the beginning of a joyous lifetime of learning, and who will take pride in finding better methods for solving the problems of the future, through creativity?

60 Some thoughts on evaluation

Related selections: 61, 62

To many persons the term "evaluation" is a synonym for testing; to others it is the equivalent of grading. In the article below, the author defines evaluation as a phase of the learning process, and points out that evaluation is done by the learner and not by the teacher. What then is the place of the teacher in the evaluative process? Weir defines for him a significant role.

If we think of learning as activity through which ideas are identified, examined, tested as solutions to problems, and incorporated into the life of the learner, then evaluation is not something incidental to or apart from learning; it is a central and ongoing phase of the process of learning itself. Although evaluation is required to complete the act of learning, it is not a terminal act, but is continuous throughout all phases of the learning process. And, like all phases of learning, evaluation is not an act performed by one person for another; it is always, in the final analysis, something which the individual does for himself. The learner must think about his activity and relate it to his own purposes if the activity is to take on meaning which can be used in future activity. Just as thought and learning remain incomplete until applied to behavior, so does the meaning of behavior remain ambiguous and productive of little learning until mind is applied to act. To learn from activity, one must experience the activity. To experience the activity, one must think about it, relate it to self, and decide whether the relationship is constructive to self-development and should be maintained and strengthened, or whether it is restrictive of self-development and should be discontinued. When we continue an activity—or abandon it—without giving evaluative attention to the meaning of the activity, we bring the learning process to a halt and inhibit the possibilities for our own growth. "For healthy, integrated adjustment, one must constantly be evaluating his experiences to see whether they require a change in the value structure. Any fixed set of values will tend to prevent the person from reacting effectively to

EDWARD C. WEIR, *Bulletin of the National Association of Secondary-School Principals*, 46 (December, 1962), 23–29. Reprinted by permission of the publisher.

DR. WEIR is Associate Professor of Secondary Education, University of Pittsburgh.

new experiences. One must be flexible to adjust appropriately to the changing conditions of life." [1]

EVALUATION IS CONTINUOUS

Evaluation, like the learning process itself, is continuous. It has been going on all the time in the activities of all the other phases of learning. As the learner sought to identify himself with the ongoing classroom activities, he was making judgments about his own current activities. To become aware of the alternative ideas present in the situation, it was necessary for him to become aware of the value of his own ideas. As he utilized data and consequence to analyze the meaning of the alternatives, he was making anticipatory judgments as to the relative merits of the alternatives. He put the ideas to work in order to test their worth. He now examines the effects of the idea-at-work upon his own experience to see if its value is in reality what he thought it would be.

What is equally important, however, is the fact that the act of evaluation is not the culminating act in the learning process. *It is an act which always leads to further learning.* If the evaluation shows that the idea is not working as predicted, we modify the idea and alter the direction and quality of our behavior accordingly. This is learning. If the evaluation shows that the idea does produce the desired results, we integrate the idea even more firmly and centrally into our living. This is learning, also, and it does not stop there. The added meaning which the evaluation has created becomes in turn a tool which the learner continues to use in discovering, analyzing, and adopting new meanings into his experience.

Evaluation, being an integral part of the process of choice in which learning occurs, is itself an act of choice. As an act of choice, it is personal. It is something the individual does for himself. The responsibility for evaluation cannot be transferred or delegated to someone else, nor can one person—no matter what his position of authority—set himself up as a judge of the actions of another. The self is the sole judge of its own performance. It is true that we do make judgments of others, and these judgments are frequently accepted and integrated into behavior. However, the acceptance of judgments made by others —regardless of how objective, realistic, or friendly the judgments may be— depends upon the decision of the evaluatee to accept. Moreover the meaning of the judgment can only be the meaning given to it by the person being judged, and this meaning may be as it was intended or it may be something very different from what was intended.

The evaluative experience consists of the individual's perception of the value of performance. As in all perception, the individual's perceptions of value are a function of the relationship which he discerns between self and experience. Experiences which are seen as directly related to self are highly valued, either

[1] Hall, Calvin S., and Lindzey Gardner. *Theories of Personality*. New York: Wiley and Sons, 1957, p. 488.

negatively or positively, and these valuations enter significantly into behavior. I "like" the meaning which one kind of experience seems to have, for it fits harmoniously into the picture I have as to the kind of person I am. I hate and fear the meaning of another experience because it brings disharmony into my own self-concept. In the words of Carl Rogers, "As experiences occur in the life of the individual, they are either (a) symbolized, perceived, and organized into some relationship to the self, (b) ignored because there is no perceived relationship to the self-structure, (c) denied symbolization or given a distorted symbolization because the experience is inconsistent with the structure of self." New perceptions, then, together with their attendant new behavior emerge as the learner engages himself in the process of making judgments as to the value of experience. We learn from experience as we judge its value. This includes the learner's "experiencing" of someone else's judgment. He must himself evaluate another's judgment and make the decision to incorporate it into himself before it can be said that evaluation has taken place.

The individual tends to make the decision to accept, ignore, or reject evaluations on the basis of whether or not he feels that the evaluation will lead to enhancement of self. The evaluation that is offered may in actuality be urging a more adequate concept of self, a reorganization of perception and performance in closer conformity to reality. But it must be seen in this way by the learner if he is to accept it. This is characteristic of all human behavior and of all phases of learning: we are receptive to those meanings which seem to contribute to the improvement of personal effectiveness; we ignore, reject, or distort the meaning of experiences which seem to be destructive to self. Our judgments of the value of experience may be completely and harmfully inconsistent with reality, but to us they *are* reality. Our decision to ignore evaluative advice may in actuality be destructive of self in its effect, and, to others, the foolishness of our decision will be obvious. But to us it is equally obvious that the decision was in our own best interest. We refused to accept the evaluation because it represented a threat to the integrity of self, a restriction upon our efforts at self-realization. Furthermore, the more often we encounter threat in the evaluative experience, the more difficult it becomes for us to evaluate ourselves and make ourselves more adequate for dealing productively with life.

> "The self builds up defenses against threatening experiences by denying them to consciousness. As it does so, the self-image becomes less congruent with organismic reality, with the result that more defenses are required to maintain the false picture held by the self. The self thereby loses contact with the actual experiences of the organism, and the increasing opposition between reality and self creates tension. Consequently the person becomes more and more maladjusted." [2]

[2] Rogers, Carl R. *Client-Centered Therapy*, Boston: Houghton Mifflin, 1951, p. 486.

EVALUATION CONTRIBUTES
TO SELF-DEVELOPMENT

The converse is equally true. As evaluations are seen by the learner as contributions, rather than threats, to his own self-development, he becomes less self-defensive, more receptive to reality, more able to adjust and re-adjust his own behavior to meet the requirements of effective living.

Does the urge to self-enhancement mean that we can only accept laudatory evaluations? Not at all. It matters not whether the evaluations are negative or positive. The question is, instead, are the evaluations valid, and are they seen by the learner as valid and useful to him in re-ordering his own experience along more productive lines. Negative evaluations, providing they are valid and providing they are viewed with objectivity by the learner, can be most helpful in bringing about improvement of performance. On the other hand, laudatory evaluations, if they are not valid and if they are not received objectively, can be most harmful, for they lead the learner in false directions.

To say that the evaluative act is a personal act of choice is not to say that it is not also a social act. Evaluation occurs in the individual's interaction with other people. The condition of being human in a social condition and the act of evaluation must encompass the realities of the social condition of man. One of these realities is that the fullest possible development of self requires the fullest possible development of others with whom the self interacts. Man becomes human in his intercommunication with his fellow men. Intercommunication exists in the sharing of goals and interests and in the acceptance of mutual responsibility for the maximum development of the human potential for intelligent, self-directed living. Narrowly selfish goals and interests and activities which lead only to immediate satisfaction tend to block the ebb and flow of intercommunication in which broader goals of human development can be acquired.

When the individual acts without taking into account the effects of his act upon others, he denies his own humanity, cuts himself off from the human resources he needs in his efforts to work out his own pattern of effective living. When the individual acts so as to cause another to draw back defensively into himself and away from reality or to strike out with equal unreality in aggressive attack upon life, then he has seriously undermined that person's capacity for productive living. In so doing, the selfish or thoughtless individual has restricted his own potentialities, for he has deprived himself of an intelligence which could have been helpful to him in evaluating his own living. Evaluation based only upon the satisfaction of the individual's immediate goals and interests is superficial and unproductive in its effects upon behavior. Such evaluation, since it is blinded to the realities of the human condition, can have little constructive effect upon the individual's attempts to relate and adjust his thought and behavior to reality. It can hardly be of help in the human task of trying to become more human.

EVALUATION IS AN ACT OF SHARING

The very fact that the evaluative act is so intensely and intimately personal is in itself the proof that it is at the same time an act of sharing. If my evaluative approach to another is one which threatens or degrades him, if I approach him as an outsider who requires that he measure up to my standards, then, as we have previously seen, it will be difficult if not impossible for him to accept my evaluation. What is required instead is a warm and mutually trusting interpersonal relationship that develops out of the recognition that each of us is caught in the human dilemma, that each has his own peculiar strengths and weaknesses, and that because we have strength and weakness, each man needs the other. The completion of the evaluative act assumes that the participants recognize each other as equally legitimate and important entities, that each in his potential and in his striving to realize his potential is an end in himself and not a means to be used for the purposes of another's self-aggrandizement.

Evaluation requires the mutual knowledge that each man seeks to become the best that he is able to become, and that, in trying to realize self, each man consistently uses whatever courses of action are psychologically available to him. This knowledge makes it more difficult for the evaluator to act as a judge of another's conduct, but easier for both to share in each other's thinking to the end that both can accomplish the purposes of evaluation—the examination of the meaning of conduct and the discovery of more adequate modes of conduct which otherwise might not have occurred to either individual alone. The question upon which evaluation focuses is no longer, "What is wrong with you that you do not measure up to my standards?" The question becomes, instead, "What are your standards, and what are mine? Where do they clash, and where do they merge? How can we together broaden our standards so that they include more of humanity and thereby more of ourselves. And how can we help each other to realize these more encompassing and more self-rewarding goals?"

IMPLICATIONS FOR INSTRUCTIONAL METHOD

If evaluation is to occur in the teaching-learning situation, *the teacher must become a participant in the evaluative process.* He involves himself with the learners in the classroom to help decide what has been learned from ideas that have been put to work and to determine what further learning is needed if performance is to continue to improve. Knowing that ultimately all evaluation is subjective, because it is a judgment made of one's own performance by oneself, the teacher's concern in evaluation is not telling his students what *he* thinks about what they have done. His concern is rather with the question, "What do *we* think about what *we* have done?"

Evaluative procedures which provide only the teacher's rating of students' performance arise out of the mistaken assumption that teaching-learning is a one-way affair, proceeding always from teacher to learner. Evaluative procedures which ask students to examine the meaning of their own experience are based upon the idea that learning is a process in which both teacher and learner join in making decisions about what they are to believe and do. Evaluation is also based upon whether what they are doing measures up to what they believe it should be.

The teacher who knows that evaluation is performed by the self will withhold temporarily his judgments of his students as he seeks to initiate evaluation. The judgments of the teacher cannot be as valid as they should be until they have taken into account the all-important evidence of the students' evaluations of their own behavior. Initially, then, the teacher devises procedures which will direct students to the question, "What do *you* think about what you have done? It is *your* living that is the primary concern here, and it is your thinking about the quality of your own living that can help you to become whatever it is you deeply wish to be."

The teacher who knows that evaluation is an act of choice will, when the time is ripe, offer his own judgments to the total array of alternatives from which the student will choose as he seeks to determine where he has succeeded or failed and what he can do to capitalize upon his strengths. The teacher's approach will invite his students to consider his opinions of their progress, if they wish to do so. In effect, he will say to them, "Here are some ideas I have formed about you as I have watched you trying to solve your problems and reach your goals. Tell me, do my estimates of what you have done seem pertinent to you, valid for your purposes? Only you can decide."

The teacher who knows that evaluation is an act of sharing will try to relate himself in a warm and friendly way with his students. He will try continuously to help the students to become aware of his feeling that he is in the same boat with them, that their successes are his successes and their failures his. He does this because he knows that, unless he can somehow touch their inner core and unless his touch is one from which they will not flinch, he will have little success in helping them to live more effectively. But this cannot be an act of continuous condescension, with the teacher giving all the help. Evaluation is interactive. The students need to know that they are needed too—by their fellow students, but more particularly by the teacher.

Knowing that they, too, are needed, that they, too, can help in very important ways, will in turn serve to create the kind of interpersonal relationship which makes for greater receptivity to evaluative help when it is offered. Moreover, the need of the teacher for the students is not a fabricated one. It is very real. If he is to learn to be a teacher, he needs above all else to know not only what the students really think about *their* learning, but also what they really think about *his* teaching. If he is to develop his own competence as a person and as a teacher, his evaluation must include the great reality of the human condition—that the development of one depends upon the development of all. Evaluation is far from being a cold and sterile thing of objective tests and grades and praise and punishment which hurts the punisher more than the punished. Evaluation, like teaching itself, is an act of love.

61 *Analyzing test results*

Related selections: 60, 62

*The administering of standardized tests is an accepted practice in
almost every school in the nation. Individual scores are duly computed and recorded, but too often these test results remain as statistics in the archives of the school and are not put to effective use in
the classroom. In the article below, Dr. Hagen gives straightforward
suggestions to the classroom teacher on how to analyze and utilize
test results.*

Standardized tests are given to obtain information about students. The information they provide must be used and used constructively to improve the teaching-
learning situation or else the tests should not be given. The classroom teacher
is the critical person in the constructive use of test results. He must be able to
analyze the test results for a group or an individual and interpret the scores in
terms of what they mean for teaching the group or the individual.

ANALYZING WHAT THE TEST MEASURES

In order to interpret the scores from a test or series of tests, the teacher must
know what the tests measure. This point may seem obvious, but many classroom
teachers do not know specifically what the tests they use are measuring. One
cannot depend upon the title to tell what is being measured by the test. For
example, reading comprehension tests differ markedly from each other both in
the range of reading skills which they measure and the emphasis they give to the
different reading skills.

The first thing that a classroom teacher should do is to analyze each test carefully both for the content being measured and the mental processes required of
the examinee to answer the items. Many of the tests published since 1955 provide
an analysis of the content in the manuals written for the classroom teacher. For
example, the *Iowa Test of Basic Skills* and the *Sequential Test of Educational
Progress* (STEP) provide an item by item analysis of the skills being measured
and classify and categorize the items for easy analysis. However, the classroom

ELIZABETH HAGEN, "Analyzing Test Results," *National Elementary Principal*,
41 (November, 1961), 11–17. Reprinted by permission of the publisher.
Copyright 1961, Department of Elementary School Principals, National
Education Association.

DR. HAGEN (1915–   ) is Associate Professor of Education, Teachers College, Columbia University.

teacher should check the test publisher's analysis by taking the test himself. He should make a note of any items that are inappropriate for his students. He should also note the kinds of skills or content not being tested so he will be aware of the limitations that must be put on his interpretation of the scores.

Only when the classroom teacher knows thoroughly the tests that his class has taken is he prepared to work with the test results. However, before he can organize the scores in some systematic way as a basis for analysis, the teacher must know what kind of scores he has.

NORMS

Since the raw score (the number of correct answers) on a test has no direct meaning in and of itself, the raw scores on a standardized test are given meaning by comparing them to the performance of a standard reference group. This standard reference group is called a norm group and the score obtained by such a comparison is called a norm.

A norm is *merely a description* of the performance of a certain group such as a sample of fifth-grade students throughout the United States; it is *not* a standard of achievement. For example, on the arithmetic computation sub-test of the *Stanford Achievement Test*, the norm for students at the beginning of the fifth grade is 21 items correct out of a total of 45 items. However, the standard of achievement that one would like to reach is 100 percent accuracy in computation. One cannot even say that the norm, particularly a national norm, represents a desirable level of achievement. A national norm group is made up of bright, average, and dull students drawn from outstanding, average, and poor schools, subjected to good, poor, and indifferent teaching. With such a heterogeneous group, one can scarcely be satisfied with the performance of the norm group when he knows that improvements in curriculum and teaching could vastly improve performance.

Three kinds of norms are usually provided for standardized tests at the elementary school level. These are age norms, grade norms, and percentile norms.

Age norms: Strictly speaking, age norms are not relevant to achievement test results because progress in school achievement does *not* depend upon chronological age, but upon exposure to the learning situation in the classroom. For this reason, age norms should not be used for achievement tests.

Grade norms: The grade norm is the most widely used and widely abused type of norm at the elementary school level. Although it is useful, the grade norm is so frequently misinterpreted that one wishes it had never been used. A grade norm merely discribes the typical performance of a specified grade group. For example, on the paragraph meaning sub-test of the *Stanford Achievement Test, Intermediate Battery,* the median score for students in the fifth month of the fifth grade in the normative sample was 30 items right; therefore, a score of 30 items right was assigned a grade equivalent score of 5.5. This means that one-half of the students in the normative sample who were in grade 5.5 scored higher than 30 and one-half scored lower than 30. Since the norm is usually defined as a median, in an unselected sample of students, one-half must fall above the norm and one-half must fall below. One can see, then, the ridiculousness of the statement that everyone in a class should be "up to the norm."

Another kind of misinterpretation of grade norms occurs with grade-equivalent scores that deviate markedly from the grade placement of the individual student. For example, consider the student in the fifth month of the fifth grade who obtains a grade-equivalent score of 11.7 on the paragraph meaning sub-test of the *Stanford Achievement Test, Intermediate Battery.* One frequently hears classroom teachers say that this student is reading at a high eleventh-grade level. This is nonsense. Eleventh-grade students have never taken this particular test. An extreme score such as this means only that this particular student is a very outstanding reader in comparison to the typical student in the fifth month of the fifth grade.

There is one other basic defect in grade norms that causes trouble in interpretation—grade norms on different tests do *not* have the same meaning. Look at the following scores for a student who took the *Stanford Achievement Test* in the second month of the fifth grade:

Test	Grade-equivalent score
Paragraph meaning	7.4
Word meaning	7.0
Spelling	6.5
Language	7.7
Arithmetic reasoning	6.6
Arithmetic computation	6.1

Looking at the set of grade-equivalent scores one would say that the student had performed best in language and poorest in arithmetic computation. However, every one of these scores equals or exceeds the performance of 90 percent of the norm sample at that particular grade level. In other words, the student performed equally well on all the tests in spite of the fact that the grade-equivalent scores are *not* the same. This phenomenon is *not* caused by a defect in this particular test or a defect in norming; it is due to the differences in variability of performance of students on the tests. There is a much greater spread of scores among students in the same class in reading and language than there is in arithmetic and spelling because these last two are more closely tied to the curriculum of the school than is reading.

Percentile norms: The lack of equivalence in meaning of grade scores from test to test is serious when one is trying to compare scores for a group or an individual on different tests. For this reason, percentile norms are preferable in most cases. A percentile tells the percentage of a group that falls at or below a particular score. For example, if a student obtains a raw score of 15 on a test and this is equivalent to a percentile rank of 20, it means that 20 percent of the norm group scored lower than 15 and 80 percent obtained scores higher than 15. The percentile norm has the additional advantage of keeping the reference point where it belongs—in a group of which the individual can be considered to be a member. That is, a fifth-grade student is compared with other fifth-grade students, not with sixth-grade or fourth-grade students.

The percentile norm would be an ideal norm except for one defect: It does not have equal units all along the scale. An increase of five percentile points from the 50th percentile to the 55th percentile does *not* represent the same increment in score as an increase in five percentile points from the 90th to the 95th percentile. This defect in percentile norms is most troublesome when one wants to measure growth or increase in achievement from year to year.

STANDARD ERROR

Up to this point, we have been concerned with two kinds of things that the classroom teacher should thoroughly understand before he attempts to analyze and interpret test scores: (1) the test itself, and (2) the kind of score that is being used to report test results. There is one additional point that the classroom teacher should keep in mind as he analyzes and interprets test scores. He should remember that when we give a test to an individual or a group of individuals we are getting an estimate of the student's performance on the items on that particular test. From this estimate, we then make an inference about the ability of the student in the area being measured by the test.

For example, suppose we had given a fourth-grade class the *Otis Quick-Scoring Mental Ability Test, Beta.* Each of the students taking the test would mark his answers in the appropriate place; then, the number of right answers that the student had marked would be counted. The number of right answers would be the individual's score, which we would call his mental ability. But the score itself is *not* the mental ability. It is a *record* of a *sample* of behavior. Any judgment regarding mental ability is an inference based on the evidence provided by the number of correct answers on this particular *sample* of behavior. In other words, we have an estimate of his performance on a series of items purportedly measuring mental ability. This estimate is *not* absolutely accurate; it contains a certain amount of error called the error of measurement.

When a classroom teacher is looking at a set of scores for an individual, he must always allow for this error of measurement. He can never consider a score obtained by a student as an unvarying point on a scale but must, instead, always think of it as a band. Suppose for example, that on the Otis test mentioned previously, an individual obtained a score that yielded him an IQ of 115 for his performance on that test at that particular time. The manual for the Otis test states that the standard error of measurement is 4 IQ points. The classroom teacher should multiply the standard error by two, which would give 8 IQ points, and think of that individual as most probably having an IQ on that test of somewhere between 107 and 123. And this is as accurate as he can be in estimating that individual's mental ability on the Otis test.

The standard error of measurement varies from test to test. The manuals for the tests usually give the standard error but, as a rough rule-of-thumb, it would be well for the teacher to estimate intelligence test score bands by adding 10 to the obtained intelligence quotient and subtracting 10 from the obtained intelligence quotient. For example, a student obtains an IQ of 103 on X intelligence test. The teacher should think of the student as having a score most probably between 93 and 113 on X intelligence test. On an achievement test when using grade-equivalent scores, a rough guide is to allow a full grade below and above the obtained score. If a student had been given a reading comprehension test and had obtained a grade score of 4.7, the teacher should think of the score as being most probably somewhere between 3.7 and 5.7. This should make the teacher very wary of interpreting small differences between scores on different tests for an individual student.

When a classroom teacher is working with average scores for a group of individuals, the error of measurement is smaller than for an individual. The reason for this is that the errors in measurement are due to chance factors; in some instances, the error of measurement will make a score for an individual higher than it should be and in other instances, it will make the score lower than it should be. When scores are averaged over a large number of individuals, these chance effects cancel each other so that the average score for a group has a smaller standard error than does the score for an individual. How much error there is in an average score for a group depends upon the number of people in the group and other factors.

Now let us suppose that the classroom teacher understands thoroughly all of the things previously mentioned. How does he organize the test data so he can obtain a better understanding of the students as a group and as individuals? The kinds of tabulations and analyses of data that the teacher makes are, of course, dependent upon the kinds of questions he is trying to answer. Although one probably cannot foresee all of the questions a classroom teacher is likely to ask about a set of test data, there are certain questions that are commonly asked and these will be discussed here.

AVERAGE SCORES MISLEADING

Let us assume that the classroom teacher has been given for the 30 students in his class an alphabetical listing of scores on a verbal group intelligence test and an achievement battery that includes tests of reading comprehension, vocabulary, spelling, language usage, arithmetic computation, arithmetic reasoning, and study skills. If the list also contains average battery scores for all tests combined or average scores obtained by averaging two or more tests—for example, an average arithmetic score obtained by combining the arithmetic computation score and arithmetic reasoning score—the teacher can ignore them since this type of score can be misleading. Consider the following students in grade 4.3 who obtained a composite average grade-equivalent score of 4.6 on the battery of achievement tests:

Test	Student 1	Student 2	Student 3
Reading comprehension	2.9	6.1	4.8
Vocabulary	3.1	6.5	4.6
Language usage	4.5	5.8	4.5
Spelling	4.8	5.1	4.3
Arithmetic computation	6.0	3.2	4.4
Arithmetic reasoning	6.5	2.0	4.9
Study skills	4.4	3.5	4.7
Composite battery score	4.6	4.6	4.6

On the basis of the composite average battery score, the three students appear to be achieving at the same level and appear to be very much alike. However, a look at the scores for each student on the separate tests shows that these students are quite different and need quite different instructional programs. Student 1 shows a definite weakness in reading and vocabulary and definite strengths in arithmetic computation and arithmetic reasoning. On the other hand, student 2 shows quite definite strengths in the verbal areas of reading, vocabulary, language usage, and spelling and very definite weaknesses in the quantitative areas of arithmetic computation and arithmetic reasoning. Student 3 shows no outstanding strengths or weaknesses but is an even performer on all of the tests. The use of an average score for all the tests obscures these differences among students; therefore, it is advisable for routine classroom use to ignore the average scores and use only the scores on the individual tests.

SCANNING FOR INCONSISTENCIES

When a classroom teacher receives a list of scores for students in his class, the first thing he should do is scan the scores for each individual pupil to see if they are internally consistent and check the scores of each individual pupil against previous test scores or other information about the student. This scanning will avoid the necessity of trying to find explanations for test performances that are internally inconsistent or are inconsistent with other data on the individual when the inconsistency may very well be due to clerical errors in scoring the test, errors in using a table to convert scores, or errors in recording the results. Test papers scored by teachers contain a large number of errors in scoring—some quite substantial. Test papers scored by outside agencies or by electronic machines can also contain errors.

To illustrate what is meant by internal inconsistencies or inconsistencies with other data, let us consider an example. Suppose you are a sixth-grade teacher and have received the following scores for an individual student in the third month of the sixth grade (6.3):

Test	Score
Verbal IQ	85
Reading comprehension	10.6
Vocabulary	10.7
Language usage	6.6
Spelling	6.8
Arithmetic computation	10.4
Arithmetic reasoning	11.7
Study skills	10.5

Before you blithely label the student as an "overachiever," it would be well to check the intelligence test to determine whether the test has been scored accurately and the intelligence quotient has been computed accurately. The intelligence test score is singled out for attention in this case because the achievement test scores are consistently high. If you can find no error in the scoring of the intelligence test or in the computation of the intelligence quotient, check against previous test data on the student. Suppose this student had been given the same intelligence test when he was in the fourth grade and had obtained an intelligence quotient of 120. The difference of 35 points between the fourth-grade testing and the sixth-grade testing is too large to attribute to error of measurement and the student should be retested. Test scores that are inconsistent or out-of-line with other evidence on the individual should never be entered on a permanent record until their accuracy has been established.

ANALYZING THE TOTAL CLASS: USE OF MEDIANS

After eliminating the inconsistent cases from consideration in the analysis, the classroom teacher is ready to organize the class data in order to obtain answers to his questions. The first question to be answered is usually, "How did the class on the whole perform on each of these tests?" To answer this question, the teacher should tabulate and list the scores on each test from the highest score to the lowest score. Then for each set of scores, he should determine the median score—the score which divides the class in half.

Having computed the median for each of the tests, the teacher is ready to look at the pattern of the medians in order to obtain an answer to the question, "What are the strong and weak points of the class as a whole?" In looking for patterns of performance, the classroom teacher should group median scores for related areas. For the achievement battery that we are using as an example, the medians for reading comprehension and vocabulary should be examined together; the medians for spelling and language usage should be looked at as a unit; the medians for arithmetic computation and arithmetic reasoning should be looked at as a unit; then, the medians for study skills. This type of pattern analysis needs to be done in order to differentiate a class disability from an individual disability. To illustrate, let us look at the following example showing medians for a fourth-grade class tested in November (4.3):

Test	Class median
Verbal IQ	105
Reading comprehension	5.1
Vocabulary	4.8
Language usage	4.5
Spelling	4.2
Arithmetic computation	3.0
Arithmetic reasoning	2.7
Study skills	2.7

This particular class shows strength in the verbal-language areas and weaknesses in the quantitative and study skills areas. Since the class shows a very marked weakness in the quantitative and study skills tests, the teacher might well ask the question, "Why are these students performing so poorly in these areas?" To obtain more specific information about what the class does and does not know in these areas, the teacher should make a sample item analysis of the arithmetic and study skills test.

ITEM ANALYSIS

In order to make an item analysis of the tests, the teacher needs the answer sheets of the students. With the answer sheets at hand, the teacher can make a tally of the number of correct answers, the number of wrong answers, and the number of omitted answers to each test question. Then, he should look at the items that have been marked correct and incorrect by a large proportion of the class.

In the school from which these data were taken, such an item analysis was made and showed three things: (1) the students on the whole were slow workers; a large proportion of students had never reached the last 20 items on the test; (2) the students tended to make mistakes on simple addition or subtraction items that were written on a line instead of under each other; most of the students missed items involving the use of decimals unless they were problems dealing with money. The teacher investigated the previous educational experiences of the students in arithmetic and found that accuracy had been emphasized; that the students had always been given their addition and subtraction problems in the same form; and that problems involving decimals other than money were a part of the curriculum for the last half of the fourth grade. With this information, the teacher could do better planning for the class in arithmetic than he could with just the scores alone.

PERFORMANCE AND EXPECTANCY

When the teacher is looking at the median scores for his class, he frequently asks, "Are these scores what they should be in light of the ability level of the class?" This question deals with the relationship between obtained scores and expected scores and poses a sticky problem. Too frequently, the classroom teacher tries to make a direct comparison between intelligence test scores and achievement test scores. However, both scores have errors in them and the correlation between intelligence and achievement is not perfect.

The level of achievement in a group depends not only upon the scholastic ability level of the group but also upon the educational experiences to which it has been exposed and the cultural backgrounds of the individuals making up the group. The judgment of whether a group is performing at the expected level can be made only if median scores for groups of like-level of ability are available for comparison. If the median level of scholastic ability for the group is average, if the median socio-economic level is about at the average for the nation as a whole, and if the curricular emphasis in the school is like schools in the United States as a whole, then and only then can the national norm be used as a reference point for judging whether the group is performing at expectancy. If the classroom group deviates from the national group on *any one* of these points, then the national norm cannot be used to judge whether a particular group is performing at expectancy, and local expectancy charts must be set up for this purpose.

IDENTIFYING NUMBER OF ACHIEVEMENT LEVELS

The last question that a teacher is likely to ask about the group as a whole is, "How many distinct levels of achievement do I have in each of the areas covered by the tests?" Again, it is better if the classroom teacher looks at patterns of scores.

If the teacher has arranged the scores for each test from high to low and computed medians for each test, he can then compute the 25th percentile and 75th percentile on each test. These three score points will divide the scores on each test into four parts: the lowest quarter, those falling below the 25th percentile; the second quarter, those falling between the 25th percentile and the median; the third quarter, those falling between the median and the 75th percentile; and the fourth quarter, those falling above the 75th percentile. He can use some simple designation for each quarter such as L (low) for the lowest quarter; LA (low average) for the second quarter; HA (high average) for the third quarter; and H (high) for the fourth quarter. The teacher can then list the students alphabetically, and rule off columns for each test and enter the appropriate symbol for each student for each test. The record would look something like this:

Student	Int.	Read. comp.	Voc.	Lang. usage	Spell.	Arith. comp.	Arith. reas.
John A	H	LA	LA	HA	LA	H	H
Anne B	LA	LA	LA	LA	HA	L	L

A record such as this not only helps the teacher to see how many groups he needs, but also helps him see the pattern of scores for the individual students and locate students who need enriched programs, remedial work, or a modified program.

INTERPRETING THE INDIVIDUAL'S SCORES

The analyses that have been proposed not only will give the teacher a picture of the group as a whole, but also will serve as a point of reference for interpreting the scores of an individual student. There are two questions concerning individual students that are frequently asked: (1) Is the student performing at expectancy according to his ability level? and (2) How much growth or progress has the student made since the last testing? Both of these questions are difficult for the classroom teacher to answer because they involve rather sophisticated statistical procedures. In both instances, we are dealing with scores that are highly related to each other and have a certain amount of error of measurement. When we make these comparisons, we are dealing with the difference between two scores and these differences are less reliable than either of the individual scores.

Let us consider the question of how well a student's performance conforms to the level of performance expected of him. The classroom teacher needs outside help in order to determine levels of expectancy of different ability levels. In large systems, the school as a whole can help the teacher by preparing expectancy charts. To do this, one needs the intelligence test scores and the achievement test scores for each individual. A large number of students is also required in order for the expectancy chart to be stable. For each achievement test, a bivariate or two-way distribution of the achievement test scores against intelligence test scores should be made. An example of a basic expectancy chart is shown on page 572.

The basic chart is made up with intelligence test scores (in broad groupings) on one axis and the achievement test scores on the other axis. Each student is tallied in the box that correctly identifies him as to intelligence test score and achievement test score. For example, a student who obtained an Otis IQ of 105 and a reading grade score of 4.7 would be tallied in row three (IQ grouping 100-109), column seven (reading grade score 4.5 to 4.9).

Once the basic expectancy chart has been prepared, one can compute the 25th percentile, the median, and the 75th percentile for each row of intelligence test

Expectancy table for end of 3rd grade
on metropolitan reading test according to Otis IQ

Reading Grade Score on Metropolitan Reading Test

Otis IQ	1.5 to 1.9	2.0 to 2.4	2.5 to 2.9	3.0 to 3.4	3.5 to 3.9	4.0 to 4.4	4.5 to 4.9	5.0 to 5.4	5.5 to 5.9	6.0 to 6.4	6.5 to 6.9	7.0 to 7.4	7.5 to 7.9	8.0 to 8.4	8.5 to 8.9	9.0 to 9.4	Total
120 & above	0	1	4	4	10	19	14	7	4	3	2	0	1	1	1	2	73
110–119	0	2	5	23	19	27	21	8	7	4	3	0	2	1	0	0	122
100–109	0	2	19	21	39	26	21	21	5	5	0	1	2	0	0	0	162
90–99	1	5	25	25	26	24	12	6	5	1							130
89 & below	1	5	19	17	10	4	2	2									60

scores. The decision about what represents the expected level of achievement is a somewhat arbitrary one. For this example, expectancy for any intelligence level was set as the middle 50 percent, below expectancy was set as the lower 25 percent, and above expectancy was set as the highest 25 percent.

The teachers in the school where this expectancy chart was made were given the following summary table to use in interpreting individual cases:

Summary table

Summary	IQ's 120+	IQ's 110–119	IQ's 100–109	IQ's 90–99	IQ's 89 & below
Below expectancy	3.9 & below	3.4 & below	3.4 & below	3.0 & below	2.6 & below
At expectancy	4.0–5.1	3.5–4.8	3.5–4.8	3.1–4.3	2.7–3.6
Above expectancy	5.2 & above	4.9 & above	4.9 & above	4.4 & above	3.7 & above

The question of how much growth an individual student has made since the last testing cannot be answered by simply subtracting the two scores. About the best judgment a teacher can make is in terms of whether a student is maintaining his relative position in the group. If he is, his progress is satisfactory. If he has improved his relative position, he has made more progress than the average child. If his relative position is lower, he has made less progress.

The analyses suggested in this article may seem to be involved and time-consuming, but they represent a wise use of time. If the classroom teacher, with the help of others in the school, will do them, he will have information about teaching problems of the coming year, about areas in which emphasis in teaching is needed, and about individuals who need special kinds of attention. With these types of information, the classroom teacher will be better able to provide appropriate learning experiences for both the total class and individual children.

62 *Is testing a menace to education?*

Related selections: 60, 61

Some people believe that today's widespread testing programs in our schools threaten to submerge the individual in a mass of group norms, attach nonvalid labels to students, and create undue anxiety in children and parents. Dyer agrees that the current emphasis can menace the educational process but lists and describes nine misconceptions about tests and charges that it is the misconceptions and not the tests that are the real threat.

The title of this talk is a question: "Is Testing a Menace to Education?" Knowing who I am and what I do for a living, you would have every reason to believe that I am going to answer the question with a resounding, "No!" But you would be dead wrong, for I am going to answer the question with a tentative, "Yes, but—" Yes, testing *is* a menace to education, *but* probably not for the reasons you think. It is a menace to education primarily because tests are misunderstood and test results are misused by too many educators. In his recent book called *The Schools,* Martin Mayer speaks of testing as a "necessary evil." I disagree. It is not *necessarily* evil. Tests *could* be a blessing to education if only teachers and counselors and educational administrators would divest themselves of a number of misconceptions about what tests can and cannot do and would learn to use test results more cautiously and creatively in the educational process.

There are nine principal misconceptions that seem to stand in the way of the appropriate use of tests.

The *first* misconception is the notion that aptitude or intelligence tests measure something called "native ability," something fixed and immutable within the person that determines his level of expectation for all time. I am not prepared to say such an inherent entity does not exist. The chances are it does. Studies in genetics certainly support the idea, and so do many psychological studies. But intelligence or aptitude tests do not *measure* such an entity—at least not directly, and certainly not in any interpretable manner.

What intelligence tests do measure is the individual's performance on certain types of mental tasks . . . a long time after the child has first entered the world.

HENRY L. DYER, "Is Testing a Menace to Education?", *New York State Education,* 49 (October, 1961), 16–19. Reprinted by permission of the New York State Teachers Association.

DR. DYER is vice president for College Board Programs, Educational Testing Service, Princeton, N.J.

The kinds of mental tasks that appear in any intelligence or aptitude test are clearly the kinds that a student *learns* to perform from his experiences in the world around him. The amount of learning based on such experiences may depend on many things that can vary enormously from one child to another— the number and quality of books available in his home, the kind of talk he hears, the richness and variety of his surroundings, the vividness and emotional quality of the thousands of happenings in his life from day to day. It is absurd to suppose that a child's score on an intelligence test by-passes all these factors, to suppose that such a score gets directly at the brains he was born with.

I prefer to think of an intelligence test as essentially indistinguishable from an achievement test—that is, as a measure of how well, at a given point of time, a student can perform certain well-defined tasks. The main difference between the tasks in a so-called achievement test and those in a so-called intelligence test is, generally speaking, that the tasks in an achievement test are usually learned over a relatively short time and those in an intelligence test are learned over a relatively long time.

The consequences of thinking of an aptitude test as measuring some immutable determiner of student performance can be pretty serious. First, such thinking encourages the dangerous idea that one can, from an aptitude score, decide once and for all at a fairly early age what kind and level of educational or vocational activity a student is fitted for. It nurtures that hardy perennial, for instance, that if a student has an IQ of 115 or better he ought to prepare for college, and if his IQ is below 115 he ought to make other plans—this, despite all the studies which have shown that an IQ may be highly variable for a given student, that colleges vary enormously in the quality of students they enroll, and that some low scorers succeed in college while some high scorers fail. I have often wondered how many educational crimes are annually committed on the strength of the theory that intelligence tests measure something they cannot possibly measure.

A second consequence, almost as serious, is the conception that a student with a high aptitude score and low achievement scores (or low grades in school) is an "under-achiever"—another hardy perennial. It was exploded 30 years ago, but it is back and can lead to some rather distressing treatment of individual pupils. The diagnosis goes that a student with a high aptitude score and low achievement scores is "unmotivated" or "lazy" or suffering from some sort of emotional disturbance. Granted there may be some grounds for such diagnoses, nevertheless they are scarcely inferable from the discrepancy in scores alone. And some new and possibly more useful insights about such students might be forthcoming if one frankly regarded the discrepancies simply as differences in performance on one kind of achievement test as compared to another.

Finally, the idea that aptitude tests are supposed to measure native ability leads to the persistent and embarrassing demand that they should be "culture free"; that if they are, as they must be, affected by the student's background of experience in school and at home, then *ipso facto*, they are "unfair" to the under-privileged. I wish we could get it *out* of people's heads that tests are unfair to the underprivileged and get it *into* their heads that it is the hard facts of social circumstance and inadequate education that are unfair to them. If educational opportunities are unequal, the test results will also be unequal.

A *second* misconception about tests is the notion that a prediction made from a test score, or from a series of test scores, or from test scores plus other quantifiable data, are, or should be, perfectly accurate, and that if they are not, the tests must be regarded as no good. This fallacy arises from a confused conception of what constitutes prediction. There are some people—maybe most people— who think of prediction as simply an all-or-none, right-or-wrong business. If a test score predicts that Johnny will get B in American history, the score is right if he actually gets a B; it is wrong if he gets a B– or a C. I suppose this is a legitimate way of thinking about prediction in certain circumstances, but it is scarcely fair to the test and it may well be unfair to Johnny. A more meaningful and useful way of thinking about a prediction is to regard it as a statement of the odds: A given test score might predict that Johnny has 8 chances in 10 of getting a grade of B or better in American history, and 3 chances in a hundred of flunking. This approach recognizes that in forecasting future events, especially human events, we never have sufficient information to be sure of being right every time, but we do have information, in the form of test scores and other data, which, if appropriately organized, can help us make better decisions than would be possible without them.

The *third* misconception is that standardized test scores are infallible or perfectly reliable. Reliability, I remind you, has to do with the degree to which the score of an individual stands still on successive testings. It rarely occurs to the uninitiated that a test can never be more than a *sample* of a student's performance and that, in consequence, the score on any test is afflicted with sampling error. To the man-in-the-street, to many teachers, school administrators and parents, who have never reflected on the problem, a score is a score is a score, and they are shocked to find that when a student takes one test today and an alternate form of the same test tomorrow, his score can change. Anyone who deals with a test score must always be conscious that such a score, like any sort of measurement whatever, is clouded with uncertainty, that it is never more than an estimate of the truth.

A *fourth* misconception is the assumption that an achievement test measures all there is to measure in any given subject matter area—that an achievement test in history, for example, measures everything a high school student should know about the facts of history and how to deal with them. It never seems to occur to some people that the content of a standardized achievement test in any particular subject matter area may be only partially related to what a specific course of study in that area may call for.

If people will only take the trouble to look critically at the insides of achievement tests and not just at their covers, they will almost certainly find that even the test best suited to their purposes still fails to sample *all* the types of learning that are sought in a given subject, or even all the most important types of learning. And it may also often include matters that the student is not expected to know. The consequence is, of course, that on a particular standardized achievement test a student may look considerably better or considerably worse than he really is, and decisions based on his score may miss the boat by a considerable margin.

A *fifth* misconception is that an achievement test can measure only a pupil's memory for facts. This used to be true. But a good modern achievement test gets at far more than a command of facts alone; it usually measures in addition the pupil's skill in reasoning with the facts he remembers and also his skill in reasoning with facts newly presented to him. It is this introduction into achievement tests of the requirement to reason, to cope with problems, to think clearly, critically and even creatively that helps to blur the distinction between aptitude and achievement tests. The modern achievement test recognizes that as students come up through the grades they are, or ought to be, learning to think as well as to know. It recognizes also that there may be many different kinds of thinking to measure, depending upon the subject matter in which the thinking is required. The result is that a well-conceived battery of achievement tests gives the same sort of information one would get from a general intelligence test plus a good deal more.

A *sixth* misconception has to do with profiles of achievement or aptitude scores, that a profile of scores summarizes clearly and efficiently a considerable amount of reliable information about the relative strengths and weaknesses of an individual. Test technicians have inveighed repeatedly against the use of profile charts on the grounds that they are often grossly misleading, that the differences they depict—even when they appear large—may be, and usually are, unreliable differences, that the score scales used for the several tests in the profile may not be comparable, that the several measures which show on the profile may have the appearance of being highly independent measures when, in fact, many of them may be highly correlated—in short, that the apparent clarity and efficiency of a test score profile is really an illusion covering up all sorts of traps and pitfalls in score interpretation which even the most wary can scarcely avoid. Yet the profile chart is still in much demand and in wide use, primarily, I suppose, because it is extraordinarily convenient. Mere administrative convenience is hardly sufficient justification for hiding confusion under a false coat of simplicity. Good test interpretation takes mental effort, a bit of imagination and some willingness to cope with complexity.

A *seventh* misconception is that interest inventories measure some kind of basic orientation of a student irrespective of the kinds of experiences to which he has been or will be exposed. Let me cite just one example. A presumably well-trained guidance counselor in a high school where the large majority of students go on to college was confronted by a girl with top-notch scholastic standing in all of the college preparatory subjects. Her parents were college-trained people, had always expected their daughter would go to a liberal arts college; the daughter had always enthusiastically entertained the same idea.

The counselor, however, was apparently bewitched by one of the girl's scores on an interest inventory which indicated her major interest was in clerical work. Disregarding all the other evidence, the counselor insisted that the girl was unfitted for the work of a liberal arts college and would be happy only in a secretarial school. Tears on the part of the child, anger on the part of the parents and hell-to-pay all around. Certainly interest test scores are useful in promoting thought and self-analysis, but certainly also the tests are scarcely capable of probing deeply enough into an individual's past and future to warrant anything approaching the dogmatism which characterized this counselor.

The *eighth* misconception is that on a personality test an individual reveals deep and permanent temperamental characteristics of which he himself may be unaware. I suppose there is nothing about the whole testing business that frightens me more than this. Anyone close to the research in personality testing who has any critical sense at all knows that we have still barely scratched the surface of a field whose dimensions are still far from defined. To put it perhaps a little too strongly, personality tests—the inventories, the projective tests, all of them— are scarcely beyond the tea-leaf-reading stage. To be sure, there is some interest- ing—even exciting—research going on in the area, but none of it yet adds up to tests that can be trusted as evidence leading to important decisions about children.

There are four major weaknesses in personality tests. First, they purport to measure traits such as introversion-extroversion, neurotic tendency, gregarious- ness, tolerance for ambiguity, and the like—all of which are highly fuzzy con- cepts, to say the least, and for none of which there are any agreed-upon defini- tions. There is not even any general agreement on what we mean by the word "personality" itself. How can you describe or classify a person meaningfully with a test whose scores do not themselves have any clear or rigorous meaning?

Secondly, it is characteristic of current personality tests that the behavior they sample is essentially superficial nonsignificant behavior. By this I mean when a subject answers such a question as "Do you often daydream?" his response of "Yes" or "No" may well be nothing more than a purely random phenomenon quite unconnected with any of his habitual behavior tendencies. The whole essence of the measurement problem is to secure reliable samples of human behavior under standardized conditions which will have strong cor- relates with the universe of behavior an individual habitually exhibits in his waking life. The personality tests currently available have yet to demonstrate that they can provide such samples.

Thirdly, even if we were able to establish some meaningful personality traits, we still know little or nothing about their stability. We still don't know whether an introvert at age 15 may not turn into an extrovert by the time he is 22.

Finally, of course, practically all personality tests can be faked. I proved to my own satisfaction how fakable such tests are when I gave one to a class I was once teaching. I asked the students to take a personality inventory twice—once to prove that they were thoroughly well adjusted people and once to prove that they were ready for a mental institution. The first set of scores showed that the whole class was a bunch of apple-cheeked extroverts; the second set showed that they were all nuts.

Please do not misunderstand me. I take a very dim view of current personality tests, and I think the general public is being much too frequently taken in by the mumbo-jumbo that goes with them. On the other hand, I am very much in favor of as much solid research as we can possibly get into the fundamental dynamics of human behavior, for we shall never be in full command of the educational process until we have far more understanding than we now have of what makes children tick. There are glimmerings of hope, but we are not out of the woods yet, and who can tell when we will be? In the meantime, let's not kid ourselves by putting our trust in gimmicks.

The *ninth* and final misconception is this: that a battery of tests can tell all one needs to know in making a judgment about a student's competence, present and potential, and about his effectiveness as a human being. The fact is that no test or series of tests now available is capable of giving the total picture of any child. Tests can illuminate many areas of his development, suggest something about his strengths and weaknesses, show in certain respects how he stands among his peers. But there are still many important aspects of learning and human development where we must still rely upon the observation and judgment of teachers if we are to get something that approaches a complete description of the child as a functioning individual. There are subtle but supremely important human elements in the teaching-learning situation that no combination of tests yet devised is able to capture. Such elements are elusive, but if ever we lose sight of them, the educational process in all its ramifications will become something less than the exciting human enterprise it should always be.

These are the nine misconceptions which I think most frequently lead to wide misuse of tests and test results. Some of our brasher critics have argued that, since tests are so widely misused, they do constitute a menace to sound education and therefore should be abolished. This argument is specious. It is the same as saying that automobiles should be abolished because they are a menace to human life when reckless drivers are at the wheel. Or it is the same as saying that teachers should be abolished because too many of them make psychometric hash out of marks and test scores.

In any case, I think it is highly unlikely that tests will be abolished any more than that textbooks will be abolished. Too many schools have discovered that, menace or not, they cannot operate effectively without them. The problem is not one of doing away with tests and testing but of getting people to use tests intelligently. When this happens testing will cease to be a mere administrative convenience or, worse still, a burden on the souls of teachers and pupils; it will become an effective instrument for vitalizing the total educational process and for helping to insure that in these days of skyrocketing enrollments the individual pupil will not be lost in the shuffle.

PROGRAMED LEARNING
AND TEACHING MACHINES

Ten years ago the literature on programed learning and teaching machines could have been collected and reproduced in a very few pages. Today, the flow of articles, textbooks, research reports, units, and other writing related to this field is overwhelming.

The six selections from that vast array which follow should be read as a unit by persons unfamiliar with the topic. It is suggested that the reader weigh carefully the opinions, arguments, and evidence presented in each of the six articles before forming his own tentative position.

Lysaught (selection 63) tells why programed learning is important to the individual classroom teacher and relates the process to a stimulus-response learning model. In selection 64, Quackenbush organizes some of the research findings so that the reader may start to examine the effectiveness of auto-instructional techniques. A vigorous case is made by Skinner in selection 65 for the use of teaching machines, and he goes somewhat deeply into the related learning theory. Selection 66 is a strong warning by Pressey that the present welter of action in programing has blurred the issues, and he describes what he sees as the crisis toward which we are moving. Thelen (selection 67) and Fitzgerald (selection 68) express strong doubts concerning the direction in which the programed learning movement is taking us.

63 *Programed learning and the classroom teacher*

In Roanoke, Va., eighth-grade students covered an entire year of algebra in one term. When they took comparative tests with ninth graders who had taken the two-term course, 41 percent of the eighth graders surpassed the average of the ninth graders. In Clinton, N.Y., logic students at Hamilton College have experienced in the past two years a rise in the class average of approximately 20 points, and a reduction in failures—almost to the zero point. In New York City, students at the Collegiate School are showing never-before-matched progress in mathematics and languages.

A common thread runs through each of these experiences. The classroom teachers in all three cases are using the techniques of programed learning to increase the learning rate and proficiency of their pupils. The results in experiment after experiment bear out the predictions of the teachers who feel that here is a powerful, new learning tool.

Programed learning, unlike many of the nostrums advanced for education today, is a development by educators, for educators, and is firmly grounded on educational theory. This should be stressed if only because the popular press has sometimes given the impression that programed learning, and its vehicle for presentation, the teaching machine, are merely one more audio-visual aid— bigger, better and technologically improved. This picture is wholly inaccurate.

Programed learning is designed to offer the teacher and the student a complete learning system which utilizes the classical Stimulus-Response learning pattern.

A typical "program" consists of a carefully constructed pattern of learning items. After each presentation of information, the student is given the immediate opportunity to answer a question, construct a solution, solve a problem or in other ways demonstrate that he has acquired mastery of the item. As quickly as he responds, he can compare his answer with the program answer to determine his own effectiveness. All of this is taking place between the individual and the program and is paced by the individual himself.

Two alternatives now follow. If the student has made the correct response to the stimulus item, confirmation of his correctness by the program serves as immediate reinforcement. And any classroom teacher knows the satisfaction and reward of a student's learning—and simultaneously knowing that he is learn-

JEROME P. LYSAUGHT, "Programed Learning and the Classroom Teacher," *New York State Education*, 48 (February, 1961), pp. 9–11, 39. Reprinted by permission of the New York State Teachers Association.

DR. LYSAUGHT (1930–) is Assistant Professor of Education at the University of Rochester. His research is in the area of programed learning, and he is the author of many articles and a book on the subject.

A sample of programed learning is shown in the excerpts below. These were taken from a course in psychology. First appears the statement in which the student supplies the missing thought; then the correct word follows.

A doctor taps your knee (patellar tendon) with a rubber hammer to test your "_____."	"reflexes"
If your reflexes are normal, your leg _____ to the tap on the knee with a slight kick (the so-called "knee jerk").	responds (or reacts)
In the knee jerk or patellar tendon reflex, the kick of the leg is the _____ to the tap on the knee.	response (or reaction)
The stimulating *object* used by the doctor to elicit a knee jerk is a(n) _____.	hammer (or mallet)

ing. On the other hand, if the student has responded incorrectly, he obtains the advantage of immediate knowledge of his error. He need not wait for a later class period or examination paper to recognize a mistake. In psychological terms, we apply immediate extinction to incorrect performance.

This describes what happens as a student responds to a single stimulus item. The learning program for a single term may consist of some 2,500 to 5,000 items. These items are so interconnected and designed that the student will constantly progress to higher degrees of complexity. At the same time the program introduces review and recall items enabling him to retain and master the course material.

In all this, the learning program is designed to be self-contained and self-sufficient so that the student can learn the material through his active interaction with the stimulus items. Many educators feel that with properly programed stimuli the student will not only master the material but do so with almost complete freedom from error since he should always be prepared by previous items to answer correctly the item next placed before him.

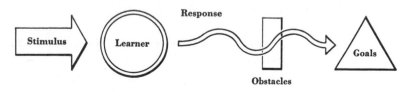

A simplified illustration of events occurring in Stimulus-Response learning.

This is a description of what takes place in programed learning. The figure reproduced here illustrates the standard Stimulus-Response learning diagram. To relate programed learning to this model, we might advance these thoughts:

A. PROGRAMED LEARNING AFFECTS THE LEARNER BY—

1. Improving "set"—learner always alert and busy.
2. Providing constant interaction between learner and program.
3. Idealizing the S-R process by individualizing each learner's experience.
4. Increasing motivation through frequent reinforcement.
5. Tending to decrease individual frustration.

B. PROGRAMED LEARNING AFFECTS THE STIMULUS BY—

1. Presenting a single stimulus at a time.
2. Presenting stimuli in selected order and relationship.

C. PROGRAMED LEARNING AFFECTS THE RESPONSE BY—

1. Providing immediate knowledge of results—feedback.
2. Providing consistent, immediate reinforcement of correct responses.
3. Providing immediate extinction of incorrect responses.
4. Assisting the student in developing correct responses through the medium of the program, i.e., cuing, review, etc.

D. PROGRAMED LEARNING AFFECTS THE OBSTACLES BY—

1. Insisting that a given point be understood before the student moves on.
2. Presenting just that material for which the student is prepared.
3. Simplifying the complexity of the learning material through the introduction of small, more easily assimilated bits.
4. Dealing effectively with the range of individual differences.

E. PROGRAMED LEARNING AFFECTS THE GOALS BY—

1. Demanding the construction of concrete goals prior to the construction of the program.
2. Accomplishing the end goal by a series of approximations.
3. Enabling the instructor to develop complex relationships through the interlocking of discrete, simple items.

F. PROGRAMED LEARNING AFFECTS THE OVER-ALL LEARNING PROCESS BY—

1. Most effectively employing the actual Stimulus-Response Learning Process.
2. Optimizing conditions for individual learning.

3. Providing constant evaluation of student progress and program effectiveness.

Now, having explored the points of relationship between programed learning and learning theory, let us go on to the very important consideration of what this means to the individual teacher.

While there are now currently available standard curriculum courses in spelling, English, algebra, languages, physics and other subjects, most teachers would agree that the first thing a teacher interested in programed learning should do is to construct some programed lessons herself. This would mean, first of all, the statement of the course goals in concrete terms, then the development of item-by-item sequences which will result in student mastery of these goals. People who have taken the plunge into programing feel that it is as challenging an exercise in teaching as any they have ever encountered. The benefits, however, seem to be just as great.

Alice L. Foley, director of instruction, Brighton District No. 1, has written, "I am certain that any teacher who does some programing will be a better teacher when he has finished the work." Dr. John Blyth, professor of philosophy, Hamilton College, has said simply that in two years of programing information for his students he has learned more about teaching than he did in all his previous 23 years of classroom experience.

These comments stem from the fact that in order to program learning materials for this new medium, the teacher must perceive again the student's approach to the subject matter. The teacher must develop a learning map to the course goal which can be followed by each student at his own pace. The various items of information must be so introduced, and fitted together, that at the conclusion of the program the student will have developed a full and complex understanding of the subject.

Programing is obviously quite different from testing. Testing is designed to unearth gaps in a person's understanding; programing on the other hand is designed to fill and to prevent gaps in understanding. In fact, experienced educators feel that programed learning, if properly constructed, should mean that any normal student would gain mastery of the content. This has been true in several experiments. In Arizona, for instance, it was found that high school students could master college statistics through the medium of the learning program. They took longer on the average than college students to complete the course, but they did achieve mastery. Interestingly enough, a few of those who successfully mastered statistics by means of programed learning had failed high school algebra the previous semester when taught by conventional methods.

Programed learning is designed to present teaching material and to bend every effort at helping the student learn. In addition to its carefully constructed features, it employs cues, prompts and other devices to help the student gain his mastery. In the final analysis, student difficulty with the program generally means that the program itself is taking too much for granted, or too large steps, or is not absolutely clear, rather than indicating student error.

Mastery, then, should be an achievable goal for almost every student. Evidence indicates that almost all students, by investing sufficient study time, can conquer the subject matter. Fast and slow learners will differ greatly on the relative speed with which they complete a programed sequence, but the slow student can look forward to success through the medium of a program which displays infinite patience and assistance.

There are other benefits that the classroom teacher can expect from programed learning. John Blyth has summarized his own experience in these words: "We wasted no class time on routine checking or drill. We wasted no class time on unprepared students. We knew in advance who had done work on the program and who had not. In the classroom we could presuppose a common background of experience. We could usually count on a working command of basic concepts and principles. There was a great increase in interest and improvement in morale."

Programed learning can supply the students the basic information of a subject matter, primarily those portions characterized by memorization and rote understanding. Here then is one of its brightest promises: the teacher, released from these more automatic, drill-types of work, is free to do more and more creative teaching and to undertake such teaching with students who come to her grounded in the fundamentals and ready to be challenged.

There will not be a programed learning revolution. In the first place, abrupt changes in educational emphasis are usually self-defeating. Secondly, a revolution is highly unnecessary. Programed learning stems from educational theory and will be developed and refined by educators. It promises tangible benefits to both student and teacher.

The future of programed learning rests with the classroom teacher. As its value to teacher and pupil becomes more widely recognized by the education profession, we can expect its contributions to be extremely significant.

64 How effective are the new auto-instructional materials and devices?

In view of the rapidly expanding attempts by publishers of programs and by manufacturers of machines to get educators to use the new "teaching machines" and "programmed texts," it seems imperative that the crucial question, "How effective are they?" be answered. A number of problems are immediately apparent in attempting to answer this very real question. First there are the varying meanings for the word *effective*. The meaning assigned to it by a teacher of elementary-school children may be widely different from the meaning imposed on the word by the college professor or school administrator. Second, if machines and programs are capable of teaching better and faster, with savings in time and money as well as in the teacher's physical effort, as has been claimed, we must report just how capable they are, not in terms of, "They are good because they fit the principles of good pedagogy so well," but in practical terms which have meaning to the classroom teacher and the administrator. What seems to be called for by many of these people is not a discussion of the design of the experiment and the theoretical background but a statement in the nature of, "When I used them in this situation they made this kind of difference over what I was able to do previously and they are therefore x times as effective"—in other words, they have a practical effectiveness as compared to a theoretical or research effectiveness.

This article attempts to report statements of this type in the hope of encouraging not a blind acceptance of them as true (for in many cases they leave something to be desired from a research viewpoint) but some feel for the potential of, and the consistent trend toward, effective teaching by the use of programs and auto-instructional devices.

In general, the format used is question and answer, and the studies are reported only in summary form, with little or no discussion about the design of the study. When information relating to subject matter, number of subjects, and duration of the study is known, it is mentioned. A brief description is also given of the teaching machine or device utilized. It is hoped that readers who become interested in a particular subject area or educational level will make use of the bibliography and seek more detailed information.

JACK QUACKENBUSH, "How Effective Are the New Auto-Instructional Materials and Devices?", *IRE Transactions on Education*, December, 1961, pp. 144–50. Reprinted by permission of the publisher.

DR. QUACKENBUSH, at the time of publication of this article, was with the Learning Research Center, Pennsylvania State University.

In an attempt to deal with the varying criteria of effectiveness, the studies are grouped according to educational level—Elementary, High School, and College—as well as into three special groups—Special Education, Armed Forces Instruction, and Industrial Uses.

To facilitate the location of studies relating to particular criteria of effectiveness see Table I.

TABLE I

Criterion of effectiveness	Studies reporting data relating to criterion*
1) Achievement, learning	
a) Equal to or better than other treatments	E-1, E-2, E-4, E-5, E-7, H-1, H-4, C-1, C-2, C-4, C-5, C-6, C-8, SE-1, AF-1, AF-2, AF-3, AF-4
b) Not compared	E-6, C-7, C-9, AF-3, AF-4
2) Course coverage	C-1
3) Course improvement	C-1, C-5
4) Course level lowered successfully	E-6, H-2
5) Discipline	H-5, C-1, C-7
6) Drill and routine	H-5, C-1, C-7
7) "Effective" (undefined)	E-3
8) Failure rate	H-5
9) Independent study	C-4
10) Motivation, attitudes, and morale	E-2, E-7, H-2, C-1, C-8, SE-1, AF-1
11) Production rate	I-1, I-2
12) Retention	E-2, E-4, H-4, AF-2
13) Teacher work with individual student	H-5, C-1
14) Time	
a) Qualitative	H-5, C-1, I-3
b) Quantitative	E-1, E-7, H-1, H-3, H-4, H-5, C-1, C-9, AF-1, AF-2
15) Vocabulary	E-6

* In some cases the relationship to the criterion is implied rather than explicitly stated in the report. On the other hand, there are also some criteria which are not listed, the major one being cost. These omissions are due to a lack of information on these points.

ELEMENTARY-SCHOOL STUDIES

How effective are these techniques when used in the first-grade to eighth-grade level? The criterion for effectiveness here may be considered in terms of what the teacher does. The typical elementary situation imposes a great deal of administrative and drill work on the teacher. The effective devices, therefore, would be those which, among other things, would lighten these burdens and permit more attention to individual students, would improve discipline, and would provide opportunities for enrichment of programs for brighter students.

E-1: A year-long study, directed by F. W. Banghart, is being conducted at the University of Virginia. The study involves the use of an "inexpensive mechanical device" and a programmed textbook in the study of fourth-grade mathematics. The textbook and device are both of the constructed-answer type. About 400 experimental subjects (using devices and programmed texts) and 400 control subjects (using standard materials) are involved in the study. A preliminary report [1] stated: "Preliminary tests suggest that the experimental subjects are doing as well as or better than the controls. . . . however, the preliminary test indicated that the experimental subjects scored higher on problem solving than did the controls." The author also reported that "fast" experimental students were able to progress approximately twice as fast as "slow" students, and that several of the "fast" students had been able to complete the course in fourth-grade mathematics, normally scheduled for one year, before Christmas. It would seem that the programs were highly effective in terms of teaching the standard subject matter, and were indeed much faster—but the teachers may now be in the rather ineffective situation of having students in the classroom for whom they have to create work. If this work is the "busy work" with which many of us are familiar, perhaps ground has been lost.

E-2: A study conducted by the General Atronics Corporation [6], a Philadelphia manufacturer of teaching machines (Atronics Tutor), asked, "Does learning occur with teaching machines?" The answer was in the affirmative, showing that two programmed groups had a greater percentage of correct answers on an achievement test plan than an equivalent control group. All groups were at the fifth- and sixth-grade levels. A total of 96 students participated in the study. The duration of the study was not reported. The device used was a mechanical multiple-choice machine. A retention retest three weeks later showed that one of the programmed groups had a loss of 11 percentage points on the test, whereas the other programmed group showed a gain of 3 percentage points on the test. This data is difficult to evaluate, as retest data for the control group was not reported.

From the motivational viewpoint, a survey of student attitude showed that only 2 of the 49 experimental subjects, reacted, unfavorably to the technique.

E-3: The present increasing trend towards earlier foreign language instruction than was formerly available is also reflected in programming efforts. The Center for Programmed Instruction in New York [5] reported on the development of a programmed text in French spelling for the sixth, seventh and eighth grades. Preliminary reports on its use seem to indicate that it is ". . . approximately twice as effective [undefined] as other spelling study methods."

E-4: Gropper and Lumsdaine, at the American Institute of Research in Pittsburgh, applied the principles of programming to a lesson in elementary science. A similar standard (nonprogrammed) lesson was also prepared, and the two lessons were broadcast over television to two groups of randomly-assigned students (six classes of seventh and eighth graders) using the television receiver as a device for presenting the programmed material. The program group were required to construct answers to the frames presented on the screen. Preliminary results [14] indicated that ". . . analyses of results from achievement tests administered to a sample class before the lesson on nuclear change went on the air (TV) revealed that the students have relatively little prior knowledge about the subject matter to be taught. Following the program, a comparison of achievement-test data for randomized groups of students who had watched the experimental (programmed) and control (nonprogrammed) versions of the prepared lesson revealed the superiority of the experimental version: that is, the students who watched the experimental version of the lesson scored significantly higher than the students watching the control or standard version." The students were then retested after a delay of a week and a half, and the initial superiority of the programmed group was still in evidence.

E-5: Working with 14 elementary-school subjects and using a mathematics program presented by filmstrips on an electro-mechanical device, Keisler [20] reported that ". . . subjects performed significantly better on a test of understanding of rectangles than did their matched controls who received no planned instruction on this topic." This use of a "no-treatment" group, which is quite common, illustrates that learning took place which was significantly greater than that which would be attained by the students in their everyday living. (In other words, students who receive instruction generally learn more about a subject than those who do not.)

E-6: Keisler later attempted to teach some understanding of molecular theory to first graders by using programs on teaching machines. An audio-visual device was used, since the children could not read the material. It utilized 2″ x 2″ slides and a tape-recorded commentary. The material covered a three-week period.

Keisler [21] reported, "First, we learned that these children do gain some understanding of the theory, but there were broad individual differences. Three out of thirteen cases did very well, with more than 90% correct on the standardized oral interview, while some others learned very little. Secondly, we learned that these children do answer many oral questions by using words they have never said out loud before." This study has a number of interesting implications. It showed that complex material in programmed form could be taught very early in a child's school experience. Of course, the author was not attempting to prove that this subject-matter should be used at this level; he was merely demonstrating a technique of teaching. The study also showed that the program differentiated among individuals; it may be possible to use it as a new type of achievement or intelligence test. Finally, there was an observed increase in vocabulary of the children.

E-7: In a study of the teaching of spelling to both sixth graders and second graders, Porter [27] reported:

An interesting aspect of the entire program was that no spoken instruction was given to students. Teaching materials paralleled standard lessons in textbooks which were used by the control group as closely as possible. The words taught were exactly the same as those received by the control group.

Twenty-two weeks of a normal 34-week program of spelling instruction were given both the sixth- and second-grade levels using teaching machines (a mechanical constructed-answer device was used). Results were measured on standardized achievement test scores. These showed the experimental group to be significantly superior.

Porter also showed that students did not lose interest in the device; learning for the second half of the course was consistent with that for the first half.

HIGH-SCHOOL STUDIES

The criteria of effectiveness at this level are similar to those which seem important at the elementary level. However, there seems to be more interest in developing independent study on the part of the student, and a greater need to enrich or accelerate the brighter students.

H-1: One of the largest controlled studies in auto-instruction was done by the American Institute for Research in Pittsburgh, under the direction of Klaus [22]. This study involved some 650 students representing 25 physics classes in 17 different high schools. The physics materials were presented to the students via a panelled program textbook which required a constructed response. The programmed material covered approximately 6 weeks of work in high-school physics.

Several different uses were made of programmed material during the study. From one substudy it is reported that: "Those students who had supplemental auto-instructional materials did substantially better on those tests than did the remaining students. . . . Our first conclusion, then, was that auto-instructional methods can produce increments in achievement even when substantial efforts had been made to maximize learning." In another substudy, classes were given regular instruction vs auto-instructional materials: ". . . in this portion of the study, we found that both groups received practically identical scores on the achievement test given. Here we found no evidence to suggest that a human teacher would provide instruction, at least with respect to materials such as physics, that could not be presented by means of an auto-instructional program."

H-2: In New York State [19] when programmed materials which had been prepared for and used with college students in a freshman logic course were presented to 22 gifted junior and senior high-school students, the examination performances of these students compared favorably with those of college students. These students were sufficiently motivated to spend several hours each week on the program, hours which normally would have been spent on extracurricular activities.

H-3: After use of a programmed mathematics course at the Collegiate School, it was reported [31] that in one case 75 students completed in two weeks a highly abstract algebra course that formerly took more than two months.

H-4: The power of programmed materials was dramatically shown by a study conducted in Roanoke, Va., in the spring of 1960 [3]. A group of eighth-grade students studied algebra, a ninth-grade course, without teacher, textbook, or homework, using only a mechanical teaching machine (Foringer, Model 2002) with programmed materials requiring constructed-answer responses. On national examinations in algebra, where the norms were developed on ninth-grade students, the average score of the program group fell in the lower end of the average category for ninth graders, but 41 per cent of the test group surpassed the average score attained by ninth graders. Only one student in the test group fell in the "very low" category. This group of eighth graders also covered the full year's work in algebra in half the time normally required.

In examination of retention of this material, Dr. Allen Calvin, psychologist-director of the Roanoke project, nearly a year later retested 25 of the students from the original group and found that the average score on the retest was 90 per cent (or higher) of the original test score.

H-5: On the basis of these results the school system in Roanoke, Va., has gone ahead with a greatly expanded high-school mathematics program for the school year 1960–1961. First reports on this expanded program are now available [11]. The results are reported for three high schools, involving approximately 900 students. Although other courses were programmed and used, only data on geometry, algebra, and trigonometry were reported. Three treatments were imposed during the study for each programmed courses and for each of three high schools, giving nine groups in all for each subject area. One group (*traditional*) received conventional teaching; a second group (*no help*) used the programmed courses with no help from the teacher in the classroom except in the form of periodic examinations; the third group (*help*) worked on the programmed material, but help from the teacher was available at all times. In addition, while the students in the traditional classes were allowed to proceed in usual fashion, the experimental groups were not permitted to do homework. For this expanded study, machines were not used and all materials were presented in programmed textbooks.

The data from this work have not been completely collected, but some indication of the effectiveness can be gathered from Table II [11], which shows the percentage of students from each high school (A, B, C) who *failed* each of the courses. In each case the most effective treatment was that which produced the *lowest* percentage of failures. For example, consider the geometry course offered in high school A. The help class (6 per cent failures) and the no-help class (8 per cent failures) had approximately the same failure rate. There was, however, a higher failure rate (15 per cent) for the traditional classes, indicating on this measure at least that the programmed materials effectively reduced failures for this particular course in this particular high school. It will be seen from examination of the table that in only two cases did the traditional group have a lower failure rate than the programmed group.

Was there any time saving as a result of use of these programmed texts? The students were permitted to proceed at their own rate, but only during their regularly scheduled class periods. From the very start, wide individual differences were noted. Starting in September, a few students had completed a full year's work in mathematics by December, whereas others had not even kept pace with the traditional class.

What does this mean in terms of effectiveness? We see that it has made highly effective use of some of the brighter students' time and abilities. However, some of the slower students appeared to be working less effectively than they would have if they had been in a traditional classroom group. It may well be that these slower students are learning better, but since some of them have not completed the program, effectiveness of learning cannot yet be evaluated for them.

Were there any other results of this study which indicate increased effectiveness? The results reported are of course preliminary and tenuous, but some Roanoke teachers are quoted [11] as feeling that the programmed classes alleviated discipline problems; routine questions were usually handled by the program, allowing teachers to concentrate on the more important ones. The teachers also reported more opportunity to work with individual students.

COLLEGE STUDIES

At the college level we have somewhat different criteria of effectiveness. The professor is of course primarily interested in having the students learn the sub-

TABLE II

Percentage of failures

Class	High school (per cent)		
	A	B	C
Geometry			
Help	6	7	6
No-help	8	0	0
Traditional	15	8	0
Algebra			
Help	21	25	4
No-help	20	29	3
Traditional	23	9*	11
Trigonometry			
Help	10	0	—
No-help	4	0	—
Traditional	18	7	—

* The only case in which the percentage of failures did not correspond to available test scores on the national standardized examination.

ject matter in his course. Therefore, *any* technique which increases the amount of material covered, as well as the student's grasp of the content, would be considered (barring individual idiosyncrasies) effective.

Savings in actual class time are also vital to the college professor and student. However, programmed materials have been shown to increase the effectiveness of the face-to-face class period qualitatively. This qualitative improvement may be one of the most important aspects of auto-instruction at this educational level. Other factors of importance are expanded opportunity for independent study and more opportunity for enrichment of course content.

Large-scale studies involving a teacher in a face-to-face situation vs auto-instructional materials are not available in the literature. However, we do have some situations which seem to be intuitively of a very similar nature. These occur when a professor who has been teaching a course for a number of years then adds auto-instruction in some form and reports his observations and impressions about the effect of the use of the new materials, whether they are used as a supplement or as the entire course.

C-1: One of the most highly publicized of these studies, reported in detail in the Lumsdaine and Glaser source book [23], was conducted at Hamilton College in Clinton, N.Y. Blyth reported [2] on the supplemental use of programs in a freshman logic course, and saw substantial saving in the quantitative and qualitative use of class time. This semester course was reduced to two hours of class per week instead of the usual three. Yet, the students covered more material more thoroughly than had ever been possible before. The antecedent conditions which led to these savings were many: elimination of routine drill or checking in class; no unprepared students; prior knowledge of areas of difficulty (via feedback from the program work the student had completed); a common background of knowledge and experience, as well as a working knowledge of the principles and concepts. In addition, there was an improvement in morale and an increased interest in the material. A secondary advantage was a reduced need for conferences with individual students. At the same time, when the student did come for a conference, the professor had a detailed summary of that individual's progress through the course as well as knowledge of the areas which were causing him difficulty.

When these students were given an hour-long examination on probability, the examination scores were approximately thirty points higher than a corresponding examination which had been given the previous year. The final examination marks were raised about ten or fifteen points to a new high average of eighty-five.

C-2: Evans, Glaser, and Homme [12] investigated a number of variations in programming formats with groups of about 5 to 20 undergraduate students, and reported, ". . . 3 In general, Ss [students] receiving learning sequence [programmed text] made higher achievement scores and exhibited less variability in performance than did Ss receiving conventional textbook presentation of the same material." The subject areas in this case were short segments of courses in statistics and music.

Since psychologists have been in the forefront of this new educational movement, it is not surprising that a number of studies have been conducted using psychology as subject matter.

C-3: On the West Coast, Coulson and Silberman [7] of the Systems Development Corporation used a simulated teaching machine with college students working on a segment of a psychology course and showed that ". . . use of the simulated teaching machine led to significant learning by Ss, as determined by comparison with the control [no treatment] group." The simulated teaching machine was an experimenter-controlled, manually-operated device.

C-4: In a small study which indicated that programs may have an indirect influence on effective use of textbooks, McCullough and Van Atta [24] added a programmed supplement to the study of some rather difficult psychology texts and reported that it aided the students in comprehension and use of the textbook contents. It was not, however, significantly better in every case than use of a regular supplement to the textbook. Because of the small number of students (six undergraduates) involved and the duration of the study (six weeks), the authors regard this only as an indication of possible use of programs for increasing effectiveness of individual study.

This report also presents an interesting sidelight which deals with the frequent question, Is it not true that programs are good only for rote memory learning? On a criterion test, students were asked to diagram the immediate effects of a gas thermostat (material which had been presented in one of the texts). The students who had used the programmed supplement had not been asked to do any work with the diagram during their study. When they (the program group) answered this question, no one reproduced the diagram given in the text; all the diagrams produced were different, yet all were perfectly correct in principle and operation, which indicates an understanding of the principles concerned.

C-5: At Harvard University programmed materials in psychology have been in use for three years with several hundred college students. On the basis of this experience, Holland [17] reported, "In summary we have been very favorably impressed with the use of teaching machine programs in the teaching of psychology. The performance on items which were taught by machine program was superior to that on lecture items." It was also reported that the students were accepting the use of machines and were, as seen in most studies, showing wide individual differences. A factor felt to be of significance was the detailed information obtained from the students' behavior on the program, insuring a *yearly improvement of the course.*

The following two studies were conducted with engineering students:

C-6: Roe from the Department of Engineering at the University of California, Los Angeles, presented programmed materials on statistics in a variety of formats, with a number of response modes and in several learning environments. The study involved 186 students who studied a program of about 200 frames. The students worked on multiple-choice machines, constructed-response machines, and programmed textbooks. Additional treatments included listening to "programmed" lectures.

Roe [28] reported that there were no significant differences among the various automated teaching methods but that there was a significant difference between programmed methods and standard methods in favor of the programmed classes.

C-7: Using the scrambled book technique, Williams at the Carnegie Institute of Technology in Pittsburgh taught some aspects of Kirchhoff's Laws to 112 engineering students. He reported [32]: ". . . (c) teaches the student to apply Kirchhoff's Laws with accuracy after the steps (a) [application] and (b) [reduction of the problem to Kirchhoff's model] have been taken. Regarded solely in the light of (c), this particular unit has been adjudged very successful; students have demonstrated their skill and it has been possible to exclude much relatively trivial drillwork from the classroom."

C-8: In a college chemistry course, scrambled books were used to teach two difficult concepts, one (molar solution) at the freshman level and the other (kinetic theory of gases) at a more advanced level. The programs were used with an entire freshman introductory chemistry class and with a junior class in physical chemistry. In both cases it was found [25] that a ". . . significantly greater amount of learning occurred." Dr. Day, Chairman of the Chemistry Department at Ohio University which used the programs, reported, however, that at the advanced level there were some student criticisms. It appeared that although the students learned the material, a few felt it was too easy and regarded it as an insult to their intelligence. This is similar to the results of a questionnaire completed by the psychology students at Harvard, where 2.7 per cent reported, "The use of machine reflected upon my dignity as a human being."

C-9: A final study at the college level was related to the teaching of German. From an initial group of 28 volunteers, data were reported [13] for six students who completed the programmed course presented in a type of workbook. The students took an average of 47.5 hours to finish the program. This is compared to the 48 hours spent in the classroom by a regularly-taught German class. Following completion of the program, the students were tested in recognition of vocabulary and in writing German sentences. The authors conclude, "The students had no instructor and were given no formal statements of grammatical principle; yet, the material succeeded in teaching inductively such conceptualizations as gender, verbs, transitivity, morphology, and syntax of the German case system, and sentence word-order."

SPECIAL-EDUCATION STUDIES

Although the properties of individual rates, careful and small-step sequences, as well as the possibility of not requiring a written response in the case of some machines, would appear to offer great potentials for special education, only one study was found in the literature utilizing auto-instructional materials for this purpose.

SE-1: Working with retarded adolescents at the Devereux Schools in Devon, Pa., Smith and Quackenbush [30] reported that when a multiple-choice teaching machine (Devereux Model 80), a battery-operated device, was used over an eight-month period to present supplemental drill and instruction in mathematics, the mean arithmetic gain for 17 subjects was more than doubled over the previous year, while gain in other subject areas remained constant. This was not a controlled experiment in terms of hours of use of materials, as each student worked on the materials as long as he needed them. However, a very significant rise in student motivation toward the subject area was noted, and often the difficulty arose that students were sneaking out of other classes to spend more time in the room where the machines were kept.

ARMED-FORCES STUDIES

The instruction of large groups of students in as brief a period of time as possible makes the criterion for effectiveness used by the Armed Forces different from that used for other situations. Typically, cost of instruction per pupil is not the major factor. The major problems are an increasing need for qualified instructors, short terms of enlistment, and rapidly changing and highly complex course material, much of which is completely new to the students. The "effective" new technique is therefore one which deals with one or more of these areas.

AF-1: A preliminary report [15] from Keesler Air Force Base in Biloxi, Miss., concerns the use of Western Design AutoTutors, a complex electronic filmstrip machine, in an electronics course. The data reported covered the first half of the course and involved six-hour days for four weeks. It was believed that some fairly significant results were obtained. This was a controlled study which utilized three groups of 15 students. One group received the material in the normal manner taught by a special instructor assigned to the project. A second group received the same course via the AutoTutor, receiving no classroom instruction; and a third group, called the "blind control group," was composed of individuals selected at random, without their knowledge, from other sections of the same course. All three groups received the instruction simultaneously. Performance score on a regularly administered Air Force proficiency examination was the behavior criterion. The performances of the three groups on this examination were virtually identical, showing increased effectiveness in terms of eliminating instructor time for one of the classes. The motivation of the students working on the program appeared to be quite high, and they often used the machines in off-hours.

AF-2: A second Air Force study reported by Hosmer and Nolan [18] gives data related to a number of the questions about effectiveness which have been raised. Multiple-choice scrambled textbooks were prepared for segments of three different courses (Air Police Training, Medical Training, and Personnel Training). There were two control and two experimental groups used in each course. On *amount learned* the experimental groups (programmed) and the control groups (normal classroom) were comparable, learning being measured by an end-of-course test. Analysis of the results also showed that the programmed students covered the material in *much less time* than the controls; in each case the controls took at least twice as long. On a *retention* test given from 11 to 38 days later, no differential forgetting was yet taking place. In the analysis of the data for the programmed group in terms of speed of learning and amount learned, it was found that those students who took longer to finish the program learned as much as or more than those students who finished the program in shorter periods of time.

AF-3: Hatch [16], using a game-like self-tutoring device in a pilot's lounge for a two-month period, reported that the experience resulted in statistically significant gains in job information (flight information) for 62 pilots voluntarily playing the device. "The statistical assurance that success of the self-tutoring approach applied to pilot training and retention by them was not accidental constitutes an important finding. The fact that improvements resulting from the application of the self-tutoring technique employed in this particular study were not large in no way detracts from it, as conditions affecting pilot participation on the device were far from ideal." This study did not actually use a program (carefully sequenced frames) in the self-tutoring device, but is reported as being typical of a large body of literature dealing with devices which could easily be adapted to program use. The particular device utilized in this study presented multiple-choice items visually, and timed and scored the subject's response automatically. For additional information of this kind, the reader is referred to two relevant bibliographies, [9] and [29].

AF-4: In a study reported by Mager [25] it was found that printed materials in programmed form (both completion type and scrambled-book type) could teach relatively complex skills. Both electronically sophisticated and electronically naive groups of subjects were trained by programs to energize and calibrate electronic equipment. Seventy per cent performed this task without error, even when they had never seen the equipment during learning.

INDUSTRIAL STUDIES

In industry is found perhaps the clearest set of criteria for effectiveness. Industry training programs are designed to produce persons capable of performing a skill which is clearly defined in behavioral terms (educators often have great problems with such a definition). The student typically is required to apply these skills immediately, and there are numerous objective measures of his level of learning in production rate, rejection rate, quality control, etc. Management is therefore concerned with the ratio between time and cost of training, and production. Any means which is found to reduce the former and increase the latter would usually be regarded as effective.

At the Eastern Psychological Association Meetings in Philadelphia, Pa., in April, 1961, Deutsch [10] reported that, from a recent survey of industry which he had conducted, there were at least 63 U.S. firms that had invested half a million dollars in automated training programs. Unfortunately, much of the information about these efforts is proprietary and not available.

I-1: Hughes Aircraft Company, one of the largest users of programmed principles, has been reported to have ". . . more than five hundred machines tutoring women on complex parts assembly with step-by-step instructions." Hughes claims that these audio-visual machines, dubbed VIDEO SONICS, have helped cut assembly rejects 70 per cent [4]. VIDEO SONICS is somewhat different from most teaching machines in that, although it presents step-by-step programmed information, there is no feedback from the learner to the machine and no confirmation of results presented to the learner.

I-2: Crumpler [8] of Applied Communication Systems, Culver City, Calif., reported, "In short order after one major electronics firm introduced audio-visual techniques [same type of device as mentioned above] productivity increased approximately 40 per cent above the work standard. Defects were reduced from thirteen per unit to one-half per unit." He further stated, "In another industry where complex products are manufactured, productivity per worker increased from two to five units per day," following the installation of the programmed device. He traced these improvements to a number of things, including increased communication between engineers and production workers, and a reduction in complex printed and graphic materials to be interpreted by the workers.

Two final notes from industry:

I-3: A major U.S. industrial firm reported that on an early trial of a programmed machine course in product service, the saving in time alone appeared to be 47 per cent over previous requirements. The opinion was expressed that this saving would be increased with better programming.

I-4: IBM, with one of the largest employee-training programs in the U.S., has been investigating the use of programmed instruction. The company has conducted some experiments with such courses, and because of the favorable results they "anticipate the future use of this new teaching method in sales, systems and computer programming." If a firm is increasing efforts in any area, it would appear that preliminary results must have shown auto-instruction to be effective.

Now, what about effectiveness in terms of reduced cost per pupil? Attempts to answer this question have been notably lacking, due to the fact that most of the work has been experimental and supported by various grants and awards, where cost per pupil was not a major concern. However, it appears that data will be available within a year; and where programmed textbooks are being used, a guess can be made that cost will be approximately the same as present instruction—since the program cost compares favorably with standard textbook cost—although there is the possibility of some reduction in instruction costs, due to reduction in the number of instructors necessary, and increase in production.

It is desirable at this point again to remind the reader that the preceding summary statements have often been lifted out of context in an attempt to present a rapid view of the nature of the results obtained thus far with auto-instructional materials. From the viewpoint of clean, controlled experimental design, many of the studies have obvious faults. Persons interested in the design aspects should consult the original study wherever possible, especially if they are attempting to experiment with these new materials.

It is never detrimental to a new idea or technique to examine it objectively. The problem is to find people who can be objective about teaching machines, programs, and related materials.

REFERENCES

[1] F. W. Banghart, "An Experiment with Teaching Machines and Programed Textbooks," presented before Am. Educ. Research Assoc., Chicago, Ill.; 1961.

[2] J. Blyth, "Teaching machines and human beings," *Educ. Record*, vol. 41, pp. 116–125; April, 1960, Reprinted in [23], pp. 401–415.

[3] D. Boroff, "The three R's and pushbuttons," *N.Y. Times Mag.*, pp. 36, 66, 68, 70, 72; September 25, 1960.

[4] "How machines do teaching job," *Business Week*, No. 1620, pp. 111–112, 114; September 17, 1960.

[5] Mimeographed report describing the organization, function, and programming efforts of the Center for Programmed Instruction, as well as brief reports on research. Available upon request from the Center for Programmed Instruction, 365 West End Avenue, New York 24, N. Y.

[6] R. W. Clark, "Research Studies in Automated Instruction," report presented to the Pennsylvania Advisory Committee on Self-Instructional Devices, Harrisburg, Pa.; 1961.

[7] J. E. Coulson, and H. F. Silberman, "Effects of three variables in a teaching machine," *J. Educ. Psychol.*, vol. 51, pp. 135–143; June, 1960.

[8] J. Crumpler, "Development of Applied Communication Systems Devices and Methodology," presented at the Teaching-Machine Conf., sponsored by the Electronics Personnel Research Group, Dept. of Psychol., University of Southern California, Los Angeles; October, 1960.

[9] C. L. Darby, "An Annotated Bibliography on the Automation of Instruction," U.S. Army Air Defense Human Research Unit, Fort Bliss, Tex., Research Memo.; July, 1959.

[10] W. D. Deutsch, "Automated Tutors in Industry," presented before Eastern Psychol. Assoc., Philadelphia, Pa.; April, 1961.

[11] "TEMAC, Programmed Learning Materials," Encyclopedia Britannica Films, Wilmette, Ill., Rept. No. 2; 1961. (Repts. No. 1 and 2 available upon request from R. P. Kroggel, Vice President, Programmed Learning Materials, Encyclopedia Britannica Films, 1150 Wilmette Avenue, Wilmette, Ill.)

[12] J. L. Evans, R. Glaser, and L. E. Homme, "A preliminary investigation of variation in the properties of verbal learning sequences of the 'teaching

machine' type," presented before Eastern Psychol. Assoc., Atlantic City, N.J.; April, 1959. Reprinted in [23], pp. 446–451.

[13] C. B. Ferster and S. M. Sapon, "An application of recent developments in psychology to the teaching of German," *Harvard Educ. Rev.*, vol. 28, pp. 156– 157; Winter; 1958. Also reprinted in [23], pp. 592–594.

[14] G. L. Gropper and A. A. Lumsdaine, "Experiments on Active Student Response to Televised Instruction. An Interim Report," Am. Inst. Research, Pittsburgh, Pa., Report AIR-CIC-60-IR-108; 1960.

[15] H. W. Gustafson, "Intrinsic Programming Developments," presented at Teaching-Machine Conf., sponsored by the Electronics Personnel Research Group, Dept. of Psychology, University of Southern California, Los Angeles; October, 1960.

[16] R. S. Hatch, "An Evaluation of the Effectiveness of a Self-Tutoring Approach Applied to Pilot Training," Wright-Patterson Air Force Base, Dayton, Ohio— Wright Air Dev. Center, WADC Tech. Rept. TR 59–320; 1959.

[17] J. G. Holland, "Teaching Psychology by a Teaching-Machine Program," unpublished mimeographed Rept.; 1960.

[18] C. L. Hosmer and J. A. Nolan, "Time saved by a tryout of automatic tutoring," *Automated Teaching Bull.*, vol. 1, no. 2, pp. 31–34; 1960.

[19] J. Jacobson, Jr., "Teaching high school students a college level course by means of a learning machine program," *Mid-Hudson Channel*, vol. 10, no. 2, p. 14; 1961.

[20] E. R. Keisler, "The development of understanding in arithmetic by a teaching machine," *J. Educ. Psychol.*, vol. 50, pp. 247–253; December, 1959. Reprinted in [23], pp. 425–436.

[21] ——, "Preliminary Report on Project to Teach Mathematics and Molecular Theory to First Graders Using Teaching Machines," presented at the Teaching-Machine Conf., sponsored by the Electronics Personnel Research Group, Dept. of Psychol., University of Southern California, Los Angeles; October, 1960.

[22] D. J. Klaus, "Some Observations and Findings from Auto-Instructional Research in Newer Educational Media," Pennsylvania State University, University Park; October, 1960.

[23] A. A. Lumsdaine and R. Glaser, "Teaching Machines and Programmed Learning: A Source Book," National Education Association, Washington, D.C.; 1960.

[24] C. McCullough and L. Van Atta, 'The use of miniature programs to supplement conventional teaching techniques," presented before Am. Psychol. Assn., Chicago, Ill.; September, 1960.

[25] R. F. Mager, "Preliminary studies in automated teaching," IRE TRANS. ON EDUCATION, vol. E-2, pp. 104–107; June, 1959.

[26] S. M. Markle, "Programer, Teach Thyself," The Center for Programed Instruction, New York, N.Y.; 1961.

[27] D. Porter, "Some effects of year-long teaching machine instruction," in "Automatic Teaching: The State of the Art," E. H. Galanter, Ed., John Wiley and Sons, Inc., New York, N.Y.; pp. 85–90; 1959.

[28] A. Roe, et. al., "Automated teaching methods using linear programs," Automated Learning Research Project, Dept. of Engrg. University of California, Los Angeles, Rept. No. 60–105; December, 1960.

[29] R. T. Root, "An Annotated Bibliography of Research on Training Aids and Training Devices," Training Methods Div., HumRRO, George Washington University, Washington, D.C., Staff Memo.; August, 1957.

[30] E. A. Smith and J. F. Quackenbush, "Devereux teaching aids employed in presenting elementary mathematics in a special education setting," *Psychol. Repts.*, vol. 7, pp. 333–336; October, 1960.

[31] "Programed Learning," *Time Mag.*, Education Section, pp. 36–38; March 24, 1961.

[32] E. M. Williams, "Programmed learning in engineering education. A preliminary study," Dept. of Engrg., Carnegie Institute of Technology, Pittsburgh, Pa., unpublished Rept. (Available upon request.)

65 *Why we need teaching machines*

Current suggestions for improving education are familiar to everyone. We need more and better schools and colleges. We must pay salaries which will attract and hold good teachers. We should group students according to ability. We must bring textbooks and other materials up to date, particularly in science and mathematics. And so on. It is significant that all this can be done without knowing much about teaching or learning. Those who are most actively concerned with improving education seldom discuss what is happening when a student reads a book, writes a paper, listens to a lecture, or solves a problem, and their proposals are only indirectly designed to make these activities more productive. In short, there is a general neglect of education method. (Television is no exception, for it is only a way of amplifying and extending *old* methods, together with their shortcomings.)

It is true that the psychology of learning has so far not been very helpful in education. Its learning curves and its theories of learning have not yielded greatly improved classroom practices. But it is too early to conclude that nothing useful is to be learned about the behavior of teacher and student. No enterprise can improve itself very effectively without examining its basic processes. Fortunately, recent advances in the experimental analysis of behavior suggest that a true technology of education is feasible. Improved techniques are available to carry out the two basic assignments of education: constructing extensive repertoires of verbal and nonverbal behavior and generating that high probability of action which is said to show interest, enthusiasm, or a strong "desire to learn."

The processes clarified by an experimental analysis of behavior have, of

B. F. SKINNER, "Why We Need Teaching Machines," *Harvard Educational Review*, 31 (Fall, 1961), 377–98. Reprinted by permission of the author and the publisher.

DR. SKINNER (1890–   ) is Edgar Pierce Professor of Psychology at Harvard University. He is an authority on the effects of reinforcement in learning and a pioneer in the application of programed learning techniques.

course, always played a part in education, but they have been used with little understanding of their effects, wanted or unwanted. Whether by intention or necessity, teachers have been less given to teaching than to holding students responsible for learning. Methods are still basically aversive. The student looks, listens, and answers questions (and, incidentally, sometimes learns) as a gesture of avoidance or escape. A good teacher can cite exceptions, but it is a mistake to call them typical. The birch rod and cane are gone, but their place has been taken by equally effective punishments (criticism, possibly ridicule, failure) used in the same way: the student must learn, or else!

By-products of aversive control in education range from truancy, early drop-outs, and school-vandalism to inattention, "mental fatigue," forgetting, and apathy. It does not take a scientific analysis to trace these to their sources in educational practice. But more acceptable techniques have been hard to find. Erasmus tells of an English gentleman who tried to teach his son Greek and Latin without punishment. He taught the boy to use a bow and arrow and set up targets in the shape of Greek and Latin letters, rewarding each hit with a cherry. He also fed the boy letters cut from delicious biscuits. As a result, we may assume that the boy salivated slightly upon seeing a Greek or Latin text and that he was probably a better archer; but any effect on his knowledge of Greek and Latin is doubtful.

Current efforts to use rewards in education show the same indirection. Texts garnished with pictures in four colors, exciting episodes in a scientific film, interesting classroom activities—these will make a school interesting and even attractive (just as the boy probably liked his study of Greek and Latin), but to generate specific forms of behavior these things must be related to the student's behavior in special ways. Only then will they be truly rewarding or, technically speaking, "reinforcing."

We make a reinforcing event contingent on behavior when, for example, we design a piece of equipment in which a hungry rat or monkey or chimpanzee may press a lever and immediately obtain a bit of food. Such a piece of equipment gives us a powerful control over behavior. By scheduling reinforcements, we may maintain the behavior of pressing the lever in any given strength for long periods of time. By reinforcing special kinds of responses to the lever—for example, very light or very heavy presses or those made with one hand or the other—we "shape" different forms or topographies of behavior. By reinforcing only when particular stimuli or classes of stimuli are present, we bring the behavior under the control of the environment. All these processes have been thoroughly investigated, and they have already yielded standard laboratory practices in manipulating complex forms of behavior for experimental purposes. They are obviously appropriate to educational design.

In approaching the problem of the educator we may begin by surveying available reinforcers. What positive reasons can we give the student for studying? We can point to the ultimate advantages of an education—to the ways of life which are open only to educated men—and the student himself may cite these to explain why he wants an education, but ultimate advantages are not contingent on behavior in ways which generate action. Many a student can testify to the result. No matter how much he may *want* to become a doctor or an engineer, say, he cannot force himself to read and remember the page of text in front of him at the moment. All notions of ultimate utility (as, for example, in economics) suffer from the same shortcoming: they do not specify effective contingencies of reinforcement.

The gap between behavior and a distant consequence is sometimes bridged by a series of "conditioned reinforcers." In the laboratory experiment just described a delay of even a fraction of a second between the response to the lever and the appearance of food may reduce the effectiveness of the food by a measurable amount. It is standard practice to let the movement of a lever produce some visual stimulus, such as a change in the illumination in the apparatus, which is then followed by food. In this way the change in illumination becomes a conditioned reinforcer which can be made immediately contingent on the response. The marks, grades, and diplomas of education are conditioned reinforcers designed to bring ultimate consequences closer to the behavior reinforced. Like prizes and medals, they represent the approval of teachers, parents, and others, and they show competitive superiority, but they are mainly effective because they signalize progress through the system—toward some ultimate advantage of, or at least freedom from, education. To this extent they bridge the gap between behavior and its remote consequences; but they are still not contingent on behavior in a very effective way.

Progressive education tried to replace the birch rod, and at the same time avoid the artificiality of grades and prizes, by bringing the reinforcers of everyday life into the schools. Such natural contingencies have a kind of guaranteed effectiveness. But a school is only a small part of the student's world, and no matter how real it may seem, it cannot provide natural reinforcing consequences for all the kinds of behavior which education is to set up. The goals of progressive education were shifted to conform to this limitation, and many worthwhile assignments were simply abandoned.

Fortunately, we can solve the problem of education without discovering or inventing additional reinforcers. We merely need to make better use of those we have. Human behavior is distinguished by the fact that it is affected by small consequences. Describing something with the right word is often reinforcing. So is the clarification of a temporary puzzlement, or the solution of a complex problem, or simply the opportunity to move forward after completing one stage of an activity. We need not stop to explain *why* these things are reinforcing. It is enough that, when properly contingent upon behavior, they provide the control we need for successful educational design. Proper contingencies of reinforcement, however, are not always easily arranged. A modern laboratory for the study of behavior contains elaborate equipment designed to control the environment of individual organisms during many hours or days of continuous study. The required conditions and changes in conditions cannot be arranged by hand, not only because the experimenter does not have the time and energy, but because many contingencies are too subtle and precise to be arranged without instrumental help. The same problem arises in education.

Consider, for example, the temporal patterning of behavior called "rhythm." Behavior is often effective only if properly timed. Individual differences in timing, ranging from the most awkward to the most skillful performances, affect choice of career and of artistic interests and participation in sports and crafts. Presumably a "sense of rhythm" is worth teaching, yet practically nothing is now done to arrange the necessary contingencies of reinforcement. The skilled typist, tennis player, lathe operator, or musician is, of course, under the influence of reinforcing mechanisms which generate subtle timing, but many people never reach the point at which these natural contingencies can take over.

A relatively simple device supplies the necessary contingencies. The student taps a rhythmic pattern in unison with the device. "Unison" is specified very loosely at first (the student can be a little early or late at each tap) but the specifications are slowly sharpened. The process is repeated for various speeds and patterns. In another arrangement, the student echoes rhythmic patterns sounded by the machine, though not in unison, and again the specifications for an accurate reproduction are progressively sharpened. Rhythmic patterns can also be brought under the control of a printed score.

Another kind of teaching machine generates sensitivity to properties of the environment. We call an effective person "discriminating." He can tell the difference between the colors, shapes, and sizes of objects, he can identify three-dimensional forms seen from different aspects, he can find patterns concealed in other patterns, he can identify pitches, intervals, and musical themes and distinguish between different tempos and rhythms—and all of this in an almost infinite variety. Subtle discriminations of this sort are as important in science and industry and in everyday life as in identifying the school of a painter or the period of a composer.

The ability to make a given kind of discrimination can be taught. A pigeon, for example, can be *made* sensitive to the color, shape, and size of objects, to pitches, and rhythms, and so on—simply by reinforcing it when it responds in some arbitrary way to one set of stimuli and extinguishing responses to all others. The same kinds of contingencies of reinforcement are responsible for human discriminative behavior. *The remarkable fact is that they are quite rare in the environment of the average child.* True, children are encouraged to play with objects of different sizes, shapes, and colors, and are given a passing acquaintance with musical patterns; but they are seldom exposed to the precise contingencies needed to build subtle discriminations. It is not surprising that most of them move into adulthood with largely undeveloped "abilities."

The number of reinforcements required to build discriminative behavior in the population as a whole is far beyond the capacity of teachers. Too many teachers would be needed, and many contingencies are too subtle to be mediated by even the most skillful. *Yet relatively simple machines will suffice.* [One such apparatus] is adapted from research on lower organisms. It teaches an organism to discriminate selected properties of stimuli while "matching to sample." Pictures or words are projected on translucent windows which respond to a touch by closing circuits. A child can be made to "look at the sample" by reinforcing him for pressing the top window. An adequate reinforcement for this response is simply the appearance of material in the lower windows, from which a choice is to be made.

The child identifies the material which corresponds to the sample in some prescribed way by pressing one of the lower windows, and he is then reinforced again—possibly simply because a new set of materials now appears on the windows. If he presses the wrong window, all three choices disappear until the top window has been pressed again—which means until he has again looked at the sample. Many other arrangements of responses and reinforcements are, of course, possible. In an auditory version, the child listens to a sample pattern of tones and then explores other samples to find a match.

If devices similar to these were generally available in our nursery schools and kindergartens, our children would be far more skillful in dealing with their environments. They would be more productive in their work, more sensitive to art and music, better at sports, and so on. They would lead more effective lives. We cannot assert all this with complete confidence on the present evidence, but there is no doubt whatsoever *that the conditions needed to produce such a state of affairs are now lacking.* In the light of what we know about differential contingencies of reinforcement, the world of the young child is shamefully impoverished. And only machines will remedy this, for the required frequency and subtlety of reinforcement cannot otherwise be arranged.

The teacher is, of course, at a disadvantage in teaching skilled and discriminative behavior because such instruction is largely nonverbal. It may be that the methods of the classroom, in which the teacher is said to "communicate" with the student, to "impart information," and to build "verbal abilities," are better adapted to standard subject matters, the learning of which is usually regarded as more than the acquisition of forms of behavior or of environmental control. Yet a second look may be worthwhile. Traditional characterizations of verbal behavior raise almost insuperable problems for the teacher, and a more rigorous analysis suggests another possibility. We can define terms like "information," "knowledge," and "verbal ability" by reference to the behavior from which we infer their presence. *We may then teach the behavior directly.* Instead of "transmitting information to the student" we may simply set up the behavior which is taken as a sign that he possesses information. Instead of teaching a "knowledge of French" we may teach the behavior from which we infer such knowledge. Instead of teaching "an ability to read" we may set up the behavioral repertoire which distinguishes the child who knows how to read from one who does not.

To take the last example, a child reads or "shows that he knows how to read" by exhibiting a behavioral repertoire of great complexity. He finds a letter or word in a list on demand; he reads aloud; he finds or identifies objects described in a text; he rephrases sentences; he obeys written instructions; he behaves appropriately to described situations; he reacts emotionally to described events; and so on, in a long list. He does none of this before learning to read and all of it afterwards. To bring about such a change is an extensive assignment, and it is tempting to try to circumvent it by teaching something called "an ability to read" from which all these specific behaviors will flow. But this has never actually been done. "Teaching reading" is always directed toward setting up specific items in such a repertoire.

It is true that parts of the repertoire are not independent. A student may acquire some kinds of responses more readily for having acquired others, and he may for a time use some in place of others (for example, he may follow written directions not by responding directly to a text but by following his own spoken instructions as he reads the text aloud). In the long run all parts of the repertoire tend to be filled in, not because the student is rounding out an ability to read, but simply because all parts are in their several ways useful. They all continue to be reinforced by the world at large after the explicit teaching of reading has ceased.

Viewed in this way, reading can also be most effectively taught with instrumental help. A pupil can learn to distinguish among letters and groups of letters in an alphabet simply as visual patterns in using the device and procedures just described. He can be taught to identify arbitrary correspondences (for example, between capitals and lower-case letters, or between handwritten and printed letters) in a more complex type of stimulus control which is within reach of the same device. With a phonographic attachment, correspondences between printed letters and sounds, between sounds and letters, between words and sounds, between sounds and printed words, and so on, can be set up. (The student could be taught all of this without pronouncing a word, and it is possible that he would learn good pronunciation more quickly if he had first done so.)

The same device can teach correspondences between words and the properties of objects. The pupil selects a printed or spoken word which corresponds in the language to, say, a pictured object or another printed or spoken word. These semantic correspondences differ in important respects from formal matches, but the same processes of programming and reinforcement can—indeed, must—be used. Traditional ways of teaching reading establish all these repertoires, but they do so indirectly and, alas, inefficiently. In "building a child's need to read," in motivating "his mental readiness," in "sharing information," and so on, the teacher arranges, sometimes almost surreptitiously, many of the contingencies just listed, and these are responsible for whatever is learned. An explicit treatment clarifies the program, suggests effective procedures, and guarantees a coverage which is often lacking with traditional methods. Much of what is called reading has not been covered, of course, but it may not need to be taught, for once these basic repertoires have been established, the child begins to receive automatic reinforcement in responding to textual material.

The same need for a behavioral definition arises in teaching other verbal skills (for example, a second language) as well as the traditional subjects of education. In advancing to that level, however, we must transcend a limitation of the device [described]. The student can *select* a response without being able to speak or write, but we want him to learn to *emit* the response, since this is the kind of behavior which he will later find most useful. The emission of verbal behavior is taught by another kind of machine. A frame of textual material appearing in the square opening is incomplete: in place of certain letters or figures there are holes. Letters or figures can be made to appear in these holes by moving sliders (a keyboard would be an obvious improvement). When the material has been completed, the student checks his response by turning a crank. The machine senses the settings of the sliders and, if they are correct, moves a new frame of material into place, the sliders returning to their home position. If the response is wrong, the sliders return home, and a second setting must be made.

The machine can tell the student he is wrong without telling him what is right. This is an advantage, but it is relatively costly. Moreover, correct behavior is rather rigidly specified. Such a machine is probably suitable only for the lower grades. A simpler and cheaper procedure, with greater flexibility, is to allow the student to compare his written response with a revealed text. [A device using this principle exists.] It is suitable for verbal instruction beyond the lower primary grades—that is, through junior high school, high school, and college, and in industrial and professional education. Programmed material is stored on fan-folded paper tapes. One frame of material, the size of which may be varied with the nature of the material, is exposed at a time. The student writes on a separate paper strip. He cannot look at unauthorized parts of the material without recording the fact that he has done so, because when the machine has been loaded and closed, it can be opened only by punching the strip of paper.

The student sees printed material in the large window at the left. This may be a sentence to be completed, a question to be answered, or a problem to be solved. He writes his response in an uncovered portion of a paper strip at the right. He then moves a slider which covers the response he has written with a transparent mask and uncovers additional material in the larger opening. This may tell him that his response is wrong without telling him what is right. For example, it may list a few of the commonest errors. If the response he wrote is among them, he can try again on a newly uncovered portion of the paper strip. A further operation of the machine covers his second attempt and uncovers the correct response. The student records a wrong response by punching a hole alongside it, leaving a record for the instructor who may wish to review a student's performance, and operating a counter which becomes visible at the end of the set. Then the student records the number of mistakes he has made and may compare it with a par score for the set.

Exploratory research in schools and colleges indicates that what is now taught by teacher, textbook, lecture, or film can be taught in half the time with half the effort by a machine of this general type.[1] One has only to see students at work to understand why this is a conservative estimate. The student remains active. If he stops, the program stops (in marked contrast with class-room practice and educational television); but there is no compulsion for he is not inclined to stop. Immediate and frequent reinforcement sustains a lively interest. (The interest, incidentally, outlasts any effect of novelty. Novelty may be relevant to interest, but the material in the machine is always novel.) Where current instructional procedures are highly efficient, the gain may not be so great. In one experiment [2] involving industrial education there was approximately a 25% saving in the time required for instruction, something of the order of a 10% increase in retention, and about 90% of the students preferred to study by machine. In general, the student generally likes what he is doing; he makes no effort to escape—for example, by letting his attention wander. He need not force himself to work and is usually free of the feeling of effort generated by aversive control. He has no reason to be anxious about impending examinations, for none are required. Both he and his instructor know where he stands at all times.

No less important in explaining the success of teaching machines is the fact that each student is free to proceed at his own rate. Holding students together for instructional purposes in a class is probably the greatest source of inefficiency in education. Some efforts to mechanize instruction have missed this point. A language laboratory controlled from a central console presupposes a group of students advancing at about the same rate, even though some choice of material is permitted. Television in education has made the same mistake on a colossal scale. A class of twenty or thirty students moving at the same pace is inefficient enough, but what must we say of all the students in half a dozen states marching in a similar lock step?

In trying to teach more than one student at once we harm both fast and

---

[1] Under the direction of Allen Calvin of Hollands College, an 8th grade class in the Roanoke School System completed all the work of a 9th grade class in algebra in one term. Test scores were comparable with a normal 9th grade performance, and a test nine months later showed a retention of at least 90% of the material learned.

[2] More recent results with the same material improved in the light of the earlier experiment were reported by J. L. Hughes and W. J. McNamara at the Annual Meeting of the American Psychological Association in New York, September, 1961. Their work concerned the use of programmed texts in industrial education.

slow learners. The plight of the good student has been recognized, but the slow learner suffers more disastrous consequences. The effect of pressure to move beyond one's natural speed is cumulative. The student who has not fully mastered a first lesson is less able to master a second. His ultimate failure may greatly exaggerate his shortcoming; a small difference in speed has grown to an immense difference in comprehension. Some of those most active in improving education have been tempted to dismiss slow students impatiently as a waste of time, but it is quite possible that many of them are capable of substantial, even extraordinary, achievements if permitted to move at their own pace. Many distinguished scientists, for example, have appeared to think slowly.

One advantage of individual instruction is that the student is able to follow a program without breaks or omissions. A member of a class moving at approximately the same rate cannot always make up for absences, and limitations of contact time between student and teacher make it necessary to abbreviate material to the point at which substantial gaps are inevitable. Working on a machine, the student can always take up where he left off or, if he wishes, review earlier work after a longer absence. The coherence of the program helps to maximize the student's success, for by thoroughly mastering one step he is optimally prepared for the next. Many years ago, in their *Elementary Principles of Education*,[3] Thorndike and Gates considered the possibility of a book "so arranged that only to him who had done what was directed on page one would page two become visible, and so on." With such a book, they felt, "much that now requires personal instruction could be managed by print." The teaching machine is, of course, such a book.

In summary, then, machine teaching is unusually efficient because (1) the student is frequently and immediately reinforced, (2) he is free to move at his natural rate, and (3) he follows a coherent sequence. These are the more obvious advantages, and they may well explain current successes. But there are more promising possibilities: the conditions arranged by a good teaching machine make it possible to apply to education what we have learned from laboratory research and to extend our knowledge through rigorous experiments in schools and colleges.

The conceptions of the learning process which underlie classroom practices have long been out of date. For example, teachers and textbooks are said to "impart information." They expose the student to verbal and nonverbal material and call attention to particular features of it, and in so doing they are said to "tell the student something." In spite of discouraging evidence to the contrary, it is still supposed that if you tell a student something, he then knows it. In this scheme, teaching is the transmission of information, a notion which, through a false analogy, has acquired undue prestige from communi-

[3] Thorndike, Edward, and Gates, Arthur. *Elementary Principles of Education*. (New York: B. Macmillan Co., 1929).

cation engineering. Something is undoubtedly transmitted by teacher to student, for if communication is interrupted, instruction ceases; but the teacher is not merely a source from which knowledge flows into the student. We cannot necessarily improve instruction by altering the conditions of transmission—as, for example, by changing to a different sensory modality. This is a mistake made by some so-called teaching machines which, accepting our failure to teach reading, have tried to restore communication by using recorded speech. The student no longer pores over a book, as in the traditional portrait; he stares into space with earphones on his head. For the same reasons improvements in the coding of information may not be immediately relevant.

The student is more than a receiver of information. He must take some kind of action. The traditional view is that he must "associate." The stream of information flowing from teacher to student contains pairs of items which, being close together or otherwise related, become connected in the student's mind. This is the old doctrine of the association of ideas, now strengthened by a scientific, if uncritical, appeal to conditioned reflexes; two things occurring together in experience somehow become connected so that one of them later reminds the student of the other. The teacher has little control over the process except to make sure that things occur together often and that the student pays attention to them—for example, by making the experiences vivid or, as we say, memorable. Some devices called teaching machines are simply ways of presenting things together in ways which attract attention. The student listens to recorded speech, for example, while looking at pictures. The theory is that he will associate these auditory and visual presentations.

But the action demanded of the student is not some sort of mental association of contiguous experiences. It is more objective and, fortunately, more controllable than that. To acquire behavior, *the student must engage in behavior*. This has long been known. The principle is implied in any philosophy of "learning by doing." But it is not enough simply to acknowledge its validity. Teaching machines provide the conditions needed to apply the principle effectively.

Only in the early stages of education are we mainly interested in etablishing *forms* of behavior. In the verbal field, for example, we teach a child to speak, eventually with acceptable accent and pronunciation, and later to write and spell. After that, topography of behavior is assumed; the student can speak and write and must now learn to do so appropriately—that is, he must speak or write in given ways under given circumstances. How he comes to do so is widely misunderstood. Education usually begins by establishing so-called formal repertoires. The young child is taught to "echo" verbal behavior in the sense of repeating verbal stimuli with reasonable accuracy. A little later he is taught to read—to emit verbal behavior under the control of textual stimuli. These and other formal repertoires are used in later stages of instruction to evoke new responses without "shaping" them.

In an important case of what we call instruction, control is simply transferred from so-called formal to thematic stimuli. When a student learns to memorize a poem, for example, it is clearly inadequate to say that by reading the poem he presents to himself its various parts contiguously and then associates them. He does not simply read the poem again and again until he knows it. (It is possible that he could never learn the poem in that way.) Something else must be done, as anyone knows who has memorized a poem from the text. The student must make tentative responses while looking away from the text. He must glance at the text from time to time to provide fragmentary help in emitting a partially learned response. If a recalled passage makes sense, it may provide its own automatic confirmation, but if the passage is fragmentary or obscure, the student must confirm the correctness of an emitted response by referring to the text after he has emitted it.

A teaching machine facilitates this process. It presents the poem line by line and asks the student to read it. The text is then "vanished"—that is, it becomes less and less clear or less and less complete in subsequent presentations. Other stimuli (arising from the student's own behavior in this case) take over. In one procedure a few unimportant letters are omitted in the first presentation. The student reads the line without their help and indicates his success by writing down the omitted letters, which are confirmed by the machine. More of the line is missing when it again appears, but because he has recently responded to a fuller text, the student can nevertheless read it correctly. Eventually, no textual stimulus remains, and he can "recite" the poem.

(If the reader wishes to try this method on a friend or member of his family without a machine, he may do so by writing the poem on a chalk board in a clear hand, omitting a few unimportant letters. He should ask his subject to read the poem aloud but to make no effort to memorize it. He should then erase another selection of letters. He will have to guess at how far he can go without interfering with his subject's success on the next reading, but under controlled conditions this could be determined for the average student quite accurately. Again the subject reads the poem aloud, making no effort to memorize, though he may have to make some effort to recall. Other letters are then erased and the process repeated. For a dozen lines of average material, four or five readings should suffice to eliminate the text altogether. The poem can still be "read.")

Memorized verbal behavior is a valuable form of knowledge which has played an important role in classical education. There are other, and generally more useful, forms in which the same processes are involved. Consider, for example, a labeled picture. To say that such an instructional device "tells the student the name of the pictured object" is highly elliptical—and dangerous if we are trying to understand the processes involved. Simply showing a student a labeled picture is no more effective than letting him read a poem. He must take some sort of action. As a formal stimulus, the label evokes a verbal response, not in this case in the presence of other verbal behavior on the part of the student, but in the presence of the picture. The control of the response is to pass from the label to the picture; the student is to give the name of the pictured object without reading it.

The steps taken in teaching with labeled pictures can also be arranged particularly well with a machine. Suppose we are teaching medical-school anatomy at the textbook level. Certain labeled charts represent what is to be learned in the sense that the student will eventually (1) give the names of indicated parts and describe relations among them and (2) be able to point to, draw, or construct models of parts, or relations among them, given their names. To teach the first of these, we induce the student to describe relations among the parts shown on a fully labeled chart. One effect of this is that he executes the verbal behavior at issue—he writes the names of the parts. More important, he does this while, or just after, looking at corresponding pictured details. He will be able to write the names again while looking at a chart which shows only incomplete names, possibly only initial letters. Finally, he will be able to supply the complete names of parts identified only by number on still another chart. His verbal responses have passed from the control of textual stimuli to that of pictured anatomical details. Eventually, as he studies a cadaver, the control will pass to the actual anatomy of the human body. In this sense he then "knows the names of the parts of the body and can describe relations among them."

([A device may be] designed to skip one or two steps in "vanishing" textual stimuli. A fully labeled chart may be followed by a merely numbered one. The student writes the name corresponding to a number in the first space. If he cannot do this, he operates the machine to uncover, not merely some indication that he is right or wrong, but additional help—say, a few letters of the correct response.)

Learning a poem or the names of pictured objects is a relatively straight-forward task. More complex forms of knowledge require other procedures. At an early point, the main problem becomes that of analyzing knowledge. Traditionally, for example, something called "a knowledge of French" is said to permit the student who possesses it to do many things. One who possesses it can (1) repeat a French phrase with a good accent, (2) read a French text in all the senses of reading listed above, (3) take dictation in French, (4) find a word spoken in French on a printed list, (5) obey instructions spoken in French, (6) comment in French upon objects or events, (7) give orders in French, and so on. If he also "knows English," he can give the English equivalents of French words or phrases or the French equivalents of English words or phrases.

The concept of "a knowledge of French" offers very little help to the would-be teacher. As in the case of reading, we must turn to the behavioral repertoires themselves, for these are all that have ever been taught when education has been effective. The definition of a subject matter in such terms may be extraordinarily difficult. Students who are "competent in first-year college physics," for example, obviously differ from those who are not—but in what way? Even a tentative answer to that question should clarify the problem of teaching physics. It may well do more. In the not-too-distant future much more general issues in epistemology may be approached from the same direction. It is possible that we shall fully understand the nature of knowledge only after having solved the practical problems of imparting it.

Until we can define subject matters more accurately and until we have improved our techniques of building verbal repertoires, writing programs for teaching machines will remain something of an art. This is not wholly satisfactory, but there is some consolation in the fact that an impeccable authority on the excellence of a program is available. The student himself can tell the programmer where he has failed. By analyzing the errors made by even a small number of students in a pilot study, it is usually possible to work a great improvement in an early version of a program. ([A machine may be] designed to supply the necessary feedback to the programmer in a convenient form. When a student punches an error, he marks the back of the printed material, which eventually carries an item-by-item record of the success or failure of the programmer. This is obviously valuable during the experimental stages of programming, but it will also be desirable when machines are widely used in schools and colleges, since publishers can then periodically call in programs to be studied and improved by their authors. The information supplied might be compared to a record showing the percentage of students who have misunderstood each sentence in a text.)

The teaching machine [described above] falls far short of the "electronic classrooms" often visualized for the schools and colleges of the future. Many of these, often incorporating small computers, are based on misunderstandings of the learning process. They are designed to duplicate current classroom conditions. When instruction is badly programmed, a student often goes astray, and a teacher must come to his rescue. His mistakes must be analyzed and corrected. This may give the impression that instruction is largely a matter of correcting errors. If this were the case, an effective machine would, indeed, have to follow the student into many unprofitable paths and take remedial action. But under proper programming nothing of this sort is required. It is true that a relatively important function of the teacher will be to follow the progress of each student and to suggest collateral material which may be of interest, as well as to outline further studies, to recommend changes to programs of different levels of difficulty, and so on, and to this extent a student's course of study will show "branching." But changes in level of difficulty or in the character of the subject need not be frequent and can be made as the student moves from one set of material to another.

Teaching machines based on the principle of "multiple choice" also often show a misunderstanding of the learning process. When multiple-choice apparatuses were first used, the organism was left to proceed by "trial and error." The term does not refer to a behavioral process but simply to the fact that contingencies of reinforcement were left to chance: some responses happened to be successful and others not. Learning was not facilitated or accelerated by procedures which increased the probability of successful responses. The results, like those of much classroom instruction, suggested that errors were essential to the learning process. But when material is carefully programmed, both subhuman and human subjects can learn while making few errors or even none at all. Recent research by Herbert S. Terrace,[4] for example, has shown that a pigeon can learn to discriminate colors practically without making mistakes. The control exerted by color may be passed, *via* a vanishing technique, to more difficult properties of stimuli—again without error. Of course we learn something from our mistakes—for one thing, we learn not to make them again—but we *acquire* behavior in other ways.

The teaching machines of S. J. Pressey,[5] the first psychologist to see the "coming industrial revolution in education," were mechanical versions of self-scoring test forms, which Pressey and his students also pioneered. They were not designed for programmed instruction in the present sense. The student was presumed to have studied a subject before coming to the machine. By testing himself, he consolidated what he had already partially learned. For this purpose a device which evaluated the student's selection from an array of multiple-choice items was appropriate. For the same purpose multiple-choice material can, of course, be used in all the machines described above. But several advantages of programmed instruction are lost when such material is used in straightforward instruction.

In the first place, the student should *construct* rather than *select* a response, since this is the behavior he will later find useful. Secondly, he should advance to the level of being able to emit a response rather than merely recognize a given response as correct. This represents a much more considerable achievement, as the difference between the sizes of reading and writing vocabularies in a foreign language demonstrates. Thirdly, and more important, multiple-choice material violates a basic principle of good programming by inducing the student to engage in erroneous behavior. Those who have written multiple-choice tests know how much time, energy, and ingenuity are neeeded to construct plausible wrong answers. (They must be plausible or the test will be of little value.) In a multiple-choice *test*, they may do no harm, since a student

[4] Terrace, Herbert S. Discrimination Learning With and Without Errors (unpublished Ph.D. Dissertation, Department of Psychology, Harvard University, 1961).

[5] Pressey, S. J. A simple apparatus which gives tests and scores—and teaches. *School and Society*, 1926, *23*, 373-376. This article and other articles concerning teaching machines by S. J. Pressey are included in Lumsdaine, A. A., and Glaser, Robert (eds.), *Teaching Machines and Programmed Learning: A Source Book* (Washington, D.C.: National Education Association, 1960).

who has already learned the right answer may reject wrong answers with ease and possibly with no undesirable side-effects. The student who is *learning*, however, can scarcely avoid trouble. Traces of erroneous responses survive in spite of the correction of errors or the confirmation of a right answer. In multiple-choice material designed to teach "literary appreciation," for example, the student is asked to consider three or four plausible paraphrases of a passage in a poem and to identify the most acceptable. But as the student reads and considers inacceptable paraphrases, the very processes which the poet himself used in making his poem effective are at work to destroy it. Neither the vigorous correction of wrong choices nor the confirmation of a right choice will free the student of the verbal and nonverbal associations thus generated.

Scientific subjects offer more specific examples. Consider an item such as the following, which might be part of a course in high school physics:

> As the pressure of a gas increases, volume decreases. This is because:
>   (a) the space between the molecules grows smaller
>   (b) the molecules are flattened
>   (c) etc. . . .

Unless the student is as industrious and as ingenious as the multiple-choice programmer, it will probably not have occurred to him that molecules may be flattened as a gas is compressed (within the limits under consideration). If he chooses item (b) and is corrected by the machine, we may say that he "has learned that it is wrong," but this does not mean that the sentence will never occur to him again. And if he is unlucky enough to select the right answer first, his reading of the plausible but erroneous answer will be corrected only "by implication"—an equally vague and presumably less effective process. In either case, he may later find himself recalling that "somewhere he has read that molecules are flattened when a gas is compressed." And, of course, somewhere he has.

Multiple-choice techniques are appropriate when the student is to learn to compare and choose. In forming a discrimination . . . an organism must be exposed to at least two stimuli, one of which may be said to be wrong. Similarly, in learning to "troubleshoot" equipment there may be several almost equally plausible ways of correcting a malfunction. Games offer other examples. A given hand at bridge may justify several bids or plays, no one of which is wholly right and all the others wrong. In such cases, the student is to learn the most expedient course to be taken among a natural array of possibilities. This is not true in the simple acquisition of knowledge—particularly verbal knowledge—where the task is only rarely to discriminate among responses in an array. In solving an equation, reporting a fact of history, restating the meaning of a sentence, or engaging in almost any of the other behavior which is the main concern of education, the student is to *generate* responses. He may generate and reject, but only rarely will he generate a set of responses from which he must then make a choice.

It may be argued that machines which provide for branching and decision-making are designed to teach more than verbal repertoires—in particular, that they will teach thinking. There are strategies in choosing from an array, for example, which require kinds of behavior beyond the mere emission of correct responses. We may agree to this without questioning the value of knowledge in the sense of a verbal repertoire. (The distinction is not between rote and insightful learning, for programmed instruction is especially free of rote memorizing in the etymological sense of wearing down a path through repetition.) If an "idea" or "proposition" is defined as something which can be expressed in many ways, then it may be taught by teaching many of these "ways." What is learned is more likely to generalize to comparable situations than a single syntactical form, and generalization is what distinguishes so-called deeper understanding.

But not all thinking is verbal. There are, first of all, alternative, parallel nonverbal repertoires. The mathematician begins with a verbal problem and ends with a verbal solution, but much of his intervening behavior may be of a different nature. The student who learns to follow or construct a proof entirely by manipulating symbols may not engage in this kind of thinking. Similarly, a merely verbal knowledge of physics, as often seen in the student who has "memorized the text," is of little interest to the serious educator. Laboratories and demonstrations sometimes supply contingencies which build some nonverbal knowledge of physics. Special kinds of teaching machines could help, for machines are not only not confined to verbal instruction, they may well make it possible to reduce the emphasis on verbal communication between teacher and student.

A more clear-cut example of the distinction between verbal and nonverbal thinking is musical composition. The composer who "thinks musically" does more than perform on an instrument or enjoy music. He also does more than use musical notation. In some sense he "thinks" pitches, intervals, melodies, harmonic progressions, and so on. It should not surprise us that individuals differ greatly in their "abilities" to do this, since the necessary contingencies are in very short supply. One might attack the problem by setting up an explicit kinesthetic repertoire in which "thinking a pitch" takes the form of identifying a position on a keyboard. A device which arranges the necessary contingencies is under development. With its help we may discover the extent to which students can in general learn (and at what ages they can learn most effectively) to strike a key which produces a tone which has just been heard. Similar devices might generate important forms of nonverbal mathematical behavior or the behavior exhibited, say, by an inventor conceiving of a device in three dimensions, as well as creative repertoires in other forms of art. Here is an extraordinary challenge to the technology of instrumentation.

There is another sense in which the student must learn to think. Verbal and nonverbal repertoires may prepare him to behave in effective ways, but he will inevitably face novel situations in which he cannot at first respond appropriately. He may solve such problems, not by exercising some mental ability, but by altering either the external situation or the relative probabilities of parts of his own repertoire. In this way he may increase the probability of an adequate response.

In this sense, thinking consists of a special repertoire which we may call self-management. For example, the student may alter the extent to which the environment affects him by "attending" to it in different ways. As one step in teaching thinking we must teach effective attending. The phrase "Pay attention!" is as common on the lips of teachers as "Open, please" on those of dentists—and for much the same reason: both phrases set up working conditions. The student may pay attention to avoid punishment and in doing so may learn to pay attention, but where aversive sanctions have been given up, teachers have resorted to attracting and holding attention. The techniques of the publication and entertainment industries are extensively invoked. Primers are usually decorated with colored pictures, and high school textbooks are sometimes designed to resemble picture magazines. Films dramatize subject matters in competition with noneducational films and television.

Attention which is captured by attractive stimuli must be distinguished from attention which is "paid." Only the latter must be learned. Looking and listening are forms of behavior, and they are strengthened by reinforcement. A pigeon can learn to match colors, for example, only if it "pays attention to them." The experimenter makes sure that it does so, not by attracting its attention, but by reinforcing it for looking. Similarly, a well-taught student pays attention to sentences, diagrams, samples of recorded speech and music, and so on, not because they are attractive but because something interesting occasionally happens *after* he has paid attention.

Most audio-visual devices fail to teach attention because they stimulate the student *before* he looks or listens closely. No matter how well a four-colored text or a dramatically filmed experiment in physics attracts attention, it prepares the student only for comics, advertising, picture magazines, television programs, and other material which is *interesting on its face.* What is wanted is an adult who, upon seeing a page of black-and-white text, will read it because it may *prove* interesting. Unfortunately, the techniques associated with captured and paid attention are incompatible. Whenever a teacher attracts the attention of a student, he deprives him of an opportunity to learn to pay attention. Teaching machines, with their control over the consequences of action, can make sure that paying attention will be effectively reinforced.

Another activity associated with thinking is studying—not merely looking at a text and reading it but looking and reading *for the sake of future action.* Suppose we show a child a picture and later, in the absence of the picture, reinforce him generously for correct answers to questions about it. If he has done nothing like this before, he will probably not be very successful. If we then show him another picture, he may begin to behave in a different way:

he may engage in behavior which will increase the probability that he will later answer questions correctly. It will be to his advantage (and to ours as educators) if this kind of behavior is taught rather than left to chance. We teach a student "how to study" when we teach him to take notes, to rehearse his own behavior, to test himself, to organize, outline, and analyze, to look for or construct mnemonic patterns, and so on. Some of these behaviors are obvious, but others are of more subtle dimensions and admittedly hard to teach. Machines have an advantage in maintaining the contingencies required for indirect or mediated reinforcement.

Other aspects of thinking, including the solution of personal problems, can also be analyzed and directly programmed. This is not current practice, however. Students are most often "taught to think" simply by thrusting them into stiuations in which already established repertoires are inadequate. Some of them modify their behavior or the situation effectively and come up with solutions. They may have learned, but they have not necessarily been taught, how to think.

Logicians, mathematicians, and scientists have often tried to record and understand their own thinking processes, but we are still far from a satisfactory formulation of all relevant behaviors. Much remains to be learned about how a skillful thinker examines a situation, alters it, samples his own responses with respect to it, carries out specific verbal manipulations appropriate to it, and so on. It is quite possible that we cannot teach thinking adequately until all this has been analyzed. Once we have specified the behavior, however, we have no reason to suppose that it will then be any less adaptable to programmed instruction than simple verbal repertoires.

Teaching machines and the associated practices of programmed instruction will have proved too successful if their practical consequences are allowed to overshadow their promise for the future. We need teaching machines to help solve a very pressing problem, but we also need them to utilize our basic knowledge of human behavior in the design of entirely new educational practices.

Teaching machines are an example of the technological application of basic science. It is true that current machines might have been designed in the light of classroom experience and common sense, and that explanations of why they are effective can be paraphrased in traditional terms. The fact remains that more than half a century of the self-conscious examination of instructional processes had worked only moderate changes in educational practices. The laboratory study of learning provided the confidence, if not all the knowledge, needed for a successful instrumental attack on the *status quo*. Traditional views may not have been actually wrong, but they were vague and were not entertained with sufficient commitment to work substantial technological changes.

As a technology, however, education is still immature as we may see from the fact that it defines its goals in terms of traditional achievements. Teachers are usually concerned with reproducing the characteristics and achievements of already educated men. When the nature of the human organism is better understood, we may begin to consider not only what man has already shown himself to be, but what he may become under carefully designed conditions. The goal of education should be nothing short of the fullest possible development of the human organism. An experimental analysis of behavior, carried out under the advantageous conditions of the laboratory, will contribute to progress toward the goal. So will practical experiments conducted in schools and colleges with the help of adequate instrumentation.

66 Teaching machine (and learning theory) crisis

For several years now, all over the country, learning theorists have been programing books and other matter into numerous little "frames" each consisting of a very easy question or statement with space for writing a one or two word "constructed" response, to be verified by turning a page or turning up a "teaching machine" roll. One learned by responding (the theory was) and the more responding the more adequate the learning. In preparing each question the effort was not so much to contribute to a larger meaning as to assure that the student "emitted" the desired response, on the ground that he learned by making correct responses and an error would tend to recur. Multiple-choice questions are not used, because they involve the presentation of wrong alternatives, and also call merely for discrimination. All this has seemed plausible theoretically, and hopes have been high for extraordinary educational advances.

NOT GAIN BUT CONFUSION

Instead, evidence has been accumulating that the above hypotheses on which the programing was being based were, *for human learning of meaningful matter*, not so! Such learners dealing with such materials may profit by seeing not only what a thing is but what it is not, may profit by mistakes, may learn to recall from learning to discriminate. Further, some half-dozen investigators have

SIDNEY L. PRESSEY, "Teaching Machine (and Learning Theory) Crisis," *Journal of Applied Psychology*, 47 (February, 1963), pp. 1–6. Reprinted by permission of the author and the publisher.

DR. PRESSEY (1888–   ) is Professor Emeritus of Psychology of The Ohio State University, and is currently visiting professor at the University of Arizona. For over forty years he has been interested in the development and use of teaching machines.

reported that as much may be learned in a given time simply by reading, as by reading *and* responding (Pressey, 1962; Silberman, 1962). In short, these theorists have independently discovered what educators have known about and been investigating for over 40 years—silent reading! Further, as programed matter has been used over a period of time, it has been realized that for skimming for main ideas, for review—for any use except that initial go-through— the programed book is almost impossible and the teaching-machine roll entirely so. Mostly, even for the first go-through, they are unsatisfactory, because most important matter to be learned has structure, which the programing destroys except the serial order, and most important learning is integrative and judgmental, so requires a looking about in what is being studied; for all such purposes a teaching machine seems about as hampering as a scanning device which requires that one look at a picture only 1 square inch at a time, in a set order. Much seems very wrong about current attempts at autoinstruction.

A possible basic factor is suggested by Hilgard (1956) when he questions

> the generalization from comparative studies that there are no differences, except quantitative ones, between the learning of lower mammals and man. . . . It is strange that the opposite point of view is not more often made explicit—that at the human level there have emerged capacities not approached by the lower animals, including other primates. . . . Language in man is perhaps the clearest of the emergents which carries with it a forward surge in what may be learned. . . . There are probably a number of different kinds of learning, following different laws. [Further, in man] the ceiling of ability itself may be modified by training. [Thus after acquiring] appropriate linguistic or mathematical tools [he can solve problems previously impossible] (pp. 460-461).

Surely that now taken-for-granted but really marvelous skill, silent assimilative reading, is such a tool. Also more important than often recognized are a variety of skills and strategies in learning usually grouped together as methods of study.

With Hilgard's position the writer would agree. He would say that the learning theorists have with notable vigor and consistency applied "generalizations from comparative studies" to problems of learning in school, and that the results have shown, more adequately than ever before, the unsatisfactoriness of those generalizations for that purpose. For a learner with reading-study skills, conventional textual matter orders and structures its contents in paragraphs and sections and chapters, exhibits that structure in headings and table of contents, makes all readily available in index with page headings and numbers. The learner thus has multiple aids to the development and structuring of his understanding. If need be he can, with a flick of the finger, move about in the material; he can skip the already known, turn back as a result of a later felt need, review selectively. As a way to present matter to be learned, the average textbook may not be best. But thousands of frames on a teaching-machine roll or strung through a programed book would seem close to the worst. To make a very bad pun, the programers have "framed" the textbook. Instead of trying to improve their programs, they might better consider very broadly how best to present matter for learning. The opinion is ventured that the best will be found closer to texts than to their programs.

But did not Socrates so teach the slave boy? The boy could not read. What about the often-cited skillful tutor? He assumed that the student had done some reading. However, both Socrates and the tutor did further learning by asking questions. The writer would contend that neither simply presented an idea and then reinforced it. Brownell's (1928) early research regarding primary school children's learning of arithmetic here seems relevant. Simply telling them that $2 \times 3 = 6$ did *not* bring about real learning of that number combination. These sturdy little empiricists had not merely to be *told*; they had to be shown, as by putting out two sets each of three pennies and demonstrating that they did indeed count to six. They had similarly to verify, and to differentiate, that $2 + 3$ was 5 and $3 - 2$ was only 1. As Piaget (1954) and others have described, children gradually develop a number system, also cognitive schema as of space, causality; and they do this not by so crude a rote process as the accretion of bit learnings stuck on by reinforcements, but by progressive processes of cognitive integration and clarification.

Moreover, such clarification is commonly by differentiation, and multiple-choice items involve just such processes. The three-choice question $2 \times 3 = 1$, 5, or 6 differentiates the correct answer from answers got by wrongly subtracting or adding. In this one concise little item are thus packed three arithmetic processes and three number combinations, and study of the item might well involve all six issues, with autoinstructional dealing with the item clarifying of all. The point will be returned to.

But first a brief summary of the position so far. The past decade has seen an extraordinary "boom" in autoinstruction; most of this work has been dominated by concepts of operant conditioning deriving directly from animal experimentation and has become stylized in terms of initial presentation of tasks in numerous frames with immediate constructed response. Because thus so special in origin and nature, as well as yielding often question raising results, a basic critical review of current autoinstructional concepts seemed called for. Doubts have been raised as to whether human learning of meaningful material can be adequately accounted for by animal based theory, programed matter is satisfactory for such learning, and reinforcement adequately accounts for the process (Gagné, 1962).

BUT WHERE FROM HERE?

When in doubt about such a theory-dominated situation, it is sometimes well to pull back and see whether a very practical analysis may helpfully reconstrue issues. If this be done, an obvious early question is this: what is the best way *initially* to present matter to be learned? The programers have been cutting it into little pieces each responded to, but now recognize that one may learn from reading without responding. Then how big may the piece be? The writer has stressed that the bigger piece may have structure which should be made evident, and that first consideration as well as review or selective use may make it desirable that the learner can move about freely in the material. Perhaps it would be granted that a questioner who interrupted the reading of this paper should be asked to wait until it was all before him—that it would be then that the discussion could be most profitable. Surely it will be granted that the paper can best be understood if seen in print so that one can glance about and see headings; rather than if heard, when one cannot thus study—as one cannot study a teaching-machine roll. So the suggestion is: that the initial presentation might most often best be a very well organized and well written substantial statement much like a chapter in a good textbook! And the autoinstruction should follow and should be like a series of questions in a very good discussion of such a chapter.

Some "autopresentation" might be helpful: a teaching-machine roll might picture two groups each of three pennies and then six and so make clear to the child mind that 2×3 does make six. *After* his number system has been somewhat established, there may be automatized drill. The printed word "house" may be thus associated with a picture of one. Sundry sorts of detail-learning and of drill may be dealt with piecemeal. But mostly (the writer believes) initial presentation of what is to be learned will be in field trip, demonstration or experiment, or most commonly a substantial unit like an incisive textbook chapter, *not* all mixed up with autoinstruction. The "autodiscussion" would follow, and its function would be (to paraphrase a statement in Ausubel's 1961 review) to enhance the clarity and stability of cognitive structure by correcting misconceptions, and deferring the instruction of new matter until there had been such clarification and elucidation.

In difficult matter such as a science text or industrial or military training manual, bits of autoinstruction may be needed more frequently; each step in the solution of a difficult problem may need such autoelucidation. But the manual or text need not be fragmented into thousands of frames. Problems may be explicated in autoinstructional matter supplementary to the text; and there, or perhaps every 3 or 4 pages in the book, clusters of autoexplicating queries may keep check on understanding. But a book's structured coherence and orderliness of presentation, and its convenience for overview, review, and reference, can be kept.

If the autoinstruction is thus to *follow* presentation of what is to be learned, then (like a good tutor or teacher) it will deal only with issues which need further clarification or emphasis. Such adjunct autoelucidation will *not* cover everything, may jump from one point to another or even back and forth. It will be very much shorter than present "programs," which attempt both to present matter to be learned and autoinstruct about it in the same aggregate. Being so different, such supplemental autoinstruction might well be given a different name, as auto-elucidation or explication.

But how would matter for adjunct autoinstruction or explication be selected? Experienced teachers would have many suggestions as to points needing special elucidation. They would be indicated in published research regarding pupils' learning of and difficulties in spelling, arithmetic, algebra, composition, science, and history. Additional research, for development and trial of such elucidative material, would suggest more items and better ways of presenting them. Some could be cleared up by making the initial presentation more lucid. But some students would still have difficulty with some items; perhaps those troubling 10% of the pupils or more would be dealt with in the adjunct autoinstruction.

The items should usually there appear (the writer is convinced) as multiple-choice questions with only such wrong alternatives as express common misunderstandings and a right answer notably clear. There is evidence that, contrary to theoretical inference, students do, after autoinstruction with such items, *less* often make the so-labeled mistakes, more often get things right, and transfer or generalize so that the gains appear on recall and yet other types of end tests (see for instance Jones, 1954; Lumsdaine & Glaser, 1960, pp. 52-93). Only half the students in a class may get such an item right on a pretest, but almost all of them do so on an end test a month later. In striking contrast, the perverse requirements of the orthodox programer make any such effectiveness impossible: the item is initially supposed to be so easy that at least 95% pass it, errors cannot be identified as such because they must not be shown, and right statements are limited to such as the student can be maneuvered into hastily formulating himself. And orthodox improvement consists of making the items yet easier! In contrast, improvement of such an item as here urged would involve making wrong alternates clearer expressions of common misconceptions and the right more clearly right so that gains would be yet greater. In addition, the ease of checking objective items, with immediate indication of correctness (as by instant change of color of the check mark on a "chemo-card" or turn to next question on a key machine) makes possible going through many more items in a given time—so presumably more learning.

RANGE OF EVALUATIONS

But what of the argument that orthodox programs have been found greatly to save time, so that for instance a college course was finished in the first 2 months of a semester, or an industrial training course similarly shortened? Independent study plans have made possible marked reduction of time in class without any such programs (Baskin, 1960). The average class and the average business training session may be very time wasting and otherwise inefficient, and a number of alternatives may be shown to be better. In a college or secondary school course with several sections, it should be feasible to have one or more taught in conventional fashion, one or more use an orthodox program, a similar number try what the writer has called adjunct autoinstruction, another venture a planned independent study procedure, and outcomes on a carefully made final examination compared. If so made, such examinations can yield some analysis of outcomes; does one method or another bring more recall, transfer, application? Experiments of this type under the writer's direction have shown adjunct autoinstruction superior to conventional classes in all these respects.

These experiments also showed the adjunct materials very useful in planned independent study: in a room set aside for such use and having all the readings, laboratory material, and adjunct autoinstructional sheets available but looked after by an assistant, the students came in and worked when they wished, in small groups or individually, consulting the assistant when they so desired. All finished the 11-week course within 6 weeks. All did well on midterm and final examinations. But informal reports and interviews indicated yet other values, as gains in ability to work independently—though the students became better acquainted than in formal classes! The opportunity to save time was motivating. Several of these students took another course by independent study during the second half of the quarter.

More broadly, appraising experiments involving considerable numbers of students with different instructors over considerable periods of time—preferably a whole school or business training course—have yet other values. Methods have to be tolerable in long continued and routine, not simply brief and special, use. In the work just described, the best all-purpose "teaching machine" was judged to be a 3 x 5 chemo-card haxing 30 lines each of four squares: on this answer card the student checked his choice of answer to each of 30 four-choice questions on a teach-test sheet, using a special red ink which instantly turned black when he marked in the right answer-box (because of an invisible chemical printed there). The student kept trying on each question until this color-change feedback told him he had the correct answer. For remedial review he had only to note where his red marks were, the sum of them was his error-score; the instructor had only to note where he saw most red on the cards for a given day to see where some corrective discussion might be desirable, and for both him and the students the cards were a compact easily-filed record.[1] In the writer's adjunct autoinstructional procedure, everything except the cards could be used over and over again, easily returned to again as for review. For long-continuing flexible use and re-use, it seemed apparent that a text or business manual plus perhaps 50 adjunct autoinstructional sheets (and some chemo-cards) was far more practicable than that manual or text cut up into 3,000 frames on a teaching-machine roll (with the machines) or strung through a programed book.

[1] Yet more convenient autoinstructional cards are possible. Instead of a pen with special ink, only a pencil may be needed; a mark with it, or a stroke of its eraser, breaks through an overprint to reveal a "c" underneath when the right answer is found. For 30-item 3-choice teach tests, a device little larger than a stop watch, and less complicated, may both teach and keep score. An apparatus little larger than an electric desk clock may both teach and provide selective review.

RÉSUMÉ AND RECOMMENDATIONS

Teaching machines and programed materials are now being used all over the country in schools and colleges and in industrial and military training. Manufacture and sale of such products are a major enterprise of many publishers and equipment makers. Ambitious young people are embarking on careers in such work. The whole subject has become an accepted topic of everyday talk. However, there is disturbing evidence that current autoinstruction is *not* up to the claims made for it, that the current "boom" might be followed by a "bust" unfortunate for those involved—and for psychology. This paper is first of all a plea that to guard against such a danger the whole situation be soon given close critical inspection, and not merely to assure (as is now being attempted) that programs are good; but critically to consider whether the whole current concept of programing may be at fault, and an almost totally different approach than now orthodox to all ideas about autoinstruction be called for.

The archvillain, leading so many people astray, is declared to be learning theory! No less a charge is made than that the whole trend of American research and theory as regards learning has been based on a false premise—that the important features of human learning are to be found in animals. Instead, the all-important fact is that human has transcended animal learning.[2] Language, number, such skills as silent reading, make possible facilitations of learning, and kinds of learning, impossible even for the apes. Autoinstruction should enhance such potentials. Instead, current animal derived procedures in autoinstruction destroy meaningful structure to present fragments serially in programs, and replace processes of cognitive clarification with largely rote reinforcings of bit learnings.

An "adjunct autoinstruction" is urged which keeps, makes use of, and enhances meaningful structure, the autoinstruction serving to clarify and extend meaningfulness. Texts, manuals, laboratory exercises, instructional moving pictures and television would be kept (though often improved), and the autoinstruction would aid in their use and increase their value. The materials would be perhaps only a tenth as bulky as present programs; and being objective, their use could be greatly facilitated by automating devices.

Evaluations should not merely (as is now projected) compare the merits of various "orthodox" programs. Those should be compared with such adjunct

---

[2] For this conclusion there is no less evidence than the whole history of civilization! Basically more significant than Skinner's brilliant research regarding animal learning may well be the almost forgotten finding of Kellogg and of Cathy Hayes that even if an ape be raised in a home like a child, it can never learn to talk. Far more remarkable than Skinner's pigeons playing ping pong is the average human scanning a newspaper—glancing about to find matter of interest to him, judging, generalizing, reconstruing, all in silent reading without overt respondings or reinforcings. Most remarkable of all is it to see learning theorists, hypnotized by the plausibilities of a neat theory, trying to teach that human as if he were a pigeon—confining his glance to the rigid slow serial peep show viewing of innumerable "frames" each demanding that he respond and be reinforced.

autoinstructional materials as here advocated. Adaptability should be compared for use with other media as books and movies and other methods as guided independent study. Convenience and cost for continuing general use should be hard-headedly appraised. The prediction is ventured that in all respects adjunct autoinstruction will be found far superior: time and work saving will be great yet more will be accomplished—courses often completed in half the usual time, years saved but nevertheless more accomplished in school and college, industrial and military training tasks reduced perhaps a third in length and all with great time and trouble saved instructional staffs. Then at long last the "industrial revolution" in education may come about which the writer predicted (Pressey, 1932) just 30 years ago. Further, somewhat as the practical testing movement from the first world war on greatly stimulated and aided research and theorizing regarding abilities, so autoinstruction may get research on learning out from under its long dominance by comparative psychology and confinement in the laboratory and evolve vigorous new theory.

67 *Programed instruction: insight vs. conditioning*

Suppose I want you to learn that the chemical symbol for Sodium is Na, for Potassium, K, for Calcium, Ca, and so on down through a list of 25 elements. By "learn" I mean becoming able, without hesitation, to respond with "Na" when I say "Sodium," with "K" when I say "Potassium."

Probably the simplest way to teach you is through drill. You would read the list of elements and symbols and would try to memorize the connections. Then I would give you a list of elements and you would try to write the correct symbols. I would correct your mistakes and you would try again. We could also drill orally, with me naming the elements, you responding, me correcting. Or we could conduct the drill on a machine which would give you immediate "feedback" of "right" or "wrong."

CONDITIONING

This sort of learning occurs through repetition and "reinforcement"—some sort of feedback or response which tends to "fix" the connection between element

HERBERT A. THELEN, "Programed Instruction: Insight vs. Conditioning," *Education*, 83 (March, 1963), 416–20. Reprinted by permission of the author and the publisher. Copyright 1963 by The Bobbs-Merrill Co., Inc., Indianapolis, Indiana.

DR. THELEN is Professor of Education at the University of Chicago.

and symbol in your mind. The objective is to develop the specific habit of associating names and symbols. This process is called "conditioning."

Conditioning is the only process through which nonsense (or near-nonsense) can be learned. It can also be used to teach pigeons to tread on the right lever in order to get grain. It is an efficient way to learn *isolated* bits of information, such as the year in which Columbus discovered America, the months of the year, and the density of lead.

It is hoped that being told your response is correct will make you want to make further effort; but, if you don't really care about it, then we will fall back on the notion that generally speaking, if a person makes a response (never mind for what reason) he is more likely to make the same response the next time the stimulus is presented. Programers say that such learning tactics "increase the verbal repertoire."

AN EXPERIMENT

Let us consider another type of task. Suppose I want you to learn the quantitative law "governing" the period of back-and-forth oscillation of a pendulum. I can give you a ball of twine, an assortment of weights (different sizes, shapes, weights, and colors), and a support from which you can hang the weights by means of the twine. I would probably also give you a yardstick and a stop-watch, although I might prefer to wait until you asked for them.

My instructions would be to play with the things I had just given you and see if you could discover what it is that determines how rapidly the pendulum will swing back and forth; and also just what the relationship is between this factor and the rate of swing.

You would probably begin by using a piece of string to hang one of the weights from the support, and you would set it in motion and notice its regular rate of swing. Your next move would probably be either to lengthen or to shorten the string and see what happened. You would soon get the notion that changing the weights (color, weight, shape) made no difference, but lengthening or shortening the string resulted in the pendulum swinging slower or faster.

You would then use the yardstick to measure the length of the string, and the watch to time the swings. You would make several measurements and you would find that the shorter the string the faster the pendulum, but not in direct proportion.

I might have to give you a hint about trying the square root of the length. But we would keep at it until you found the relationship that worked—which would also mean you would have to realize that you had to measure from the "middle" (center of gravity) of the weight rather than from the hook on its top.

We would discuss what you had done, and I would be interested both in your findings and in your strategy. I would probably want to see next if you could make use of the law you had discovered to work some problems, and if you could use the strategy of controlled experimentation more efficiently in another discovery situation.

"INSIGHT" LEARNING

The kind of learning process I have been describing is "insight" learning. You explore various hunches and at some point you are aware of the principle. Then you move systematically to demonstrate the principle. You cannot make "mistakes" because each "mistake" furthers your inquiry by eliminating an unfruitful possibility.

This sort of insight learning is most effective for the learning of principles (the law of the pendulum) as distinguished from discrete bits of information (how many seconds a 12-inch pendulum requires to swing back and forth once). Principles learned through this sort of discovery tend to be "internalized"; they can be used in many unfamiliar or different situations later.

If I had merely told you the principle, you would memorize my words, but all you would have learned is the answer to the specific question: What is the law of the pendulum?

If I had told you the principle and then given you some problems to work, you would learn to use the formula for making calculations, but it would not necessarily be useful to you for any other purpose.

If I had tried to develop the principle through question and answer discussion with you, you might develop the insight required to use it as part of verbal expositions, but you would not be very likely to "see" its operation in a wide range of situations in nature later (when I was not there).

Eighty per cent of present programs (those using Skinner-linear and Crowder-branching rules) teach by the first method, conditioning. The remaining twenty per cent teach by a miscellaneous variety of rules, but tend more toward their authors' conceptions of insight learning. There is considerable controversy about the worth and usefulness of the eighty per cent. (The twenty per cent have mostly not been available to the public. Their turn will come later.)

THE MAJOR ISSUE

It seems clear to me that the major issue concerning programed learning is primarily the large educational issue of conditioning versus insight. This issue, unresolved for two thousand years, is still unresolved. Teaching programs, educational television, the place and nature of achievement tests, the differences between education for the masses and for the elite—answers to these questions hinge on one's position about conditioning versus insight learning as the means of education.

To say this does not mean that there isn't plenty to criticize about present learning programs even for conditioning, but I do not think that is the main issue. The issue is whether "increasing the verbal repertoire" is a legitimate educational objective; whether conditioned learning of a very large number of fragments of information can in any way contribute to the development of character, ability to think critically, ability to apply principles, development of interests, and so on.

This is yet to be demonstrated; and it will be hard to demonstrate because we do not have the sort of evaluation devices and techniques we need to assess most of these major educational objectives.

THREE COURSES OF ACTION

Not having the necessary assessment instruments to measure the significant objectives, what shall we do? Three courses of action are possible.

One is to develop the instruments, but the present pattern of "achievement tests" is so well entrenched at present that I don't have much immediate hope.

The second course of action is to give up our educational mission and settle for a lesser one. For the most part this is what the programers are trying to persuade us to do: a good program, they would have us believe, is one that does as good a job as an average teacher in teaching the things that are typically measured on achievement tests. This seems to me to be a cynical view, the counsel of despair.

The third alternative is the oldest and best; it is actually the basis of most teaching. This is to study the experiences of the children *during* the learning activity. Thus one may assume that if students work absorbedly, come up with ideas that are new to them, try to build on each other's ideas, think up alternative ways to do things, offer and evaluate conclusions drawn from experiences they can describe—in such a case we would probably say they were having "worthwhile educative experiences" even though we have *not* yet given them a "test."

What we are working from is a model in our minds of what productive study looks and feels like. As long as a classroom full of students fits the teacher's model (even though he doesn't know he has one) the teacher simply tries to maintain interaction as it is; but the moment the experiences begin to lose their thrust or go sour, the teacher acts to change the situation and get back on the track.

The best model for classrooms is that of educated people utilizing knowledge effectively to conduct inquiries into problems, questions and issues that they feel are important. This model assumes that one becomes educated by acting more and more like an educated person.

The teacher is satisfied if he believes the children are doing this as well as they can, given their immature status, lack of experience, and present skills. If the teacher has no sound internalized image of such an operation, then he will act in accordance with some non-educative substitute, such as simply being comfortable and polite, becoming an audience for his play-acting of the expert or executive, becoming a congregation for his moralizing, becoming glibly informed with a lot of talk about (rather than understanding of) phenomena, becoming "independent" (which usually boils down to getting over being immobilized in an anarchic situation).

As I say, the big question is what we really *mean* by education—as shown by our actions as teachers. What is the nature of an educative situation?

THE BEST POLICY

There is little doubt that most competent opinion by people who have no vested interest in particular materials or in the sacred traditions of public schools is that we should maximize insight learning and minimize conditioned learning as much as possible.

There are both theoretical and practical objections to conditioned learning as the way to useful and utilizable knowledge (even though most attitudes and many skills are learned through conditioning in the family). There are only practical objections (too much work) to insight learning.

SOME HELPFUL DEDUCTIONS

As applied to programing of materials, the following deductions may serve as a starting set:

1. The student would be able to define his purpose in using the materials in terms of a question to be answered, a relationship to be sought, a skill to be learned, and he would have solid reasons which, for him, justify his learning of these things.

2. The materials would present reasonably large or molar "situations" containing many elements, and the student would devise his own path through these elements, taking them in any order he chooses, going back and forth among them, having free choice.

3. Each of these molar situations would involve at least two phases: discovery of the pattern followed by immediate application, summarizing, prediction, or raising of further questions that occurred to the student as he was working.

4. During the "search" phase, the student would get immediate feedback when he had classified each element appropriately.

5. During the application or assimilation phase, feedback could not be built into the program because any of a large number of speculations or answers might be right—at least from the point of view of the student. The feedback for this phase would have to be reserved for a non-material third phase: class discussion which begins with the testimony of several students.

6. The programed materials thus would lead into class discussion; the reported speculations and difficulties of the students during the second phase would be testimony from which the agenda for discussion is generated.

7. The discussion would be concerned both with the students' speculations and conclusions and with the way in which the students arrived at these answers.

8. Diagnosis of the discussion would lead into the formulation of what the students need to study next, and a variety of activities as appropriate, including further work with programed materials, would then be initiated.

68 Teaching machines: a demurrer

There is a new force in American education, coming up fast and strong: teaching machines. A number of educators have already claimed that this innovation shows great promise in helping to solve the current national "crisis" in education. By now, most people have heard about teaching machines (programmed instruction), but there has been remarkably little public discussion about the issues involved in their use or, from what one can learn from talking to people, little private thinking.

For those who have not had any contact with one, a teaching machine is any one of a rapidly increasing variety of desk-sized devices that presents a student, first, with a printed item of information, a statement, or a fact (a "prompt") and then with a question about that information. The student answers the question by writing a word or a group of words in a space on the blank or by selecting one of a series of multiple-choice answers or by punching a key. He then presses a button or a slide to reveal the correct answer to the question and compares it with his own. If his response is the same as that revealed by the machine, he presses another button for the next prompt and question. If his answer is incorrect, he goes back to review previous steps or to a branch that tells him why his choice was incorrect. A series of several hundred to several thousand closely graduated, interlocking question-and-answer frames are required to cover a particular subject, such as elementary principles of logic or basic inorganic chemistry. The student works at his own pace but cannot proceed to a new frame until he has successfully answered the question in the preceding frame. The machine may also be equipped to time the student, to score his errors, and to compute his standing in relation to other students. The student also may simultaneously listen over earphones to recorded instructions. After he has completed the program, a new roll of paper, filmstrip, tape, or set of cards is installed in the machine for the next sequence, and the student goes on to more data, more questions, and more answers.

With various mechanical and electronic elaborations, these machines are based on a well-known principle of learning first demonstrated with laboratory animals: the conditioning of behavior through reinforcement and repetition. But instead of the rat and pigeon psychologist's pellet of food or negative electric

H. T. FITZGERALD, "Teaching Machines: A Demurrer," *School Review,* 70 (Autumn, 1962), 247–56. Reprinted by permission of the University of Chicago Press. Copyright 1962 by The University of Chicago.

MR. FITZGERALD is Director of Education and Training in the automotive industry in Flint, Michigan.

shock, praise and the satisfaction of getting correct answers provide reinforcement for human students. Also, humans are capable of learning their way through
much more complicated mazes and of memorizing an incredibly greater number
of correct responses than laboratory animals are. Therefore, learning a subject
like fundamentals of electricity is largely a matter of learning (or giving) a large
number of correct responses to logically related sequences of questions that constitute the subject. Or, to put it in another way, once a subject has been carefully
divided ("programmed") into a series of many small bits of information
("steps"), a student has only to learn by repetition and reward ("rapid and
frequent reinforcement") the correct answers to a series of questions about the
small bits of information. Instrumentation of the sort described here makes it
possible to shape a wide variety of verbal and non-verbal behaviors of students.
In short, since this is a behaviorist view, learning is conditioning, learning is
behavior. Even thinking is a behavior that can be analyzed and produced to
specification.

All this may sound rather surprising, presented as it is here so baldly, but it
represents the learning theory of the psychologists who have developed programmed instruction. However, the companies that are now hard at work building, improving, and marketing teaching machines will not stress the conditioning
aspect because of its uninspiring connotations. Rather, public school boards and
educational administrators are being presented with a long list of advantages
that these machines offer.

First, they will save money and help solve the teacher shortage. Even though
a single machine costs several hundred dollars and hundreds of machines will
be required to program a school, they will save on teachers' salaries in the long
run, since one classroom teacher can supervise many more students. Students
work (study) in separate booths, so that problems of discipline and cheating are
greatly reduced. A missed lesson can easily be made up, and even slow learners
eventually complete the course.

Advantages are also seen in the impersonal nature of machine learning, especially for the hard core who have the wrong attitudes toward schooling and the
conventional classroom situation. Machines are patient; they do not shame or
disparage as human teachers might do, or be perceived to do. Skinner of Harvard
University, a pioneer and the most important single figure in the field, argues
that "adversive" practices (failing, punishing) are one of the worst features of
conventional teaching, while programmed learning is always affectively positive,
since machine instruction insures mastery at every stage. Solving problems successfully encourages even poor students, and the gadgetry involved in operating
the machine is said to be intrinsically interesting. When mass production reduces
the cost, families of school-age children will be able to afford a teaching machine
to provide an opportunity for self-instruction in the home.

A student learns more rapidly and more thoroughly from programmed courses
because he is forced to concentrate on the material before him and because he

gets immediate feedback on his progress. The quality of education in the schools will improve because students will be exposed to programs that reflect the methods of the nation's best teachers, rather than suffering under the possibly mediocre teachers of their own community. The time saved by both teacher and superior pupil can be used for individual counseling and creative work. The uniformity of instruction and the elimination of the factor of subjectivity in grading are also held to be advantages. Finally, in return for his greater productivity, the teacher can ask society to improve his economic position.

Like much earnest, unreflective salesmanship, some of this scarcely merits argument. Besides, with all this consensus and cheering, one feels reluctant to criticize, especially before the system has been given a fair chance to demonstrate its merits in actual operation. So let us be satisfied here with raising a few skeptical questions on the possibility of disadvantages.

Take, for example, the problem of rigidity, or lack of flexibility. Programmed learning by its nature requires plodding, step by minute step, across the expanse of a subject or sub-subject. The machines do not readily lend themselves to skimming for an over-all view, to dipping into a future chapter to anticipate development or returning to an earlier chapter to check points already made to weigh and compare information. Programmed learning also resists changes and growth of subject matter. A great deal of effort must be spent in developing any single program, and the result is a logically integrated unity. It reminds one of a piece of close hand knitting that cannot be altered anywhere once it is completed, without unraveling the whole garment. Knowledge, however, and our approach to it are dynamic and change slowly or rapidly. A live instructor can supplement his syllabus with references to recent research, critical reviews or articles, and related information from other fields. Styles change, too. Those who have worked with educational films know how quickly they become dated and how distracting this aging is to content. But because of the investment by producers and film libraries, prints are often not revised or withdrawn from circulation until they become antiquated.

Yet perhaps the worst rigidity of programmed learning is its natural tendency to infallibility. Despite all the assurances of the authors, their stance of pious open-mindedness, their denial of dogmatism, we can expect that in a short time, when the machines get out into boroughs and parishes, we will repeat the experience we have had with intelligence, aptitude, personality, and scholarship testing. When there is a choice between "A, B, C, D, or E (none of these)" and the manual says that "C" is the correct answer, there is no appeal. You may write to the organization that publishes the test, but your protest will be lost in the endless baffles of educational bureaucracy. The most you can hope for is a note expressing an "appreciation of your interest" and a promise of possible revision "at some future date, pending further research in this and related areas." Meanwhile, the machines go blindly on, scoring "C" as correct and deducting fractional points for answers marked "A, B, D, or E (none of these)."

In attempting to apply the principles of animal learning to human learning, the programmers have made a false analogy, a technical error. A word rarely has the semantic specificity of reference and effect to persons that a grain of corn or a flashing light has to laboratory animals. Yet even if the answers were completely free of error and the wording devised so as to be unambiguous and capable of only one interpretation, the single-answer approach to education remains objectionable in principle. This approach assumes that our knowledge of the world is a fixed and orderly body of facts and conclusions. It implies a concept of reality wrapped up in separate little packages and tied with string, stacked neatly on the shelves of a vast warehouse. But the task of intelligence is more than that of a warehouse employee picking stock down the aisles, more than that of a novitiate reciting a long catechism of correct answers. Education is also inquiry, insight, emergence, the development of a critical faculty and an intuition of the web of interdependent hypotheses and inferences, the structure of abstractions about the seen and the unseen that comprises our understanding of the physical world. Learning is also exploring, conceptualizing, experimenting, interacting, valuing. Reality is also process, flow, a great running together, a barely intelligible, absurd, endless poem, a brilliant light at the entrance to our cave.

Perhaps all this sounds like rhetorical arm-waving, but even on a flatly pragmatic basis the problem of content must be faced. A number of companies are now manufacturing teaching machines and are beginning to compete with one another in the same way that the textbook and audio-visual people compete. High-volume sales are important to reduce cost; and in cultivating as wide a market as possible, there will be a tendency to oversimplify subjects, to eliminate anything extraneous (and therefore connected with other subjects), to boil the day's lesson down to a few definite points that we can trust the student to carry away with him. This approach is what makes the package programs frequently used in conference training programs in industry so dull. Each problem selected is neatly resolved by a school solution. Similarly, the play for markets and the fear of offending anyone—no controversy—is what makes many textbooks and commercial educational films mediocre, infrequently stimulating.

Admittedly, the best people are now pioneering in the field of programmed learning, and they are laboring with the best of intentions. As the field grows, however, they will be supplemented by the hacks and hawkers whom we have already met in the testing companies whose sales representatives gladly offer a whole series of superficial personality traits to schools and employers so that they may determine who is introverted or extroverted, socially mature and adjusted. (Do you drive a car rather fast? Do you have a low-pitched voice? Were you bashful when you were a child? Do you like fishing?)

Moreover, in making a choice between the Apex programmed course in basic economics and the Zenith programmed course in basic economics—both of which claim to be rigorously, systematically correct—someone or some group in the local school system will have to work through the content of each to decide which is more correct. Such a comparison, interesting as it may be, will be unavailable to individual students or teachers, who can now review various available textbooks. The child will get either economics by Apex or economics by Zenith; but, because his learning is based on conditioning, he will not be able to benefit from both. And if the student does not agree with one or more of the machine's positions, it is just too bad: he cannot argue with the machine, ask it questions, or request further clarification. He will have to accept and give back the wanted answer, or it will not let him proceed with the remainder of the course. But if the child has started his education on the machines in the primary grades (as is also proposed), by the time he gets to economics he will not be in the habit of asking questions. "I'm really awfully glad I'm a Beta because . . . ."

In spite of these demurrers, one can expect that teaching machines will achieve a fair amount of currency in the coming years. The cold war has enlisted education as part of our national policy (for example, the National Defense Education Act) and has provided new money along with new pressures. In this country, a typical political response to any given problem is to spend more money to solve it. But money will not increase the supply of people with good minds, at least not in the short run; and money cannot guarantee to eliminate the ambiguities, the random undependability of people. Jones, with a wide grasp of his subject matter, may not give so good a lecture as Brown, and even Brown's performance may vary in quality from day to day. Even deciding whether Brown is better than Jones requires study and the exercise of personal values and judgment, something that has not been too popular since the advent of the tenure system. Small wonder, then, that spending money for hardware—new buildings, equipment, gadgets—provides an appealing solution to the public demand for more education, while allowing the administrator to feel that he has left no stone unturned in providing the most up-to-date, the best facilities.

Efficiency and the solution of immediate, practical problems are difficult to argue against, especially in public forums. A prominent example is the gradual spread over the years of government control and surveillance in many phases of what was once considered the private life of private citizens. Each legislative act, each administrative interpretation, has been justified at the time of its inception by expediency, by the need for the efficient solution of specific problems. And by these imperceptible steps, personal freedom has been constricted. It would be no surprise, as the next possibility, during a really serious military crisis, to see the introduction of a national system of identification cards. Many salient reasons would be advanced for their need; they would greatly simplify the work of government agencies, the police, the tax people, insurance companies, and banks. Almost everyone would benefit, and what really good arguments could be offered in opposition?

In the same way, teaching machines have the magical attraction of efficiency, of solving one of the country's pressing problems, and in their own small way, they lead to the slow spread of—if not authoritarianism as such—authoritarian thinking. We are certainly a long way from state control of education, as in the USSR, but we already show tendencies toward centralization and away from pluralism, especially as we become a mass society and the problem of order, of dealing with sheer numbers of people, becomes acute.

Programmed instruction may turn out to be only a passing fad, but we have seen other movements that did not pass away. The problem of scholarship and college-entrance testing, for example, has already been largely turned over to IBM scoring machines. Teaching machines are admittedly based on the theory of reinforcement, of rote learning, of stimulus-response, of a mechanical one question–one answer. This is an intrinsically undemocratic—worse, an anti-intellectual—theory of learning. The next step should be to strengthen "rapid and frequent reinforcement" by, let us say, a mild electric shock for incorrect answers. To this, of course, the student would voluntarily submit because he has been convinced of its efficiency, just as wholly innocent people submit to polygraph tests to most efficiently prove their innocence.

Finally, there are some of us who will find a deeper, more personal distaste for learning from a machine, from interacting with it. This is a rather quaint, almost archaically humanistic idea, but it is there, nevertheless. We spend entirely too much time with machines these days. The most prominent example is watching television as a passive substitute for an active, emotional life with real people, but other examples come to mind. The difficulty is that, taken one at a time, all our interactions with machines have some value (television is educational), but the total effect in our lives is more than the sum of its parts. Interaction with is not the same as using a machine, such as an electric drill or a vacuum cleaner, but involves being somehow part of the machine or being subjected to it. A year or so ago I attended a twenty-four-hour reading improvement course that was built around the use of an automatic projector that flashed on a screen words and sentences of varying lengths at varying speeds. When the machine is in operation, one is paced by it, with the sense of being harnessed to it. I did best when I achieved the proper mental set, by turning off conscious thinking and allowing the images direct access to a sort of blank mind.

There are many, I know, who do not experience any distaste in living among and through machines, just as there are many who feel perfectly at home with plastic furniture, synthetic flavored food, and tranquilized affect; and to such as those, of course, these remarks will have little relevance, except as an opportunity for an ascription of questionable motives. Such is the temper of the times! Nevertheless, I find the thought of millions of children spending hours each day with millions of machines in millions of separate cubicles an appalling prospect.

Perhaps an analogy will explain. One may compare the merits of paper roses with real roses, but all the good arguments, all the advantages—economy, durability, accuracy, availability, habituation, and relativity of taste—are on the side of paper roses. There's not much one can say in favor of a live rose, except to

assert lamely, naively, that it is true, that it does not betray. And any good dia-
lectician has a ready answer for that kind of romantic subjectivity. There is not
much one can say for learning from a live teacher either, considering all his imperfections, or for learning in the company of other live students, considering
the distractions of their greater imperfections. One can merely suggest, hope for
the occasional nuances, the sparks, the candor, the possibility of sharing perceptions and intelligence and experience, the possibility of learning humanity from
humans. Teaching machines only teach (condition) machines.

Correlation of this book with
educational psychology texts

CORRELATION OF THIS BOOK WITH
EDUCATIONAL PSYCHOLOGY TEXTS

Bigge & Hunt
PSYCHOLOGICAL
FOUNDATIONS OF
EDUCATION
Harper & Row, 1962

Blair, Jones, & Simpson
EDUCATIONAL
PSYCHOLOGY, 2D ED.
Macmillan, 1962

Cole & Bruce
EDUCATIONAL
PSYCHOLOGY, REV. ED.
Harcourt, Brace &
World, 1958

Text chs.	*Related selections*	*Text chs.*	*Related selections*	*Text chs.*	*Related selections*
1	48	1	54	1	23, 27, 28, 34, 35, 45, 47, 48
2	2, 17, 18, 39	2, 3, 4	13-23, 34, 35	2, 3	13-19
3	2, 3, 8, 13, 14, 17-19	5	1-7, 65, 66	4	20-30
4	21, 23, 27, 28, 32, 34, 35	6	24-30	5	31-40, 45-59
5	20-24, 27, 60-62	7	16, 29, 33, 34	6	
6	13, 14	8	17, 23, 26-28, 30, 31-35	7	11, 12, 36-40
7	2, 3, 36, 37, 65, 67	9	8-12, 24-26, 41-44	8, 9, 10, 11	1-7, 9, 63-68
8	19, 27, 33, 35	10		12	8, 9, 10, 41-44
9	17, 18, 33, 38	11	23, 28, 45-50, 59	13	
10	1, 6, 8	12	20-22, 27, 28, 30, 32, 33, 49, 50	14	
11, 12	1-3, 5, 7, 8, 10-12, 15, 16, 29, 65-67, 94	13	17, 31, 36-40, 52-58	15	59-62
13	63-68	14	49, 50, 58, 59	16	49, 50, 51
14	4, 5, 7, 20, 45-48	15	7, 27-40, 49, 50		
15, 16, 17, 18	3-16, 21, 24, 29, 30, 32, 34, 41-44, 51, 54-62	16			
19	12, 27, 28, 30, 32, 33, 35, 39, 40, 46-50, 52, 53, 55-57	17, 18	60, 61, 62		
		19	46, 51		
		20			
		21			

Cronbach
EDUCATIONAL
PSYCHOLOGY, 2D ED.
Harcourt, Brace &
World, 1962

Text chs.	Related selections
1	12
2	8, 10, 27, 28, 30, 32-35, 39, 40, 55-57
3	1-11
4	13-16, 18, 29, 35, 45, 47
5	17, 23, 27, 28, 30, 32, 39, 40
6	15, 16, 20-26, 29, 30, 34, 60-62
7	41-44, 46, 51
8	
9	3-5, 63-68
10	20, 23-26, 41
11	7-11, 23-26, 41-44
12	4, 59, 63-68
13	27, 30, 32, 33, 37-40, 45-50, 52-58
14	34, 45-47, 51, 53, 58
15	45-51, 54-59
16	60-62
17	7, 12, 20, 27, 28, 31, 32, 34, 35, 40
18	23, 27, 30, 32, 33, 35, 38, 46

Frandsen
EDUCATIONAL PSYCHOLOGY
McGraw-Hill, 1961

Text chs.	Related selections
1	
2	1-7, 54, 65
3, 4	13-30, 60-62
5	45, 47, 48
6	11, 12, 15-17, 29, 34, 51, 58
7	8-10, 41-44
8	63, 68
9	
10	
11	
12, 13	27-40, 46, 49, 50, 52, 53, 55-58
14	23, 34, 35, 45, 47
15	60-62

Garrison, Kingston, & McDonald
EDUCATIONAL PSYCHOLOGY
Appleton-Century-Crofts,
1955

Text chs.	Related selections
1	
2	
3	13-19, 34, 35
4	20-23
5	8-10, 24-26
6	30-35
7	1-7, 15, 16, 29, 51, 63-68
8	
9	
10	41-44
11	8-10, 24-26
12	35-40
13	21, 59-62
14	
15	27
16	20-23, 27-35, 47, 49-51, 56-59
17, 18, 19	17-19, 28, 30, 36-40, 45-53, 55-57

Jordan
EDUCATIONAL
PSYCHOLOGY, 4TH ED.
Holt, Rinehart &
Winston, 1956

Text chs.	Related selections
1	
2	20-23, 34
3	13-19
4	20-40
5	1-11, 65, 66
6	27-35, 45-59
7	
8	
9	31-40, 46-59
10	20-26, 41-44
11	
12, 13, 14	20, 60-62

Kingsley & Garry
THE NATURE AND
CONDITIONS OF
LEARNING, 2D ED.
Prentice-Hall, 1957

Text chs.	Related selections
1	
2	
3, 4	1-7, 60-62, 65-68
5	11, 12, 13-30, 51
6	
7	63-68
8	23-25, 28, 34, 37, 45-48, 51, 57, 58
9	
10	5
11	4, 20, 37
12	63-68
13	30, 41
14	8-10, 24-26, 41-44
15	2, 30-35, 46, 51, 55-57
16	11, 12, 36-40, 46-53
17	
18	

Klausmeier
LEARNING AND
HUMAN ABILITIES
Harper & Row, 1961

Text chs.	Related selections
1	1-7, 20-23, 65, 66
2	
3	13-30
4	49, 50
5	32, 45-48, 51, 55-59
6, 7	5, 8-10, 23-26, 41-44
8	13, 14, 18
9, 10	17, 19, 27-40, 44-59
11	15-17, 29, 30, 65
12	
13	7, 20-28, 32, 34, 45-47, 51
14	63-68
15, 16	59-62
17	

Kolesnik EDUCATIONAL PSYCHOLOGY McGraw-Hill, 1963		*Lindgren* EDUCATIONAL PSYCHOLOGY IN THE CLASSROOM, 2D ED. Wiley, 1962		*McDonald* EDUCATIONAL PSYCHOLOGY Wadsworth, 1959	
Text chs.	*Related selections*	*Text chs.*	*Related selections*	*Text chs.*	*Related selections*
1		1		1	36-38
2		2	13, 14, 17, 20, 27, 28, 36-38, 40, 53, 55-57	2	
3		3	13-19, 22, 33	3	
4	13-19, 21, 23, 34	4	21, 23, 27, 34, 35	4	11, 17, 23, 27, 29, 30, 34, 46, 51
5	17, 19, 31, 35	5	45-48	5, 6	8-10, 24-26, 41-44
6, 7	20-23	6	31-35, 39, 40	7, 8	12, 31-35, 46-53
8	22-27, 51	7, 8	1-12, 65	9	3, 5, 65
9	1-12, 65	9	15, 16, 27, 29, 58	10	8, 9, 10, 41-44
10	63-68	10, 11	45-48, 53, 55-58, 63-68	11	13-19
11		12		12	36-40
12	8-10, 25, 26, 41	13	45, 47, 48	13	30, 32, 45-59
13	24-26, 42-44	14, 15	59-62	14, 15, 16	60-62
14	15-17, 29, 34, 51	16	20-30	17	
15, 16	59-62	17	7, 46	18	
17	34, 35, 45-48	18	56		
18, 19	30-40, 46-50, 52, 53, 55-58				
20					
21					

Pressey, Robinson, & *Horrocks* PSYCHOLOGY IN EDUCATION Harper & Row, 1959		*Sawrey & Telford* EDUCATIONAL PSYCHOLOGY Allyn & Bacon, 1958		*Skinner* et al. ESSENTIALS OF EDUCATIONAL PSYCHOLOGY Prentice-Hall, 1958	
Text *chs.*	*Related* *selections*	*Text* *chs.*	*Related* *selections*	*Text* *chs.*	*Related* *selections*
1		1	15-19, 23, 29, 30, 34, 51	1	10, 45, 47, 48
2	13-19			2	54-62
3	20-24	2, 3, 4	1-7, 65, 66	3, 4	13-19, 35
4		5		5	20-30, 59-62
5	27, 28, 30-35, 53-58	6	59-62	6	46, 47, 49-51
6	35, 46-48	7	31	7	1-7, 65, 66
7	16, 29, 51	8	13-19	8	15-17, 51
8		9	20-30, 34, 45, 47, 60-62	9	65
9		10	11, 27, 34	10	41-44, 54
10	6, 35, 45-48	11	2, 7, 31-35	11	8-10
11	1-7, 65	12	36-40, 49-58	12	23-26
12		13	34, 45-48	13	30-40
13	59-62	14	36-40	14	27-30, 34, 35, 39, 53, 55-57
14		15	7	15	20-30
15				16	32, 37, 38, 40, 46-48, 52, 56
16	7, 37, 38			17	60-62
17				18	7
18				19	
19	40				

Smith & Hudgins EDUCATIONAL PSYCHOLOGY Knopf, 1964			Sorenson PSYCHOLOGY IN EDUCATION, 3D ED. McGraw-Hill, 1954			Stephens EDUCATIONAL PSYCHOLOGY, REV. ED. Holt, Rinehart & Winston, 1956	
Text chs.	Related selections		Text chs.	Related selections		Text chs.	Related selections
1			1	60, 61, 62		1	
2	60-62		2	59		2	
3, 4, 5	27-40		3			3	
6	34, 45-48		4	13-19		4	13-19
7	49-51, 54-59		5	17		5	20-30
8	46-48		6	27-35		6	41-44, 59-62
9	48, 51, 58		7	36-40		7	20-30, 34, 41-44
10	1-7, 65, 66		8			8, 9	1-7, 11, 12, 65, 66
11	11, 54, 57		9	34, 35, 45, 47, 48		10	15, 16, 28-30, 45, 47, 48, 51, 52
12	8-10, 20-30, 41-44		10			11	34, 65
13	65		11	20-26		12	5, 8-10, 23-26, 41-44
14	31-40, 55, 56, 65		12	20, 21, 22		13	
15	54-68		13	23-27		14	
			14			15	46, 48, 54-59
			15	21, 22		16	36-40, 50, 51
			16			17	31-35, 52-58
			17	1-7, 65		18	47, 48
			18	15, 16, 29, 30, 34, 51		19	27, 28, 36, 37, 40
			19			20	46, 52-58
			20			21	
			21			22	
			22				

Stroud		Thompson et al.		Trow	
PSYCHOLOGY IN EDUCATION, 2D ED. McKay, 1956		EDUCATIONAL PSYCHOLOGY Appleton-Century-Crofts, 1959		EDUCATIONAL PSYCHOLOGY, 2D ED. Houghton Mifflin, 1950	
Text chs.	*Related selections*	*Text chs.*	*Related selections*	*Text chs.*	*Related selections*
1		1	13, 14, 15	1	
2	20-23	2	16-19	2	55-57, 59
3		3	23, 34, 51	3	21-23, 27, 28, 30, 34, 35, 45-48
4	11	4, 5	60-62	4	15-17, 29
5	63-68	6	20-30	5, 6	27, 28, 30-40, 46, 47, 49, 50, 52, 53, 55-57
6	28	7	27	7	13-19
7	20, 21, 23	8	49, 50	8	20-30
8	13-19, 22-30, 60-62	9	47, 48	9	60-62
9	22, 23, 27, 28, 32	10		10	1-7
10	1-7, 65	11	1-10, 65, 66	11	63-68
11	20, 21, 23, 27, 28, 34, 45-50	12	15-18, 23, 29, 30	12	8, 9, 10
12	49, 50, 54-62	13		13	
13		14	8-10, 41-44	14	
14		15	41, 42	15	
15	7-40, 46-48, 51-53, 59	16	23, 27, 28, 30, 33, 40, 53, 55-58	16	23-26
		17		17	21, 31-35, 46, 47, 51, 55-58
		18, 19, 20, 21	27-35, 36,40, 46, 47, 49, 50, 52, 55-58		
		22	45-48		
		23			
		24